GREAT LIVES
FROM
HISTORY

GREAT LIVES FROM HISTORY

Renaissance to 1900 Series

Volume 4
Mir-Scha

Edited by

FRANK N. MAGILL

SALEM PRESS

Pasadena, California   Englewood Cliffs, New Jersey

1/90

Library of Congress Cataloging-in-Publication Data
Great lives from history. Renaissance to 1900 series /
edited by Frank N. Magill.
    p.   cm.
Includes bibliographical references.
Summary: This five-volume work examines the lives
of 495 individuals whose contributions greatly influenced the world's cultures that flourished from the Renaissance through 1900. An annotated bibliography ac-
companies each entry.
1. Biography. 2. World history [1. Biography. 2. World
history.] I. Magill, Frank Northen, 1907-
CT104.G68   1989
920'.009'03—dc20
[B]
[920]   89-24039
ISBN 0-89356-551-2 (set)   CIP
ISBN 0-89356-555-5 (volume 4)   AC

PRINTED IN THE UNITED STATES OF AMERICA

LIST OF BIOGRAPHIES IN VOLUME FOUR

LIST OF BIOGRAPHIES IN VOLUME FOUR

GREAT LIVES
FROM
HISTORY

COMTE DE MIRABEAU
Honoré-Gabriel Riqueti

Born: March 9, 1749; the Estate of Mirabeau, Bignon, near Nemours, France
Died: April 2, 1791; Paris, France
Areas of Achievement: Government and politics
Contribution: Mirabeau was a bridge between the aristocracy and the people, and between the variously named legislatures and the king. He led the fight to establish the National Assembly out of the Estates-General to bring order in the then-named National Constituent Assembly and to save the monarchy as one of the two agents of the people.

Early Life

Honoré-Gabriel Riqueti, Comte de Mirabeau, was christened Gabriel-Honoré and called Gabriel in the family. Many of his works were first published anonymously, and he seldom used his title. In the legislature, he was mostly referred to as Mirabeau and sometimes as "the Tribune of the People."

The Riquetis have been traced to the small town of Digne, near Marseilles. Family members accumulated wealth in Marseilles through commerce. Mirabeau's father, Victor Riqueti, Marquis de Mirabeau, anxious to increase the family estate and to ensure a long and distinguished family line, sought and finally found an heiress with great financial potential, Marie-Geneviève de Vassan, who was sixteen years old at their marriage in 1743. In six years, she produced two daughters and a son who died in an accident. The marquis was overjoyed when his son and heir, Comte de Mirabeau, was born, but he was immediately appalled to see the child's huge head, two teeth, misshapen foot, and malformed tongue. That harsh blow was intensified three years later, when the child was struck by smallpox.

As the young count grew, he seemed more and more to resemble the Vassan side of the family, which his father came more and more to detest. The birth of two normal children, who resembled the Mirabeau side of the family, worsened the situation. Nevertheless, the marquis, who bravely pursued his wife's fortune, devoted himself to saving his son and heir. The marquis gave his son an excellent tutor and three years of study with the famed Abbé Choquard in Paris and found for him a position in the regiment of the Marquis de Lambert in 1768.

When the young Mirabeau quarreled with Lambert and fled, his father saved his son with the first of many personal orders of the king. These orders, or *lettres de cachet*, permitted imprisonment without a (possibly humiliating) public trial. He was released to join an expedition to Corsica, which France had purchased from Genoa and which, under the famed Pasquale Paoli, was in revolt. Mirbaeau served with distinction. Returning home in 1770, he spent time occupied with various projects on family estates. He married Marie-Marguerite-Émilie de Covet de Marignane on June 23, 1772.

Life's Work

Mirabeau's career began with bankruptcy, for which he was jailed under another *lettre de cachet*. While in prison, he met and fell in love with Marie-Thérèse-Richard de Ruffey, the Marquise de Monnier, a married woman. Mirabeau escaped from prison, and the couple fled the country; Mirabeau was eventually arrested in the Netherlands and imprisoned under yet another *lettre de cachet*.

During this period of about ten years, Mirabeau wrote his most important works. His *Éssai sur le despotisme* (1775; essay on despotism) eloquently advocated representative government and a strong executive through the monarchy, but opposed an upper chamber of aristocrats. The essay revealed a knowledge of history and contributed to the later view of Mirabeau as an authority on government and an advocate of the people. *Des lettres de cachet et des prisons d'état* (wr. 1777, pb. 1780; of *lettres de cachet* and of state prisons) was a more technical work, ranging over French constitutional history and developing the theme that personal liberty is the liberty essential to all other liberties. Thus, not even the national interest should be invoked to violate it. This work, with impressive citations, considering Mirabeau's confinement, came to be admired in England and contributed to the growing conviction in France that the monarchy needed restraint.

Mirabeau managed to write many other works and letters while in prison, although he complained that his paper was rationed. He wrote a French grammar and a work on mythology for the Marquise de Monnier (who gave birth to his only child, Sophie-Gabrielle, while he was in prison), a study on inoculation, and several translations. He was passionate and ambitious and, like the philosophes, confident of reason, law, and virtue. He supported the American colonists and detested the Church.

If prison served as a graduate school for Mirabeau, it was in court cases in 1782 and 1783 that Mirabeau realized his vocation, or at least his greatest talent—moving people through the spoken word. Two cases received wide public attention. In 1782, he won cases of the government against him. In 1783, he defended himself against suits brought by his wife's wealthy family in Aix-en-Provence. He lost the judgments and the acceptance of his own class, but he won the hearts of the people with his oratory. Six years later, the people would remember and elect him overwhelmingly as a deputy of the Third Estate (Commons).

During the next several years, Mirabeau took a mistress (Henrietta-Amélie de Nehra, who had a good influence on him), traveled to England, and adopted a son, Lucas de Montigny. Mirabeau was not successful in England. Returning to France in March, 1785, Mirabeau fought off his debts by writing pamphlets for speculators on the Paris Bourse, including famous persons such as Étienne Clavière, who was later Minister of Finance, Pierre-Samuel du Pont de Nemours, who was later chairman of the finance committee of the National Assembly, and Talleyrand, then Abbé Périgord, who was later to serve every revolutionary government. Mirabeau also antagonized other famous persons such as Jacques Necker, who was a three-time finance minister, and Pierre-Augustin Caron de Beaumarchais, a playwright.

Mirabeau's attempts at employment as secretary of the Assembly of Notables, a blue-ribbon panel called by the king at the request of his finance minister to endorse his package of fiscal reforms, failed. The 144 notables refused to endorse any reforms, and the minister was dismissed and replaced by a minister who prepared a similar reform package. This reform package was signed by the king and placed before the law courts, which refused them on the grounds that, by taxing privileged classes, the reforms violated the constitution and so could be approved only by the Estates-General representing the three social classes. The Estates-General, however, had three votes, and the two privileged classes expected to defend their interests by a two-to-one vote. The issue from May 4 through July 15 was the revolution of the three-vote Estates-General into the one-man-one-vote National Assembly. Mirabeau led this struggle, although he was absent when the Bastille was captured on July 14, because of his father's funeral. When the deputies had been ordered to disperse on June 23, Mirabeau had responded, "go tell the king that we are here by the will of the people and we will leave only by the points of bayonets."

After the king canceled troop movements and accepted the National Assembly, the problem was to control the assembly. Mirabeau sought to do that with a responsible ministry. The assembly, however, would not go along with him, even though he proposed that he himself be excluded from that ministry. Next, Mirabeau attempted an alliance with the Crown, and there were tortuous negotiations through the summer of 1790. Mirabeau was rejected by the court and attempted personal control of the assembly. He became president of the Jacobin Club on November 30 and president of the National Assembly on January 29, 1791, and he was widely praised for his leadership. Then his health failed. His last speech, on March 27, was as fierce as ever. He then took to his bed and died on April 2, 1791.

Summary

After Comte de Mirabeau's death, a leading centrist (liberal monarchist) of the assembly, Pierre-Victor Malouet, said of Mirabeau, "his death, like his life, was a public misfortune." Generally regarded as scandalous, his past may have been a handicap in relationships with others, but Mirabeau showed no regrets. He devoted the last week of his life to the preparation of his papers. All Paris and the government showed affection for him at his death. His personal life, including the prison time, the court cases, and the voluminous writings, justified his claim to being "the Tribune of the People" and caused him to appear as a lonely combatant standing against the establishment. He could intimidate both the Left and the Right and was correct in perceiving more threat to his objectives from the Left than from the Right. Jean-Sylvain Bailly said, "it cannot be denied that Mirabeau was the moving force in the National Assembly. . . . Whatever may have been his moral character, when he was aroused by some eventuality, his mind became ennobled and refined, and his genius then rose to the heights of courage and virtue."

The history of the National Assembly through March 28, 1791, can be traced in Mirabeau's speeches. Called a politician without a party, he was also a minister without a king, an officer without an army, and a teacher without a class. Experience has since confirmed the value of his emphasis on personal liberty and on balance between the executive and the legislature. Yet, after Mirabeau, there were still the Marquis de Lafayette, Talleyrand, and Emmanuel-Joseph Sieyès; the constitution was completed; and the Legislative Assembly (1791-1792) did function and was terminated only in war panic. Whether constitutional monarchy was a necessary failure in the construction of a responsible and stable government or a tragic failure augmenting the bloodshed, no one saw better than Mirabeau the potential advantages and the dangers of the executive and the legislature. Scholars disagree on Mirabeau's personal ambition and venality, although his motion to exclude himself from the ministry seems sincere; few had more faith than did Mirabeau in nation, law, and king.

Bibliography
Aulard, Alphonse. *The French Revolution: A Political History, 1789-1804.*
  Vol. 1, *The Revolution Under the Monarchy, 1789-1792.* Translated with
  a preface by Bernard Miall. New York: Russell & Russell, 1965. Aulard
  was biased toward democracy and republicanism but recoiled from the
  excesses of both. Contains a full chronology.
Connelly, Owen. *French Revolution: Napoleonic Era.* New York: Holt, Rinehart and Winston, 1979. An up-to-date modern survey. Chapters 2 and 3
  describe Mirabeau's period in the Revolution, and later chapters tell what
  happened next. Connelly is a Napoleonic scholar, and in this book politicians do not loom as large as in more political surveys. The treatment of
  Mirabeau and other politicians is clear and reasonable.
Higgins, Earl L., ed. and trans. *The French Revolution as Told by Contemporaries.* Boston: Houghton Mifflin, 1938. This work, under the general
  editorship of William L. Langer, contains extracts of Mirabeau's speeches
  on the veto and the exclusion of ministers and several contemporary views
  of Mirabeau.

Nezelof, Pierre. *Mirabeau: Lover and Statesman*. Translated by Warre Bradley Wells. London: Robert Hale, 1937. One of the best of many older works on Mirabeau, this book reads like a novel, with much conversation and drama. An easy introduction to Mirabeau.

Welch, Oliver J. *Mirabeau: A Study of a Democratic Monarchist*. Reprint. Port Washington, N.Y.: Kennikat Press, 1968. The best biography in English. Based on original sources, this study handles the sensationalism prudently and struggles through Mirabeau's controversial career to craft a sympathetic and reasonable judgment.

Frederic M. Crawford

MOHAMMED I ASKIA

Born: c. 1442; probably near Gao, Songhai Empire
Died: 1538; near Gao, Songhai Empire
Areas of Achievement: Monarchy and statecraft
Contribution: Mohammed I Askia greatly expanded and consolidated the Songhai Empire, which dominated much of West Africa in the fifteenth and sixteenth centuries. His policies resulted in a rapid expansion of trade and the imposition of the stamp of Islamic civilization on Songhai.

Early Life

Mohammed I Askia was born Mohammed Ture ibn Abi Bakr, probably of parents of the Soninke people. Although the Soninke frequently are cited as the source of the royal lineage of ancient Ghana, a large West African kingdom that flourished before A.D. 1000, most Soninke, including Mohammed's clan, were subject in the fifteenth century to the Songhai Empire, centered at the Niger River entrepôt of Gao. Mohammed's family was of a military caste, providing soldiers and officers for the Songhai cavalry regiments. His childhood and education no doubt reflected that experience. He probably received systematic religious instruction in some Islamic institution as a child. In early adulthood, Mohammed became a trusted lieutenant in the service of the Songhai Emperor, Sonni Ali. Mohammed's early years were a time of unprecedented expansion and turmoil for Songhai. Although oral dynastic history of Songhai goes back to the eighth or ninth century, prior to the fifteenth it had been only a small principality.

Sonni Ali's leadership transformed Songhai into a regional influence. Taking advantage of the progressive disintegration of its powerful western neighbor Mali, after 1450, his forces swept westward, capturing the fabled city of Tombouctou, pushing back the Saharan nomads who menaced the river towns, and punishing recalcitrant Mossi chieftains to the south. In the process of forming an empire, however, Sonni Ali revealed a streak of barbaric cruelty. Further, many of the newly conquered areas west of Songhai proper were heavily Islamic and culturally more sophisticated than Songhai itself, and often related more to North African than sub-Saharan ethnic types. Sonni Ali's vicious temperament and cavalier attitude toward Islam set his subjects to plotting. His death in 1492, before consolidation of Songhai's considerable territorial gains could be completed, prepared the way for Mohammed to emerge as a national leader.

Life's Work

In April, 1493, Mohammed allied himself with the Muslim clerics and disaffected Muslim portions of the empire against Sonni Ali's son and would-be successor, whose support lay primarily in the Songhai homeland. Ethnic and religious divisions ran deep in the ranks of the large Songhai army. Mohammed avoided what otherwise might have become a bloody and pro- longed civil war by staging a coup, seizing the capital, and forcing Sonni Ali's son into exile. He took the dynastic title of Askia (*askiya*).

Mohammed's first task was to obtain recognition as the legitimate ruler of Songhai. That he achieved, at least initially, by purging or deporting as many members of earlier Songhai dynastic lines as possible. His long-term strategy, however, involved cultivation of tighter alliances with Muslim in- tellectuals and clerics. Mohammed viewed Islam as the logical counterpoint in Songhai to the power and influence of the traditional priesthood and politi- cal leadership. He lavished attention, gifts, and titles upon Muslim notables, particularly those in the newly conquered, western part of the empire. He also strove to develop the city of Tombouctou—already known for its con- centration of Muslim clerics and scholars—into a first-rate center of learn- ing, a cultural focus that could rival the traditional religious center of Kukia in the eastern Songhai homeland.

Mohammed must have perceived the enormous advantages of Islam in transforming Songhai from a peripheral state into a partner in what was, in the sixteenth century, the world's most diverse and extensive civilization and commercial network. Songhai, and its predecessors Ghana and Mali, de- pended upon the export of gold and ivory to North Africa for hard currency and crucial imports such as horses for cavalry. There is evidence too that, by Mohammed's time, the presence of European trading stations on the West African coast was beginning to affect traditional commercial networks in the region.

For these reasons, doubtless also as an expression of his own piety, Mo- hammed in late 1496 undertook the hajj, or pilgrimage, to Mecca. The expedition was a stupendous effort to eclipse the pomp and splendor of the pilgrimage by Mansa Musa some 175 years earlier. In Egypt, the titular Abbasid caliph bestowed upon Mohammed the title Caliph of the Blacks. In addition to donating enormous amounts of gold to the poor and needy, Mohammed endowed a hostel for future pilgrims from West Africa. Mo- hammed was away nearly two years, which suggests that he was firmly in control of affairs in Songhai.

Mohammed's hajj was a boon to the fortunes of Islam in West Africa. He established visibility for the kingdom and returned determined to purify the practices of West African Muslims and bring them into line with orthodoxy. The hajj attracted scholars and religious notables from all over the Middle East; many accompanied Mohammed back to Songhai and greatly strength- ened the scholarly community there. Tombouctou, in particular, developed an international reputation as an academic and religious center. Farther to the west, amid the serpentine courses of the Niger floodplain, protected from invasion by the annual inundation, the city of Djenné developed a reputation throughout West Africa comparable to that of Tombouctou.

Mohammed continued to expand Songhai's frontiers, often in the cause of a jihad, or holy war. His soldiers battled the Mossi tribes of modern Burkina Fasso to the south and captured most of the important salt mines and oases in the Sahara as far as the frontiers of modern Algeria and Libya. Even some of the powerful Hausa city-states of northern Nigeria fell under Mohammed's sway. The Songhai army featured a mobile cavalry and levies of conscripts, very likely the first such standing army in Africa, supported by a strong riverine navy on the Niger. (Firearms, however, though apparently known, were not used by the Songhai forces.) By the end of Mohammed's active reign, these forces had created what most likely was the largest political entity in African history to that time.

The administrative structure of Songhai shows little of the Islamic influence so pervasive in other facets of the state. It was a simple system of provincial governors responsible to Mohammed. There was a ministerial council of sorts but with little real power and usually dominated by members of the royal family in any case. The court protocol that was reported by foreign travelers—among them the famous Leo Africanus—suggests that Mohammed continued to behave as a traditional West African king, wielding almost absolute power. Despite his commitment to Islam, there is no evidence of persecution of unbelievers. Gao, in fact, became a haven for Jewish refugees from the Saharan oases when persecution broke out there in the early sixteenth century. Many of Mohammed's gestures toward traditionalism may have resulted from the fact that the people of the Songhai capital of Gao continued to resist Islamic influence.

Signs of despotism reappeared in Mohammed's later years. Moreover, the large and unprecedented administrative apparatus of the court and provincial government had to be supported by a growing system of landed aristocrats, a network of royal estates producing food and military supplies through slavery and forced labor. Newly conquered peoples found themselves assigned to the production of weapons and armor or to service to the army. Others plied the Niger to produce fish for the court.

In his declining years, Mohammed lost his grip on the empire. In order to foster the continued growth of Islam, the king had designated a western governor as successor, but his ambitious sons were determined to seize power. In 1528, they deposed Mohammed, who was already blind and infirm, exiling him to an island in the Niger. Nearly a decade of turmoil elapsed before the Askia rivals settled on a system of succession and power sharing.

Summary

Mohammed I Askia belongs to a tradition of warrior-kings who periodically unified and integrated the Niger basin and adjacent areas, beginning perhaps as early as A.D. 800. This periodic unification greatly affected the economic history of lands around the Mediterranean, especially with respect to the export of gold and other precious commodities. In the Niger region itself, it established a level of political order and stability necessary for commerce to thrive. In the period of Mohammed, as well as in earlier decades when Mali was prominent, Islam made important advances, which conferred a measure of cultural unity upon the region and also stimulated interaction with the outside world.

Mohammed himself was among the foremost of the unifiers, administrators, and purveyors of Islam. Evidence from the era of his predecessor, Sonni Ali, strongly suggests that Islam was in decline, actively challenged by pagan and traditional elements in West African society. Given the importance of Muslim merchants in the economic life of the region, it is also likely that the Niger basin was in a state of economic disarray owing to the disintegration of Mali and growing hostility to outsiders. These trends Mohammed dramatically reversed, restoring and greatly expanding commerce and drawing the Niger basin closer than ever before to the world economy. His contributions toward an Islamic cultural order laid the foundations for the eventual emergence of Islam as a mass religion in West Africa.

Mohammed's Askia dynasty continued after his death. His sons ruled ably for fifty years in the mid-sixteenth century, during which time Songhai maintained relations with the newly established Ottoman Empire in North Africa, and Songhai was able to withstand some of the commercial turmoil resulting from increased European activity on the African coast.

On the other hand, the limits of Mohammed's Islamic campaign in Songhai are clear. Neither he nor his successors managed to close the gap between the predominantly Muslim west and the still-pagan Songhai heartland in the eastern part of the empire. Civil war eventually resulted in a disastrous reverse for Mohammed's Islamic edifice in 1588. Three years later, an invasion from Morocco brought the empire crashing down and the Askia dynasty to a humiliating close.

Bibliography
Boahen, A. Adu, Jacob F. Ade Ajayi, and Michael Tidy. *Topics in West African History*. 2d ed. Burnt Mill, England: Longman Group, 1986. An excellent description of Songhai within the wider context of medieval West African history.
Bovill, E. W., and Robin Hallet. *The Golden Trade of the Moors*. 2d ed. London: Oxford University Press, 1968. An excellent treatment of medieval West African history and its connections with European events. Gives a detailed account of the rise of Songhai and the contributions of its major rulers.
Hunwick, J. O. "Religion and State in the Songhay Empire." In *Islam in Tropical Africa*, edited by I. M. Lewis. London: Oxford University Press,

1966. Discusses the tensions between Islamic and pagan religious and philosophical ideas in Songhai and how the major rulers borrowed and elaborated upon ideas from both sources to organize and administer the empire.

Kaba, Lansine. "The Pen, the Sword, and the Crown: Islam and Revolution in Songhay Reconsidered, 1464-1493." *Journal of African History* 25 (1984): 241-256. Traces the rise of Songhai to changing trade patterns and discusses Sonni Ali's antagonism toward Muslim elites which, by contrast, Mohammed supported and used to build his administration.

Pardo, Anne W. "The Songhay Empire Under Sonni Ali and Askia Muhammad: A Study in Comparisons and Contrasts." In *Aspects of West African Islam*, edited by Daniel F. McCall. Boston: Boston University Press, 1971. An unusually critical treatment of chronicles and other sources in an effort to determine the precise ideological and religious attitudes of Sonni Ali and Mohammed.

Saad, Elias. *A Social History of Timbuktu: The Role of Muslim Scholars and Notables, 1400-1900*. New York: Cambridge University Press, 1983. An important study of social and intellectual life in precolonial West Africa. Provides extensive coverage of the zenith of Songhai civilization in the early sixteenth century, using indigenous chronicles and a wide variety of other documentary sources.

Trimingham, J. Spencer. *A History of Islam in West Africa*. New York: Oxford University Press, 1962. One of the most painstaking studies of the development of Islamic influence and practices in the region. Particularly harsh on Sonni Ali and critical of other accounts suggesting a high level of Islamic intellectual activity in Songhai and the center of learning in Tombouctou.

Ronald W. Davis

MOLIÈRE
Jean-Baptiste Poquelin

Born: January 15, 1622 (baptized); Paris, France
Died: February 17, 1673; Paris, France
Areas of Achievement: Theater and drama
Contribution: By grafting character study and social commentary upon traditional farce, Molière became the creator of modern French comedy and continues to be ranked as France's finest comic playwright.

Early Life

Jean-Baptiste Poquelin was born in Paris, France, and was baptized on January 15, 1622, the eldest child of Marie Cressé Poquelin and Jean Poquelin, who came from well-to-do families, prominent for two generations as merchant upholsterers. Jean-Baptiste was followed by five other children, only three of whom survived. When he was ten years of age, his mother died, and his father remarried and moved to a house in the cultural and social center of Paris. Meanwhile, Poquelin was assuring his son's future. He sent Jean-Baptiste to the Jesuit College of Clermont, an excellent school which was attended by students of the most prominent families, and then had him begin the study of law in Orléans. In 1641, Jean-Baptiste became a notary.

In a society whose center was the king, anyone who was ambitious needed court connections. In 1631, Jean Poquelin had purchased from his brother the largely honorary office of valet and upholsterer to the king. Six years later, he had obtained hereditary rights to the position for Jean-Baptiste and had him take the oath of office. Given his family background, his education, his profession, and his future court position, Jean-Baptiste's pathway to prosperity seemed clearly marked.

Jean-Baptiste, however, had fallen under the influence of the actress Madeleine Béjart, and in 1643 he renounced his court position, abandoned his social status, and even risked damnation, according to the clerics of his time, in order to become an actor. Béjart, her brother Joseph, her sister Geneviève, Jean-Baptiste (now calling himself Molière), and nine other actors formed a theatrical company, rented a theater, and, at the beginning of 1644, began to produce their plays. They were, however, unsuccessful. Their financial condition was so poor that Molière, who had become the manager of the troupe, was twice imprisoned for debt and had to be rescued by his father.

In 1646, Molière and the three Béjarts, along with several other actors, began a tour of the provinces. During the next twelve years, Molière learned his craft as an actor, who before long was regularly cast in leading roles; as a producer and financial manager; and as a writer, who practiced his skill in farcical sketches before proceeding to full-length plays. By 1658, Molière and his troupe of seasoned actors were ready once again to attempt the conquest of Paris. With his self-discipline, his energy, and his dedication to the theater, Molière was to prove a brilliant leader. Although his hatred of hypocrisy, which he expressed in telling satire, would earn for him enemies, his genius would bring him friends to defend him, not the least his king. While he was uncompromising in principle, Molière was tolerant in practice and equipped with consistent good humor. It was fortunate that Molière possessed such qualities, for there would be adversities during the last fifteen years of his life that must have made him yearn for the carefree, vagabond days in the provinces.

Life's Work

On October 24, 1658, Molière and his troupe gave the performance that would determine their future. They appeared at the Louvre before the young King Louis XIV, his brother Philippe, or "Monsieur," and the court. Although the king was unenthusiastic about their major play, a tragedy by Pierre Corneille, he enjoyed Molière's farce. As a result, the troupe was granted permission to play at the royal Petit-Bourbon theater, where they shared performance days with the Italian Comedians until the Italians went back to Italy in July, 1659. Because they were under the patronage of Philippe, Molière's troupe was called the *troupe de Monsieur* (Monsieur's troupe).

It is not surprising that the king preferred Molière's comedies to other plays that the company performed. Although they were based on Italian comedies and farces, Molière's plays were superior in language, in wit, in the inventiveness of their plots, and, above all, in the realistic depiction of character. Soon the company was reviving Molière's earlier full-length plays, written when he was in the provinces, *L'Étourdi: Ou, Les Contretemps* (1653; *The Blunderer*, 1678) and *Le Dépit amoureux* (1656; *The Love-Tiff*, 1930). Molière followed them with his first comedy of manners, *Les Précieuses ridicules* (1659; *The Affected Young Ladies*, 1732), which satirizes the affectations of Parisian society. This play was then followed by *Sganarelle: Ou, Le Cocu imaginaire* (1662; *Sganarelle*, 1755), a complicated story of love and misunderstanding, which became one of Louis' favorites.

A contemporary portrait of Molière at breakfast with Louis XIV reveals the strength of character which was one of the playwright's dominant traits. Molière's sharp features, hawklike nose, and firm chin reflect his determination; barely resting on the chair, he is all nervous energy, a creative artist temporarily restrained only by the presence of his monarch.

Unfortunately, the approval of the king and the adulation of the public aroused the jealousy of rival troupes, who intrigued against him and in 1660 succeeded in having his theater torn down without notice, supposedly because it was in the way of a new façade for the Louvre. Unwilling to interfere with the plans formulated by his own officials, Louis instead permitted Molière's actors to use the theater of the Palais Royal. This was to be the home of Molière's company for the rest of his life.

The first play to be produced in the Palais Royal was a failure. The second, *L'École des maris* (1661; *The School for Husbands*, 1732), was very popular. The play is based on the situation in a comedy by Terence, in which two boys receive very different kinds of education. In Molière's play, however, the children are girls. Molière's audience was delighted with the success of the heroine, who foils her severe guardian in his plans to wed her and even tricks him into helping her into the arms of the young man with whom she is in love.

Probably to strengthen his position at court, in 1660, when his brother died, Molière resumed his rights to the court office of his father and later performed the quarterly duty of making the king's bed. In 1661, Molière also produced the first of a number of comic ballets, which was presented at an entertainment in the king's honor. Critics have lamented the fact that thereafter Molière spent so much of his time on various court entertainments; yet without the king's favor Molière would have been in serious trouble during the years to come.

Although Molière's greatest works were still ahead of him, so were his greatest difficulties. In 1662, when he was forty, Molière married the charming, spoiled actress Armande Béjart, who was the twenty-year-old sister of Molière's friend and mistress Madeleine Béjart. Scholars do not credit the persistent rumor that Armande was really Madeleine's daughter, perhaps by Molière. They do, however, agree that Armande brought Molière more misery than joy. It is obvious that the themes of jealousy and infidelity, so often arising from the marriage of an older man to a young woman, as in *L'École des femmes* (1662; *The School for Wives*, 1732), reflected Molière's own unhappy experience with a girl much like the coquettish Célimène of his *Le Misanthrope* (1666; *The Misanthrope*, 1709).

The more successful Molière became, the more his enemies sought to destroy him. Calling Molière godless, they attempted to suppress *The School for Wives*, the story of a country girl made vulnerable by her own innocence. In 1663, in a series of essays, verses, and plays, Molière and his friends battled against those who traduced the playwright, calling him a cuckold and charging him with incest. In 1664, Molière was forbidden to perform *Tartuffe: Ou, L'Imposteur* (1664; *Tartuffe*, 1732), the story of a pious hypocrite; because of objections from religious fanatics at court, the play was not approved until 1670. Meanwhile, in 1665, pressure on Molière forced the withdrawal of his play *Dom Juan: Ou, Le Festin de Pierre* (1665; *Don Juan*, 1755), which dealt with the legendary seducer.

In 1666, Molière's troupe performed the work that many critics consider his masterpiece, *The Misanthrope*, which, significantly, relates the difficulties encountered by an outspoken, honest man in a dishonest society. The play was only moderately successful. By now, Molière's troubles with his wife had become worse, his father's business was in difficulty, and his own health was declining. Yet he continued to produce plays, including *Le Médecin malgré lui* (1666; *The Doctor in Spite of Himself*, 1672), *Amphitryon* (1668; English translation, 1755), *L'Avare* (1668; *The Miser*, 1672), and *Le Bourgeois Gentilhomme* (1670; *The Would-Be Gentleman*, 1675).

Despite the success of most of his plays, Molière's last years were dark. In 1670, his father died in poverty, and in 1672 a newborn son died. Molière himself was desperately ill and forced to depend on the doctors whom, as his plays indicate, he deeply distrusted. Meanwhile, Molière's enemies triumphed: He lost the right to stage musical entertainments for the king, and finally he was refused permission to stage a play at court. Molière's play *Le Malade imaginaire* (1673; *The Imaginary Invalid*, 1732) was about a healthy man who imagined himself to be ill. On February 17, 1673, Molière, who was playing the title role, became ill onstage. Although he managed to finish the performance, he died later that night. Even then, the clergy were not done with him; they insisted that he should not be buried in consecrated ground. The king intervened, and, during the night of February 21, Molière was quietly interred in the cemetery of Saint-Joseph in his native Paris.

Summary

Molière is generally said to have created modern French comedy. Examined carefully, Molière's plots are farfetched, with the farcical situations of his dramatic predecessors. Yet he develops them masterfully, piling complication on complication and reversal on reversal, until, in the denouement, he resolves the difficulties which he has so carefully created. More important was his handling of character. Misers and misanthropes, foolish women and greedy doctors, court flatterers and pious hypocrites were familiar types in earlier plays. Although his comic characters, like those of Ben Jonson in England, were still types, Molière individualized them. In *Tartuffe*, for example, the autocratic father Orgon, who is so easily deceived by the hypocrite, is not only a fool; he is a middle-aged man, married to a young wife, who does not believe that he can control her, his domineering mother, his rebellious children, or even his outspoken maid. Thus, Molière converts a standard character into a realistic and complex person, with whom the audience can sympathize, even while they condemn his folly.

By providing a serious basis for comic drama, the satirical denouncement of hypocrisy, vice, and folly, Molière changed the nature of French comedy. His influence spread through the Continent and across the Channel to England, where the Restoration Wits imitated his plays. In later centuries, his popularity has persisted; his plays are frequently performed throughout the world, and his characters have become immortal.

Bibliography

Chapman, Percy Addison. *The Spirit of Molière: An Interpretation*. Edited by Jean-Albert Bédé. Princeton, N.J.: Princeton University Press, 1940. A portrait of Molière in the context of his times, written by a scholar who knew the period extremely well. Includes critical chapters on half a dozen of the major plays. Sections on the court and the theater provide valuable material which is difficult to find elsewhere.

Frye, Northrop. *Anatomy of Criticism: Four Essays*. Princeton, N.J.: Princeton University Press, 1957. With references to works by various comic playwrights, Frye propounds his own theories as to the structure of comedy. His comments on the use of proofs and ordeals, the movement toward reconciliation, and the methods of eliminating the characters who attempt to block a happy ending are all applicable to various Molière plays.

Gossman, Lionel. *Men and Masks: A Study of Molière*. Baltimore: Johns Hopkins University Press, 1963. In seven brilliant essays, five major plays are studied in detail, with particular emphasis on the issue of identity in Molière's characters. The last two chapters survey criticism of Molière in his own period and in subsequent centuries.

Mander, Gertrud. *Molière*. Translated by Diana Stone Peters. New York: Frederick Ungar, 1973. A book in the World Dramatists series, Mander's study is well organized and thorough. Sections are devoted to fourteen of the major plays. Includes a detailed and useful chronology, excerpts from reviews of twentieth century productions, and an extensive bibliography. Useful for the general reader.

Moore, Will G. *Molière: A New Criticism*. Oxford: Clarendon Press, 1949. This work is directed specifically toward the resolution of certain difficulties in the interpretations of Molière's plays. The approach is analytical, based on close study of the works themselves. Readers will also be interested in Moore's discussion of the several levels of comedy in Molière's plays. A major work in Molière criticism.

Nicholas, Brian. "Is Tartuffe a Comic Character?" *Modern Language Review* 75 (1980): 753-765. This essay replies to Moore's analysis of Molière's most controversial character. Nicholas' theories of the purpose and nature of satire in comic drama are the basis for his discussion of Tartuffe.

Rosemary M. Canfield Reisman

THEODOR MOMMSEN

Born: November 30, 1817; Garding, Schleswig
Died: November 1, 1903; Charlottenburg, Germany
Area of Achievement: Historiography
Contribution: Mommsen transformed the study of Roman history by correcting and supplementing the literary tradition of the ancient historians with the evidence of Latin inscriptions. Going beyond the usual focus on the generals and emperors, Mommsen championed study in all aspects of ancient societies.

Early Life

Now considered a German historian, Theodor Mommsen was born a Danish subject in Garding, Schleswig, on November 30, 1817. The eldest son of a poor Protestant minister, Mommsen was reared in Oldesloe, where he was educated by his father until 1834, when he attended school in Altona, outside Hamburg. In 1838, he entered the University of Kiel to study jurisprudence, which at the time involved a thorough grounding in Roman law. Under the influence of Friedrich Karl von Savigny's writings on the interrelationship of law and history, Mommsen's interest shifted to Roman history by the time he completed his doctorate in 1843. Equally influential were Otto Jahn's lectures on epigraphy, the study of inscriptions, which convinced Mommsen of the need for a complete collection of Latin inscriptions.

With a grant from the Danish government, Mommsen traveled through Italy from 1844 to 1847, collecting inscriptions and studying ancient Italian dialects. At the suggestion of the Italian scholar Bartolomeo Borghesi, he concentrated on Naples, and his subsequent monograph, *Inscriptions regni Neapolitani Latinae* (1852; inscriptions of the Latin Neopolitan kingdom), impressed scholars with its philological method and organization.

When Mommsen returned to take a post in Roman law at the University of Leipzig in 1848, Schleswig was agitating for union with Prussia. An ardent German patriot, Mommsen was caught up in the revolutionary nationalism, and his academic career was momentarily interrupted. Slightly injured in a street riot, Mommsen stayed behind when his brothers took up arms against the Danish crown, and instead he furthered the cause as editor and writer for the *Schleswig-Holsteinische Zeitung*.

In the reaction after the failed uprising, Mommsen was eventually dismissed from his teaching post in 1851. After a period of what he termed exile in Zürich, he returned to Germany in 1854 to teach at the University of Breslau, before settling permanently in Berlin, first with the Berlin Academy of Sciences and then with the University of Berlin.

Life's Work

Nineteenth century scholars, Germans in particular, applied scientific methods to the humanities in the belief that just as Charles Darwin had demonstrated the laws of natural selection, they could discover the laws of historical and social evolution. Unfortunately, some scholars were led by the evolutionary analogy, with its emphasis on the survival of the fittest, to dismiss questions of morality in their desire to establish the inevitability of historical development. This was especially true in Germany, where the nationalistic yearning for a unification had been building ever since Napoleon I's power over the German states was broken. Consequently, German scholars often found it easy to let supposedly objective science serve political ends.

Mommsen never overtly subverted scholarship to nationalism; however, the tendency was manifest in his most famous work, *Römische Geschichte* (1854-1856; *The History of Rome*, 1862-1866), which covers Roman history up to the end of the Republic. Never intending to write for a general audience, Mommsen was approached in 1851 by his future father-in-law, the publisher Carl Reimer, who convinced him to undertake the project.

Immediately famous, even notorious, *The History of Rome* was not only the first comprehensive survey of Roman history but also a passionate narrative of the rise and fall of the Republic, brought to life by Mommsen's vivid and partisan portraits of historical personalities. With a dynamic, journalism-influenced style, Mommsen drew on familiar political and historical incidents and presented even abstract ideas in concrete imagery to make Roman history accessible to a wide audience.

The History of Rome impressed the scholarly community with its rigorous questioning of the ancient historians, but it was faulted for not citing sources or acknowledging any possible differences in interpretation. Moreover, many believed that he went so far in his demythologizing that he falsely recast Roman history in terms of his biased perspective of German politics.

These critics feared that *The History of Rome*'s adulatory depiction of Julius Caesar as the savior of Rome dangerously glorified power and buttressed Prussian militarism. Despite a belief in the generally progressive and civilizing effect of the emergence of powers such as Rome or Germany, Mommsen was not authoritarian so much as elitist, believing that the best government was that of an intellectual aristocracy in support of an enlightened leader such as Caesar. Because the closest example in German history was Prussian leadership in the tradition of Frederick the Great, Mommsen initially supported Prussia's central role in German unification.

Yet when other Germans surrendered to, even welcomed, outright domination, masterfully managed by the German Chancellor Otto von Bismarck, Mommsen felt betrayed. He opposed the extralegal and self-interested ambitions of Bismarck in Germany and of Napoleon III in France, though *The History of Rome* was often used to justify their actions. Mommsen served in both the Prussian and German legislatures, where he resisted Germany's colonial and economic policies. When he denounced protectionism as a swindle, Mommsen was brought into court by Bismarck on a charge of libel. Though acquitted, Mommsen largely withdrew from politics after 1884.

It was in the calmer arena of the university that Mommsen made his more important though less famous contributions to scholarship. Mommsen's collection of Neapolitan inscriptions had made it obvious that he was the man to undertake a more comprehensive cataloging of all Latin inscriptions, a project already begun by the Berlin Academy. He was appointed editor in 1858 and worked on the project the rest of his life, demonstrating the highest standards of scholarly and organizational brilliance. To eliminate any possibility of forgery or error, he insisted on the examination of the actual inscriptions instead of secondhand reports. With the first volume of the monumental *Corpus inscriptionum Latinarum* (1863-1902; collection of Latin inscriptions), Mommsen transformed Roman historiography by providing it with an extensive factual basis. At the time of Mommsen's death, *Corpus inscriptionum Latinarum* comprised 130,000 inscriptions in fifteen volumes, six of which he edited himself.

Though this would have been the life's work of other men, Mommsen also reconstructed Roman law in *Römisches Staatsrecht* (1871-1888; Roman constitutional law) and *Römisches Strafrecht* (1899; Roman criminal law). In the tradition of Savigny, Mommsen examined Roman law not as an abstract system but as a cultural and historical development determined by power struggles in the Roman Republic and Empire.

Despite reiterated plans to continue *The History of Rome*, Mommsen did almost no work on a narrative history of the Empire. Instead, he published *Das Weltreich der Caesaren* (1885; *The Provinces of the Roman Empire from Caesar to Diocletian*, 1886), which, though termed a continuation of his *The History of Rome* and accessible to the nonscholar, is very different from the earlier work. Nonnarrative and nonpartisan, *The Provinces of the Roman Empire* is a study based on the Latin inscriptions gathered from the areas that were once under Roman domination, revealing the Empire to have been far more stable than the traditional focus on dynastic struggles suggested.

Over the years, Mommsen became a well-known character in Berlin. Active up to his death at eighty-five, he worked late each night but arrived at the university each morning at eight, even using the tram ride to read. Although he was neither a graceful man nor, with his shrill voice, a particularly good lecturer, he commanded absolute respect. Mesmerized by his piercing blue eyes and intellectual authority, his students sat in total silence as Mommsen raced through prepared lectures. Rigorous in his criticism, he was equally generous in his assistance to his former students and left a lasting legacy with the generation of scholars he trained to his own exacting standards of research. At a time when solitary labor was still normal for scholars, Mommsen contributed to many cooperative efforts, started several international journals, and helped found the International Association of Academies in 1901.

Said by some to be intolerant of equals, Mommsen was no recluse, surrounding himself with students, friends, and a large family. Marie Reimer, to whom Mommsen was married in 1854, bore him sixteen children and for nearly fifty years provided her husband with a comfortable and supportive domestic life.

Summary

Theodor Mommsen is universally acknowledged as one of the nineteenth century's most important historians. In his own lifetime, Mommsen's eminence was recognized when he was awarded the Nobel Prize in 1902. Because so much of his work dealt with matters of interest only to scholars, however, his fame is overshadowed by that of the great narrative historians, such as Leopold von Ranke.

With his amazing capacity for work, Mommsen put his name to more than a thousand published articles in his nearly sixty-year career. Highly regarded for an imaginative handling of voluminous statistics and detail as well as memorable epigrams and pithy summations, most of Mommsen's writing is still of interest mainly to specialists. Except for his *The History of Rome*, he wrote little narrative history, focusing instead on gathering and interpreting the inscriptions on stone and coins left by the Romans and correcting the less reliable written tradition. The *Corpus inscriptionum Latinarum*, which continues to grow, is indispensable for Roman studies, as are his studies of Roman law; yet much of his other work was superseded even in his own lifetime as others built on his pioneering work and methodology.

Throughout his career, Mommsen represented the very best in humanistic scholarship. Dedicated to putting all studies on the most rigorous scientific footing, Mommsen never lost sight of the human element, which transcends national and racial considerations. Despite the controversy still surrounding *The History of Rome*, Mommsen's positive estimation of Caesar is shared by most scholars today, and his animated style exerted a beneficial influence on later German writing. His emphasis on the nonliterary sources encouraged scholars to shift their attention away from dynastic history to many areas of ancient societies. Welcoming innovative ideas and methods regardless of their political or personal consequences, Mommsen was always more interested in forwarding scholarship than in preserving his preeminence.

Bibliography

Broughton, T. Robert S. Introduction to *The Provinces of the Roman Empire*, by Theodor Mommsen. Chicago: University of Chicago Press, 1968. Provides biography with an overview of Mommsen's major works and a discussion of reasons for his not finishing *The History of Rome*. Examines

Mommsen's innovative scholarship and traces his influence on historiography into the mid-twentieth century. Contains a bibliography.

Gooch, George Peabody. "Mommsen and Roman Studies." In *History and Historians in the Nineteenth Century.* London: Longmans, Green, 1913. Chronological overview of Mommsen's life and his major work, detailing his many interests and activities along with contributions to the work of others. Conceding Mommsen's historical biases and tendency to esteem the victorious too highly, Gooch ranks Mommsen along with Ranke for demythologizing Roman history and encouraging new trends in scholarship. Contains valuable bibliographical footnotes.

Haverfield, F. "Theodor Mommsen." *The English Historical Review* 19 (January, 1904): 80-89. An obituary assessing Mommsen's character and contribution. In a review of Mommsen's main works, Haverfield analyzes the historian's remarkable combination of imagination, hard work, and organizational brilliance. Stresses Mommsen's pioneering use of inscriptions and cooperative projects in scholarship.

Kelsey, Francis W. "Theodore Mommsen." *Classical Journal* 14 (January, 1919): 224-236. A comprehensive biographical and character sketch with attention to the influences of Mommsen's teachers and colleagues. Argues that Mommsen was not so much an innovator as a brilliant and diligent realizer of the innovations of others. Details Mommsen's helpfulness as a teacher and includes a portrait of his happy domestic life.

Thompson, James Westfall, and Bernard J. Holm. *A History of Historical Writing.* Vol. 2. New York: Macmillan, 1942. Contends that through mastery of scholarship and a scientific approach to evidence, Mommsen revolutionized the study of Roman history. Examines Mommsen's elitist views and adulation of Caesar, dismissing their connection to German militarism and anti-Semitism. Includes a biographical sketch, a physical description, and a good bibliography.

Philip McDermott

CLAUDE MONET

Born: November 14, 1840; Paris, France
Died: December 5, 1926; Giverny, France
Area of Achievement: Art
Contribution: Monet is central to the development of Impressionist painting
in the 1870's. In the 1890's, Monet developed the concept of multiple
views of one subject, and in the 1940's and 1950's the abstract Impres-
sionism of Monet's late water lily paintings provided a stimulus for the
American abstract expressionists.

Early Life
Although Claude Monet was born in Paris, he grew up on the Normandy
coast at Le Havre. Yet the first intimations of his future vocation came not
with landscape paintings but with a series of caricatures of local personalities
which earned for him a considerable reputation by age sixteen. His direction
changed after meeting the marine painter Eugène Boudin in 1858. Boudin,
who was already a devotee of working outdoors, introduced Monet to plein
air painting, which would eventually become the touchstone of the Impressionist landscape approach.

Monet used the proceeds from his lucrative caricature business to finance
his first art studies in Paris in 1859, where he met the future Impressionist
Camille Pissarro at the Académie Suisse. A photograph of Monet at age
twenty suggests a romantic sensitivity, but later photographs portray a more
rugged, stockier individual, with a square-cut, curly beard emphasizing his
square face. Monet's studies were interrupted in 1861 by obligatory military
service, but in 1862 he became ill and was sent home, after which his
parents bought an exemption from his remaining service.

Returning to Paris, Monet enrolled in the studio of the academic painter
Charles Gleyre. His year there was notable only because three of his future
colleagues and friends, Pierre-Auguste Renoir, Alfred Sisley, and Frédéric
Bazille, were fellow students; all four quickly became disillusioned with the
academic curriculum. Henceforth they developed on their own, discovering
for themselves the Forest of Fontainebleau and the Barbizon landscapists
who had worked there since the 1830's.

In the spring of 1865, Monet had two large landscapes of the Normandy
coast accepted by the salon (the official government-sponsored exhibitions),
achieving considerable success with them, as well as with the figure painting
sent the next year, although some reviewers confused Monet with the slightly
older painter Édouard Manet, who was creating scandals with the exhibition
of such precedent-shattering paintings as *Déjeuner sur l'herbe* (1863; luncheon on the grass). Manet's revolutionary technique, which aimed, by the
elimination of halftones, to produce the effect of forms seen in a blaze of

light, was an additional stimulus toward Monet's development as an Impressionist.

Life's Work

Those early successes at the salon were almost the only official ones for Monet. As he became more individualistic, his paintings were increasingly refused by the tradition-bound salon juries. The first refusal was in 1867 of a major work, *Women in the Garden*, which has since been hailed as the first large whole-figure composition to be painted entirely outdoors. Though not a true Impressionist painting, since the treatment of light is static, it represents a major milestone in the stages leading toward the development of Impressionism.

The Impressionist movement actually began when Monet and Renoir painted together in the summer of 1869 at a suburban pleasure spot on the Seine, la Grenouillère, where the moving current of the river sparked the new approach and vocabulary of Impressionism, with its interest in transitory effects of light, color, and atmosphere. To capture these effects, the painters developed a broken technique of swift, small, separate strokes of pure color. Monet and Renoir also began developing the so-called rainbow palette, eliminating earth tones and bitumens to enhance the effects of prismatically refracted light. Throughout the 1870's, this interest in capturing the moment was of paramount interest for the Impressionists. To achieve the effect they wanted, they required the plein air approach and subjects which lent themselves to a casual treatment, such as riverbank scenes, fields, the railway, and the crowded, newly created great boulevards of Paris.

In 1870, Monet went to London to escape the Franco-Prussian War and had a chance to study at first hand the paintings of John Constable and J. M. W. Turner, whose interests in atmosphere prefigured those of the Impressionists. Upon his return, Monet moved with his family to Argenteuil, a Paris suburb on the Seine, where many of his most famous Impressionist landscape paintings were produced. Although Monet and his friends were now mature artists, the problem with salon juries did not improve, and the precarious financial situation of most of them was exacerbated by the depression that began in 1873. Therefore, in 1874, Monet, Pissarro, Renoir, and Edgar Degas executed a plan they had been considering for some time: to bypass the salon altogether and mount their own juryless Exhibition, to which each would contribute a sum for expenses. Thirty artists, not all of them Impressionists, took part in what has come to be known as the First Impressionist Exhibition, which was held from April 15 to May 15. There would be eight Impressionist exhibitions, the last one held in 1886; Monet took part in all but three. While at first the exhibitions were greeted mainly with derision (indeed, the name "Impressionism" comes from a sneering remark in a satirical review by the critic Louis Leroy, commenting on a Monet painting entitled

Impression, Sunrise), this approach finally proved to be the most viable way for avante-garde artists to get their work shown.

Monet painted many views of the St. Lazare station in 1877, showing eight of them together at the Third Impressionist Exhibition that April; the simultaneous showing may have provided the germ for his later series paintings. In the early 1880's, all the Impressionists went through a crisis in reaction to all the criticism of "carelessness" and "formlessness." While Monet does not seem to have reacted as much as Renoir, he was nevertheless affected by the criticism and attempted henceforth a more fully actualized treatment.

In 1890, Monet began to paint his first deliberate series of paintings: views of haystacks. These were produced at different seasons of the year and from different points of view, with different aspects of light, but in 1891 he showed fifteen of them in an exhibition at the dealer Paul Durand-Ruel's; the series proved to be surprisingly successful. In 1892 and 1893, Monet painted the famous sequences of views of the façade of Rouen Cathedral, in which his serial procedure is fully developed. For these paintings, Monet worked on several canvases during the course of one day, moving from one to another as the light changed. To appreciate fully this serial progression, one must see several of the canvases in sequence.

After 1900, the majority of Monet's paintings were done in and around Giverny, on a tributary of the Seine halfway between Paris and Rouen, where he had lived since 1883. Monet gradually acquired the status of the dean of living painters, and Giverny became a mecca, especially for two types of visitors: young American Impressionists and young Symbolist writers, such as Gustave Geffroy, who became Monet's biographer, and Octave Mirbeau, who elucidated one of the major reasons for Symbolist interest in later Monet works when he praised Monet for expressing the inexpressible and seizing the unseizable. Perhaps even more significant were Monet's numerous contacts with the great Symbolist poet Stéphane Mallarmé, beginning in the mid-1880's.

Once Monet had created his Japanese water garden on his Giverny property, he began, in 1899, to produce the stunning series of paintings of the pond that formed his chief endeavor in the twentieth century. Most of the sequences show the surface of the pond, its water lilies, its overhanging willows, and its reflections. These paintings, which Monet called "waterscapes," tend increasingly toward a form of abstract Impressionism, partly because of Monet's treatment of the entire surface of the canvas, which negates the idea of focus, and partly because of his elimination of the horizon line in his paintings after 1905, which meant that he painted the surface of the pond only, providing no clear sense of direction. A further impetus toward abstraction may have been provided by Monet's increasing eye problems (cataracts in both eyes were diagnosed in 1912; in 1923, he underwent a partially successful operation on his right eye), which necessitated greater breadth of technique and the use of stronger color. Yet these bold, free strokes are still intended to record the specific nuances of Monet's visual impressions of light and color.

The greatest of all the water lily series is the huge cycle housed in two large oval rooms in the Orangerie in Paris, a project originally suggested to Monet by Georges Clemenceau during World War I and intended as a donation to the state. Much of the painting was done during World War I, but Monet continued to rework and revise the sequence until close to his death in 1926. The cycle was dedicated in May of 1927, a fitting tribute to one of the most extraordinary artists of the modern era. The viewer, standing in the middle of each oval space engulfed by the huge size of the panels, is himself put into the picture. It is, as André Masson described it in 1952, the "Sistine Chapel of Impressionism . . . one of the summits of French art."

Summary

Through the years, Claude Monet has come to be considered the leading Impressionist painter, a position which is strengthened by the fact that he, unlike Renoir or Pissarro, who had periods when they retreated from the Impressionist approach, remained largely faithful to the Impressionist goal of transcribing every nuance of changing optical sensations for the whole of his exceptionally long career, which spanned a full sixty years. This mammoth oeuvre, consisting of approximately two thousand paintings, was not codified until the 1970's and 1980's in a definitive four-volume *catalogue raisonné* by Daniel Wildenstein, *Claude Monet, biographie et catalogue raisonné* (1974-1985). Monet's vision remained remarkably consistent throughout the developments in his style.

It is, rather, outside judgments that have varied: Supporters in the 1870's stressed the element of direct observation; Symbolist champions of the late 1880's and 1890's sensed an affinity with their aims in the infinitely nuanced transcription of his series paintings. In the wake of formalist movements of the early twentieth century, Impressionism was often judged as a short-lived, limited phenomenon and late Monet paintings, in particular, as a dead end. That was before the large "action paintings" of artists such as Jackson Pollock suddenly revealed the relevance of the late Monet works. Somewhat later, the interpretations of social historians stressed the contemporaneity of Impressionist themes in the 1870's, such as the railroad, and questioned the famous judgment of Paul Cézanne, who became one of the foremost challengers of Impressionism, that "Monet is only an eye . . . but what an eye." Most scholars, however, continue to stress the aspect of observation over interpretation, emphasizing that the Impressionists never comment on what they observe. In Monet's case, the central importance of his essentially visual focus is amply supported by many of his own statements. Whether one's interest in

Monet centers on pure observation, on social concerns, or on the affinities with Symbolism, Monet's central position in the late nineteenth century seems secure, and Giverny, refurbished and restored, has once again become a mecca for pilgrims.

Bibliography
Belloli, Andrew P. A., ed. *A Day in the Country: Impressionism and the French Landscape.* Los Angeles: Los Angeles County Museum of Art, 1984. This scholarly exhibition catalog provides a considerable treatment of Monet which enables one to see his work in the context of the Impressionist movement. Consists of a series of articles on different aspects of Impressionism, notes on each of the paintings exhibited, a bibliography, and an index.
House, John. *Monet: Nature into Art.* New Haven, Conn.: Yale University Press, 1986. An excellent, detailed study of aspects of Monet's themes, composition, techniques, and the like, as well as a discussion of the evolution of his series concept. Includes a chronology, footnotes, bibliography, and index. Amply illustrated.
Isaacson, Joel. *Claude Monet: Observation and Reflection.* Oxford, England: Phaidon Books, 1978. This study consists of a succinct essay chronicling the major phases of Monet's career and stylistic development, followed by individual notes on each of the plates, a chronology, a bibliographical note, and an index.
Rewald, John. *The History of Impressionism.* Rev. ed. New York: Museum of Modern Art, 1973. This exhaustively detailed chronological treatment of Impressionism remains the most essential work on the movement. The treatment of Monet is interwoven throughout the volume to give a thorough presentation of his place in the Impressionist group. Excellent footnotes, a chronology, a superlative chronological bibliography, and an extensive index are included. Contains many plates.
Stuckey, Charles F., ed. *Monet: A Retrospective.* New York: Park Lane, 1985. Consists of seventy-seven selections from a series of books and articles on Monet (dating from 1865 to 1957), a number of them eyewitness accounts, some translated from the French for the first time. Includes an index and plates.

Dorathea K. Beard

GASPARD MONGE

Born: May 10, 1746; Beaune, France
Died: July 28, 1818; Paris, France
Areas of Achievement: Mathematics, chemistry, physics, and engineering
Contribution: Monge founded modern descriptive geometry (essential to mechanical and architectural drawing) and revitalized analytic geometry (essential to many fields of physics and mathematics). An enthusiastic supporter of the French Revolution, he helped establish the metric system and the École Polytechnique, an important engineering school.

Early Life

Gaspard Monge was born on May 10, 1746, in Beaune, a small town 166 miles southeast of Paris. He was the eldest son of Jacques Monge, an itinerant peddler and knife-grinder, and Jeanne Rousseaux, a woman of humble Burgundian origin. Jacques deeply respected education and sent his three sons to the local school run by the Oratorian religious order and to their Collège de la Trinité in Lyons. Although all three brothers eventually made successful careers in mathematics, Gaspard was clearly the genius. He was the golden boy of the Oratorians, and he regularly won academic prizes and became, at the age of sixteen, a physics teacher at Lyons.

In the summer of 1764, during a vacation to Beaune, Monge used surveying instruments of his own invention and construction to make a detailed map of the town. A military officer who later saw the map was so impressed by the boy's ability that he recommended Monge to the commandant of the military school at Mézières. Created in 1748, the École Royale du Génie had become a prestigious institution for the training of officers, who derived mostly from the nobility. Upon his arrival at Mézières in 1765, Monge learned that he would not study with the officers but would be trained as a draftsman to do the routine work of military surveying. Within a year, however, he had an opportunity to show that his mathematical skills were vastly superior to those of the officers. He was assigned the problem of computing the best places to locate guns in a proposed fortress at Metz. At the time, the calculation of positions shielded from enemy firepower in intricate fortifications was a long and arduous arithmetic procedure, but Monge developed a geometric method that obtained results so quickly that the commandant was initially skeptical. Upon detailed inspection by skilled officers, the advantages of Monge's invention, which formed the basis of what later came to be known as descriptive geometry, became evident. In fact, Monge's method was so highly valued that it was preserved as a military secret for twenty-five years.

Life's Work

Monge spent the first fifteen years of his career at the military academy of Mézières, where he was at first répétiteur to the professor of mathematics, then a teacher of mathematics, and finally a royal professor of mathematics and physics. Through his excellent teaching, he was able to improve the French engineering corps and influence several students who went on to brilliant military careers. His lectures on descriptive geometry (then called stereotomy) allowed him to develop his ideas about perspective, the properties of surfaces, and the theory of machines. Descriptive geometry is basically a way to represent three-dimensional figures on a plane. Albrecht Dürer, the German painter and engraver, had used the idea of orthogonal projection of the human figure on mutually perpendicular planes in the early sixteenth century, and in 1738 A. F. Frézier had suggested a method of representing solid objects on plane diagrams, but Monge developed descriptive geometry into a special branch of mathematics. He systematized its principles, developed its basic theorems, and applied this knowledge to problems of military engineering, mechanical drawing, and architecture.

Documents from his Mézières period reveal that Monge did extensive research in several areas of mathematics. He wrote memoirs on various curves and studied their radii of curvature. He analyzed evolutes (the loci of centers of curvature for a given curve) and systematically applied the calculus, in particular partial differential equations, to his investigations of the curvature of surfaces. In 1775, he presented to the French Academy of Sciences in Paris a paper on a developable surface, that is, a surface that can be flattened on a plane without distortion, a subject of great interest to mapmakers.

During the middle 1770's, Monge's interests began to switch from mathematics to physics and chemistry. In physics, he helped develop the material theory of heat (he called the heat substance "caloric"). This theory was useful to physicists and chemists in the eighteenth century (it was replaced by the kinetic theory of heat in the nineteenth century). Working alone at Mézières and with Antoine Lavoisier on his trips to Paris, Monge carried out experiments on the expansion, solution, and reaction of various gases. To enable him to carry out his research in chemistry and physics better, Monge established a well-equipped laboratory in the late 1770's at the École Royale du Génie.

In 1777, Monge married a twenty-year-old widow, Catherine (Huart) Horbon, for whose honor he had earlier tried to fight a duel with one of her rejected suitors. The couple had three daughters. Since she owned a forge, Catherine had an indirect influence on her husband's interest in metallurgy. Supervising its operation led Monge to study the smelting and properties of metals. His outstanding work in mathematics and the physical sciences led to his election to the Academy of Sciences in 1780. This honor forced him to divide his time between Paris and Mézières. During his stays in Paris, he taught hydraulics (the science and technology of fluids) at the Louvre, and during his time at Mézières he taught engineering to the military officers and prepared memoirs on physics, chemistry, and mathematics for presentation at the Academy of Sciences.

Monge's researches in chemistry consumed so much of his time that he arranged for a substitute to deliver many of his lectures at Mézières. In the summer of 1783, he carried out his famous experiments on the synthesis of water from its component elements. Monge mixed hydrogen and oxygen gases (then called inflammable air and dephlogisticated air) in a closed glass vessel and ignited the explosive reaction between the gases by an electric spark from a voltaic battery. He found that the weight of the pure water he obtained was very nearly equal to the weights of the two gases. These studies became part of the so-called water controversy over the first discoverer of the compound nature of water. Monge deserves credit for showing quantitatively that water is composed of two elemental gases, but he did not formally publish until 1786. Henry Cavendish, the English physicist who published his results in 1784, showed that water is produced when inflammable air is burned in dephlogisticated air, but he interpreted his experiments in terms of the confusing phlogiston theory. Lavoisier correctly interpreted the reaction as the oxidation of hydrogen.

In the fall of 1783, Monge accepted yet another responsibility in Paris— the examiner of naval candidates. For a while, he tried to continue his professorship at Mézières along with this new position, but this proved impossible; in December, 1784, he resigned from the school where he had spent nearly twenty years of his life. His post as examiner also required him to make tours of inspection of naval schools outside Paris, and this enabled him to reform the teaching of science and technology in the provinces. His time in Paris was spent participating in the activities of the academy and conducting research in chemistry, physics, and mathematics. During the 1780's, he did important work on the composition of nitrous acid, the liquefaction of sulfur dioxide, the nature of different types of iron and steel, and the action of electricity on carbon dioxide gas. In these chemical researches, he interpreted his results through Lavoisier's new oxygen theory rather than the outdated phlogiston theory. In physics, he did research on the double refraction of Iceland spar (a transparent calcite); he also studied capillary action. In mathematics, he continued his work on curved surfaces and partial differential equations.

When the French Revolution began in 1789, Monge was one of its most ardent supporters. His humble birth and his negative experiences with aristocrats gave him firsthand knowledge of the poverty of the masses and the corruption of the *ancien régime*. In 1791, he served on the committee that established the metric system. In 1792, he became Minister of the Navy and played a significant role in organizing the defense of France against the counterrevolutionary armies. In 1793, he voted in favor of the death of King Louis XVI. After all this, he was still bitterly attacked for not being revolutionary enough. These attacks forced him to resign from his ministerial post. Nevertheless, he continued to support the republic, and as a member of the committee on arms and munitions he worked hard to improve the extraction and purification of saltpeter and the construction and operation of powderworks in Paris and in the provinces. He also became involved in establishing a new system of scientific and technical education. It was during his teaching at the short-lived École Normale that his work on descriptive geometry was finally published.

Monge was very much concerned about preserving the nation's cultural and intellectual heritage during this time of revolutionary turmoil. He was convinced of the value of a national school for training civil and military engineers. As an influential member of the Commission of Public Works, he helped institute the École Polytechnique in 1794. Monge became an important administrator and popular teacher at this school. His textbook on analytic geometry, which appeared in 1795, was used in the course he taught on the application of algebra to geometry. In pursuing the correspondence between algebraic analysis and geometry, Monge recognized that families of surfaces could be described both geometrically and analytically. He founded a school of geometers at the École Polytechnique, who would exert a powerful influence on the development of mathematics in the nineteenth century.

The last stage of Monge's career began in 1796 and was dominated by his fascination with—some have called it his mesmerization by—Napoleon I. Monge had actually met Napoleon earlier, when he cordially welcomed the young artillery officer from Corsica to the military school at Mézières. Though Monge had forgotten this meeting, Napoleon remembered and called Monge to Italy as a member of the committee supervising the selection of the paintings, sculptures, and other valuables that the victorious army was to bring back to France. Although this looting disturbed Monge's conscience, he accepted it as a way to finance Napoleon's military campaigns. Monge's duties took him to many cities throughout Italy and gave him the opportunity to become Napoleon's confidant and friend.

In the fall of 1797, Monge returned to Paris to begin his new post as director of the École Polytechnique, but his stay was brief, for Napoleon called him back to Rome to conduct a political inquiry. Monge also participated in the creation of the Republic of Rome and in the preparations for Napoleon's Egyptian adventure. Monge arrived in Cairo on July 21, 1798, the day after Napoleon's victory at the Battle of the Pyramids. Napoleon made Monge president of the Institut d'Égypte, modeled on the Institut de France, the revolutionary organization intended to replace the royal academies. Monge was heavily involved in many of the projects of the Institut d'Égypte. He was also a companion of Napoleon on a trip to the Suez region, on his disastrous Syrian expedition, and on his secret voyage back to France in 1799.

Upon his return to Paris, Napoleon rewarded Monge for his services. These favors continued throughout the period of the consulate as well as during Napoleon's reign as emperor. Monge was given more powerful administrative responsibilities along with extensive land grants. Napoleon created Monge Count of Péluse, an honor he accepted gratefully, although he had once voted to abolish all titles. Napoleon also named Monge a senator, and by accepting the position Monge became publicly and irrevocably tied to Napoleon. A representation of Monge at this time depicts him in a powdered wig, looking slightly uncomfortable in the trappings of nobility. His strong and stocky build seems awkwardly confined by the expensive clothes, but his piercing eyes radiate intelligence and confidence, showing him to be a man ready to meet any challenge.

During these Napoleonic years, Monge divided his time among his duties in the senate, at the École Polytechnique, and in the Academy of Sciences. At the École Polytechnique, Monge influenced many young French mathematicians in various kinds of geometry—synthetic, analytic, and infinitesimal. Monge's great contribution to synthetic geometry was his *Géométrie descriptive* (1798; *An Elementary Treatise on Descriptive Geometry*, 1851), a summation of his life's work in descriptive geometry and a book that proved useful not only to mathematicians but also to artists, architects, military engineers, carpenters, and stonecutters. In 1801, Monge published a book on analytic geometry that revealed how useful geometry could be for algebra, and vice versa. In the same year, he published an expanded version of his lectures on infinitesimal geometry, his favorite subject, in which he used ordinary and partial differential equations to study complex surfaces and solids.

Monge's health began to decline in 1809, when he stopped teaching at the École Polytechnique. His health worsened during the autumn of 1812, when Napoleon's army suffered great losses on its retreat from Moscow. Monge deliberately fled Paris and did not participate in the senate session of 1814 that dethroned Napoleon. Seeing Napoleon as the standard-bearer of the revolutionary ideals of liberty, equality, and fraternity, Monge refused to condemn him, and during the so-called Hundred Days in 1815, when Napoleon tried to recover his throne, Monge pledged his allegiance to the emperor, remaining loyal even after Napoleon's defeat at Waterloo and his abdication. When the Bourbons were restored to the French monarchy in 1815, Monge, who refused to modify his anti-Royalism, was deprived of all of his honors and positions, even his membership in the Academy of Sciences. The last years of his life were filled with further humiliations and greater physical sufferings. Following a stroke, he died on July 28, 1818. Many students at the École Polytechnique asked to attend his funeral, but the king refused permission. Although they observed the king's refusal, the next day the students marched *en masse* to the cemetery and laid a wreath on the grave of their beloved teacher.

Summary

Gaspard Monge's reputation derives from his work in geometry, and there is no doubt that he was responsible for the revival of interest in geometry that occurred in the late eighteenth and early nineteenth centuries. As a result of his inspiration, a golden age of modern geometry began, and his methods flourished first in France and later throughout Europe, blazing the way for such nineteenth century mathematicians as Carl Friedrich Gauss and Georg Friedrich Bernhard Riemann. Though Monge was not strictly the inventor of descriptive geometry, he was the first to elaborate its principles and methods and to detail its applications in mathematics and technology. He also made valuable contributions to analytic and infinitesimal (or differential) geometry.

Despite his reputation as a geometer, Monge's accomplishments were actually much broader. Besides his exceptional sense of spatial relations, he was also an insightful analyst who could transform geometric problems into algebraic relations. For Monge, geometry and analysis supported each other, and in every problem he emphasized the close connection between the mathematical and practical aspects. His treatment of partial differential equations has a geometrical flavor, and he believed that problems involving differential equations could be solved more readily when visualized geometrically. On the other hand, some problems involving complex surfaces led to interesting differential equations. Many historians of mathematics ascribe to Monge the revival of the alliance between algebra and geometry. René Descartes may have created analytic geometry, but it was Monge and his students who made it a vital field.

Monge was a Renaissance man in the Age of the Enlightenment. He possessed a broad combination of talents: He was a creative mathematician, an excellent chemist, and a talented physicist and engineer. Furthermore, he was an adroit politician, a capable administrator, and an inspiring teacher. His skill as a teacher can be seen in his distinguished pupils, some who continued on paths he had opened and others who created new paths. Charles Dupin applied Monge's methods to the theory of surfaces. Victor Poncelet, the most original of Monge's students, became the founder of projective geometry. Jean Hachette and Jean Baptiste Biot developed the analytic geometry of conics and quadrics.

Throughout his career, Monge was interested in the practical consequences of his work in science and mathematics. At Mézières and at the École Polytechnique, he was interested in the structure and functioning of machines. He took his work on such practical problems as windmill vane design as seriously as the highly abstract problems of differential geometry. He believed that technical progress helped to augment human happiness, and, since technical progress depended on the development of science and mathematics, he supported France's efforts to improve education in these basic fields. In his unified view, science freed man's intellect with the truth about the world, and this was the only valid way to social progress.

Bibliography
Bell, Eric T. *Men of Mathematics*. New York: Simon & Schuster, 1937. Bell, who spent most of his teaching career at the California Institute of Technology, was a skilled writer in unraveling the mysteries of mathematics for the general reader. In this book, he uses the lives of the men who created modern mathematics to explain some of the most important ideas animating great areas of mathematics as it exists today. Monge and Joseph Fourier are treated together in a chapter entitled "Friends of an Emperor." Bell's book is widely available, very readable, and assumes only a modicum of mathematical knowledge.
Boyer, Carl B. *History of Analytic Geometry*. New York: Scripta Mathematica, 1956. Reprint. Princeton Junction, N.J.: Scholar's Bookshelf, 1988. An important study of the development of analytic geometry from ancient times to the nineteenth century. Boyer's approach is conceptual rather than biographical, but Monge's work on analytic geometry is extensively analyzed. Boyer's emphasis is on the history of mathematical ideas, and some knowledge of algebra and geometry is assumed.
_____. *A History of Mathematics*. New York: John Wiley & Sons, 1968. A textbook for college students at the junior or senior level. Though he assumes an understanding of calculus and analytic geometry, much of the material is accessible to readers with weaker mathematical backgrounds. Boyer analyzes both Monge's contributions to mathematics and his involvement in politics. The book contains extensive bibliographies after each chapter and a good general bibliography following the final chapter.
Kline, Morris. *Mathematical Thought from Ancient to Modern Times*. New York: Oxford University Press, 1972. Monge's contributions to descriptive geometry and partial differential equations are extensively discussed. Kline's book is aimed at professional and prospective mathematicians, and a knowledge of advanced mathematics is necessary to understand his analysis of Monge's contributions.
Partington, J. R. *A History of Chemistry*. Vol. 3. London: Macmillan, 1962. This volume, dealing with the seventeenth, eighteenth, and early nineteenth centuries, contains an excellent analysis of chemistry in France during the time of Monge's career. Discusses Monge's contributions to chemistry in depth, with extensive references to original documents, some of which are translated into English. Accessible to the general reader.
Taton, René, ed. *The Beginnings of Modern Science*. Translated by A. J. Pomerans. New York: Basic Books, 1964. This work, the third volume in Taton's History of Science series, covers the period from 1450 to 1800.

Monge's contributions to geometry and chemistry are discussed in their historical contexts, but this book is best used as a reference rather than for narrative reading.

Robert J. Paradowski

MICHEL DE MONTAIGNE

Born: February 28, 1533; Château de Montaigne, Périgord, France
Died: September 13, 1592; Château de Montaigne, Périgord, France
Areas of Achievement: Philosophy, politics, and literature
Contribution: In an age of violent religious and political struggles, Montaigne mediated for tolerance. His gift to literature was the invention of the essay.

Early Life

Michel Eyquem de Montaigne was born in his father's château in Périgord, a French county east and north of Bordeaux, which became a part of France in 1607. His father, Pierre Eyquem, held many important posts, including that of Mayor of Bordeaux, and afforded an unusual model of religious tolerance by heading a Catholic family that included a Protestant wife of Spanish and Jewish blood and two Protestant children.

Montaigne dearly loved his father, who was responsible for his receiving a gentle and cultured life. At age six, he was sent to the finest school in Bordeaux, where he completed the twelve-year course in seven years. Sometime during the next eight years, he very likely studied law.

From 1557 to 1570, Montaigne was a councillor in the Bordeaux Parlement and took numerous trips to Paris. During this period, he made a close and erudite friend, Étienne de La Boétie, who in the remaining four years of his life came to be more important to Montaigne than anyone else and influenced Montaigne throughout his life. It was La Boétie's stoic acceptance of suffering and his courageous death, at which Montaigne was present despite the danger of contagion, that turned Montaigne toward Stoicism and probably inspired him to begin writing.

In 1565, Montaigne married Françoise de La Chassaigne. He seldom mentions her in his writing. Of his six children, only one, Léonor, survived childhood.

About 1567, Montaigne's father had him translate a work which was strongly opposed to Protestantism and atheism: *Theologia naturalis, sive Liber creaturarum* (1485; the book of creatures: or natural theology), written in medieval Latin by a fifteenth century Spaniard, Raymond Sebond. His father, although terminally ill, arranged for the publication of the translation.

After his father's death, Michel became Lord of Montaigne, owner of the château and the estate, and at thirty-eight years of age retired to what he hoped would be a life of quiet study and composition. Much of his time was spent in the tower, which he asked to be added to his castle, and which even his wife was forbidden to enter. There he wrote his life's work, *Essais* (1580, 1588, 1595; *The Essays*, 1603), which was placed on the Index in 1676 but was viewed favorably by the Vatican in Montaigne's day.

Life's Work

Over a period of thirty years, Montaigne dealt with every conceivable aspect of man's life by describing in detail his own thoughts, beliefs, experiences, and habits of living. Nothing was too abstruse to be tackled or too insignificant to be mentioned. His essay titles range from "Sur des vers de Virgile" ("On Certain Verses of Virgil") to "Des coches" ("Of Coaches"). His early essays were compilations of views followed by a brief moral, often showing the influence of Seneca the Younger or Plutarch, both of whom he admired immensely. These were followed by what is called his skeptical period, during which he coined his motto: "What do I know?" The years from 1578 onward are termed his Epicurean period, wherein he endeavored to find his own nature and to follow its dictates. His hero during this period was Socrates, and life was a great adventure to be lived as happily as possible, with due regard for the rights of others and guided by common sense. He counseled moderation in all things, freedom with self-control, and honesty and courage.

In the essay "De la prœsumption" ("About Presumption"), Montaigne describes himself as below average height but strong and well-set, with a face not fat but full. A portrait of him in the Condé Museum at Chantilly depicts a handsome man with regular features, fine eyes, short-cropped hair, a small mustache, and a neat beard. Evidently he was not given to vanity. He enjoyed horseback riding, travel, and conversation with intelligent men. He also enjoyed the company of his "covenant daughter," Marie de Gournay, who became his literary executrix.

After Montaigne's retirement, all of his time was not spent in seclusion: Between 1572 and 1576, he attempted to mediate between his friend Henry of Navarre (later Henry IV) and the extremist Catholics of the Holy League. At the accession of Henry III in 1576, Montaigne was made a Gentleman of the Bedchamber, an office that gave access to the king without requiring residence at court. His disgust at the excesses of the Wars of Religion gave him a strong distaste for government, and, while he loved the city of Paris, he avoided the royal court.

In 1580, Montaigne journeyed to take the waters at Lucca on the west coast of Italy. He hoped, but probably did not really believe, that the baths could cure his recurring misery caused by a kidney stone. Accompanied by his younger brother, two nobles, and a secretary, he left on horseback with no planned itinerary.

En route to the baths, he visited Paris, Switzerland, and Germany. In Rome, he was declared a citizen of that city, an honor which he greatly coveted. During his second stay in Lucca, he learned to his dismay that he had been elected Mayor of Bordeaux. He tried to refuse the responsibility but finally capitulated and arrived home after an absence of seventeen months.

Montaigne served two terms as mayor, from 1581 to 1585, and without showing undue zeal managed to initiate some reforms that included improving the lot of foundling children and imprisoned women and helping the poor by refusing to allow the rich to be exempt from taxation. He showed his concern for education by improving the Collège des Jésuites and also his own old school, the Collège de Guyenne. He left office somewhat ignominiously, tendering his resignation outside the city, which was at that time stricken by the plague.

Although no longer mayor, Montaigne was unable to avoid for long his involvement in the turbulent political situation. After a peaceful year at home working on *The Essays*, he found his unprotected estate overrun by soldiers and himself suspect to both the Catholics and the Protestants. In early 1588, he was sent to Paris on a secret mission to Henry III from Henry of Navarre. En route, he was detained by Protestants and a few months later found himself briefly imprisoned in the Bastille by the Catholics. After nearly a year spent in following the king from Paris to Chartres to Rouen and attending the Estates-General at Blois, Montaigne returned home and helped to keep Bordeaux loyal to the king. In his remaining years, he continued to add passages to *The Essays*. There is no eyewitness account of his death, but numerous contemporaries claim that he died peacefully while hearing Mass in his room.

Summary

Michel de Montaigne's writing style is vivacious and strong, with unexpected images, picturesque details, and often ironic humor. He reaches his highest level when he discusses the interdependence of mind and matter; modern psychologists and even psychiatrists might well claim him as their forefather. It is said that Sigmund Freud was interested in *The Essays*. Perhaps it is the surprising intimacy that Montaigne creates that is the most novel characteristic of his work: The reader believes that he knows the author better than he knows his closest friends or his family and maybe better than he knows himself. This kind of writing was new to literature.

In politics and in religion, Montaigne was opposed to change; his aim was peace, and he worked toward that end. Despite personal reservations, he remained a loyal subject of the Crown and a practicing Catholic, proclaiming that one ought to accept the government of one's country and its religion.

In education, Montaigne was centuries ahead of his time: In his essay "De l'institution des enfants" (on children's schools), he advocated training a child to be an efficient human being by exposing him not to pedants but to men of all social stations. The child must be taught to observe and to judge for himself.

In literature, Montaigne established the great principle of the seventeenth century: respect for and imitation of the classics. He insisted that the only subject suitable for man's study is man himself. There is no doubt that his essays influenced Francis Bacon, François de La Rochefoucauld, Blaise Pascal, Jean de La Bruyère, and Joseph Addison.

While Montaigne was describing himself in his writings, he was also depicting man in general; in fact, he was dealing with the human condition. In the twentieth century, Albert Camus, André Malraux, Jean-Paul Sartre, and a host of other eminent writers in Europe and the United States have devoted their talents to examining the human condition. Whether they acknowledge it, directly or indirectly, they are all indebted to Montaigne.

Bibliography
Burke, Peter. *Montaigne*. New York: Hill & Wang, 1981. Each of the ten chapters is devoted to a special aspect of Montaigne. Each chapter has its own bibliography, and there is an index. The style is straightforward, the information accurate. For students and general readers.
Frame, Donald M. *Montaigne's Discovery of Man: The Humanization of a Humanist*. New York: Columbia University Press, 1955, 2d ed. 1967. An account of the life of Montaigne and the development of his thought as conveyed in *The Essays*.
_____. *Montaigne's Essais: A Study*. Englewood Cliffs, N.J.: Prentice-Hall, 1969. A detailed study of Montaigne's life and an erudite examination of the evolution of his talent as revealed in *The Essays* as well as an estimate of his impact during the last four centuries. Contains a chronology, a bibliography, and an index.
Montaigne, Michel de. *The Essays of Michel de Montaigne*. Translated by George B. Ives. 4 vols. New York: Limited Editions Club, 1946. Introduction by André Gide and an accompanying handbook, which includes notes on the text by the translator and a series of comments on *The Essays* by Grace Norton. Highly readable and informative.
Sichel, Edith. *Michel de Montaigne*. London: Constable, 1911. Divided into "Montaigne the Man" and "Montaigne the Philosopher," this is a leisurely and rather personal view of his times, his life, and his work based largely on quotations from *The Essays*. Facsimiles of portraits and manuscript and bibliographical notes. Pleasant, easy reading.

Dorothy B. Aspinwall

MONTESQUIEU
Charles-Louis de Secondat

Born: January 18, 1689; La Brède, near Bordeaux, France
Died: February 10, 1755; Paris, France
Areas of Achievement: Philosophy and political theory
Contribution: Montesquieu's most lasting contribution was his defense and development of the theory behind separation of powers in government. His work in this area significantly influenced the framers of the United States Constitution. Philosophically, he is best known for positing history as the basis for normative judgment. Before Montesquieu, normative judgment had always been based on nature.

Early Life

Montesquieu's youth was a strange mixture of luxury and scarcity. His family was of noble heritage, yet his parents wanted him to be sensitive to the needs of the poor. His godfather was a beggar, and his first three years were spent nursing with a peasant family. His mother died when he was seven, which contributed to his shy and withdrawn manner.

At age eleven, Montesquieu was sent to school at Tuilly, where he spent the next five years. The school, which was maintained by the Congregation of the Oratory, provided him with a solid classical education. He was a good student who took a special interest in language. Drawn especially to Latin, Montesquieu acquired a special interest in Stoic philosophy. In 1705, Montesquieu, fulfilling the wish of his uncle, began to study law. Three years later, he received his license and became a legal apprentice in Paris. In 1713, he returned to Bordeaux, in the same year his father died, which forced him to settle down and assume the responsibilities of head of the family.

In 1716, when his uncle died, Montesquieu inherited wealth, land, and office. The office was the presidency of the Parliament of Bordeaux, a chief judgeship in the local court. He worked hard at his legal duties but did not enjoy them. After ten years, he sold his position to pursue his true interests in science, literature, and the more theoretical aspects of law.

Life's Work

Once he was freed from his judicial responsibilities, Montesquieu moved back to Paris to enjoy the literary fame acquired by publication of his *Lettres Persanes* (1721; *Persian Letters*, 1722). The *Persian Letters* were initially published anonymously and were a fictitious account of two Persians touring Europe. The book focused on the corruption of humanity. The accounts cited in the letters were critical of both French and Parisian society. For this reason, they proved to be a mixed blessing when Montesquieu was identified as the author. The instant fame he received was accompanied by the French court's displeasure. While Montesquieu considered his comments a reflection on European society at large, the court blocked his initial proposal to the French Academy.

Montesquieu spent the years from 1728 to 1731 traveling in Europe. The last two years of his travels were spent in England; this period greatly influenced his later works. His admiration for the English government made him a favorite at the court of Queen Caroline, which led to his election to the Royal Society. It is believed that this is where he first recognized the virtues of separation of powers. Many commentators on his work note the curiosity of his basing so much on a misreading of the British system of government.

When Montesquieu returned to France, he spent considerably more time at his family estate in La Brède. At this point in his life, he settled into more scholarly pursuits. His next major work was his *Considérations sur les causes de la grandeur des Romains et de leur décadence* (*Montesquieu's Considerations on the Causes of the Grandeur and Decadence of the Romans*, 1882). Published in 1734, this work developed his notion of historical causation. This book also set the groundwork for his more famous political writing, *De l'éspirit des loix: Ou, Du rapport que les loix doivent avoir avec la constitution de chaque gouvernement, les mouers, le climat, la religion, le commerce, . . .* (1748; *The Spirit of Laws*, 1750). Montesquieu's examination of the history of Rome led him to conclude that the strength of the Roman republic could not be sustained by the larger and more authoritarian Roman Empire. At the heart of his argument was his commitment to a free society. Much like Niccolò Machiavelli and William Shakespeare, Montesquieu believed that the tensions and conflicts that characterize free societies are the key to their political stability and strength. According to Montesquieu, tranquil republics are not as free as turbulent and divided ones.

The Spirit of Laws is Montesquieu's best-known work. Montesquieu had spent some twenty years on this book. In his preface to *The Spirit of Laws*, Montesquieu indicates that this is at least his most and possibly his only mature work. This book is often criticized for its lack of organization. Yet Montesquieu claimed that there was a method to the work and that he chose to keep the method obscure so that he could present unorthodox views without being punished by church or state. After Montesquieu's death, Jean Le Rond d'Alembert supported this thesis, claiming that the book was designed with two audiences in mind and that the structure of the book allowed Montesquieu to address both audiences at once.

The Spirit of Laws is certainly one of the most detailed and sweeping examinations of law ever attempted. Montesquieu's historical approach permitted him to make vast generalizations about human nature and its consequences on society, generalizations that were unheard of in previous works on law. For him, law was the application of human reason, and, therefore, the range of law must parallel the range of human reason. All things are governed by laws, and human laws must be understood in the light of this fact.

Montesquieu's goal was to establish a social science that would rival the natural sciences; this aim led to his abandonment of spirituality as a basis for human activity. In spirituality's place, he put history: All human activity was assessed in the light of historical studies. According to Montesquieu, history was the only key that could unlock the mysteries of causation; it was history that would make sense of the relationship between theory and practice.

The hallmark of Montesquieu's teachings was his conviction that laws can only be understood in relationship to the form of government that produced them. This assertion led to his detailed examination of the different types of political structures. Montesquieu identified three species of government: republican, monarchical, and despotic. He believed that a republican government can be either democratic or aristocratic and that types of government are distinguished by the passions and prejudices that are permitted to guide the political institutions. He also considered moderation to be one of the most important civic virtues. According to Montesquieu, the principles of a government are what shape and direct the actions of the government.

Montesquieu believed that republics place power in the hands of many of its citizens or in only a few and that this distinction determines whether a republic is a democratic-republic or an aristocratic-republic. In either case, for Montesquieu, virtue is the guiding principle of republics. It is important to remember that his was not a Christian understanding of virtue but a political one. Montesquieu understood virtue as a kind of patriotism that is derived from love of one's republic and the laws that are produced by the republic. Montesquieu believed that the main strength of republics is their ability to maintain the devotion of their citizens and that such devotion is best maintained in a political society wherein there is not great wealth. Montesquieu understood republican virtue to be strongest when a fair degree of equality exists among the citizens. For this reason, he argued that the natural place for a republic is a small society. He considered the history and development of Rome a good example of a small, healthy republic that outgrew its basic principle. In contrast, Montesquieu believed that the principle behind monarchy is honor and that the principle behind despotism is fear. Thus honor and fear are the respective principles that integrate these types of societies as virtue integrates republics. While Montesquieu did not consider any particular political system the best purely and simply, he did harbor a decided preference for republican government.

Montesquieu's political and social trademark was his unswerving commitment to liberty. Liberty, as he described it, is the right to do whatever the law permits. For Montesquieu, the key element to liberty is that it helps produce a stable, well-ordered society. His devotion to the separation of powers derives from these ideas, for only a restrained government could guarantee the liberty he so strongly desired.

Montesquieu's adult life was largely consumed by his writings, so much so that some biographers have complained that even his appearance remained a mystery to many outside his immediate circle of friends. Yet it is known that he had blue eyes, a long pointed chin, and a prominent nose—features that were rumored to make him appear much older than he really was.

Summary

Although some have criticized Montesquieu for placing greater faith in history than in nature, his approach to social and political matters is now commonplace. He may not have been an inventor in the purest sense, but there is little question about his intellectual independence. It would probably be an exaggeration to call him one of the great political thinkers of the Western world, yet his impact on practical politics—especially in the United States—is without question. Despite the confusion over the organization of *The Spirit of the Laws*, few works of political theory have had such a lasting impact on political practice.

Montesquieu's thoughts on commerce may help illustrate this point. He was the first theorist to consider commerce a topic deserving of serious consideration in a major political treatise. He believed that commerce is an important form of communication for modern societies and that it not only draws people together but also forges links between nations. Like separation of powers, commerce is another device that complicates social systems, which, to Montesquieu, is one of commerce's great virtues. Montesquieu further argued that commerce is one of the main social forces that encourage the arts and sciences. Montesquieu believed that the industry created by commerce serves every aspect of life, mental as well as physical. This broad perspective is characteristic of Montesquieu's prescient political thought.

Bibliography

Jones, W. T. "Charles Louis de Secondat, Baron de Montesquieu." In *Masters of Political Thought: Machiavelli to Bentham*. Boston: Houghton Mifflin, 1947. After a short biography, this essay mixes selections from Montesquieu's writings with commentary. Though limited in scope, it does highlight Montesquieu's key political teachings.

Lowenthal, David. "Montesquieu." In *History of Political Philosophy*, edited by Leo Strauss and Joseph Cropsey. Chicago: Rand McNally, 1963. A concise but thorough topical breakdown of Montesquieu's political teachings covering topics such as nature, commerce, religion, and political liberty.

McDonald, Lee Cameron. "Montesquieu." In *Western Political Theory: The Modern Age*. New York: Harcourt, Brace & World, 1962. A standard short essay that mixes biographical information with some analysis. The analysis is presented in a topical format with an especially long section on separation of powers. Not as probing or complete as the Lowenthal essay.

Montesquieu, Baron de. *The Spirit of the Laws*. Translated by Thomas Nugent. New York: Hafner Press, 1949. A complete volume of Montesquieu's most important work. This edition includes a useful introductory essay by Franz Neumann.

Pangle, Thomas L. *Montesquieu's Philosophy of Liberalism*. Chicago: University of Chicago Press, 1973. A book-long commentary on *The Spirit of Laws*, this work examines Montesquieu's thought in a complete and objective manner. Pangle is especially strong on Montesquieu's understanding of nature and normative reasoning.

Shackleton, Robert. *Montesquieu: A Critical Biography*. Oxford: Oxford University Press, 1961. The most complete biography on Montesquieu available in English. Presented in chronological order, this book is a mix of biographical data and analysis. A wonderful resource work on every aspect of Montesquieu's life and writings. Includes a complete bibliography of Montesquieu's works.

Donald V. Weatherman

CLAUDIO MONTEVERDI

Born: May 15, 1567; Cremona, Duchy of Milan
Died: November 29, 1643; Venice
Area of Achievement: Music
Contribution: Monteverdi was the outstanding Italian composer of his age, which bridged the periods of the Renaissance and the Baroque. He made equally important contributions to the fields of sacred and secular music, especially in the genres of opera and the madrigal, and forged for himself and his successors an expressive musical style by combining the established techniques of his predecessors with the innovations of his contemporaries.

Early Life

Claudio Giovanni Antonio Monteverdi was the eldest child of Baldassare Monteverdi, a chemist and barber surgeon, and his first wife, Maddalena (née Zigani). Claudio and his brother Giuleo Cesare studied music with Marc'Antonio Ingegneri, the *maestro di cappella* of Cremona Cathedral. In 1582, Claudio published a book of three-part motets entitled *Sacrae cantiunculae* in Venice, and the next year he published a book of sacred madrigals for four voices in Brescia. These were followed in 1584 by a book of canzonettas for three voices, again published in Venice. As was the custom at the time, many of Monteverdi's early works were modeled on specific pieces by older composers. In addition to his compositional talent, he developed his skills as a string player.

After an interval of three years, Monteverdi published his first book of madrigals in 1587. These works for five voices illustrate the grasp of structural organization and contrapuntal technique that he had acquired from Ingegneri as well as the more modern approaches to text setting of the Ferrarese composer Luzzasco Luzzaschi and the Roman Luca Marenzio.

Monteverdi's second book of five-part madrigals, published in 1590, displays even more clearly the influence of Marenzio. This book also shows the new influence of Giaches de Wert, especially in the setting of amorous but not emotionally charged texts by Torquato Tasso. This book was the last publication in which Monteverdi acknowledged himself to be a pupil of Ingegneri, and he was clearly hoping to follow in the footsteps of other Cremonese composers, such as Benedetto Pallavicino, Giovanni Gastoldi, and Costanza Porta, by seeking work outside his hometown. After an unsuccessful attempt to land a job in Milan in 1589, he soon accepted another as a string player in the musical establishment of the Gonzaga court at Mantua. He was then nearly twenty-five, with five publications to his name and in command of a highly polished compositional technique.

Surviving portraits of the young Monteverdi show a handsome youth of above-average height, with an oval face and penetrating eyes. In most of the portraits of Monteverdi as an older man, his face is lined and somewhat haggard, perhaps a legacy of his ill health in the years following his wife's death. He was clearly embittered by his dealings with the Gonzaga family and was a difficult man at times, but in his later years he was capable of a certain amount of happiness. His character was essentially serious, and he made few concessions either to his colleagues or to his audiences, but he was a good provider for his family and a generous teacher.

Life's Work

The Gonzagas were active patrons of the arts and maintained a spirited rivalry with their neighbors the Estes at Ferrara. Peter Paul Rubens, Tasso, and Battista Guarini were all resident at Mantua at different times, and Duke Vincenzo I was responsible for several large-scale performances of the latter's tragicomedy *Il pastor fido* (1590; *The Faithful Shepherd*, 1602). The musical establishment was smaller than that at Ferrara but hardly less distinguished. Under the direction of Wert the *cappella* included the composers Pallavicino, Francesco Rovigo, and Salomone Rossi, while Lodovico Viadana was organist at the cathedral and Giovanni Gastoldi was director of music at the ducal chapel of Santa Barbara. Monteverdi's initial duties included participating in the weekly concerts in the ducal palace, at which the court singers attempted to rival the exploits of the famous "three singing ladies" (*concerto delle donne*) of Ferrara.

Almost immediately, Monteverdi published his third book of madrigals, heavily influenced by the essentially serious style of Wert. The book included a number of texts from Tasso's *Gerusalemme liberata* (1581; *Jerusalem Delivered*, 1600), in direct emulation of Wert's Tasso settings of the 1580's, and an even larger number of madrigal texts and excerpts from Guarini's *The Faithful Shepherd*. The collection was popular enough to be reprinted two years later in 1594. Monteverdi continued to compose madrigals throughout the 1590's but did not publish another collection until 1603. He traveled with the duke on the duke's military expedition to Austria and Hungary in 1595 and again on a visit to Flanders in 1599, returning from each voyage richer only in experience. He had hoped to succeed Wert when the latter died in 1596 and was disappointed when the post went to Pallavicino. He may have sought employment at Ferrara and was certainly about to dedicate a book of madrigals to Duke Alfonso II d'Este, when that nobleman died in 1597.

On May 20, 1599, Monteverdi married one of the Mantuan court singers, Claudia Cattaneo, who bore him three children in rapid succession. Only the two sons survived infancy: Francesco, who eventually became a singer in the choir at St. Mark's, Venice, and Massimilione, who became a medical doctor in Cremona. Finally, in 1601, on the death of Pallavicino, Monteverdi was appointed *maestro di cappella* of the Mantuan court, and in April, 1602, he and his family were given Mantuan citizenship.

Monteverdi's madrigals of the 1590's had circulated in manuscript, and several were attacked in print by the theorist Giovanni Maria Artusi in 1600, instigating a controversy that continued for some years. Artusi objected specifically to Monteverdi's use of certain harmonic idioms and of unprepared or unresolved dissonances. Monteverdi defended these devices as being necessary to express the meaning and emotional content of the text rather than merely to reflect the syntax of the poem and graphically to depict certain key words through the use of stylized musical formulas.

In 1603, Monteverdi published his fourth book of madrigals, to be followed the next year by his fifth. These two largely retrospective collections contain some of his most original and emotionally intense music, especially in the settings of epigrammatic texts by Guarini in book 4. The last six madrigals of book 5, however, show an increased interest in formal musical structure, in contrast to direct expression of the emotional content of the text, with the introduction of an obligatory *basso continuo*, or "figured bass," in which the figures indicated chords to be played by a keyboard or plucked string instruments. Thus, in a symbolic way, book 5 marks the boundary between Renaissance and Baroque music.

An even more striking and clearly Baroque technique was monody, which permitted the flexible musical declamation of a text by a solo voice to the accompaniment of a *basso continuo*. This technique had been developed at Florence in the late 1590's and led directly to the creation of opera. For a variety of reasons, the Gonzagas had become interested in Florentine activities around 1600, and these latest musical developments were well known at Mantua, at least by report. This knowledge led to the composition and performance in early 1607 of the opera *La favola d'Orfeo*, with music by Monteverdi and a libretto by Alessandro Striggio, the Younger. Both parties were clearly inspired by the Florentine opera *Euridice* of 1600, with music by Jacopo Peri and a libretto by Ottavio Rinuccini.

La favola d'Orfeo was performed before the Accademia degli Invaghiti in a room in the ducal palace in February, 1607. Although it employed a large orchestra, the vocal and staging requirements were modest by the standards of court operas—presumably because it was not composed to celebrate a state occasion. In the music, Monteverdi combined the new Florentine monody, in particular Peri's development of theatrical recitative, with various techniques from his own *a cappella* and *continuo* madrigals, with the instrumental forms with which he was familiar, and with his own sense of formal structure, to produce the first full-fledged opera.

La favola d'Orfeo was well received and was repeated at the command of the duke. Although it was published in 1609 and again in 1615, no further performances were forthcoming. Meanwhile, Monteverdi had returned to

Cremona to be with his seriously ill wife. She died in September, leaving him desolate. He briefly refused to return to Mantua but changed his mind when another opera was required of him. This opera was *L'Arianna*, with a libretto by Rinuccini, commissioned by Vincenzo to celebrate the wedding of Prince Francesco Gonzaga to Margherita of Savoy in early 1608. Again, the composer was confronted with tragedy, for the young singer Caterina Martinelli, whom he had taught for several years and who had lived in his household almost as an adopted daughter, died of smallpox in March, 1608, while preparing the title role. The opera was postponed while another singer was found and was finally given on May 28 to an enthusiastic reception.

L'Arianna was Monteverdi's most renowned opera, and it was later performed at Naples and, as late as 1640, at Venice. The famous lament, in particular, was widely admired and served as the model for the string of laments written by other composers in the 1620's and 1630's. The lament was printed in several different forms by Monteverdi himself, and is the only piece of music to survive from the opera.

After the festivities, to which Monteverdi also contributed a ballet in the French style entitled *Il ballo delle ingrate* (1608) and a prologue to Guarini's pastoral play *L'idropica* (1609), he returned to Cremona in a state of physical collapse and deep depression. He blamed the climate of Mantua for his wife's death and his own ailments; he blamed Mantuan officials for withholding his salary while paying exorbitant sums to visiting musicians such as the Florentine composer Marco da Gagliano; and he requested release from Gonzaga service. In the end, his salary was increased, and he was granted an annual pension, which he had difficulty collecting for the rest of his life.

In 1610, Monteverdi published a collection of church music in a variety of styles and forms, both archaic and modern, generally referred to as the *Vespers of 1610*. Although much of the music may have been intended for use at Mantua, and the motets in particular were clearly designed for virtuoso singers, the publication seems primarily to have been an advertisement of his suitability and availability for a new position involving church music, perhaps at Rome or Venice. He remained at Mantua until (following the death of Vincenzo) he was dismissed by the new Duke Francesco in July, 1612, along with a number of Mantuan artists, including his brother Giuleo Cesare. He then returned to Cremona for a year before being appointed to the prestigious and remunerative position of *maestro di cappella* at St. Mark's in Venice on August 19, 1613.

Monteverdi's first task at St. Mark's was to restore the standards of the musical establishment. That involved recruiting and training singers, regularizing the pay structure of the choir and instrumental ensemble, and introducing new music. He must have contributed new works of his own, but few were published. He gradually appointed younger men, many of whom had been his students, to take over some of the responsibilities for the music program; most prominent among these were Francesco Cavalli, Alessandro Grandi, the Elder, and Francesco Rovetta. Monteverdi continued to compose secular works throughout the next two decades. Among the products of this period was his last commission from Mantua, the opera *La finta pazza Licori*, projected for 1627 but never performed. Of Monteverdi's late Mantuan stage works, only the music for the ballet survives.

All musical activity decreased in Venice during the early 1630's as a result of the plague and related financial difficulties, and Monteverdi, who was already in his sixties and preparing to take holy orders, seems to have composed less himself. The opening of the first public opera houses at Venice in 1637, however, prompted him to undertake a final series of stage works. The opera *L'Arianna* was revived in 1640, to be followed the same year by *Il ritorno d'Ulisse in patria*. In 1641, Monteverdi composed a ballet, *La vittoria d'amore*, on commission from the Count of Parma for performance at Piacenza. Finally, in 1642 he produced his last opera, *L'incoronazione di Poppea*, which contains music of an astonishing variety (some of which may have been added posthumously by other composers for subsequent performances outside Venice). He died in Venice, after a final visit to Cremona, and is buried in the Church of the Frari.

Summary

Claudio Monteverdi's career demonstrates both his versatility and his adaptability. His first two books of madrigals and first book of canzonets are essentially student works, but they display his grasp of the musical idioms and techniques of the 1580's. The madrigals of books 3-6 show an increased interest in selecting poetry with serious emotional content and expressing those emotions through a heightened use of dissonance, contrast, and rhetorical declamation. These books mark the zenith of the madrigal as an expressive musical form.

The opera *La favola d'Orfeo* offered Monteverdi the chance to draw upon all the techniques he had mastered in his madrigals and incorporate with them the newer developments of monodic song and recitative developed by the earliest Florentine opera composers. *La favola d'Orfeo* thus stands as Monteverdi's first attempt to consolidate conflicting musical styles into a musical and dramatic whole, and is rightly considered the first great opera.

Monteverdi's enduring works are memorable for their expression of human emotions, depiction of individual characters, and sheer beauty of sound. His first six books of madrigals mark the culmination of a great Italian tradition of secular polyphony. Of his operas, *La favola d'Orfeo* was the first fully formed, *L'Arianna* the most influential, and *L'incoronazione di Poppea* arguably the greatest opera of the seventeenth century. The remarkable variety of styles in the *Vespers of 1610* provides an overview of Italian sacred music at the beginning of the Baroque era as interpreted by the composer who was largely responsible for the introduction of secular style to sacred music. Monteverdi was recognized as a giant by his contemporaries, and, although he had little direct influence on the music of succeeding generations, that status was recognized anew in the twentieth century.

Bibliography
Arnold, Denis. "Claudio Monteverdi." In *The New Grove Dictionary of Music and Musicians*, edited by Stanley Sadie. London: Macmillan, 1980. The standard music reference article on Monteverdi. Contains a complete list of works and an extensive bibliography.
_____. *Monteverdi*. Edited by J. A. Westrup. Rev. ed. London: J. M. Dent & Sons, 1975. The standard biography of the composer in English. Contains a summary list of works and a select bibliography. Part of the Master Musicians series.
Arnold, Denis, and Nigel Fortune, eds. *The New Monteverdi Companion*. London: Faber & Faber, 1985. An excellent collection of essays on Monteverdi's musical environment, his own compositions, and questions of performance practice. Contains an extensive bibliography.
Monteverdi, Claudio. *The Letters of Claudio Monteverdi*. Edited and translated by Denis Stevens. Cambridge: Cambridge University Press, 1980. The authoritative English translation of Monteverdi's extensive correspondence, with detailed annotations by the editor. Select bibliography.
Schrade, Leo. *Monteverdi: Creator of Modern Music*. New York: W. W. Norton, 1950. Reprint. New York: Da Capo Press, 1964. The first full-length biography of Monteverdi in English and the most detailed. Contains a select bibliography.
Stevens, Denis. *Monteverdi: Sacred, Secular, and Occasional Music*. Rutherford, N.J.: Fairleigh Dickinson University Press, 1978. A brief introduction to Monteverdi's works, treated categorically rather than chronologically. Calls attention to many of the lost works and their place in his output. Contains a select bibliography.
Tomlinson, Gary. *Monteverdi and the End of the Renaissance*. Berkeley: University of California Press, 1987. An insightful discussion of the development of Monteverdi's musical style and his place in Italian cultural and intellectual life of the period. Contains numerous musical examples and an extensive bibliography.
Whenham, John, ed. *Claudio Monteverdi: "Orfeo."* Cambridge: Cambridge University Press, 1986. One of the Cambridge Opera Handbooks, this is a collection of essays on the composition, production, and reception of the opera *La favola d'Orfeo*. Includes reprints of several articles and much new material. Contains a bibliography and discography.

Graydon Beeks

MONTEZUMA II

Born: 1467; Tenochtitlán, Aztec Empire
Died: June 30, 1520; Tenochtitlán, Aztec Empire
Area of Achievement: Monarchy
Contribution: Montezuma II expanded the Aztec Empire to its greatest size and died as his empire crumbled under the pressures of Hernán Cortés.

Early Life

Axayácatl named his fourth son Montezuma, the Younger, after the child's great-grandfather. Montezuma I was the Mexica *Uei Tlatoani* (great speaker, or emperor) of the Aztec Empire, centered in Anahuac, an intermontane valley in central Mexico. At Montezuma the Younger's naming ceremony, held four days after his birth in 1467, the priests dedicated the infant to Quetzalcóatl, that year's patron deity, and prophesied that he would earn greatness as both ruler and priest.

The prophecy was not a guarantee. Young Montezuma was born into an oligarchy called the *Pipiltin* (sons of lords) that was composed of the putative descendants of Acamapichtli, founder of the Mexica state, and a princess of the fading Culhuacán dynasty. The office of emperor was not hereditary. A council of *Pipiltin* elders elected a successor on the basis of merit rather than on degrees of kinship to the deceased emperor. For Montezuma to become emperor when his generation came of age, his accomplishments would have to set him apart from his brothers and cousins.

After spending five years in the *Calmécac*, an elite preparatory school, twelve-year-old Montezuma moved into the barracks for a two-year apprenticeship before joining the warriors in combat. He soon excelled in battle and captured enough enemies to be inducted into the exclusive Order of the Eagle. In 1483, at age sixteen, he resumed religious studies and became a priest of the war god Huitzilopochtli (Blue Hummingbird). The next year, Montezuma had to decide whether to take an oath of celibacy and devote his entire life to the priesthood or to marry and continue his military career.

He chose the middle route and became a warrior-priest. He took, eventually, four legitimate wives and participated in most of the major military campaigns until his installation as emperor in 1503. Through his first wife, he inherited the title *Tlatoani* (speaker, or ruler) of the city-state Ehecatepec. Prowess in war made him an army commander at age thirty, and later he became *Tlacochcalcatl* (prince of the house), one of the four closest advisers to the emperor. He also retained his priestly office and rose through clerical ranks to become high priest of Huitzilopochtli.

Life's Work

This warrior-priest bore the markings of both professions on his body.

Among warriors he was a *Tequihua* (master of cuts) and had the sides of his head shaved, leaving on top a stiff tuft bound with a red thong. A sizable plug through his lower lip and large studs through extended ear lobes identified him as an aristocrat. A band of black paint across his face signified his priestly status, as did the streaks of cuts and scars on his ears, arms, and thighs. Montezuma had made these cuts with cactus thorns as he propitiated the deities with his own blood. He was of average height, slight but of wiry build; he had little wisps of hair on his upper lip and chin and a yellowish-brown skin color. In demeanor he was grave, reserved, almost aloof. To his reputation of bravery was added respect for his soft-spoken advice on political and religious affairs of state.

The Aztec Empire was relatively young. The Mexica themselves were the last branch of the Aztec tribe to leave the ancestral home of Aztlán. They had arrived in Anahuac in 1258. Called *Chichimeca* (sons of dogs) by the remnants of the disintegrating Toltec-Culhuacán civilization, the Mexica had been treated as outcasts for a century. In 1375, Acamapichtli had secured recognition as a fellow *tlatoani* from the rulers of the city-states around Lake Texcoco. Having risen from abasement to parity, Acamapichtli and his three successors had forged alliances and waged wars until the Mexica dominated Anahuac.

Montezuma I, the fifth *tlatoani*, had sent conquering armies down the slopes of the central valley in all directions and built an empire that reached the oceans to the east and west, the deserts to the north, and the tropical forests to the south. His next three successors, his grandsons—the father and uncles of Montezuma II—had inherited the title *Uei Tlatoani* and continued the policy of constant expansion.

The Aztec Empire was built by war and sustained by blood. Conquered nations paid annual tributes of young men and women who were sacrificed to gods that consumed human hearts. The victims' beating hearts were ripped out of their chests, heads severed then stacked in enormous pyramids, and bodies butchered for consumption by the victorious Mexica.

When Emperor Ahuitzotl died in 1502, Montezuma's piety and prowess persuaded the council of elders that he was preferable to his elder brother Macuilmalinaltzin. Following his election, Montezuma II spent a brief time in prayer and meditation, and then he led an invasion of two neighboring provinces. He brought back fifty-one hundred prisoners to be sacrificed and eaten as part of the enthronement festivities the following year. As emperor, Montezuma had to let his hair grow to shoulder length, wear a thin gold tube through his nose, and exchange his copper lip and ear plugs for larger, golden plugs. He wore a half-miter crown and gold sandals. Once installed, he launched a series of startling actions.

He purged from all government positions *Pipiltin* supporters of his brother and dissolved the council of elders. He then directed the massacre of Macuilmalinaltzin, two younger brothers, and twenty-eight hundred Texcoco warriors. With his power consolidated, Montezuma turned his attention to the empire's subject states. He required all conquered nations to send their nobles to Tenochtitlán, where they replaced the commoners in Montezuma's palace as servants. Tribute payments were increased, and each nation had to erect its own temples to Huitzilopochtli. He then sent armies to the south to add new territories to the empire and to bring more oblations to Huitzilopochtli. By 1519, Montezuma's empire encompassed about 200,000 square miles and contained more than twenty million people. Montezuma had created a chasm between himself and commoners by surrounding himself with only nobles. He had elevated Huitzilopochtli in importance throughout the empire and had identified himself more closely with Huitzilopochtli. Soon, however, his patron god Quetzalcóatl overtook the war god in importance for Montezuma and his empire.

The principal deities of the primitive Mexica had been their tribal goddess Mexitli and Huitzilopochtli. When the Mexica arrived in Anahuac, the principal Toltec deity was Quetzalcóatl, the god of divine wisdom who had taught humans agriculture and all the other arts of civilization. The Toltecs had an elaborate cosmogony that included a cyclical theory of time and a conviction that quarrelsome gods had created and destroyed the world four times. At a reconciliation, some of the gods had created a fifth world by immolating themselves. Quetzalcóatl traveled to the netherworld and collected the bones of humans who had lived in the previous worlds. He then ground the bones into powder and re-created humanity by mixing his own divine blood into the powder.

In the ninth century, three hundred years before the Mexica began their trek, the Toltecs were ruled by a high priest who had taken Quetzalcóatl as his own name. This Quetzalcóatl introduced radical religious reforms. He ended human sacrifice, took a vow of celibacy, and sought spiritual unity with his divine namesake through prayer, meditation, and penance. When the priest was an old man, three sorcerers gave an intoxicant, which they called a medicine, to Quetzalcóatl. When the priest was inebriated, the sorcerers put him in bed with a princess, who successfully tempted him to break his vow of chastity. Upon awakening, Quetzalcóatl felt his disgrace so keenly that he fled the Toltec nation, which promptly restored human sacrifice. When Quetzalcóatl reached the Gulf of Mexico, he sailed eastward on a magic raft and vowed to return once he found the place of perfect wisdom.

In their cyclical reckoning of time, the Toltecs and their successors calculated the possible return of Quetzalcóatl and the possible destruction of the fifth world. In the third year of Montezuma's reign, 1506, a fifty-two-year cycle of time was completed. A campaign to Oaxaca garnered twenty-three hundred captives, who were sacrificed en masse in a petition for fifty-two more years of life. If Quetzalcóatl were to return in this new cycle, the light-skinned, bearded priest would return from the East on a magic raft in 1519.

While Hernán Cortés and his five hundred Spaniards sailed up the Yucatán coast in early 1519, Montezuma received regular reports of their activities. After consulting with his priests, Montezuma concluded that the Spaniards were either Quetzalcóatl himself and his entourage or emissaries of the fabled priest. The return of Quetzalcóatl not only was predicted by the calendar but also explained the series of fantastic events that had baffled the Mexica since 1489. There had been earthquakes, a solar eclipse, a flood, and comets that appeared both in the day and at night. Grotesque people and wondrous animals mysteriously appeared and magically disappeared. Huitzilopochtli's temple burst spontaneously into flames, and its replacement was struck by lightning. A woman rose from the dead and told Montezuma that he was the last emperor, and a disembodied woman's voice frightened residents of Anahuac by wailing in lament at night. To Montezuma, the arrival of Cortés gave meaning to these bizarre events; they foretold the return of Quetzalcóatl, who would reclaim the empire he had left years ago.

Reluctant to face the religious reformer who had ended human sacrifice, the high priest of Huitzilopochtli tried to hold onto the throne without defying Quetzalcóatl. Montezuma sent Cortés rich gifts, pledged his fealty, exaggerated the difficulties of the journey from the coast to Anahuac, and asked the Spaniards to return to the East. When Cortés led his Spaniards and six thousand Indian allies across the mountains, Montezuma desperately tried to have Cortés ambushed. When all efforts failed, Montezuma accepted his fate and on November 8, 1519, greeted Cortés with these words: "Thou hast arrived on earth; thou hast come to thy noble city of Mexico. Thou hast come to occupy thy noble mat and seat, which for a little time I have guarded and watched for thee. . . . [N]ow it is fulfilled: thou hast returned."

Montezuma's advisers were appalled at their emperor's behavior. They regarded the Spaniards as dangerous aliens that should be repulsed rather than welcomed. The Spaniards' Indian allies were the rebellious Cempoalans and the intransigent Tlaxcalans who already had encouraged the subject states to renounce their loyalty to the empire. Sensing danger, Cortés arrested Montezuma and hoped that his royal hostage would guarantee the Spaniards' safety. When the Spaniards massacred the priests of Huitzilopochtli and placed crucifixes in the temples, Montezuma tried to secure his freedom through intrigue, but it was too late. The *Pipiltin* deposed Montezuma, replaced him with his brother Cuitláhuac, and assaulted the Spaniards. When Cortés had Montezuma taken to the rooftop to restore calm, the infuriated warriors threw stones at their former *Uei Tlatoani* and wounded him seriously in the head. Montezuma died three days later, on June 30, 1520. That night, the Spaniards fought their way out of the city and vowed to return. When the *Pipiltin* found Montezuma's body, they first threw it into a sewage canal and then burned it in a trash heap.

Summary

Since the time of the Spanish conquest and the destruction of the Aztec culture, Montezuma II has entered the world of symbolism. For centuries, he was seen as the embodiment of barbarism, cruelty, and evil. His image was rehabilitated by *indigenistas* (admirers of Indian culture) during the Mexican Revolution of 1910, and he has been portrayed as the epitome of an innocent America violated by a corrupt, greedy, ruthless Spain. With the waning of *indigenista* fervor by the mid-twentieth century, the name Montezuma has come to be associated with the concept of "authentic" Mexico.

Bibliography

Brundage, Burr Cartwright. *A Rain of Darts: The Mexica Aztecs*. Austin: University of Texas Press, 1972. A careful chronicle of the Aztecs, based on intensive study of the codices. Brundage concludes that Montezuma was insecure, bloodthirsty, and morbidly religious.

Burland, C. A. *Montezuma: Lord of the Aztecs*. New York: G. P. Putnam's Sons, 1973. This biography, richly illustrated with photographs of Mexico and the Aztec codices, is somewhat melodramatic and error prone.

Díaz del Castillo, Bernal. *The Discovery and Conquest of Mexico*. Translated by A. P. Maudslay, with an introduction by Irving A. Leonard. New York: Noonday Press, 1956. First written in the 1560's and first published in 1632. Díaz wrote his vivid memories of the conquest of Mexico and his observations of the Aztecs and of Montezuma.

Fagan, Brian M. *The Aztecs*. New York: W. H. Freeman, 1984. This copiously illustrated work is a topical examination of Aztec society that updates older studies by George C. Vaillant, Jacques Soustelle, and Nigel Davies.

Madariaga, Salvador de. *Hernan Cortes: Conqueror of Mexico*. Garden City, N.Y.: Doubleday, 1969. A lively work that is much more than a biography of the Spanish conqueror. Gives extensive, sympathetic treatment to Montezuma.

Padden, R. C. *The Hummingbird and the Hawk: Conquest and Sovereignty in the Valley of Mexico, 1503-1541*. Columbus: Ohio State University Press, 1967. One of the narratives of the conquest of Mexico. Padden concludes that Montezuma was reaching for divinity and lost his grip on humanity and reality.

Paul E. Kuhl

JACQUES-ÉTIENNE MONTGOLFIER
and
JOSEPH-MICHEL MONTGOLFIER

Jacques-Étienne Montgolfier

Born: January 6, 1745; Vidalon-les-Annonay, France
Died: August 2, 1799; Serrières, France

Joseph-Michel Montgolfier

Born: August 26, 1740; Vidalon-les-Annonay, Ardeche, France
Died: June 26, 1810; Balaruc-les-Bains, France

Areas of Achievement: Aeronautics, invention, and technology
Contribution: The Montgolfier brothers contributed to the invention, improvement, and flying of lighter-than-air craft. Their greatest achievement was their successful coordination in the invention and flying of the first balloon.

Early Lives

The Montgolfier brothers were born at Vidalon-les-Annonay to Pierre Montgolfier, a paper manufacturer, and Anne Duret. Joseph-Michel Montgolfier, the elder of the two brothers, showed an early inclination toward creativity and inventiveness when, at the age of twelve, he glided from the second floor of the family residence to the ground, supported by umbrellas, which he held in his hands. He was sent to the College of Touron in the Rhone Valley from which he twice ran away. The second time he fled to Saint-Étienne, where he developed a new process for making Prussian blue dye, which was used for a long time in his father's paper-making industry. Joseph-Michel returned to Vidalon to work with his father in the family paper mill but then joined another brother, Augustine, at Rives to aid in the development of another Montgolfier plant.

Jacques-Étienne was sent at a very early age to the College of Saint Barbe in Paris. From 1755 to 1763, he studied science, since he had a particular taste and aptitude for precision and exactitude. Upon completion of his secondary studies, he became a student of architecture and had as his professor the famous Jacques-Germain Soufflot. He succeeded remarkably in his chosen field.

From 1763 to 1772, Jacques-Étienne studied and practiced architecture in Paris and its suburbs. His father, however, asked Jacques-Étienne to return to Vidalon to aid him in the management of the family business. Although he had been happy and successful in Paris, he conceded to his father's desires. From the moment of his return to Vidalon until his death, he strove to become very competent in his new profession. Initially he was named as technical adviser to his father. By 1777, Jacques-Étienne was recognized by the French authorities as the inventor of vellum paper.

In about 1780, Joseph-Michel went to Avignon under the pretext of acquiring a degree in law. By 1782, he received his degree, but during this time his dominant interest remained in science and invention. Following the discovery of hydrogen by Henry Cavendish in 1766 and the publication of Joseph Priestley's book on the different types of air, Joseph-Michel and his brother Jacques-Étienne had toyed unsuccessfully at Vidalon with small paper bags that they filled with hydrogen. Although these experiments had proved quite unfruitful, they were the beginnings of the Montgolfiers' invention.

Life's Work

On November 15, 1782, while still at Avignon, Joseph-Michel pondered several of his scientific readings and considered the discoveries of Cavendish and Priestley. One day, he buttoned his shirt and proceeded to hold it over the fire in his fireplace. The shirt filled with the heated air and rose toward the ceiling. Returning to Vidalon, Joseph-Michel and his brother constructed a taffeta vessel and filled it with warm air from a fire of paper mixed with wool and damp straw. This lighter-than-air craft rose to a height of thirty meters. Believing in the outstanding importance of their adventure, the Montgolfier brothers contacted the Academy of Sciences in Paris.

A vessel three times as large ascended on December 14, 1782. It subsequently fell unharmed on the nearby hills of Grattet. This experience was repeated successfully several times and provided Joseph-Michel and his brother occasion to calculate the characteristics of a "globe" considerably greater in size.

The new balloon was about twelve meters in diameter and made of sections of thin paper of several layers. It was fortunate that the Montgolfier family owned a paper mill. The different parts were held together and strengthened with ropes and metal wires. The base was held open by a wooden form two and a half meters wide, to which was attached a metallic stove, in which straw and pieces of vine were burned to produce the necessary heat. The whole machine weighed more than 225 kilograms.

After several experiments, June 4 was chosen by the Montgolfier brothers as the official date for the public presentation of their new invention. The event was to occur in the center of Annonay, in the Place des Cordeliers. The whole experience was to be witnessed by the General Council of the Vivarais region, whose meeting coincided with this auspicious aerial adventure.

On June 4, 1783, at about five o'clock in the afternoon, the spectators, almost suffocated by the smoke, could see a strange contraption begin to take shape and start to rise from the earth. On the command of Joseph-

Michel and his brother, the restraining ropes were released and the balloon was freed. It rose without any difficulty over the heads of the admiring spectators and attained an estimated altitude of one thousand meters. The south wind carried it more than two kilometers from the center of Annonay. Upon the request of the inventors, the senators of the Vivarais who had witnessed the event signed a succinct report of all that had occurred.

Jacques-Étienne had written to the Academy of Sciences in Paris in December, 1782. He confided the discovery of the balloon to the geologist Nicolas Desmarest. Yet Desmarest did not bring it to the attention of the academy, whose members learned of it by the official version describing the event at Annonay on June 4, 1783.

A commission of the academy was formed to invite Jacques-Étienne to Paris in order to demonstrate the new finding to the Parisians. It was normal that Jacques-Étienne be chosen rather than Joseph-Michel, since the former had studied and worked previously in the French capital. Socially and professionally he was a well-known personage in the Parisian world of that time. The decision was taken to allocate academy funds to the Montgolfiers' project. The king also decided to give a small sum of money to the scientists. Jacques-Étienne undertook in his Paris demonstration to have a lamb, a chicken and a duck as passengers in the ascent of the newest balloon. This larger craft was made by Jacques-Étienne at the factory of a good friend. On September 19, 1783, the latest version of the Montgolfier craft was shown to King Louis XVI, the representatives of the academy, and the court at Versailles. Jacques-Étienne directed the whole operation with great success, and all the royal assistants witnessed the ascension of the new balloon to an estimated altitude of five thousand meters. After eight minutes of flight, the craft descended about three and a half kilometers from Versailles. Its passengers were slightly shaken, but only the chicken suffered an injury: a broken beak.

Joseph-Michel and Jacques-Étienne communicated faithfully all during these new experiences. They now decided that it was time to have one of their balloons transport two human beings. The two men chosen were Marquis François d'Arlandes and Jean-François Pilâtre de Rozier. Yet it is certain that on October 12, prior to the ascent of the two chosen airmen, Jacques-Étienne received his aerial baptism during a ten-minute ascent. This would be his first and last flight. With its new basket large enough for two passengers, Pilâtre de Rozier and Arlandes ascended in the attached container on November 21, 1783. Jacques-Étienne had improved, for this memorable event, the method of heating the air within the balloon.

During this time, Joseph-Michel had brought his aerial experience to Lyons. After several improvements in technique, he completed, on November 18, a flight of fifteen kilometers from Lyons. The Lyonnais no longer were envious of the flights directed by Jacques-Étienne near Paris.

Jacques-Étienne next established his new point of departure for the first free balloon flight of Pilâtre de Rozier and Arlandes. It was to take place from the grounds of the Château de la Muette, in Paris. After a few unsuccessful attempts, Jacques-Étienne made a final inspection and permitted this historic departure. The two valiant airmen rose majestically above Paris, floated over the Seine, Saint Sulpice, and the Luxembourg Gardens. Finally, the landing took place at the Butte aux Cailles, ten kilometers from the Château de la Muette. The Montgolfiers had succeeded in their dream. Two days later Jacques-Étienne was invited by another aeronautical engineer to christen the latter's hydrogen-fueled balloon. Within two days the first human flights in lighter-than-air craft had taken place. The Montgolfiers, however, won the lion's part of the prize.

On December 10, 1783, the Montgolfier brothers were named to the French Academy of Sciences. Jacques-Étienne received the Order of Saint Marcel; Joseph-Michel received a royal pension as well as gifts conferred by the king and Marie Antoinette. Other gifts and honors also were profferred to these successful inventor brothers.

Joseph-Michel then proceeded in his typically impetuous fashion to launch the largest balloon in the world from Lyons on January 19, 1784. Joseph-Michel himself ascended in this balloon, which was 31 meters in diameter and 38 meters in height. The so-called Fleselles did not successfully complete the trip from Lyons to Paris as planned. Jacques-Étienne returned to the paper mill at Vidalon and continued to produce inventions in that industry. Joseph-Michel returned to the responsibility of the paper mill at Rives.

Summary

The Montgolfier brothers worked successfully at the invention of hydraulic machines for use in the paper-making industry and at other innovations in this field. Yet their most outstanding achievement was the invention of the lighter-than-air balloon.

While Jacques-Étienne was at home assisting his father in the family paper mill, Joseph-Michel returned to Vidalon to seek the partnership of his brother. The two young men, though very different from each other, had from very early childhood a marked, fraternal affection that made them most compatible in their future invention endeavors. A distracted though remarkably scientific genius, Joseph-Michel was responsible for many other types of inventions in paper making, hydraulics, and chemistry. Yet his invention of lighter-than-air craft remains his outstanding contribution to the advancement of science. He was successfully seconded by his younger brother, Jacques-Étienne, who was educated formally earlier than Joseph-Michel. The stabilizing effect of Jacques-Étienne on the more impetuous genius of Joseph-Michel produced a very well-balanced inventive team.

The Montgolfier brothers had been the original inventors and the primary moving force in the development of lighter-than-air craft. Later inventors, in turn, would build on the Montgolfiers' elementary findings, perfect their balloons, and advance into the new forms of lighter-than-air craft called dirigibles.

Bibliography

Dwiggins, Don. *Riders of the Wind: The Story of Ballooning*. New York: Hawthorn Books, 1973. A historical approach to the invention and development of ballooning. Includes narration by balloonists from different countries who participated in the evolution and practice of ballooning. Includes pictures, diagrams, and outlined maps of flights in various parts of the world. Rather elementary and narrative in style, it is intended for younger readers.

Gillispie, Charles Coulston. *The Montgolfier Brothers and the Invention of Aviation, 1783-1784*. Princeton, N.J.: Princeton University Press, 1983. The most comprehensive book in English on the family history of the Montgolfiers and the inventions of Joseph-Michel and Jacques-Étienne. Sources are all in French. Each subject is treated very thoroughly. Includes copious notes and illustrations, some in color. The details of the Montgolfiers' other inventions are very well integrated.

Jackson, Donald Dale. *The Aeronauts*. Alexandria, Va.: Time-Life Books, 1980. A fine presentation of the history of aeronautics including events, inventions, and persons from the early nineteenth century through the use of aerostats. Includes a good section on the use of balloons and dirigibles in war. Contains excellent illustrations and pictures, black-and-white as well as color, a bibliography, and an index.

Marevalas, Paul. "Joseph Montgolfier: The Ballooning Pioneer." *Ballooning*, September/October, 1981: 59-63.

_____. "The Montgolfiers' Moment in History." *Ballooning*, May/June, 1981: 59-63. Two good articles by a twentieth century balloonist who writes briefly on the invention of lighter-than-air craft. The author makes interesting contrasts with modern methods and frank statements regarding the limitation of practical uses of balloons and dirigibles. Provides a modern point of view on the state of the art of ballooning.

                                                              William C. Marceau

WOLFGANG AMADEUS MOZART

Born: January 27, 1756; Salzburg, Austria
Died: December 5, 1791; Vienna, Austria
Area of Achievement: Music
Contribution: Along with Joseph Haydn and Ludwig van Beethoven, Mozart represents the fullest achievement of the Viennese classical style. Prolific and precocious, Mozart worked in a wide range of musical forms, from court dances and chamber music to symphonies and operas, producing some of the most enduring and masterful compositions in each.

Early Life

Johan Crysostom Wolfgang Amadeus Mozart was born in Salzburg, Austria, on January 27, 1756, the second of the seven children born to Leopold and Anna Maria Mozart to survive infancy. He and his older sister, Maria Anna ("Nannerl"), received the full benefit of the musical education bestowed on them by their father, himself a composer. Although both children proved to be musically precocious, greater attention was lavished on young Mozart. By 1762, both he and Nannerl were attracting much attention, both in their native Salzburg and in the musically more prestigious capital city of Vienna. In 1763, the family set off for Paris and London, with the young Mozart giving performances along the way, both to extend his reputation and to help defray the family's expenses.

Mozart's early European travels were especially important to his development. He was able to display his talent and skills and thereby dispel any doubts held by those who had not heard him. More important, he was exposed to a wide variety of styles, which he would master and synthesize into a personal style at once imitative and distinctive. Still more important was the trip father and son took seven years later to Italy, then a hotbed of musical experiments. Already a precocious and prodigious composer of a wide variety of musical forms, Mozart now added opera to his growing list of accomplishments, as well as five new symphonies in a newly adopted Italian style. Exactly how much of the work attributed to this child prodigy was actually and solely composed by him is impossible to determine. Many of the surviving manuscripts survive only in Leopold's hand or in texts heavily corrected by him.

Nevertheless, it is clear that Mozart's talent was far in excess of the opportunities available to him in Salzburg, whose archbishop considered the young musician little more than a servant. Realizing that his son's prospects would be brighter elsewhere, Leopold traveled with him to Vienna. Mozart came under the influence of the Viennese classical style which characterizes the symphonies written during this period. The works he wrote during his stay in Vienna mark his leap from precocity to mastery, even genius. By

1777 the situation in Salzburg had deteriorated so much that Leopold asked for his son's release from service, which, after some initial reluctance, the archbishop granted. Whether that release was the consequence or the cause of Mozart's growing independence is difficult to determine. While traveling with his mother to Mannheim, he fell in love with Aloysia Weber (whose sister, Constanze, he would later marry), much to his father's displeasure. When his mother died on July 3, 1777, Mozart was suddenly on his own, and when his father summarily ordered him home, he made the return trip slowly and reluctantly. Still under his father's influence and once again in the archbishop's service, Mozart, on temporary leave from the latter, traveled to Munich to write the opera *Idomeneo, rè di creta* (1781; *Idomeno, King of Crete*, 1951); when he returned to Vienna, he made his decisive break both from home and from the archbishop.

Thus began Mozart's Vienna period, which lasted from 1781 until his death a decade later. It was to be a period of triumph and frustration, of independence and decline. It began with the success of the opera *Die Entführung aus dem Serail* (1782; *The Abduction from the Seraglio*, 1827), written in German rather than the more conventionally accepted Italian, and this was soon followed by his marriage to Constanze, which Leopold opposed and which may well have been orchestrated by the bride's conniving mother. For better or worse, Mozart had in a sense come of age.

Life's Work

One may say that Mozart matured either very early or very late, depending on whether one defines maturity along musical or psychological lines. Short, slightly built, and pallid, perhaps sickly, yet energetic and prodigiously talented, Mozart had to face a host of difficulties during his Vienna period: a strained relationship with the father, who has alternately been described as a tyrant and as a selfless, tireless promoter of his son's career; financial problems exacerbated by marital responsibilities which Mozart may have been poorly prepared to handle; a love of artistic independence that put him at odds with the very people upon whom his success and financial well-being depended; and, corollary to this last, his failure ever to obtain positions and pay commensurate with his talent. Clearly the picture of Mozart ruined by an uneducated spendthrift wife who was herself the cause of the rift that occurred between father and son is far too simplistic, particularly in the way it absolves Mozart of all responsibility and elevates the greatest of all the composers of the classical period into a caricature of legendary Romantic genius.

The sheer variety of forms in which Mozart was able to compose so many works of incomparable distinction during this period proves not to be surprising when one considers his early training and exposure. More surprising is the fact that Mozart seemed never to tire of experimenting, borrowing from others yet transforming their works and styles into something new and entirely his own. One detects in the six string quartets he composed from 1781 to 1784, modeled on the works of Franz Joseph Haydn (and dedicated to him), a new sense of strength and discipline. Mozart simultaneously sought to make his music—his piano concertos in particular—able to please both musical connoisseurs and less sophisticated listeners. Although Mozart wrote only four symphonies during the 1781-1784 period—and one of these, *Haffner* (1782), originated as a serenade—the piano concertos of the mid-1780's differ from the earlier ones chiefly in their being decidedly symphonic in structure and effect. The experiments in style and structure that he undertook at this time indicate that Mozart was reaching a turning point. He was done with that desire to synthesize existing forms and styles which had characterized his earlier work. In the works composed from 1785 to 1788, the change becomes especially noticeable; the style is freer, the texture deeper and more sensuous. Yet even this change would not be Mozart's last. By 1789, his style had changed again, becoming, as one critic noted, "more austere and refined, more motivic and contrapuntal, more economical in its use of materials and harmonically and texturally less rich."

The second half of the decade witnessed the growth not only of Mozart's reputation throughout Europe but of his financial difficulties as well. Even as he sought ways to supplement his income, he managed to produce many of his greatest works: two of his three DaPonte operas—*Le nozze di Figaro* (*The Marriage of Figaro*) in 1786 and *Don Giovanni* in 1787 (the year of his father's death)—the three final and greatest of his forty-one symphonies, *Die Zauberflöte* (1791; *The Magic Flute*, 1911), in which he successfully combined serious music and subject matter with the popular form of the German singspiel, all for production on the stage of Emanuel Schikaneder's theater, located in a working-class suburb. Despite its popular success, *The Magic Flute* had one especially unfortunate result. Interpreted by some as a betrayal of the secret rituals of the Order of Freemasons, which Mozart had joined in 1784, the opera led to his estrangement from one of his few remaining sources of income, his fellow Masons in general and Baron von Swieten in particular, who had long served as one of Mozart's most ardent champions and most consistent patrons.

Not surprisingly, Mozart's remarkable achievements as well as his untimely death at age thirty-five have given rise to a number of equally remarkable legends, many of which focus on his final year. In was in that year, 1791, that he received from Count Walsegg-Stuppach a commission to write in secret a requiem mass, which the count planned to have performed as his own composition. While working on the requiem (a work he would not live to complete), Mozart had premonitions of his own death, or so goes the legend retrospectively concocted by certain imaginative biographers. The facts are that Mozart died on December 5, 1791, of rheumatic fever, not, as some have speculated, of uremia brought on by years of alcoholic (as well as sexual) excess or of poison administered by his "rival," Antonio Salieri, whose generosity toward many of his contemporaries is a matter of record. However odd by modern standards, the circumstances of Mozart's burial conform to the Viennese practice of the time: The corpse went unaccompanied to the cemetery and was buried in a mass grave. Yet that did not prevent others from seeing in it further evidence of Mozart's having been a romantic outcast whose genius went unrecognized and unrewarded in his own time. Similarly, although Mozart's precocity is a fact, the claim that he could effortlessly compose first and only drafts of some of the most brilliant music ever written is less true. Mozart, it seems, did revise on occasion, and although he did often compose rapidly (and often out of financial necessity), he generally did so less rapidly that his adulators have claimed. Available evidence suggests, for example, that he did not write *La Clemenza di Tito* (1791; *The Clemency of Titus*, 1930) in eighteen days—some of it in a carriage—though he may have composed all of its arias in so short a span.

Finally, dramatic as it may be for a biographer (as recently as Wolfgang Hildesheimer in 1982) to claim a significant Oedipal relation between the death of Leopold and the composition of *Ein musikalischer Spass* (1787; a musical joke) a short time after, scholarly research makes clear that Mozart could not have conceived it as a joke aimed at his dead father because most of it was written before Leopold died. This is not to say that certain of the conclusions drawn by Mozart's most responsible Freudian critics do not have a certain validity. Brigid Brophy, for example, is surely right in seeing Mozart as a deeply divided figure in revolt against, as well as paradoxically obedient to, not only his father but also all figures and forms of authority: archbishop, emperor, Church, Masons, and other, usually more established and generally older composers, as well as the musical traditions Mozart absorbed, mastered, and transformed.

Summary

Wolfgang Amadeus Mozart's reputation is rivaled by only a handful of composers and surpassed by none. His work is as renowned for its melodic beauty, rich texture, innovativeness, and formal perfection as Mozart is for his virtuosity, improvisation, and ability to imitate and combine popular and serious forms. Above all, one must be impressed by the sheer variety of Mozart's compositions, as well as by the excellence of the music he created in each of the many forms in which he worked: sacred, chamber, orchestral, keyboard, and both serious and comic opera. Even in the composition of works in an admittedly minor form, such as the dances he wrote in his capacity as court *Kammermusicus* (to which position he was appointed in 1787 at less than half the salary of his predecessor, Christoph Gluck), he displays the same variety and craftsmanship evident in his quartets, concertos, symphonies, and operas.

Although his reputation has grown immensely in the twentieth century, his genius did not go unrecognized during his own lifetime. Genius, however, did not necessarily translate into either financial security or popular acclaim, especially in the case of a composer who was often believed to put too many demands on his listeners and who tended toward innovation rather than predictability and conventionality. Although his preeminence among composers is universally accepted and his operas generally recognized as having changed the very nature of that form, both the man and his art remain at least partly shrouded in legend. The popularity of Peter Shaffer's brilliant play *Amadeus* (1979) and the 1984 film version by Miloš Forman will, when balanced by the meticulous scholarship of researchers such as Alan Tyson, ensure greater understanding of Mozart and his art.

Bibliography
Biancolli, Louis. *The Mozart Handbook: A Guide to the Man and His Music*. Cleveland, Ohio: World Publishing, 1954. An especially useful work for those in need of convenient summaries of Mozart's major works, of his technical achievements, and of available scholarship dealing with these and other areas of Mozart studies. Discussion of Mozart's life and works is, however, necessarily limited in scope.
Blom, Eric. *Mozart*. London: J. M. Dent and Sons, 1935. Rev. eds. 1962, 1974. Surely the most authoritative, balanced, and accessible study of Mozart's life and works. Designed for all who are interested in the composer, from the lay listener to the music scholar. This "standard" work, one of the volumes in the Master Musicians series, makes excellent use of available scholarship. Blom devotes half of his book to Mozart's life and half to discussion (rather than detailed technical analysis) of the music.
Brophy, Brigid. *Mozart the Dramatist: The Value of His Operas to Him, to His Age, and to Us*. London: Libris, 1988. An unabashedly psychoanalytical reading of Mozart and his operas, but one which sheds surprising light on Mozart and on works such as *The Marriage of Figaro*, *Don Giovanni*, and *The Magic Flute* (the latter's internal contradictions, in particular).
Deutsch, Otto Erich. *Mozart: A Documentary Biography*. Translated by Eric Blom, Peter Branscombe, and Jeremy Noble. Stanford, Calif.: Stanford University Press, 1965. This treasure trove of Mozart-related materials is chronologically arranged and annotated where necessary but without any intrusive interpretive editorializing. Includes petitions, church records, death certificates, diary entries, title pages from Mozart's published works, newspaper items (including reviews), and letters from the Mozart family circle. (For letters from the composer himself, see *The Letters of Mozart and His Family*. London: Macmillan, 1938, 2d ed. 1966, edited by Emily Anderson.)

Einstein, Alfred. *Mozart: His Character, His Work*. Translated by Arthur Mendel and Nathan Broder. New York: Oxford University Press, 1922, 2d ed. 1945. Einstein makes no attempt to retell Mozart's life in detail; he chooses instead to define Mozart's character in terms of the events and people that exerted the greatest influence on him. In the book's latter half, he discusses Mozart's music according to general type (orchestral, vocal, operatic). The emphasis throughout this enthusiastic study is on Mozart's development.

Hildesheimer, Wolfgang. *Mozart*. Translated by Marion Faber. New York: Farrar, Straus & Giroux, 1982. The most readable, perhaps the most compelling, and certainly the most unreliable biography of Mozart. The author, a German novelist, views Mozart psychoanalytically. He chips away at the musical mask Mozart chose to hide behind in order to expose the doomed figure Mozart actually was. Mozart emerges as a man totally frustrated in his attempts to win the favor of a public incapable of understanding his music.

Jahn, Otto. *Life of Mozart*. Translated by Pauline D. Townsend. 3 vols. London: Novello, Ewer, 1891. Although now dated, Jahn's work remains an indispensable source for the facts of Mozart's life. Later biographers have not so much supplanted Jahn's work as supplemented it, adding certain new facts or reading them in a different light. Lamentably, Herman Albert's revised and expanded edition of Jahn's biography (*W. A. Mozart*, 2 vols., 1919-1921) has not been translated into English. The most helpful modern synthesis of biographical facts is Stanley Sadie's long Mozart entry in the *New Grove Dictionary of Music and Musicians*.

Landon, H. C. Robbins. *1791: Mozart's Last Year*. New York: Macmillan, 1988. Landon does not so much offer new material as bring together material unearthed by previous scholars. In doing so he manages to demystify Mozart's final year, which has been the subject of so many legends. Landon is particularly interested in correcting what he believes are the errors popularized by Hildesheimer and Peter Shaffer.

Landon, H. C. Robbins, and Donald Mitchell, eds. *The Mozart Companion*. New York: Oxford University Press, 1956. An excellent and comprehensive selection of essays by diverse hands on a wide variety of topics: Mozart's style and influence, keyboard music, wind serenades, chamber music, symphonies, smaller orchestral works, concertos, operas, concert arias, church music, and even Mozart portraits.

Shaffer, Peter. *Amadeus*. New York: Harper & Row, 1980. Shaffer's popular and controversial play, first performed in London and later made into a film directed by Miloš Forman, closely follows Hildesheimer's psychoanalytical reading of Mozart's character except that Shaffer presents his story less in a biographical than in a theatrical, or even fictional, manner, from the point of view of Mozart's "rival," Antonio Salieri. The play is not biography (nor does it claim to be); it is, rather, a brilliant meditation on genius.

Tyson, Alan. *Mozart: Studies of the Autograph Scores*. Cambridge, Mass.: Harvard University Press, 1987. A detailed and fascinating study of Mozart's manuscripts which enables Tyson to redate a number of works. As a result, he proves that Mozart did not always compose his works completely in his head before he set them down on paper. Many of the works, especially the later ones, were composed in distinct stages over a considerable length of time. Scholarly yet readable, Tyson's essays will have a profound impact on Mozart studies.

Robert A. Morace

MUHAMMAD 'ALĪ PASHA

Born: 1769; Kavala, Macedonia
Died: August 2, 1849; Alexandria, Egypt
Areas of Achievement: The military and government
Contribution: By applying strong-arm techniques so as to assure central-government control, Muhammad transformed Egypt from its eighteenth century status as an ungovernable and unproductive province of the Ottoman Empire into a largely autonomous state supported by an impressive military apparatus. That was done by combining Ottoman "new order" reform priorities with European technical contributions, especially in the areas of military and agricultural modernization.

Early Life

Although Muhammad 'Alī Pasha's family originated in Albania, it was in the Ottoman Turkish province of Macedonia (in modern Greece) that the first biographical information concerning him was recorded. His father's position as a ranking Ottoman bureaucrat serving the sultanate of Selim III (who ruled between 1789 and 1808) was very significant for the future career of Muhammad. One of Selim's main goals was to use loyal servants of the state to create, in the place of the by then severely inefficient Janissary corps and imperial administrative system, an army and government of "the new order" (*nizam-ul Cedid*). Without actually being members of the new order elite military unit which Selim had consciously copied from contemporary European models, both his father and the young Muhammad were heavily influenced by the visible efficiency of new order Ottoman institutions.

When the sultan needed a capable lieutenant to accompany a force of irregular Albanian troops sent to reoccupy the Ottoman province of Egypt (after the retreat of Napoleon I's famous 1798-1802 expeditionary force on the Nile), he chose Muhammad. The future governor of Egypt entered history in early adulthood, not as an Albanian and certainly not as an Egyptian, but as a loyal Ottoman military officer.

Life's Work

Muhammad's rise to power as an Ottoman governor and then a virtually independent ruler of Egypt between 1805 and 1848 was tied to his ability to centralize (in typical Ottoman new order fashion) governmental control over military, bureaucratic, and economic functions. He began this process in Egypt by befriending rival local groups and playing each against the others. Then he gradually and systematically reduced each of his temporary allies to dependence on his sole will. In stages, for example, the army under the new governor's command ceased to be Albanian and was replaced by trainees under new order officer candidates selected by Muhammad. Some of those selected to take the place of Albanian irregulars and residual (pre-1798) *mamluk* (foreign slave elite) military grandees were already Ottoman professionals. Others were retrained *mamluks*. Any elements likely to resist Muhammad'$ restructuring of the province's military forces were eliminated either by being reassigned (the case of Albanians sent to combat Wahhabi tribes in Arabia after 1811) or by being mercilessly killed (the fate of many *mamluk* beys in 1811).

Once he was in firm political and military control over Cairo's governorate, Muhammad proceeded to introduce a series of major internal reforms which would help strengthen his position. First, Egypt's old *mamluk*-dominated tax farm system (*iltizamat*) was replaced by a single tax (*ferda*) collected by direct salaried agents of the governor. Proceeds from taxes were used not only to expand and train the new military establishment (by bringing more professionals, including, after 1815, retired Napoleonic officers) but also to invest in publicly sponsored agricultural innovations. These included new irrigation canals engineered to increase productivity during the low Nile season and the introduction of new internationally marketable crops. The latter, especially silk and cotton, were brought under cultivation according to strictly controlled governmental terms.

By the early 1820's, the effectiveness of Muhammad's authority as Governor of Egypt was so obvious that his sultanic sovereign, Mahmud II, called on him (in 1826-1827) to send troops to help subdue Greek insurrectionists. Had this expedition been successful, Muhammad might well have been named to the high imperial post of Ottoman grand vizier. Instead, the Concert of Europe powers, worried about Ottoman repression of the Greek independence movement but also very seriously concerned about Muhammad's dominant, monopolistic control over the conditions of cash-crop trade (especially cotton) in Egyptian ports, intervened militarily at Navarino in 1827 and forcibly removed him from the Ottoman theater. Sultan Mahmud was thus robbed of the possibility of having a grand vizier and military commander capable of reversing Istanbul's obvious decline.

The result was that Muhammad redoubled his determination to make Egypt strong. State monopolistic controls over agricultural production methods and marketing were increased (in a specifically agricultural-labor code, or *ganun al filahah*, in 1829), and the army was expanded to include, for the first time, large numbers of Egyptian peasant recruits. In 1831, this army, under the command of Muhammad's son Ibrahim, seized control of Mahmud's Syrian province, including the key Levant trade subzones of Lebanon and Palestine. Egypt's governor then extended to Syria the same iron-handed controls over taxes, agricultural production, and trade that applied in Egypt, creating a sort of mini-empire, this time at Mahmud's expense.

For eight years, Muhammad and Ibrahim reigned supreme over this expanded Arab state of Egypt, Greater Syria, and the Red Sea coast province of Arabia. By 1839, it was clear that the European powers that had intervened at Navarino in 1827 were determined that an even greater show of force against Muhammad might be necessary. When the Battle of Nezib occurred in June, 1839, the Ottomans were so roundly defeated that Mahmud's successor Abulmecid might very well have been removed by Muhammad. That would have made it possible to put the revolutionary reform methods of the latter in place throughout the Ottoman Empire. To avoid this, the London Convention of 1840 produced an international ultimatum to Muhammad: either withdraw to a hereditarily guaranteed Egyptian governorate and abandon commercial monopolies over the Levant zone as a whole or confront a joint European force.

Muhammad's decision to save his Egyptian governorate (which eventually became the hereditary possession of his family, a situation that ended only with the overthrow of King Faruk in 1952) saved him from a nearly certain military disaster in 1840. The terms which the Ottoman sultan imposed on Cairo during the last eight years of his rule, however, made it clear that the new order principles that had built Muhammad's power would not survive long. Egypt's cotton monopoly was dismantled and its army cut back to a mere eighteen thousand men. By the time of his death in 1849, Muhammad had begun to rely on practices of ruling patronage (private land grants for privileged political supporters and members of the ruling family, decentralization of taxation with benefits for privileged elements, and the like) that would characterize Egypt's decline and eventual chaotic drift toward foreign colonial domination in the third quarter of the nineteenth century.

Summary

Muhammad 'Alī Pasha's governorate in Egypt represented a successful application of Ottoman imperial new order reform priorities to a single regional province. Once the old forms of inefficient military and fiscal organization were removed and restored state authority became unchallenged, the productive potential of Egypt became very promising. Because of what proved to be possible in Egypt under the right conditions, future prospects for the eastern Mediterranean basin as a whole took on new importance. From a position of relative unimportance until 1798, Egypt emerged in the brief span of twenty years, between 1820 and 1840, to occupy a key position of international strategic importance that it would hold throughout the nineteenth and into the twentieth century.

Muhammad's strongly autocratic reforms may have been necessary to assure the maintenance of order and expanded productivity in the local context of the Egyptian province. When they were expanded beyond this local context, however, it became apparent that parties who were accustomed to the Ottoman status quo prior to 1798, especially where open trade in Levantine agricultural and transit trade products were concerned, were not keen to see other areas of the empire fall under Muhammad's control. The effects of his expanded governorate over Syria and Lebanon proved to be very controversial, both for the interests of internal social and economic subgroups (especially the Maronite Christians) and, ultimately, for the foreign powers who drafted the 1840 London Convention on the "Egyptian crisis." Once the latter decided to intervene to reverse Muhammad's gains, a pattern was set for the future intermingling of foreign imperial priorities and vested (if not to say reactionary) local interest groups leery of centrally imposed government reform priorities.

Bibliography
Abdel-Rahim Mustafa, Ahmed. "The Breakdown of the Monopoly System in Egypt After 1840." In *Political and Social Change in Modern Egypt*, edited by Peter M. Holt. New York: Oxford University Press, 1968. Deals specifically with the internal and international consequences of the Concert of Europe's decision, in 1840, to force free-market conditions on Muhammad's governorate. Particularly useful for its discussion of the terms of the Anglo-Ottoman Commercial Treaty of 1838, which became after 1840 the basis for European dealings, not only in cotton but also in other agricultural products which Muhammad's monopoly system had defined as the basis of a nationalistic (or protectionist) economy for the Egyptian province as early as the 1820's.
Baer, Gabriel. *A History of Landownership in Modern Egypt, 1800-1950*. New York: Oxford University Press, 1962. Baer's study contains perhaps the best-documented examination of the pre-Muhammad decentralized tax farm (*iltizam*) system and its linkages with land ownership and patterns of cultivation. The chapter on Muhammad's reforms examines his success not only in boosting administrative efficiency by replacing the *iltizams* but also in the effect such changes had on agricultural productivity.
Holt, Peter M. *Egypt and the Fertile Crescent, 1516-1922*. Ithaca, N.Y.: Cornell University Press, 1966. Deals with the general history of Egypt and its relations with surrounding Ottoman provinces. Contains a chapter on Muhammad's governorate in part 3: "The Last Phase of Ottoman Rule." Because both Syria and Lebanon are part of Holt's general history, this book makes it possible to place the phenomenon of the Egyptian occupation of 1831-1841 in a comparative historical context.
Hunter, F. Robert. *Egypt Under the Khedives, 1805-1879*. Pittsburgh: University of Pittsburgh Press, 1984. Part 1 of this book is devoted to a concentrated analysis of Muhammad's reign, which the author characterizes as "the emergence of the new power state." In addition to its concise synopsis of Muhammad's governorate, this work contains the most comprehensive coverage, in one book, of the reigns of his immediate suc-

cessors, Abbās the Great, Saʿīd Pasha, and Ismāʿīl Pasha. The study of these successors is important in order to gauge the long-term effects, both positive and negative, of what Muhammad had accomplished, both in the area of political institutions and in their supporting social and economic structures.

Sayyid-Marsot, Afaf Lutfi. *Egypt in the Reign of Muhammad Ali*. New York: Cambridge University Press, 1984. Deals not only with the close circles of elites, both Egyptian and foreign, who had a hand in the construction of Muhammad's state system but also with the measurable effects of the changes which he introduced. Very valuable, for example, for its investigation of the industrial and commercial sectors of Egypt's economy under Muhammad, which complemented developmental efforts in agriculture.

Byron D. Cannon

MODEST MUSSORGSKY

Born: March 21, 1839; Karevo, Pskov, Russia
Died: March 28, 1881; St. Petersburg, Russia
Area of Achievement: Music
Contribution: Mussorgsky, a major figure in the Russian national school, was the most original composer among the so-called Mighty Five. He excelled in creating dramatic works and songs in which natural speech inflections determined the vocal line, thus creating a striking realism, or naturalism.

Early Life

Modest Petrovitch Mussorgsky was descended from wealthy landowners. Modest's father, Peter, and his mother, Julia Chirikova, had four sons. The first two died in infancy; the third, Filaret, survived the youngest, Modest, by some twenty years. Much of what is known about the composer's early years is drawn from some drafts (one in Russian, two in poor French) which he wrote himself and from the scattered recollections of his brother. Mussorgsky's familiarity with Russian folklore is attributed to the family nurse, while his skill at the piano is credited to the lessons he took from his mother and, during the period 1849-1854, from Anton Herke in St. Petersburg. Mussorgsky, according to his own account, was able to play some small pieces by Franz Liszt by age seven and a concerto by John Field at age eleven.

In August, 1849, Modest and Filaret were taken by their father to St. Petersburg. There, Modest entered a preparatory school while studying with Herke; in 1852, he followed Filaret to the School for Cadets of the Guard. In this environment, the embryonic military man was exposed to a life of drinking, gambling, dancing, and debaucherie. Although serious study was not a highly prized virtue at the institution, Mussorgsky seems to have taken an interest in history and German philosophy. His musical inclinations resulted in the dedication of a piano piece, *Porte-Enseigne Polka*, to his fellow students; it was published at the expense of his proud father, who died in 1853. Mussorgsky participated in the school choir and made a cursory study of old Russian church music, including some of the works of Dmitri Bortnyanski, though he did little composition.

In 1857, however, a year after leaving the cadet school, he met Aleksandr Dargomyzhski and César Cui; through them, he became acquainted with Stasov and Mili Balakirev. At musical gatherings of these men and other artists, Mussorgsky was exposed to the music of such luminaries as Hector Berlioz, Franz Liszt, Robert Schumann, and Mikhail Ivanovich Glinka, much of it performed on the piano. He then sought Balakirev as a teacher of composition. Shortly thereafter, he resigned his commission. Under Balakirev's guidance, the youthful creator produced various early pieces, some of which were later lost.

Nervous disorders, at least in part attributed to excessive drinking, appeared as early as 1858. A visit to the estate of family friends near Moscow in 1859 for a rest resulted in a turn from a cosmopolitan outlook to a Russian orientation. On January 23, 1860, Anton Rubinstein conducted the orchestral version of Scherzo in B-flat Major, thus marking Mussorgsky's public debut as a composer. Another nervous crisis ensued, but after spending the summer at the estate of friends, the composer pronounced himself cured of the "mysticism" with which he had been afflicted.

Life's Work

In 1861, an imperial decree declared the emancipation of the serfs, and Mussorgsky was immediately enmeshed in family difficulties associated with the change in the social order. Over the next two years, he was obliged to spend considerable time aiding his brother in managing the family estate. Mussorgsky, however, was not musically inactive during this period. The *Intermezzo in modo classico* (1860-1861) for piano and such songs as "Tsar Saul" (1863) manifest a musical maturity. The opera *Judith* by composer-critic Aleksandr Serov, performed on May 28, 1863, and a reading of Gustave Flaubert's *Salammbô* (1862) that autumn, impelled the composer to write a libretto based on *Salammbô*. Mussorgsky's mélange of verse, with liberal borrowings from Russian poets and from Heinrich Heine, took its stage directions from Flaubert's work. The accompanying music, which occupied his attention until 1866, contains borrowings from his earlier piece *Oedipus in Athens*, and some portions of *Boris Godunov* are prefigured.

In December of 1863, as a consequence of a major downturn in his financial status, Mussorgsky took a position as collegiate secretary in the engineering department of the Ministry of Communications, and, on February 1, 1864, he was elevated to the post of assistant head clerk in the barracks section of the same department. In December, 1866, Mussorgsky was made titular councilor, but, on May 10, 1867, he was fired. In late 1863, the composer joined a commune with five other young men, lived together with them in a flat, and engaged in discussions on life and art. The group was strongly influenced by the novel *Chto delat'?* (1863; *What Is to Be Done?*, c. 1863), by Nikolai Chernyshevski, written during the author's imprisonment in the fortress of St. Petersburg. The burning issue with which Mussorgsky wrestled from this point onward was the subordination of art to life, as proposed by Chernyshevski. Musical works which exemplify this turn in his creative thinking are the two-piece *From Memories of Childhood* and *Rêverie* (both compositions dating from 1865). That year was, indeed, a pivotal one. Following his mother's death, Mussorgsky's alcoholism became so serious that a case of delirium tremens caused the severing of his ties with communal life. His recovery at his brother's flat allowed him to resume work, but the seeds of destruction were sown.

Salammbô was abandoned, probably because Mussorgsky had come to grips with his technical deficiencies and his lack of empathy, at the time, for the Eastern coloration the work demanded; however, in January, 1867, *The Destruction of Sennacherib* for chorus and orchestra was completed, and, late in 1866, such songs as "Darling Savishna," "You Drunken Sot," and "The Seminarist" flowed from his pen. Naturalism and irony were by then mainstays of the composer's vision, and, as he provided his own texts to each of these three efforts, there is a distinctly personal level embodied therein. A modest degree of recognition was bestowed on the beleaguered artist when, with the earlier "Tell Me Why" (1858), "Darling Savishna," and "Hopak" were published in 1867, Mussorgsky's first creative efforts to appear in print since the youthful *Porte-Enseigne Polka*.

In 1866, Mussorgsky, who had for some years been interested in Nikolai Gogol's tale "St. John's Eve" even to the point of considering it for an opera, wrote a piece based on the tale as a tone poem for orchestra. This work became *Night on Bare Mountain* (popularized in the film classic *Fantasia*, 1940). The unusual tonalities, intentionally "foul and barbarous," disturbed the sensibilities of his more conventional contemporaries, and the work was never performed in Mussorgsky's lifetime. During this same period, an orchestral setting of the *Intermezzo in modo classico* (with an added trio) and an unfinished tone poem inspired by the Pan-Slav Congress, *King Poděbrad of Bohemia*, give witness to the several directions in which Mussorgsky was moving.

After a hiatus of several years, Mussorgsky returned to the Dargomyzhski circle at a time when "Dargo" was working on *The Stone Guest*, based on Aleksander Pushkin's play. By this time, he was officially a member of what Vladimir Stasov called "The Mighty Handful," known familiarly as "The Five." He also rejoined the ranks of the employed by accepting an appointment as assistant head clerk in the forestry department in the Ministry of Imperial Domains. Early in 1868, he busied himself with song composition, composing "The Orphan" and "Eremushka's Lullaby." In June of 1868, he set the first act of Gogol's comedy *The Marriage*, and a few months later he commenced composition on *Boris Godunov*, based in part on a play by Pushkin, and with a libretto fashioned by the composer. Unlike the usual fits and starts that accompanied many of his large-scale works, Mussorgsky's energy and intensity were such that *Boris Godunov* was completed by December 15, 1869. Although Dargomyzhski died on January 5 of that year, his influence is notable. The Imperial Theatre rejected *Boris Godunov* for its "extraordinary modernism": The piece departed from custom and operatic tradition; for example, it lacked a major female character. Undeterred, Mussorgsky set about to revise by excising politically objectionable material and by adding two "Polish Scenes" that included a female character, Marina, and a closing "Revolutionary Scene." Individual portions, such as the "Coronation Scene" and the "Polonaise," received favorable receptions, but the Committee of the Theater remained implacable in their shortsightedness. On February 17, 1873, Eduard Nápravník directed the "Inn Scene" and the "Polish Act" at the Marinsky Theatre. Cui reported that the ovations were unprecedented. A full production was finally mounted on February 8, 1874, with Nápravník again on the podium. While the public was enthusiastic (Mussorgsky took some thirty curtain calls), the critics were, for the most part, unmoved. The composer could take solace in that the public had at last recognized his immense talent. The realism and the intensity of the drama struck a nerve in the audience of the time that set into motion a new way of thinking about opera.

While *Boris Godunov*'s travails occupied several years of his lifetime, Mussorgsky, nevertheless, busied himself with other grand projects. During much of 1873 and 1875-1876, he devoted his attention to *Khovanshchina*, another historial opera; sustained periods of heavy drinking prevented uninterrupted work, however, and his last efforts on this work date from 1880. Nikolay Rimsky-Korsakov completed the work in 1886.

During the summer of 1873, Mussorgsky began to share living quarters with a distant relative, the amateur poet Count Arseny Golenishchev Kutuzov. The latter provided the texts to two song cycles, *Sunless* (1874) and *Songs and Dances of Death* (1875-1877). The six *Sunless* songs, reflecting a morbid text, contain much of Mussorgsky's characteristic melodic recitative, but with increased attention to subtle shadings in harmony reflective of changes in mood. The piano is used in a most original manner to evoke or to suggest the appropriate atmosphere. In the *Songs and Dances of Death*, there emerges a series of vividly painted dramas in cameo. The vocal declamation, now at a level of perfection, is blended with a melodic line that grips and sustains the listener's attention. Golenishchev-Kutuzov provided the texts for two more individual songs, "Forgotten" (1874) and "The Vision" (1877). Mussorgsky wrote the texts to his remaining songs, "Epitaph" (1874), "The Nettle Mountain" (1874), and "Sphinx" (1875); only the latter was actually completed.

Stasov, who was growing increasingly alarmed at Mussorgsky's dementia, encouraged the latter to visit Liszt, who had made known his admiration for *The Nursery*, a song cycle published in 1872. Mussorgsky declined; instead, he devoted his energy both to composition and to his civil service position. In June of 1874, he created the piano suite *Pictures from an Exhibition*, inspired by the architectural drawings and paintings of his friend Victor Hartmann, who had died only the year before. The musical depiction of such drawings as *The Gnome*, *The Old Castle*, *The Hut of Baba-Yaga*, and the concluding *Great Gate at Kiev*, unified by a recurring "Promenade" theme, include bold and unconventional harmonies which unsympathetic critics referred to as "crude" and "barbaric."

Mussorgsky and Glinka's sister were involved in the jubilee celebrations for Osip Petrov, the bass whose role of Varlaam in *Boris Godunov* set the standard for others to follow; during this general time frame (spring 1876), the composer returned to a projected comic opera based on Gogol's "Sorochintsy Fair," which he had begun two years earlier. By 1878, he had abandoned the work once again. Another regression in his battle with the bottle caused Stasov to intercede with the state controller for the purpose of transferring Mussorgsky to his own control department. As the state controller was a devotee of folk songs and an admirer of "The Five," he complied willingly with the entreaty; furthermore, he gave Mussorgsky permission to take a three-month leave in order to accompany the contralto Darya Leonova on a concert tour through central Russia and the Crimea. Delighting in the scenery, Mussorgsky composed some pleasant but inconsequential piano pieces and the popular "Song of the Flea."

In November, 1879, Rimsky-Korsakov conducted excerpts from *Khovanshchina* in St. Petersburg. As the new year began, however, Mussorgsky was relieved of his duties in the Control Department. Friends came to his rescue by providing funds, with the stipulation that he complete *Khovanshchina* and *Sorochintsy Fair.* Neither composition was completed. Leonova provided him with employment as her accompanist and as a teacher of theory and arranger of duos, trios, and quartets for use by students in her singing school. At her summer residence at Oranienbaum, Mussorgsky conceived a plan for a suite for orchestra with harp and piano based on motives from folk tunes he had collected on his tours.

On February 15, 1881, Mussorgsky received the applause of the audience at a performance of *The Destruction of Sennacherib* given by Rimsky-Korsakov at the Free School of Music. Only eight days later, he suffered an apparent stroke on a visit to Leonova, and, on the following day, he was taken unconscious to the Nikolaevsky Military Hospital. Periods of lucidity enabled the noted portrait painter, Ilya Repin, to produce, in four sittings, the most frequently reproduced painting of the unruly genius; in it, he appears haggard and disheveled. According to Repin, a misguided attendant gave Mussorgsky a bottle of brandy to help celebrate his impending birthday. Craving the alcohol, Mussorgsky disobeyed doctor's orders and, at five in the morning on March 28, 1881, he died.

Summary

In his last year of life, Mussorgsky provided a statement of his artistic principles: "Art is a means of communicating with people, not an aim in itself." Only artist-reformers, he stated, such as Giovanni Palestrina, Johann Sebastian Bach, Christoph Gluck, Ludwig van Beethoven, Berlioz, and

Liszt, create art's laws, but these laws are not immutable. Art for its own sake was anathema to Mussorgsky; he believed that art should reflect life and communicate the common experiences of the human condition. Mussorgsky had particular empathy for the peasant class, despite his privileged early years; this earthiness, in fact, becomes a distinguishing feature of some of his most profound musical utterances.

During Mussorgsky's formative years, the many and varied influences of Glinka, Balakirev, Schumann, and Liszt, among others, are readily identifiable, as are the technical deficiencies which created a host of detractors and which caused Rimsky-Korsakov and others to rework some of Mussorgsky's pieces. Later, Mussorgsky aimed at the musical representation of human speech, but, from time to time, elements of Russian folk song are discernible, and they establish the lyrical quality which gives his work its unique blend of antipodal musical forces. His gift for satire is most observable in the songs, revealing Mussorgsky as a keen observer of all aspects and stations of life. His extraordinary talent for penetrating the inner recesses of the soul is nowhere better demonstrated than in *Boris Godunov*; because of this ability, the harmony, which would otherwise appear to be amateurish, seems perfectly suited to the requirements of dramatic expression.

Starting with the best intentions, "the fixers," such as Rimsky-Korsakov, were determined to complete, to reorchestrate, and to revise much of Mussorgsky's corpus. It has been argued that these refurbishings made the compositions accessible to audiences at large and contributed to their publication; however, the prettification of such masterworks as *Boris Godunov* and *Night on Bare Mountain* have stripped them of their raw, rough-hewn strength. Now that the original versions are available, there is no justification for automatically opting for the well-known revisions.

Bibliography
Brown, Malcolm Hamrick, ed. *Musorgsky: In Memoriam, 1881-1981*. Ann Arbor, Mich.: UMI Research Press, 1982. A collection of essays dealing with various aspects of Mussorgsky's life and music. Among the most informative and revelatory are "Musorgsky and the Populist Age," by Richard Hoops; "Musorgsky's Interest in Judaica," by Boris Schwarz; "Musorgsky's Choral Style," by Vladimir Morosan; "Editions of *Boris Godunov*," by Robert William Oldani; and "Musorgsky and Shostakovitch," by Laurel E. Fay.
Calvocoressi, Michael D. *Modest Mussorgsky, His Life and Works*. London: Rockliff, 1956. A major biographical study, this work contains musical illustrations, portraits of "The Five," and a catalog of Mussorgsky's compositions. A chronological account of the composer's life and works is followed by two excellent chapters devoted to "Technique and Style."
_____. *Mussorgsky*. London: J. M. Dent & Sons, 1946. This book,

part of Dent's Master Musicians series, presents the salient facts about Mussorgsky and his music. There are fine musical illustrations to highlight the descriptive analyses of important compositions. The appendices are of practical value; they include a calendar of Mussorgsky's life with an adjoining column relating to contemporary musicians.

Leyda, Jay, and Sergei Bertensson, eds. *The Musorgsky Reader: A Life of Modest Petrovich Musorgsky in Letters and Documents.* New York: W. W. Norton, 1947. Essentially, this valuable source is a life of Mussorgsky in letters and documents. They are presented in chronological order and appear in their entirety in English translations. The footnotes provide excellent explanatory data.

Montagu-Nathan, M. *Mussorgsky.* Reprint. New York: AMS Press, 1976. This book, part of the Masters of Russian Music series, is divided into four parts: career, Mussorgsky as operatic composer, choral and instrumental works, and songs. Emphasis is placed on what the author perceives as the high points in the composer's career. A brief commentary is provided on all the major works.

Orlova, Alexandra. *Musorgsky's Days and Works.* Edited and translated by Roy J. Guenther. Ann Arbor, Mich.: UMI Research Press, 1983. This work contains an exhaustive day-by-day account of Mussorgsky's life; it is, in effect, a biography in documents. Material is drawn from letters, diaries, newspaper and journal articles, and reviews, and the like. Sheds much new light on Mussorgsky's travels with Darya Leonova.

Riesemann, Oskar von. *Mussorgsky.* Reprint. Translated by Paul England. New York: AMS Press, 1970. This popular biography encompasses all aspects and phases of the composer's life. Despite occasional errors in small details, the book has much to admire, and the material is presented in a logical and orderly manner.

David Z. Kushner

NĀNAK
Rāi Bhoi dī Talvandī

Born: 1469; Talwandi, Punjab
Died: 1539; Kartārpur, Punjab, Mughal Empire
Area of Achievement: Religion
Contribution: Nānak was a religious reformer who synthesized the fundamental principles of Islam and the tradition of Hinduism into a new universal religion, Sikhism. His teaching emphasizes equality of all human beings and regards responsible social action as integral to true spiritual practice. Monism and the rejection of excessive ritual are the basic tenets of this religion.

Early Life

The historical facts of Nānak's life can be gleaned only by sifting them carefully from the embellishments of myth and legend. The essential story of his life, however, seems fairly clear. Nānak was born in 1469 in the West Punjab in a small town, Talwandi. His father, Kalu, was a relatively well-to-do person and commanded influence in the area. Nānak was a precocious and gifted child possessing unusual intelligence and an extraordinarily pronounced concern for the well-being of everyone with whom he came into contact. He had a contemplative nature with a strong inclination toward otherworldly preoccupations. Stories about his childhood and the years toward adulthood indicate these qualities. It is said that even when Nānak was an infant his heart would melt at the sight of others' suffering. At play, he would devise games imitating holy men and involving mental concentration to achieve a perception of God.

Nānak's intellectual abilities and spiritual insights had already developed phenomenally before he was old enough to start school, although the story of his questioning the teacher on the first day of school about the significance of the letters of the alphabet and his composing on that occasion an acrostic on each letter is almost certainly apocryphal. The same must be said about his discussion with the family Brahmin when the latter came to invest him with the sacred thread. Nānak rejected the thread, thus refuting the importance of the external trappings of religion. A hymn by Nānak ascribed to this occasion must be of later date.

Nānak was married at a very young age and soon had children, but to his father's dismay he did not settle down to a regular occupation. If Kalu sent him on a trip to buy merchandise for business, Nānak gave away the money to holy mendicants and called it a "true transaction." Asked to work at the family farm, he left things unattended. Stories about this period of his life relate several supernatural occurrences. For example, one hot, sunny day while herding cattle, he fell asleep under the shade of a tree. The shade did not move with the sun's movement. Another time, a cobra was seen shading his head with its hood while he slept in the sun.

Life's Work

At the age of eighteen, Nānak moved to Sultanpur, where his father and brother-in-law procured for him employment as storekeeper and accountant at a government store. He stayed there for about ten years, settling down to a well-regulated life. He maintained his family with only a small portion of his salary, giving the rest away to the poor. He spent his spare time meditating or discussing metaphysics with holy men and continued thus to progress steadily in his spiritual search. One morning, when he went for his daily bath in the Bein, a nearby stream, he disappeared, some thought in the Bein. During his disappearance, he had a spiritual experience. Soon after he reappeared, he proclaimed that he was neither Hindu nor Muslim, left his family and all other worldly belongings, and set out on worldwide travels.

Popular accounts of Nānak's travels are filled with fantastic occurrences. He is described as traveling to distant places, often by a supernatural process of instant self-transportation. These stories do have a basis in history, however, and they are also quite meaningful in another way, for they convey in a veiled manner aspects of his teaching. Primary biographical sources, such as they are, claim that he went as far as Assam in the east, Ceylon (modern Sri Lanka) in the south, Tibet and China in the north, and the Middle Eastern countries and Turkey in the west. On many of these journeys he was accompanied by his Muslim disciple, Mardana. Wherever Nānak went, many people became his followers. Hindus regarded him as their guru and Muslims as their *Pir*, and eventually his followers came to be known as "Sikhs," meaning "disciples." Thus started Sikhism, a new religion transcending the boundaries of the other religions.

The religion that Nānak preached emphasized a monistic metaphysics and the importance of social and moral responsibility. The elements of his teaching are illustrated by various incidents during his peregrinations. According to one account, Nānak pointed out the difference between the wholesomeness of honest living and the corruption of ill-gotten wealth by squeezing in separate hands two morsels of food, one from a hard-working carpenter with whom he stayed and the other from a rich man whose banquet he had refused. From his host's food poured milk and from the rich man's, blood. In another story, Nānak reformed a highway thug whose name, "Sajjan," meant "friend." With his hospitality and show of piety, Sajjan enticed travelers to stay with him and robbed them while they slept. Nānak shocked Sajjan into realizing the true meaning of his name and the karmic consequences of evil deeds. Sajjan mended his ways. At Hardwar, on the banks of the Ganges, Nānak stood in the river and started to splash water toward the west. Asked by the Hindu pilgrims what he was doing, he said that he was watering his fields in the Punjab. When they laughed, he asked how they expected the water they threw up toward the sun to reach the sun, thus pointing out the futility of rituals. Similarly, in a dialogue with a pundit, he expounded on the vanity of learning devoid of the inner experience of true reality. Inner peace, he insisted, is obtained by contemplation, not mere reading. During his sojourn in the Himalayas, he met some yogis. He reprimanded them for hiding from the social and political turmoil of the time, saying that is was their duty to guide and help oppressed humanity. The best-remembered story about Nānak's travels is one about his visit to Mecca. It is said that upon reaching the Kaaba, Nānak lay down with his feet toward the shrine, the holiest in Islam. Outraged, the keepers of the shrine admonished him to move his feet away from the Kaaba. He refused and told them to turn his feet to where there was no God. As they dragged him around, the Kaaba moved in the same direction as his feet, the moral being that God is everywhere. In the turmoil caused by Bābur's invasion of India, Nānak was taken prisoner. It is believed that Bābur, whose interest in religion was deep, heard about Nānak and met with him. Nānak is said to have given him instruction and conveyed to him his concern for people's suffering.

In about 1526, Nānak ended his travels and settled down at Kartarpur, on the bank of the river Ravi in central Punjab. There he consolidated his life's work and laid down the essential organizational bases of the Sikh religion — the institutions of guruship, prayer, *sangat* (congregation), *langar* (communal meal and sharing), and family. He returned to the life of a regular householder, considering it far superior to renunciation as a means of spiritual realization. Before his death, in 1539, he chose his best disciple, Angad, as the next guru in preference to his own sons.

Throughout his life, Nānak regularly recorded his observations about life in poetical compositions which over time added up to a large volume. These compositions, or hymns, articulate with intense feeling Nānak's views on theology and ethics, and on social, political, and economic issues. Used as recitations for prayer from the very time of their creation, Nānak's hymns comprise the nucleus to which the verses of the later Sikh gurus and other saints were added to make the Sikh scripture, the *Ādi Granth*. Nānak's verses contain the essence of the Sikh religion. They are gathered in various sequences. Most important among these sequences is the *Japji*, meaning "recitation," the daily morning prayer. Its recitation is also central to prayers for many other occasions. In a sense, *Japji* contains the gist of the whole scripture. The root mantra of the Sikh religion is *Japji*'s opening verse. Because of its quintessential character, the verse is also a complete prayer by itself and figures at the start of other major compositions. It reads:

> There is one God
> Whose name is Truth

> He is the Creator
> Devoid of fear
> Without rancour
> Of eternal form
> Beyond birth and death.
> Self-existent,
> By the Guru's grace He is obtained.

The root mantra has its further summation in "There is one God" (*Ek Onkar*)—oneness including all other attributes of divinity.

In Nānak's teachings, as Creator, the divine Self produces creation from within Itself. Creation, therefore, is part of the divine reality, emerging from and merging back into the eternal oneness of Being. There is no duality between the Creator and the created. As creatures, however, human beings suffer from the illusion that they have an existence of their own as separate individuals. This separateness from the source, regardless of whether they know it, causes grief and suffering for them. The state of being an all-encompassing unity is alone a state of unqualified happiness. God is that state; God is perfect bliss. Nānak explained that to free themselves from the sorrows of the endless cycle of birth, death, and rebirth, human beings must regain union with God. One cannot achieve this goal only by the performance of outward acts of piety or by learning. Spiritual realization requires sincere devotion to God and detachment from worldly desires. One must bring to this devotion complete self-surrender to God's will and a total renunciation of the ego. Nānak often described the relation between God and the human soul as one between the bride and the bridegroom. He prescribes the recitation (*simran*) of God's Name (*nam*) as a necessary means for expressing as well as winning the love of God. *Nam* comprehends all compositions (*bani*), such as Nānak's hymns, so that *simran* involves not mere mechanical repetition of words but concentration on their meaning and application of this meaning in one's daily conduct.

The process by which, with *simran*, one overcomes the ego, achieves mental calm, and becomes disciplined in action is slow and gentle (*sahaj*). Nānak rejected extreme asceticism as a means to spiritual development. He rather recommended a life of moderation—one that includes normal worldly activities but shuns attachment to the world. One should be like the lotus, which stays dry amid water. Progress on this path of spiritual growth requires personal guidance by a teacher (guru), the true guru being one who has realized truth. Also necessary for progress is the company (*sangat*) of others who are on the same quest. *Sangat* not only provides mutual mental reinforcement but also is the arena for right social action, without which there can be no spiritual life. It represents the equality, community, and mutual interdependence of all humanity. In Nānak's teaching, God, guru, and humans are one. The road to God realization lies squarely in the human world. A loving acceptance of this world fills Nānak's compositions with such enchanting poetry and music as make the face of the earth a window on the divine.

Summary

Nānak's teaching was part of the religious reform that swept India during the fifteenth and sixteenth centuries. By that time, Muslims had ruled the country for about three hundred years and made a deep impact on it. On one hand, Islam and its social egalitarianism had spread widely, but on the other the strictly defined character of the Muslim religion and the Muslim state's discriminatory policy toward Hindus caused extreme religious conflicts and social strife. Communal antagonism bred bigotry and an excessive preoccupation with the external forms of religion, leading to frequent oppression of non-Muslims. That tended to tear asunder the fabric of society. There was a dire need for a resolution of this conflict, for the creation of unity and harmony. Sufis, the mystics of Islam, who emphasized love of God instead of works of religion, many of whom were active in India, helped prepare the way toward such a resolution. The full answer to the problem came with the rise of the *Bhakti* movement, which spontaneously overwhelmed India on all sides toward the fifteenth century. *Bhakti*, which means "love of God," rejected all outward forms of religion and found the universal meaning of religion in intense devotion to God. It considered the love of God inseparable from the love of humanity and the rest of creation, thus combining the quest for the divine with active involvement in the world.

Indian Sufism and the *Bhakti* movement reached a culmination in Nānak's teaching. He preached a universal religion based on the oneness of God and the sameness of human beings everywhere. Because of the force his message had for unifying people of widely divergent backgrounds, he left a deep imprint on Indian civilization. His picture—a man with a long, white, perfectly rounded beard, his large eyes half closed in quiet bliss, and his whole aspect exuding a deep friendliness and tranquillity—hangs prominently in the homes of Indians, and his image lives in their minds.

Bibliography

Anand, Balwant Singh. *Guru Nanak: His Life Was His Message*. New Delhi, India: Guru Nanak Foundation, 1983. A lucid biographical account.

Banerjee, Anil Chandra. *Guru Nanak and His Times*. Patiala, India: Punjabi University, 1971. About half of the volume is devoted to the historical context of Nānak's life and work.

McLeod, W. H. *Guru Nanak and the Sikh Religion*. Oxford, England: Clarendon Press, 1968. A major work by a non-Indian. The focus is on Nānak rather than on Sikhism as a whole. The book has aroused some controversy.

Nānak. *Hymns of Guru Nanak*. Translated by Khushwant Singh. New Delhi, India: Orient Longmans, 1969. A judicious selection of hymns from Nā-nak's works. Translated with literary sensitivity.

——————. *Hymns of Guru Nanak*. Translated by S. Manmohan Singh. Patiala, India: Language Department, Punjab, 1972. Contains all of Nānak's compositions. Gives the original in Punjabi, an English translation, and an explanation of the meaning in Punjabi prose.

Singh, Ganda, ed. *Sources of the Life and Teachings of Guru Nanak*. Patiala, India: Punjabi University, Department of Punjab Historial Studies, 1969. Compiled by a foremost scholar of Sikh history, it is a basic work.

Singh, Harbans. *Guru Nanak and Origins of the Sikh Faith*. New York: Asia Publishing House, 1969. Examines Nānak's work as the foundation of Sikhism.

Singh, Kartar. *Guru Nanak Dev: Life and Teachings*. Ludhiana, India: Lahore Book Shop, 1969. Tells the story of the Guru's life and concludes with a review of his teachings.

Singh, Trilochan. *Guru Nanak, Founder of Sikhism: A Biography*. Delhi, India: Gurdwara Parbandhak Committee, 1969. This book is a standard, well-documented work.

Talib, Gurbachan Singh. *Guru Nanak: His Personality and Vision*. Delhi, India: Gur Das Kapur, 1969. A comprehensive and analytical survey of Nānak's thought.

Surjit S. Dulai

NAPOLEON I

Born: August 15, 1769; Ajaccio, Corsica
Died: May 5, 1821; Saint Helena Island
Areas of Achievement: Government, politics, and the military
Contribution: One of the greatest generals in history, Napoleon I also made
   lasting contributions to the laws and civil administration of France and
   other lands. His darker legacy is to have developed a dictatorial rule that
   is the precursor of modern Fascism.

Early Life

Although a native of Corsica, Napoleon Bonaparte was sent to French
military schools in Brienne and Paris, where he became known as "the little
corporal" because of his small stature. Commissioned to the artillery in
1785, he later took part in fighting on behalf of the French Revolution. In
1793, he was promoted to brigadier general, but he was imprisoned the next
year when the forces in power changed from the radical Jacobins to Ther-
midorean reactionaries intent on stopping the reign of terror that had made
the Revolution turn on its own members. He was soon released, however,
and back in favor in October, 1795, when he dispersed a Parisian mob
threatening the government.

A politically helpful marriage and victories in the field, especially in
northern Italy, increased Napoleon's prestige. Other spectacular victories in
Egypt, coupled with a weak government at home that was overthrown in
1799, led to his elevation as first consul in the new government. A plebiscite
was held confirming his enormous popularity, and by 1801 (the year in
which he made peace with the Roman Catholic church, one of the Revolution's greatest enemies) he was the supreme dictator of France.

Napoleon's remarkable early success was in part a matter of good fortune
and in part the product of an unconquerable will and energy that took the
maximum advantage of every political and military opportunity. Given the
chaos of the revolutionary years, it is not surprising that a military man with
political prowess should do so well. With France under siege and surrounded
by hostile powers, Napoleon's victories could be viewed (rather romantically) as having saved the Revolution from destruction. At the same time,
his own steadiness of purpose prevented warring factions from destroying
the Revolution from within.

Life's Work

Napoleon I was to keep France in the paramount position to which he had
brought it in only a few years. If France were to be secure, it had to dominate the European continent. Thus Napoleon intervened successfully in
Austria, Italy, and Germany—all enemies of the Revolution. England, with

its control of the sea, was a major target, but Napoleon repeatedly failed in attempts to destroy British military power in Egypt and on the European continent.

By 1804, Napoleon had himself proclaimed emperor. What had once been a man of humble origins, whose energies and talents had been released by revolutionary actions, now increasingly became an individual identifying his personal successes with the glory of the state. England, Austria, Russia, and Sweden formed an alliance against him, but on December 26, 1805, he overwhelmingly defeated their armies at Austerlitz. By 1808, he was master of the Continent, with only the sea power of England to thwart his imperial plans.

Although Napoleon had made significant legal reforms in France, he relied increasingly on the force of his own personality to rule. Rather than developing some kind of governmental structure that might perpetuate his rule or forming a strong general staff that could carry through with his military plans, he relied almost exclusively on his own genius. As a tireless worker and supremely organized person, he counted on being able to switch rapidly from one issue to another or from one field of battle to another. He had a detailed grasp of both civil and military matters that was awesome, and he refused to delegate the authority that accrued from his command of the components of power.

Napoleon thought, mistakenly, that he could use members of his own family as extensions of his will. Thus he conferred the thrones of Holland and Westphalia on his brothers Louis and Jerome. He made his stepson, Eugène, a viceroy of Italy and his third brother, Joseph, King of Naples and later of Spain. Few of these familial appointments were successful, either because his relatives were incompetent or because they acted independently of his wishes. Yet he continued to act as though he could invent a royal line for himself, having his marriage to Joséphine (who was unable to bear his child) annulled in 1809 so that he could marry the daughter of the Austrian emperor Francis II, Marie-Louise, who bore him a son.

Between 1808 and 1814, Napoleon continued to triumph in war, but at great cost to his country. A defeat he suffered in May, 1809, in a battle with the Archduke Charles at Aspern, demonstrated his vulnerability. Yet he drove his forces on, invading Russia in June, 1812, with an army of 500,000 men, the largest collection of troops ever mobilized in Europe. Although he made it to Moscow, the Russians had devastated their own country along the route of his advance, depriving him of the sustenance of the land and exacerbating his problems with supply lines that became overextended. With winter overtaking him, the Russians struck back, reducing his huge army to one-fifth of its original size, so that he had to hasten back to Paris to prepare a defense against an invasion. When Paris fell on March 31, 1814, Napoleon abdicated and was exiled to Elba.

A much lesser man might have accepted the verdict of history. It was a measure of the esteem Napoleon could still compel that he was able to escape and rally France once more. In his effort to reconstruct his empire, he liberalized certain features of the French constitution, but, before he could truly mobilize public opinion, he was forced into battle at Waterloo (June 12-18, 1815), the decisive defeat of his career. In exile on Saint Helena Island, Napoleon assiduously built up the myth of himself as the Revolution's man, the conqueror who had meant to liberate Europe from reactionary elements.

Summary

Napoleon I's impact on his time and on subsequent events has been extraordinary. First, there was his conceit that Europe could be unified under the rule of one man. Napoleon established a cult of the personality, a disturbing phenomenon that would be repeated in the bloody rules of Joseph Stalin and Adolf Hitler in the twentieth century. Hitler, in particular, suffered from delusions of grandeur that had their precedent in Napoleon. Both leaders, in fact, were bold military strategists who imagined that if only they took over the details of command the world could be shaped according to their desires. Napoleon established the modern model for the world-historical individual who believes in the triumph of his will.

The great Marxist critic Georg Lukács has argued that Napoleon's movement of masses of men across a continent resulted in the development of a historical consciousness in which millions of men suddenly saw their fate linked to the fate of millions of others. Even when Lukács' Marxist bias is discounted, his evocation of Napoleon's ability to motivate millions of people takes on an inspiring and frightening aspect. Napoleon took the ideas of democracy, of popular rule, and of government by the majority and turned them into another tool of the dictator. At the height of his own popularity, at crucial periods in his career, Napoleon used plebiscites to legitimate his military and imperial ambitions.

Historians of various biases continue to argue over Napoleon's significance, for they recognize in his example a powerful lesson on personality and politics. At the beginning of his career, Napoleon was seen as the outcome of a revolutionary movement and as the very type of man the forces of history had shaped to rule. Yet by the end of his career, large parts of Europe regarded him only as a dictator who camouflaged his tyranny in the rhetoric of the Revolution.

The comparison with Hitler is, again, apposite. There is virtually nothing in Hitler's record that can be salvaged, no vision of a united Europe worth contemplating. The difference between him and Napoleon can be gauged by imagining what would have happened if each man had been able to conquer all of Europe. Hitler's ideology was founded on excluding and exterminating various groups of people. Napoleon's ideology was based on the principle of inclusion. Armies were defeated in the field, and, though civilian populations also suffered in the Napoleonic Wars, the emperor had no final solution, no master plan, to rid Europe of undesirable elements. If Napoleon did betray much of the Revolution, he also left a code of law and an enviable legacy of civil administration. He is not the monster Hitler was precisely because Napoleon evolved from the context of a revolution, which in practice he may have subverted but which he also supported in a way that still influences scholars of this period.

Bibliography
Cronin, Vincent. *Napoleon: An Intimate Biography.* London: Collins, 1971. As the title suggests, this biography aims to give a close-up view of the man. Written in a clear, conversational style, this is by no means one of the classic works on Napoleon, but it is an accessible way of studying a figure who has been layered with so many different interpretations. The notes and the index sections are helpful guides to further research.
Geyl, Pieter. *Napoleon, For and Against.* London: Jonathan Cape, 1949. This study by a great Dutch historian is essential reading. With great clarity and impartiality he relates the various reactions to Napoleon that still govern writing on him today. Geyl is an acute student of nationalism and shows how nationalistic reactions to Napoleon color much of the writing that has been done on him.
Hobsbawm, E. J. *The Age of Revolution: Europe, 1789-1848.* London: Weidenfeld & Nicolson, 1962. Napoleon cannot really be understood apart from his age. This classic history by one of the most important British historians of the century brilliantly evokes a sense of the historical period and of social and political change.
Jones, R. Ben. *Napoleon: Man and Myth.* London: Hodder & Stoughton, 1977. Should be read after consulting one of the standard biographies of Napoleon. Divided into chapters on historical background, Napoleon's civil and military career, and the impact of his myth, this is a very useful study that includes maps, bibliographies, and chronologies of important periods and events.
Kircheisen, F. M. *Napoleon.* New York: Harcourt, Brace, and Co., 1932. One of the standard biographies of Napoleon, condensed in this edition from nine volumes and more than five thousand pages of text. Based on extensive archival research and reading in sources in many languages, but still a readable and informative study. Well indexed with maps and illustrations.
Lefebvre, Georges. *Napoleon: From 18 Brumaire to Tilsit, 1799-1807.* New York: Columbia University Press, 1969.
_____. *Napoleon: From Tilsit to Waterloo, 1807-1815.* New York:

Columbia University Press, 1969. These volumes are a translation of what is generally considered to be the greatest biography of Napoleon. While it focuses on the man, the biography opens with a first chapter that helpfully situates him in the context of his revolutionary times.

Palmer, R. R. *The Age of Democratic Revolution: A Political History of Europe and America, 1760-1800.* 2 vols. Princeton, N.J.: Princeton University Press, 1959-1964. This is a particularly lucid overview of the Napoleonic period. Palmer's balanced prose and helpful bibliography are essential and should be read in conjunction with Hobsbawm's classic study.

Stendhal. *The Red and the Black.* Translated by C. K. Scott Moncrieff. New York: Modern Library, 1929. Stendhal served in Napoleon's army and was his great admirer. In this novel, his masterpiece, he traces the career of Julien Sorel, a young man of Napoleonic ambitions. There is no finer source for appreciating the power of Napoleon's myth on his generation and on the generations to follow.

Thompson, J. M. *Napoleon Bonaparte: His Rise and Fall.* New York: Oxford University Press, 1952. A standard biography relying extensively on Napoleon's correspondence. It is somewhat unusual for being structured in chapters strictly devoted to the many countries on which Napoleon had an impact. Contains notes and an index.

Tolstoy, Leo. *War and Peace.* Translated by Constance Garnett. London: Heinemann, 1914. No student of Napoleon should overlook this great novelist's attack on the "great man" theory of history. The novel is an epic view of Napoleon's invasion of Russia and of the inexorable historical forces in which Tolstoy's characters find themselves immersed.

Carl Rollyson

NAPOLEON III

Born: April 20, 1808; Paris, France
Died: January 9, 1873; Chislehurst, Kent, England
Areas of Achievement: Government and politics
Contribution: Napoleon III, nephew of Napoleon I, was President of the Second French Republic from 1848 to 1852 and Emperor of the Second Empire from 1852 to 1870. He was one of the key figures, sometimes unwittingly, in the political unification of both Italy and Germany, and was also greatly responsible for the rebuilding of Paris.

Early Life

Louis Napoleon Bonaparte was born in Paris in 1808. His father, also Louis Napoleon, was a younger brother of Napoleon I, and his mother, Hortense, was the daughter of the emperor's first wife, Josephine, from an earlier marriage. The marriage of Louis Napoleon and Hortense was not a success, and rumors persisted regarding the child's paternity. After Waterloo and the exile to St. Helena, all the Bonapartes were forced out of France. Hortense, having separating from her husband, settled in Switzerland, where Louis Napoleon was educated to the dual heritage of the French Revolution and the imperialism of Napoleon I. Both traditions formed his character.

As a young man, Louis Napoleon was a romantic figure. Of average height for the day, about five feet, five inches, he had a pale complexion and dark, curly hair. Women were greatly attracted to him, perhaps because of his name. It is impossible to ascertain when his own political ambitions first matured, though it is probable that he saw himself as a man of destiny at a very early age. Louis Napoleon's older brother died in 1831, and Napoleon I's son by his second wife, the so-called Duke of Reichstadt, died in 1832, leaving Louis Napoleon as the political head of the Bonaparte family. In 1836, he attempted his first *coup d'état* against the French government of King Louis-Philippe. It failed ignominiously, and after his arrest he was exiled, first to the United States and then, after his mother's death, to London.

In 1840, the British government consented to the return of Napoleon I's body to France from St. Helena, where he had died in 1821. Hoping to take advantage of the Bonaparte legend, Louis Napoleon again attempted a coup against Louis-Philippe. It, too, utterly failed, and he was sentenced to imprisonment for life. During the next few years, Louis Napoleon wrote and studied. He authored various works, identifying himself with the heritage of Napoleon I. In 1844, he published "Extinction du paupérisme" (the extinction of poverty), which, contrary to the laissez-faire ideology of the times, advocated government intervention in the economy. In 1846, he escaped from prison and within a few hours was back in England, but no closer to power.

Life's Work

The year 1848 was a revolutionary year in Europe and in France. In February, Louis-Philippe was overthrown. Initially, Louis Napoleon was unable to profit by the change, but after a working-class uprising in May and June, which alarmed the middle and upper classes, his opportunity came. Abandoning the monarchy, the French established the Second Republic, and Louis Napoleon was elected president, receiving almost 75 percent of the vote. His uncle's reputation, his own activities against the former regime, his economic program, the divisions among his opponents, and perhaps merely the times made Louis Napoleon President of France.

The government of the Second Republic was modeled after the American presidential system rather than the parliamentary form of England. Louis Napoleon lacked a political party of his own and the newly elected French assembly owed him little loyalty. In addition, the presidential term was for four years with no immediate reelection allowed. Finally, there were Louis Napoleon's own ambitions and his heritage. Those factors guaranteed still another revolution, this time, ironically, by Louis Napoleon against his own government. "Operation Rubicon" was successful, in December, 1851, but at the cost of many arrests, 370 lives lost, and twenty thousand exiled, damaging the legitimacy of his rule. Yet, in a carefully worded plebiscite, the voters approved the *coup d'état*, and a year later, in another plebiscite, they overwhelmingly voted to abolish the Second Republic and replace it with the Second Empire, with Louis Napoleon as Emperor Napoleon III.

The creation of the Second Empire caused considerable fear among other European governments as possibly portending the revival of the military imperialism of Napoleon I. Napoleon III, however, publicly stated that his empire would be an empire of peace; as president, he had proposed to the British and Prussian governments that naval and land armaments be reduced, although nothing came of it. Early in his reign, Russian pressure on the Turkish Ottoman Empire ignited the fears of both France and England about Russia's territorial ambitions and its perennial quest for warm-water ports. The result was war in the Crimea in 1854. For Napoleon, the determining factor was his desire for an alliance with England, the old enemy, more than fear of Russia. The war itself was a stand-off, but the emperor reaped credit for his diplomacy which led to peace.

In the nineteenth century, national unification was perceived by many to be both logical and necessary. Napoleon was sympathetic toward Italian unity. Yet it was easier for Napoleon to become involved in Italian affairs than to get out of them. In 1849, he had alienated both Italian nationalists and Catholics when he intervened in Roman affairs. Expecting to be welcomed, instead the French were opposed both by liberals on the Left, who had recently established a republic in Rome, and by conservative Catholics on the Right. In spite of Napoleon's support of Italian national aspirations, for some Italian patriots he moved too slowly, and in 1858 there was an attempt to assassinate him. Napoleon supported Sardinia's aim of eliminating Austria from Italy, but he envisioned not a strong united Italy but a federated state which would look to France and himself for guidance. His decision to wage war against Austria was risky, lacking as it did the support of most European governments, and after initial victories, Napoleon agreed to peace. Sardinia was not pleased, but France obtained Savoy and Nice as a result of the newest Napoleon's imperialism. Italian unification remained for the future, and Napoleon's intervention had failed to satisfy any of the participants.

Perhaps the major accomplishment of the Second Empire was the rebuilding of Paris. Here, too, Louis Napoleon was inspired by his uncle's accomplishments. Even as late as 1848, Paris was in many ways a medieval city, but, with the assistance of Georges Haussmann, Napoleon made Paris into one of the first modern and planned cities in Western civilization. The Seine River was no longer a public sewer, the city streets were widened, trees planted, parks provided, and gas lights added, making Paris the famous City of Lights. Undoubtedly, the emperor wished to create a monument to his rule—he saw himself as a second Caesar Augustus building a new Rome—but there were economic and strategic considerations. Jobs would be created, and the wider, straighter streets would make it more difficult for the Parisians to rebel against his regime.

As emperor, Napoleon faced the responsibility of providing an heir. After canvassing several European princesses, the imperial eye fell upon Eugenie de Montijo, daughter of a Spanish nobleman and his part-Scottish wife. For Napoleon, it was a love match, unpopular with many of his advisers; yet Eugenie, for all of her beauty and charm, was ultimately not a suitable consort. She gave birth to a son, the prince imperial, in 1856, but she and the emperor were not close and Eugenie often pursued policies independent of those of Napoleon. In particular, she was a strong supporter of the Papacy during the era of Italian unification, and she was the energetic sponsor of French adventure in Mexico whereby the Austrian Archduke Maximilian was placed on the throne of that unwilling country. In time, Maximilian's position became untenable, and the Austrian was executed by his Mexican subjects.

The 1860's saw a change in policy as the emperor slowly began moving toward the creation of a more liberal empire. The earlier high tariff policies, which had benefited French industrialists, were modified and freer trade with Great Britain instituted. The assembly was given additional powers, and in elections republican and Royalist opponents of the imperial regime, although still in the minority, improved their numbers. Napoleon III had claimed to be a socialist, and in the 1860's he allowed the development of labor unions, but his policies and approaches were more paternalistic than democratic. By the end of the decade, the empire was more liberal than at its beginning but in reality still more despotic than democratic. If given sufficient time, Napoleon's empire might have evolved into something approximating the constitutional monarchy of Victorian England, but it faced many obstacles. Its violent birth in 1851 and its opposition from both the Left and the Right—from republicans and from Royalists—created problems which were difficult to surmount. Napoleon's advisers were often marginal political figures who lacked prominence and political stature. Napoleon's health was poor, and his own personality was more suited to the seeking of power than to the wielding of it. He remained more the conspirator than the statesman.

It was Napoleon's ultimate misfortune to face one of the most astute statesman of modern European history. Otto von Bismarck of Prussia desired a united Germany, a Germany created by blood and iron. In 1866, Prussia defeated the Austro-Hungarian Empire in only six weeks, which led the northern German states into a federation. In 1870, Bismarck turned his talents against Napoleon. The vacant Spanish throne was offered to a Catholic prince of the Protestant ruling house of Prussia. The French feared that they would find themselves encircled by Germans. Napoleon's government demanded that the Prussian king apologize for the affair, but Bismarck made the diplomatic conversations appear that the Prussian rejection of the French demand was harsher and more dismissive than it was in reality. The French public, including Eugenie, demanded war with Prussia, and against his own inclinations Napoleon weakly succumbed. War was declared in 1870. It was an unmitigated disaster. Napoleon III was captured by the Prussians and soon abdicated. The Second Empire was over.

Summary

Napoleon III chose exile in England. In France, the war against Prussia continued briefly, but ultimately Germany prevailed and the French were forced to surrender the provinces of Alsace and Lorraine. The Second Empire was replaced by the Third Republic. Napoleon III died in his English exile in 1873. His son and heir, the prince imperial, the hope of the Bonaparte dynasty, joined the British army in South Africa. He was killed in action against the Zulus in 1879. Eugenie survived until 1920; she lived long enough to see Alsace and Lorraine restored to republican France after World War I.

Although Napoleon's diplomatic accomplishments were sometimes significant and his economic policies showed vision, the ease with which he was swept away in the events of 1870 suggests that his hold upon France was extremely superficial. He ruled for more than twenty years—longer than his famous uncle—but other than on Paris, his ultimate impact was slight. He remained the political adventurer and the dreamer to the end.

Bibliography

Bury, J. P. T. *Napoléon III and the Second Empire*. London: English Universities Press, 1964. Bury, also a biographer of Leon Gambetta, a leading republican opponent of Napoleon III, has here written one of the best introductions to the Second Empire.

Corley, T. A. B. *Democratic Despot: A Life of Napoleon III*. New York: Clarkson N. Potter, 1961. This study notes two of the elements found in Napoleon, the popular and the autocratic, and the emperor's attempt to reconcile them. The author takes Napoleon's intellectual attempts seriously, arguing that he was the first modern politician but failed as a statesman.

Gooch, Brison D., ed. *Napoleon III, Man of Destiny: Enlightened Statesman or Proto-Fascist?* New York: Holt, Rinehart and Winston, 1963. This volume is a compendium of excerpts by various historians of Napoleon, allowing the reader to sample differing interpretations of the emperor and his regime. The subtitle captures its scope.

Pinkney, David H. *Napoleon III and the Rebuilding of Paris*. Princeton, N.J.: Princeton University Press, 1958. The author concentrates upon the creation of modern Paris under the leadership of the emperor and Georges Haussmann. The City of Lights is perhaps the major monument to the Second Empire, showing both its strengths and its weaknesses.

Thompson, J. M. *Louis Napoleon and the Second Empire*. New York: Noonday Press, 1955. This analysis of Napoleon ultimately finds the emperor lacking the necessary qualities to succeed in the inheritance left to him by Napoleon I. Suggesting the author's interpretation, each chapter begins with a quote from *Hamlet*.

Eugene S. Larson

JACQUES NECKER

Born: September 30, 1732; Geneva
Died: April 9, 1804; Coppet, Helvetia
Areas of Achievement: Business, government, and politics
Contribution: Necker was the best-known and perhaps most successful financier, financial writer, and reform minister during the reign of King Louis XVI—at a time when all three fields were in their pioneer stage. Controversies about his abilities and policies have not ceased, and he is a major figure in the continuing debates over mercantilism and Physiocracy.

Early Life

Jacques Necker's early life was short and sweet—short in the telling and sweet to him. His father, Karl Friedrich Necker, born in Kostrzyn, Pomerania, in 1686, was serious and hard-working, as probably were generations of north German Neckers, many of them Lutheran pastors. Of considerable intellect, Jacques's father was trained in law, gained political appointments, published on international law, and was elected professor of public law in 1726 at the Genevan Academy, where he flourished in a serious and respectful environment. He became a Genevan citizen and married Jeanne-Marie Gautier of a prominent Genevan family. Their first son, Louis, later known as Louis of Germany for the estate he purchased, was serious and bright.

Jacques was a precocious student. He completed his secondary curriculum when he was fourteen, and although he wished to pursue literature, he followed his father's wishes and went to work in the banking firm of Isaac Vernet, brother of a colleague of Jacques's father. Jacques pleased his employer and in 1750 was transferred to the Paris branch. There he served a long apprenticeship. Vernet retired in 1756, and a new company, Thelluson and Necker, was formed. Apparently, George-Tobie de Thelluson, the son of a Genevan banker, supplied most of the capital, and Necker supplied most of the hard work and banking skills. The apprenticeship continued; modest profits and valuable experience were gained in making government loans during the Seven Years' War (1756-1763).

Life's Work

Necker turned thirty-one in 1763, began to date (it was called courting), and began to establish his fortune. He made money in speculation in grain, Canadian notes, and the Company of the Indies, as many did, although few retained their fortunes. Famines, the loss of Canada in the Treaty of Paris (1763), and the reorganization of war debts made these three areas lucrative. Critics tried to prove shady dealings on Necker's part, but at worst it could be said that he exploited the practices and standards of the times. His activities left him with the lifelong conviction that "business enterprise should be left to businessmen," a belief contrary to the dictates of mercantilism, to which Necker was believed to adhere, because he opposed the allegedly Physiocratic reform minister Anne-Robert-Jacques Turgot.

In 1763, Necker began to court Germaine de Vermenoux, a well-to-do widow; her sister was married to Necker's partner, Thelluson. Probably concerned about their different social status, Germaine resisted Necker's attention. Escaping to a health spa near Geneva with her young son, she met Suzanne Curchold, a governess of unusual wit and charm, and took her back to Paris in 1764 as companion-governess. Suzanne and Necker fell in love and married at the end of the year. Germaine forgave her former suitor and her employee, and remained a friend of the Neckers until her death in 1785. Necker acknowledged the great help he had received from "the companion of his life." Suzanne rapidly became a fashionable hostess in Paris; her "Fridays," by 1768, were well frequented by *lumières* (bright, famous, and promising persons). The unfriendly accused her of entertaining (and living) only to advance her husband's career; the generous, including Voltaire, Denis Diderot, and Jean-Jacques Rousseau, found her to be a genuine *lumière*.

Necker retired from Thelluson and Necker in 1772. He then devoted most of his time to writing and to his political appointments and showed little interest in increasing his personal fortune. He had enough to live comfortably all of his life. Necker won the prize of the Académie Française in 1773 for his *Éloge de Jean-Baptiste Colbert* (eulogy of Colbert). In 1775, Necker published an essay on legislation and the grain trade, which attacked Finance Minister Anne-Robert-Jacques Turgot's free-trade policy and fixed the view of Necker as a mercantilist and anti-Physiocrat and therefore antiphilosophe. Actually, Necker was more of a pragmatist than a theorist, as is fitting to a finance minister, which is what he was to become. He was first placed in complete control of France's finances when he was named director of the Royal Treasury in 1776. The following year, he was made finance minister.

Necker faced enormous difficulties in his first administration. Turgot had commenced reform, but the main result had been to awaken the opposition of the special interests and to establish the inconsistency of the king. Five months of inattention increased the disorder, and Necker had to struggle to meet current obligations. He managed enough loans to finance participation in the American Revolution and institute reforms to lessen the cost of those long-term obligations. Special interest groups mounted a pamphlet offensive against him; his appeals to the king for support were ignored. He issued his famous *Compte rendu au roi* (1781; *State of the Finances of France*, 1781) and resigned amid consternation in the financial community.

Finances worsened. Even conservative ministers such as Charles-Alexandre de Calonne and Étienne-Charles de Loménie de Brienne were forced to recommend reforms. Facing the refusal of the Assembly of Notables to endorse reforms and the Law Court of Paris to enregister reform edicts, and lacking the resolve to call out troops, Louis XVI, in August, 1788, recalled Necker to head finances, quibbling over his title, and announced a meeting of the Estates-General for May, 1789. The market value of government securities surged.

Contrary to public belief, Necker was not in command; in fact, the king, the ministers, and the court paid little attention to him. The Estates-General paid little attention to him when it met on May 5. Leaders of the clergy and leaders of the nobility were intent on the protection of their privileges; leaders of the Third Estate (Commons) were equally intent on changing the composition of the Estates-General and on clarifying the constitution, or on writing one (they disagreed on whether there was one), so few deputies were able to concentrate on Necker's three-hour presentation. While he received some praise and support, mostly he was blamed for not being able to communicate. The king expected Necker to control the Commons, but neither king nor Commons listened to Necker. At court, Necker's party, looking toward a British type of constitution, pressed Louis to meet major demands, and the queen's party pressed the king to bring in troops to disperse the legislature. The queen won. Necker was dismissed and left Paris on July 11. By July 13, Paris was not only "in a fury but roaring drunk." On July 14, the Bastille fell, and on July 15 a letter of reappointment was sent to Necker at Basel.

Necker's concern in his third ministry was to restore the moral authority of the king to the public mind. The National Assembly did not respond to his numerous financial reports and recommendations, and was not moved by his eloquence. He concluded that the deputies wanted to enjoy all the power and prestige as representatives of the nation but none of the responsibility for government. The greatest problem was the disposal of the property that had been confiscated from the Church during the Revolution. The National Assembly issued *assignats*, or interest-bearing bonds; Necker urged that nothing be spent until land was sold, lest speculation, inflation, and depreciation of the *assignats* mushroom. Again, the assembly did not listen. Necker resigned in September, 1790.

Necker's retirement is usually forgotten, but it is instructive. He lived at Coppet for fourteen years. He cared for his ailing wife and, after her death, arranged and published her writings in five volumes. He published a study of the executive power in large states in 1792 and a three-volume history of the Revolution in 1796. A fifteen-volume edition of his works by his grandson was published in 1820-1821.

Summary

A patient, line-by-line analysis of Jacques Necker's personal and professional financial dealings substantiates the claim that Necker was the most experienced and knowledgeable financier of the late eighteenth century. One of the reasons he has not had more acclaim is that so few then (or later) understood finances well enough to judge. Many, such as Comte de Mirabeau, believed Necker to be "full of wind." His presentation on the opening day of the Estates-General was long and frustratingly detailed, and the reaction to his speech was not positive. He did, however, advise the assembly well when he concluded, "You will not be envious of what time can achieve and will leave something for it to do. For if you attempt to reform everything that seems imperfect, your work itself will be so."

Necker offered advice to many friends. He urged the émigrés to make peace with the Revolution. He deplored the absence of executive power of the king and recoiled in horror at the evidence of violence against persons and property. He likened himself to the sixteenth century chancellor of Queen Regent Catherine de Médicis, Michel de l'Hospital, who had tried to mediate between Catholics and Protestants; forty years of violence followed.

Bibliography
Bosher, J. F. *French Finances 1770-1795: From Business to Bureaucracy.* Cambridge: Cambridge University Press, 1970. Convincingly contradicts the older view that bankruptcy was a terminal illness of the Old Regime and that the royal administration was beyond reform. Includes a helpful table of French terms, five organization charts, five tables of expenses and revenues, a list of treasurers, treasurers general, and receivers general, and a bibliography.
Doyle, William. *Origins of the French Revolution.* New York: Oxford University Press, 1980. Part 1 describes writings on revolutionary origins since 1939. Page 39 clearly contrasts the old and the new judgments of Necker. Part 2 is a thirteen-chapter topical study of the breakdown of the Old Regime and is a good supplement to Egret's narrative.
Egret, Jean. *The French Prerevolution, 1787-1788.* Translated by Wesley D. Camp. Introduction by J. F. Bosher. Chicago: University of Chicago Press, 1977. The best study of the period. This work reaps the financial effects of the reaction to Necker's first ministry and sets the stage for his second.
Gershoy, Leo. *The French Revolution and Napoleon.* New York: F. S. Crofts, 1933. The best-organized and most clearly written of the many older surveys. Presents the older view of Necker in chapter 4, "The Reform Movement During the Old Regime," and chapter 5, "The Destruction of the Old Regime."
Harris, Robert D. *Necker: Reform Statesman of the Ancien Régime.* Berkeley: University of California Press, 1979. The first four chapters describe Necker's early life and professional career up to his first appointment as finance minister. Contains a bibliography and a list of terms.

_____. *Necker and the Revolution of 1789*. Lanham, Md.: University Press of America, 1986. A continuation of Harris' study of Necker's political career. Analyzes royal administration in the 1780's, finance ministries between Necker's first and second terms, and Necker's second and third terms. Contains a complete twenty-page bibliography.

Herold, J. Christopher. *Mistress to an Age: A Life of Madame de Staël*. Indianapolis: Bobbs-Merrill, 1958. As close to a biography of Necker as is available in English. Part 1, "The Neckers," is most germane to Necker, but he is an important figure throughout the book because Madame de Staël, Necker's daughter, was unusually devoted to her father and unusually influenced by him.

Frederic M. Crawford

SAINT PHILIP NERI

Born: July 21, 1515; Florence
Died: May 26, 1595; Rome
Area of Achievement: Religion
Contribution: As a priest living in Rome during the Counter-Reformation, Saint Philip Neri stood apart from the religious politics of his time and influenced countless Catholics to reform their lives and return to traditional spirituality. Called the "Apostle of Rome," he founded the Congregation of the Oratory, which inspired both laymen and clergy to lead lives of holiness and charitable works.

Early Life

Saint Philip Neri was born in a poor section of Florence, ruled at that time by the Medicis. His father, Francesco Neri, was unsuccessful in his career as a notary and thus turned to alchemy, losing the family's financial security through his improvidence. When Philip was five years old, his mother, Lucrezia da Mosciano, died shortly after giving birth to her fourth child. The household, by all reports a happy one, was thereafter managed by a woman who was either the mother-in-law of Francesco, or his second wife.

Young Philip, unlike many other saints, showed no evidence of a precocious interest in religion. Yet even as a child he was noted for his charm and sweetness of disposition, personal qualities which would characterize his relationships with others throughout his life. His nickname was "Pippo Buono" (good little Philip). His formal schooling with the Dominican fathers probably ended when he was about sixteen, and thereafter he was self-educated. In 1532, he went to San Germano to work for his father's cousin Romolo Neri, with the understanding that he would eventually take over the family business. Instead, during a period of intense prayer and meditation, he decided to give his life to God. He had no plans to enter the priesthood but to live in poverty and offer his service to humankind. Accordingly, in 1533 he left San Germano and traveled to Rome, where he lived in the home of Galeotto Caccia, a customs official from Florence, serving as tutor to Caccia's two young sons.

Life's Work

Although Philip would not be ordained a priest until he was thirty-six years old, in 1533 he quietly began the work to which he would dedicate the rest of his life. Philip lived during the Counter-Reformation, thus called by those who consider it to have been a response to the Protestant movement; it is also known as the Catholic Revival by those who consider it to have been an internal revitalization of the Church begun in the previous century in Spain.

Rome, sacked during an invasion by the French in 1527, was noted for its atmosphere of licentiousness and low moral standards, and was ripe for reform. To Catholic observers, the influence of classical, or "pagan," authors was responsible for the weakness of faith in the Church. Abuses within the Church were flagrant, with the Medicis using their political power to control church elections and corrupt clergymen neglecting the spiritual needs of the people. The Council of Trent, meeting from 1545 to 1563, would reform the abuses and clarify church teaching but would be unsuccessful in the attempt to reunite with the Protestants.

Philip, his life newly dedicated to God, became one of the many hermits of the streets of Rome, preaching informally to anyone who would listen. At night, however, he went to the catacombs outside the city to pray and meditate in solitude, beginning his life as a mystic. He also took courses in philosophy and theology at the university but, realizing that he had no calling to the scholarly life, sold his books and gave the money to the poor. He continued to live with the Caccia family, in a small attic room, eating a meager diet of bread and olives.

Soon Philip's gift for influencing others came to public attention. With his good humor, he succeeded in converting many young men who had come at first to mock his preaching. He also took up charitable work in the public hospitals, offering spiritual comfort to the dying. Although he met Saint Ignatius of Loyola during this time, Philip was not attracted to the Jesuit priesthood and had no intention of seeking ordination himself, even though many of the young men he converted became priests.

In 1544, on the eve of Pentecost, Philip underwent an unusual experience while praying in the catacombs. He reported that a ball of fire entered his mouth and lodged in his heart, creating a swelling or malformation that was visible to others. The autopsy report of his death showed an enlarged heart that had broken several ribs. Whatever the explanation for this phenomenon, observers noticed throughout his life that his heartbeat could be heard across a room and that he would tremble violently when overcome by a mystical experience.

In 1548, Philip laid the foundation for the organization that would eventually become the Congregation of the Oratory. With Father Persiano Rossi, he formed a confraternity of laymen that met at the Church of San Girolomo to pray, read the Scriptures, and discuss the lives of the saints and church history. In 1551, at the insistence of Father Rossi (and probably because the Church disapproved of lay preachers), Philip was ordained. At that time, no special education was required for ordination, although the Council of Trent was to found the system of seminaries that would educate priests in the future.

Given the power to hear confessions, Philip, contrary to the custom of the time, insisted that his followers receive this sacrament frequently. He was noted for his insights as a spiritual adviser, reportedly knowing what the penitent was thinking before any words were spoken. Despite his need for solitude, he made himself available at all hours, even during the night, to those who asked for his guidance.

Philip's meetings became famous in Rome, attracting many followers. After the spiritual exercises, the followers would make the pilgrimage to the Seven Churches, a special devotion in Rome, stopping to eat and drink with the enthusiasm of picnickers. Among his followers were the historian Cesare Baronio, Cardinal (later Saint) Carlo Borromeo of Milan, Pierluigi da Palestrina, and Giovanni Animuccia. These last two composed sacred music for the prayer meetings, originating the musical form of the oratorio, which takes its name from this group.

In 1575, Pope Gregory XIII formally recognized the Congregation of the Oratory. Although Philip had not intended to found a religious congregation, his movement spread to several other cities in Italy. The Congregation of the Oratory differed significantly from other religious organizations in that, although the priests lived in community, they took no vows, kept their personal property, and were free to leave at any time. The pope gave Philip the property of Santa Maria in Vallicella, where he had a new church constructed and lived for the rest of his life. Since he had no wealth of his own, he apparently depended upon contributions from the faithful to carry out his work.

Philip's reputation for clownish behavior might seem at first to contradict his saintly vocation. He often ordered strange penances, such as requiring a follower to sing or dance in the streets or perform humiliating work such as sweeping the church steps while dressed in an outlandish costume. Once, when a penitent asked permission to wear a hair shirt, Philip commanded him to wear it outside his clothing, visible to all. With his belief in the virtue of humility, Philip saw these penances as a way of puncturing the egos of sinners full of self-love. Although he was personally fastidious, his appearance was sometimes laughable. Once he appeared in the streets with half his beard shaved, and sometimes he wore his clothes inside out. When the pope offered him the red hat of a cardinal, Philip took this honor as a joke and tossed the hat around like a ball. This good-humored mockery of his own dignity was taken by Romans as evidence of his saintliness and increased their affection for him.

Throughout his life, Philip wrote poetry, although little remains, as he destroyed his papers before death. As his reputation for sanctity grew, so did stories about his mystical experiences while celebrating Mass. He would often lose himself in contemplation and go into a trancelike state, reportedly rising in the air, then collapse in a state of exhaustion. His followers increased, including not only ordinary people but also cardinals and even several popes.

In his old age, Philip had a luxuriant white beard and bright, childlike blue eyes. His frail appearance became more pronounced; always an ascetic, he ate barely enough to sustain life and in his last years withdrew entirely to a life of contemplation. Philip died in 1595. Popularly acclaimed as a saint during his lifetime, he was canonized by Pope Gregory XV in 1622.

Summary

Saint Philip Neri is an example of the power of a humble man, devoid of any desire for public acclaim or political power, to exert a significant influence on the events of his time. A priest of the Roman Catholic church during the turbulent years of the Counter-Reformation, his example of personal holiness, balanced with a whimsical (at times eccentric) sense of humor, persuaded countless Romans, from ordinary workers to highly placed churchmen, to reform their lives. He is called the "Apostle of Rome."

The most significant event during Philip's lifetime was the Council of Trent, which clarified the doctrines of the Catholic church, set down the rules for the reform of the clergy, and called upon the faithful to lead disciplined lives under the spiritual direction of the Church. Although Philip took no part in the deliberations of the council, he founded the Congregation of the Oratory (Oratorians), a loosely organized group of laymen and priests who gathered to pray, read and discuss the Scriptures, and exhort others to a life of holiness. Some of Rome's most notable clerics, public figures, and musicians attended these meetings. The Oratorians, unlike members of other religious orders, took no vows.

As is often the case in reports of saints' lives, controversy arises over the contemporary biographers' records of miraculous occurrences (ecstasies, prophecies, medical cures) as manifestations of Philip's holiness. Interpretation of the meaning of these phenomena is a matter of faith. Yet there can be no question that, in a time when the Church produced both illustrious and notorious public figures, Philip stands out as a man who, through his considerable personal magnetism and holiness, became a model for personal reform for the countless people who sought his spiritual guidance.

Bibliography

Bouyer, Louis. *The Roman Socrates: A Portrait of St. Philip Neri*. Translated by Michael Day. Westminster, Md.: Newman Press, 1958. Offers insight into Philip's spiritual life from the viewpoint of a modern French priest who belongs to the Congregation of the Oratory.

Butler, Samuel. "St. Philip Neri." In *Butler's Lives of the Saints*, edited by Herbert Thurston and Donald Atwater. New York: P. J. Kenedy and Sons, 1956. An updated edition of an indispensable reference work, which gives a concise overview of Philip's life and contribution to the history of the Catholic church.

Daniel-Rops, Henry. *The History of the Church of Christ.* Vol. 5, *The Catholic Reformation.* Translated by John Warrington. London: J. M. Dent & Sons, 1962. A detailed scholarly study, especially useful in placing Philip's life and work within the framework of the Catholic Revival, which influenced him and was influenced by him, because so many of his followers were church officials.

Harney, Martin P. "Religious Orders, Old and New." In *The Catholic Church Through the Ages.* Boston: Daughters of St. Paul, 1974. A highly readable account of church history for those without scholarly knowledge of the times. Valuable in describing the Congregation of the Oratory against the background of the Council of Trent.

Maynard, Theodore. *Mystic in Motley: The Life of St. Philip Neri.* Milwaukee: Bruce Publishing, 1946. A lucid biography that draws on sources from Philip's own time as well as earlier biographies not generally available. Sifts through the technical accounts of canonization procedures and miracles to provide a readable, balanced explanation for many events in Philip's life.

Schamoni, Wilhelm. "Philip Neri, the Apostle of Rome." In *Face of the Saints.* Translated by Anne Freemantle. New York: Pantheon Books, 1947. A fascinating collection of death masks and portraits of the saints painted during their lives, along with brief biographies. The introduction has a useful explanation of the canonization process for the lay reader.

Marjorie J. Podolsky

MICHEL NEY

Born: January 10, 1769; Saarlouis, France
Died: December 7, 1815; Paris, France
Area of Achievement: The military
Contribution: Ney was arguably the most celebrated of the twenty-six marshals who served Napoleon I and the French Empire throughout the
   1804-1815 period. Ney is primarily remembered for his leadership during
   the retreat from Moscow and at Waterloo.

Early Life
   Michel Ney was born in the French city of Saarlouis in 1769, twenty years
before the outbreak of the French Revolution. Michel was the second son of
Pierre Ney, a barrel cooper, and Marguerite Grevelinger. Michel received
training as a notary public and as an overseer of mines but discovered that
his inclinations lay in martial pursuits. In 1788, one year before the Revolution, he joined the light cavalry and from 1789 fought in the French republican armies.
   Ney underwent his baptism of fire from 1792 to 1794, when he rose to the
ranks of sergeant major and subsequently of captain. The tall, sturdily built,
blue-eyed Ney was already a superb horseman and swordsman and was
skilled in drill and maneuver. He had also acquired the reputation for reckless courage and a hot temper, which, combined with his flaming red hair,
earned for him the nickname of "Le Rougeaud," or "the red-headed one."
   From 1794 to 1799, Ney advanced steadily to the rank of general of
division. His military talent was complemented by an immense personal
charisma. He led his men from the front rank, an exposure to danger that
endeared him to the soldiery of France. Already, he had been wounded three
times and had been temporarily captured. In 1800, Ney contributed to the
French victory at Hohenlinden. Thereafter, the future Emperor of France,
Napoleon, took an interest in him. In 1802, Ney was further connected to
Napoleon through marriage to Aglaé Louise Auguié, a friend of Napoleon's
wife. When Napoleon was crowned in 1804, he elevated Ney to the distinguished position of marshal.

Life's Work
   From 1804 to 1815, the French Empire under Napoleon fought successive
wars against seven coalitions of enemies. The foundation of Napoleon's rule
was the military, and at the top of the military was his personally created
body of twenty-six marshals. Ney was France's most celebrated marshal and
the one most remembered by posterity, even if he was not its most consistently talented member. During the 1805-1807 campaigns in Central Europe,
Ney demonstrated both his talents and his weaknesses. One of his greatest

victories was the Battle of Elchingen, during which he surrounded an Austrian army at Ulm. Ney then subdued the Austrian Tyrol. Against the Prussians at Jena, however, he attacked too precipitously, nearly cutting off his VI Army Corps. The impetuous Ney then provoked a foraging incident in eastern Prussia in January, 1807, which developed into the Battle of Eylau. Eylau was the first real check to Napoleon's Imperial Grand Army, but Ney partially redeemed himself by staving in the Russian right flank and causing their withdrawal. Ney's redemption was completed after the Battle of Friedland, wherein his advance led to a decisive defeat of the Russian army and directly to the Treaty of Tilsit. Out of gratitude, Napoleon created Ney Duke of Elchingen in June, 1808.

Ney's years in Spain, from August, 1808, to March, 1811, were less happy. Spain, the scene of a bloody guerrilla war, damaged many French officers' reputations, and Ney's was no exception. Initially, Ney led his VI Army Corps to minor victories, and in 1810 he participated in the invasion of Portugal under Marshal André Masséna. Ney captured the fortress of Ciudad Rodrigo and fought, indecisively, at Bussaco. The French high-water mark was reached at Torres Vedras, and, thereafter, the British, Spanish, and Portuguese armies slowly rolled back the French. Ney's gallantry and inspiration held the exposed rear guards together, but another side to his personality was revealed: a general lack of cooperation with his fellow marshals and with his superior. That resulted in his being dismissed by Masséna in 1811.

Napoleon, however, was seldom disturbed when his marshals drew daggers against one another, and he lost no time in appointing Ney head of the military camp of Boulogne, a post he held from August, 1811, to February, 1812. In April, 1812, Ney was put in charge of the III Army Corps in the greatest French army yet assembled, which was preparing to invade Russia and bring Czar Alexander I back into an economic line more favorable to Napoleon's continental system. Instead, it was the French who were brought to heel in the beginning of the end for the French Empire.

Conversely, however, Ney's reputation prospered. On August 17, Ney was the first to go into Smolensk, where he was again wounded; at Borodino, on September 7, he pushed back Prince Pyotr Ivanovich Bagration's troops. The French occupied Moscow a week later. Yet the Russian field army had not been decisively beaten, and the czar would not come to terms. Moreover, a mysterious fire in Moscow robbed the French of their winter quarters. The cataclysmic French retreat began on October 19. As in Spain, Ney was placed in command of the dangerous rear guard. There, amid snows, harassed by Cossacks, and low on supplies, Ney led by such heroic personal example and élan that Napoleon respectfully named him "the bravest of the brave." Ney was reportedly the last Frenchman to have left Russian soil. Next to Napoleon, Ney had emerged the most renowned soldier of France.

In recognition, Napoleon created Ney Prince of the Moskowa, in March, 1813.

After the disaster in Russia, much of Europe rallied against the French, and Ney fought a series of battles in German states in 1813. After receiving yet another wound and achieving an indecisive victory at Lützen, Ney blundered at Bautzen, where he had been in command of several corps. Briefly recovering at Dresden, Ney was defeated at Dennewitz and failed to take Berlin. His critics would note that his effective span of control was one corps and that he was not usually successful with a larger body. Defeated at last in 1813, Napoleon and Ney fell back on France, engaging in some of their most classic if smaller battles in an effort to keep their country from being overrun. Sensing the end, Ney was one of the first marshals to call for Napoleon's abdication. That set the stage for Ney's increasing political involvement, which went so much against his temperament and natural ability.

When Napoleon was exiled to Elba, the returned Royalist government under Louis XVIII eagerly employed such a preeminent marshal as Ney on its own behalf. Complicating events, Napoleon escaped in February, 1815, and began raising a new army with which to conquer France and, ultimately, Europe. That put Ney in a terrible quandary, for he owed Napoleon his career and owed nothing to the aristocrats, who looked upon him as a mere upstart. Although Napoleon's chances seemed dim, Ney could see that the army rank and file largely longed for a return to the former days of glory. Ney deserted to Napoleon, an act for which he would later pay with his life.

During the Waterloo Campaign in June, 1815, Ney commanded the left wing in the Battle of Quatre-Bras. Uncharacteristically, Ney's actions on June 16 were dilatory. He incorrectly assessed the situation and failed to take the strategic crossroads. Napoleon's own choice of ground at the Battle of Waterloo on June 18 was unfortunate, and his method of frontal attack was equally so. Further, even though Ney's capabilities in the grander scale had already been tested and found not to be his strongest feature, Napoleon chose to entrust to him the conduct of the main assault at Waterloo. Repeatedly and courageously, Ney charged against the well-prepared British defenses, exhausting the French cavalry. Unable to break through to Brussels, the French were themselves struck in the right flank by the Prussians. As a word, "Waterloo" has become synonymous with defeat. Napoleon was exiled to the remote island of St. Helena, and Ney was tried and executed by the Bourbon Royalists on December 7, 1815. Out of respect for France's hero, "the bravest of the brave" was allowed to conduct his own firing squad beside the wall of the tranquil Luxembourg Gardens in Paris.

Summary

Michel Ney's life may be considered a failure if one only reflects that the cause he served failed. If, above all, the age symbolized the drift away from monarchy, the seeds had at least been planted. From a personal view, Ney's career was spectacular. Few have risen from completely obscure origins to become a marshal and a prince. Ney was a successful man before Napoleon chose him as one of the elect, but Ney largely owes his historical reputation to his service in Napoleon's French Empire while under the banner of the Imperial Grand Army. Had there been no Napoleon, Ney might well have been marked by posterity as no more than one of the many newly promoted republican generals.

Ney's career as a marshal of France was made more because of his outstanding bravery than from any qualified skill as a military strategist. That is not to belittle Ney's overall martial talent. Ney's personal example, energy, charismatic inspiration, and willingness to share risks made him an exceptional leader of men and France's greatest period soldier second only to Napoleon.

From 1815 to 1848, France struggled between her traditions of monarchy and her increasingly republican leanings. The Bourbons understandably forbade the erection of a statue to Ney's memory, until their own downfall in 1848. In 1852, however, the nephew of Napoleon secured by plebiscite the mantle of hereditary emperorship, and the following year a statue of Ney was commissioned. The statue stands in the Carrefour de l'Observatoire in Paris as an eternal tribute to a national military hero of France.

Bibliography

Chandler, David G. *The Campaigns of Napoleon*. New York: Macmillan, 1966. This work is the best single-volume work on the period. Ney appears in the index, and his name covers an entire column of entries. Invaluable for understanding Ney's position in the Imperial Grand Army. Excellent maps indicate where Ney fought. Although it is appreciative of Ney's role throughout, the chapters concerning Russia and Waterloo are especially rewarding.

——————. *Dictionary of the Napoleonic Wars*. New York: Macmillan, 1979. The entry on Ney fills approximately two pages and includes a picture. The subject is covered chronologically. Key events are set off by asterisks, which permit cross-referencing and therefore a more complete explanation.

——————, ed. *Napoleon's Marshals*. New York: Macmillan, 1987. This is the best account of the twenty-six marshals so far published. Each marshal is presented in a separate section authored by a separate period scholar and includes a picture of the subject. Ney is covered by Peter Young. A map and analysis of the Battle of Elchingen sheds light on Ney as a commander. His talents may be easily compared and contrasted to those of his fellow marshals.

Delderfield, R. F. *The March of the Twenty-Six: The Story of Napoleon's*

Marshals. London: Hodder & Stoughton, 1962. The book is illuminating because it deals with the interactions of the marshals in a chronological sequence. Thus, it is complementary to works that adopt a sectional subject approach. Ney is indexed throughout the text.

Esposito, Vincent J., and John Robert Elting. *A Military History and Atlas of the Napoleonic Wars*. New York: Frederick A. Praeger, 1964. The atlas is without doubt the best military atlas on the Napoleonic period and, because of the rising cost of publication, may stand indefinitely as the definitive work. The maps offer a complete understanding of Ney's positions during the campaigns. Coverage is comprehensive, and each map is supported by an oversize page of linking narrative.

Marshall-Cornwall, Sir James. *Napoleon as Military Commander*. London: B. T. Batsford, 1967. This book offers a literate exposition that is well-illustrated with detailed maps and a chronological table. Presents a balanced account of Napoleon's career. Ney is frequently referenced in the index and may be briefly related against the larger background of his leader.

Morton, John Bingham. *Marshal Ney*. London: Arthur Barker, 1958. Only two chapters cover the 1812-1815 period. Three chapters review the politics of the second restoration or the events surrounding Ney's trial. The work adequately portrays the ineptitude of Ney in the climate of shifting politics.

Young, Peter. *Napoleon's Marshals*. New York: Hippocrene Books, 1973. The section on Ney is not as comprehensive or informative as Young's section in Chandler's edited *Napoleon's Marshals*. Four pictures of Ney and a color-plate of the marshal in uniform provide the finest single, illustrative coverage, but the Chandler book is to be preferred in most respects.

David L. Bullock

NICHOLAS I
Nikolay Pavlovich

Born: July 6, 1796; Tsarskoye Selo, Russia
Died: March 2, 1855; St. Petersburg, Russia
Areas of Achievement: Government and politics
Contribution: As Czar of the Russian Empire, 1825-1855, Nicholas I partially succeeded in restoring the historic power and position of the autocracy in Russian life and European affairs. His reign marks the high point of Russian conservative reaction to the French Revolution, Napoleonic Europe, and the Decembrist Revolt.

Early Life

Nikolay Pavlovich, known in the West as Nicholas I, was born on July 6, 1796, in Tsarskoye Selo, the third surviving son of Emperor Paul I and Empress Maria Fyodorovna, a former Princess of Württemberg. Being the third son, Nicholas was not expected to rule in his own right but rather to serve one of his elder brothers, the future Czar Alexander I or the Grand Duke Constantine Pavlovich. Consequently, Nicholas was not initially prepared to rule but rather was given a traditional, conservative, military education. What liberal training Nicholas did receive probably came from one of his tutors, the German economist Heinrich Storch. Nicholas proved to have no mind for abstraction; he was interested in science and technology and was especially talented in mathematics. Like his father before him, he took a strong interest in military affairs.

Nicholas' natural conservatism was profoundly deepened during the last years of Alexander's reign, after 1812-1814, and as a result of the Decembrist Revolt in 1825. After he returned from the Congress of Vienna, Alexander—and Russia through him—came under the sway of conservative German mystical Romanticism from the West. Opposition arose from young reform-minded noble military officers and civil servants, who staged demonstrations in St. Petersburg to influence the new czar, Constantine, upon the somewhat sudden death of the childless Alexander in 1825. Unbeknown to the Decembrists, however, Constantine secretly had renounced his right to succeed in 1822, in favor of Nicholas, when he had married a Roman Catholic Polish aristocrat. When they realized that Nicholas was the new emperor, the Decembrists went into rebellion in St. Petersburg and Kiev. The Decembrist Revolt was thoroughly crushed, and Nicholas I saw it as a manifestation of the liberal treason of much of the nobility, an attitude which set the tone for his entire reign at home and abroad.

Life's Work

Not only did the Decembrist Revolt strengthen Nicholas' conservative resolve, but also it forced him to rebuild the historic power of the Russian

autocracy and concentrate on internal affairs over foreign relations throughout most of his reign. To do this he surrounded himself with reasonably
talented conservative and reactionary advisers in key positions, many of
whom came from military backgrounds. Together they created and enforced
the state ideology of official nationalism, with its four-pronged attack: autocracy, orthodoxy, nationality, and legitimacy. Autocracy meant the historic
direct, divine-right absolutism of the czar; orthodoxy reaffirmed Russian
Orthodoxy as the one true faith and condoned the persecution of all dissenters, especially Roman Catholics, Muslims, and Jews; nationality called for
the protection of the unique Russian character from the decadence of the
West; and legitimacy was a guide for foreign policy, allowing for intervention abroad to preserve the antirevolutionary status quo.

To create a degree of bureaucratic efficiency, Nicholas did not reform the
bureaucracy as such; rather, he added yet another layer, His Majesty's Own
Imperial Chancery, which was more directly responsible to him. It contained
six sections: Sections 1 and 6 dealt with charity and welfare, respectively.
Section 2, under Count Michael Speransky, very successfully carried out the
codification and some modernization of Russian law from 1833 to 1835, a
prelude to the judicial reforms to come under the reign of Alexander II in
1864. Section 4 managed the conquest of the Caucasus Mountains region,
which began under Nicholas and continued in the reigns that followed. Part
of Armenia was secured in a war with Persia in 1826-1828 and the eastern
shore of the Caspian Sea in a war with Turkey in 1828-1829. Section 5,
under General Paul Kiselyov, considered the reform of serfdom. Nicholas
wanted to do something about this pressing problem, which had kept Russia
economically and socially backward, had in large part precipitated the Decembrist Revolt, and had constantly fueled debate and dissent in the Russian
Empire. As with so many important matters, however, he never committed
himself to doing anything about it.

The most infamous of these sections, though, was the third, the secret
police, under General Alexander Benckendorff. Based on French Revolutionary and Napoleonic models, it was a modern, professional police establishment through which Nicholas controlled dissent, monitored public opin-
oin, propagandized his people, and otherwise enforced his will. Through the
third section, censorship was maintained, and famous troublesome intellectuals such as Peter Chaadayev, Alexander Pushkin, Nikolai Gogol, Vissarion
Belinsky, and Aleksandr Herzen were hounded and controlled. Nevertheless,
under Nicholas, dissent (especially that dissent inspired by the West) continued to grow.

Nicholas did not see art as propaganda but believed that it was able to
portray attitudes; he was therefore determined that the attitudes portrayed be
the correct ones. He fancied himself as an artist and an architect, and he
played a personal role in the rebuilding of the Winter Palace and the comple-

tion of St. Isaac's Cathedral in St. Petersburg.

Section 3 acted and reacted efficiently and helped Russia to suppress the Polish uprisings of 1830-1831 and move against Russian dissidents to prevent trouble in 1848; Russia and Great Britain were the only two major European countries not to experience upheavals in 1848. Nicholas' Russia even sent troops abroad to quell a rebellion in Hungary in 1848. With section 3, Nicholas laid the basis for the modern Russian and Soviet police states. In this regard, Nicholas eventually came to be known as the "gendarme of Europe."

Nicholas reenergized the pattern of "defensive modernization" for the Russian Empire first set by Czar Alexei Mikhailov and his son Peter the Great in the late seventeenth and early eighteenth centuries. Russia did not have an original industrial revolution, and Nicholas believed it necessary for Russia to modernize cautiously to protect itself from the aggressive tendencies of the West and to avoid coming under the sway of Western decadence. Western expertise and capital therefore were allowed to come into Russia only very slowly and selectively. For example, under Nicholas the first railroad in Russia was completed in 1838, not primarily to foster internal economic development but to move troops more efficiently between Moscow, St. Petersburg, and Kiev to control possible social disorder.

Meanwhile, intellectuals of opposing Slavophile and Westernizer groupings debated the past, present, and future of Russia and sought to influence the czar and his policies. Slavophiles such as Sergei Khomyakov and the Aksakovs usually were supportive, while Westernizers such as Belinsky were much more critical. Through its control of government spending, it was really the Ministry of Finance under the reactionary Count Yegor Kankrin that was in charge of modernization and reform during much of Nicholas' reign.

A haphazard commitment to improve education also was made. A heavy emphasis was placed on science and technology. New schools and curricula were established and the older ones expanded by Minister of Public Instruction Sergei Uvarov in the years 1833-1848, marking the end of the period of reaction to the Decembrist Revolt. Soon, however, the educational system, especially as manifested by the universities, was seen as responsible for stimulating the development of a radical intelligentsia. The universities came to be distrusted, greater centralized control was instigated, and the period of post-1848 reaction ensued.

Despite the efforts at reform and modernization, the Russian defeat in the Russian-provoked Crimean War (1854-1856) at the end of Nicholas' reign showed how far the Russian Empire had declined from great power status and how backward it was. The defeat spurred Nicholas' son and successor, Alexander II, to initiate a major era of reform, beginning with the emancipation of the serfs in 1861.

Summary

Nicholas I was the last Russian czar to embody the historical definition of the autocrat. Through the strength of his conservative character and the power of his will, he reconstructed the autocracy of Ivan the Great, Ivan the Terrible, and Peter the Great in his own image. Unfortunately, in the process of this atavistic quest he retarded and often hurt Russia and its people. His stifling of progressive development, furthering of bureaucratic absolutism, expensive militarism and foreign adventurism, and general lack of progressive accomplishment left those who followed in his footsteps with a growing number of aggravated problems with which to cope.

Yet, while Nicholas did not stop Russia's slide from greatness, he did prepare the way for some of the accomplishments of his successors. The addressing of the problems of serfdom and the codification of law facilitated the later reforms of Alexander II. He furthered the march of the Russian Empire across Eurasia and into China. Defensive modernization helped bring on the Russian Revolution, and modernization continues through the Soviet period of Russian history to the present. Nicholas was a strong ruler but not a positive one, and his antireform reactionary conservatism was out of step with the needs of his country, the times in which it existed, and the modern world. In trying to strengthen the Russian Empire, Nicholas actually weakened it severely.

Bibliography

Blackwell, William L. *The Beginnings of Russian Industrialization, 1800-1860*. Princeton, N.J.: Princeton University Press, 1968. Largely a study of the very important period under Nicholas in the history of Russian industrialization prior to the actual Russian industrial revolution. Very good on the role of the state in stimulating Russian industrialization and modernization.

Golovin, Ivan. *Russia Under the Autocrat Nicholas the First*. London: H. Colburn, 1846. A critical account of the first two decades of Nicholas' reign written by a member of one of Russia's more important aristocratic families. A valuable primary source on the life and times of Nicholas and his Russia.

Grunwald, Constantin de. *Tsar Nicholas I*. Translated by Brigid Patmore. New York: Macmillan, 1955. Somewhat romanticized and very traditional, but for years the standard biography of Nicholas. Stresses foreign affairs.

Ingle, Harold N. *Nesselrode and the Russian Rapprochement with Britain, 1836-1844*. Berkeley: University of California Press, 1976. Centering on the activity of Nicholas' principal foreign minister, Count Karl Nesselrode, this work addresses the Cold War relationship that developed between Russian and Great Britain in the nineteenth century. A good study of Nicholas' unsuccessful attempt to transfer his conservative values to European affairs.

Kohn, Hans, ed. *The Mind of Modern Russia: Historical and Political Thought in Russia's Great Age*. New York: Harper & Row, 1955. Commentary and documents on Russian intellectual history in the nineteenth century. The first seven chapters deal with the reign of Nicholas. A classic text.

Leatherbarrow, W. J., and D. C. Offord, eds. *A Documentary History of Russian Thought: From the Enlightenment to Marxism*. Ann Arbor, Mich.: Ardis Publishers, 1987. In many ways an expanded modernization of Kohn, but sadly lacking in his commentary and insight. Parts 2, 3, and 4 center on the activities during the years of Nicholas.

Lincoln, W. Bruce. *Nicholas I: Emperor and Autocrat of All the Russias*. Bloomington: Indiana University Press, 1978. Largely synthetic, but very good and readable. A definitive and up-to-date standard biography of Nicholas.

Monas, Sidney. *The Third Section: Police and Society Under Nicholas I*. Cambridge, Mass.: Harvard University Press, 1961. Excellent on the third section and its various activities and on the early modern Russian police state of Nicholas. An unmatched standard.

Pinter, Walter McKenzie. *Russian Economic Policy Under Nicholas I*. Ithaca, N.Y.: Cornell University Press, 1967. A study of Russian "defensive modernization" under Nicholas I. Especially good on the philosophy and activities of Nicholas' Minister of Finance, Count Kankrin.

Riasanovsky, Nicholas V. *Nicholas I and Official Nationality in Russia, 1825-1855*. Berkeley: University of California Press, 1959. An excellent study that concentrates on the construction of the conservative Russian state ideology of official nationality by Nicholas and his advisers. Reveals in part the complex personality of Nicholas I.

Dennis Reinhartz

NICHOLAS V
Tommaso Parentucelli

Born: November 15, 1397; Sarzana, Republic of Genoa
Died: March 24, 1455; Rome
Areas of Achievement: Diplomacy, church reform, and patronage of the arts
Contribution: Nicholas V restored church unity by ending the schism between the Papacy and the conciliar party in Basel. He initiated serious efforts at church reform, helped bring peace to Italy, and sponsored architectural and literary projects in Rome.

Early Life

Tommaso Parentucelli, the future Pope Nicholas V, was born a physician's son at Sarzana in the Republic of Genoa. Orphaned early, he was forced in his youth to withdraw from the University of Bologna to earn a living as a tutor in Florence. There he met Humanist scholars and artists who enhanced his interest in the classical studies then gaining popularity among the educated classes of northern Italy. In 1419, he was able to return to complete a doctorate in theology. The impressive academic record and serious demeanor of the young priest caught the eye of Niccolò Albergati, the Bishop of Bologna, who offered him a position as his assistant. This association, which lasted twenty years, provided Parentucelli with a valuable apprenticeship in church politics.

He accompanied Albergati on many trips, within Italy and beyond. He visited the papal court under Martin V, the first pontiff to reign unchallenged in Rome in more than a century. Parentucelli used every opportunity on his travels to acquire the classical manuscripts that had become his passion. Then, in 1439, his skills in settling a dispute with Greek churchmen at the Florence Council so impressed Pope Eugene IV that, upon Albergati's death in 1443, the pope named Parentucelli to succeed him as Bishop of Bologna.

In late 1446, the pope elevated Parentucelli to the cardinalate for his performance as papal diplomat among the German princes. Finally, when Eugene died in March, 1447, Parentucelli was elected his successor by the College of Cardinals. He had been only four years a bishop and less than four months a cardinal, but his spirituality and conciliatory temperament seemed most to have recommmended him as a compromise candidate. He took the papal name Nicholas V in honor of his patron Niccolò Albergati. The new pope was a small, homely man of delicate constitution, but he had a driving sense of purpose to confront the problems inherited from Eugene.

The Roman church was in crisis. The Council of Basel, convened half a generation before, continued to reject papal authority, recognizing only its own creation, the antipope Felix V. In Germany, most princes remained either hostile to Rome or neutral in the papal-conciliar struggle. They found effective political leverage in the mutual antagonism of pope and council. In addition, the Church suffered across Europe from scandals and corruptions that went largely unchecked. Simony and concubinage were rife among the clergy, while exotic superstitions beguiled many among the general populace. Some secular lords ruthlessly exploited church property and appointments in their lands. In Italy, the major city-states seemed incapable of peaceful coexistence. Also, the last years of Eugene IV's troubled pontificate had left Rome and the Papal States dangerously vulnerable and in a state of decay. The papal treasury was empty. The extent to which Nicholas met such challenges and the means that he chose would define his place in papal history.

Life's Work

Nicholas intensified at once the negotiations with the German princes begun by Eugene IV. Within a year, the new pope had reached a milestone agreement with Austrian Emperor Frederick III and most of the princes. The Concordat of Vienna of February, 1448, conceded official imperial recognition of Nicholas V as head of the Church and acknowledged specified papal rights to church revenues and appointments in Germany. In return, the pope accepted certain limits to his taxing and investiture privileges in the German church.

By recognizing the Austrian state as an equal in political negotiations, the pope probably surrendered in the long term more than he received. Yet the Concordat of Vienna in effect sounded the death knell of the Basel Council. With the crumbling of its last major political support, the council declared itself dissolved in April, 1449. Nicholas, the skilled diplomat, had already persuaded the antipope Felix to abdicate in exchange for a generous pension and the official rank of cardinal-bishop, second in honor only to Nicholas himself. All spiritual penalties were annulled, and most conciliarists were reconciled with Rome. On the model of the Vienna agreement, the pope proceeded to individual understandings with the kings of Portugal, Castile, and Poland, as well as with lesser princes.

To celebrate the restored unity of the Western church, Pope Nicholas declared 1450 a jubilee year in which Christians everywhere were invited to Rome. They were offered the spiritual benefits of a rich indulgence (a release from penalties for sins) and the opportunity to visit the sacred places there. The donations of the thousands of pilgrims who swarmed to the papal city filled church coffers to overflowing, which provided Nicholas with the financial means to pursue other major policies.

First, to confront the spiritual neglect, corruption, and schism plaguing the Church at large, the pope in 1450 dispatched a number of cardinal-legates. They were instructed to bring the jubilee indulgence to those unable to come to Rome and, above all, to reform in the name of the Papacy such spiritual deformities as they found. Prominent were the missions to France, northern Italy, and the German empire, including Bohemia.

Most extensive of all was the reform legation through the Germanies of Cardinal Nicholas of Cusa; however, the pope's conciliatory style served more to undermine Nicholas of Cusa's efforts than to reinforce them. The legate found his decrees against the most serious abuses, such as the cult of bleeding hosts, modified or rescinded by a pontiff fearful of offending German princes and prelates so recently partisans or sympathizers of the Basel Council. Nicholas of Cusa's legation, the last major reform attempt within the German church before Martin Luther, came to little. The other missions achieved only marginal success.

In providing for the security of Rome and the Papal States, however, Nicholas proved strikingly successful. Recognizing that peace and order at home were the essential preconditions to substantive actions elsewhere, he moved energetically in a number of directions. He built new walls around the city, then dismissed the disruptive mercenaries who had controlled Rome for nearly a decade. They were replaced by strategically located fortifications, manned by new troops under officers chosen for their loyalty and competence. Nicholas imposed similar changes in the Papal States, appointing new governors, usually drawn from the local population. Finally, he granted effective self-government to the city of Rome, conceding rights of taxation and of appointment to civil office to influential local nobles. In such ways, Nicholas peacefully defused the sometimes-furious resentment that the Roman aristocracy had felt toward his predecessor.

With these considerable political and ecclesiastical achievements realized over the first four years of his pontificate, the pope turned full attention to still another realm, the cultural and intellectual. It is for his achievements here that Nicholas would be called the first "Renaissance pope." Nicholas had once commented that, after God, his greatest love lay in buildings and books. Because of the jubilee donations, he now had the funds to pursue his passions.

It was to proclaim in more visible ways the return of greatness and dignity to the papal city that Nicholas commissioned a sweeping program of architectural construction and renovation. He built new bridges and aqueducts and completed the repair of more than forty dilapidated churches. Most impressive, Nicholas put together an elaborate plan for a project of urban renewal that would encompass both the renovation and the new construction of buildings in the Borgo region adjacent to the Vatican palace and within the palace itself.

In the neoclassical style of the designs, including porticoed streets, round towers, triumphal arches, lush gardens, and fountains, there is evident the close influence of the renowned architect Leon Battista Alberti. Although Nicholas was able to complete only the refurbishing of the Vatican Palace, his plan provided the general framework for future projects, including the completion in the early sixteenth century of the new St. Peter's Basilica. Fra Angelico and Piero della Francesca were among the painters commissioned by Nicholas to decorate various Vatican buildings, including the walls of his private chapel.

Nicholas also regarded himself as the patron of all who laid claim to Humanist achievement, and he delighted in the company of scholars. He spared no expense in making the papal court a lively center of the new learning and literature. For example, distinguished Humanists such as Lorenzo Valla and Poggio were amply compensated for translating the Greek classics of Homer and Thucydides, among others, into a fluid Latin for Western readers.

Nicholas was determined as well to restock a papal library that had in the previous century been dispersed beyond recovery by the upheavals of papal exile and schism. He searched for rare manuscripts, had copies made of others, and donated his private collection. Nicholas left some 1,150 manuscripts, both Latin and Greek, patristic as well as classical. He thereby laid the original foundations of the Vatican library, one of the cultural treasures of Western civilization. After 1453, the pope's health deteriorated rapidly, marked by recurring and agonizing attacks of gout. To the end, he remained actively engaged in his various endeavors. He was buried in St. Peter's Basilica, close to the tomb of his predecessor, Eugene IV.

Summary

The pontificate of Nicholas V constitutes something of a turning point in papal history. His diplomatic successes in ending the conciliar threat, regaining the allegiance of the German princes, and bringing peace to much of Italy portended at least a partial recovery of papal authority and prestige. Further, as a Christian Humanist scholar, bibliophile, and patron of the arts, Nicholas enjoyed considerable success in making Rome for a time the center of art, architecture, and literature in the West. He provided a major stimulus to cultural distinction on the model of the classical past.

The greatest disappointment of his pontificate was the failure after the first few years to carry forward the ambitious program of church reform that he had launched. Particularly discouraging to him was the cold response of the Western states to his plea for a crusade to liberate the Byzantine Empire from the Ottoman Turks.

Yet the reign of Nicholas was, overall, a time of peace, prosperity, and promise after generations of conflict and upheaval in the Church. As the peacemaker pope, Nicholas sought to use all the weapons of papal diplomacy and Renaissance culture he could mobilize to signal the restoration of an unchallenged papal monarchy in Rome and the revived glory of the Western church.

Bibliography

Creighton, Mandell. *History of the Papacy During the Period of the Refor-mation*. Vol. 3, *The Italian Princes, 1464-1518*. London: Longmans, Green, 1882. Based largely on published sources of the time. The balanced, even-handed treatment has withstood well the test of subsequent scholarship. Especially enlightening on Nicholas' relations with the Basel Council and with the German Empire, as well as the discussion of the Papacy in its Italian setting.

Pastor, Ludwig von. *History of the Popes from the Close of the Middle Ages*. Vol. 2. Edited and translated by F. I. Antrobus. St. Louis: Herder Book Co., 1892. By far the most detailed study in English of the full range of Nicholas' activities, including his achievements in cultural patronage, political negotiations, and especially in the extensive reform mission of papal legates in the German empire and neighboring lands. Pastor, among the first scholars granted access to the secret Vatican archives, bases his account largely on manuscript evidence. That makes the work indispensable, despite its often highly partisan tone.

Stieber, Joachim W. *Pope Eugenius IV, the Council of Basel and the Secular and Ecclesiastical Authorities in the Empire: The Conflict over Supreme Authority and Power in the Church*. Leiden, the Netherlands: E. J. Brill, 1978. Shows how Nicholas, over the crucial first two years of his pontificate, continued closely certain policies of his predecessor, Eugene IV. Above all, he sought through major concessions to enlist the support of Europe's secular powers against a conciliar party that sought to reduce the Papacy under the authority of general church councils. In a valuable appendix, Stieber provides a thorough discussion of the main documentary sources for Nicholas' pontificate.

Stinger, Charles L. *The Renaissance in Rome*. Bloomington: Indiana University Press, 1985. Provides in separate segments a clear, recent overview of the main facets of Nicholas' cultural activities. Updates Pastor's standard position not only that Nicholas was the first true Renaissance pope but also that his pontificate represents a major turning point in the recovery of the Papacy.

Vespasiano da Bisticci, Florentino. *Renaissance Princes, Popes, and Prelates*. Translated by William George and Emily Waters, with an introduction by Myron P. Gilmore. New York: Harper & Row, 1963. Contains a lively and very readable short biography of Nicholas by a close friend, the Humanist bibliographer Vespasiano. While the account is invariably laudatory, it offers personal details that provide a vivid sense of the pope's personality.

Westfall, Carroll W. *In This Most Perfect Paradise: Alberti, Nicholas V, and the Invention of Conscious Urban Planning in Rome, 1447-55*. University Park: Pennsylvania State University Press, 1974. Contends that Nicholas' vast scheme of renovation for the city of Rome began with the architect Alberti's concept of urban renewal. Westfall suggests that Alberti's general designs were adapted by others to specific projects. In the collaboration of pope and architect, Westfall sees a remarkable breakthrough toward a conscious and comprehensive urban design. The bibliography is excellent.

Donald D. Sullivan

NICHOLAS OF CUSA

Born: 1401; Kues, Upper Lorraine
Died: August 11, 1464; Todi, Papal States
Areas of Achievement: Philosophy and religion
Contribution: Nicholas of Cusa contributed to preserving the hierarchical authority and unity of the Roman church while at the same time advocating Humanism and lay participation in both sacred and secular government during the early years of the Renaissance. His most lasting contribution has been to Western philosophy.

Early Life

Nicholas Kryfts (Krebs) was born in the village of Kues, between Trier and Bernkastel, on the Mosel River in the German Rhineland. His moderately prosperous father operated a barge on the busy river, which served as a major commercial waterway in Northern Europe. Young Nicholas was first sent to a school administered by the Brothers of the Common Life at Deventer on the Lower Rhine. Nicholas was inspired by the new learning that the brothers emphasized, and they also encouraged him in a spirit of church reform centered on the idea of the Roman church as a community of clergy and faithful.

In 1416, at the age of fifteen, Nicholas registered at the University of Heidelberg. Although Nicholas only remained at Heidelberg for one year, here, too, he was exposed to modern learning. Nominalistic philosophy—rejection of universals as myths and a turn toward philosophizing based on individualism—left its mark on young Nicholas. He began to question truths arrived at through pure deduction and based on traditional authority. The Scholasticism of the late Middle Ages was giving way to a Humanistic thinking in both theology and philosophy.

Nicholas of Cusa next enrolled at the University of Padua in Italy. Padua was a major center for the study of canon law in Europe. In its lecture halls, scholars of science, mathematics, astronomy, and the humanities rigorously challenged established sacred and secular dogma. Yet the revival of Neoplatonism—envisioning a hierarchy of knowledge extending from a perfect and infinite God to an imperfect and finite world—also played a crucial role in Nicholas' education. It was at Padua that young Nicholas had an opportunity to observe at first hand the government of Roman city-states, many of which inherited the idea of citizen participation from Greek antiquity. Nicholas studied at Padua for six years, earning a doctorate in canon law in 1423.

Nicholas' early education shaped his later life's work within the Roman Catholic church; it reflected the change in worldview in the transition years from the late Middle Ages to the early Renaissance years. The medieval notion that God governed the world through unchallenged hierarchical authority was tempered by growing acknowledgment that the Creator provided all of his creatures with freedom and responsibility, subject to divine judgment. The dialectic of God's transcendence and His immanence in the world dominated the thought and life of Nicholas of Cusa; he sought in his philosophy and in his daily life to reconcile these views of God and world.

Life's Work

Nicholas of Cusa returned to Germany in 1425 to embark on his life's work as papal diplomat, theologian, and philosopher. At first he enrolled at the University of Cologne to lecture and to continue his research. There he attracted the attention of Cardinal Giordano Orsini, who was impressed by a legal document prepared by Nicholas at his request. Cardinal Orsini was a noted Humanist and progressive within the Roman church; he played an important role in Nicholas' ordination as a priest in 1426. Orsini's influence was also instrumental in securing an appointment for Nicholas as a legal adviser to the Council of Basel in 1432.

Nicholas' career in church politics began in earnest at the Council of Basel. The debate centered on the issue of the pope's authority. Nicholas sided with those who believed that the Roman church ought to be governed by a general council representing clergy and congregations. The council was to be superior to the pope, who would remain the Church's religious and administrative head but who could be discharged by the council. Nicholas' conviction was that it was through conciliar government that church unity would be best preserved. The congregation ought to be the source of church law, with pope and hierarchy serving the general council.

Nicholas expanded his thinking on church government in a philosophical treatise. This work, *De concordantia catholica* (1433; on unity), sets forth what has been called the conciliar theory of government, based on Nicholas' belief that authority of the ruler must rest on consent granted by the ruled. His main thesis was that this governmental form would bring about unity within the Church.

The controversy over conciliar government continued after the Council of Basel. Subsequently, Nicholas of Cusa modified his antipapal stance. Three reasons have been offered to explain this turnabout. First, Nicholas was displeased with the turmoil between members of the council and the Holy See. Second, Nicholas' highest priority was church unity. Finally, Nicholas was motivated by the opportunities for his own career within the church hierarchy.

Nicholas was rewarded with a papal appointment. In 1437, Nicholas was a delegate to a meeting between the Roman and Eastern Orthodox Christians in Constantinople. There he invited Greek representatives to attend a scheduled council in Italy on reunification of the Greek and Roman churches. Although his efforts failed, Christian unity and reform continued to motivate

Nicholas throughout his life, in his dealings with church politics as well as in his philosophical writings.

Nicholas continued to accept diplomatic posts from the Vatican. From 1438 to 1448, he was a papal delegate to Germany, where he worked for both reform and unity within the Church. As a reward, in 1449 Pope Nicholas V made Nicholas of Cusa a cardinal of the titular Church of Saint Peter in Chains in Rome. In 1450, he was named Bishop of Brixen, in Austria. During his tenure as bishop, Nicholas encountered the growing conflict between the Church and secular politics. It was a difficult phase in his life.

His later years were spent in a bitter struggle with the secular ruler of Austria, Archduke Sigismund. Nicholas set out to reform corrupt practices among the priests and monks of his diocese, but his efforts met with apathy and hostility among the clergy. At one point, he sought to reform a convent at Sonneburg, and there Bishop Nicholas ran into bitter opposition from secular authorities because many of the nuns had been recruited from noble families. Archduke Sigismund assumed the role of protector of the nuns.

Added to this controversy was one which concerned ecclesiastical appointments. Sigismund was unhappy over several of Nicholas' choices for church posts; the bishop had bypassed candidates supported by the duke. Open conflict between the bishop and the duke resulted in negotiations, appeals to the Vatican, and, ultimately, compromise. Nicholas was recalled in 1459 to Rome.

As a reward for his services to the Holy See, Nicholas was appointed to the high post of vicar-general for temporal affairs; he was Governor of Rome and the papal territories. It was Nicholas of Cusa's last and highest office. Unfortunately, Cardinal Cusa was not freed from conflict with the Austrian duke. Now the controversy turned into a dispute between Sigismund and the Church over certain property rights in Austria. Claims and counterclaims intensified.

On one occasion, the duke's soldiers surrounded and fired their guns upon a castle in Austria in which Nicholas was temporarily residing as the pope's representative in the dispute. The cardinal surrendered and was put under house arrest. Pope Pius II, humiliated by this treatment of his representative, intervened directly and sought to punish the duke. Nicholas was extricated from the affair. He returned to Italy to live his final days in relative peace and contemplation.

During his many years of church diplomacy, Nicholas of Cusa continued his theological and philosophical research and writing. He wrote about forty-six books and manuscripts. In addition, he was an enthusiastic collector of literary and philosophical works. His two most influential works are *De docta ignorantia* (1440; *Of Learned Ignorance*, 1954) and *De coniecturis* (1442; on conjecture); together they make up a complete outline of his philosophy.

In *On Learned Ignorance,* Nicholas sets forth the doctrine that man knows God only through whatever God chooses to reveal and through human experience. Human reason reaches its limitations in its knowledge of God, for man is finite and God is infinite. Reason is applicable to this finite world, but it is a stumbling block to knowing God. Man will be the more learned the more he grasps his own ignorance of the unknown God. The infinite God is not accessible through reason, but His awareness is present in men's minds. Through man's recognition of reason's limits, a realization which is itself reached through reason, the wisdom of learned ignorance is achieved. For Nicholas' speculative metaphysics, man's highest stage of knowledge is his recognition that he cannot attain a comprehensive knowledge of God.

In *De coniecturis,* Nicholas expands his philosophy of learned ignorance. Here Nicholas argues that God is prior to the opposition of being and nonbeing. God is unity transcending the coincidence of all opposites; He transcends and confines in Himself all distinctions and oppositions. God is thus the unity of opposites, of the finite and the infinite. He transcends man's understanding, and thus man cannot form a full and accurate concept of His nature. God transcends the world, but the world is His mirror. God is the unity of world and cosmos. These statements lead into Nicholas' theology, which concludes that because God is beyond human intellect, learned ignorance opens the way to Christian faith.

Nicholas of Cusa died in 1464. He is buried in the Chruch of Saint Peter in Chains in Rome. Inside the church there is a statue of Nicholas kneeling before Saint Peter. His best monument, however, is the home and hospital for the poor that he and his family founded in his native Kues. The attached library contains many of Nicholas' original manuscripts and his collection of books. It remains in operation as a center for scholarly research.

Summary

Nicholas of Cusa is an outstanding example of a philosopher who was active in practical affairs; he combined a life of contemplation with one of action. Throughout his life, Nicholas attempted to resolve the conflict between old and new views of God and mankind while he remained an obedient member of the church hierarchy. His later writings and practical work reflected his moderation: He sought reform within the context of order and continuation. In philosophy and ecclesiastical politics, Nicholas advocated gradual development and progress, not rebellion and revolution. Nicholas lived his life according to the fundamental principles of his thought; he remains an exemplar of the unity of thought and practice in a human being's life. As such, his life captured the spirit of the Golden Rule. Above all, Nicholas' life reflected his deep devotion to the ideal of the unity of all being in God, of harmony between reason and faith, theology and philosophy, church and state.

Scholars do not agree on whether Nicholas of Cusa was the first modern thinker or a transitional figure standing between the Middle Ages and the Renaissance. It is clear that he combined traditional elements of Neoplatonism and the Scholastic tradition with postmedieval nominalism and Humanism. Evidence is inconclusive as to whether Nicholas contributed original ideas or dressed the thought of Plato, Saint Augustine, and others in the modes of his era. It is certain, however, that Nicholas of Cusa must be included in any list of the world's great philosophers. He forged a speculative metaphysics that influenced Gottfried Wilhelm Leibniz, G. W. F. Hegel, Martin Heidegger, and the existential philosophers. Nicholas' philosophical legacy remains his enduring contribution to Western civilization.

Bibliography
Bett, Henry. *Nicholas of Cusa.* London: Methuen, 1932. Standard biography, presenting detailed account of Nicholas' life coupled with a discussion of his writings and a critique of his philosophy. Stresses Nicholas' consistent thought throughout his political, philosophical, and theological writings; this thought culminates in the unity of all existence in the hidden God.
Cassirer, Ernst. *The Individual and the Cosmos in Renaissance Philosophy.* Translated with an introduction by Mario Domandi. Oxford: Basil Blackwell, 1963. An advanced critique of Nicholas' philosophy. Argues that he was a systematic thinker who presented a totally new philosophical orientation and that the beginning of modern philosophy cannot be understood without a consideration of Nicholas' work. Nicholas offered the foundations for a new theory of knowledge and history; his greatness is enhanced because he achieved this major contribution to Renaissance philosophy from within the religious ideas of the Middle Ages.
Copleston, Frederick Charles. "Nicholas of Cusa." In *A History of Philosophy,* vol. 3. London: Burnes, Oates and Washbourne, 1946. 3d ed. Garden City, N.Y.: Doubleday, 1985. Concise treatment of Nicholas of Cusa's philosophy from the perspective of the contemporary Roman Catholic church. Author's theme is that Nicholas' work and writings aimed at reconciliation, harmony, and unity in difference.
Hopkins, Jasper. *A Concise Introduction to the Philosophy of Nicholas of Cusa.* Minneapolis, Minn.: Arthur J. Banning Press, 1978, 3d ed. 1986. Includes a text in Latin and English of Nicholas' *De possest* (1460; *On Actualized-Possibility,* 1978). Hopkins contends that this short essay contains an excellent summation of Nicholas of Cusa's philosophy; he recommends that first-time students begin here. The long introductory interpretation serves as a useful reader's guide. Excellent bibliography containing a list of the English translations of Nicholas' works as well as a list of secondary interpretations.
Jaspers, Karl. "Nicholas of Cusa." In *The Great Philosophers,* edited by

Hannah Arendt and translated by Ralph Manheim, vol. 2. New York: Harcourt, Brace and World, 1966. A detailed critique of the metaphysics of Nicholas of Cusa. Jaspers considers Nicholas' philosophical writings from the perspective of his own existentialist philosophy. He finds Nicholas' major contribution in keeping alive the idea of individual freedom in human relations and in relation to God.

Nicholas of Cusa. *Unity and Reform: Selected Writings of Nicholas de Cusa.* Edited with an introduction by John P. Dolan. Notre Dame, Ind.: University of Notre Dame Press, 1962. Selected excerpts from Nicholas' major philosophical and theological writings. Text is supplemented by editor's informative introduction, which serves as an excellent reader's guide.

Sigmund, Paul E. *Nicholas of Cusa and Medieval Political Thought.* Cambridge, Mass.: Harvard University Press, 1963. Concentrates on Nichoalas' political theory, emphasizing the foundational principle of government by consent. The philosophical and legal antecedents of Nicholas' political philosophy are traced. Good bibliography of secondary sources from the political philosophy perspective.

Gil L. Gunderson

BARTHOLD GEORG NIEBUHR

Born: August 27, 1776; Copenhagen, Denmark
Died: January 2, 1831; Bonn, Prussia
Areas of Achievement: History and philology
Contribution: An extraordinarily able historian, Niebuhr, through meticulously researched as well as voluminous books and published lectures,
founded the modern German school of critical historical scholarship, one
objective of which was regeneration of the Prussian state.

Early Life

Son of the noted German philologist and Arabian traveler Karsten Niebuhr, Barthold Georg Niebuhr was born on August 27, 1776, in Copenhagen, Denmark. Despite the appearance of being Danish, the Niebuhrs
regarded themselves as German by virtue of having lived in Denmark's Dith-
marschen district, where for centuries Germans maintained separate, nearly
independent rights, within the disputed duchies of Schleswig-Holstein. Self-
described, Barthold's childhood was that of a physically weak, almost
chronically ill, and dreamy boy who lived in worlds of his own imaginative
creation, which throughout life he regarded as dangerous to thought, justice,
and morality. Indeed, from child to adult, he remained short, thin, and con-
stitutionally nervous and excitable. Not surprisingly, having seldom passed
beyond his house and garden, and being the only son of a then-famous
father, he was precociously studious by disposition almost from infancy.
He evinced predilections for ancient and modern languages, mathematics,
geography, history, and political economy. Yet, until he was an adolescent ready for university he received his education at home.

Already formidably equipped intellectually, Barthold entered the University of Kiel eager to avoid narrow specialization and to master everything
available in Kiel's curriculum, from philosophy to mathematics, physics,
chemistry, natural history, additional languages, Roman law, European constitutions, and antiquities. The purpose of this ambitiously catholic intellectual
immersion was preparation for public service: Niebuhr wanted to become,
on his father's advice, not an academician but a man of practical affairs.

Life's Work

Impatient to get on, Niebuhr thus abandoned the university in January,
1796, to serve as secretary to the Danish minister of finance, a post for
which he seemed well adapted, considering his early and continuing interest
in Danish-German land tenures (hence finance), curiosities that bent increasingly toward Europe's classical origins. After two years' service at the
ministry, Niebuhr left to spend 1798-1799 between London and Edinburgh.
These were years that generated interesting, if superficially critical, observa-

tions on British life and institutions to his father and the Moltke family. Although Niebuhr later developed immense admiration for most things British, particularly their practicality and liberties, his encounters at the time left him feeling that the quality of German conversation and thought was far superior.

Consequently Niebuhr returned to Denmark, married in 1801, and resumed various high-status official positions: assessor in the East Indies Company's commerce department and director of the Copenhagen Royal Bank as well as of the Commercial Company of the East Indies. The great Prussian statesman-reformer Freiherr vom Stein soon drew him into Prussian service, initially to negotiate Dutch and English loans (essential during Prussian participation in the Napoleonic Wars), then as Frederick William III's privy councillor during the Saxony campaign of 1813, and finally, from 1816 to 1822, as Prussian ambassador to Rome.

Although Niebuhr's responsibilities in Prussia's wartime officialdom were complex and onerous, his relations with Stein and State Chancellor Karl von Hardenberg became strained. Stein had misread Niebuhr both as a practical man of affairs and as a politician; accidentally, Stein had recruited a pedant. "Niebuhr," Stein remarked, "is no use save as a dictionary whose leaves one turns over." Yet these were mismatches made in Heaven, for Niebuhr, a staunch Protestant, regarded Hardenberg as immoral and complained repeatedly that he detested the public duties that he executed for Stein. Essentially what he preferred all along was an exclusive devotion to historical scholarship.

Time and fortune favored him. Selecting faculty for the newly founded University of Berlin in 1810, Prussia's distinguished philologist, educational reformer, and, at the time, Minister of Education Wilhelm von Humboldt appointed Niebuhr professor of ancient history, a position with singular requirements for philological genius. Although dedicated to free research, the university's faculty was also dedicated to Prussia's internal reformation and enhancement of the state's power against the powerful menace posed by France under Napoleon I. Niebuhr was second to none in his advocacy of these objectives. Prussia's great field marshal Helmuth von Moltke described young Niebuhr as a true representative of the Prussian mind.

Popular as a lecturer with students, savants, and colleagues alike, Niebuhr, drawing upon years of previous research, converted these lectures into the first two volumes of the *Römische Geschichte* (1811-1812; *The Roman History*, 1827). Combined, the brilliance of his lectures and the fresh contributions of his first major publications solidly established his professional reputation. In these works, Niebuhr was the first scholar to attack the arcane problems of ancient Italian ethnology; to illuminate the lasting importance of the legends of ancient kings passed down to the Roman historian Livy, not as historically evidential but, through his novel philological, legal, and religious evidence, as persisting social beliefs among subsequent generations of Rome's plebeian populace; and to concentrate upon the social consequences of economic and political questions such as the Roman state's agrarian problems: that is, to unravel the complexities of Rome's agrarian laws, thereby differentiating public from private ownership uses and rights. Perhaps equally important were his efforts, born of intense empathy with his materials, to perceive interrelationships between ancient institutions and to develop a pragmatic sense for their everyday operations.

Outstanding as a historian, Niebuhr nevertheless returned to public life in 1813, reassuming a role in financial negotiations with the Dutch, witnessing Prussia's humiliation at the passage of Napoleon's troops through Berlin and defeat at the Battle of Bautzen, and suffering exhaustion as well as the burden of his wife's serious illness.

Prompted in 1815 by the deaths of his wife and father and the nearly simultaneous settlement of Napoleon's fate at Waterloo, he quickly remarried and, through appointment as Prussian ambassador to the Vatican, left Berlin for Italy which, though central to his scholarship, he had never visited. Though loathing Italians generally, much as he did the French, he vastly enriched his scholarship during his seven-year "exile" in Italy. At Verona Cathedral, he unearthed the manuscript find of a lifetime: the corpus of the legal textbook by second century Roman legist Gaius, from which subsequent knowledge of early Roman law derives. Similarly, despite the chaos of the Vatican Library, he found and published fragments of Marcus Tullius Cicero's speeches. With such professional triumphs and a growing, happy family life, he cheerfully abandoned Italy in 1823 for a resumption of professorial duties in Bonn, where, despite occasional commands from Berlin for consultations, he established residence. There he revised and republished two volumes of his Roman history, plus, in three volumes, his *Vorträge über die römische Geschichte* (1828-1830; *Lectures on Roman History*, 1850), and delivered what became his three-volume *Vortäge über altbekannt Geschichte* (1829-1830; *Lectures on Ancient History*, 1852). Drawn into the December cold of 1830 to seek late news on the French revolt—and deposition—of Charles X, Niebuhr, who had lived in fear of Napoleon's revolutionary France, contracted pneumonia and died in Bonn on January 2, 1831.

Summary

Notwithstanding his precocious erudition as applied to the attempts of Stein and Hardenberg to strengthen Prussia in confrontations with the aggressive expansions of Napoleon's revolutionary France and not discounting his successful and complex financial, consultative, and diplomatic services to Prussia, Barthold Georg Niebuhr was too passionate, excitable, physically vulnerable, and moral to earn renown in the political arena. A supporter of liberal reformers in the Prussian sense, Niebuhr, like those whom he served, mistrusted the general public's capacities either to strengthen the state or to contribute directly to German unification under the aegis of Prussia. Rather, unlike the popular origins of revolutions in France, which Niebuhr and most liberal Germans abhorred, he believed that a strong, unified Prussian state would have to extend liberalism from above.

In this context, the focus of his historical work on classical societies, on Rome particularly, was not entirely fortuitous. Rome and its institutions had been a great unifying force in Western civilization; thus, to dissect and explore Rome's evolution, strengths, and weaknesses was to instruct—or remind—intelligent Germans how better they might proceed with their own nation-building. In that didactic sense, his work would be followed by many of his colleagues, disciples, and immediate successors.

Unquestionably, Niebuhr's critical historical methodology and his penchant for solid documentation and detailed philological scrutiny of the ancient institutions upon which his work was focused distinguished him from his predecessors. Justifiably, he deserves foremost rank as a founder of modern historical methodology and as the first historian to illuminate the institutional, legal, religious, and popular recesses of ancient and classical Roman history particularly. Unfortunately his writings are so densely detailed and he so lacked the gift of broad conceptualization that he was sharply criticized by Theodor Mommsen, Leopold von Ranke, and others of his more famous, if indebted, successors. Seldom read or cited by twentieth century historians in his field, he nevertheless was recognized as a major historian during the nineteenth century for his influence on the development of scientific history.

Bibliography

Barnes, Harry Elmer. *A History of Historical Writing*. Norman: University of Oklahoma Press, 1938. Written for nonspecialists, this is a clear general exposition of the evolution of modern historical craftsmanship. Niebuhr is appropriately cited in context but is not a principal subject. His influences, however are well noted. Contains a brief index.

Croce, Benedetto. *History: Its Theory and Practice*. New York: Harcourt, Brace, 1921. Croce, a great Italian philosopher, presents a sophisticated synthesis of historical craftsmanship over the past two centuries, differentiating modern approaches to older, less evidential narrative, often fictional, styles. Niebuhr is briefly placed in context. Contains a brief index.

Fowler, W. Warde. *Roman Essays and Interpretations*. Oxford, England: Clarendon Press, 1920. An able, if sympathetic, scholarly narration of Niebuhr's career. This is a very useful and sound account. Clearly written for nonspecialists. Contains a few notes.

Gooch, G. P. *History and Historians in the Nineteenth Century*. New York: Longmans, Green, 1913. A clear and authoritative account, which in chapter 1 deals effectively with Niebuhr's minor predecessors and amply with Niebuhr's own critical contributions. Niebuhr is only cited in reference to other nineteenth century historians throughout Gooch's study. Contains footnotes.

Guilland, Antoine. *Modern Germany and Her Historians*. Reprint. Westport, Conn.: Greenwood Press, 1970. While there are minor errors, this work does an especially able job in chapter 1, "The Forerunners: Niebuhr." Contains footnotes and a useful, double-columned index.

Thompson, James Westfall. *A History of Historical Writing*. Vol. 2, *The Eighteenth and Nineteenth Centuries*. New York: Macmillan, 1942. Written brilliantly for both specialists and nonspecialists by a distinguished historian and historiographer, this extensive study is the best recent assessment of the subject. Footnotes are extensive and informative, and substitute for the lack of an overall bibliography. Contains a superb twenty-six-page double-columned index.

Clifton K. Yearley

NICÉPHORE NIÉPCE

Born: March 7, 1765; Chalon-sur-Saône, France
Died: July 5, 1833; Chalon-sur-Saône, France
Areas of Achievement: Invention and technology
Contribution: Niépce was a tenacious researcher who, despite rural isolation, succeeded in creating first a method of photomechanical reproduction and subsequently the earliest method of permanently recording the
image of the camera obscura.

Early Life

Nicéphore Niépce was born in 1765 in Chalon-sur-Saône, a city located
southeast of Paris, in the French department of Saône-et-Loire of the Burgundy region. His was a prosperous bourgeois family with several estates in
the area. His father, Claude, was a lawyer who, suspected of sympathy for
the king during the upheavals of the French Revolution, had to flee his home
for a time. Four children were born to Claude and his wife. Their firstborn
was a daughter and the second was a son, also named Claude, who was born
in 1763. Though Claude was a lifelong friend and collaborator of his younger brother Nicéphore, a third brother, Bernhard, born in 1773, appears to
have had no part in their photographic research.

Nicéphore and Claude were educated at a Catholic seminary in their
hometown. Nicéphore is thought to have been intended by his father for the
priesthood, and he taught briefly at the seminary following his studies there
until the Revolution caused the religious order to be dispersed. In 1792, not
long after the death of his father, Nicéphore joined an infantry regiment of
Napoleon I's army, an act that may have been conceived partly as a way of
allaying suspicions about his own political sympathies; in any case, military
service was mandatory for a man of his age. Achieving the rank of lieutenant
in May, 1793, he traveled to Italy and participated in the campaign there in
the following year but soon fell victim to typhoid fever. Resigning his commission, he returned to France, living in the Mediterranean city of Nice,
where he was employed by the district administration.

Nicéphore married in Nice in 1795, and two years later, while he pursued
family business affairs in Cagliari, the capital of the island of Sardinia, a
son, Isidore, was born to the young couple. Claude had accompanied his
brother on this trip, and it appears that they had conducted some unsuccessful experiments in an attempt to capture the image created in the camera
obscura, an optical device consisting of a lens and a box, or chamber, within
which an image could be viewed. The camera obscura had been used for
centuries both as a technical aid for draftsmen and as a popular entertainment, but the Niépce brothers' experiment was perhaps the first such use
of the apparatus. Only a few years later, Thomas Wedgwood and Sir

Humphry Davy were to attempt a similar experiment in England, also without success.

Both brothers returned to their home in Chalon-sur-Saône in 1801. The family's remaining wealth allowed them to continue pursuing a variety of research. From their childhood, Claude and Nicéphore had shown a penchant for experimentation, making working-scale model machines together. In the next few years, they worked on an ambitious invention that they called the "Pyréolophore," an ancestor of the internal-combustion engine. Pyréolophore is a coinage based on Greek words that translates roughly as "producer of wind and fire." Air was mixed in a piston cylinder with lycopodium power, a highly flammable plant spore, producing a controlled explosion powerful enough to propel a boat up the Saône River at twice the speed of the current. This invention, remarkable for its time, was patented by decree of Napoleon on July 20, 1807, from Dresden, Germany. The Niépce brothers continued to refine the Pyréolophore over the next twenty years with the hope of exploiting it commercially, but documentation does not suggest the importance of this endeavor relative to the work in photography, which occupied their attention during many of the same years.

It is known that the Niépce brothers conducted work in the cultivation of textile plants and the extraction of indigo dye but without creating successful business ventures based upon their efforts. Much of the work of Nicéphore and Claude seems to have been motivated more by curiosity than hope of financial gain. Nicéphore has been referred to by modern commentators as "a modest provincial amateur scientist" and as "a dilettante inventor (in the best sense of the word)," and it is certain that the prestige given to science and technology by the European Enlightenment exerted an influence upon him. Even the few existing published images of Nicéphore bear witness to his ties to the rational outlook of the eighteenth century, though they date from a much later period: His portrait is rendered in the neoclassical style, the reserved, formal kind of art typical of the latter half of the century, instead of in the more expressive and emotional Romantic style of the years of his maturity. These portraits, consisting of a sketch by his son, Isidore, a sculpture from 1853 by Jean August Barre based upon it, and a drawing from 1795 by C. Laguiche, depict Niépce as having a long but well-proportioned face and aquiline nose, and also possessing unmistakably gentle eyes that evoke a kindly personality.

Life's Work

Niépce conducted various researches at his country estate, Le Gras, in the village of Saint-Loup-de-Varennes, just south of Chalon-sur-Saône. Claude moved to Paris in 1816 to be better able to promote the Pyréolophore, but by then the brothers had begun to experiment in earnest with light-sensitive materials. The path to resuming the project that they had begun in 1797-1798 began with Nicéphore's interest in lithography, a new method of reproduction of drawings that had been introduced by Aloys Senefelder in 1798 in Munich, Germany. In 1812, a French nobleman had attempted to make the method better known in France, and by 1813, a craze for it had swept the nation. Nicéphore had begun by etching the stones drawn upon by his son, Isidore, but because the stones were of indifferent quality, he tried using pewter plates instead. Soon after father and son began this project, Isidore joined the army. Nicéphore, having little aptitude for drawing, turned from reproducing drawings to a search for a method of copying engravings onto his lithographic plates. The technique that he tried involved first oiling or waxing an engraving in order to make it transparent, then placing it atop a plate that had been coated with a light-sensitive material. These early experiments do not seem to have been successful, but in 1822, employing a form of asphaltum called bitumen of Judea as the light-sensitive coating, his efforts resulted in an effective method he named "heliography," derived from the Greek roots meaning "sun" and "drawing." In the early instances, these copies were made upon glass plates. The emulsion-coated plate was then exposed through the oiled engraving to the light of the sun for two or three hours. The areas of the asphaltum emulsion that had received ample exposure through the transparent paper alone were hardened by the action of light, but the areas of the emulsion lying under the dark areas of the print remained unhardened and were readily washed away by a solvent of lavender oil and turpentine.

Niépce's first attempts to record the image of a camera obscura began in April of 1816. A sheet of paper sensitized with silver chloride was exposed in one of three small cameras for an hour or more, resulting in a faint negative image. These negatives were treated in nitric acid in an attempt to fix them, but Niépce knew that the acid was bound to attack the image. A second problem with this method was the reversal of the values of the original scene, which he tried to solve by making a print using the camera negative in much the same way that he had used an engraving in his first attempts at photolithography. Some of these prints seem to have survived in a faded condition into the 1860's.

Two other approaches to recording the camera image were the use of substances that bleach in the presence of light and the attempt to capture an image on metal and lithographic stone in order to use it for printing plates, but neither of these was successful. In the next several years, Nicéphore experimented with other light-sensitive emulsions, communicating his research in guarded letters to Claude, who had moved to London in August of 1817. Little of Nicéphore's side of the correspondence survives, apparently because Claude destroyed the letters in order to forestall discovery of their line of inquiry.

As Nicéphore's method of heliography became more refined, the possibility of using it to record the camera obscura image presented itself. The first partial success in this endeavor dates from 1824 and is reported in an optimistic letter to Claude dated September 16, 1824, which mentions images captured on stone and glass. Nicéphore's attempt to etch the stones ended in failure, however, because the image was too faint. The following year, Nicéphore experimented with zinc and copper plates and in 1826 tried pewter. Aided by improved optics and by accumulated expertise in the preparation and handling of plates, in 1827—probably in June or July—Niépce produced the image that is today regarded as the first photograph, in the accepted sense of "a permanent image of a natural scene made with a camera." It is a view taken from an upper-story window at Le Gras, showing a courtyard of the estate with a wing of the main building on the left, some trees and a low building described as a bake house in the center, and a tower on the right. Judging from the somewhat contradictory lighting of the objects in the picture, the exposure probably lasted about eight hours. This 6½-by-8-inch plate, which lay undiscovered in England until 1852, is part of the Gernsheim collection at the University of Texas, a legacy of the indefatigable historian who tracked it down. There is no conclusive proof that it is the first photograph, but since most of Nicéphore's trials were made from the same upper-story window of the house, it can be little different from other results achieved at this time that may have been lost; presumably, it is one of the best examples of his work, since it is one that he took to England with him in 1827 on a visit to see his ailing brother, Claude.

In early 1826, Niépce had ordered a camera obscura from the noted Paris opticians Charles and Vincent Chevalier, and he asked a cousin, who was to visit there, to buy the instrument for him. In conversation with Charles Chevalier, the cousin described the intended use of the specially equipped camera and even showed him an example of heliography. This unauthorized revelation soon reached another customer of the Chevaliers, the painter and scenic designer Jacques Daguerre, an ambitious man who was known principally as the proprietor of the diorama, a popular entertainment that simulated famous places and events by means of the manipulation of illusionistically painted scrims, lighting, auditory effects, and other theatrical devices. Daguerre had been conducting experiments toward fixing the image of the camera obscura—though without documented results—and upon hearing of the work of Niépce, wrote to him to gain information about his processes. Daguerre's first inquiries were all but rebuffed; Niépce was perhaps justifiably suspicious of a stranger whose motives he could not assess. After more than a year of correspondence, however, Daguerre won a response from Niépce by sending him a drawing. Niépce replied with a heliographic printing plate showing the Holy Family and a proof from it. The two men met for the first time in Paris in September, 1827, while Niépce was en route to London to visit his brother, and they met again in early 1828 on the return journey. During 1829, Daguerre slowly won Niépce's confidence, and when Niépce decided to write a handbook explaining his research, it was Daguerre's advice that Niépce should attempt to find a way of getting a large profit out of the invention before publication, apart from the honor it would gain for him. Niépce then invited Daguerre to become a partner in perfecting heliography, and in December, 1929, they signed a ten-year contract to perfect and exploit the process.

The partnership was, in many ways, an unequal one, with Niépce supplying a far greater portion of the combined technical experience. Daguerre's potential contribution, however, was far from negligible; he was a man of great energy, a skilled entrepreneur who was perhaps perfectly suited to direct the commercial exploitation of a successful photographic process (although in this episode of photographic history, as in many later ones, the financial value of the technology was surprisingly elusive). Niépce had attempted to launch heliography in late 1827, during his visit to London. While staying at Kew, near the Royal Botanical Gardens, Niépce had become acquainted with Francis Bauer, a well-known botanical draftsman. Bauer, recognizing the importance of Niépce's experiments, suggested that Niépce address a meeting of the Royal Society on the topic of heliography. A notice on heliography, accompanied by several examples, was prepared but was never presented, ostensibly because Niépce was unwilling to disclose the entirety of his work and was himself disqualified by the society's rules from making a presentation.

Niépce returned to France in early 1828, disappointed by the lack of interest in his work and saddened by the death of his brother, who seems in his last months to have suffered from delusions, including one in which he regarded the Pyréolophore as a kind of perpetual-motion machine. These personal setbacks may well have helped pave the way for Niépce's partnership with Daguerre, to whom the burden of experimentation began to pass in the early 1830's. Little physical evidence remains of the work of either Niépce or Daguerre from these years. A glass plate picturing a still life of a table set for a meal, known only from a mediocre halftone reproduction of 1891, was smashed in 1909 by a demented professor who was supposed to conduct scientific tests on it. This object may have been the work of Niépce, of Daguerre, or even of Niépce's cousin Abel Niépce de Saint-Victor, who took up the heliographic process again in 1853.

By 1829, Niépce felt ready to write a book about his discoveries. Several drafts of an outline exist, and they are quite logical, showing that Niépce was putting his photographic experiences into useful form, perhaps with some thought of his posthumous reputation. Although his partnership with Daguerre remained valid, his productive contribution to it clearly appears to have diminished in the period immediately following its inception. On July 5, 1833, Niépce died of a stroke; he was sixty-eight years old.

Summary

Nicéphore Niépce was neither an artist nor a scientist but made a contribution to each field at a time when art and science were more naturally related than they became during the Industrial Revolution. His research was less systematic than that of the scientists of his day, and he appears not to have had productive contacts with specialists who could aid his experiments. Yet, as a generalist, he succeeded where better qualified people had failed. One reason for this may have been his determination, another is surely that he had the leisure and the resources, over a long period of time, to let his accumulated experiences coalesce into practical steps toward his goals.

It is interesting to speculate on how events might have developed if particular circumstances had differed. In the case of Niépce's inability to publish his notes in England during his sojourn there, there is strong justification for the view that, had he been successful in publicizing heliography in 1827, a series of communications between various noted individuals would almost certainly have resulted in the development, before 1830, of a photographic method based upon paper negatives. Not only would Daguerre's partnership with Niépce have been forestalled, along with the daguerreotype process that was its legacy, but also the great intellectual gifts of the Englishman William Henry Fox Talbot might not have been directed into photography. Whether this course of events would have had any truly lasting effect upon the art or technology of photography is, however, debatable, especially since both Niépce and Daguerre were cognizant of the possible advantages of emulsions coated upon glass plates, the method that was soon to triumph over both Daguerre's and Talbot's processes.

Though there is scant evidence of artistic intention in Niépce's research, his photograph from the window at Le Gras has assumed a monumental significance within the art of photography; as an item of photographic incunabula, it has taken on an aura that is more than sentimental. Technically primitive, it nevertheless announces the beginning of a new era in communication and a new dimension of artistic sensibility.

Bibliography

Braive, Michel F. *The Era of the Photograph: A Social History*. London: Thames & Hudson, 1966. In addition to a brief memoir of Niépce by his descendant, photographer Janine Niépce, this book offers several illustrations of Niépce memorabilia not found elsewhere.

Daval, Jean-Luc. *Photography: History of an Art*. New York: Rizzoli, 1982. This book treats Niépce only in passing, but it offers a rare reproduction of one of his heliographs that represents his experiments more accurately, perhaps, than the enhanced and even retouched illustrations available in other sources.

Fouque, Victor. *The Truth Concerning the Invention of Photography: Nicé-*

phore Niépce, His Life and Works. Translated by Edward Epstean. New York: Tennant and Ward, 1935. This difficult-to-find translation of a work originally published in 1867 contains the correspondence between Claude and Nicéphore Niépce, but the material is adequately available in the standard modern sources.

Gernsheim, Helmut. "The 150th Anniversary of Photography." *History of Photography: An International Quarterly* 1 (January, 1977): 3-8. An indication of Gernsheim's eminence in the study of the history of photography is given by the fact that this personal memoir is the lead item in the inaugural issue of this journal. The article is an account of his discovery in 1952, by scholarly instinct and luck, of the image now recognized as the first photograph.

Gernsheim, Helmut, and Alison Gernsheim. *The History of Photography from the Camera Obscura to the Beginning of the Modern Era*. New York: Oxford University Press, 1955. Rev. ed. London: Thames & Hudson, 1969. For years this was the standard detailed survey of the history of photography. This book displays both the authors' thoroughness and their affection for the subject. There are hundreds of excellent illustrations as well as notes, an index, and a bibliography meeting high scholarly standards.

_____. *The Origins of Photography*. New York: Thames & Hudson, 1982. Essentially an adaptation of material from the Gernsheims' 1969 history of photography, this volume covers the photographic medium only until the end of the era of the calotype and daguerreotype. This book is better designed than its predecessor but contains fewer illustrations pertaining to Niépce.

Newhall, Beaumont. *Latent Image: The Discovery of Photography*. Garden City, N.Y.: Doubleday, 1967. This is the best survey of the technical research pursued by Niépce, Daguerre, Talbot, and others. Written in an entertaining narrative style, this book by a leading historian of photography tells the human side of the story as well.

_____, ed. *Photography: Essays and Images, Illustrated Readings in the History of Photography*. New York: Museum of Modern Art, 1980. The rather dry documentation of material that survives from Niépce's experiments was understandably omitted from this collection, but the book vividly shows the cultural context of the search for a photographic technology. Indispensable to students of the early history of photography is the reprinting of the entire text of an 1857 article by Lady Elizabeth Eastlake, who affectionately calls Niépce the "philosopher of Chalon."

Scharf, Aaron. "The Mirror with a Memory." In *Pioneers of Photography: An Album of Pictures and Words*. London: British Broadcasting Corporation, 1975. This chapter contains generous excerpts from Niépce's diaries and correspondence as well as a highly amusing chart showing his linguistically oriented attempt in 1832 to derive a name for "photography" from Greek roots.

C. S. McConnell

FRIEDRICH WILHELM NIETZSCHE

Born: October 15, 1844; Röcken, Prussian Saxony
Died: August 25, 1900; Weimar, Germany
Areas of Achievement: Philosophy and literature
Contribution: Though mostly ignored during his lifetime, Nietzsche's writings became a bellwether in the twentieth century for radical philosophical, psychological, linguistic, and literary critiques of Western culture. Through a series of remarkable works of German prose, Nietzsche sought to smash the idol of Christian morality and liberate the few who might follow after him into a triumphant and tragic this-worldly life.

Early Life

Friedrich Wilhelm Nietzsche—named for the reigning king of Prussia, Friedrich Wilhelm IV, whose birthday was also October 15—was born in a parsonage. His father, Karl Ludwig Nietzsche, was a Lutheran pastor; his mother, Franziska Nietzsche (née Oehler), was the daughter of a Lutheran pastor. (The union produced two other children, Elisabeth in 1846 and Joseph in 1848, who died shortly before his second birthday.)

With the death of his father in 1849, Friedrich would spend most of his early life surrounded by women: his mother, his sister, his paternal grandmother, and two maiden aunts. The family moved in 1850 to Naumburg, in Thuringia, where the young Nietzsche attended elementary school and a private preparatory school. In 1858, he entered Germany's most renowned Protestant boarding school, the Schulpforta, on a scholarship. There he met Paul Deussen, also a student, who became one of his few lifelong friends; Deussen found Nietzsche to be deeply serious, "inclined to corpulence and head congestions," and extremely myopic.

Nietzsche was graduated from the school at Pforta in 1864 with a classical education; that same year, he entered the University of Bonn to study theology and philology, the latter under Friedrich Wilhelm Ritschl. Unable to fit into the rowdiness of student life at Bonn—despite his entertaining students on the piano—Nietzsche abandoned any pretense of theological studies and transferred in 1865 to the University of Leipzig, where his friend Ritschl had gone. Writing to his sister Elisabeth about his abandonment of the Christian faith, Nietzsche told her that he had become a disciple of the truth, wherever it led; he could not be content with a religious happiness. That same year, the serious Nietzsche told Deussen that a recently published "life of Christ" by David Strauss was disingenuous in its removal of the miraculous Christ from the Gospels while holding on to his precepts. "That can have serious consequences," said Nietzsche; "if you give up Christ you will have to give up God as well."

The year 1865 was remarkable for two other reasons. As Deussen later wrote, Nietzsche had told him that a street porter, asked to take him to a restaurant in Cologne, instead had delivered him to a brothel. Speechless, Nietzsche soon left. Deussen speculated that his friend remained a lifelong virgin. There is much scholarly debate on the subject, but it seems likely that Deussen was wrong. Since there is no indication in Nietzsche's correspondence that he ever had sexual relations with a woman of his own class, it is probable that in 1865 or later Nietzsche acquired syphilis at a brothel. Early in 1889, he would collapse into insanity.

It was in 1865 that Nietzsche encountered the works of the pessimistic philosopher Arthur Schopenhauer, and though Nietzsche was later to renounce his allegiance to Schopenhauer's perspective, and his anti-Semitism, by late in 1865 he had announced that he had become a follower. The Leipzig years, from 1865 to 1869, saw Nietzsche taken under Ritschl's wing as his protégé, the development of his friendship with Erwin Rohde, and the entrance of composer Richard Wagner into his life. After hearing Wagner's music in 1868, Nietzsche became a convert; meeting with the composer that same year, Nietzsche found that Wagner, too, loved Schopenhauer. Yet, as he would do with Schopenhauer, Nietzsche would one day reject Wagner.

Nietzsche entered into the cavalry company of an artillery regiment in October of 1867, but in March of the next year he suffered a serious chest injury while trying to mount a horse. On extended health leave from the military, Nietzsche resumed his studies in Leipzig; in 1869, the university (on Ritschl's recommendation) conferred a doctorate on Nietzsche on the strength of his published philological writings and without the customary examination and dissertation required for a German degree. That same year, Basel appointed Nietzsche to the chair of classical philology; he was twenty-four, no longer a citizen of Prussia, now a resident of Switzerland.

Life's Work

In the two decades of sanity that remained to Nietzsche, he would battle often against long periods of ill health, especially after 1870, when he fell victim to dysentery and diphtheria while serving as a medical orderly with the Prussian army in the Franco-Prussian War (1870-1871). On his return to Basel to resume his teaching chores in philology (he was an unsuccessful applicant to the chair of philosophy), Nietzsche was plagued with frequent bouts of nausea and exhaustion.

For a time, his one surcease was his friendship with Wagner. From 1869 until Wagner moved to Bayreuth in 1872, Nietzsche visited the composer and his wife, Cosima, some twenty-three times at the Wagner residence at Tribschen, near Lucerne. The composer welcomed a disciple; yet his increasing use of Christian images, especially in his last opera, *Parsifal*, sickened Nietzsche, as did Wagner's anti-Semitism. By 1878, their friendship had been sundered.

Nietzsche's first book broke with tradition. *Die Geburt der Tragödie aus dem Geiste der Musik* (1872; *The Birth of Tragedy Out of the Spirit of Music*, 1909) was far from being a classical philological study burdened by arcane footnotes. Instead, Nietzsche had written a speculative treatment of what he found to be two competing forces in ancient Greek life—the Dionysian, representing potentially destructive passion, and the Apollonian, representing reason and restraint. Greek tragedy had fused the two, but, with the triumph of Socrates, the Apollonian was in the ascendant. (Much later Nietzsche would redefine the Dionysian impulse as a sublimated or perfected "will to power" and would ally himself with Dionysus.)

Nietzsche was granted a leave of absence from Basel in 1876 because of ill health, but his continued headaches, vomiting, and deteriorating eyesight led to his resignation in May, 1879, with a pension of three thousand Swiss francs a year for six years. From that time onward, Nietzsche increasingly became an enigma to his friends. His publication of the aphoristic *Menschliches, Allzumenschliches: Ein Buch für freie Geister* (1878; *Human, All Too Human*, 1910, 1911) was characterized by Wagner as the beginning of Nietzsche's slide into madness. Nietzsche cut his intellectual mooring to Schopenhauer as well, writing a friend that he no longer believed what the philosopher had said.

In the decade beginning in 1879, Nietzsche, moving from boardinghouse to boardinghouse, always seeking new curatives, lived in the French Riviera, Italy, and Switzerland, a virtual recluse. His letter writing was a substitute for most human contact. Suffering almost ceaseless pain, Nietzsche turned within—as if the pain itself were a spur to creativity, or as if, through his project of revaluing traditional Christian values, his literary genius would master his physiology.

There was much emotional pain as well. His friendship with philosopher Paul Rée (who was investigating the psychological basis of religious belief), which had begun in 1873, was marred when in 1882 both men met Lou Salomé (later the wife of Orientalist F. C. Andreas, friend of Sigmund Freud, and mistress of the poet Rainer Maria Rilke) and both proposed—Nietzsche apparently through Rée. Declining both requests, Salomé counterproposed a platonic ménage à trois; Nietzsche's sister Elisabeth learned of the plan, took him to task for his immorality, and informed their mother of Nietzsche's behavior. The three continued in one another's company, but by November, with Salomé and Rée having departed, Nietzsche realized that he had been abandoned.

In January, 1883, in only ten days, Nietzsche penned the first part of what was to become his literary masterpiece, *Also sprach Zarathustra: Ein Buch für Alle und Keinen* (1883-1885; *Thus Spake Zarathustra*, 1896). His only work of fiction, the book (completed in 1885, the fourth and final part privately printed from Nietzsche's own funds) brings a biblical narrative style to parody the Socratic and Christian wisdom teachings, and to bring to "everyone and no one" (the subtitle) the teachings of the *Übermensch* (variously translated "superman" or "overman"). A more explicit elucidation of Nietzsche's philosophical orientation came in 1886 with *Jenseits von Gut und Böse: Vorspiel einer Philosophie der Zukunft* (*Beyond Good and Evil*, 1907), and, in 1887, *Zur Genealogie der Moral* (*On the Genealogy of Morals*, 1896). Books streamed from Nietzsche's pen. In the last year of his sanity, 1888, he wrote five of them, including *Der Antichrist* (1895; *The Antichrist*, 1896) and *Ecce Homo* (1908; English translation, 1911), the last a semiautobiographical overview of Nietzsche's published works.

Several months of euphoria preceded Nietzsche's descent into madness, but following his collapse in the Piazza Carlo Alberto, in Turin, Italy, on January 3, 1889—he had seen a cab driver beating his horse and had flung himself around the horse's neck—the darkness was complete. For the next eleven years, Nietzsche was variously cared for in a Basel asylum, by his mother in Naumburg (until she died in 1897), and by his sister in Weimar.

Elisabeth, married in 1885 to anti-Semite Bernhard Förster (who committed suicide in 1889), managed to gain control of Nietzsche's literary estate and began zealously to refashion her brother's image into that of a proto-Nazi. She withheld *Ecce Homo* from publication for twenty years after Nietzsche had written it, established a Nietzsche archive, and compiled and published a series of notes Nietzsche himself had never intended for publication. She edited it and titled it *Der Wille zur Macht* (1901; *The Will to Power*, 1910).

Only in the last year of his sanity did Nietzsche begin to receive important public notice, a result primarily of the philosophy lectures given by Georg Brandes at Copenhagen. It seems ironic that the first commercial successes of the man who wanted to be understood came at the hands of his sister, who carefully crafted a mythical Nietzsche. Poignantly, it was the ever-prescient Nietzsche who had written in *Ecce Homo*, "I have a terrible fear I shall one day be pronounced holy. . . ." Nietzsche died in Weimar on August 25, 1900, not yet fifty-six, his mane of hair and his shaggy mustache still dark brown.

Summary

There is much scholarly dispute over the nature of Friedrich Wilhelm Nietzche's philosophy, and even over whether he intended to have one. In his mature works, from *Thus Spake Zarathustra* on, many themes seem important to Nietzsche, from the concept of the overman, the idea of eternal recurrence, of a man being in love with his own fate and thus triumphant in it, to the psychological origins of traditional morality, the nature of the will to power in human affairs, and the death of God, the last announced by a madman in section 125 of *Die fröhliche Wissenschaft* (1882, 1887; *The Joy-*

ful Wisdom, 1910). Yet in Nietzsche's modified aphoristic style, his themes receive no systematic exploration; scholarly interpretations are legion.

Nietzsche's analysis of the psychology of the priest, and of Christian morality, anticipated Freud. Traditional morality has quenched the instinct for life, and has pronounced sexuality, nobility of self, and intellect to be evil; the afterlife is promised only to those who submit to the priest, to the slave morality, the *ressentiment* of those who are weak. Nietzsche's message was that the sickness, the life-denying morality of the Church, must be replaced by the message of the overman; though perhaps an unachievable ideal, the overman is able to fall in love with every aspect of his fate and, without self-deception, to will the eternal repetition of every part of his life. God is dead—the new learning killed Him—but the late nineteenth century slumbered on in its nihilism, unaware of the consequences. Nietzsche's message of triumph and tragedy fell on deaf ears during his lifetime.

Yet his insights, often not fully developed, have been mined by twentieth century existentialists such as Albert Camus, deconstructionists such as Jacques Derrida and Michel Foucault, phenomenologists such as Martin Heidegger, religious thinkers such as Paul Tillich and Martin Buber, novelists such as Thomas Mann and Hermann Hesse, and playwright George Bernard Shaw; Sigmund Freud and Carl Jung also felt Nietzsche's influence. As a man "born posthumously," Nietzsche is a key to understanding the twentieth century's most influential and most deeply perplexing currents of thought.

Bibliography
Gilman, Sander L., ed. *Conversations with Nietzsche: A Life in the Words of His Contemporaries*. Translated by David J. Parent. New York: Oxford University Press, 1987. Fully aware of Elisabeth Förster-Nietzsche's tendencies to mythologize her brother, this anthology draws carefully on her letters, and those from dozens of other correspondents and writers, to paint a picture of Nietzsche as others knew him. Accessible to the general reader, who will be struck by the varying impressions Nietzsche made on those around him.
Hayman, Ronald. *Nietzsche: A Critical Life*. New York: Oxford University Press, 1980. A chronological account of Nietzsche's life and work. Includes a helpful timeline and a section of photographs. Hayman draws extensively upon Nietzsche's letters, especially in detailing Nietzsche's many illnesses. Attempts to integrate the man with his philosophy but is sometimes murky and cryptic.
Higgins, Kathleen. *Nietzsche's Zarathustra*. Philadelphia: Temple University Press, 1987. A cleanly written and accessible exploration of the book Nietzsche considered his best. Higgins finds thematic and structural unities when the book is considered from a literary standpoint. The first chapter draws on Nietzsche's life and letters during the time of the com-

position of *Thus Spake Zarathustra* to reveal Nietzsche's serious concerns behind the sometimes-mocking prophet. The twelve-page bibliography is useful.

Hollingdale, R. J. *Nietzsche: The Man and His Philosophy*. Baton Rouge: Louisiana State University Press, 1965. A sympathetic chronological and interpretive narrative, contending that, in the end, one is left with Nietzsche the man and not with some movement or philosophical system. A standard work by one of Nietzsche's English-language translators.

Kaufmann, Walter. *Nietzsche: Philosopher, Psychologist, Antichrist*. Princeton, N.J.: Princeton University Press, 1950, 4th ed. 1974. A standard and important account of Nietzsche's life and thought by one of his modern English-language translators. The extensive thirty-page annotated bibliography of primary and secondary sources is invaluable. Included are samples of Nietzsche's handwriting. Kaufmann attempts to smooth Nietzsche's rough edges even as he removes the onus of Elisabeth's manufactured image of her brother. Somewhat dated, as it takes issue with many works on Nietzsche published early in the twentieth century.

Solomon, Robert C., and Kathleen M. Higgins, eds. *Reading Nietzsche*. New York: Oxford University Press, 1988. Based on papers presented at a 1985 seminar on Nietzsche at the University of Texas at Austin. Twelve Nietzsche scholars in the Anglo-American tradition provide insightful interpretations of most of the Nietzsche canon. A ten-page bibliography of primary and secondary sources, including works on specific texts, is extremely valuable in directing first-time readers of Nietzsche into the mountain of Nietzsche studies. Works in the continental tradition are also cited in the bibliography.

Dan Barnett

NIKON
Nikita Minin

Born: 1605; Veldemanovo, Russia
Died: August 27, 1681; en route to Moscow, Russia
Areas of Achievement: Religion and politics
Contribution: Nikon contributed to the liturgical reforms in the Russian Orthodox church, the introduction of Western intellectualism in Russia, and the definition of the role of the church in the Russian state.

Early Life

Nikita Minin, the future patriarch of the Russian Orthodox church, was born in the Nizhni-Novgorod province of northern Russia to landless peasants. Minin, or Nikon, as he would come to be known, was born during a period in Russian history called the Time of Troubles. This historical era was marked by a succession crisis which resulted from the death without an heir of Czar Fyodor I. Nikon was educated in a local school until the age of twelve. After this, because of parental abuse, he ran away to the Makariev Monastery.

Nikon's parents persuaded him to leave the monastery and be married. In 1625, at the age of twenty, he became the village priest of Kolychevo. A year later, Nikon assumed control of a parish in the Moscow province, where he remained for the next ten years. He had three sons during this time, all of whom died. In 1634, Nikon persuaded his wife to enter a Moscow convent, thus clearing the obstacles for Nikon to go to the north and live as a hermit.

For several years, Nikon lived in utter solitude, preparing himself to become a monk. He entered the monastery at Kozheezero, in the Kargopol district in the northern tundra region. Between 1641 and 1646, Nikon was the administrator for the monastery. In 1646, while on monastery business in Moscow, Nikon met Stepan Vonifatiev, the confessor of Czar Alexis I. Through Vonifatiev, Nikon, a six-foot, six-inch-tall, forty-two-year-old monk from the north, met and awed the seventeen-year-old ruler of Russia with his spiritual bearing. Alexis was so impressed with his newfound friend that he named Nikon to the position of archimandrite (head) of the Novo-Spasski Monastery in Moscow. Nikon soon became involved with church reform. A group led by Vonifatiev established a printing press in Moscow for the purpose of increasing the number of religious texts available. The aim of the reformers was to increase the level of intellectual life in Russia by raising the literacy level of the clergy. Members of this reform group were first to support and later to disassociate themselves from Nikon's ideas concerning church reform.

Life's Work

In 1648, serious riots erupted in Moscow. The surface cause of the riots was a higher salt tax, but the root of the popular disturbances was the inefficiency of the state. The modern Russian state was formed in 1613, amid the debris accumulated from years of internal conflict (the Time of Troubles). Alexis inherited the problems of the fledgling state: debts from years of warfare, a state without a consistent form of collecting taxes, and rulers who relied on others to make decisions. In 1648, Alexis replaced his boyar adviser with Nikon. This rise in station of a religious man to the position of the czar's adviser initiated the struggle between church and state which dominated Russian history until the rule of Peter the Great.

The Metropolitan of the Novgorod Church district died in 1649. Using his power as the secular head of the Russian Orthodox church, Alexis appointed his friend Nikon to the vacant post. Nikon proved his loyalty to and gratitude for the czar's confidence during an armed uprising in Novgorod in 1650. This revolt was against the power of the czar to absorb Moscow's former great rival, the free city-state of Novgorod, into the ever-expanding Russian state. Nikon, appointed as the czar's overseer in Novgorod, brutally repressed the rebelling Novgorodians in Alexis' name. In 1652, Nikon returned to Moscow after the death of Joseph the patriarch (spiritual leader) of the Russian Orthodox church. Alexis begged Nikon to become Joseph's successor and to help guide the czar in secular decisions. Nikon accepted the patriarchy on condition the czar give him a free hand in the reordering of the Russian Orthodox church.

As Patriarch of the Russian Orthodox church, Nikon's first reform was to bring uniformity to the worship service. He accomplished this by publishing service books to be used by all the clergy. As patriarch, Nikon controlled the printing press, and through it he was able to direct the mission of the church. The *Kormchaia Kniga* (the pilot book), published in 1650, was not only a polemic against Judaism and other religions deemed to be false but also was a work based on canon law. Nikon used this book as the basis for the Russian Orthodox mission to become the center of all religious life in the East.

During the previous two centuries, since the fall of Constantinople in 1453, the Russian Orthodox church had remained in an intellectual vacuum from the Western world. Through isolation and ignorance, two centuries of silence had led to many alterations in the way in which Christianity was practiced in Russia. Indeed, the fall of the Byzantine Empire, after the earlier fall of the western Roman Empire, led to the idea that pure Christianity and the legacy of Rome itself continued to survive only in Russia, an idea that is known as the Third Rome.

In his efforts to purify Russian religious texts, Nikon invited scholars from Kiev to aid him. Unlike Russian religious leaders, the Kievan scholars had been trained in both Latin and Greek, which enabled them to correct the Russian deviations from Western and Greek developments. The Nikonian corrections were intended to standardize the texts and in so doing to eliminate the various heresies being practiced as a result of differing versions of the psalter.

Nikon also reformed church services. He changed not only the form but also the substance of church rituals. He added theatrical dimensions to the worship service with expensive robes for the clergy, a grand processional, and a featured sermon given weekly. The Palm Sunday procession of Christ's entrance into Jerusalem before Easter became an important ritual of the church, with the czar leading a donkey on which the patriarch was seated. This ritual was repeated in towns and villages throughout the empire with the civil leaders in attendance to the spiritual leaders of each community.

Another reform of the church service was the change from three fingers to two while making the sign of the cross. Nikon also changed the number of loaves of bread consecrated for communion from seven to five. He altered the common people's traditional perspective on the Holy Trinity: God became the Lord, the name of Jesus was spelled differently from the way it had been spelled in previous texts, and the Holy Spirit was openly discussed instead of implied in the service.

The purpose of all the Nikonian reforms was to increase the power and authority of the patriarch. Indeed, Nikon agreed to become patriarch only after the czar and the boyars had taken an oath of loyalty to him. The oath was traditional in the Orthodox church and had been handed down to the Russian state as part of their Byzantine heritage, but Nikon took their oath of loyalty much more seriously than prior Russian patriarchs. He thought and acted under the assumption that their oath was indeed made in the original Byzantine context. Nikon had read and understood the ninth century Byzantine document that stated that the patriarch and the emperor were corulers and answerable only to God. The emperor was to be the secular leader and the patriarch the spiritual leader of the state. The patriarch was always to put the salvation of souls first, even if he had to go against the will of the emperor. Nikon thus used his position as patriarch, defined by the ancient Byzantine law, to become coruler with Alexis.

Nikon's downfall was not the result of his reforms in the Russian Orthodox church but of his attempt to garner more power for the office of the patriarch. During the Polish conflict (1652-1655), the czar went to the front, leaving Nikon as the sole ruler. The patriarch acted as an autocrat, becoming repressive and domineering toward everyone, including the czar's wife, the boyars, and influential monastic leaders. Nikon acted as both czar and patriarch, no longer concerned with the separate spheres of power defined in Byzantine law. He condemned boyars and church leaders alike whenever they opposed his ideas. By 1655, the reformers with whom Nikon had associated in the 1640's disassociated themselves from his policies, which were more radical than they were prepared to support. The czar, growing older, preferred increasingly to rule on his own. A crisis between the two men emerged and sharpened. When Alexis stopped attending church services, Nikon retreated to the Voskresenskii Monastery he had built outside Moscow. He vowed not to set foot in Moscow until the czar declared confidence in him and his reforms. Eight years later, Nikon returned to the nation's capital but not in the glory he dreamed. He was brought before a church council, stripped of his title, and sent to a monastery in the north. In 1681, Nikon died on his way back to Moscow after having received a partial pardon from the czar.

Summary

Nikon attempted to elevate the office of Russian patriarch to the same height as that held by the Byzantine patriarch in the original Orthodox church that had converted the Ukraine and Russia after 988. He worked throughout his career as metropolitan and patriarch to duplicate within the Russian state the splendor and pomp of the Byzantine Empire, in which religion and politics were so intimately linked. Nikon believed that Russia was the true inheritor of the glories of Constantinople. All of his programs of reform were aimed at creating a Russian state in which the religious sphere would be equal to the secular sphere in all matters. The conflict which resulted between church and state was ended in 1701, when Peter the Great declared that he was secular head of the church and replaced the office of patriarch with a Holy Synod, a group of officials appointed by the czar to make church decisions.

Although a failure in the realm of politics, Nikon was successful in the area of church reform. The changes he introduced in church texts and worship services were to have lasting importance. In the short run, the Church Council of 1666 found in favor of Nikon's religious reforms, while condemning his political aspirations. It upheld and mandated his religious modifications, which were then given the force of law by the czar. Yet the practice of generations was not so easily discarded. Led by the Archpriest Avvakum Petrovich, many devout Russians refused to adopt the revolutionary religious laws. The resulting break is known as the Church Schism. The dissenters contravened state law and thus rejected not only the authority of the church but also that of the czar. The Russian traditionalists viewed Nikon's reforms as Western impositions—foreign impurities thrust upon the pure faith of Russia. Nikon himself was condemned by them as the Antichrist. Avvakum's supporters, known as the Old Believers, were ruthlessly persecuted as religious heretics and dangerous political subversives.

Nikon's religious reforms thus led to a serious split and to a conflict that still provokes discussion in Russian Orthodox circles to this day. The political objectives sought by the Russian patriarch between 1652 and 1658, when he was head of the church and coruler with Alexis, resulted in the firm subordination of the church to the state which characterized relations between the two until the Bolshevik Revolution of 1917.

Bibliography
Billington, James H. *The Icon and the Axe: An Interpretive History of Russian Culture*. New York: Alfred A. Knopf, 1966. Section 3, "The Century of Schism," is not only a detailed account of Nikon's historical role but also an excellent source for discussion of the religious and social debates of seventeenth century Russian history.
Florinsky, Michael T. *Russia: A History and an Interpretation*. Vol. 1. New York: Macmillan, 1953. Florinsky provides an excellent discussion of the social development of the Russian state. Nikon's reforms are set against the backdrop of social unrest.
Kluchevsky, V. O. *A History of Russia*. Vol. 3. Translated by C. J. Hogarth. Reprint. New York: Russell & Russell, 1960. The second half of this volume explains the various reasons for the Church Schism and the role played by Nikon's reforms. Kluchevsky's discussion of the people and events is the best nineteenth century Russian work available on the subject. He examines the roots of the notion of Moscow as the inheritor of Byzantium and the incipient problems created by it for the Moscow state.
Miliukov, Paul, Charles Seignobos, and L. Eisenmann. *History of Russia*. Vol. 1, *From the Beginnings to the Empire of Peter the Great*. Translated by Charles Lam Markmann. New York: Funk & Wagnalls, 1968. This work is a collection of essays written by Miliukov before he became leader of the Cadet Party in 1905. Although Miliukov writes about Nikon the man, he discusses the Nikonian reforms as preparation for the later reforms of Peter the Great.
Spinka, Matthew. "Patriarch Nikon and the Subjection of the Russian Church to the State." *Church History* 10 (1941): 347-366. A most valuable contribution to the argument over how Moscow believed itself to be the Third Rome. Spinka explains Nikon's use of Byzantine law and Alexis' response in the Church Council of 1666.
Vernadsky, George. *The Tsardom of Moscow, 1547-1682*. Vol. 2. New Haven, Conn.: Yale University Press, 1969. An excellent source for Nikon's activities as metropolitan and patriarch. This work contains more information on Nikon's contemporaries than can be found elsewhere in English. The conclusions about Nikon's impact on Russian history are tied to Vernadsky's own prejudice that Russia was a copy of the Byzantine state.

Linnea Goodwin Burwood

ALFRED NOBEL

Born: October 21, 1833; Stockholm, Sweden
Died: December 10, 1896; San Remo, Italy
Areas of Achievement: Invention, technology, and philanthropy
Contribution: Although Nobel is remembered for inventing dynamite and the
  blasting cap that ignites it, and although he held 355 patents for his inventions, he will be most remembered for the provision he made in his
  last will for the distribution of the income from the bulk of his estate to
  provide annual prizes to those who confer upon humankind the greatest
  benefits in the fields of physics, chemistry, physiology or medicine, literature, and peace.

Early Life

Alfred Bernhard Nobel spent his life in one sort of pursuit yet is enshrined
in history for something quite different. Born in Stockholm to Immanuel and
Andriette Nobel, Alfred was the fourth of their sons. His father was a visionary, an inventor whose fortunes swung from one extreme to another. When
the family's fortunes were reduced, his mother operated a food shop to
supplement their income.

Just before Alfred's birth, Immanuel's business in Sweden foundered. In
1837, Immanuel made an attempt to reestablish himself in Finland but failed.
By 1842, however, he was a modestly successful manufacturer of mechanical devices in St. Petersburg, Russia. He flourished there until 1858, when
the Russian government canceled its contracts, creating for him a new round
of financial difficulties.

During his time in Russia, Immanuel had become fascinated with the
explosive qualities of nitroglycerin, realizing that if the substance could be
controlled it would have tremendous potential as military weaponry as well
as for use in heavy industry and mining. Alfred, frail, colorless, and thin,
was a sickly child with a spinal defect, who early shared this interest in
nitroglycerin with his father. Often he was too ill to attend school, and, in
Russia, he was taught exclusively by tutors. He showed a natural gift for
languages, acquiring them as he traveled. He had lived in Finland and Russia, and he spoke Swedish at home. Between the ages of seventeen and
nineteen, Nobel traveled in Germany, France, and the United States, learning languages as he went. Nobel, always dedicated to work, was a perfec-
tionist, always demanding more of himself than more healthy people do.

Nobel and his brothers Ludvig and Robert worked in their father's plant in
St. Petersburg. When it faced an impending financial disaster in 1858, Nobel, because of his fluency in English, was sent to England to try to negotiate
financing for the business. He failed in this attempt, however, and in 1858,
his defeated father returned to Sweden. Nobel and his brothers remained in

Russia, but in 1863, Nobel returned to Sweden to work with his father. Granted his first patent in 1857, Nobel was now on the way to discovering how to control nitroglycerin for commercial use. His invention of the blasting cap changed forever the way mining, massive construction, and war would be conducted.

Life's Work

Liquid nitroglycerin is among the world's most volatile substances. Nobel's device for igniting it, the blasting cap, consisted of a charge of gunpowder that could be ignited by a fuse and was attached to liquid nitroglycerin. This blasting cap gave workers who set the device time to seek shelter from the ensuing explosion. So revolutionary was this invention that Nobel gained fame in a matter of months, but his life was not free from sorrow, difficulty, and loneliness.

Just a year after the blasting cap was invented, Nobel's younger brother, Emil, a twenty-one-year-old student who worked in his brother's laboratory making detonators, was in the laboratory when it caught fire and exploded, killing five people who were working there, including Emil. The loss of this young son was so devastating to Immanuel that he soon suffered a paralytic stroke, from which he never recovered. Nothing, however—not even Emil's death—could shake Nobel's belief in what he was doing, and he proceeded to open explosives factories across Europe and in the United States.

So great was his confidence that Nobel yielded his patent rights when he opened foreign factories, agreeing that instead of receiving royalty payments he would receive a substantial share of the proceeds from each factory. It is this arrangement that caused him to be numbered among the world's wealthiest people by the time he died.

Nitroglycerin is a dangerous substance because it decomposes quickly; this decomposition inevitably leads to explosions. Few people realized in the 1860's and 1870's just how dangerous nitroglycerin was to work with. Two years after Nobel's laboratory exploded in 1864, a ship carrying nitroglycerin exploded and capsized near Panama, killing seventy-four people. Within months of that explosion, a San Francisco warehouse, in which liquid nitroglycerin was stored, exploded, killing another fourteen people. Nobel's factory near Hamburg, Germany, was completely destroyed by an explosion less than a year after it opened.

Continuing disasters impelled Nobel to find a safe way to store and ship nitroglycerin. Ever the inventor and thinker, Nobel knew that he had to find a way to turn nitroglycerin into a solid substance. He realized that he had to combine the liquid with something that could absorb it, and he finally settled on a siliconlike substance, kieselguhr, which was porous and would not add anything chemically to the substance with which it was mixed. Once nitroglycerin was mixed with kieselguhr, it could be formed into shapes, wrapped in paper, then transported or stored. The result was dynamite, so named by Nobel from the Greek word for power, *dunamis*.

With this advance in the latter part of the 1860's, Nobel was able to establish factories all over the world to mass-produce one of the world's most destructive substances. The production of his plants increased from a mere eleven tons in 1867 to more than three thousand tons in 1874, and to almost 67,000 tons produced by ninety-three factories—in all of which he had a financial interest—by the year of his death. Everyone connected with the production of dynamite was becoming rich; Nobel, however, because he shared in the profits of every dynamite factory in the world, was quickly gaining a financial position unheard of in Europe since the days of the Medicis.

Nobel's interest in invention never waned. After he invented dynamite, he invented an explosive gelatin more powerful than nitroglycerin, virtually impervious to shock and unaffected by moisture, which predated the sophisticated plastic explosives now available. Before Orville and Wilbur Wright flew their airplane at Kitty Hawk, North Carolina, in 1903, Nobel was experimenting with aerial photography as an expedient and accurate means of cartography, mounting his cameras on rockets. He was involved with experiments to find ways of synthesizing silk, rubber, and leather far in advance of the synthetic production of nylon, synthetic rubber, and vinyl a half century after his death. His smokeless gunpowder, *balliste*, first patented in 1887, was in great demand by armies throughout the world and added considerably to Nobel's coffers.

Through all this time, Nobel wandered from one place to another, buying houses in Paris, where he spent a considerable amount of time; at San Remo, Italy, where he bought the villa in which he eventually died; and in Sweden at Bofors, where he spent the last summer of his life. Nobel never married and his romantic involvements were never notably fulfilling, although he had a long, quite distant relationship with an Austrian, Sofie Hess, much his junior, to whom he wrote nearly daily and whom he supported during the later years of his life even though she had been married to someone else.

Summary

In his final years, Alfred Nobel speculated that he would die alone, unattended by anyone who loved him; his prediction was accurate. He spent the summer of 1896 at his home, Björkborn in Bofors, after which he went to his home in Paris, and then to San Remo. His health was failing, but he continued to work, write to his friends, and plan. On December 10, 1896, Nobel collapsed in his laboratory, and that evening, with only his servants present, Nobel died of heart failure.

On November 27, 1895, Nobel had drafted a holograph will, replacing one that left his vast fortune essentially to relatives, servants, and friends. The new will, for which Nobel will be forever remembered, substantially reduced his personal bequests. It directed that his residual estate be invested conservatively and that the income from these investments be used to establish annual prizes to be awarded with no reservations regarding nationality to those people whose activities are deemed to be of the greatest benefit to humankind in the fields of physics, chemistry, physiology or medicine, literature, and peace.

Nobel's will was contested and was in litigation for more than three years. Afterward, however, a system was established for the distribution of the income in the form of Nobel Prizes, the first set of which were awarded in 1901. As the income from the Nobel trust has increased, the size of each award has grown to the point that in 1985 the typical prize was worth over $350,000, ten times what the same award was worth thirty years earlier.

The list of Nobel laureates, which has now been expanded to include a sixth field, economics, contains the names of international giants in their fields: scientists of the stature of Albert Einstein, Marie Curie, and Linus Pauling, writers such as William Faulkner and T. S. Eliot, physicians and physiologists such as Ivan Pavlov and Sir Alexander Fleming, and advocates of world peace such as Woodrow Wilson and Albert Schweitzer. The Nobel legacy is great because of the endowment he established to recognize those who contribute most to the benefit of humankind.

Bibliography
Bergengren, Erik. *Alfred Nobel: The Man and His Work*. New York: Thomas Nelson and Sons, 1962. This brief overview of Nobel's life is supplemented by a list of Nobel institutions and of the awards that have been granted. It is particularly valuable for its discussion of Nobel's inventions and for its detail about the growing use and sales of dynamite. The research is extremely careful.

Evlanoff, Michael, and Marjorie Fluor. *Alfred Nobel: The Loneliest Millionaire*. New York: Ward Ritchie Press, 1969. This book is a study of Nobel's personal isolation and of his attempts to escape from his loneliness. It relates his establishing the Nobel Prizes to his guilt about the destructive effects of dynamite. Nobel is portrayed as a sensitive man with few roots, one whose intellect was a chief and isolating concern. Contains a list of all Nobel laureates from 1901 to 1968.

Jackson, Donald Dale. "The Nobility of Alfred Nobel." *Smithsonian* 19 (November, 1988): 201-224. This substantial article, both meticulously researched and extremely well written, focuses on Nobel's pessimism and loneliness and on their causes, relating these conditions to his establishing the Nobel Prizes. Jackson has intriguing notions concerning Hess, the young woman in Nobel's life.

Nobelstiftelsen. *Nobel: The Man and His Prizes*. Rev. ed. New York:

Elsevier, 1962. This authorized biography has chapters by eminent representatives from the five fields in which the awards were originally granted as well as a biographical chapter by Henrick Schück and a chapter on Nobel and the Nobel Foundation by Ragnar Sohlman. This book is a good starting point for those wishing to know more about Alfred Nobel.

Pauli, Herta E. *Alfred Nobel: Dynamite King, Architect of Peace*. New York: L. B. Fischer, 1942. This early assessment of Nobel is outdated, although in its time it made a valuable contribution to Nobel scholarship. The book is strongest for its biographical information, including extensive materials on Nobel's business affairs as they expanded rapidly.

Sohlman, Ragnar. *The Legacy of Alfred Nobel: The Story Behind the Nobel Prizes*. Translated by Elspeth Harley Schubert. London: Bodley Head, 1983. This book was published originally in Swedish under the title *Ett Testamente* in 1950. Sohlman was Nobel's assistant in the last three years of his life and served as one of the executors of his will, giving him a significant role in establishing the Nobel award mechanism. Sohlman knew intimately the details of Nobel's business and life, and he presents these details clearly and directly in this excellent book, which also contains a copy of Nobel's will.

R. Baird Shuman

ODA NOBUNAGA

Born: June, 1534; Owari Province, Japan
Died: June 21, 1582; Kyōto, Japan
Areas of Achievement: The military, government, and politics
Contribution: The greatest soldier of his time, Oda started a process through diplomacy and war that put an end to political fragmentation in Japan and paved the way for the unique feudal system that governed Japan during the Tokugawa period (1602-1867).

Early Life

Oda Nobunaga lived during the Sengoku Jidai, or Age of the Country at War (sixteenth century), when both the shogun and the emperor were figureheads and a multitude of warlords, known as daimyo, held sway over the provinces. In addition to the secular warlords, there were militant Buddhist organizations with standing armies often allied to some of the daimyo. The country may thus be viewed as a patchwork quilt of power centers.

Oda was born in Nagoya Castle in Owari Province. His father, Oda Nobuhide, was a lesser official of the Shiba family serving in Owari. Nobunaga's original name was Kitsubōshi, but it was changed at age thirteen. While still a teenager, Nobunaga began to adopt eccentric dress and behavior, which earned for him the nicknames "Great Fool" and "Idiot." It has been suggested by some scholars that he chose to play the fool as part of a ploy for surviving the pending fratricidal struggle that ensued upon the death of his father in 1551, when Nobunaga was seventeen years old. Despite the fact that he learned to use firearms from a very early age and that much of his military reputation hinged on guns, he was alleged to have favored the spear.

Among those who served the young Nobunaga was his sandal-bearer Kinoshita Tokichiro, who is more popularly remembered as Toyotomi Hideyoshi and who became Nobunaga's most valuable military follower; ultimately Toyotomi took over the reins of power. From 1551 until 1560, Oda fought a series of campaigns to gain control of his home province of Owari. As many members of the Oda clan were reluctant to follow him because of his youth, he used a band of one thousand low-ranking soldiers to gain a foothold in the initial period of clan infighting. In 1556, Oda managed to displace a number of his rivals in Kiyosu, which became his first "capital." Oda's younger brother posed a challenge when he gained support from some of his father's retainers. The rivalry ended with the death of the younger brother. In the year 1560, Oda became daimyo of Owari Province.

Oda was quite adept at splitting his opponents' defensive efforts. For example, he would try to make an alliance with daimyo whose territory bordered on that of an enemy of Oda. In that manner, the enemy was then compelled to divide his forces to deal with an attack on two fronts. One of the most expedient tools for cementing diplomatic and political alliances was the arranged marriage. Marriages were often used to facilitate alliances, but they remained fragile agreements at the best of times. Oda himself married the daughter of Saitō Dōsan, the daimyo of neighboring Mino Province, which lay between Owari and the capital. In 1556, while Oda was still trying to consolidate his own power in Owari, Saitō was killed by his son Tatsuoki, Oda's brother-in-law. The murder gave Oda the pretext for invasion on the grounds of avenging his father-in-law's death.

Life's Work

During June of 1560, Oda had a chance to prove his mettle to other daimyo. Imagawa Yoshimoto, the daimyo of Suruga, Totomi, and Mikawa Provinces, was on his way through Owari to Kyōto at the head of a vast army of twenty-five thousand. Although Oda could muster no more than eighteen hundred men, he nevertheless decided to give battle. His opportunity came when his enemy was encamped in a narrow sheltered valley. Taking advantage of a violent rainstorm, he launched a surprise attack, routing his enemy in the furious but brief Battle of Okehazama.

In contrast, the operations against Saitō Tatsuoki, for control of Mino, dragged on for years. Nevertheless, by 1564, Oda had reduced Saitō's fortress of Inabayama, and, by 1567, at the age of thirty-three, he had finally defeated Saitō. He decided to use Inabayama as his own capital and renamed it Gifu. At the same time, he adopted the motto *Tenka fubu*, incorporating it into his personal seal. *Tenka fubu* is translated variously as "the realm covered in military glory," "the realm subjected to the military," or "rule the realm by force." Alarmed by Oda's increasing strength, his enemies banded together to form an anti-Oda league. To bolster his position, Oda decided to espouse the cause of Ashikaga Yoshiaki, heir to the Ashikaga shogunate. After defeating limited opposition, Oda entered Kyōto with Ashikaga on November 9, 1568. The latter was installed as the shogun, the last of the Ashikaga line. The stormy relationship between Oda and the shogun was to last five years.

Much of Oda's energy during the last ten years of his life was absorbed in attempts to suppress the military power of the Buddhists. Various Buddhist groups had evolved powers that paralleled those of the daimyo, and their temples became centers of political, economic, and military activity. First, Oda dealt with the Enryakuji, the temple of the Heian school on Mount Hiei, which had been labeled "The Indestructible Light of the [Buddhist] Law." In 1571, Oda's forces stormed their stronghold and the mountainside became a killing ground as men, women, and children were killed, and the temple complex put to the torch. Between three and four thousand priests were killed; the orgy of bloodletting lasted a week.

Then Oda turned his attention to the Shinshu Buddhists (also known as Ikkō), whose sectarian strongholds were strewn across the land. Their headquarters was located at Hongan-ji, an impregnable fortress situated on highly defensible terrain and ringed by more than fifty forts and outposts. In seeking to reduce the Hongan-ji, Oda found that he had first to dispose of the threat of the shogun and the powerful daimyo Takeda Shingen. In July, 1574, Oda laid siege to the Ikkō stronghold of Nagashima, located on an estuary of the Kiso-gawa. The captive population tried to surrender but to no avail. Oda ordered the fortress to be burned to the ground, and anyone who sought to escape was shot. It is estimated that as many as twenty thousand people died inside the burning fort.

The Battle of Nagashino, against Takeda Katsuyori (Shingen's son), in 1575, demonstrated Oda's military insight. The battle grew out of Oda's efforts to relieve the siege of Nagashino Castle in Mikawa Province. The Takeda forces had surrounded the castle, which was within the territory of Oda's trusted follower Tokugawa Ieyasu. Oda had a combined force of up to thirty-eight thousand troops, of which ten thousand were armed with matchlocks. From those troops, three thousand of the best sharpshooters were selected for deployment. The Takeda clan relied on mounted samurai, which epitomized the art of the cavalry, but Oda denied the enemy a chance to utilize his horsemen effectively. Oda's men were arranged behind wooden barriers, or a palisade, which served to channel the Takeda attack. The lack of a single clear-cut objective meant that the horsemen had to thread their way through the deadly obstacles that concealed the sharpshooters. The peasant footsoldiers, or *ashigaru*, were trained to fire in ranks, which allowed a steady rate of fire as the weapons were fired and loaded in sequence.

Although the majority of sixteenth century Japanese wars were the domain of the samurai, there were also naval operations involved in Oda's rise to power. The siege of the Hongan-ji fortress was prolonged for years, because Kennyo Kōsa, who commanded the Hongan-ji force, had arranged for resupply to be provided by the Mōri clan, who shipped men and supplies from Ōsaka up the Inland Sea. Oda ordered his vassal daimyo to prepare a fleet to intercept the Mōri navy. The three-hundred-ship force assembled for Oda was outnumbered by more than two to one by the Mōri vessels. The destruction of Oda's fleet in August, 1576, compelled him to build a new navy. This naval reconstruction program resulted in the delivery of seven ironclads, complete with cannons, in July, 1578. The new navy sailed into Ōsaka and effectively cut Hongan-ji from its supply line when it destroyed the six-hundred-vessel Mōri fleet on December 4, 1578. Despite all the time and effort to reduce the Hongan-ji temple, the affair ended in a rather anticlimactic fashion, when the emperor negotiated a peace to end the Ishiyama Hongan-ji War in 1580.

Toyotomi, who had been assigned to pacify western Japan, had become bogged down, and he was compelled to request assistance from his superior. Oda dispatched the bulk of his troops to Toyotomi's aid. With a small band of only two to three hundred men, Oda took shelter at the Honnoji temple in Kyōto before joining the main force. While there, he was attacked by thirteen thousand troops led by one of his most trusted vassal daimyo, Akechi Mitsuhide. The death of Oda on June 21, 1582, at the hands of the renegade Akechi is known as the "Honnoji Incident." Toyotomi made peace with his opponents almost immediately, and thirteen days later he avenged his master's death by defeating Akechi at the Battle of Yamazaki. Akechi is referred to in some texts as the "Thirteen Day Shogun." Toyotomi eventually prevailed as the heir to Oda's efforts, and he also inherited the conquest of the Buddhist armies.

Summary

Despite Oda Nobunaga's reputation as a warlord, he did make contributions to other aspects of Japanese life and culture. Oda declared a number of free trade centers, which helped to break up the economic stagnation of a tradition-bound economy. He also sought to alter the role played by guilds in market centers. There was no blanket policy but rather a series of adjustments made to derive greater economic benefit. In some cases, guilds were abolished, while in other circumstances they were established. Oda also sought to modernize the economy by banning barter trade and replacing it with currency exchange to promote a true money economy. To prevent unfair practice, he also established currency regulations that set official standards for exchange and for the value of copper, silver, and gold. Oda took steps to simplify land ownership and encourage single-party control of estates. That went hand in hand with his implementation of cadastral surveys, which were designed to expedite administration, taxation, and assessment of land productivity.

Oda's policies had the effect of altering the role of Buddhism in Japanese society. The changes evoked include the elimination of military power, the limitation of economic power, and the subjugation of religious authorities to the central administration. Despite the tremendous amount of energy and resources expended against the Buddhists, Oda was not anti-Buddhist. Oda patronized certain temples, had Buddhist military allies, and had even relied on Zen priests as military advisers on occasion.

The Sengoku period was dominated by a warlord society, and even Oda's followers feuded. On occasion, there was treachery, and Oda had to execute some of those daimyo who sought to betray him. Yet such action was not particularly abnormal in a warlord society. The fact that Oda indulged in such behavior did not prove that he was more bloodthirsty than any other daimyo. Oda was responsible for the initial military operations that altered the balance of power and led to the centralization of power in Japan. Eventually, the process culminated in the Tokugawa shogunate, which lasted until the nineteenth century, a period of Japanese modernization known as the Meiji Restoration.

Bibliography
Hall, John Whitney. *Government and Local Power in Japan, 500 to 1700: A Study Based on the Bizen Province.* Princeton, N.J.: Princeton University Press, 1966. This study actually focuses on Bizen Province. Yet chapter 10 has relevant information on Oda. This book establishes Oda's efforts within the realm of the evolving political scene and is useful as a brief overview for those new to the subject.
Hall, John Whitney, Nagahara Keiji, and Kozo Yamamura, eds. *Japan Before Tokugawa: Political Consolidation in Economic Growth, 1500 to 1600.* Princeton, N.J.: Princeton University Press, 1981. Although the entire volume is worthwhile from the standpoint of historical context, there are two specific chapters of interest: chapter 5, "The Political Posture of Oda Nobunaga," and chapter 7, "The Commercial and Urban Policies of Oda Nobunaga and Toyotomi Hideyoshi." The work gives opportunity to focus on the nonmilitary side of the warlord.
McMullin, Neil. *Buddhism and the State in Sixteenth Century Japan.* Princeton, N.J.: Princeton University Press, 1984. An advanced examination of the relationship between Oda and the Buddhists. Despite the omission of Oda's name from the title, the work is to a large degree centered on him. This volume used by far the greatest number of original documents from which to draw information. Central to the thesis is the concept that Oda does not deserve the heinous reputation he has received.
Perrin, Noel. *Giving Up the Gun: Japan's Reversion to the Sword, 1543-1879.* Boston: David R. Godine, 1979. Primarily concerned with Japan's adoption and then later rejection of firearms. Although the chapters concerning Oda are few, this book is excellent for those seeking to understand the cultural implications of Oda's use of firearms. The author also used a number of historic Japanese texts for his research, so his bibliography is noteworthy for those studying the history of technology.
Sansom, George. *A History of Japan, 1334-1615.* Stanford, Calif.: Stanford University Press, 1961. This remains one of the standards in the field. The chapters devoted to Oda are 17, 18, and 19. It remains the best single volume for those attempting to deal with this warlord on a one-time basis. The author, however, remains firm in his conviction that Oda was a brute. An effective balance between chronology and analysis.
Turnbull, Stephen. *Samurai Warriors.* London: Blandford Press, 1987. Chapter 5 is the most relevant. As the title implies, this is a study of Oda the warlord. The emphasis is on military achievements, and the chronology of battles, combined with technical information, is useful. Although

somewhat explicit, the illustrations serve to make this the most colorful of the works listed.

Randolf G. S. Cooper

JACQUES OFFENBACH
Jacob Eberst

Born: June 20, 1819; Cologne, Prussia
Died: October 5, 1880; Paris, France
Area of Achievement: Music
Contribution: Over the course of one hundred operettas and a major opera, Offenbach virtually defined this form of musical theater through his characteristic mixture of gaiety, spontaneity, and infectious melody and thus became the first great influence in the process of internationalizing the operetta.

Early Life

Jacques Offenbach, one of the greatest figures in the history of operetta, was born Jacob Eberst, the second son of a peripatetic Jewish cantor and music teacher. Isaac Eberst, Jacob's father, was a poor man who, when not singing in the synagogue of his hometown, Offenbach-am-Main, Germany, supplemented his income as a music teacher by playing the fiddle in local cafés. Called "the Offenbacher" on his travels, Isaac thus adopted "Offenbach" as his legal surname.

Jacob clearly inherited more than his father's name, for the boy, along with his brother Julius, early showed a marked talent for music. Offenbach himself noted that he had learned to play the violin by the time he was seven, but by age ten he discovered the cello and it was with this instrument that the young man became a professional musician. Frail and thin throughout his life, Offenbach belied his appearance by playing the cello with the same high-spirited vivacity that was to characterize his music.

Offenbach's talent was in need of greater nourishment than that which could be obtained in Cologne, so in October, 1833, Isaac arranged for his son to go to Paris to enroll in the conservatoire, the pinnacle of musical opportunity. The story goes that Offenbach was at first denied admission on the grounds that he was not French, upon which he took up his cello and began playing a piece at first sight. The admissions committee did not let him finish but took his hand and welcomed him as a pupil. Offenbach began to study the violin, but within a year the young man left the conservatoire, probably from the need to earn a living. At fifteen, Jacob, now Jacques, Offenbach secured a job as cellist in the orchestra of the Opéra-Comique.

The business of music in Paris of the late 1830's was primarily a theatrical enterprise. Composers often conducted their own works and promoted them as well, and it was not uncommon for a composer of waltzes and social music to lead a sixty-piece orchestra in cafés along the boulevards. The young Offenbach submitted several of his waltzes to the leading composer-impresarios of the day, and one of his first, "Fleurs d'hiver" ("Winter Flowers"), was a popular success. By January, 1839, Offenbach, at age nineteen, gave his first public concert. Soon thereafter, he was asked to write the music for a vaudeville, *Pascal et Chambord*. Produced in March, 1839, the piece was a failure.

Undaunted, Offenbach continued to perform as virtuoso cellist and to teach. Over the next few years, he composed a number of cello works and performed in Germany and before the Queen of England. Thus, the salon and the drawing room—not the theater—dictated both the setting and the style for the compositions of Offenbach during the 1840's. His music was light, simple, generously diverting, and, above all, well crafted. The ballads and songs of this period are interesting in at least two respects. First, they often contain the melodic germs of his later work, for Offenbach had a lifelong practice of recasting earlier material. For another, they often contain elements of humor—such as the cello simulating a kazoo—that were to make his great operettas so distinctive.

It was, indeed, just this element of humor bordering on impertinence that—more than even the local musical politics—probably kept Offenbach from serious notice. Though he was known throughout the 1840's as a cellist and minor composer of songs and other salon pieces, his own ambition to write a musical work for the Opéra-Comique was spurned by the management of that theater. Meanwhile, Offenbach converted to Catholicism and married Herminie d'Alcain in 1844.

Life's Work

The Revolution of 1848 which made France, nominally at least, a republic, precipitated Offenbach's departure to Germany. The father of a young girl, he was as poor as a free-lance composer of dance music could be, but he continued to pursue his ambition of writing for the musical stage and had his first work of this kind produced in Cologne. The work went virtually unnoticed. Now approaching thirty, Offenbach returned to Paris to see Louis Napoleon, nephew of Napoleon I, installed as Emperor of France. The so-called Second Empire had begun and with it the rising fortunes of Offenbach.

During his career as cellist and salon composer, he had met the director of the Théâtre-Français, the serious theater for all state-approved tragedies and comedies. In 1851, the director appointed Offenbach conductor of the house, hoping that the young cellist's musical abilities and vivacious personality would bring back the audiences lost to administrative and artistic chaos. As conductor, Offenbach presented not only the music of other composers but also, more pertinent to his own career, his own compositions. Before long, his own incidental music to plays and his *entr'actes* (music played during the intermissions) began to gain attention.

Now in a position to write the kind of light, witty theater music that he perceived as lacking on the French stage, he dedicated himself unceasingly to the task. From this period of the early 1850's, Offenbach began to compose an astonishing number of "little operas." In 1855 alone, he produced no less than twelve one-act operettas. This was the year in which he left his official post at the Théâtre-Français and opened his own theater, the Bouffes-Parisiens. Restricted now only by his own cleverness, Offenbach flourished. By his own admission, his major vice now and throughout the rest of his life was work. He wrote incessantly, steadily, and quickly. In 1856, eight operettas came from his fecund pen, and in 1857 seven more. These early operettas, such as *Ba-ta-clan* (1855), *La Bonne d'enfants* (1856), and *Les Deux Pêcheurs* (1857), possess a lyrical charm and freshness that characterize much of the composer's best music, but they fall victim to clumsy and dated librettos and are thus seldom heard or performed.

After producing almost thirty operettas in five years, Offenbach composed what was to be his first, and perhaps best-known, major work. Unlike his previous compositions, *Orphée aux enfers* (1858) is more ambitious in scope (two acts), more serious in the variety of musical types, and, above all, more witty in its parody of some of French society's most cherished traditions. Offenbach's chief librettist for the work was Ludovic Halévy, who, along with Henri Meilhac, was to write the book for Georges Bizet's *Carmen* (1875). Together, they provided Offenbach with the librettos for his finest operettas. Offenbach's love of satire and parody infused the music of *Orphée aux enfers* with the sparkling wit and innocent naughtiness that became the composer's hallmark and a distinctive element of French operetta for the remainder of the century. Taking the Greek myth of Orpheus and Eurydice as its source, the operetta pokes fun at the pantheon of gods who talked not like Greek divinities but Second Empire boulevardiers, ladies and gentlemen of mid-nineteenth century French society. Along the way, there are musical parodies of Christoph Gluck, composer of the 1762 serious version of the Orpheus and Eurydice story, and of scenes from Italian opera. The finale consists of the famous cancan, during which the gods and goddesses cavort in a frenzied bacchanal.

Orphée aux enfers made Offenbach famous and rich, though money was never his constant companion. His generosity, love of luxury, and overall beneficent prodigality always kept the composer within view of his creditors. Still, his prodigality of money was at least equaled by his prodigality of genius as one after another operetta reached the stage. Between *Orphée aux enfers* in 1858 and his next great operetta, *La Belle Hélène* of 1864, Offenbach composed another twenty-eight works, including a ballet, *Le Papillon* (1860), and a three-act parody of medieval France, *Geneviève de Brabant* (1859). The latter contained a famous section that was later adapted by the United States Marine Corps for its well-known hymn.

When in 1860 the Opéra-Comique at last commissioned a work from him,

Offenbach offered *Barkouf*. A ridiculous libretto about a dog that becomes head of state was coupled with music which the public, for once, did not understand. The work drew the disdain of music critics and composers such as Hector Berlioz, who attacked Offenbach's use of strange and awkward harmonies. *Barkouf* represents one of the few times Offenbach overextended himself and clearly illustrates the fatality of musical stage works in thralldom to a bad libretto. Offenbach was not to make the same mistake again. *La Belle Hélène* is regarded by many as his most brilliant operetta. For his source, the composer once again returned to Greek mythology, this time to the legend of Helen of Troy. Although conservative critics condemned the work for its blasphemy of Homer, the public knew better. With *La Belle Hélène*, Offenbach reached the zenith of his career. His orchestration now bore a richer chromatic harmony, evidence of Richard Wagner's influence, and the music sparkled with a brilliant libretto.

La Belle Hélène was followed by a series of witty and gently mocking operettas. Offenbach had become the darling of the Second Empire, even as he gaily laughed at it. With the Franco-Prussian War of 1870, however, the Second Empire tottered, and when it fell Offenbach's own success and the quality of his work soon also declined. He continued to write operettas, but he began imitating himself, revising earlier productions and depending increasingly on the spectacular and the impressive rather than on spontaneity.

Always pressed for money because of lavish spending, Offenbach accepted an offer to conduct concerts in the United States as part of the centennial celebration of 1876. During a three-month tour, he played excerpts from his work in New York, Philadelphia, and Chicago. Despite some critical reserve at the naughtiness of some of his operettas, Offenbach impressed many by his personality, and the tour was an ultimate success. His impressions of his American experience were published in Paris the following year.

By the late 1870's, however, two conditions had altered Offenbach's life, one physical, the other artistic. Afflicted by gout for a number of years, Offenbach was enduring more continuous pain as his ailment wracked his already frail body. Additionally, his dream of being taken seriously as a composer now manifested itself in his determination to write a masterwork of opera. He had been making sketches for a work based on stories by the German Romantic writer E. T. A. Hoffmann since 1875, but he wrote with uncharacteristic deliberation, signifying a more serious commitment rather than a decline in creative powers.

By 1880, Offenbach completed the score of his masterpiece, *Les Contes d'Hoffmann*. By October of that year, however, the disease precipitated heart failure, and Offenbach died on October 5, 1880. The orchestration of his great opera was completed by a family friend, Ernest Guiraud. Offenbach's masterpiece was thus performed in 1881, after his death, at the Opéra-Comique, the very theater in which he first dreamed of being recognized.

Summary

Though Jacques Offenbach did not actually invent the operetta, he did infuse the form with those elements of gaiety and good-natured fun that became the model for subsequent works of the kind. His influence on later masters such as W. S. Gilbert and Sir Arthur Sullivan and the Viennese composer Johann Strauss—whom Offenbach first urged to write operettas— is indelible; Offenbach must thus be regarded as a seminal figure in making operetta an international art form.

Gioacchino Rossini, himself an operatic master, referred to Offenbach as "the Mozart of the boulevards." The similitude is apt not only because Wolfgang Amadeus Mozart was Offenbach's idol—Offenbach kept a book of Mozart's music always by his bedside—but also because, like Mozart, Offenbach had a unique gift for melody and for lucidity of style. Like Mozart's, Offenbach's music is almost always perfectly suited to the context in which it is placed and which it thus defines. His melodies are among the most infectious ever written.

The connection with Rossini, who lived in Paris during Offenbach's greatest triumphs, is also pertinent in an artistic sense. Like Rossini, Offenbach understood the dramatic excitement generated at the end of a scene by the use of a galloping rhythm combined with a crescendo. His use of brass instruments particularly heightened the vitality of the melodic line. Finally, Offenbach's music epitomizes the saucy, high-spirited, and supremely confident atmosphere of Paris during the middle years of the nineteenth century.

Bibliography

Bordman, Gerald. *American Operetta: From "H.M.S. Pinafore" to "Sweeney Todd."* New York: Oxford University Press, 1981. Contains a brief history of the popularity of Offenbach in the United States, particularly citing his *La Grande-Duchesse de Gérolstein* (1867) as an influence on later American operetta formats.

Faris, Alexander. *Jacques Offenbach*. New York: Charles Scribner's Sons, 1980. This is probably the best biography in English. Himself a conductor, Faris presents a well-balanced, though often too minutely detailed, study. Includes liberal examples of musical notation and technique. Contains an excellent bibliography, including a complete chart of all Offenbach's work, published and unpublished.

Kracauer, Siegfried. *Offenbach and the Paris of His Time*. London: Constable, 1937. A sociological study of the theatrical and artistic traditions within which Offenbach lived and worked. Though accurate, the study tends to emphasize the political and revolutionary aspects of Offenbach's works.

Mordden, Ethan. *The Splendid Art of Opera: A Concise History*. New York: Methuen, 1980. Contains an excellent chapter on musical comedy that credits Offenbach with internationalizing operetta and examines the "remarkably innovative" *Les Contes d'Hoffmann*.

Offenbach, Jacques. *Orpheus in America: Offenbach's Diary of His Journey to the New World*. Translated by Lander MacLintock. Bloomington: Indiana University Press, 1957. Offenbach's memoirs about his American concert tour. His breezy prose serves as a revealing correlative to his musical style. Contains an excellent brief biographical introduction by the translator.

Edward Fiorelli

OGATA KŌRIN

Born: 1658; Kyōto, Japan
Died: 1716; Kyōto, Japan
Area of Achievement: Art
Contribution: Kōrin worked within traditional Japanese aesthetic forms to produce an art of originality and universality that for many epitomizes Japanese taste. His screen of irises is one of the most widely known of all Japanese paintings.

Early Life

Ogata Kōrin was the son of Ogata Sōken, a wealthy textile merchant and owner of the shop called Kariganeya ("Golden House of the Wild Goose"), which specialized in the design and weaving of brocades. Kōrin studied painting first with his father and then with Yamamoto Sōken of the Kyōto branch of the Kanō school of painters. The Kanō school represented aristocratic taste in the era before Kōrin, and the Kariganeya's chief customers were the aristocracy and the feudal lords (daimyo). The daimyo were forced, because of court pressures, to spend enormous sums on clothing, frequently leading to their financial ruin. When the Ogata family's most important customer, the Empress Tofukumon-in, died in 1678, the Kariganeya's fortunes began to decline. The Ogata family had lost money in making loans to the daimyo, loans which proved to be uncollectable. An attempt to attract customers from the lower merchant class failed, and by 1697 family bankruptcy had resulted.

The Ogata family moved in aristocratic circles and the world of learning and the arts, while deriving its livelihood from a business establishment that called for the highest artisan designs and skills. Kōrin continually drew and sketched, studied calligraphy and garden design, and observed the processes and techniques of the textile business. He epitomized the Japanese ideal of a man of learning and refinement, an amateur of the arts, accomplished in painting, poetry, theater, and the tea ceremony. He was a *bunjin*, or man of letters, and the concept of a dilettante was a positive one.

Life's Work

When his father, Sōken, died in 1687, he left an equal share of his still valuable property to each of his sons: Tozaburo, the eldest, who succeeded Sōken as the head of the family and the business, Kōrin, and Kenzan. For a decade, Kōrin lived the life of a wealthy heir, no definite profession being required of him. Yet the life-style of Kyōto's upper-middle-class merchants and artisans, intimates of the aristocracy who shared their taste for art and the Nō theater, had ended. The new rising merchant class was less artistic and mostly preoccupied with profit. In 1697, Tozaburo left the cloth business, moved to Edo (modern Tokyo), and entered the service of a leading feudal lord. The two younger sons realized that they had to earn a living. Kōrin at first designed textiles and lacquerware, while Kenzan, who had studied with the master potter Nonomura Ninsei, began to produce pottery. Kōrin next assisted Kenzan by painting designs on his brother's pottery, a collaboration of great artistic harmony. Kenzan is renowned today as one of the most important potters in the history of Japanese art.

The greatest influence on Kōrin's mature style was the work of another pair of collaborators: Honami Kōetsu, a calligrapher and maker of raku tea bowls, and Tawaraya Sōtatsu, head of the Tawaraya, a decorative painting atelier. It is no exaggeration to say that the Japanese consider this quartet—Kōetsu, Sōtatsu, Kōrin, and Kenzan—as representative of the pinnacle of Japanese painterly and calligraphic achievement. These four were related by family as well, and the Ogata family had a home in Takagamine village, a community of artisans founded by Kōetsu.

In 1701, Kōrin achieved the title of *hokkyo*, an official rank of mastery in painting; by 1704 Kōrin's finances were failing, and he moved to Edo, the seat of the shogunate government, to try his luck there. In 1707, he entered the service of a daimyo, which secured for him a substantial income, but he returned to Kyōto two years later and began working with his brother Kenzan. Kenzan was forced to close his kiln in 1712. After further financial difficulties from 1713 on, Kōrin died a poor man in 1716. Yet these years of his mature style saw the completion of his two masterpieces, the *Irises* and the *Red and White Plum Blossoms*, both folding screens.

Kōrin's small ceramic wares and fan paintings, as well as his large, twelve-panel folding screens, all show the importance of calligraphy to Japanese art. His sure, crisp, swift line, revealing both elegance and energy, is related to his character; in his character, the Japanese see an expression of themselves. In his work, his calligraphic training is evident in a complex interplay of spatial relations, scale and proportion, space intervals, similarities and resemblances, repetitions, sweeping climaxes, abrupt halts, changes of direction, speed, thickness and thinness, accents and silence, and empty spaces. Kōrin used the traditional Japanese themes of "flowers and grasses," poetry, and classic secular literary works as well as Sōtatsu's composition and "wet on wet" technique, Zen "black ink" style, Kanō school drama and power, and the textile techniques of dyeing and stenciling. Continuity with the past, interpreted in a personal style, has long been a Japanese ideal.

The Japanese admire the combination of the powerful and the delicate as an expression of their belief in nonduality, as in Kōrin's *Irises* screen, where a resolution of the sharp aggressive leaves in the soft yielding flowers on a gold ground that is both solid and void is found. Expressions of the unity of man and nature, the macrocosm and the microcosm, permeate Kōrin's works and capture the Shinto concept of *kami*, or the inner living energy of all natural phenomena and space.

Summary

The rise of the style of *ukiyo-e* ("pictures of the floating world"), with its exuberant genre painting and color woodcuts that depict the world of courtesans, Kabuki actors, and the pleasure quarters, caused the momentary eclipse of Ogata Kōrin's reputation; eventually, however, the innate preference of the Japanese for works that combine traditional Buddhist values of nonduality and traditional Shinto values of the sacredness of all forms of natural life prevailed. It is this preference, more than any twentieth century appreciation for bold abstract design, that lies behind the Japanese evaluation of Kōrin as central to their concept of a way of life. By the 1820's, a style of painting called *Rimpa* (a word meaning "school of Kōrin") had arisen largely as the result of the efforts of the painter Sakai Hōitsu, who painted in the manner of Kōrin and published books on Kōrin, making Kōrin once again well known.

Bibliography

Elisseeff, Danielle, and Vadime Elisseeff. *Art of Japan*. New York: Harry N. Abrams, 1985. A general survey in the Abrams series, very well illustrated, with a section on Kōrin.

Grilli, Elise. *The Art of the Japanese Screen*. New York: John Weatherhill, 1970. A history and analysis of the Japanese screen as well as a study of key artists and examples. The large color details are exceptional, and Grilli's compositional and formal analyses of the works are uniquely perceptive.

Leach, Bernard. *Kenzan and His Tradition: The Lives and Times of Kōetsu, Sōtatsu, Kōrin, and Kenzan*. New York: Transatlantic Arts, 1967. An informative study, with translations of many original documents, by a writer who is himself a master potter. The author's insight gives his remarks on Kenzan special meaning, but his consideration of Kōrin is also acute.

Link, Howard, and Toru Shimbo, eds. and comps. *Exquisite Visions: Rimpa Paintings from Japan*. Honolulu: Honolulu Academy of Arts, 1980. A catalog of the exhibition shown at the Honolulu Academy of Arts in the fall of 1980 and at Japan House House Gallery in the winter of 1980-1981. An extensive discussion of the *Rimpa* style and its followers.

Mizuo, Hiroshi. *Edo Painting: Sōtatsu and Kōrin*. New York: John Weatherhill, 1972. A study of the four principal artists of the *Rimpa* style—Kōetsu, Sōtatsu, Kōrin, and Kenzan—with fine illustrations. Mizuo, however, overstresses the dubious concept that the *Rimpa* style was a kind of quiet artistic rebellion against the crudity of the shogunate and *chonin*

tastes. Instead, the daimyo taste encompassed both *bu* and *bun*, the aggressive and the aesthetic, exemplifying the Asian belief in nonduality.
Shimizu, Yoshiaki, ed. *Japan: The Shaping of Daimyo Culture, 1185-1868.* Washington, D.C.: National Gallery of Art, 1988. The catalog of the extraordinary exhibition held at the National Gallery of Art in Washington, D.C. Important for the background of this period and its clear exposition of the coexisting acceptance of warrior traditions (*bu*) and civilian arts, or the arts of peace (*bun*).

Karl Lunde

BERNARDO O'HIGGINS

Born: August 20?, 1778; Chillán, Chile
Died: October, 1842; Peru
Areas of Achievement: The military and social reform
Contribution: Widely regarded by Latin Americans as the George Washington of Chile, O'Higgins, inspired by both the American and the French revolutions, followed the lead of the great Argentine general José de San Martín and helped Martín liberate Chile from Spanish colonial rule. Although he was not a political administrator, O'Higgins was able to inspire both the troops under his command and the Chilean civilian population to overthrow a long-detested regime.

Early Life

The illegitimate son of an Irish father, Ambrosio O'Higgins, who distinguished himself in the Spanish government's Chilean bureaucracy and as Viceroy of Peru, and a Chilean mother of impoverished background, Bernardo O'Higgins went to primary school in Lima, Peru, and London, England. The latter school was important because, while in London, O'Higgins, a bright and energetic student, met Latin American anti-Spanish revolutionaries whose liberation ideas stayed with him, greatly influencing his later military career.

When his father died, O'Higgins went back to Chile in order to oversee lands that his father had willed him. From all appearances, he was but one of many wealthy, ambitious young Chileans who, benefiting greatly from the hacienda system of landholding, would spend the rest of his life overseeing a large estate. Yet, perhaps as a result of the revolutionary contacts he had made in England, O'Higgins grew increasingly bitter about the ongoing Spanish occupation of Chile, resolving to help free the country from these bonds in a future struggle for independence.

Together with other patriotic, anti-Spanish aristocrats of liberal tendencies, O'Higgins in 1810 joined a group of delegates to Chile's congress, which was attempting to decide the country's political future. Unfortunately for all concerned, the congress was violently divided over which kind of governmental system Chile required. Some wanted a return to old ways of doing things, instituted centuries earlier by the conquering Spanish; others favored a republican form of government; still others hoped for a complete transformation of society which would do away with the past. Those who were not interested in the radical approach decided that working with others in the Santiago congress who failed to share their utopian vision of Chile was futile; thus, they left the congress, an act which allowed their political foes, calling themselves the Executive Power, to claim control of the Chilean government.

The rebels were ruthlessly defeated by José Carrera, who had fought against Napoleon I's army in Spain. Carrera, in a manner confusing to friend and enemy alike, supported constitutional reform while continuing allegiance to Spain's King Ferdinand, the latter action having been to camouflage true anti-Spanish intent.

The new constitution created a ruling triad, which included O'Higgins, who zealously believed in the reform of both society and government and in the creation of a benevolent state encouraging the betterment of the human condition. O'Higgins' first efforts were quashed by Peru's viceroy when the combined forces of O'Higgins' and Carrera's armies were routed in 1814, a rout that allowed the capture of Santiago, Chile, by Spanish forces and a setback to the budding revolution that resulted.

O'Higgins narrowly avoided being executed by the vengeful government forces; he took his army—what remained of it—over the Andes Mountains to Argentina, in itself a heroic feat. Discouraged by this untimely defeat, O'Higgins appeared to have become merely one more victim of the Spanish occupation, which was victoriously reasserting itself in the New World. In this defeat, Chile was joined by other countries elsewhere in Spanish America—Guatemala, Mexico, and Peru—that unsuccessfully battled oppression.

Life's Work

O'Higgins is often referred to as the liberator of Chile as well as a kind of George Washington figure. Like Washington, O'Higgins suffered early defeats, only to pull together his beaten forces and win the war. After the loss in 1814 to Spanish and loyalist troops, O'Higgins, like Washington, had the good fortune to have help from outside his nation. Argentina's San Martín, Governor of Cuyo Province, was able to give O'Higgins the right sort of assistance when he most needed it. Actually, without San Martín's expertise in military matters as well as his experienced army, the liberation of Chile would most likely have remained a dream unfulfilled. This tall, handsome man was clearly a classic leader who, like O'Higgins, had the respect of his troops. San Martín became O'Higgins' mentor and friend.

The campaign for the independence of Chile began in 1817 at Mendoza, Argentina, where San Martín gathered together great amounts of ammunition and guns for the coming war. Buenos Aires was in the mood to supply what O'Higgins needed—another bit of good fortune.

In O'Higgins, San Martín recognized a strong, purposeful young leader, with whom he could share military leadership. Yet what faced them both was the daunting prospect of moving an army across Andean passes much more than three thousand meters in elevation. Nevertheless, supplies, including equipment designed for traversing gullies and ravines, were readied, though O'Higgins was not certain that they would take them where no army had gone.

Using the Los Patos and Uspollata passes in the Andes, the troops united under San Martín and O'Higgins met the Spanish and Chilean loyalists near Santiago at the town of Chacabuco. It was O'Higgins, however, who achieved the greatest triumph in that battle: He rose from relative obscurity that day to be numbered among Latin America's most illustrious liberators. San Martín also added to his already impressive reputation as a military genius.

Bravely, with little thought to his personal safety, O'Higgins led two sweeping cavalry charges into the Spanish ranks, causing the latter considerable losses and creating confusion in the ranks. These great attacks set the stage for San Martín's being offered the supreme directorship of Chile, as the new title was known. San Martín, however, graciously declined the position. The title was given to O'Higgins, an honor he happily accepted.

The independence of Chile was proclaimed by O'Higgins on February 12, 1818. Because of Spanish and loyalist entrenchment in the southern part of the country, however, the war was not over. It took San Martín's brilliant defense of Santiago and the repulse of counterforces at Maipu, near the capital on April 5 of that year, before O'Higgins could truly announce that Chile was free of its long Spanish occupation.

Deeply indebted to San Martín, who took over the Maipu battle after O'Higgins himself had fallen ill, O'Higgins returned the favor by assisting his friend in the battle to liberate Peru, the astute O'Higgins realizing that if the fledgling Chilean government were to survive, it would require that Peru and other neighboring states be free from Spanish enslavement. To this end, he joined San Martín once more, this time in acquiring a flotilla of ships, which were presented to a Scottish sailor, Thomas Cochrane, who created a Chilean fleet that was superior to anything operating in the Southern Pacific region. On August 20, 1820, the fleet left Valparaiso, and it included at least eight well-armed men-of-war and various other vessels. In September of 1820, the army under San Martín's command invaded Southern Peru while Cochrane blockaded the Peruvian coastline, attacking several Spanish ships in the process.

For O'Higgins, however, the main arena was no longer battle, but warfare of the political sort, wherein he would have to take charge of a newly free nation without any Latin American precedents to follow that would suit Chile's unique situation. To O'Higgins, the only workable way to govern a turbulent, newly freed country such as Chile was for him to declare himself a virtual dictator, which he did.

It was O'Higgins' and Chile's misfortune—since O'Higgins was a man of tremendous ability—that he could not be as successful a leader as he had been a soldier. It may have been that he lacked the skills that were needed to govern effectively, and it may have been the case that he simply was not interested in politics. Whatever the cause, history records that after trying to force various liberal social reforms on unwilling Chileans, O'Higgins was forced to resign as supreme director. In 1823, O'Higgins was deposed peacefully and sent into exile in Peru, where he stayed until he died.

O'Higgins was a true reformer by nature, his most pressing interest being in educational reform, for he believed that Chileans deserved to have widespread—even universal—public education. Thus, he re-created the once-defunct Instituto Nacional in Santiago and opened a number of schools for the people under the auspices of the English educator James Thompson.

Yet he also ordered that aristocratic titles and coats of arms be abolished and asked that estate entailment, the backbone of the hacienda system, be destroyed, measures that infuriated the rich landlords of Chile, who became convinced that O'Higgins was a threat to their pleasant, tradition-bound lifestyle. Other high-minded ideas of O'Higgins' outraged more than the elite members of Chilean society, for he wanted to do away with cockfighting and bullfighting, both highly popular pursuits among the poor. The enslavement of black people, another popular institution, was also declared immoral by O'Higgins, much to the general consternation of the populace. To add to his problems, it was not only the rich who were angry but also the liberals and moderates from whose ranks O'Higgins himself had risen. Moreover, powerful military men found the director's ideas intolerable, and this turned out to be O'Higgins' undoing, for the military, under the leadership of Ramón Freire, led the revolt that ousted him in 1823 and sent him into Peruvian exile.

It was Chile's misfortune to lose one as capable as O'Higgins in its national infancy, when it needed a strong leader. After his departure, more than ten different directors came to and left office, each of them trying in his own way to keep Chile from disintegrating completely. Although stability did eventually come to Chilean government, it was a long time in coming.

Summary

Whatever ill might be said of Bernardo O'Higgins' last years in Chile, he remains that nation's greatest hero and its political benefactor supreme. Without him, Chile might have languished under Spanish rule for several more decades than it did. O'Higgins knew that the time had come for Latin American nations in general to rise up against their colonizers.

He, along with Simón Bolívar, San Martín, and, more recently, Fidel Castro, is one of the Latin American men of destiny who profited from a political and social climate in which revolutionary thought and action could flourish. The lessons drawn from France's bloody revolution and from the inspirational American experience in its war with England taught people of intellect and patriotism living after those revolutions had triumphed that it was possible to fight against and eventually conquer the most powerful of tyrannies. Notions also drawn from the French and American conflicts that became current in Latin America's revolutionary period—freedom, liberty, and self-direction—helped O'Higgins fight against Spanish oppressors, for older notions about being subservient to foreign masters seemed stale and lifeless. Although it was not transformed immediately from a distant province of New Spain into a modern nation after O'Higgins and San Martín won the war of independence, Chile would eventually become known as one of Latin America's most reliably democratic nations. O'Higgins was shrewd enough and sufficiently visionary to realize that an opportunity had finally presented itself. He alone was able to take appropriate actions that would lead to the destruction of Spanish power in his part of the world. If he was not a dynamic politician or even a well-loved one, he created the new Chile almost single-handedly, and for that Chileans owe him much.

Bibliography
Collier, Simon. "The Story or Part of It at Least." In *From Cortes to Castro: An Introduction to the History of Latin America, 1492-1973*. New York: Macmillan, 1974. An insightful and reevaluative history of the political, social, religious, and economic currents shaping Latin American history over several centuries. A valuable account of the liberation movement led by O'Higgins and San Martín.
Eyzaguirre, Jaime. *O'Higgins*. 3d ed. Santiago, Chile: Editorial Zig Zag, 1950. An excellent biography that is very likely the finest one about O'Higgins. The author has at times an overinflated opinion of O'Higgins' attributes, yet the book does full justice to his seminal role in Chile's struggle for independence.
Kinsbruner, Jay. *Bernardo O'Higgins*. New York: Twayne, 1968. An invaluable contribution to O'Higgins scholarship that goes into considerable depth about O'Higgins' revolution and how he achieved all that he did in such a short time. Includes a selective bibliography.
Mehegan, John J. *O'Higgins of Chile: A Brief Sketch of His Life and Times*. London: J & J Bennett, 1913. One of the better general introductions to the life and times of O'Higgins.
Worcester, Donald E., and Wendell G. Schaeffer. "The Wars of Independence in the South." In *The Growth and Culture of Latin America*. 2 vols. New York: Oxford University Press, 1970-1971. Discusses how Chilean society evolved during and after the revolution O'Higgins helped lead. Also good for placing O'Higgins in a historical context.

John D. Raymer

JOHAN VAN OLDENBARNEVELT

Born: September 14, 1547; Amersfoort, Bishopric of Utrecht
Died: May 13, 1619; The Hague, United Provinces
Areas of Achievement: Government and statesmanship
Contribution: Oldenbarnevelt was the founder-lawgiver of the United Provinces of the Netherlands, whose statesmanship set the constitutional libertarian course that the modern Netherlands has followed. He was one of the greatest statesmen and diplomats in early modern Europe and in all Dutch history. Oldenbarnevelt served the United Provinces as Pensionary of Rotterdam and Advocate of Holland.

Early Life

Johan Gerrit Reyerszoon van Oldenbarnevelt was born on September 14, 1547, in Amersfoort, the second town in the Bishopric of Utrecht, one of seventeen Netherlandic provinces in the possession of the Habsburg dynasty; thus, he was born a subject of Emperor Charles V. Johan belonged to the regent class, the burgher-oligarchy and provincial nobility of the Netherlands who governed locally by hereditary right on town councils and provincial representative assemblies that were called the states, or estates. The regent class was jealous of its position and privileges, and defended them against both the populace below and the Habsburgs and their lieutenants, called stadtholders, above.

Johan inherited the traditions of both his father's family and his mother's, the Weedes, traditions of burgher-oligarchy and provincial nobility, but he would not proceed directly to eminence. His father appears to have suffered mental incapacitation, and therefore he never served on the Amersfoort town council let alone on a council of the States of Utrecht, Holland, and Zealand, which were in very close political relations, or for the States-General of the Netherlands, the representative assembly of all the provinces. Because of this family crisis, Johan did not go directly from the Amersfoort Latin school to university or on the customary grand tour of France, Germany, and Italy. Instead, in 1563, Johan served a sort of apprenticeship with a lawyer at The Hague. Between 1566 and 1570, Johan combined university study and grand tour and traveled through Louvain, Bourges, Cologne, Heidelberg, Italy, and perhaps Padua, studying arts and the law.

When Oldenbarnevelt returned to The Hague in 1570, the Duke of Alva for the Spanish Habsburgs tyrannized the Netherlands, which had begun the War of Independence in 1569. Oldenbarnevelt established law practice in the courts at The Hague, where he specialized in feudal law and law concerning dykes, drainage, and land reclamation. Because much of the Netherlands, the polders, had been reclaimed from the sea, and questions about title, responsibility for maintaining dykes, and similar matters were many, Oldenbarnevelt's practice grew quickly and soon became very lucrative. The Revolt of the Netherlands swept up Oldenbarnevelt. Though he had become a moderate Calvinist while a university student at Heidelberg, at The Hague he became a partisan of William the Silent.

War interrupted Oldenbarnevelt's legal practice and brought him onto the battlefield in the cause of Netherlandic independence. He saw action as a soldier in the disastrous attempt to relieve the Siege of Haarlem in 1573 and as supervisor of breaching the dykes in order to flood the polders for the celebrated relief of the Siege of Leiden in 1574. He also served William the Silent and his family in a legal capacity at this time.

In 1575, Oldenbarnevelt was married to Maria van Utrecht, the illegitimate daughter of a noble family, who had become a wealthy heiress when Oldenbarnevelt's legal shrewdness secured her legitimation. His courtship of Maria seems not to have been entirely mercenary, for they remained happily married for forty-three years, until his execution, and had two daughters, two sons, and grandchildren. Meanwhile Oldenbarnevelt had regained his rightful place in the regent class, demonstrated considerable legal ability, gained a fortune by his law practice and marriage, and made important friends in the House of Orange. Oldenbarnevelt was a moderate in religion and politics, a believer in liberty of conscience, and a constitutionalist who saw the necessity of balancing particularism and centralism in order to secure freedoms. He shared William the Silent's vision of an independent, united Netherlands.

Life's Work

In 1576, Oldenbarnevelt became Pensionary of Rotterdam, the legal representative and political secretary of the town, and entered the politics of Holland. Because Holland was the leading province, he thus became prominent in Netherlandic politics. Oldenbarnevelt promoted the Union of Utrecht of 1579 and the Act of Abjuration of 1581, which together became the declaration of independence and the constitution of the seven United Provinces of the Netherlands. Tensions between centralism and particularism remained, and at first the States-General thought to confer the sovereignty, which Spain had forfeited by its bloody tyranny, on the Duke of Anjou and then the Earl of Leicester, an action that would have made the United Provinces a satellite of France or England. Oldenbarnevelt led the States of Holland in opposition to such centralizing policies and in 1585 secured the appointment of Maurice of Nassau, son of William the Silent, who had been assassinated in 1584, as stadtholder and captain general. So long as the war against Spain continued, the advocate and the stadtholder collaborated in harmony—Oldenbarnevelt strengthened the United Provinces politically and diplomatically, and supported Maurice with revenue and political cooperation, and Maurice won military victories. Oldenbarnevelt led the United Provinces during the celebrated "Ten Years" (1588-1598), when the provinces achieved full self-government, balancing centralism among the States-General, the stadtholder and captain-general, and the councils, with particularism in the provincial states and the town councils, thus transforming the loose defensive alliance of seven sovereign provinces into the United Provinces of the Netherlands. It was in this that Oldenbarnevelt's leadership proved decisive. He scored the diplomatic triumph of the Triple Alliance in 1596 with France and England against Spain and thus gained international recognition of the independent United Provinces.

In 1598, France made peace with Spain, in 1604 England did the same, so in 1605 Oldenbarnevelt decided to make peace. Spain was exhausted and wanted peace, and Oldenbarnevelt knew that a peace treaty would mean at least de facto recognition by Spain and the Spanish Netherlands (the ten provinces not in the Union of Utrecht) of the independence of the United Provinces. Oldenbarnevelt's peace policy was opposed by Maurice and by his war party, which distrusted Spain's intentions, by the orthodox Calvinists who saw the war in apocalyptic terms, and by commercial interests who wanted economically to penetrate the West Indies. Oldenbarnevelt himself had an energetic commercial policy. He had in 1602 chartered the Dutch East India Company, but he was reluctant to charter a Dutch West India Company, which would jeopardize the peace with Spain. In the face of such opposition to make peace with Spain, Oldenbarnevelt characteristically compromised and negotiated the Twelve Years' Truce. Yet the truce was disturbed by religious conflict within the United Provinces. This conflict had originated in an academic theological debate between two professors at the University of Leiden, the strict Calvinist Franciscus Gomarus and the revisionist Jacob Arminius, over the Calvinist doctrine of predestination. The orthodox Calvinist Gomarists regarded the moderate Arminians, whom Oldenbarnevelt favored, as religious traitors worse than papists.

In 1617, Maurice declared for the Gomarists and rallied all parties that opposed Oldenbarnevelt over the Twelve Years' Truce. Oldenbarnevelt responded with the Sharp Resolution of August 4, 1617, which attempted to remove the military in Holland from the stadtholder and captain-general and to place it under control of the States of Holland and towns of the province. Maurice mobilized the other six provinces in the union against Holland and moved quickly and decisively. On August 28, 1618, the States-General conferred dictatorial powers on Maurice, and on August 29, 1618, Maurice ordered the arrest of Oldenbarnevelt and a few of his followers. In February, 1619, the States-General created an extraordinary tribunal to try Oldenbarnevelt and three codefendants, who included his protégé the great jurist and political philosopher Hugo Grotius.

Oldenbarnevelt's trial lasted from November, 1618, to May, 1619, but he was given neither writing materials nor access to books, documents, witnesses, or counsel. Yet he conducted an eloquent and dignified defense. The judges that were picked were his personal and political enemies, and the tribunal found Oldenbarnevelt guilty of vaguely defined capital crimes, despite his age and long service to the United Provinces. From the scaffold on May 13, 1619, Oldenbarnevelt addressed the crowd, "Men, do not think me a traitor; I have acted honestly and religiously, like a good patriot, and as such I die." After the headsman had done his work, the crowd pressed forward and, for relics of the martyred Oldenbarnevelt, dipped handkerchiefs in his blood.

Summary

Johan van Oldenbarnevelt founded the United Provinces of the Netherlands and its traditions of constitutionalism and libertarianism. While William the Silent and his sons won Dutch independence on the battlefields of the Eight Years' War against Spain, Oldenbarnevelt preserved independence through lawgiving, statesmanship, and diplomacy. He spent his long life serving his country, and he died an old man beheaded in 1619 by a Dutch special tribunal, a martyr for his vision of Dutch republican liberty. As Pensionary of Rotterdam and Advocate of Holland, Oldenbarnevelt was architect of the United Provinces of the Netherlands, which lasted until 1795, and the Dutch libertarianism which has thrived since. His leadership fostered moderation, freedom, enterprise, toleration, peace, and prosperity, and began the great cultural florescence of the United Provinces during the seventeenth century. The United Provinces became a refuge for intellectual freedom in an age of persecution. Oldenbarnevelt's diplomatic triumphs were the Triple Alliance with France and England in 1596 and the Twelve Years' Truce with Spain and the Spanish Netherlands, which gave the new United Provinces both a respite from war and international recognition. Ironically, it was Oldenbarnevelt's peace policy and religious moderation that led to his fall in 1618, and in 1619 his Dutch political enemies sentenced him to execution on very vague and unfounded charges of official misconduct and treason. On the scaffold at The Hague, the venerable statesman died as he had lived—brave and proud for the cause of liberty.

Bibliography

Geyl, Pieter. *History of the Low Countries: Episodes and Problems*. London: Macmillan, 1964. An important collection of essays, several of which supply very useful background on Oldenbarnevelt; contentious in tone.
_____. *The Revolt of the Netherlands, 1555-1609*. 2d ed. London: Ernest Benn, 1958. An admirably clear and cogent narrative, somewhat tendentious about the historical contingency of the divided Netherlands and hence inevitably ambivalent about Oldenbarnevelt's founding of the United Provinces.

Motley, John Lothrop. *The Life and Death of John of Barneveld*. 2 vols. New York: Harper & Brothers, 1874. A classic history, despite its strong Protestant and liberal bias, that is still well worth reading for its drama, eloquence, and insights into Oldenbarnevelt.

Rowen, Herbert H., ed. *The Low Countries in Early Modern Times*. New York: Walker, 1972. Includes well-selected key documents that are edited, translated, and commented upon judiciously. Sections 4 and 6 present such texts as the Union of Utrecht, the Act of Abjuration, the Treaty of the Twelve Years' Truce, and several of Oldenbarnevelt's letters.

Tex, Jan den. *Oldenbarnevelt*. Translated by R. B. Powell. 2 vols. Cambridge: Cambridge University Press, 1973. The standard scholarly biography, this work is appreciative of the great statesman but not uncritically so. Better on the public than on the private man. The book makes a peculiar defense of the special court that condemned Oldenbarnevelt.

Terence R. Murphy

NIKOLAUS AUGUST OTTO

Born: June 10, 1832; Holzhausen, Nassau
Died: January 26, 1891; Cologne, Germany
Areas of Achievement: Invention and technology
Contribution: Otto invented the first internal-combustion, four-stroke engine. His engine is the forerunner of modern gasoline automobile engines.

Early Life

Nikolaus August Otto was born in the small village of Holzhausen auf der Heide, on the Rhine. His father, postmaster and innkeeper in the village, died shortly after Nikolaus' birth. Nikolaus was a bright child who did well in school, and his mother wanted, at first, to enter her son in higher education. The unrest of 1848 changed her mind, however, and she decided that the business world would provide a better future for him. Accordingly, he gave up high school (where he had been a star student) and went to work.

Otto's first job was as a clerk in a small-town grocery store. From there he moved to a job as a clerk in Frankfurt, and eventually became a traveling salesman for a wholesale grocer, working out of Cologne. In 1860, still a traveling salesman, Otto read a newspaper account of a gas engine built by a Frenchman, Étienne Lenoir. The Lenoir engine was well known at this time, and Otto studied it carefully. As the piston of the Lenoir engine moved down the cylinder, it drew in a mixture of gas and air. An electric spark ignited the air/gas mixture halfway through the stroke, creating the power necessary to push the piston to the bottom of the cylinder. Each piston was doubled-sided, so the piston returned to its original position when the same steps were repeated on the opposite side. It is important to note that this engine did not compress the air/gas mixture and that it relied on illuminating gas (used in homes and street lamps) for its fuel. Lenoir had trouble getting it to run smoothly under a load.

Life's Work

With strong links to rural regions both in his boyhood and in his job, Otto was bothered by the fact that the Lenoir engine relied on a fuel which was available only through a system of pipelines found in the cities. He saw that the internal-combustion engine had the potential to become an important source of power in a wide variety of applications, and he determined to make an engine that could be used in city and village alike. He devised a carburetor for the Lenoir engine which enabled the engine to receive fuel from a tank rather than a pipeline. Although his patent application for the carburetor was rejected, he continued to work on the internal-combustion engine.

In 1861, Otto commissioned Michael Zons, an instrument maker and machine-shop owner in Cologne, to build a Lenoir engine. Otto studied this engine carefully in an attempt to make it run smoothly under a load. The main problem with the engine was the shock of detonation on the piston. While he was experimenting with this engine, Otto stumbled across a phenomenon which would later pay him great dividends. He drew in the air/gas charge and then, instead of allowing the piston to continue down the cylinder, he moved it back up toward the cylinder head, compressing the charge. Otto was surprised to find that the detonation was so violent as to turn the engine through several revolutions. This was the principle upon which he would later base the four-stroke cycle. After continued experimentation with the Lenoir engine, Otto decided that the difficulties were too great and turned to a new type of engine: the atmospheric engine.

The atmospheric engine resembled an upward-pointing cannon with gears and levers attached. As the motion of the flywheel pulled the piston up, air and gas were drawn in beneath the piston. At the same time, the piston pushed the air above it out of the cylinder and into a tank, where it was stored at above-atmospheric pressure. The combustion of the air/gas mixture pushed the piston up at high velocity to the top of the cylinder, creating a vacuum in the cylinder below the piston. The piston's own weight and the pressure difference between the air in the holding tank and the vacuum in the cylinder then returned the piston to the bottom of the cylinder.

Zons built a one-half horsepower model of the atmospheric engine for Otto in 1863. In order to develop the engine, Otto obtained financial backing from Eugen Langen, son of a wealthy industrialist, and they entered into a formal business agreement in March of 1864. With Langen's help, Otto refined the atmospheric engine. After three years of work, the Otto and Langen engine was shown at the 1867 Paris Exposition, winning the grand prize. Having built a successful engine, Otto and Langen now needed to manufacture and sell their product. They found more capital, created the Gasmotorenfabrik Deutz corporation in 1872, and shortly thereafter were selling their engines around the world.

The Otto and Langen engine proved to be popular; five thousand were eventually built. The engine's reliance on atmospheric pressure (the final version did not have the holding tank for air) posed a serious limitation, however, by limiting its output to a maximum of three horsepower. Furthermore, it was extremely noisy and vibrated strongly when in operation. In response to these shortcomings, Otto began to think about a new type of engine (possibly reviewing his earliest experiments with the Lenoir engine) in which the air/gas mixture was compressed in the cylinder before ignition. The engine then used one stroke each for the intake, compression, ignition (and expansion), and exhaust functions. In such an engine there was only one power stroke for every four piston strokes, hence the name "four-stroke cycle." This was a bold step, considering that the double-acting steam engine—the dominant power technology of the time—used each stroke as a power stroke.

Otto was concerned that detonation of the compressed air/gas mixture would produce a violent explosion capable of damaging the engine. To lessen the shock of detonation, he devised a concept known as the "stratified charge," in which the richest mixture would be farthest from the piston, with successive layers of air and exhaust gases filling the remainder of the cylinder. Otto believed that this would create a gradual burning instead of a violent explosion. The stratified charge was so important to Otto that it constituted the main claim in his patent, rather than the four-stroke cycle or the compressed charge.

Otto built the first of these engines in 1876 at the Gasmotorenfabrik Deutz works. Even the rough prototype demonstrated the many advantages of the four-stroke engine to Otto and his partners. Compared to the atmospheric engine (and others of the time) the four-stroke engine produced, for the same displacement and engine weight, far more horsepower. In addition to erasing the three-horsepower ceiling of the atmospheric engine, the new engine operated with much less noise and vibration, earning the nickname "Silent Otto." Gasmotorenfabrik Deutz refined the prototype and eventually marketed the engine with great success. By the turn of the century, Otto's firm had built twenty-four thousand engines.

In 1882, the first of several claims against Otto's patent rights arose. He was to spend the rest of his life defending himself against these claims. The most damaging came from a competitor who wanted to void Otto's patent on the four-stroke cycle on the basis of an obscure pamphlet written in 1862 by the French engineer Alphonse-Eugène Beau de Rochas. Rochas had clearly stated the principles of the four-stroke cycle in his pamphlet, but apparently he never realized its significance and never built an engine operating on those principles. Nevertheless, in 1886 Otto lost his German patents on the four-stroke cycle. He considered the patent suits an attack upon his honor, and the defeat in 1886 left him an embittered man. The legal battle continued until 1890, when the last appeal ended. On January 26, 1891, Nikolaus Otto died of heart failure in Cologne.

Summary

Automobiles using Nikolaus August Otto's engine appeared on the roads of Europe only ten years after he built the prototype, and less than two decades later the Wright brothers' aircraft was propelled by a four-stroke engine. The predominant type of automobile engine today is a direct descendant of Otto's 1876 engine. Nor is its use limited to transportation. One asset of Otto's engine is its flexibility, thanks to its small size, low weight, and the multitude of possible configurations (vertical, horizontal, single or multiple cylinders, ability to run on many kinds of fuels, and the like). Although Otto placed more faith in the stratified-charge concept than was probably warranted, he did, nevertheless, build the first successful engine to operate on the four-stroke cycle. For his persistence in solving the problems he encountered and for seeing them through to their respective solutions, he deserves the credit as that engine's inventor.

Bibliography
Bryant, Lynwood. "The Origin of the Automobile Engine." *Scientific American* 216 (March, 1967): 102-112. This article concentrates on the intellectual process by which Otto arrived at the 1876 engine. Bryant notes that Otto believed in the stratified charge to the end, although most other experts believed that the charge should be as homogeneous as possible. The many illustrations and photographs are a great help in understanding the technical details of Otto's engines. No documentation.
_____. "The Origin of the Four-Stroke Cycle." *Technology and Culture* 8 (April, 1967): 178-198. Examines Otto's claim to inventing the four-stroke cycle. In a carefully documented and reasoned argument, Bryant shows that while others had the idea of a four-stroke cycle, credit for invention should go to Otto. The section on Rochas, the cause of much grief to Otto, is of special interest.
_____. "The Silent Otto." *Technology and Culture* 7 (Spring, 1966): 184-200. Asks why Otto was successful after so many others had been trying to assemble an internal-combustion engine for seventy-five years. Traces his thought through fifteen years of development; points out that only in 1876, having gained much practical experience, was Otto ready to accept the four-stroke cycle he had discovered accidentally in 1862. In addition to the usual sources, Bryant has assembled evidence directly from the patent records.
Cummins, C. Lyle, Jr. *Internal Fire*. Lake Oswego, Oreg.: Carnot Press, 1976. Written by the son of the founder of the Cummins Engine Company, this book is an absorbing account of the internal-combustion engine from the seventeenth century to the present. While explaining each engine in this long tradition with plentiful technical detail (aided by line sketches and photographs), Cummins manages to place these developments in a broader context as well. Chapters 8 and 9 deal specifically with Otto. Cummins is not afraid to differ with other historians and generally provides good support for his argument. Despite sketchy footnotes, it is clear that he has consulted a wide range of sources.
Goldbeck, Gustav. "Nikolaus August Otto, Creator of the Internal-Combustion Engine." In *From Engines to Autos: Five Pioneers in Engine Development and Their Contributions to the Automotive Industry*, by Eugen Diesel, Gustav Goldbeck, and Friedrich Schilderberger. Chicago: H. Regnery, 1960. Goldbeck effectively puts together the highlights of

Otto's life and his accomplishments in the development of his engine. Lacks documentation but appears reasonably accurate. Is less sterile than many sources in that Goldbeck tries to reveal a more human side to the successes and failures Otto experienced.

Brian J. Nichelson

AXEL OXENSTIERNA

Born: June 16, 1583; Fanö, near Uppsala, Sweden
Died: August 28, 1654; Stockholm, Sweden
Areas of Achievement: Government and politics
Contribution: Combining intellect, courage, humor, and integrity, Oxenstierna
mastered every aspect of state service and helped Gustavus II Adolphus to
produce Sweden's age of greatness. As chancellor for Queen Christina, he
was largely responsible for New Sweden on the Delaware.

Early Life

Axel Oxenstierna was born on June 16, 1583, at Fanö, near Uppsala,
Sweden. His parents, Gustavus Oxenstierna and Barbro Bielke, came from
ancient noble families. During his youth, Oxenstierna experienced a Sweden
torn by conflict between the monarchy and the aristocracy. His father died
early in 1597, and since civil war had broken out, young Axel was sent to
Germany to study. He studied history, languages, and practical politics. In
1602, he returned to Sweden and swore allegiance to Charles IX. His diplomatic skills were rewarded with a post on the exchequer. He married Anna
Boot in 1608 and in the following year became a member of the Swedish
Council of State.

Life's Work

Oxenstierna began his forty-two-year career as chancellor in 1612, following the death of Charles IX in 1611. Gustavus II Adolphus, Charles's successor, appointed Oxenstierna, who had confirmed him as king and convinced him to issue a charter protecting against royal abuses. Oxenstierna's
appointment came at a time of great internal and external unrest. On the
domestic front, he represented the aristocracy in its struggle against the
monarchy—his success already demonstrated by the king's protective charter. Oxenstierna's skill as a diplomat also began to surface in his interactions
abroad.

Oxenstierna spent the next several years negotiating war settlements with
Denmark, Russia, and Poland. The Peace of Knäred was signed with Denmark in 1613. By 1617, the Peace of Stolbova was agreed to by Russia,
cutting that country off from the Baltic by extending Swedish control around
the Gulf of Finland. Poland's interests in using Russia to place Sigismund's
heirs on the Swedish throne were effectively delayed at this time, keeping
that war in abeyance.

Oxenstierna now turned his attention toward domestic reform. He wrote
the *riksdagsordning* (parliamentary law) in 1617. Development of towns to
increase the middle class and commerce was the focus of his work in 1619,
followed by local government reform in 1623. He was behind the reorgani-

zation of the nobility into three classes in 1626.

Meanwhile, diplomatic negotiations continued with Poland and Denmark. In 1626, the king shifted his war against Poland to Prussia and appointed Oxenstierna governor-general of the newly occupied territory. Oxenstierna organized the collection of the tolls from the Baltic ports, which provided much needed financial support for the Swedish war efforts up to 1635. It was clear that the Swedish dynastic struggles had become deeply involved in the European conflicts of the Thirty Years' War. In 1629, Oxenstierna negotiated peace with Poland, resulting in the Truce of Altmark.

Oxenstierna entered a new phase of his career when he was called to Germany by Gustavus Adolphus in 1631. He organized and led the army that brought relief to the king at Nürnberg in August of 1632. This military success allowed him to add revenues from occupied territory to port tolls and foreign subsidies to finance Sweden's war efforts. The string of victories came to an end with the death of Gustavus Adolphus at the Battle of Lützen in November of 1632. Leadership of Swedish affairs was assumed by Oxenstierna in Germany.

In 1633, he went to Saxony to create the Protestant league that Gustavus Adolphus had planned. The gathering at Heilbronn was led by Oxenstierna, but the Northern German princes never joined. After the military defeat at Nördlingen in 1634, Sweden's allies were disunited and disloyal, and many signed the Peace of Prague in 1635. Sweden was deprived of large parts of German territory, which had largely subsidized the war. Renewal of a truce with Poland meant relinquishing the Prussian port tolls, also in 1635. These revenue losses, along with military reverses as imperialist forces recovered, forced Oxenstierna to overcome severe difficulties. At one time, he was the prisoner of mutinous troops who had not been paid.

When Oxenstierna returned to Sweden in 1636, he was the prime ruler of the country, the major power in the council and the regency. He tutored the young Queen Christina (Gustavus Adolphus had made him her principal guardian before his death), who proved to be an apt pupil. He spent three hours each day discussing foreign and domestic affairs and explaining Sweden's international position and European politics. Christina described him as a tall, proper, straight, handsome man with a sober and fixed countenance and a grave and civil carriage. He is described as being very human in his conversation with Christina. They both derived great pleasure from their study sessions, although their relations were not always harmonious as she grew older.

Conflict between the two first came as a result of Oxenstierna's acceptance of French alliance and support in order to continue the war after 1638. The opposition of the Holy Roman Emperor, Ferdinand III, and the imperialist forces had forced Oxenstierna into this alliance, but his enemies in Sweden accused him of prolonging the war for personal gain. Christina was also dissatisfied with Oxenstierna's actions and wanted peace. This rift pleased Oxenstierna's opponents in the council. The queen took an active role in all proceedings after this time.

Relations between the queen and Oxenstierna continued to be capricious. Christina, who had begun to rule independently in 1644, made Oxenstierna a count, granting him several estates and high commendation in an assembly of the Estates following his attack of and subsequent peace with Denmark in the Treaty of Brömsebrö in 1645. Friction resurfaced, however, after the Peace of Westphalia (terminating the war with the emperor and the German princes) was signed on October 24, 1648. This friction was caused in part by Christina's growing fondness for France. Oxenstierna had never trusted Cardinal de Richelieu, nor, after Richelieu's death in 1642, did he trust Jules Mazarin. Swedish aristocrats despised and feared anything, such as French culture, that they considered unnatural and highbrow. Oxenstierna and Mazarin would continue to disagree over foreign policy and over the issue of succession through 1650, when their relations improved.

Oxenstierna's ongoing efforts to improve Sweden and increase its holdings and wealth were exemplified by his negotiations in the New World. Gustavus Adolphus had been presented with the opportunity to take advantage of trade with the New World as early as 1624. Oxenstierna was looking for a way to increase exports of Swedish copper to help finance the war effort, and, with the help of Peter Minuit, a Dutch colonial official, Oxenstierna's attention was riveted on the New World. The New Sweden Company was formed, and two vessels left early in November, 1637, entering the South Bay (Delaware River) early in March, 1638. They moved up the river and established Fort Christina, in honor of the twelve-year-old queen. Thus began the Swedish settlement on the Delaware. Trade supplies were slow in arriving, since Sweden's major attention was focused on the war in Germany. The Dutch in New Netherlands formed a serious threat, finally overcoming the Swedes and Finns in 1655.

Oxenstierna did not live to see the end of New Sweden. He died on August 28, 1654, in Stockholm. The position of chancellor under the new king, Charles X Gustav, who became king upon Christina's abdication, went to Oxenstierna's son, Erik.

Summary

Axel Oxenstierna was a great statesman of the seventeenth century. He mastered all aspects of state service, from local government reform to finances. He was successful in organizing and executing military campaigns. Known for his courage, intellect, humor, honesty, and devotion to the Vasa family, he, along with Gustavus Adolphus, pushed and pulled Sweden into an age of greatness, moving her from the edge of European society to center stage in the Thirty Years' War. He continued his work faithfully as Sweden's chancellor for forty-two years. It is possible that his most lasting memorial lies along the Delaware River, spreading throughout the United States: the heirs of the New Sweden Company.

Bibliography
Andersson, Ingvar. *A History of Sweden*. Translated by Carolyn Hannay. London: Weidenfeld & Nicolson, 1956. A valuable review of Sweden's place in history and an assessment of Oxenstierna's role in Swedish as well as European history. Chapters 16-19 focus on Oxenstierna's life, with chapter 18 especially valuable on his rule of Sweden in the regency period of Queen Christina.
James, G. P. R. *Lives of the Cardinal de Richelieu, Count Oxenstiern— Count Olivarez, and Cardinal Mazarin*. 2 vols. Philadelphia: Carey, Lea, and Blanchard, 1836. The material on Oxenstierna is in volume 2 and reviews his life with extensive attention to activities during the Thirty Years' War and Oxenstierna's efforts on behalf of Sweden after the death of Gustavus Adolphus.
Losman, Arne, Agneta Lundström, and Margareta Revera, eds. *The Age of New Sweden*. Translated by Bernard Vowles. Stockholm: Livrustkammaren for the Royal Armoury, 1988. There are five essays in this volume and some excellent illustrations, including one of Oxenstierna's chapel and his residence, Tidö, in Västmanland. The essays are helpful in presenting Sweden's developing culture and learning and social change in the seventeenth century.
Roberts, Michael. *Gustavus Adolphus: A History of Sweden, 1611-1632*. 2 vols. London: Longmans, Green, 1953-1958. This definitive biography of Gustavus Adolphus details his lifelong friendship with Oxenstierna, showing how these two extraordinary men changed the course of Swedish and European history. There are extensive illustrations, maps, and a bibliography. The index is very helpful. Roberts' work is required reading for understanding this period.
Stolpe, Sven. *Christina of Sweden*. Edited by Sir Alec Randall. New York: Macmillan, 1966. Intended for the general reader. Many of the myths about Christina are dispelled and the role of Oxenstierna during the regency period is shown. Contains an excellent review of the literature on Christina.
Weslager, C. A. *New Sweden on the Delaware, 1638-1655*. Wilmington, Del.: Middle Atlantic Press, 1988. This was written for the general public for the 350th celebration of the founding of New Sweden. Very readable, with excellent sketch maps and sketches, but no list of illustrations or index. It does contain a list of place names and a selected reading list.
_____. *The Swedes and Dutch at New Castle*. Wilmington, Del.: Middle Atlantic Press, 1987. This work by an eminent scholar and histo-

rian covers the Dutch-Swedish rivalry for control of the Delaware Valley in North America from 1638 to 1664. There is an excellent sketch map of the Delaware River area and eleven other illustrations. Contains a helpful glossary, an index, notes, and an appendix.

Mary-Emily Miller

ANDREA PALLADIO
Andrea di Pietro della Gondola

Born: November 30, 1508; Padua, Republic of Venice
Died: August, 1580; Vicenza, Republic of Venice
Area of Achievement: Architecture
Contribution: Palladio was the first great professional architect and one of
the most influential the world has ever known. Possibly the most imitated
architect in history, he was responsible for fusing classical proportions
and harmony with Renaissance exuberance, thus creating an architectural
manner that has endured into the twentieth century.

Early Life
Andrea Palladio was born in Padua to Piero, a miller, and donna Marta,
called "the cripple." Very little is known of his early years; the record of his
activities begins with his apprenticeship in 1521 to a stone carver in the local
trade corporation of bricklayers and stonemasons. His master at the corporation of Mount Berico has been identified as Bartolomeo Cavazza de Sossano,
the artist responsible for the altar in the Church of Santa Maria dei Carmini
in Padua. In 1523, Andrea ran away to Vicenza, where he was followed by
Cavazza, who forced him to return to Padua to serve out the rest of his
apprenticeship. A year later, the sixteen-year-old Andrea broke his bond and
returned to Vicenza, where for the next fourteen years he was first apprentice
and then assistant to two sculptors, Giovanni da Porlezza and Girolamo
Pittoni, both of the Pedemuro workshop, who had a near-monopoly on commissions, both private and public, to create many of Vicenza's monuments
and ornamental sculptures in the then-popular mannerist style. Records show
that in 1534 Andrea married Allegradonna, the daughter of a carpenter; the
union produced five children. Working with the Pedemuro masters gave
Andrea a thorough grounding in the techniques of stonework and sculpture,
and he might have remained a craftsman for the rest of his life had he not, at
age thirty, met Count Gian Giorgio Trissino.

Trissino hired the young stonecarver to work on a new loggia and a few
additions he had designed for his Villa Cricoli on the outskirts of Vicenza.
Trissino took Andrea under his wing, housing and educating him with a
group of young aristocrats who studied mathematics, philosophy, music, and
classical literature. During this period, Andrea was given the appropriately
classical name of Palladio by Trissino. Under Trissino's tutelage, the newly
christened Palladio embarked on a far-reaching study of architecture—
especially that of Vitruvius—and engineering, as well as ancient topography.

Palladio may have joined Trissino on an extended stay in Padua in the late
1530's; perhaps it was then that Palladio encountered the work of Alvise

Cornaro, whose influence is evident in Palladio's elegantly simple and clear writing style and in the economy of ornamentation in his designs. In 1541 and in 1545, Palladio visited Rome with Trissino. During these journeys, Palladio acquired a firsthand knowledge of classical architecture by sketching and measuring the ancient buildings—baths, arches, bridges, temples—whose remains could be seen above ground, and by studying and copying from the sketchbooks of other architects.

Shortly after Palladio returned to Vicenza, he won a commission to refurbish the Palazzo della Ragione, a vast Gothic structure that served as the meeting hall of Vicenza's Council of the Four Hundred. Whatever the council's reasons, their choice of Palladio in 1549 brought him instant recognition, and thereafter he was kept busy with commissions for palaces, villas, and churches.

Trissino died in 1550—a loss not only to Palladio but also to Vicenza's intellectual and artistic community—but by then Palladio was firmly established as an architect with several villas and public buildings under commission. Furthermore, in 1554 he published the results of his study tours in *L'antichità di Roma* (the antiquities of Rome), a small but reliable guidebook to the ancient ruins of Rome which became the standard guidebook to Roman antiquities for two centuries.

Life's Work

Ever an active student of architecture, Palladio published his ideas and theories in several works issued throughout his career. In 1556, he collaborated with Daniele Barbaro in an edition of Vitruvius. Palladio's greatest piece of writing, *I quattro libri dell'architettura* (1570), was published late in his career, after he had devoted two decades to design and building. Using many drawings of his own buildings to exemplify the principles of design to which he tried to adhere, Palladio created an architectural pattern book that dictated building practice throughout Western civilization for four centuries. His last book, *I commentarî di C. Givlio Cesare* (1575), is an edition of Julius Caesar's *Commentaries*, with illustrations by Palladio's sons Leonida and Orazio.

Palladio's architectural legacy can be classified loosely into three categories: villas, palaces and public buildings, and ecclesiastical buildings. Contrary to a popular misconception, there is no such thing as a typical Palladian villa. Palladio was far too innovative an architect to rely on one standard design, and his villas display the variety and inventiveness of his work. All the villas, however, share, as James Ackerman writes, "a common conception of architectural harmony and composition" and a fusion of the practical and the ornamental, the commonplace and the luxurious, modernity and antiquity. Unlike the typical villas of the day, Palladio's villas were nearly all built for gentlemen farmers, men of wealth, culture, and sophistication.

In the mid-sixteenth century, many of the great families moved inland to their vast estates to supervise their new ventures. These families needed homes for themselves and for their workers, shelter for their livestock, and storage for their crops. Palladio, already committed to the blending of the utilitarian and the majestic, was the perfect architect to create the new style which had no single architectural ancestry but which would integrate the traditional, the classical, and the innovative.

Palladio believed in a hierarchy of functions in design and architecture, and in one of his most famous metaphors he compared a well-designed building to the human body: In both, the noble and beautiful parts are exposed and the unattractive but essential portions are hidden. Accordingly, his villas are completely functional structures or structural complexes, created both to accommodate the day-to-day business of a large agricultural venture and to disguise that practicality with a grand design drawn from classical architecture. In another departure from common practice, these villas were situated not in walled gardens but central to the activities of the great estates. Palladio's signature element, which appeared on all the villas except Sarego (c. 1568-1569), is a pedimented temple front that appears in some buildings as a porch, in others as a relief. Although this feature appeared in classical architecture only on religious structures, Palladio incorporated it into nearly all of his domestic buildings.

None of the palaces for which Palladio created designs was completed; in some cases, only the façades and entrances were built. Only one public building was ever completed. The Veneto region in the mid-sixteenth century was subject to much financial and political instability which hampered the building of the grand structures envisioned by Palladio's patrons in Vicenza. Modern knowledge of Palladio's intentions comes from the finished façades and sections and from the detailed illustrations of specific designs in *I quattro libri dell'architettura*. Produced between about 1540 and the early 1570's—with a break of a few years in the late 1560's—the palace designs share with the villas Palladio's distinctive combination of mannerist elements with classical proportion and repose; indeed, four of the palace designs in *I quattro libri dell'architettura*, of which only the Palazzo Antonini (c.1556) was even partially built, resemble nothing so much as Palladian villas adapted to narrow city building sites and already crowded streets.

While Palladio's villas and palaces are all in the Veneto region, his churches are all in Venice, in which he was increasingly spending much of his time. It is clear that he traveled often in the 1560's: to Turin, to Provence, to Florence, where he became a member of the Academy of Design, and to Venice, where he met Giorgio Vasari, who became his friend. In 1568, Palladio was so busy that he was forced to decline an invitation to visit the Imperial Court of Vienna.

In his fifties by the time he began to design churches, Palladio believed strongly that church architecture should both glorify God and ornament the city. His commissions—private or civic or monastic, rather than from the Church—reflected his belief that religious architecture, like secular design, should surpass the achievement of earlier builders. Palladio, as well as two contemporaries, Galeazzo Alessi and Giacomo Barozzi da Vignola, developed a church design that took into account both the needs of the liturgical revival and the demands of architectural unity. This new ecclesiastical space combined a substantial nave with large side chapels, all joined but not restricted or blocked by a majestic central space that rose to a dome.

In 1558, Palladio's first ecclesiastical commission (which does not survive) was a design for the façade of San Pietro di Castello in Venice. During the next decade, he worked on a cloister for Santa Maria della Carita; the refectory and cloister and then the Church of San Giorgio Maggiore; and the façade of San Francesco della Vigna, all in Venice. In the decade before his death, Palladio produced four more designs: the Zitelle church (c. 1570) in Venice, considerably altered by the architects who finished it after Palladio's death; a chapel for the Villa Valmarana in Vicenza (c. 1576); Il Redentore in Venice (c. 1576-1577); and the Tempietto at the Villa Maser (c. 1579-1580). In the Tempietto, Palladio found his opportunity to design a central-plan church, modeled on his ideas for reconstructing the Pantheon in a modern idiom. The Tempietto retains the symbolic cross structure, which is integrated with a unified interior space enclosed by wall masses that support a dome. Palladio's last project was the Teatro Olimpico in Vicenza. Commissioned by the members of the Accademia Olimpica for their regular and elaborate stage performances, the theater is an interpretive reconstruction of an ancient Roman theater in France. Palladio did not live to see the theater completed, although most of the construction was done by the time he died in August, 1580.

Summary

Appealing more to austere Protestant sensibilities than to Catholic preferences, which favored the exuberance of the Baroque, the restrained Palladian style enjoyed its greatest popularity in the northern European cultural centers. Andrea Palladio's ideas and designs first traveled to England through the work of Inigo Jones in the seventeenth century, although the true flowering of the Palladian style had to wait for the eighteenth century and Lord Burlington, who was responsible for the popularization of Palladianism in England. The style spread to Ireland and then to the American Colonies, where the simple lines and harmonic proportions of Palladianism dominated in both domestic and public architecture. Not until the classical and Gothic revivals of the nineteenth century would the Palladian style be challenged, but its popularity remained high even in the twentieth century.

Palladianism has been interpreted variously. To some it means restraint and simplicity; to others it signals correct proportions and cool detachment; to the great majority of people it denotes a pediment plus a portico on a public building. Basically, the Palladian style is symmetrical, harmonically proportioned, majestic, and based on reason. At the same time, it is classical in its form and in its use of ornamentation. It conforms to Palladio's goals of composition: hierarchy, or the movement of subordinate elements to a dominant focal point; integration of part to part, and part to the whole; coordination between the exterior design and interior structure; and consistency of proportion.

Bibliography

Ackerman, James S. *Palladio*. Harmondsworth, England: Penguin Books, 1966. A good general study detailing both Palladio's uniqueness and his borrowings from the past and from his contemporaries. Describes his education, his era, and the physical and cultural environment in which he worked. Provides brief critical introductions to Palladio's major buildings. The text is copiously illustrated with both photographs and line drawings.

Constant, Caroline. *The Palladio Guide*. Princeton, N.J.: Princeton Architectural Press, 1985. Although technically belonging to the genre of the architectural guidebook, this volume is a presentation of the theory that Palladio's buildings share an integral relationship with and a spatial attitude to the site. Begins with a brief biography and introduction, followed by a chronological listing of the buildings. The body of the book is a series of articles, each devoted to a single villa and arranged chronologically. Features a selected bibliography and maps. Probably too confusing to be used as a guidebook, but the interpretive commentary is most informative.

Guinness, Desmond, and Julius Torusdale Sadler, Jr. *Palladio: A Western Progress*. New York: Viking Press, 1976. A brief account of Palladio's life and achievement, followed by several chapters describing the influence of Palladianism on architecture in England, Ireland, North America, and the West Indies. Very informative; profusely illustrated, primarily with photographs.

Kaufmann, Emil. *Architecture in the Age of Reason: Baroque and Post-Baroque in England, Italy, and France*. Cambridge, Mass.: Harvard University Press, 1955. The first chapter, "English Baroque and English Palladianism," offers a good introduction to Palladio's principles of design and their application in the architecture of eighteenth century England. An extensive bibliography is provided for each chapter.

Puppi, Lionello. *Andrea Palladio*. Boston: New York Graphic Society, 1975. An extensive, exhaustive, and profusely illustrated critical study of Palladio's life and work. The detailed and well-documented catalog of works makes up half of the volume and provides a thorough introduction

to Palladio's achievement. An excellent bibliography includes works by
Palladio and commentators on his work and covers material from the
sixteenth century to the 1970's.
Wittkower, Rudolf. *Architectural Principles in the Age of Humanism.* London: Warburg Institute, 1949. An essential work that laid the foundations
of modern Palladian criticism. Discusses Palladio's cultural development,
analyzes style in the villas and the ecclesiastical buildings, and provides
analyses of Palladian principles.

Edelma Huntley

DENIS PAPIN

Born: August 22, 1647; near Blois, France
Died: c. 1712; probably London, England
Areas of Achievement: Invention and technology
Contribution: Papin was one of the first to realize the potential of steam for the production of power in a piston engine.

Early Life

Denis Papin was born in 1647, in a farmhouse a few miles from Blois, France, into a Huguenot family. In 1661 or 1662, he enrolled at the University of Angers to study medicine, a profession already practiced by several members of his family. He was graduated with a medical degree in 1669. Papin also possessed a strong interest in mechanics and natural philosophy, however, and by 1671 he was in Paris, working for Christiaan Huygens, the well-known Dutch mathematician and astronomer. Huygens had helped Papin get an appointment as the curator of experiments in the laboratory of the French Royal Academy of Sciences in Paris. The academy had been established in 1666 by Louis XIV, and Huygens had been a founding member; thus, he wielded considerable influence. Once installed, Papin began a series of experiments under Huygens' guidance. Included in this extensive series of examinations were experiments on producing a vacuum, on determining the weight of air, and on the force of gunpowder. From his experiments with the vacuum, Papin constructed his own air pump, a feat indicative of his mechanical bent.

In 1674, Papin published a memoir of his work with a vacuum, *Nouvelles Expériences du vuide: Avec la description des machines qui servent à les faire*. He also wrote, with Huygens, a series of five papers about his experiments, which Huygens communicated to the Royal Society of London. In 1675, they were published in the Royal Society's *Philosophical Transactions*. In that same year, Papin left Paris, in the hope of finding a better position, but possibly to escape religious persecution as well. With the help of a letter of introduction from Huygens, he obtained employment with Robert Boyle in London.

Life's Work

In London, Papin found steady work and a place in which to continue his studies, especially in pneumatics and hydraulics. Thus settled, he embarked on the most productive period of his life. Boyle quickly capitalized on Papin's experience by initiating his own series of experiments on pneumatics. A key factor in this research was a double-barreled air pump of Papin's design. The pistons in each barrel were connected to stirrups, into which a man stepped in order to move the pistons. These experiments under Boyle continued from July, 1676, to February, 1679.

In May, 1679, Papin demonstrated to the Royal Society of London a new use of steam: his so-called digester, or what would now be called the pressure cooker. Indicative of his concern for practical ends, the digester occupied Papin's mind sporadically for many years. The Royal Society published Papin's book on the digester in December, 1680. In 1682, he even cooked a dinner with his digester for the Royal Society; it was well received, according to contemporary accounts.

Following his work with Boyle, Papin worked for the Royal Society, performing secretarial duties until the society terminated the position in December, 1679. During 1680, he may have returned to Paris to assist Huygens with work on a gunpowder engine, in which a flash of gunpowder pushed most of the air out of a cylinder beneath a piston, thereby allowing the weight of the atmosphere to push the piston down. In late 1680, he became a Fellow of the prestigious Royal Society.

In 1681, Papin traveled to Venice at the request of Ambrose Sarotti, whom Papin had met when Sarotti had been in London as the Venetian senate's representative to the English court. Sarotti, a Fellow of the Royal Society since 1679, was establishing his own scientific academy in Venice, and he hired Papin as curator of experiments. Papin stayed until 1684, when he once again returned to London, this time as a temporary curator of experiments for the Royal Society. As such, he was required to prepare experiments for each meeting of the society.

He was very good at preparing and conducting experiments and demonstrations, and his own work began to reflect the expertise he thus gained. He also continued to publish papers in the society's *Philosophical Transactions*, but he left many others unpublished.

During this stint with the Royal Society, Papin began working on various methods of raising water. By now he had almost fifteen years of experience with pneumatics and hydraulics, and he began applying that knowledge to practical ends. His first scheme, which he presented to the Royal Society in June, 1685, was little more than a toy, in which he used the force of air to raise water. By June, 1686, he published a method for lifting water, which could have been used to drain water from mines or to supply a municipal water system with river water. This second proposal still offered a pneumatic means of lifting water, the power coming from a vertical waterwheel placed in a river.

The next iteration of his pneumatic engine for lifting water used the power of the waterwheel to create a vacuum under large pistons. The weight of the atmosphere then pushed the pistons down, thus doing work. This was the first attempt to use the weight of the atmosphere to provide a continuous effect (in this case the transmission of power). It does not appear that any such machine was ever built.

A few months later, in October, 1687, Papin turned to the use of gunpowder to evacuate a chamber below a piston of air. He was following Huygens' earlier idea, but he claimed to have made important improvements. In this proposal, the explosion of a small charge of gunpowder inside a cylinder (beneath a moving piston) forced much of the air in the cylinder out through one-way valves. The cylinder being thus evacuated, the weight of the atmosphere drove the piston down, doing work in the process. Although this plan had its merits, the gunpowder left a residue inside the cylinder, and Papin's tests showed that the explosion evacuated only about 80 percent of the air.

Shortly after presenting these ideas to the Royal Society in late 1687, Papin moved once again, this time to Germany, where he took the mathematics chair at the University of Marburg. His work suffered little interruption as a result of the move, and in August, 1690, he published a brief memoir of perhaps his most important technological innovation: production of a vacuum under a piston by condensation of steam. Papin built and demonstrated a small model engine working on this principle. At the bottom of the cylinder, he placed a fraction of an inch of water and then pushed the piston down the cylinder until it touched the water. He then placed a flame under the cylinder. As the water boiled, the pressure of the steam forced the piston up the cylinder; the steam condensed as the cylinder cooled, leaving a vacuum beneath the piston. As in his earlier engines, the weight of the atmosphere then pushed the piston down, performing work as it went. This scheme solved the major problems of the gunpowder engine, but Papin does not seem to have built a full-size engine of this type.

Papin moved in 1695 or 1696 from Marburg to Cassel, where his patron, Landgrave Charles of Hesse, employed him as an engineer. Among his many tasks was the job of draining the landgrave's mines. In 1705, still in the landgrave's employ, he received a drawing of Thomas Savery's engine for draining mines. This engine also used a vacuum created by the condensation of steam, but not in conjunction with a piston. Papin attempted to improve upon Savery's engine, but by all accounts the engine he built was inferior to Savery's.

By late 1707, Papin was again in London, but not without mishap. Precipitating his departure from Cassel was the explosion—resulting in fatalities—of an experimental cannon, which was to have used steam rather than gunpowder to propel a projectile. He departed with his family on a small experimental boat propelled by a steam engine, although the exact type of engine remains unclear. Fearing competition from this new mode of transportation, rivermen on the Fulda River pulled the boat ashore and wrecked it. Papin's luck did not change when he reached London. Most of his friends from the Royal Society, especially the influential ones, were dead, and Savery held the patent rights for the steam engine. As a result, he lost his most important means of livelihood. Papin's last years are shrouded in obscurity. He apparently lived for a few years on small payments from the Royal Society for services rendered, but the exact time and place of his death are unknown.

Summary

Denis Papin was a thinker first and foremost. Although he had a very practical bent, he was not inclined to pursue one line of thought from the original conception to the construction of a working machine. Perhaps he was not capable of following a project from start to finish. Trained as a medical doctor, he had neither business expertise nor an engineering education. Papin also suffered from the lack of a strong supporter and financial backer. Without being able to market and profit from his inventions and without strong financial backing, he had little chance of completing projects that required substantial capital (such as a full-size steam engine). Finally, it is important to remember that Papin never established a solid reputation. By moving frequently, especially as a younger man, and by failing to publish all but a few of the many papers he wrote, Papin failed to make himself and his ideas widely known.

Clearly, Papin was the first man to think of producing a vacuum under a piston by the condensation of steam and letting the weight of the atmosphere perform work. This was the idea behind the early steam engine. It is not so clear what Papin actually contributed to the first engine; it may well be that Thomas Newcomen, whose famous steam engine worked on the same principle, arrived at the idea independently.

Bibliography

Barr, Scott E. "Denis Papin." *American Journal of Physics* 32 (1964): 290-291. This short article provides a concise overview of Papin's life and accomplishments. It correctly brings to light that he devised many original ideas—or, in some cases, new twists on old ideas—but that he lacked thoroughness. As a result, he left many papers unpublished and many inventions unnoticed.

Bernard, Paul P. "How Not to Invent the Steamship." *East European Quarterly* 14 (Spring, 1980): 1-8. Bernard focuses on the claim that Papin invented a steamship. He briefly examines the work that led to the supposed steamship Papin sailed down the Fulda as well as the obstacles he encountered, including the Fulda rivermen and the politics within the Royal Society. Bernard also shows that Papin's reputation has suffered since, largely as a result of nationalistic debates between German and French historians.

Dickinson, H. W. *A Short History of the Steam Engine*. Cambridge, England: Cambridge University Press, 1938. Reprint. New York: Augustus M. Kelley, 1965. Dickinson considers only Papin's contributions to the development of the modern steam engine. Thus, although he briefly mentions Papin's work on the digester and the force of gunpowder, among other things, he concentrates on the steam engine that Papin first proposed in 1690. His explanation of how this engine worked is quite clear and includes one simple illustration. An introduction by A. E. Musson places Dickinson's work in its proper historiographical setting and also supplies a few illuminating comments on Papin.

Galloway, Robert L. *The Steam Engine and Its Inventors: A Historical Sketch*. London: Macmillan, 1881. Although quite old, this work is perhaps the best English-language account of Papin's work in pneumatics and hydraulics. Galloway briefly treats Papin's early life in chapter 1. Chapters 3 and 4 deal exclusively with Papin and his inventions. Includes illustrations and numerous informative footnotes.

Robinson, H. W. "Denis Papin (1647-1712)." *Notes and Records of the Royal Society of London* 5 (1947): 47-50. Based on the records of the Royal Society, this brief narrative is especially good, as one would expect, on Papin's relationship with the society. Provides a good overview of Papin's inventive life.

Brian J. Nichelson

PARACELSUS
Philippus Aureolus Theophrastus Bombast von Hohenheim

Born: November 10, 1493; Einsiedeln, Swiss Confederation
Died: September 24, 1541; Salzburg, Austria
Areas of Achievement: Biochemistry, chemistry, medicine, and philosophy
Contribution: Paracelsus has been hailed as the founder of biochemistry.
  He also made major contributions to the development of modern chemistry and made revolutionary changes in Renaissance medical theory and practice.

Early Life

Philippus Aureolus Theophrastus Bombast von Hohenheim, known to the world as Paracelsus, was born in 1493 in the village of Einsiedeln, Swiss Confederation. He was the only son of a physician, Wilhelm of Hohenheim, who came from a noble Swabian family whose original seat was at Hohenheim, near Stuttgart in northern Germany. Paracelsus' mother, Els Ochsner, came from a family of peasants living on land belonging to the local Benedictine Abbey, and she worked as a nurse's aid. Because his illegitimate father had no legal right to the family heritage, Paracelsus was reared in poverty. Yet he said that his home environment was quiet and peaceful, although his mother apparently suffered from manic depression and committed suicide when he was nine.

Following his wife's death, Wilhelm and his son moved to Villach, Austria. Paracelsus probably attended the mining school of the Fuggers at nearby Hutenberg, where his father was a tutor. In Paracelsus' writings, he pays generous tribute to his father, who played a large part in his son's education. Paracelsus also states that he learned from experts, including bishops and an abbot. It is therefore likely that he received what was considered to be a universal education, including cabalistic, alchemical, and magical traditions, as well as orthodox religion and philosophy. It is clear, however, that Paracelsus neglected many of the formal aspects of his education. His Latin was not good, and he never acquired elegance in either speech or writing.

In 1507, at the age of fourteen, Paracelsus became a traveling student, attending universities in Germany, Italy, France, and Spain. He studied for a bachelor's degree at Vienna between 1509 and 1511, and between 1513 and 1516 he traveled and studied medicine in Italy, notably at Ferrara. Yet he was a restless, pugnacious, and rebellious student, and he soon found himself completely dissatisfied with the education that was offered by the universities he attended. From 1517 to 1524, he again traveled extensively throughout Europe. He was employed as a military surgeon in Venice and was involved in three wars of the period. He traveled to Moscow when the Grand Duke Basil invited Western physicians and Humanists to the Russian

court, accompanied a Tatar prince on a diplomatic mission to Constantinople, and visited the Holy Land and Alexandria. In all of his journeys, Paracelsus was building the knowledge that would enable him to revolutionize
many aspects of Renaissance medicine.

Life's Work

With his fame spreading rapidly and many of his cures being regarded as
miraculous, Paracelsus reached Salzburg in 1524. Yet the following year he
was arrested for siding with the peasants in the Peasants' War of 1524-1526
and was forced to flee. In 1526, he arrived in Strasbourg and was entered in
the city register as a surgeon. He apparently enjoyed great popularity there
and was consulted by many prominent men. Yet he left after less than a year,
for unknown reasons. During this period, he wrote eleven treatises on various diseases, ranging from tuberculosis to gout.

From Strasbourg, he traveled to Basel, where he cured the famous and
influential printer Johann Froben. Through Froben, he was introduced to the
intellectual elite of Basel, the result being his appointment as municipal
physician and professor of medicine at Basel in March, 1527. This influential
position proved to be the highlight of Paracelsus' professional life. Yet he
made no attempt to moderate his habitually aggressive and combative manner. He challenged the established medical system by saying that he would
not accept the authority of Hippocrates or Galen. Instead, he would form his
theories from his direct experience in dealing with the sick. In a famous
incident, he put Avicenna's classical works on medicine to the bonfire. The
authorities retaliated by refusing him the right to lecture and disputing his
medical qualifications. Yet Paracelsus continued his work. Defying all tradition, he lectured in German rather than Latin, and he drew large and appreciative audiences. Many were attracted by his credo: "The patients are your
textbook, the sickbed is your study."

Yet having made so many enemies, Paracelsus' fortunes soon took a turn
for the worse. His benefactor, Froben, died suddenly in October, and shortly
afterward a malicious lampoon of Paracelsus appeared. He counterattacked
in typical fashion, denouncing past authorities and his colleagues in extreme
language: They were all liars, cheats, and fakes, according to him. The
situation came to a head when Paracelsus accused the town magistrate of
ignorance and bias after a legal suit in which Paracelsus had attempted to
collect a promised fee from a patient he had cured. Facing arrest and severe
punishment for insulting a high official and with most of the town against
him, Paracelsus fled in February, 1528.

After this debacle, he embarked on a new set of journeys, to Alsace,
Germany, Switzerland, Bohemia, and Austria, rarely staying more than a
few months in one place. In 1529, he was in Nürnberg, but professional
doors were closed to him. He responded by proposing to cure any patient

who had been declared incurable, and he is reported to have succeeded in nine out of fifteen cases involving lepers. In Nürnberg, he also wrote much, particularly on the disease of syphilis, the most pressing medical problem of the day.

In 1530, he was in Beratzhausen, where he again wrote copiously, including one of his best-known works, the brief *Paragranum* (1530; *Against the Grain*, 1894), in which he claimed that medicine should be based on four pillars: natural philosophy, astronomy, alchemy, and virtue. In 1531, he reached Saint Gall, where he wrote *Opus paramirum* (1531), which contains the fundamentals of his medical doctrine. During this period, he also focused strongly on the inner life, writing more than one hundred religious tracts, and he also took to religious preaching.

Facing poverty and adversity wherever he went, he came in 1533 to Appenzell, Switzerland, and to the mining districts of Hall and Schwaz, where he wrote a treatise on the miner's disease—the first ever written on an occupational disease. From Switzerland, he went again to Austria and in 1534 to Sterzing and Meran, living all the time like a beggar and rarely sleeping two nights in the same bed. In 1536, he was in Ulm and Augsburg, where his book on surgery, *Grosse Wundarzney* (1536; *Great Surgery Book*, 1894), was first printed; it said far more about how to avoid surgery than about surgery itself. In 1537, Paracelsus reached Munich and Bohemia, where he began work on his philosophical magnum opus, the *Astronomia magna* (1537-1538; *Great Astronomy*, 1894), which was an attempt to write a comprehensive system of natural philosophy. Highly eclectic but disorderly and inconsistent, it covers a vast range of topics, including man and the universe, salvation, magical lore, such as the healing power of stones, physiognomy, phrenology, meteorology, and Paracelsus' vision of the development of new technologies.

The best-known and most reliable likeness of Paracelsus, in a portrait by Augustin Hirschvogel, dates from 1537. It shows him clean-shaven and bald on the top of his head, with long unruly hair at the sides. Stern-faced, with deep-set eyes, his solemn expression tells the story of a hard but determined life. Of Paracelsus' last three years, little is known. From August, 1540, he was again in Salzburg, summoned by Archbishop Prince Ernst of Bavaria. On September 21, 1541, he suffered a stroke and died three days later.

Summary

From Paracelsus' own day to the present, a fierce debate has raged about his contribution to the development of Western science. Some people in his time denounced him as a charlatan, and his modern detractors have argued that his fame is more the result of his colorful and controversial life than any original contributions he made to human thought. On the other hand, his supporters argue that he was a great medical reformer who made substantial achievements in the development of modern chemistry, that he was the founder of biochemistry, and that he also made contributions to gynecology, psychiatry, and even psychotherapy.

In chemistry, it can certainly be said that he worked toward a systematic classification of all known chemical substances and that he devised a method of detoxifying dangerous chemical compounds, which he was then able to use for therapeutic purposes. He also introduced new laboratory methods. The methods of early chemists such as Andreas Libavius, Oswald Croll, and Jan Baptista van Helmont are clearly linked to those of Paracelsus. In medicine, he left accurate descriptions of diseases and had much success in the treating of wounds and chronic ulcers.

Yet if his contributions to modern knowledge are overemphasized, the picture of his work as a whole becomes distorted. He belongs firmly in the Renaissance. His belief in the correspondence between the microcosm and the macrocosm was a commonplace of the period, but it has been rejected by the modern world. Without it, however, much of Paracelsus' work would become unintelligible. He always viewed man in terms of man's relationship with nature and the cosmos as a whole, believing that everything in the inner world corresponded to something in the outer world and that knowledge of this relationship was vital for the healer. The philosophical bases of his views were the esoteric systems of Gnosticism and Neoplatonism. It is this unique coexistence of contradictory elements in his thought, the ancient and the modern, that makes Paracelsus a man of such enduring fascination.

Bibliography
Jung, Carl G. "Paracelsus" and "Paracelsus the Physician." In *The Spirit in Man, Art, and Literature*. Translated by R. F. C. Hull. New York: Pantheon Books, 1966. The first essay is the text of an address delivered by Jung in 1929 at the house in Einsiedeln where Paracelsus was born. Some of the biographical information is inaccurate, but Jung's insights into the essence of Paracelsus, although full of broad generalizations, remains valuable. The second, longer essay, originally given as a lecture in 1941, is one of the best short introductions in English to Paracelsus' thought.
Pachter, Henry M. *Magic into Science: The Story of Paracelsus*. New York: Henry Schuman, 1951. A lively and very readable biography. Pachter tries to rescue Paracelsus from what he sees as an attempt by esoteric groups, including faith healers, mystics, occultists, and homeopaths, to claim Paracelsus as one of their own. Instead, Pachter gives most prominence to those aspects of Paracelsus' work that show his contribution to the development of modern science, including chemistry, chemotherapy, biochemistry, gynecology, and psychiatry.
Pagel, Walter. *Paracelsus: An Introduction to Philosophical Medicine in the Era of the Renaissance*. New York: S. Karger, 1958. One of the best and

most comprehensive examinations in English of Paracelsus' work. Excellent on his philosophy, his medical theories and practice, and his sources. Resists viewing Paracelsus exclusively as a forerunner of modern science and medicine, and as a result serves as a useful corrective to Pachter, above. Instead, shows how Paracelsus forged mystical, magical, and scientific elements into a new synthesis based on personal experience.

Paracelsus. *Selected Writings*. 2d rev. ed. Edited with an introduction by Jolande Jacobi. Translated by Norbert Guterman. Princeton, N.J.: Princeton University Press, 1969. One of the best anthologies in English of Paracelsus' writings. Extracts from his works are arranged under thematic headings; references are comprehensive, although only German titles of the works are given. Jacobi's introduction to Paracelsus' life and work, from a Jungian point of view, contains valuable insights. The detailed glossary of Paracelsan terms is an exceptionally valuable aid to study. Includes many illustrations and a bibliography of primary and secondary sources.

Shumaker, Wayne. *The Occult Sciences in the Renaissance: A Study in Intellectual Patterns*. Berkeley: University of California Press, 1972. Extremely useful for understanding the intellectual and cultural milieu in which Paracelsus lived. Shumaker examines five areas of Renaissance thought: astrology, natural or white magic, witchcraft, alchemy, and the body of occult writings associated with the name Hermes Trismegistus. Includes extensive quotations from primary sources, many of which are unavailable in translation elsewhere, many illustrations, and an annotated bibliography.

Bryan Aubrey

BLAISE PASCAL

Born: June 19, 1623; Clermont-Ferrand, France
Died: August 19, 1662; Paris, France
Areas of Achievement: Religion, philosophy, and mathematics
Contribution: Pascal was a man of genius in many areas, who made important contributions to mathematics and physics and invented an early form of the calculator. His major contribution, however, is the record of his religious and philosophical struggle to reconcile human experience, God, and the quest for happiness and meaning.

Early Life

Blaise Pascal was the third child of Étienne Pascal, a government financial bureaucrat, and Antoinette (Begon), who died when Pascal was about three. After his mother's death, Pascal and his family moved to Paris. Pascal's father decided to educate his children himself, rather than making use of either tutors or schools. Étienne Pascal was associated with the intellectual circles of Paris and thereby exposed Pascal to the best scientific and mathematical thought of his time.

While still a teenager, the precocious Pascal attracted the attention of the court and, in 1640, published his first mathematical treatise. In 1642, he began working on a mechanical calculator to help in his father's work. He continued improving the device for the next ten years and in 1652 sent a version of it to Queen Christina of Sweden. In 1646, Pascal and his two older sisters first came under the influence of Jansenism, a strict, pietistic movement within the Catholic church that stressed a life of devotion, practical charity, and asceticism. Pascal experienced what is usually called his "first conversion," feeling the need for religious renewal but not wanting to give up his scientific and mathematical endeavors. His scientific work at this time included experiments with vacuums, an important area of exploration in seventeenth century physics.

Life's Work

By his mid-twenties, Pascal had assumed a pattern of life that he would continue until his death. In 1647, he entered into the first of the public religious controversies that would preoccupy him on and off for the rest of his life. He also continued his scientific work on the vacuum, exchanging information with the great philosopher René Descartes and publishing his own findings. In 1648, he wrote a mathematical essay on conic sections. Throughout this period, Pascal was afflicted with serious illness, as he would be for the remainder of his life.

Pascal's sister Jacqueline continued to be influenced by Jansenism, and during this time she expressed her desire to enter the Jansenist religious community at Port-Royal. Both Pascal and his father objected, but after her father's death in 1651 Jacqueline entered the convent the following year. Pascal began a brief phase in which he indulged himself in the pleasures and pursuits of French society, finding the experience empty but also finding no other direction for his life at this time.

Pascal experienced a growing disillusionment with the skeptical worldliness of society life and greatly desired something more meaningful. During the middle of the night of November 23, 1654, he had an intense, mystical religious experience that lasted about two hours and changed the direction of his life. During this experience, Pascal felt powerfully and unmistakably the truth of God's existence and the blessing of His love and forgiveness. Pascal had been provided with the kind of experiential certainty for which his scientific mind yearned and, consequently, saw everything thereafter in spiritual terms. In reaction to this experience, Pascal went to Port-Royal, the center of Jansenism, for a two-week retreat in early 1655 in order to begin the reformation of his life that he now sought. He was particularly concerned with overcoming the willful pride that had marked his life since his spectacular intellectual accomplishments as a boy and the selfishness that showed itself in his resistance to his sister Jacqueline's entrance into the community at Port-Royal.

Jansenism was to dominate his life for the next few years. In 1653, Pope Innocent X had condemned the writings of Cornelius Jansen, Bishop of Ypres, upon which the Jansenist movement in the Catholic church was based. The great enemies of the Jansenists were the rationalistic Jesuits, and in January of 1656 Pascal wrote the first of a series of anonymous letters now entitled *Lettres provinciales* (1656-1657; *The Provincial Letters*, 1657). These letters, eighteen in all, came out until May, 1657, and are masterpieces of satire, wit, analytic logic, and French prose style. Especially in the early letters, the fictitious writer adopts a pose of objective, naïve curiosity about the controversy between the Jesuits and Jansenists, which he is purportedly trying to explain to his fellow provincial back home. In reality, the letters are an impassioned defense of the principles and principals of the Jansenist movement and a stinging attack on the Jesuits. The letters were enormously popular, and the local authorities went to great lengths to try to suppress them and discover their author. Pascal's letters have been admired ever since as masterpieces of French prose.

Pascal was not satisfied, however, merely to defend a particular movement within the Catholic church. He desired to write a great defense of Christianity as a whole at a time when religious faith was increasingly under attack by skepticism, on the one hand, and rationalism, on the other. Prompted in part by what he took to be the miraculous cure of his young niece, Pascal began in 1657 to take notes for this work, which he once said would take ten years of steady effort to complete. As it turned out, Pascal never completed the work or even a draft of it. Instead, he produced approximately one thousand notes, some only a few words, others pages long and substantially revised. The majority of these notes were written in 1657 and 1658, after which time he fell into the extremely painful and debilitating illness that would largely incapacitate him until his death. They were first published in abbreviated form as *Pensées* (*Monsieur Pascal's Thoughts, Meditations, and Prayers*, 1688; best known as *Pensées*) in 1670 and have become one of the classic documents of Western culture.

Although Pascal never wrote his great apology for the Christian faith, he did organize many of his notes into groups, from which scholars have speculated as to his ultimate intentions. As enlightening as these speculations sometimes are, the timelessness of *Pensées* comes not from the tantalizing promise of some irrefutable defense of religious faith but from Pascal's compelling, often painful insights into the human condition and from the process of watching one of history's great minds struggle with eternal questions of faith, spirit, and transcendence.

Many of Pascal's most powerful entries poignantly explore the tragedy and folly of the human condition if there were no God. He depicts humankind as lost in an alien and inhospitable world, given over to the empty baubles and distractions of society. Pascal portrays the world as a psychologically frightening place. Men and women are caught between the infinitely large, on the one hand, and the infinitely small, on the other. They are torn by a divided nature which is neither angel nor beast, to use one of his images, but is capable of acting like either. Human beings yearn for something sure and permanent but find only illusion and transience. Pascal finds the solution for the human dilemma in the grace of God as manifested in Jesus Christ. Only by knowing who created them, Pascal argues, can humans know who they are and how they can be happy. He does not, however, offer this solution as an effortless one. Part of Pascal's enduring appeal is his very modern awareness of the difficulty of religious faith in a scientific and skeptical world.

Pascal was seriously ill much of the last four years of his life, but that did not prevent him from at least sporadic efforts on a variety of projects. In 1658, he made further mathematical discoveries on the cycloid and publicly challenged the mathematicians of Europe to a contest in solving problems in this area. He was drawn briefly into the Jansenist controversy once again but then withdrew from it altogether. His concern for the poor led him to invent and launch a public transportation system in Paris in March of 1662. Additionally, when health permitted, he worked on his defense of Christianity that became *Pensées*. After much suffering patiently borne, Pascal died on August 19, 1662, at the age of thirty-nine.

Summary

Blaise Pascal is one of those handful of individuals in history whose wide range of accomplishments shows evidence of a fundamental genius that expressed itself wherever it was applied. Proof of his greatness is given by the number of different fields of intellectual effort which claim him. He is considered a mathematician of the first rank, an important physicist at the early stages of that science, an inventor, a literary master of French prose, and, most important, a philosopher and religious thinker who has written brilliantly about fundamental questions of the human condition.

Pascal was a man standing at the beginning of the modern age who felt keenly the call of reason and science but who realized the price to be paid if one lost a sense of the spiritual and transcendent. He felt caught between two contrary forces: the rationalism of rising seventeenth century science, and the skepticism about all human efforts, reason included, as epitomized by his French predecessor, Michel de Montaigne. He sought an approach to life that avoided the arrogance and materialism of the former and the cynicism and moral passivity of the latter. In this sense, Pascal's situation anticipates the modern one. How does one find meaning, values, and faith in a rationalistic, skeptical world where most traditional guidelines are called into question? For more than three hundred years, men and women have found insight and inspiration in Pascal's answers.

Bibliography
Coleman, Francis X. J. *Neither Angel nor Beast: The Life and Work of Blaise Pascal*. New York: Routledge & Kegan Paul, 1986. A somewhat poorly organized but still-insightful overview of Pascal's life and work. Good at placing Pascal in the context of thought of the seventeenth century. Detailed account of the Jansenist controversy. Also useful on Pascal's style. Contains biographical overview, chronology, and bibliography.
Davidson, Hugh M. *Blaise Pascal*. Boston: Twayne, 1983. A good first introduction to Pascal. Short but adequate overview of his life and discussions of all of his major and most of his minor works, including detailed discussion of his mathematical contributions. Includes a chronology, index, and annotated bibliography.
Krailsheimer, Alban. *Pascal*. New York: Hill & Wang, 1980. Part of the very helpful Past Masters series, which provides short (less than one-hundred-page) but serious overviews of the lives and work of central figures in Western culture. Brief but helpful summary of Pascal's mathematical and scientific accomplishments. Good on the cultural context and central concerns of the *Pensées*. Short bibliography.
Nelson, Robert J. *Pascal: Adversary and Advocate*. Cambridge, Mass.: Harvard University Press, 1981. One of the more comprehensive and ambitious studies of Pascal. Takes a psychological approach to Pascal's biography and work and offers extensive critical study of individual works. Includes a detailed bibliography.

Pascal, Blaise. *Pensées*. Translated by A. J. Krailsheimer. London: Penguin Books, 1966. One of the better of the many translations of Pascal's great work. Follows the ordering of the fragments that has become the standard, though work still goes on as to the best ordering of Pascal's fragments. Others who have translated Pascal into English include W. F. Trotter, E. B. Thayer, John Warrington, H. F. Stewart, E. Cailliet, and John Blankenagel.

Daniel Taylor

LOUIS PASTEUR

Born: December 27, 1822; Dôle, Jura, France
Died: September 28, 1895; Saint Cloud, near Paris, France
Areas of Achievement: Chemistry and biology
Contribution: Pasteur, by his pioneering work in crystallography, established the discipline of stereochemistry (left-handedness and right-handedness in organic structures). He spent the bulk of his career founding modern microbiology and making exciting discoveries in immunology.

Early Life

Louis Pasteur was born in Dôle on December 27, 1822, but he grew up in Arbois, a nearby and smaller town in which his father, Jean-Joseph, a veteran of Napoleon I's army, operated a tannery. His mother, Jeanne-Étiennette Roqui, was a gardener's daughter. The best portraits of his parents were done in pastels by young Louis himself, who was an excellent artist. He, like them, was of medium height and dark-haired with a high forehead. His nearsightedness was said to have enhanced his ability to see close up and tiny things. In his maturity, he wore the beard and mustache of most males of his time.

Louis was a late bloomer, and his grades in school were only slightly above average. He attended the Collège d'Arbois, and late in his career there, he became inspired and desired to enter the prestigious École Normale Supérieure in Paris. He left Arbois in 1838 and entered Barbet's preparatory school in Paris but became so homesick that his father had to bring him home. In 1839, Louis enrolled in the Collège Royal at Besançon, in his home province of Franche Comté. Away from home but not far from it, the young scholar partially supported himself with a student assistantship and received his bachelor of science degree in 1842. Although accepted to the École Normale Supérieure, Pasteur believed that he was not yet ready to enter, and thus he spent a year at Barbet's preparatory school before finally matriculating in the fall of 1843.

Pasteur did well at the École Normale Supérieure, passing high on the teachers' examination in 1845 and quite high in his comprehensive exams the following year. In 1847, he received his doctorate in chemistry and soon found employment as a professor, first at the University of Dijon, where he taught physics for a semester, and then at the University of Strasbourg, where in 1849 he obtained a position in the chemistry department. It was also in Strasbourg that Pasteur met Marie Laurent, the twenty-two-year-old woman whom he soon made his wife. Their marriage lasted a lifetime and produced five children, although three of the daughters died early from typhoid. Throughout his life, Pasteur was politically conservative except for a youthful involvement in the Revolution of 1848, and he was a thoroughgoing supporter of the Second Empire under Napoleon III. Indeed, he received considerable grants and recognition from the emperor and empress personally.

Life's Work

As early as 1848, Pasteur was publishing his work on crystals, which he had begun for his doctoral research. Working with tartaric acid, he searched for the solution as to why one form of the acid twisted to the right the light rays passing through it, while another form (paratartaric or racemic acid), did not rotate the plane of the light rays. The two forms of the acid were chemically identical, but Pasteur discovered that racemic acid had crystals which were either left-handed or right-handed—each the mirror image of the other. Using tweezers, he laboriously hand-separated the dried crystals into left and right piles. Then he dissolved each pile and found to his satisfaction that the left-handed crystal solution rotated light rays to the left and the right-handed to the right. When the two solutions were then mixed in equal amounts, no rotation occurred—the mixture was optically inactive. This breakthrough established Pasteur's reputation as a scientist, because it opened the door to stereochemistry, a new way of studying the molecular composition of substances. Pasteur had begun to understand dissymmetry, which characterizes not only organic forms but most inorganic forms as well.

Pasteur, as he continued his research on crystallography, moved to the University of Lille, where he served as a dean as well as a professor from 1854 to 1857. While at Lille, Pasteur was approached by a man seeking expert help in explaining why some of his vats of sugar-beet juice, which he was fermenting prior to distilling alcohol from the mash, had been going bad. Pasteur had been urged by his superiors to serve practical ends as well as pure science, and, as it happened, Pasteur's own research into the composition of organic molecules had caused him to want to know how fermentation modified those molecules. Pasteur was eager to use the sugar-beet industry as a laboratory.

The scientist examined the vats and took samples. Under his vertically mounted microscope, Pasteur detected small, round globules of yeast from the "good" samples but found that the "bad" ones contained rodlike microorganisms, bacilli. He assumed that the yeasts, which he observed multiplying by budding, were the cause of fermenting beet sugar into the desired alcohol, but the rods were a mystery.

After considerable effort, he succeeded in formulating a soup in which he was able to culture the bacilli. After introducing only a few of the rods into the sterile solution, he saw them multiply into millions of vibrating germs. They were alive, and they were what crowded out the yeast and transformed the sugar into lactic acid—the acid of sour milk. Pasteur wrote a paper on his discovery entitled "Mémoire sur la fermentation appellée lactique" (memoir on the fermentation called lactic), which was published by the French Academy of Sciences in 1857. This paper was hailed as the initial proof that germs cause fermentation.

Pasteur's article of 1857 was the second great stride of his career, and as a result he was called to Paris and made director of scientific studies at the École Normale Supérieure. His elevated post, however, did not provide him with his own laboratory, so he created one for himself in two rooms in the attic. There he proceeded to demonstrate the extreme complexity of the processes involved in alcoholic fermentation. Chemists had previously expressed the conversion of sugar into ethyl alcohol and carbonic acid by means of a simple, inorganic formula, but Pasteur detailed the complex role of brewer's yeast in digesting the sugar into a number of compounds, of which alcohol was only the most important.

Continuing his work on microbes, Pasteur found that some bacteria required the absence of oxygen in order to survive, whereas others needed oxygen to live. The former he termed "anaerobic," and he named the latter "aerobic"—nomenclature used by science to the present day, as Pasteur was the first to bring to scientific and public attention the two different kinds of bacteria. Antoni van Leeuwenhoek and Lazzaro Spallanzani had earlier observed anaerobic bacteria but had failed to attract much notice to the discovery.

Pasteur then conducted a lengthy experiment on the canning of food, a process discovered by his fellow countryman François Appert in the time of Napoleon I. Pasteur showed conclusively that the heating of sealed containers killed the microbes that caused fermentation and putrefaction. That was the secret of food preservation. He explained that microbes are necessary for decomposition of organic matter into its inorganic components and that without such microbes all the plants and animals that had ever lived would have their dead remains choking the surface of the planet.

Pasteur also proved that microbes came only from other microbes, that life came from life, and that there was no spontaneous generation. Leeuwenhoek two hundred years earlier had disproved spontaneous generation, but few had been willing to listen. Pasteur was so insistent that he forced people to pay attention. To illustrate that microbes can be carried through the air, Pasteur and his assistants exposed many sterile cultures briefly to the air of a deep basement in Paris, the surface-level air in Paris, the air of a vineyard on a hill of the Jura Mountains, and finally the air high on the slopes of Mont Blanc. Pasteur found that the higher and more rural the area the lower the percentage of cultures that were contaminated. The only low-lying location that had pure air was the nearly draft-free deep cellar in Paris.

Next Pasteur and his chief assistant, Émile Duclaux, set up a makeshift field laboratory in Pasteur's hometown of Arbois. Wine producers in the area had been having difficulty, as their output was sometimes ropy, acid, oily, or bitter. Looking through his microscope, Pasteur startled the vintners by correctly pronouncing what was wrong with each sample without tasting it. To prevent the spoilage, Pasteur recommended a treatment that came to be known as "pasteurization"—heating the wine, once fermentation was complete, to a certain temperature below boiling and holding it there for a specified period of time. The temperature could be lower if the time were lengthened and vice versa. When farmers objected to cooking their wine, Pasteur explained that the natural acidity of their product made it less hospitable to germs and that the required temperature was really quite low. Milk, beer, cider, and other liquids could be similarly preserved, and Pasteur designed special equipment for commercial pasteurization.

One of Pasteur's former professors, J. B. Dumas, begged Pasteur to investigate a disease of silkworms, pébrine, a blight that was devastating a main industry in south central France. Between 1865 and 1870, Pasteur spent several months of each year in and around Alais (modern Alès), the center of the nation's silk culture. Pasteur's confusion about what ailed the silkworms was compounded, as he eventually discovered, by the fact that the worms were suffering not from a single disease but from two different microbial infections.

Before he attained a breakthrough in the silkworm diseases, however, Pasteur suffered a cerebral hemorrhage in October, 1868, at the age of forty-five. Many thought that he would surely die; his left side was completely paralyzed. Yet he regained partial use of his left side, and he walked, though with a severe limp. He depended on his assistants to do much of the manipulation required by his experiments, but his mind remained keen, and he never relinquished control over his laboratories. He had finished the rescue of the silk industry by 1870.

Pasteur, whose name was a household word in France and who had greatly assisted the French sugar-beet, wine, vinegar, silk, and beer industries, moved comparatively late in his career into the field of immunology. He confirmed the work of Robert Koch in Germany, who had discovered the complete life cycle of the anthrax bacillus, the cause of the animal (and sometimes human) disease anthrax, but he greatly desired to outdo the German. After considerable experimentation with animals, Pasteur announced that he had invented a vaccine, composed of weakened bacilli, which if injected into an animal would confer immunity against anthrax.

It was something Koch had never done. Skeptical French veterinarians in 1881 challenged Pasteur to a dramatic public experiment to test the immunization. Pasteur's assistants cautioned against accepting, as the vaccine had not been field-tested and a public failure could be devastating. Pasteur was adamant, however, and they caught the train for Pouilly-le-Fort, a village near Melun, southeast of Paris. Twenty-four sheep, one goat, and six cows were immunized, it was hoped, by Pasteur's assistant, the physician Émile Roux, with two injections of serum twelve days apart. Two weeks later, those animals and an equal-sized control group of animals were injected with a powerful culture of anthrax bacilli. All the immunized animals survived; all the others died; France went wild with the news.

Pasteur next turned to conquer rabies, probably motivated by childhood memories of an attack on his town by a rabid wolf. Sucking foam from the mouths of caged mad dogs, Pasteur and his men never found a responsible microbe, as hydrophobia is caused by a virus—something too small to be seen with a light microscope—but the scientists made a vaccine and used it successfully on animals. Then a mother brought in her son, bitten by a mad dog and sure to die. Pasteur ordered the child inoculated, and the child lived. Soon others came, even from distant Russia and the United States, and, except where too much time had elapsed, the cure was effective.

It was fitting climax to a brilliant career. On his seventieth birthday, a great celebration was held to honor Pasteur. Pasteur's son had to deliver his father's speech, in which Pasteur said that it gave him immense happiness to "have contributed in some way to the progress and good of humanity."

Summary

Louis Pasteur is best known for his work in bacteriology, a field which he virtually founded. His discoveries contributed greatly to the control and treatment of cholera, diphtheria, tetanus, tuberculosis, and other diseases. His studies of the transmission of infection also contributed to the development of antiseptic procedures in surgery. His discovery of vaccines to prevent anthrax and other diseases of animals had an enormous impact not only in France but also worldwide. Although less widely known than his contributions to immunology, Pasteur's pioneering researches in crystallography were of fundamental importance. Among the many great scientists of the nineteenth century, Pasteur stands in the first rank.

Bibliography

Compton, Piers. *The Genius of Louis Pasteur.* New York: Macmillan, 1932. A readable and thorough account of Pasteur's life and contributions, this book has several interesting photographs of people, places, and events in his life.

Cuny, Hilaire. *Louis Pasteur: The Man and His Theories.* Translated by Patrick Evans. London: Souvenir Press, 1965. This book provides detail without being overwhelming. Cuny's explanations of the technical aspects of Pasteur's work are readily comprehensible to the layperson.

De Kruif, Paul. *Microbe Hunters.* New York: Pocket Books, 1950. Although more superficial than the full-length biographies, this book has two exquisitely entertaining chapters on Pasteur that convey the excitement inherent in making scientific breakthroughs that result in saving lives and industries.

Dubos, René. *Louis Pasteur: Free Lance of Science*. Translated by Elizabeth Dussauze. New York: Charles Scribner's Sons, 1976. This book is thorough and gives a good perspective on Pasteur. Includes a large photographic section.

Duclaux, Émile. *Pasteur: The History of a Mind*. Translated by Erwin Smith and Florence Hedges. Philadelphia: W. B. Saunders, 1920. Reprint. Metuchen, N.J.: Scarecrow Press, 1973. Written by a man who studied and worked under Pasteur, this book provides many insights into Pasteur's thinking. Duclaux deals exclusively with Pasteur's professional life and not with his personal life, and gives a balanced treatment with proper credit to Pasteur's rival researchers.

Vallery-Radot, René. *The Life of Pasteur*. Translated by R. L. Devonshire. Mineola, N.Y.: Dover, 1960. This is the standard biography of Pasteur and was written by Pasteur's son-in-law. The book provides many quotations from documentary sources and gives an inside look at Pasteur, his life and his work.

Allan D. Charles

PAUL III
Alessandro Farnese

Born: February 29, 1468; Canino, Papal States
Died: November 10, 1549; Rome
Area of Achievement: Religion
Contribution: Pope Paul III was the last of the Renaissance popes, aristo-
cratic, educated in the classics, with the concerns of his family often
paramount. Yet he was also the first pope of the Catholic or Counter-
Reformation, and it was he who summoned the Council of Trent, whose
decisions governed the Church in subsequent centuries.

Early Life

Alessandro Farnese was born in 1468 into an old aristocratic family whose
lands in central Italy were located between Rome and Florence. Generally
supportive of the Papacy in its struggles with the Holy Roman Empire, over
time the family owned a large amount of land. Yet it was not until early in
the fifteenth century that the Farneses succeeded in becoming important in
Rome, an event occasioned by a successful marriage. Educated in classical
studies in Florence in the establishment of Lorenzo de' Medici, Farnese
entered the Church, and inasmuch as it was the era of Renaissance Humanism, the choice was probably more for social than for spiritual reasons.

His sister Giulia, the favorite mistress of Alexander VI, head of the
Borgia family, was able to further Farnese's career, and when he became a
cardinal in the Church at the age of twenty-five, many claimed that it was a
result of her influence. He well might have succeeded anyway; members of
his class often rose to the highest positions in the Church during that era. He
was properly educated; he was intelligent and shrewd; and his manner was
pleasing. After becoming a cardinal, he maintained one of the most opulent
palaces in Rome. Although as a cleric he could not marry, he did father
several children out of wedlock, which was not unusual among the clergy at
that time. He subsequently supervised their upbringing and furthered their
careers.

Although Farnese had been a cardinal for many years, it was not until he
was about fifty that he took holy orders and became a priest. His abilities and
ambition had long been recognized. In 1521, he was one of the alternative
candidates to Clement VII, and afterward Farnese became Clement's chief
adviser. It was predicted that he would succeed to the papal throne after
Clement, and he did so in 1534, against little opposition, at the advanced
age of sixty-seven. He took the name Paul III.

Life's Work

Paul's accession was acclaimed among most factions in Christendom. Because of his age, many believed that his reign would be brief and his impact upon events slight. As a Roman, he was popular among the city's populace. As he was an aristocrat, his selection was no threat to the hierarchical social order. Because of his humanistic education, many felt assured that those values would be maintained. Unlike many previous popes, Paul was not tainted with much of the corruption associated with the papal office, this in spite of his own illegitimate children.

It was a complex and difficult time. Paul would probably have preferred to continue in the tradition of most then-recent popes, focusing mainly on secular concerns and pleasures. In 1517, however, Martin Luther began his public criticism of the Catholic church, and by 1534 the demands of the Protestant Reformers were threatening to tear apart the fabric of the Church and the unity of Christendom. In addition, there were military and political struggles which often impinged upon the security of Italy and the Papal States, and even, it seemed, the survival of the Church itself. In 1527, the forces of Emperor Charles V had captured and sacked Rome, a traumatic event not only for the Romans but also for the Papacy. It is probable that Paul was chosen pope as much for his diplomatic and political abilities as for his spiritual commitments. If so, it was a good choice; in the years which followed Paul succeeded in maintaining his, and the Church's, independence, and the Papacy did not become merely a pawn in the game of power politics, a possibility which seemed likely at the time of his accession.

Paul believed that, in order to resist the various religious and political threats to the Catholic church, it was necessary to make changes in the papal court itself. The transitional nature of Paul's reign can be seen by his choice of new cardinals. Two were his teenage grandsons, but others, such as John Fisher, Reginald Pole, Gasparo Contarini, and Gian Pietro Caraffa, proved to be significant selections. Pope Paul also appointed a commission of cardinals to make recommendations regarding possible reforms. When the report was submitted in 1537, it was critical of many past clerical appointments. The buying and selling of church offices and legal decisions from the various church courts was condemned, as were the abuses in the sale of indulgences. It was argued that even the absolute authority of the popes needed to be changed and that Rome itself should be cleansed of corruption. Paul refused to have the report published, but soon unauthorized editions were circulating throughout Europe. Most Protestants were in the process of weakening the authority of the clergy, but the cardinals, and Paul, were more concerned with strengthening the clergy through reform.

Progress was slow. Paul, cautious and conservative, was unwilling to alter the existing system radically, but in 1540 he ordered the banishment of numerous church officials who were improperly residing in Rome. Paul also entertained the possibility of summoning a general church council to reform the Catholic church, but he was opposed to any weakening of papal authority, and in the past councils had often attempted to place limits upon the Papacy. There was no unity on the matter of a council outside the Church. The Protestants were as reluctant to accept a council's authority and its decisions as to follow papal demands. Various European rulers, in an age of rising nationalism, were unwilling to compromise their freedom of action to any supranational body such as the Church had been in the Middle Ages. Charles V was especially in a difficult position. He was a loyal Catholic, but by the 1530's many of his German subjects had become fervent Protestants. His need for peace within Germany and for support against both Francis I of France and the invasion by Muslim Turks, however, meant that he had to make peace with his Protestant citizens. He desired compromise in a world of increasing polarization. An attempt was made in 1541, at Ratisbon, but little was accomplished. The differences between the two factions was already too great.

Many doubted Paul's own commitment to reform. He had, against considerable opposition, made his illegitimate son a duke from lands of the Papal States, and he continued to further the private interests of his own family, including negotiating the marriage of a grandson to the illegitimate daughter of Charles V. Could such a figure of Renaissance Rome be taken seriously as a religious reformer? He was committed, but only under the condition that the council remain under the firm leadership of the Papacy. Finally Paul called for a general council to meet in northern Italy at Trent, a compromise location not too far from Rome but also within the lands of the Holy Roman Empire. For a number of reasons—military, political, diplomatic, and personal—the council was postponed and did not formally begin until December, 1545. Although meeting only sporadically over many years, it was to prove to be a momentous event in the furthering of the religious reformation of the Catholic church itself as well as countering the accomplishments and appeals of Luther, John Calvin, and other Protestants.

Paul also gave his support to two other significant events of the Counter-Reformation. In 1540, he gave his consent to the formation of a new religious order, the Society of Jesus, under the leadership of Ignatius Loyola. Loyola had been a controversial figure and had been imprisoned by Catholic officials in Spain before moving to Paris and then to Rome in 1538. Initially Paul was reluctant to grant Loyola's request: Too much fanatical enthusiasm was suspect by the Farnese aristocrat. Yet one of his own cardinals, Gasparo Contarini, convinced him to charter the Jesuits, who then owed allegiance directly to the Papacy itself. Under Loyola and his successors, the order, in its commitment to missionary activity and to the teaching of approved Catholic doctrine, became one of the most important elements in the Counter-Reformation.

In 1542, Paul granted to Cardinal Gian Pietro Caraffa, another of his appointments to the curia, the office of Inquisitor-General of the Inquisition, giving Caraffa full authority in Italy. Influenced by the earlier Spanish Inquisition, Caraffa soon made his mark in rooting out Lutherans and other heretics within and without the clergy. Under Paul, a man of the Renaissance, Caraffa's Inquisition was somewhat limited, but when Caraffa was elected pope as Paul IV in 1554, the Inquisition became more threatening to the unorthodox in religious belief and practice.

Paul reigned as pope for fifteen years in spite of his advanced age. In 1545, somewhat reluctantly, he gave Parma and Piacenza to his illegitimate son, Pier Luigi. The lands belonged to the Papal States, but it was argued that they could be better defended by their own ruler. It was an extravagant example of papal nepotism. Pier Luigi became the first duke. The decision was not popular, and Pier Luigi was assassinated in 1547. The Emperor Charles V demanded the cession of Parma, and when Paul considered instead making a member of the Orsini family the new Duke of Parma, his own grandchildren, fearing a loss of their recently achieved patrimony, began negotiations with the emperor. The rebellion of his family was too much for the eighty-one-year-old pope, and he died in Rome on November 10, 1549.

Summary

In 1543, Titian painted the portrait of Paul III. The pope was then in his mid-seventies, a formidable age. In the artist's rendition, however, Paul still shows his qualities of authority and perseverance. His white beard and aged wrinkles are countered by the focus of his eyes, which appear to be concentrating upon one of his many concerns—Charles V, Francis I, Loyola, or Caraffa. His years as pope were as momentous as any in the long history of the Catholic church. A man of the Renaissance, he was forced to confront an era of spiritual renewal that was perhaps foreign to his essential nature. As leader of the church universal, he faced a world of rising nationalism. Nevertheless, Paul, while remaining a product of his immediate past, also transcended it.

By cautiously committing himself to the reform of the Church, he helped pave the way for its rehabilitation. At one time, it seemed as if the Protestants would totally replace the Roman church with a reformed church, or churches, but that was not to be. For his support of change within the papal curia, his willingness to countenance the activities of new Catholic reformers such as Loyola, his support of the Inquisition under Caraffa, and most of all his summoning of the church council which met at Trent, Paul, in spite of his secular background, his family concerns, and his conservative nature, must rank among the most important of the popes during the early modern period.

Bibliography
Burns, Edward McNall. *The Counter Reformation*. Princeton, N.J.: D. Van

Nostrand, 1964. The author has combined a brief narrative of the events and figures of the era with a selection of documents. There is no biography of Paul III in English, but Burns gives a succinct account of his life and activities.

Dickens, A. G. *The Counter Reformation*. New York: Harcourt, Brace & World, 1969. Dickens, an English academic, is one of the most influential historians of religion in the sixteenth century. This volume is an excellent survey, with many illustrations, of the era of the Counter-Reformation.

Mullett, Michael A. *The Counter-Reformation and the Catholic Reformation in Early Modern Europe*. London: Methuen, 1984. This brief pamphlet not only covers the major events but also provides a bibliographical account of the various interpretations by historians of the Catholic reformation and the era of Paul III.

Ranke, Leopold von. *The History of the Popes During the Last Four Centuries*. Translated by E. Foster. London: George Bell & Sons, 1907. Ranke, the great German historian of the nineteenth century and the father of scientific history, portrays Paul III as a secular figure, diplomatically and politically astute, whose support for the religious reform of the Catholic church had little to do with any deeply felt spiritual concerns.

Solari, Giovanna R. *The House of Farnese*. Translated by Simona Morini and Frederic Tuten. Garden City, N.Y.: Doubleday, 1968. The author has written a popular history of the Farnese family, beginning with the life of Alessandro Farnese, Paul III. The volume focuses primarily upon personalities and family activities.

Eugene S. Larson

JOHANN HEINRICH PESTALOZZI

Born: January 12, 1746; Zurich
Died: February 17, 1827; Brugg, Switzerland
Area of Achievement: Education
Contribution: Pestalozzi spent his life seeking ways to help students improve their learning skills so that they could develop into effective adults. His method was based upon imparting an awareness of and encouraging direct interaction with objects, progressing from simple steps to more complex ones in an orderly pattern, thereby achieving harmonious organic development.

Early Life

The Pestalozzis, Italians who immigrated to Switzerland from Locarno in the sixteenth century, settled in Zurich. By 1746, when Johann Heinrich Pestalozzi was born, the family had been in Zurich for two hundred years and had been accorded the full rights of citizens—a privilege in a city of 145,000, only 5,000 of whom were citizens. Heinrich was the youngest of Johann Baptist and Suzanne Hotz Pestalozzi's three children. Johann, a surgeon, died in 1751 at the age of thirty-three, leaving the family in straitened circumstances. Because Pestalozzi was a sickly child, his mother sheltered him, seldom allowing him to play with other children or to do chores. He was exposed to the poor when he visited his paternal grandfather, a clergyman near Zurich. The young Pestalozzi developed an interest in and sympathy for the poor.

At Zurich's Collegium Carolinum, Pestalozzi, an indifferent student, developed a consuming love for his country that led him to join the Helvetic Society and to write articles about the poor and suffering for its publication. Upon graduating from Collegium Carolinum, Pestalozzi entered the University of Zurich but abandoned his university studies soon after starting them. Having read Jean-Jacques Rousseau, Pestalozzi was particularly affected by *Émile: Ou, De l'éducation* (1762; *Emilius and Sophia: Or, A New System of Education*, 1762-1763). Rousseau's glorification of the natural life led Pestalozzi to spend the year 1767 studying agriculture. In 1768, he bought acreage near Birr and devoted himself to cultivating it. The failure of this venture in 1774 caused him to lose everything he owned except the house, Neuhof, which dominated his property, and a plot on which he raised food for his wife, Anna, whom he had married in 1769, and their son, Jean-Jacques, named for Rousseau.

By 1773, Pestalozzi had turned Neuhof into a school where he taught poor and unfit children to become cotton spinners. He taught them mathematics and catechism as they worked, and after work the boys gardened while the girls learned sewing and cooking. Pestalozzi also taught them the skills of basic literacy. The school attracted more than fifty unkempt students, ages six to eighteen. Pestalozzi, a slim, gentle man with a kind, understanding smile, reformed many of them, serving simultaneously as teacher and surrogate father. Nevertheless, in 1779 the school closed for lack of funds.

Life's Work

Pestalozzi was a dreamer, a true idealist, motivated primarily by his concern for those less fortunate than he and by his intense loyalty to Switzerland. He felt a deep personal commitment to make life better for his fellow humans, and he went through life seeking ways to bring about such an outcome as a way of improving society.

Pestalozzi's exposure to teaching during the five years at Neuhof suggested to him ways to create a better society and convinced him that social amelioration, his highest goal, proceeded from the bottom up by enabling the children of the poor to find a means of sustaining themselves, of gaining self-respect through productive work such as the cotton spinning that he taught them. He was not satisfied, however, for these students to be merely cotton spinners. He expected them to work with their minds, to elevate their thinking, and to imbue their lives with a dimension that typical workers lack. His ultimate aim was to make them functioning, effective members of the ideal democratic society that he envisioned for Switzerland. He thought education was society's obligation to all of its young. His ideas were precursors of the universal free education that was later widely accepted in developed nations.

Ruined financially by the failure of his school, Pestalozzi sought to make money by entering literary contests and thus began his career in writing. He first published *Abendstunde eines Einsiedlers* (1780; *Evening Hours of a Hermit*, 1912), which articulated his notion that human beings must work at developing their inner powers and that such development can be accomplished best within a wholesome family environment supplemented by a well-designed educational program free to everyone.

The publication of *Lienhard und Gertrud: Ein Buch für das Volk* (1781; *Leonard and Gertrude: A Popular Story*, 1800), in which Gertrude reforms her heavy-drinking spouse and, aided by the local schoolmaster, saves her community from corruption, brought Pestalozzi great attention. With this book, Pestalozzi invented the biographical novel. Before 1787, the initial novel was followed by three sequels, the most important of which is *Christoph und Else lesen in den abendstunden das Buch "Lienhard und Gertrud"* (1782; Christopher and Elsa read the book *Leonard and Gertrude* in the evening), in which Pestalozzi attempts a less sentimental, more socially critical appeal than that in the earlier book, which a sentimental reading public had misinterpreted.

It was not until two decades later, however, that *Wie Gertrud ihre Kinder*

lehrt (1801; *How Gertrude Teaches Her Children*, 1894), consisting of fourteen letters about education, appeared, making its mark as the most coherent
expression of Pestalozzi's educational tenets. If his books had brought him
recognition, they brought him neither job offers nor money. He struggled
to survive. He even made a desperate attempt to publish a newspaper, *Ein
Schweizer-Blatt*, but this weekly soon failed. Nevertheless, the venture was
important to Pestalozzi's development because, as editor, he wrote about
how the state should deal with criminals, proposing the same sort of humane
treatment for prisoners that he had accorded his students at Neuhof.

It was not until Pestalozzi was past fifty that he had another opportunity to
work with children. The French invasion of Stans was a wholesale slaughter.
When the French retreated, orphans had to be cared for. The Swiss government established a residential school for them, with Pestalozzi as head.
Starting with fifty children, the school soon had eighty in residence. Pestalozzi worked with these students, assisted only by a housekeeper. The operation went reasonably well, even though the canton's dominant Catholic
population viewed Pestalozzi, a Protestant, with suspicion.

After six months, the orphanage was taken over by the French, who again
invaded the city, as a hospital. Pestalozzi, who was emotionally and physically spent, did not return to the orphanage when the facility was returned to
that purpose. Instead, at age fifty-two, he became an assistant teacher in the
poorest school in Burgdorf, where again he instituted his radical methods of
discouraging rote learning, emphasizing understanding, and having students
learn from observing and working with objects.

Not long after his initial assignment in Burgdorf, Pestalozzi was appointed
sole teacher in a school of about sixty students from poor families. He could
now implement the methods in which he most believed. Soon, the government helped him establish in Burgdorf Castle a school that attracted children
from affluent families, not the kinds of students that most interested Pestalozzi. It was during this period that Pestalozzi published *How Gertrude
Teaches Her Children*, the book that more than any other established his
reputation.

When the government requisitioned Burgdorf, Pestalozzi was finally in a
position to establish his own experimental school. After a brief, abortive
attempt to work with Philipp Emanuel von Fellenberg at Hofwyl, Pestalozzi
established his school at Yverdon in 1805. The school became important not
only as an institution where children learned by novel methods that emphasized discovery, the understanding of concepts, and proceeding from the
simple to the complex but also as a school that provided teacher training for
hundreds of prospective teachers. Soon, governments from surrounding nations subsidized study at Yverdon for their most promising teachers.

Pestalozzi's methods were controversial throughout his lifetime. He was
convinced that education is a growing and changing process, not a fixed one.

At its best, education, thought Pestalozzi, could address and cure most social ills. He believed that education must be secular rather than religious. He valued the senses over the intellect, perhaps moving further in that direction than was prudent. Not all Pestalozzi's methods worked to the best advantage of students. For example, employing his idea that one should proceed from the simple to the complex, Pestalozzi had beginning readers learn small syllabic constituents of words before they read whole words. He had them memorize an imposingly large "syllabary" consisting of hundreds of items such as *am*, *em*, *im*, *om*, and *um* before they tackled words. Methods of this sort, although hypothetically interesting, proved counterproductive. In addition, the methods were applied to fields such as drawing, in which Pestalozzi had students draw constituent shapes—curves, lines, and circles—in isolation rather than drawing entities. His obsession with formal analysis limited his students and frustrated some teacher trainees at Yverdon, a number of whom, including Friedrich Froebel, became critical of Pestalozzi's method. When Yverdon closed in 1825, however, two years before its founder's death, it had made a significant impact upon education in the Western world. Objection to some of the specifics of Pestalozzi's pedagogy in no way diminishes the effect it had upon education, particularly at the elementary level.

Summary

Johann Heinrich Pestalozzi succeeded at little during his first fifty years. Had he not founded Yverdon, his books would document his social and educational philosophy. His influence, however, would be less far-ranging than it was after he gathered around him a coterie of disciples who would help propagate his work after Yverdon's closing and his death.

Had Pestalozzi died at fifty, he would not have had the opportunity to practice in any sustained way the pedagogy that he developed. Yverdon became his laboratory. If Pestalozzi had a salient shortcoming, it was that he refused to admit the ineffectiveness of some of the methods in which he believed. This shortcoming, however, was more than counterbalanced by his devotion to children and by the sincerity of his effort.

The Pestalozzi legacy points in several directions. His school at Yverdon became a model for laboratory schools and for teacher-training institutions throughout the world. The normal school in the United States is an outgrowth of Yverdon. Pestalozzi's emphasis on having children learn by doing rather than by reading or hearing about things leads directly to John Dewey and other progressive educators who came indirectly under Pestalozzi's influence.

Maria Montessori's object-centered education, which led to the establishment of Montessori schools throughout the world, employs the Pestalozzi method of learning through observing objects and arriving at generalizations from those observations. The notion of engaging the senses in learning activities can be traced to Pestalozzi and such contemporaries of his as Johann Bernhard Basedow, Froebel, and Rousseau.

Pestalozzi's idea that education is the right of all children, not widespread in his time, is a prevailing tenet in most countries today, as is the separation of schools from religious authority, a radical view in the early 1800's. Few educational theorists have had the diverse effect upon modern educational practices that Pestalozzi had, though much of his significant work came after he had experienced a lifetime of failure.

Bibliography

Downs, Robert B. *Heinrich Pestalozzi: Father of Modern Pedagogy*. Boston: Twayne, 1975. This brief biography is well researched and well written, although its bibliography of primary sources is slightly disappointing. The chronology at the beginning of the book is a helpful, ready resource.

Green, J. A. *The Educational Ideas of Pestalozzi*. New York: W. B. Clive, 1914. Reprint. New York: Greenwood Press, 1969. A small book that reproduces well-selected samples of Pestalozzi's most significant writing. Provides an excellent overview of the intellectual development of the man and his ideas.

Gutek, Gerald Lee. *Pestalozzi and Education*. New York: Random House, 1968. This fascinating book is the most comprehensive account of the development of Pestalozzi's educational philosophy. An indispensable source.

Mueller, Gustav E. "Heinrich Pestalozzi: His Life and Work." *Harvard Educational Review* 16 (1946): 141-159. A brilliant article that places Pestalozzi in a broad cultural context and demonstrates how his influence has pervaded most aspects of modern educational thought. Carefully researched and well reasoned.

Pestalozzianum and the Zentralbibliothek, Zürich, ed. *Pestalozzi and His Times: A Pictorial Record*. New York: G. E. Stechert, 1928. This handsome book contains a fine introduction that goes deeply into Pestalozzi's background before presenting nearly one hundred pictures of the man, his family, places he lived and worked, and manuscript pages. An extraordinary book.

Silber, Käte. *Pestalozzi: The Man and His Work*. London: Routledge & Kegan Paul, 1965. A good treatment of Pestalozzi and the range of his ideas. This book supplants the earlier works and brings to light some of Pestalozzi's writing about topics other than education.

R. Baird Shuman

PETER THE GREAT

Born: June 9, 1672; Moscow, Russia
Died: February 8, 1725; St. Petersburg, Russia
Areas of Achievement: Politics and social reform
Contribution: Borrowing both ideas and technology from the West, Peter the Great modernized Russian society, introduced significant military reforms, and built a navy almost from scratch. He won important territories on the Baltic coast from Sweden and transformed Russia into a great European power.

Early Life

Peter was born on June 9, 1672, the first child of Czar Alexis' second wife, Natalia Naryshkin. From his first wife, Maria Miloslavskaya, Alexis had several daughters, the eldest of whom was Sophia, and two sons, Fedor and Ivan. Inevitably, even while Peter's father was still alive, the court factions centering on the Miloslavskys and Naryshkin families contended for power and influence. On Alexis' death in 1676, the eldest son Fedor, though physically weak, became the czar. Yet he too died in 1682 without leaving an heir.

Thus Peter was only ten years old when the Kremlin saw an open and violent struggle of power between the Naryshkins and Miloslavskys, who were now supported by the *streltsy*, the special regiments created in the sixteenth century by Ivan IV. Peter witnessed the brutal killings of several members of the Naryshkin faction, including his mother's former guardian, Artamon Matveyev. Although the struggle ended in the making of Peter and his mentally handicapped half brother Ivan co-czars, these unnecessary and savage killings created a deep hatred in Peter against the *streltsy* and a permanent revulsion against the Kremlin and its politics.

During the next seven years, when Sophia acted as a regent, Peter spent most of his time in the nearby village of Preobrazhenskoe. Because of neglect, he had failed to get a good education even before the 1682 events; this continued to be the case. Yet Peter used his own devices to acquaint himself with military matters and Western technology. While in Preobrazhenskoe, he amused himself with live "toy" soldiers and later organized them in two well-trained battalions. He learned, at least on a rudimentary basis, about Western science, military technology, and shipbuilding from foreigners, mainly German and Dutch, who lived in the nearby German settlement.

In 1689, a number of events affected Peter. In January, his mother married him to Eudoxia Lopukhin, a court official's daughter, by whom he had a son, Czarevitch Alexis, a year later. In August, 1689, as he lay asleep at Preobrazhenskoe, he was awakened and told that the *streltsy*, at the orders of Sophia, were on their way to kill him. He ran to take shelter at the Monastery of the Trinity in the northeast, where he was joined by his "toy" regiments and his mother and the patriarch. Sophia quickly lost support and was imprisoned in the Novodevichy Convent in Moscow. Peter's mother now served as a regent. Her death in 1694, and that of Ivan in 1696, left Peter as the sole ruler of Russia.

Eager to acquire Western knowledge and to seek European allies against Turkey, Peter undertook a long journey to the West in 1697-1698. Traveling with a large Russian delegation as an ordinary member, he spent several months in the Netherlands, learning how to make ships. He also visited England, Austria, and Prussia, and was about to go to Italy when he learned of the revolt by the *streltsy*. Although the revolt had already been crushed, he hurried home to destroy the force forever. Besides executing thousands of the *streltsy* savagely and publicly so that no one would dare oppose him in the future, Peter forced Sophia to become a nun. Peter now enjoyed unchallenged power.

Life's Work

A very important part of Peter's work consisted of acquiring territories on the Black Sea in the south and on the Baltic in the north in order to establish direct links with Central and Western Europe. Just before he left for his European journey in 1697, he had captured Azov on the Black Sea from the Turks. This acquisition was now formalized in a treaty that the two countries signed in July, 1700.

Although Peter had failed to acquire allies against Turkey during his stay in Europe, he did enter into an alliance with Poland-Saxony and Denmark, against the youthful Swedish ruler, Charles XII. Yet while Poland-Saxony and Denmark entered the Great Northern War in early 1700, Peter waited until after the signing of his treaty with Turkey to join the fray. Charles XII, however, proved a tough adversary. He forced Denmark out of the war and then inflicted a humiliating defeat on the Russian army at Narva. It would be very hard to predict what the outcome would have been had he decided to continue his march toward Moscow, but he suddenly turned toward Poland first.

Charles XII's decision to turn first against Poland became a blessing for Peter, which he exploited to the fullest with great determination, inexhaustible energy, and imagination. From melting church bells (to replace lost artillery) to making it necessary for individuals of noble background to rise in the military ranks only after the proper training (as well as enabling the commoners to become officers), Peter soon succeeded in recruiting and training a large and efficient army.

As Charles XII remained entrenched in his struggle against Augustus II of Poland, Peter used his new army skillfully and effectively in making inroads into Livonia and Estonia and inflicted defeat on the Swedes at many points, thus firmly establishing his predominance over the Gulf of Finland. In 1703, he founded the city of St. Petersburg on the Neva as his future capital, and, in order to protect it, he ordered the construction of a fortress on Kronstadt Island. He also rapidly built a navy in the Baltic Sea.

Having defeated Poland in 1706, Charles was now free to turn toward Moscow. Rather than attack from the north, he decided to go southward into the Ukraine, hoping to get the support of the Cossacks and the Ukrainians. The Russians succeeded, however, in interrupting and destroying some of his supplies as at Lesnaia in September, 1708. Though the Cossack leader Ivan Stepanovich Mazepa did support him, the majority of the Ukrainians still remained loyal to Peter. The two armies finally faced each other at Poltava in the Ukraine in July, 1709. At this historic battle, a depleted Swedish army met Peter's larger force and was defeated. Both Charles and Mazepa had to escape into Turkey.

Peter's great victory at Poltava was complicated by Turkey's entry into the war. Rather than making peace with the Turks, at a time when he was still at war with Sweden, Peter, in an overconfident mood, entered the Balkans hoping to incite Turkey's Christians against their masters. He soon decided to extricate himself by returning the hard-won Azov to Turkey in the Treaty of Pruth of 1711.

Peter could now concentrate on the north, where his army was already active in acquiring new territories on the Baltic. War with Sweden finally ended in 1721. In the Treaty of Nystadt, Peter obtained more than what he had hoped for when he first went to war against Sweden in 1700. In addition to the territories known today as Latvia, Lithuania, and Estonia, Russia annexed Ingria and part of Karelia with the strategic Viborg.

Peter's success in foreign affairs was not confined to his acquisitions from Sweden. His efforts to establish links with China would result in the Treaty of Kiakhta in 1727, establishing important trade links with Beijing. He encouraged further exploration of Siberia and obtained, from Persia, territory along the Caspian Sea, including the important Port of Baku.

His efforts to modernize Russia, which initially appeared haphazard and were often undertaken more to facilitate his war efforts than with a clear vision to change Russian society, finally began to take shape toward the latter part of his reign. While his efforts to force the Russians to surrender their beards and traditional long dresses had only a limited impact, steps taken to develop industry and make the Russian language more simplified (making it possible to translate a large number of European scientific works into Russian) would have lasting positive results.

One of Peter's most interesting—as well as very effective and useful— innovations was the creation of a table of ranks. Providing for fourteen categories in a hierarchical order for all officials, including officers in the military, the device enabled Peter to reward individuals of nonnoble background, even allowing them to become nobles. In this manner, without abolishing the institution of serfdom, he was able to get the services of all talented individuals. A very important administrative reform, undertaken in 1711 when he was away fighting Turkey, also proved lasting. So the work of the government could continue in his absence, he created a senate to supervise all judicial and administrative functions. Its head, the ober-procurator, served as his direct agent, a kind of modern prime minister. In 1717, he created colleges for different governmental functions as foreign affairs, finance, and navy. Here, again, this was the creation of something like the modern ministries. Significant, but less successful, attempts were also made in the area of local government.

Although the church in Russia had gradually come under the control of Muscovite rulers since the days of the Mongolian rule, it was still led by a patriarch who might undermine the czar's wishes. Peter wanted to abolish that anomaly, and, in line with the model of state-church relations existing in the German Lutheran states, he wanted the state's absolute primacy over the church. When Patriarch Adrian died in 1700, he decided not to appoint any other individual to that post. After intense personal interest and painstaking work over a number of years, he, in 1721, decided to create a synod consisting of members of the Orthodox clergy to replace the office of the patriarch and to be headed by a lay official: The church administration almost became a function of the government.

Summary

A man of inexhaustible energy and determination, Peter the Great succeeded, in a span of only a quarter of a century, in fulfilling all of his ambitions on the Baltic. Russia now came to replace Sweden as a great European power. Flopan Prokopavich, Peter's adviser on church affairs, in his funeral oration was not amiss when he said that Peter had "found but little strength" in Russia but succeeded in making its "power strong like a rock and diamond." On the territory he won from Sweden, he built his new capital as a living symbol of his orientation toward the West, and even today it stands as one of the most beautiful cities of Europe.

While there is hardly any dispute regarding the significance of his accomplishment in creating a modern army and navy and his remarkable military victories made possible by them, the nature and impact of his reforms aroused much controversy in his own time. Even in the later period, when the problems of change and modernization still concerned the Russians, Peter aroused both deep hatred and admiration, as, for example, in the bitter debate between the Slavophiles and the Westernizers in the nineteenth century. Peter's policies raised a very fundamental question: Which path should Russia take in order to modernize itself and create a better society and political system?

In one respect, though, Peter followed the old Russian tradition. He did not hesitate to use maximum force, as was the case in his treatment of the rebellious *streltsy*, in order to suppress the opposition. He remains the only Russian ruler who did not even hesitate in torturing and eventually causing the death of his only son, Czarevitch Alexis. In his total dedication to the welfare of his country, he also remains one of the earliest examples of an enlightened despot. Russia, in a very fundamental way, was a changed country when Peter died in 1725.

Bibliography

Anderson, M. S. *Peter the Great*. London: Thames & Hudson, 1978. A standard biography, pointing both to Peter's failures and to his successes. Written by a British historian, it makes liberal use of the observations of foreign visitors to Russia and of the dispatches sent by foreign diplomats in the Russian capital. Includes an annotated bibliography of both Russian and Western works.

De Jonge, Alex. *Fire and Water: A Life of Peter the Great*. New York: Coward, McCann & Geoghegan, 1979. Attempts to place Peter and his work in the context of Russian historical traditions. The author has no hesitation in linking the nature of Petrine Russia to the subsequent periods in Russian history, including the Soviet era. Includes a short bibliography.

Massie, Robert K. *Peter the Great: His Life and World*. New York: Alfred A. Knopf, 1980. A recent popular biography. Presents an admiring and somewhat uncritical portrait of Peter. What distinguishes this biography from others is its attempt to give the readers a picture of the European world so Peter's accomplishment can be seen in a larger context. Contains an excellent but unannotated bibliography.

Oliva, L. Jay. *Russia in the Era of Peter the Great*. Englewood Cliffs, N.J.: Prentice-Hall, 1969. Avoids the temptation of linking Petrine Russia to later periods, including the Soviet era. The emphasis is on the heritage of Peter's Russia and on the eighteenth century environment in which Peter tried to shape his work. Includes a good, briefly annotated bibliography.

Riasanovsky, Nicholas V. *The Image of Peter the Great in Russian History and Thought*. New York: Oxford University Press, 1985. Starting with the image of Peter in the Russian Enlightenment during the period from 1700 to 1826, the author covers the nineteenth century as well as the Soviet period. Contains a long and very useful bibliography.

Surendra K. Gupta

PHILIP II

Born: May 21, 1527; Valladolid, Spain
Died: September 13, 1598; El Escorial Palace, Spain
Areas of Achievement: Government, politics, and religion
Contribution: Philip II was one of the most dominant monarchs in Europe during the late sixteenth century. Guided by his deep religious faith, Philip was involved in virtually every major event in the last half of the sixteenth century.

Early Life

Philip was born into the most influential family in sixteenth century Europe—the Habsburgs. His father, Charles V (Charles I of Spain), was the most powerful Holy Roman Emperor to that date. Philip's first years were spent under the guidance of his mother, Isabel of Portugal, as Charles traveled on imperial business. Isabel's religious and serious nature had a pronounced effect on her son. In 1535, Charles established a separate household for Philip, who was taught such arts as riding and hunting. In addition, Philip received a formal education, excelling in language skills. He could speak and write Latin, understand French and Italian, and speak French, but he was most comfortable with the language of his homeland.

Philip's physical appearance was similar to that of his ancestors. Having the famous Habsburg jaw, a large protruding under jaw and lip, he wore a short and pointed beard early in life and allowed it to grow longer and wider as he grew older.

Philip had an unusual married life. He had four wives, and he outlived each of them. At age eighteen, he married Maria of Portugal, the mother of a son who died later under questionable circumstances. Philip's next wife was the English queen Mary I. In 1558, Mary died without heirs, and that broke all connections Philip had with England. His third wife was Elizabeth of Valois, who bore him two daughters before dying in 1568. His last marriage was to Anne of Austria, the daughter of his cousin, Emperor Maximilian II. Anne bore Philip four sons and one daughter before she died in 1580.

Life's Work

Philip ruled many lands. Although Charles V gave the Austrian lands to his brother, Ferdinand, he reserved for Philip the Spanish lands in the New World and Europe. The New World lands were most important as sources of revenue. Among his holdings, however, Philip loved Spain best. Indeed, he never left his homeland after his return from Northern Europe in 1559. He built for himself a palace, El Escorial, which became a monument to his reign; some called it a monastery.

One of the most disturbing problems Philip faced throughout his rule was the Protestant Reformation. Indeed, the fight against the heretics colored almost every aspect of his reign. He had been reared as a Catholic and was devoted to the Church. When the Council of Trent finished its work, he attempted to enforce its decisions. He believed that it was his duty to restore Europe to the true Church. He did not always agree, however, with the popes and often fought with them over authority in church-state issues. In turn, the popes resented Philip's control over the Spanish church. The Spanish clergy, however, supported Philip.

Philip's reign was usually dominated by affairs outside the Iberian Peninsula. The situation in the Netherlands created much difficulty. The Dutch were growing wealthy and were gaining a sizable Protestant population. Although they had been restless under Charles V, they did not create major problems for him; they paid their taxes and, as a result, were low in funds when Philip assumed control. Philip expected the Dutch not only to pay their taxes but also to maintain a defense against his northern enemies, while promoting the Roman Catholic church.

Philip attempted several different approaches to the Netherlands. He first tried to rule through a regent, his half sister Margaret, and a close adviser, Antoine Perrenot de Granvelle, Bishop of Arras (after 1561, Cardinal Granvelle). The cardinal actually controlled the government and attempted to carry out Philip's orders. The Dutch Protestants, led by William the Silent, insisted that they had certain privileges that had to be respected. William finally forced Philip's recall of Granvelle, only to discover that Granvelle had been following orders. When the Protestant militants began to destroy churches and other property, Philip sent troops to end the rebellion. Several thousand people were executed for heresy. Taking control of the northern provinces, William demanded religious freedom, along with the removal of troops and restoration of rights. Philip could never allow religious freedom, so this civil war continued throughout his reign. While there were a few periods of Spanish success, the northern provinces gained their independence, although Spain refused to recognize the loss until 1648.

England prevented Philip from pursuing the revolt in the Netherlands as actively as he might have wished. Throughout the sixteenth century, Anglo-Spanish relations had seen peaks and valleys. When Philip married Mary in 1554, it had only been after careful consideration. Many in the English Parliament opposed the marriage and relented only after ensuring that Philip would have little to do with English government. Philip was unhappy about the situation but accepted his father's advice to rule England through Mary. Unfortunately for this goal, Mary died soon after the marriage.

Problems constantly beset the two countries during the Elizabethan years. One of the most vexing was the English "Sea Dogs" (privateers), who preyed on Spanish New World trade. Although Philip beseeched Elizabeth to control her sea captains, she never did. She also angered Philip by providing

English troops to aid the Protestant cause in the Netherlands.

Convinced that diplomacy was not going to control the English, Philip plotted an invasion. His plans originally called for assembling a large armada and sending it to the Netherlands, where it would board troops and cross the Channel to capture England. This Spanish Armada quickly ran into problems. In 1587, an English sea captain, Francis Drake, surprised the Spanish fleet in port and inflicted considerable damage. Determined, even at great financial costs and administrative difficulties, Philip repaired the Armada and sent it to sea in 1588. As it arrived in the Channel, a combination of English ships and Channel weather seriously crippled the fleet, and only a small portion managed to limp back to Spain. While Philip never gave up the idea of conquering England, the idea remained only a dream.

Spain was in the middle of a war with France when Philip assumed the mantle of leadership from his father in 1555-1556. It was not until 1559 that the Treaty of Cateau-Cambrésis was negotiated with the King of France, Henry II, ending the conflict. After the death of Henry II, there was a struggle for control of the French throne. The French Huguenots demanded their religious rights as well as certain political ones. Wars frequently raged between the Catholic and Huguenot factions. Philip carefully watched the situation and in December, 1584, signed the secret Treaty of Joinville with the Catholic League. The goals of the treaty were to keep a Huguenot off the throne and to suppress heresy in France. When the next in line to the throne seemed to be Henry of Navarre, a Huguenot, Philip forced the reigning King Henry III to proclaim an elderly uncle, Charles, Cardinal of Bourbon, as his successor. When Charles died in 1591, Philip advanced his daughter, Isabella Clara Eugenia, by Elizabeth of Valois, the eldest daughter of Henry II's eldest daughter. These claims failed, and Henry of Navarre assumed his place on the French throne; Philip could not dislodge him.

During the last few years of his life, Philip suffered from crippling arthritis and usually had to be carried from place to place. He accepted what comfort he could from his religion. He was a man of faith, and his religious beliefs, which carried him throughout his life, were with him when he died.

Summary

Philip II was one of the most dominant forces in the second half of the sixteenth century. He touched the lives of many both in the New World and in Europe. In his own fashion, he established a Spanish colonial governance that lasted well into the nineteenth century. In Europe, he fought with his fellow monarchs for control, even seizing the Portuguese crown when it became vacant in 1580. He rarely retreated from any position, because he was usually convinced that God had ordained him to undertake a mission.

Philip would not make decisions quickly. Some argue that he was being prudent, while others say that he was timid. Perhaps his procrastination was caused by his lack of funds. Despite the riches of the New World, Philip had such staggering debts that his reign was bankrupt in 1557, 1575, and 1596. He collected money from every possible source to meet his needs. Another reason for his procrastination could have been his habit of employing ministers with widely varying views, even ones opposed to his own, and then demanding that they express themselves. Council meetings, such as the Council of State, often became battlegrounds for rival factions.

Because of his absolute faith and strong convictions, Philip became part of the Black Legend, or anti-Spanish view, that surfaced in the English-speaking world. Philip's connection with the legend began when William the Silent, deep in battle over the Netherlands, branded Philip a murderer. Two major contributions to the Black Legend's growth were books by Antonio Perez and John Lothrop Motley. Perez, who had been close to Philip and had fallen from power, tried to destroy Philip's name to avenge himself. Motley, a noted Protestant historian, used the distorted documents of Perez and others to paint Philip as evil. More balanced accounts have since emerged, and Philip has been placed in a more appropriate perspective.

Bibliography

Mattingly, Garrett. *The Armada*. Boston: Houghton Mifflin, 1959. A readable book about one of the major issues of Philip's reign—the defeat of the Spanish Armada. Contains a good, but outdated, bibliography. This work is considered a classic.

Merriman, Roger Bigelow. *The Rise of the Spanish Empire in the Old World and the New*. Vol. 4, *Philip the Prudent*. New York: Macmillan, 1918. Reprint. New York: Cooper Square, 1962. While Merriman's work might be considered an old source, it is still excellent for information on Philip's life. This is a balanced account and a good starting point for a serious study of Philip. Contains bibliographic information.

Parker, Geoffrey. *Philip II*. Boston: Little, Brown, and Hutchinson, 1978. While the documentation herein is not what many historians would like to see, the book still presents a good view of Philip.

_____. "Philip II of Spain: A Reappraisal." *History Today* 19 (1979): 800-847. Parker, who has written several articles on Philip, provides the reader with a close examination of Philip in this short article. Contains comments on the physical problems that Philip had toward the end of his life and addresses the problem of the Black Legend, briefly explaining Philip's role in it.

Pierson, Peter. *Philip II of Spain*. London: Thames & Hudson, 1975. A superb short biography. Pierson covers each major section of Philip's life and work. He tries to make the point that Philip thought in terms of dynasty and religion and not of nation state.

Rule, John C., and John J. TePaske, eds. *The Character of Philip II*. Boston: D. C. Heath, 1963. An excellent source for trying to determine what Philip was really like. Includes selections from authors representing several nationalities.

Eric L. Wake

PHILIP THE MAGNANIMOUS

Born: November 13, 1504; Marburg, Hesse
Died: March 31, 1567; Cassel, Hesse
Areas of Achievement: Monarchy and church reform
Contribution: Philip the Magnanimous was perhaps the most significant single political supporter of the Protestant Reformation during the critical early years of the movement in the sixteenth century.

Early Life
Philip succeeded his father, Landgrave William II, on the throne of Hesse in 1509, when he was not yet five years of age. For half a century, the principality of Hesse had been riven by dynastic feuds and minority administrations, which had allowed the estates to obtain considerable influence. In 1509, a conflict for control of the regency erupted between the mother of young Philip, Anne of Mecklenburg, and the estates, which resulted in civil war and the intervention of neighboring princes, especially the rival Ernestine and Albertine branches of the House of Saxony.

These conflicts continued throughout the minority of Philip, providing an extremely strife-filled youth for the prince, who was often the object of contention and was shuffled about from one faction to another. Anne was supported by the Albertine Duke George the Bearded of Saxony and arranged for the marriage of Philip to George's daughter, Christine. The Ernestine Elector Frederick the Wise of Saxony, on the other hand, supported Anne's opposition. In 1518, when Philip was but fourteen years old, Emperor Maximilian I proclaimed Philip of age in an effort to restore peace, but the landgrave's mother continued to dominate the government, and civil conflict would continue until Philip assumed personal control of the Hesse throne in the mid-1520's.

In 1521, Philip attended the Diet of Worms, at which Martin Luther's teachings were condemned, and left with a strong attachment to the Wittenberg professor. During the following years, he took part in suppressing the uprising of imperial knights led by Franz von Sickingen and Ulrich von Hutten, and the peasant uprising led by Thomas Münzer.

Philip was a prince of considerable personal charm, with a handsome physique. At least during his youth, he was dynamic and outspoken, even to a fault. At the Diet of Speyer in 1526, for example, he was so eager to testify publicly to his new faith that he dined on an ox on a Friday. His activist nature, joined to the caution of his Saxon allies, often led to divided command in the Protestant camp. Despite the obvious sincerity of his adherence to the Reformation, Philip had strong sensual desires which would lead him into bigamy in 1540. On May 12, 1525, his mother died, and Philip became, for the first time, master of his own house.

Life's Work

By the time of his mother's death, Philip was effectively master of his principality and was committed to the Lutheran Reformation. During the winter of 1525-1526, Philip reached an agreement with the elector John of Saxony, cousin and rival of his mother's supporter, to pursue a common policy in defense of the Reformation at the upcoming Diet of Speyer. At that meeting, the princes, led by John and Philip, were able to prevent the enforcement of the decrees against Lutheranism, obtaining instead an agreement that each prince would act in his own lands "in such a way as everyone trusted to justify before God and the Imperial Majesty." This gave the princes a free hand in their own territories, setting the precedent for the later principle of state supremacy—*cuius regio, eius religio*—adopted by the Peace of Augsburg in 1555.

With this mandate, Philip called a synod of the Hessian church at Homburg in October, 1526, which adopted the *Reformatio ecclesiarum Hassiae*. This plan, primarily the work of François Lambert of Avignon, a Franciscan friar trained at Wittenberg, would have provided the Hessian church with a democratic structure, consisting of elected clergy and annual synods. On the advice of Luther, this model was rejected in favor of that being developed in neighboring Saxony, under which Philip became the effective head of the new church administration.

Twelve months later, Philip summoned the estates of Hesse for the first time in nine years to consider the disposition to be made of the confiscated monastic properties. This parliament agreed that 41 percent of these revenues were to be used by the prince, while the remaining 59 percent were to serve pious, educational, and ecclesiastical purposes, including the foundation of the University of Marburg to train future clergymen and officials. It was Philip's liberal endowment of the new university and various pious and charitable institutions which earned for him the sobriquet "the Magnanimous."

In the atmosphere of mutual suspicion following the rapprochement between Emperor Charles V and Pope Clement VII in 1528, Philip fell prey to the forgeries of Otto von Pack, a discredited councillor of Duke George. Pack persuaded him that Catholic forces were assembling to exterminate the new heresy, whereupon Philip formed an alliance with John, sent feelers to the emperor's enemies in France and Hungary, and assembled a significant armed force. Although no actual fighting ensued, Philip's precipitate action in appealing to the enemies of the emperor weakened the Protestant cause at the next diet, also held at Speyer, where in April, 1529, a new law revoked the concessions made three years earlier, halting all ecclesiastical innovations and restoring the jurisdiction of Catholic bishops. Philip joined with six other princes and fourteen cities in the Protest of Speyer in rejecting this decision, from which the adherents of Luther were known as "Protestants."

By this time, voices other than Luther's had been raised demanding the reform of the Church, resulting in divided councils among the Protestants. The major controversy was between Luther and Huldrych Zwingli over the doctrine of the Eucharist. Believing that a common front was necessary to defend the Protestant cause, Philip sponsored the Marburg Colloquy from October 1 to 3, 1529, in an effort to promote harmony. The disputants agreed on fourteen points, but their failure to achieve full agreement on the fifteenth article, on the Lord's Supper, was also the failure of the Protestant movement to achieve unity.

In 1530, Philip took part in the Diet of Augsburg, where an attempt was made to reach agreement between the Lutherans and the Catholics, and was one of the seven princes to subscribe to the Augsburg Confession presented there. With the failure of these negotiations, the emperor ordered the complete restoration of Catholicism. To defend themselves against this threat, the Protestant princes and the cities of Magdeburg and Bremen formed the military League of Schmalkalden in February, 1531. This league became the major political expression of German Protestantism for a generation.

Philip became the leading spirit in the Schmalkaldic League, overshadowing his more cautious cousin Elector John Frederick of Saxony. With French support, in 1534 Philip made the first significant territorial gain for Lutheranism in southern Germany when he conquered Württemberg from the Habsburgs, restoring the previous ruler, the Lutheran Duke Ulrich. Philip then gave support to the Prince-Bishop of Münster in his conflict with the radical Anabaptists, assisting in the siege of the city, which fell on June 25, 1535. Thus, during the 1530's, Philip was at the height of his influence.

At the age of nineteen, Philip had married Christine of Saxony, a daughter of his mother's ally, Duke George. The marriage was not successful. Influenced by Luther's statement that bigamy was not as serious an offense as divorce, he entered into a second union with Margaret von der Saal, which was soon made public. This not only caused dissension among the members of the league but also, because bigamy was a crime against imperial law as well, gave the emperor considerable leverage with Philip.

A confrontation in Germany had been avoided since 1530, largely because of the emperor's desire to obtain the support of the princes in his wars with the French and the Turks, and because of disagreements with the Papacy. In 1544, with the Treaty of Crépy, peace was concluded with France, and in 1545 the Council of Trent began its deliberations. After failing to convince the Lutherans to attend the council, Charles determined on war. At the Diet of Regensburg in 1546, Philip and John Frederick were placed under the ban of the empire.

In the War of the League of Schmalkalden, the dynamic Philip and the cautious John Frederick shared the command with other allies, which was the major cause of their defeat at Mühlberg on April 24, 1547. John Frederick was captured, and Philip was summoned to surrender, with the promise that his life would be spared; he would not suffer perpetual imprisonment, but he would have to pay a substantial fine of 150,000 gulden. Philip consulted his estates, which advised accepting, and they pledged their loyalty to their prince. A regency under Philip's eldest son was established, which governed during his five-year imprisonment. Taken to the Netherlands, he was not released until after the Truce of Passau in 1552.

The Peace of Augsburg (1555) ended the wars of religion in Germany for this generation. Chief among its provisions was the principle of *cuius regio, eius religio*, confirming the authority of the German princes over the Church in their lands. During the remaining years of his life, Philip devoted himself primarily to the governance of Hesse, but he strove to promote unity among the Protestants of Germany and to support the Huguenots of France. After his death in 1567, his lands were partitioned among the four sons of his first marriage.

Summary

Philip the Magnanimous, building on the foundations laid during the regency of his mother, broke the power of the estates of Hesse, creating the strong princely authority which would allow his descendants to play an important role in German affairs into the nineteenth century. More important, his early, ardent, and consistent support for the Protestant cause contributed to its spread and eventual acceptance in large parts of Germany. Although the sincerity of his religious convictions is manifest, so also are the limitations placed upon his contributions by the strength of his emotions. His precipitate action in the Pack affair contributed to the Protestant setback at the Diet of Speyer in 1529. His bigamous marriage in 1540 caused scandal for and within the Protestant forces, while politically neutralizing him for a time. His inability to work in harmony with the more cautious John Frederick contributed to the Protestant defeat in 1547.

Despite these failures, Philip undoubtedly contributed significantly to the success of the Lutheran movement. The Protest of Speyer of 1529, the Augsburg Confession of 1530, and the League of Schmalkalden of 1531 were signed by only seven princes. Other than Philip, the only significant signatory was John Frederick. Without Philip's support, the Lutheran movement in Germany might have been overwhelmed at this critical time in its development. This, alone, is sufficient to justify the inclusion of Philip the Magnanimous among the leading figures of the Reformation.

Bibliography

Bainton, Roland H. *The Reformation of the Sixteenth Century.* Boston: Beacon Press, 1952. This work by one of the premier twentieth century scholars of the Reformation is a significant contribution to the interpretation of the Protestant movement. It contains a brief but insightful discussion of the impact of Philip's actions on the Diet of Speyer in 1529, and of his bigamy.

Carsten, Francis Ludwig. *Princes and Parliaments in Germany, from the Fifteenth to the Eighteenth Century.* Oxford: Clarendon Press, 1959. This seminal work on the estates of the lesser German principalities contains an extremely useful discussion of the troubled regency period in Hesse, of the relations of Philip with his subjects, and of the unilateral actions of the landgrave in introducing the Reformation into his principality.

Grimm, Harold J. *The Reformation Era, 1500-1650.* 2d ed. New York: Macmillan, 1973. Grimm's masterful study of the Reformation remains unsurpassed among traditional interpretations for its breadth and objectivity. Contains excellent analyses of the character of Philip, his role in the political events of the age, the Sacramentarian controversy and Marburg Colloquy, and the impact of his bigamous marriage.

Holborn, Hajo. *A History of Modern Germany.* Vol. 1, *The Reformation.* New York: Alfred A. Knopf, 1959. This classical study of German history is especially useful in placing Philip in his historical context and in developing the influence of individual political actions on the course of the Reformation.

Wright, William John. *Capitalism, the State, and the Lutheran Reformation: Sixteenth Century Hesse.* Athens: Ohio University Press, 1988. This more recent work utilizes developments in modern historiography to place both the individual prince and the Protestant movement as a whole securely in their socioeconomic setting.

William C. Schrader

PIERO DELLA FRANCESCA

Born: c. 1420; Borgo San Sepulcro
Died: October 12, 1492; Sansepulcro, Tuscany
Areas of Achievement: Art and mathematics
Contribution: Though admired selectively for centuries, Piero della Francesca's paintings were not placed among the world's masterpieces until the twentieth century. His *Baptism of Christ*, *Resurrection*, *Legend of the True Cross*, and *Nativity* are now seen as crucial to the development of the characteristic forms and methods of Italian Renaissance painting.

Early Life

Partly because of his being born and reared—and later choosing largely to remain—in a provincial Tuscan market town, almost nothing is known of Piero della Francesca's life up to the age of about twenty. For this reason, the date of his birth, and consequently his age at the time of his dated works, have been subjects of considerable debate. This debate is more significant than such things normally are, for Piero was active during the formative period of the high Italian Renaissance. For a long time, his role in this development was obscured by ignorance, and influences originating in him were attributed to others; later, the pendulum swung the other way. Now his genius is firmly established.

He was born into the Dei Franceschi family (della Francesca is a feminine variant of the name), locally prominent leather merchants, dyers, and farm owners, in Borgo San Sepulcro (modern Sansepulcro, Italy), near Arezzo. The first notice of him appears on September 7, 1439, as an assistant to Domenico Veneziano in a series of now-ruined frescoes in the Church of Sant'Egidio in Florence. Later, in 1442, Piero became one of the Priori (town councilmen) of San Sepulcro, an office he kept for the remainder of his life, though he did leave the town periodically to work in Florence, Milan, and Urbino.

This provincial, rustic upbringing supplied an essential element in Piero's mature technique, for the arid, desolate masses of the Apennine foothills provide the brooding, static backgrounds of his scenes of secular and religious history. In this respect, he adapted the scene-framing techniques of Fra Angelico and his master Domenico Veneziano, going beyond them in using natural settings to shape the emotional and iconological contexts of the foreground subjects. That is, he was one of the first to create thematically integrated compositions, in which every detail contributed to the dominant effect. He undoubtedly received the initial impetus toward this totally unified vision during his apprenticeship to Veneziano in Florence, at a time when the dominant artists were, besides his master, Leon Battista Alberti, Luca della Robbia, Lorenzo Ghiberti, Fra Angelico, Masaccio, and Andrea del

Castagno. Piero had the good fortune to mature at the very moment that advances in perspective theory, form, light, and color seemed to call for fusion in a new technique. In the course of his career, Piero forged that technique.

Life's Work

Piero's first known work, an altarpiece commissioned in 1445 for the charitable company known as the Misericordia in his hometown, at first seems to show little evidence of this fusion. This commission, intended to replace an existing work in several segments of different sizes, required him to use the existing panels and frames, thus limiting him to what was by then an antique format. This format dominates the work; at first viewing, the observer is likely to believe that the painting dates from the preceding century, so stiff and compartmentalized do the figures represented appear. Fire damage and overpainting during attempted restorations do not correct the impression. Further study, however, reveals that Piero is here experimenting with novel treatments of light as a means of defining and disclosing form. His light is flushed with color, subtly varied from surface to surface, pervading even the shadows from which it emerges. This is the light of Angelico and Veneziano, but immensely refined in that it takes on and projects texture, in the process inhabiting form. His figures, the clothes they wear, and the volumes they create become tactile, almost palpable. Further, the whole breathes an appropriate, and characteristic, solemnity.

Around 1450, Piero created his first masterwork, *Baptism of Christ*, for a priory in San Sepulcro. The large panel centers on Christ standing in the ankle-deep flow of a translucent stream winding its way down a Tuscan hillside; John strides out from the right to perform his ministry, while three angels watch from the left, under the arch of a small poplar springing improbably from the very bank of the stream, and a postulant in the middle distance pulls off his tunic to become the next candidate. The painting is an arresting combination of strength and subtlety. The Christ is severe, stark, almost repulsive; his features are harsh, peasantlike, rather brutal, certainly common. He stands resolute, firm, determined to take what is coming to him, even if against or beyond his will. The angels lounge idly yet ceremonially, as if they were paid attendants, early altar boys. The event may inaugurate a revolutionary mission, yet no one is paying much attention to it; it is simply another baptism, and even John seems to be merely resigned to it, going through a formality.

Still, this Christ is as vulnerable as he is determined. His contours swell softly: His skin would quiver to the touch, and his transparent loincloth reveals his essential humanity. Further, his white, columnar body precisely parallels the trunk of the poplar, as if the two were of one kind, two manifestations of the same spirit, sprung from the same root. Similarly, the dove centered above the vessel from which John pours, representing the Third Person of the Trinity, is almost indistinguishable from the adjacent clouds. More remarkable, and in defiance of artistic tradition, God the Father does not appear, not even by disembodied hand. Piero seems to suggest that the Father, nevertheless, is there, as much as Son and Holy Spirit. He is simply more immanent than they, as the Son is also in the tree and the Spirit in the clouds. This revelation of theme in seemingly accidental yet completely integrated detail is the signature of Piero. Typically, every naturalistic detail—like the inverted reflection of landscape in the stream—is rendered with the utmost fidelity to the natural phenomena.

The *Resurrection* fresco (c. 1453) is Piero's best-known work. The subject was the official symbol of the town—hence its name—and Piero deliberately represents the event as taking place while the sun rises in the rocky hills above the town. Christ mounts the sarcophagus with his left foot, grasping a red-cross standard which unfolds above him. His pale rose-colored robe opens to expose the spear wound. The face is as compelling as that in the *Baptism of Christ*, but these eyes are simultaneously harrowing—they have experienced everything—and compassionate, probing into the soul of the viewer. Four soldiers sprawl in front of the tomb, dozing, the back of one resting against the frontal plane of the painting. Though apparently disposed at random, the figures combine with that of the risen Christ in a pattern of interlocking and embedded triangles, creating an impression of great strength and endurance.

In the middle background, the landscape on the left—luminous in the shimmering light of dawn—is withered and barren, while that on the right is in full leaf. This is the iconographic equivalent of Christ's remark on the way to Calvary: "If they do these things in a green tree, what shall be done in the dry?" (Luke 23:31), referring to the persecution that would follow upon his execution. There was a further association of green and withered trees with the Trees of Life and of Knowledge in the Garden of Eden, the second of which in legend became both symbolically and actually the agent of human redemption, by furnishing the wood for Christ's cross. In this painting, Piero created an image in which all of the details fuse in a vision of total integrity, in which psychological intensity and doctrinal content reinforce each other.

Piero's only major fresco cycle, the *Legend of the True Cross* (1452-1457), is the most ambitious project he attempted: a series of twelve frescoes setting forth a pious medieval legend of complex, and improbable, fantasy. Unfortunately, the entire chancel, on which the frescoes were done, has suffered from water seepage over the ensuing centuries, and much of the surface has been lost and ineptly restored. These restorations have recently been removed, so that what remains of the original can now be seen. What is there is astonishing. The panels narrate major episodes in the legend, from the fetching of a branch from Eden by Seth to cure his father Adam through Solomon's burying of a beam and Helena's discovery of the cross fashioned from it to its recovery from Chosroes by the Emperor Heraclius. Piero arranged them not chronologically but in order to focus on visual, symbolic, and thematic resonances. Thus, for example, scenes dominated by women are set on opposite walls, as are those of battles and those involving visions of the Cross. Further, each panel consists of two paired scenes representing two incidents within a single episode. Independently, these paintings serve as illustrations of rhythmic group composition, Albertian perspective, and visual and thematic integration; together, they constitute one of the most magnificent sequences of painting ever composed, truly remarkable especially for the fidelity of its coloring, so that the landscapes and people represented take on tangible reality.

In the middle of his career, Piero occasionally left San Sepulcro to do some of his most significant work at Urbino, Milan, and Florence. In Urbino, for example, he painted a mysterious *Flagellation of Christ* (probably 1463-1464), the thematic content of which has only recently been convincingly interpreted. The dignity of his figures, however, the delicacy of light and color, and the austere sincerity of the work have never been in doubt. Also in Urbino, Piero composed complementary portraits of *Count Federico da Montefeltro* and his wife, *Battista Sforza* (after 1474), which bear allegorical triumph scenes on their reverses. The portraits show to the highest degree Piero's fusion of austerity of vision and revelation of character, and the triumphs disclose a blend of imaginative landscape with mythological content. His last known painting, *Nativity* (1480), reveals modulations of color and light that have never been surpassed; Piero almost makes the air visible.

Though he lived on for some twenty years, he seems not to have returned to painting, busying himself instead in theoretical studies, which included the first Renaissance treatise on perspective and a book on geometry. According to legend, he became blind in the last years of his life.

Summary

Up to the twentieth century Piero della Francesca and his work were believed to be remote and somewhat primitive; at best, he was considered a "provincial master" and treated somewhat condescendingly. At this point, it is difficult to understand that neglect. His work is always compelling, particularly in his rare union of force and subtlety. Even when disfigured by time or made to appear crude by clumsy overpainting, his scenes are honest, direct, forthright, and sincere. Further study always reveals what can only be called marvelous hidden harmonies underlying fully integrated compositions. It is almost as if Piero thought out each painting completely and then executed what he saw in his mind's eye. Every detail falls into its necessary place, supporting and subordinated to the whole.

Probably the most striking aspect of Piero's painting is a quality not immediately perceptible, since the underlying unity and harmony of his work is accomplished by means of subtle geometric patterns; abstract shapes — triangles, parallelograms, rhomboids — emerge through the living figures of the surface. These anchor his compositions, creating weight and mass, imparting a solid dignity rivaled only by Masaccio and Castagno. These geometrical patterns contribute to the formal emphasis of his work, giving it almost palpable substance, as if his scenes have more body than real life. It is easy to understand why the abstract painters and formalists of the early twentieth century should have made a hero out of Piero; he anticipated many of their interests.

Other qualities of his work also had to wait until the twentieth century for proper appreciation. Among them is his creation of human characters who, though outwardly commonplace, even crude, are absolutely convincing in their individuality and humanity. For this reason, reproductions of his incidental figures became favorites of painters and art students during the ascendancy of Georges Braque and Pablo Picasso. Still, there are elements in Piero's work that stand independent of such fashionable revivals. The lyricism of his colors, for example, is a pure joy, transcending the accomplishments of everyone before Leonardo da Vinci. Coincident with that is his use of light, especially in the way he combines the two to bring out the solidity and mass of his figures. Finally, there is his use of landscape to integrate the composition of his paintings and to unify them thematically. No one had done this kind of thing before him; no one ever did it better.

Bibliography
Battisti, Eugenio. *Piero della Francesca*. University Park: Pennsylvania State University Press, 1972. This text is the standard academic study of Piero, fully documented, with excellent reproductions, a complete bibliography, and thorough discussions of the paintings and their artistic and historical contexts. The explanations of the paintings are outstanding, particularly because the quality of the plates is so high.
Baxandall, Michael. *Painting and Experience in Fifteenth-Century Italy: A Primer in the Social History of Pictorial Style*. New York: Oxford University Press, 1974. One of the standard reference works for Quattrocento art, this offers a particularly incisive account of Piero's pivotal role in the development of painting. Also contains useful insights into his failure to attract general appreciation until the twentieth century.
Clark, Kenneth. *Piero della Francesca*. New York: Phaidon, 1951. An early account of Piero's work and development, this is perhaps the most accessible study of the paintings. Some of the material and the plates are dated, requiring correction and amplification in later studies.

Gilbert, Creighton. *Change in Piero della Francesca*. Locust Valley, N.Y.: J. J. Augustin, 1968. This is a groundbreaking account of Piero's stylistic development, offering a more thorough technical analysis of his methods than any other source. Some of the arguments seem forced, but in general this is an indispensable work for an appreciation of what Piero really accomplished.

Hartt, Frederick. *History of Italian Renaissance Art: Painting, Architecture, Sculpture*. 3d ed. New York: Harry N. Abrams, 1989. Hartt gives an excellent account of Piero's position in the development of Italian Renaissance art; in short space, he sketches the essential qualities of his work, focusing on formal and thematic integrity. His writing is eminently readable, making this the best available introduction.

Longhi, Roberto. *Piero della Francesca*. 2d ed. Milan, Italy: Hoepli, 1946. One of the first revisionist studies of Piero's formal qualities and of his role in the evolution of Italian painting. It is still vital and convincing, but the reproductions are inferior and many of the interpretations need to be updated

Vasari, Giorgio. *Lives of the Most Eminent Painters, Sculptors, and Architects*. 10 vols. Translated by Gaston du C. De Vere. London: Macmillan and The Medici Society, 1912-1915. In this edition of a famous volume of biographical sketches by a near-contemporary of Piero, Vasari includes many details which would otherwise have been unrecorded; he is thus the source of most of what is known, though much is based on hearsay. Vasari also shows what was thought of Piero during the sixteenth century.

James Livingston

CAMILLE PISSARRO

Born: July 10, 1830; Charlotte Amalie, St. Thomas, Danish West Indies
Died: November 12, 1903; Paris, France
Area of Achievement: Art
Contribution: Pissarro contributed to the formation of Impressionist techniques and thus to the Impressionist movement in France in the last half of the nineteenth century. In addition, he played an instrumental role in establishing a series of exhibitions to promote the work of the Impressionist artists.

Early Life
Born in Charlotte Amalie, the capital of St. Thomas, Jacob Camille Pissarro was the third of four sons of Jewish parents, Frédéric Pissarro and Rachel Manzano-Ponie Petit. His father's family had left Bordeaux, France, in search of a better life and settled on St. Thomas, where they established a family-operated trading store. To his father's displeasure, Camille spent his youthful years roaming the luxurious paths of the island, preferring to sketch and paint rather than work in the family business. At the age of twelve, Camille was sent to school in Passy, a suburb of Paris.

In Passy, the young Pissarro was encouraged by his schoolmaster to nurture his obvious talent, despite explicit instructions from his father that he was to be educated in business. After five years in Passy, his father called him home. The time in France, however, had left its mark on Pissarro. For the next five years, Pissarro preferred to sit by the docks, drawing and sketching the ships, or to hike across the island in search of suitable motifs for his sketchbook. During one of these excursions, he encountered Fritz Melbye, a Danish marine and landscape artist who encouraged Pissarro in developing a method of working outside, "in the fresh air" (*en plein air*), which he continued throughout most of his career. In 1852, the two artists moved to Caracas, Venezuela, where Pissarro remained for two years, painting continuously and interacting with the energetic artistic community in the capital. The years in Venezuela awakened Pissarro to his own ignorance of technique and of new directions then being taken in art. He left for France in 1855, never to see his homeland again.

Pissarro was twenty-five when he arrived in Paris, enthusiastic but naïve and already sporting the full, Old Testament prophet beard for which he became famous among his friends. While attending the Universal Exhibition, he discovered the work of Camille Corot, whose reputation, as both a painter and a teacher, was then at its height. Despite his youth and inexperience, Pissarro managed to show his work to the great master. Corot was favorably impressed, encouraging Pissarro to focus on developing what he termed values, or the harmony between two tones, in his work.

Life's Work

The meeting with Corot in 1855 set Pissarro on a path which he was to follow, with only occasional digressions, for the remainder of his artistic career. Heeding Corot's advice, he began to pay particular attention to the importance of tonal values in creating a truly harmonious work. He practiced a lifelong attention to the importance of drawing, to self-discipline manifested in daily exercising of his craft, to *pleinairisme* ("plain-airism"), to painting what he felt, and to painting not bit by bit but rather working on the whole canvas at once. In all of this he followed the tenets established by Corot. This focus on sensation ultimately became the basis of Pissarro's work.

In 1858, Pissarro moved to Montmorency in order to paint the landscape *en plein air.* This first move to the country announced Pissarro's lifelong struggle to reject the bourgeois oppressiveness of the city in favor of simpler, rural settings. Although later in life he was often to return to Paris, staying in various hotels and painting views of the city from his window, in his early years, he preferred the bucolic setting of the countryside to the bustle of urban life. During his frequent trips to the city, he developed friendships with most of the young avant-garde artists of the time, such as Paul Cézanne and Pierre-Auguste Renoir. Because of his natural ability to offer criticism and guidance without offending the delicate egos of his colleagues, Pissarro quickly became a trustworthy and articulate spokesman for the diverse group of artists soon to be known collectively as the Impressionists.

In 1871, Pissarro married Julie Vellay. Their first of seven children, Lucien, became an accomplished artist in his own right. Although much in love in the early years of their marriage, the couple's constant financial struggles turned Julie into a sharp-tongued, unsupportive partner in later years. From all accounts, except those of Julie, Pissarro was a loving father. Nevertheless, his financial responsibility to his children never deterred him from resolutely continuing his painting even in the worst of times.

Firmly established among the Impressionists in Paris by 1863, Pissarro exhibited three paintings at the Salon des Refusés, an exhibit organized for those artists whose work had been refused by the judges for the official Salon exhibit of that year. The system of exhibitions was tightly regulated at the time by official judges (under the auspices of the emperor himself), who sought to establish national, and thus conservative, tastes in art. The Salon des Refusés was approved by the emperor in response to the artistic outcry against the conservatism of the official Salon art. Here were presented the most revolutionary works of the day. The exhibition drew desultory remarks from critics, derision, and the laughter of incomprehension from the general public. Pissarro's works went virtually unnoticed as all attention was focused on Édouard Manet's scandalous masterpiece, *Luncheon on the Grass* (1863), which depicted a naked female model accompanied on a picnic by two clothed gentlemen.

Infuriated by the public's total disinterest in his work, Pissarro was nevertheless convinced of the rightness of the new direction he was taking with his compatriots. Unlike the realistic artists whose works were being shown in the grand Salons, Pissarro and the other Impressionists sought first to capture the fugitive effects of light on a subject at a particular moment in time. Through the use of bold colors, slashing brushstrokes, and motifs chosen from everyday life, these young iconoclasts attempted to transform on canvas an effect of an impression of reality into a visually more personal, thus in their view more realistic, representation of the world.

By 1874, Pissarro was one of the acknowledged leaders of the Impressionist movement and assisted in organizing An Exhibition of the Society of Painters, Sculptors, Engravers, etc., the first of eight Impressionist exhibitions. The show included the works of Edgar Degas, Claude Monet, Berthe Morisot, Renoir, Alfred Sisley, and Cézanne. Although his work elicited only negative reactions, during the late 1870's and early 1880's he continued to paint in the Impressionist mode, experimenting with colors and different brushstrokes. Gradually he developed a highly personal and easily identifiable style, known as "Pissarro's *tricotage*" (knitting), consisting of parallel cross-hatchings of varying dimensions, which give his work of this period a distinctive sense of movement and textural unity.

Pissarro's art took a dramatic turn in October, 1885, after a meeting with the painter Georges Seurat. Influenced by then-current scientific theories of color and its perception by the human eye, Seurat departed from the Impressionists to develop a pointillist, or divisionist, style of painting using small dots of color rather than brushstrokes. Seurat's neo-Impressionist work announced a dramatically new intent to make visible the subjective rather than, as the Impressionists had sought to do, to make the objective world subjective. Pissarro exhibited his divisionist work alongside that of Seurat in May, 1887, but without success.

Pissarro's neo-Impressionist phase lasted about five years, although strictly pointillist technique distinguishes only part of his work of this period. While his works sold poorly, he made many new friends, particularly among the Symbolist poets and writers who regarded neo-Impressionism as a visual translation of their quest toward verbal fluidity and musicality. He was also developing a strong sense of the social function of art as a supportive statement of the need for societal change, as professed by the active group of anarchists in Paris with whom he was acquainted. Melding politics and aesthetics, his work contains numerous scenes of peasants working cooperatively and serenely in the fields, content in their distance from the harsh realities of industrialization. By the late 1880's, Pissarro had found the divisionist methods tedious and abandoned the technique.

A retrospective exhibit of his work in January, 1892, proved popular with critics and public, particularly a series of landscapes and landmarks painted during a trip to London. All seventy-one works exhibited were sold, finally establishing the artist's commercial success at the age of sixty-two. His continued association with various revolutionary groups resulted in his having to flee to Belgium in 1894. In his final years, however, Pissarro enjoyed the rewards of a lifetime of hard work. Financial security came with an exhibition in 1896 of a series of paintings of the Seine executed in Rouen. Two final series of works, one of the Parisian Grands Boulevards, the other of the Avenue de l'Opéra, capped his career with critical and public acclaim. Having rented in 1900 a small apartment in Paris, he spent his last years focusing his vision on urban motifs: views of the Louvre, the Pont-Neuf, and the Tuileries Gardens. At the age of seventy-three, he developed an abcess of the prostate gland. Having always believed in the country wisdom of homeopathic medicine, he refused the necessary operation and succumbed to septicemia in 1903.

Summary

Camille Pissarro never produced a signature painting which critics regard as his masterpiece. One may speak of a series of masterful works, yet no single work stands clearly above the rest. Perhaps this is true, as one critic has suggested, because Pissarro saw art as "a continual search after the eternally changing." His love of fall and winter scenes—for example, his fascination with light playing on snow-covered hills and streets—led him to paint dozens of canvases of Pontoise and its environs, each distinctive yet most effectively viewed as one part of a corporate vision of the village.

The internal coherence of each painting was supremely important for Pissarro. His son Lucien identified the dominant characteristic as a concern for *les valeurs rapprochées* (closely related values of color). Viewing Pissarro's work over a forty-year period from 1863 to 1903, one notes that while the artist often adjusted his style to his subject, he was always ruled by the immediacy of sensations brought into direct experience with his motif, sensations which he then struggled to order into an "idea of unity." Although his work was generally not appreciated in his own lifetime, critical consensus has established his rightful place among the giants of the Impressionist movement.

Bibliography

Adler, Kathleen. *Camille Pissarro: A Biography*. London: B. T. Batsford, 1978. A short, 190-page biography, which was the first to reconstruct Pissarro's life for the English reader. The work contains numerous illustrations and photographs of the artist and his family. The useful combination of endnotes and bibliography into one document provide the reader with easy access to secondary sources, arranged chronologically.
Lloyd, Christopher, ed. *Studies on Camille Pissarro*. New York: Routledge

and Kegan Paul, 1986. A series of essays covering diverse aspects of Pissarro's life and work, authored by some of the most imminent of modern Pissarro critics. Several previously unexplored aspects of Pissarro's work are examined, such as the link between his political philosophy and his art, and the possible influence of Rembrandt on Pissarro's etchings.

Rewald, John, ed. *Camille Pissarro*. New York: Harry N. Abrams, 1963. Perhaps the best of the relatively few collections of Pissarro's work in print, included in the Library of Great Painters series. A short introduction highlights the principal events in the artist's life and identifies major influences. Historical and aesthetic commentaries accompany each color plate.

Shikes, Ralph E., and Paula Harper. *Pissarro: His Life and Work*. New York: Horizon Press, 1980. A thorough and sensitive rendering of Pissarro's life in the context of his artistic evolution. The work contains twenty-one color plates and black-and-white reproductions. Drawing from material previously unpublished, the authors seek to reveal the complex and contradictory character of the artist. A current bibliography and detailed index assist both the casual and serious reader.

Stone, Irving. *Depths of Glory: A Biographical Novel of Camille Pissarro*. Garden City, N.Y.: Doubleday, 1985. Although a biographical novel, Stone's work scrupulously follows the documented details and spirit of Pissarro's life. A splendid evocation of the times by the author of similar works on the lives of Vincent van Gogh and Michelangelo. The serious reader will not be deterred by the novel's six hundred compellingly written pages.

William C. Griffin

PIUS II
Enea Silvio Piccolomini

Born: October 18, 1405; Corsignano, Republic of Siena
Died: August 14/15, 1464; Ancona
Areas of Achievement: Religion and politics
Contribution: Through his elegant rhetoric and skilled diplomacy, Pius II reconciled differences among Christians to bring some peace to Western Christendom and tried vainly to mobilize a crusade to liberate Constantinople from the Turks.

Early Life

Enea Silvio Piccolomini—better known by the Latin version of his name, Aeneas Silvius Piccolomini—was born in the village of Corsignano (which changed its name to Pienza when its most famous son was elected to the papacy), near Siena, of a noble but poor family. Piccolomini left home to begin his studies at the University of Siena in 1423, but he really began his career in 1431, when he accompanied Domenico Capranica to the Council of Basel. For the next four years, Enea learned his trade, polishing his rhetorical skills in speaking and writing and earning the trust of others, for whom he conducted many diplomatic errands. On one of his missions to Scotland, he fulfilled a vow to walk barefoot for ten miles to a shrine; as a result, he froze his feet so badly that he was a semi-invalid for the rest of his life.

In 1436, he obtained a seat on the Council of Basel, which soon moved to Florence. At Florence he participated in the election of Amadeus VIII of Savoy as Pope Felix V. As ecclesiastical conflicts raged and Felix was declared an antipope, Piccolomini left Rome in 1442 to enter into the diplomatic service of Emperor Frederick III. Welcomed by this Holy Roman Emperor, who promptly named him poet laureate, Piccolomini wrote most of his pagan poetry and prose during this time. Writing in the style of Giovanni Boccaccio's *Decameron: O, Prencipe Galeotto* (1349-1351; *The Decameron*, 1620), Piccolomini wrote a play, *Chrysis* (1444), and a more substantial prose romance, *De duobus amantibus Eurialo et Lucresia* (1444; *The Tale of Two Lovers*, 1560), which endeared him to the literary Humanists of the Italian Renaissance.

All this activity ended, to the skepticism of his peers, when in 1446, Piccolomini announced that he was "forsaking Venus for Bacchus," by which he meant that he was renouncing sexual license for the wine of the Eucharist. He took holy orders as a deacon and was reconciled to the church hierarchy by Pope Eugene IV. After that, ascent was swift. Pope Nicholas V appointed him Bishop of Trieste in 1447 and promoted him to the bishopric of Siena in 1449. Callistus III made him cardinal in 1456. Finally, on August 19, 1458, a sharply divided College of Cardinals looked for a peacemaker and elected

Aeneas Silvius Piccolomini pope; he boldly chose the name of a second century saint, Pius, to be "reminiscent of pious Aeneas."

Life's Work

Pius II faced an enormous challenge. Surrounded on all sides by rivals and enemies, he would need all of his diplomatic skills to play his enemies against one another. From the northeast there was the Papacy's oldest rival, the empire—which people had long since declared to be neither "holy" nor "Roman" nor an "empire," but which remained powerful. Pius relied upon his previously congenial diplomatic service with Frederick to defuse this threat. From the northwest there was the Papacy's most dangerous enemy, the kingdom of France, which nearly fifty years earlier had been forced to give up its Avignon antipope and which, a half century hence, would invade Italy. Pius would fight his fiercest battle with King Louis XI. On the Italian peninsula itself, in the north the commercial city-state republics of Venice, Florence, and others defied papal pretensions; in the south, the shaky throne of Naples was attracting the covetous attention of both Spanish Aragon and French Anjou. Pius could ignore the northern threat; he tried to mediate between the latter claimants. Overriding all other threats for the leader of Western Christendom, however, were two supreme challenges: one from within—conciliarism—and one from without—the calamitous fall of the capital of Eastern Christianity, Constantinople, to the Turks in 1453.

During the first four years of his reign, Pius persuaded France's new king, Louis XI, to withdraw his support for the Pragmatic Sanction in order to gain papal support for the French claim to the kingdom of Naples. This diplomatic coup was designed to nullify simultaneously the conciliarism and the enmity of France. The Pragmatic Sanction of 1438 represented the high point of the conciliar movement, the ecclesiastical movement to subordinate the pope to the church councils. The French kings and most French clergy had supported the sanction because they hated the clerical power of Rome. Pius had inherited his predecessors' policy, which supported the Aragonese claim to Naples, but he suggested to the French king that he could back the Angevin claim in exchange for some concessions. This diplomatic feat was Pius' only political success, and he was unable to capitalize on it.

The diplomatic situation was complicated because there were other players in the game. In fact, Louis' repudiation of the conciliar movement stemmed more from his fear of his own clergy in France (called "Gallicans") than from any foreign policy consideration. The Gallican clergy opposed many aspects of monarchical rule. Louis was also fighting the Burgundian duke who claimed the French throne. Unfortunately, Pius was unable to follow through on his bargain with Louis. Finding that he needed Spanish support for his greater enterprise, the pope was compelled to turn to Burgundy, making concessions which solidified French hostility. The conciliar movement, however, was mortally wounded, and Pius deserves partial credit for administering its *coup de grâce*.

For the last two years of his reign, Pius prepared for the Crusade to liberate Constantinople from the Ottoman Turks. Eight centuries of fighting had culminated in the city's capture only five years before Pius' election. In his eyes, a crusade was essential to vindicate his life, his career, and his faith. At the personal level, a crusade was the only way that Pius could prove to his public, to his skeptical Humanist peers—who were angry at his desertion—and to the anxious religious constituents who were not yet convinced of his piety and faith, that he was what he professed to be: a true Christian. At the political level, this was the best way that Pius could protect the Papacy from its internal enemies. In *Commentarii* (1464; *The Commentaries of Pius II*, 1936-1937), which he wrote in the last years of his life, Pius had four themes, which are largely political. On the Italian peninsula, to recover papal territory and support the anti-French candidate to the throne of Naples, Sigismondo Malasta of Rimini must be fought. On the Continent, the pope must not only curb France but also intervene judiciously in the turmoil of the empire, where Frederick III is embattled. In the moral realm, there is the nonreligious materialism of the Venetians, Florentines, and even Sienese—as dangerous as the outright heresy of the Hussites in Bohemia. Finally, there is the greatest menace of all: the Turk.

Pope Pius' Crusade was a failure. Providentially finding alum mines in Italy to help raise money, he decided to lead the crusade himself. Carried on a litter because of his ruined feet, he embarked on June 18, 1464. Accompanied by a handful of loyal troops from Rome, Pius crossed to the shores of the Adriatic Sea. At the rendezvous, there were virtually no Italians. Louis XI from France did not come or his army; the Aragonese from Spain and Naples, the Burgundians, and Emperor Frederick III did not come. During the night of August 14/15, at Ancona on the Adriatic Sea, far from Constantinople, Pius died.

Summary

The question still lingers: Who was dominant? Aeneas Silvio Piccolomini, Renaissance Humanist and man of letters, or Pope Pius II, Crusader and would-be martyr? The man was not a mystic like Joan of Arc, whose accomplishments and martyrdom streaked across the European landscape when he was in his twenties. He was not a poet or scholar like his idols and peers, whose literary achievements were transforming Europe throughout his lifetime. He was not a charismatic reformer capable of cleansing the Church from the inside. All he had learned from his formal education was to write elegantly and speak persuasively to educated people. All he had inherited from his medieval profession was the desire to protect the papal office and to start a crusade.

History has not remembered either the Humanist or the pope, and scholars who study him in the context of other pursuits have not been kind. In a speech to a group of cardinals, Pius frankly observed that the Europe of his day had rejected the medieval concept of a crusade without having yet awakened to the Turkish threat to Western civilization. When he said this in 1462 (before he was committed to his futile project), he was aware of his own variety of motives, both practical and idealistic. Nevertheless, he did decide to mobilize the gigantic defense operation necessary to save Christian Europe from the Turk—although he did not know how to proceed. All he could manage was to be carried in the direction of the battle and wait for either natural or supernatural intervention. He waited in vain.

What remains, then, are his writings. Although he ranks as a second-rate writer of the Italian Renaissance, being neither as good a storyteller as Boccaccio nor as incisive politically as Niccolò Machiavelli nor as philosophically profound as Giovanni Pico della Mirandola, he was adept enough to rise from poverty in a world of elegant Humanists. In addition, he was concerned enough to perceive that the greatest peril of the day emanated not from antipopes but from materialism in the West and the Turks from the East. He was brave enough to act upon his observations with courage and commitment to the very end.

Bibliography
Ady, Cecilia M. *Pius II (Aeneas Silvius Piccolomini) the Humanist Pope*. London: Methuen, 1913. This older study was written by an authority on late medieval and Renaissance Italy. It is favorable and sympathetic to a man caught in the predicament of being both a Humanist intellectual and a political leader of an institution not respected by Humanist intellectuals. Outdated.
Gragg, Florence A., and Leona C. Gabel. *Memoirs of a Renaissance Pope*. New York: Putnam Publishing Group, 1959. Gragg and Gabel delineate four major themes in the introduction to this abridged translation of *The Commentaries of Pius II*: Italian political conflicts, both between the pope and secular opponents and between two factions for the throne of Naples; France's malevolent presence; the disintegration of the amorphous Holy Roman Empire; and the planned Crusade against the Ottoman Turks, who had conquered Constantinople in 1453.
Rowe, John Gordon. "The Tragedy of Aeneas Silvius Piccolomini," *Church History* 30 (1961): 288-313. A savage critique of the man as a Humanist and as pope. This review is valuable to balance the usually positive view of Pius II. Unless the pope was spectacularly villainous—as many were in this period—most are sympathetically treated by both popular and academic critics. Since the literature in English on Pius is limited, this critique must serve. Ample bibliography.

Woodward, William Harrison. *Vittorino da Feltre and Other Humanist Educators: Essays and Versions*. Cambridge, England: Cambridge University Press, 1897. Woodward devotes most of his attention to Vittorino da Feltre. Although Pius is fitted into his historical context, he is portrayed as not very important. Woodward's pedagogical moralism will strike most students as old-fashioned. No bibliography.

David R. Stevenson

PIUS V
Antonio Ghislieri

Born: January 17, 1504; Bosco, Duchy of Milan
Died: May 1, 1572; Rome
Areas of Achievement: Religion and church reform
Contribution: Pius V effected the reforms dictated by the Council of Trent, attempted to stem the spread of Protestantism, participated in the Inquisition, and was largely responsible for the naval defeat of the Ottoman Empire at Lepanto. His piety, religious zeal, and dedication to the Church eventually resulted in his canonization.

Early Life

Antonio Ghislieri, who would become Pope Pius V, was born in Bosco, a small town near Alessandria, in the Duchy of Milan. His parents, Paolo and Dominica (née Augeria), were poor, and the future pope worked as a shepherd as a youth. Through the generosity of a more prosperous neighbor, he was put under the tutelage of the Dominican friars at Bosco; two years later, at fourteen, he was sent to the Dominican convent at Voghera. After beginning his novitiate at the Convent of Vigevano, he received his Dominican habit in 1520 and assumed his religious name, Michael, the following year. During this time, he developed his scholarly talent and practiced the monastic ideals of austerity, simplicity, and self-denial. His character and conduct as a pope were shaped in large part by his early life in the monastery.

An avid student, Ghislieri attended the University of Bologna, and he later became an equally successful teacher of philosophy and theology, which he taught at several Dominican friaries. In 1528, he was raised to the priesthood at Genoa and for the next several years served at various Dominican convents, where his piety, humility, and dedication won for him the respect of his colleagues—he was elected prior at four of the friaries. During this time, he also became confessor to many important people, among them the Governor of Milan, yet he remained humble and, unlike many of his clerical peers, traveled everywhere by foot.

In 1542, the humble priest's life was changed by an act which ultimately led to his elevation to the Papacy. As a result of religious schism, notably the spread of Martin Luther's doctrine, a papal bill instituted the Roman Inquisition. Because of Ghislieri's skill at refuting the Lutheran "heresies"—he had been summoned to Parma in 1543 to combat Lutheran doctrine and attacks on pontifical authority—he became inquisitor in the diocese of Patvia in 1543. It was his zealous role in the Inquisition that brought him to the attention of church leaders and his eventual election as Pope Pius V.

Life's Work

Although he was almost forty years old when he began his inquisitorial career, Pius' life's work and place in history are inextricably related not only to his pontificate but also to the Inquisition. In the relentless pursuit of his duties, he was often embroiled in disputes with a populace, including clergy, that was sympathetic to Luther. After he confiscated twelve bales of "heretical" books and excommunicated the guilty parties in Como, he barely escaped an enraged crowd. He was vindicated in Rome and as Inquisitor of Bergamo dealt severely with a Luther supporter, Bishop Vittorio Soranzo, who was subsequently imprisoned, convicted, deposed as bishop, and exiled to Venice. In 1551, he became, despite his objections, Prefect of the Palace of the Inquisition, and in 1558 he became the first and the only Grand Inquisitor of the Roman Catholic church. Ecclesiastical advancement accompanied his increasing role in the Inquisition. In 1556, he became Bishop of Sutri and Nepi, then Bishop of Mondovi; in 1557, he was named Cardinal Alessandrino (after the large city near his birthplace). So secure was his position that the 1559 election of Pope Pius IV, which adversely affected other cardinals, left him untouched. In fact, he demonstrated that his principles were more important than politics when he opposed Pius IV's elevation of a relative youngster to a position of authority in the Church.

Upon Pius IV's death, Cardinal Alessandrino became, through the efforts of Cardinal Borromeo, Pope Pius V. While his papacy lasted only six years (1566-1572), he presided over a church under siege from without and undermined from within. The Turks of the Ottoman Empire were a constant threat, and the Reformation sects in Germany, France, England, and the Lowlands were rapidly gaining converts, a disturbing development since church and state were one in the sixteenth century. Unfortunately, the Catholic princes—Philip II of Spain, Maximilian II of Germany, and Sigismund Augustus of Poland—were protective of their own power, unwilling to offend powerful Protestants, or bent on achieving their own ends. Pius also had to contend with clergy who did not share his enthusiasm for the reforms of the recently concluded Council of Trent (1545-1563) and with clergy who had been tainted by Lutheran doctrine.

Pius moved quickly to effect the reforms dictated by the Council of Trent, reforms that were consistent with his monastic life, his idealism, and his piety. During his papacy, the *Catechismus Romanus* (for pastoral use) appeared, the reform of the Breviary was completed, the *Missale Romanum* was printed, and three new masses were composed. Besides the liturgical reforms, he brought about an improvement in public morals in a Rome accustomed to the luxury-loving Renaissance popes. His internal reforms, which can be seen as a Counter-Reformation or reaction to Reformation inroads, can also be regarded as the Church's efforts to reform itself, efforts that had begun before Luther's break with the Church.

In Germany, where the Reformation was solidly established, Pius' efforts to influence Maximilian II (who was also the Holy Roman Emperor) were unsuccessful, for the emperor pursued a policy of conciliating the Catholics without alienating the Protestants. Despite the efforts of Commendone, the pope's nuncio (representative) to Germany, Maximilian was unwilling to move beyond the Augsburg Confession of 1555, which was unacceptable to the pontiff, and the emperor continued to let his Protestant subjects practice their religion. When his numerous concessions to Maximilian proved fruitless, Pius responded with an action that angered the emperor because it encroached on political matters. In an attempt to recapture the ancient rights of papal authority, which had been diminished by his predecessors, Pius crowned Cosimo I as Grand Duke of Tuscany in 1569.

The same erosion of papal authority had occurred in Spain, where Philip II shared Maximilian's concern about the threat to "Caesaropapistical" rights, rights that political rulers had gained at the expense of the Papacy. Philip II was reluctant to have the imprisoned Archbishop Carranza moved to Rome for his heresy trial, and Pius succeeded in moving Carranza only after making financial concessions and conducting protracted negotiations with Philip. Though, like Maximilian II, Philip vowed his support of Pius, the Spanish king was equally reluctant to grant the pope's request that he send his troops to subdue the rebellious Netherlanders. The political/ecclesiastical conflict was heightened by Pius' unpopular papal bull prohibiting bullfighting, but Philip was also guilty of making civil inroads on papal authority. When Pius attempted to curb civil authority in his papal bull of 1568, *In Coena Domini*, Philip essentially ignored it and never really relinquished his regal rights to Pius V.

Even in Poland, a Catholic stronghold, there were problems. Although the Catholics were able to prevail over the Protestants at the 1570 Diet in Warsaw, Pius' nuncio to Poland could not persuade Sigismund Augustus to reform the monasteries or to join the league against the Turkish threat. The Polish monarch's recalcitrance was caused in part by the pope's unwillingness to grant him a divorce from Queen Catherine.

In England, where Henry VIII's divorce had caused a break with Rome, Pius failed in his attempt to return the country to the Catholic faith. Unsuccessful in gaining support for Mary, Queen of Scotland, from Philip or from the Duke of Alba, Pius excommunicated Elizabeth in 1570. His *Regnans in Excelsis*, which also freed Catholics from the obligation to obey her, was countered by Elizabeth's repressive anti-Catholic measures. Elizabeth was the last monarch to be excommunicated by a pope.

Only in the Netherlands and in France did Pius win convincing victories for the Church. Philip finally dispatched the Duke of Alba to crush the revolt in the Netherlands; the duke was only partly successful, and his brutality was notable even when judged by sixteenth century standards. In France, the civil war was ended in 1569 at Jarnac, where the Catholics won a decisive victory.

The pope's greatest achievement, however, was the defeat of the Turkish forces at Lepanto in 1571. Although the Ottoman Empire had invaded Hungary and threatened not only Venice but also Italy, only Pius seemed aware of the danger. Through the pope's negotiating skills and his financial commitment to the cause, Philip was persuaded to join Venice against the Turks. Under the command of Don Juan of Austria, the Christian fleet sailed to battle against the Ottoman forces, which had already overrun Nicosia and Famagusta in Cyprus. The Christian victory at Lepanto marked the high point of Pius' efforts for the Catholic church.

Soon after the battle the pope's health, which had never been good, deteriorated, and he died on May 1, 1572. One hundred years later, Pope Clement X beatified Pius V, and on May 22, 1712, he was canonized by Pope Clement XI.

Summary

The fact that no pope had been canonized in the 350 years that preceded Pius' canonization vividly demonstrates the esteem that he enjoyed within the Catholic church. His efforts to effect the reforms dictated by the Council of Trent, his own monastic piety, his missionary zeal (during his papacy many missionaries were sent to South America, especially Brazil), and his lack of personal ambition—these traits reflect the saintliness of the pope known as "The Pope of the Holy Rosary." History, however, has not been kind to the "Inquisition Pope," whose redemption of Sixtus of Siena must be measured against the strict censorship and the brutal torture of the Inquisition he endorsed and supported.

Pius was motivated by his ambition for the Catholic church, threatened by the Turks and the Protestant Reformers, beset by internal apathy, and undermined by the political ambitions of rulers whose expanding powers eroded traditional papal authority. From the Church's perspective, church and state were the same, and political threats were religious threats (England, the Ottoman Empire, the Protestant German states) that ultimately threatened a civilization synonymous with the Church. Given the besieged condition of such an integrated world, Pius' extreme measures can be understood, if not justified.

The Western world was, however, irrevocably fragmented politically and theologically, and Pius' attempts to return to an earlier unified age were futile. In fact, his efforts to restore lost papal authority were not realistic, given the religious ferment and the political ambitions of rulers. Philip ignored Pius' papal bull of 1568, and Elizabeth's response to her excommunication revealed that weapon to be futile and obsolete. The world was effectively divided between the temporal and spiritual realms, and even the glorious victory at Lepanto was followed by apathy and dissension among the Catholic allies. Although he did not restore the Church's power and did not prevent the spread of Protestantism, Pius did achieve some success at reforming the Church and did enhance the image of the Papacy, which had been in decline.

Bibliography
Antony, C. M. *Saint Pius V: Pope of the Holy Rosary.* New York: Longmans, Green, 1911. A short biography from a Roman Catholic perspective, the book was one of the sources for Browne-Olf's *The Sword of St. Michael* (1943). The book is rich in anecdotes and provides information about the details of the pope's canonization.
Daniel-Rops, H. *The Catholic Reformation.* Translated by John Warrington. New York: E. P. Dutton, 1962. An evenhanded evaluation of Pius that praises his reforms, summarizes his relations with Maximilian and Elizabeth, and discusses his "draconian orders for the hunting down of heresy, free thinking, and the faintest scent of Protestant sympathies." Daniel-Rops describes Pius' outlook as "largely medieval."
Olf, Lillian Browne-. *The Sword of Saint Michael: Saint Pius V, 1504-1572.* Milwaukee: Bruce Publishing Co., 1943. One of the few biographies in English, the book vindicates Pius and suffers from such a Roman Catholic bias that it equates World War II with the Reformation and Adolf Hitler with Martin Luther. Nevertheless, the book is helpful at showing the Reformation in context. Contains a select bibliography.
Seppelt, Francis X., and Clement Löffler. *A Short History of the Popes: Based on the Latest Researches.* St. Louis: B. Herder Book Co., 1932. A short overview of the pope's most important achievements, which are seen as church reform and monastic life. His role in the Inquisition is virtually ignored except for an observation that he could be "harsh and severe when offenses were committed against ecclesiastical discipline."
Von Ranke, Leopold. *The History of the Popes During the Last Four Centuries.* 3 vols. London: G. Bell & Sons, 1913. The first volume contains an overview of Pius from the perspective of a German Protestant. While granting the pope's achievements, the author does portray Pius as an obstinate zealot who insisted on obedience and as a persecutor of innocence and purity. Consequently, Pius' role in the Inquisition is stressed, and his sainthood is not mentioned.
Walsh, William Thomas. *Characters of the Inquisition.* New York: P. J. Kenedy & Sons, 1940. Examines the inquisitorial spirit from the time of Moses to the twentieth century. Walsh focuses on the relationship between Philip and Pius, discusses the Carranza affair, and concludes that Spain ruthlessly trampled on the rights of the Catholic church.

Thomas L. Erskine

PIUS IX
Giovanni Maria Mastai-Ferretti

Born: May 13, 1792; Sinigaglia, Papal States
Died: February 7, 1878; Rome
Area of Achievement: Religion
Contribution: Pius was elected pope in 1846, on the eve of the year of revolutions (1848). His was to be the longest papal reign in history. He led the Church through a difficult period into the era of Italian unity; in spite of the bitter conflict between church and state, he left the Church stronger at his death.

Early Life

Giovanni Maria Mastai-Ferretti was born into a family of lesser nobility in the Marches only a few years before Napoleon I marched into Italy. He studied at Viterbo and at a seminary in Rome, where he developed a vocation for the priesthood. He suffered from epilepsy in his youth and consequently his application for service in the Swiss Guard was refused. He later recovered and was ordained as a priest in 1819. He was sent on a papal mission to Chile (1823-1825), his only experience of foreign travel. He was director of a Roman orphanage, Tata Giovanni, from 1825 to 1827, thereafter serving in the Papal States as Archbishop of Spoleto (1827-1832) and Bishop of Imola (1832-1840). Gregory XVI elevated Mastai-Ferretti to cardinal in 1840. In these early years, Archbishop Mastai-Ferretti gained a deserved reputation as a devoted leader of his flock, and he was remembered with gratitude by his congregations as a man of sincere spiritual humility who set aside time to visit the poor and showed a special devotion to children. He also observed directly the consequences of the reactionary rule of Pope Gregory, and his recognition of the need for reform in the Papal States earned for him the reputation of a liberal.

At Imola, he formed a friendship with the liberal Count Giuseppe Pasolini, who introduced him to Vincenzo Gioberti's *Del primato morale e civile degli Italiani* (1843; of the civic and moral primacy of Italians). Gioberti was a Turinese priest whose earlier enthusiasm for Giuseppe Mazzini's ideas about Italian unity had raised suspicions about his orthodoxy. His thesis was that only the pope had the authority to bring unity to Italy, and the solution to the burning question of the Risorgimento was a federation of states under the presidency of the pope. At this period of Mastai-Ferretti's life, the reformist ideas of Gioberti were appealing, and he took a copy of the book with him when he was summoned to Rome for the conclave upon the death of Gregory XVI in 1846.

Life's Work

Mastai-Ferretti was elected pope on the fourth ballot, on June 16, 1846.

He was the compromise candidate, between a liberal cardinal, to his left, and the former secretary of state to Gregory XVI, the reactionary Luigi Cardinal Lambruschini, to his right. He adopted the name of Pius for his revered Pius VII, once Napoleon's prisoner, who had helped the young Mastai-Ferretti enter the priesthood. Roman and European opinion was ecstatic. A liberal pope had been chosen, and it was widely believed that the days of absolute papal control of the Romagna were numbered.

One of Pius' first acts as pope was to grant amnesty to political prisoners and exiles. He granted freedom of the press, introduced street lighting to Rome, and established a new Roman Council (composed of an overwhelming majority of laymen, many of whom held openly republican views). He finally bent to the temper of the times and conceded a constitution in March, 1848. These reforms, however, were more the result of popular pressure than spontaneous concessions granted freely from above. The new pope was worried that he had unleashed forces beyond his control. When Venice and Milan, followed by Charles Albert of Piedmont, rose against the Austrian occupation, the pope refused to assume the symbolic leadership of the national struggle. In his allocution of April 29, 1848, he stated that, as the vicar of Christ on earth, he would not wage war on another Catholic power. That was the moment when the Papacy and the secular leaders of the Risorgimento parted company.

When the pope's prime minister, Count Pellegrino Rossi, was murdered on November 15, 1848, Pius was forced to flee Rome in disguise and seek asylum in Gaeta under the protection of King Ferdinand of Naples. A republic was declared in Rome, and Mazzini was summoned to lead it, with Giuseppe Garibaldi in charge of the defenses. From Gaeta, the pope appealed to the Catholic powers to overthrow the insurgents, and the French government (under the republican president Louis Napoleon) found itself in the embarrassing position of sending a small force to challenge a sister republic. The Roman republic collapsed in July, 1849, but the pope did not return until the following April.

Henceforth all pretense at accommodation with secular reformers was abandoned. Under the stewardship of the astute secretary of state, Giacomo Cardinal Antonelli, the Papal States prepared for a return to paternalism. The groundwork was laid for a growing conflict between church and state as Charles Albert of Piedmont, under King Victor Emmanuel II of Savoy and his chief minister Count Cavour, assumed the initiative in the final struggle for Italian unity. In Piedmont, the pope had to endure the spectacle of the sequestration of church property, the abolition of religious orders, and the assumption of all educational responsibilities by the state. In Cavour he found a far more formidable adversary than Mazzini and Garibaldi, for Cavour was a brilliant and occasionally unscrupulous politician prepared to impose his will. As the power of the secular state expanded, so papal territory shrank. As the Piedmontese drove the Austrians out of Lombardy in 1859, Cavour sent forces into the Romagna to wrest it from the rule of the Papacy. The loss of the Papal States was a heavy blow, for Pius considered this territory an essential part of the Church's patrimony, granted by God in perpetuity. For Cavour and most Western European leaders, however, the Papal States were a thorn in the side of modern progress, a medieval impediment in the path of the secular future.

In the two decades after 1850, the pope presided over a great international expansion and revival of the Catholic church and the spread of its teachings. In 1864, he published the encyclical *Quanta Cura* along with the Syllabus of Errors, denouncing virtually every social and moral belief that had achieved general acceptance since the French Revolution. The gesture was intended to be an assertion of papal authority in spite of the loss of the Romagna and adjoining territories. Between 1860 and 1870, Rome was defended by French troops provided by Napoleon III, who was acting under pressure from French Catholics; he found himself now in opposition to Charles Albert of Piedmont, whose ambitions he had earlier, as president of a republic rather than emperor, supported. The outbreak of the Franco-Prussian War in July, 1870, however, led to the withdrawal of the French occupational force and the collapse of papal resistance to the government of King Victor Emmanuel. The last obstacle to Italian unity was removed and the pope retreated to the Vatican Palace.

It was Pius who cast himself in the role of "the prisoner of the Vatican," but only after he rejected a generous offer of settlement from the government (the Law of Guarantees). He thus set the pattern for his successors by refusing to come to terms with the secular institutions of power and attempting to persuade Catholics not to participate in the political life of the state. It is not a coincidence that the Vatican Council summoned by Pius in 1869 proclaimed the pope infallible in all declarations on faith and morals in order to regain a hegemony in the spiritual sphere which had been lost in the temporal. Outbreaks of anticlericalism in Europe culminated in the abrogation of the concordat with Austria in 1874, followed by the aggressive anti-Catholic campaign (*Kulturkampf*) launched by Otto von Bismarck in Germany in 1875, which included the expulsion of Jesuits and a dissolution of Catholic schools. In spite of his isolation and doctrinally intransigent stance toward the modern world, Pius retained until the end not only the affection of the faithful but also that of the Roman populace in general, as well as the esteem of his opponents. Pius died peacefully on February 7, 1878.

Summary

While Pius' reign may be viewed as a disaster politically, ecclesiastically it recorded some major successes. Since he was not a skillful diplomat or an experienced politician, these occurred in the area of doctrine. Three events above all stand out. In 1853, Pius set about defining the dogma of the Virginity of Mary. Demands for such a definition were initially received from the lower ranks of the religious orders and the Catholic laity. The pope then requested advice from his bishops, after which the doctrine was defined by a panel of experts. It was the pope himself (who had played an active role in all the proceedings) who read the proclamation at a ceremony in St. Peter's on December 8, 1854.

The Syllabus of Errors—published ten years to the day after the proclamation on Mary—is a trenchant expression of orthodoxy, setting the Church consciously at odds with a heterodox world which it deplores. Eighty propositions are listed and condemned in the syllabus, including pantheism, rationalism, liberalism, socialism, and communism. All the "principles of '89"—the heredity of the French Revolution—that had infiltrated themselves into the myriad struggles for reform in the nineteenth century and had contributed to the secularization of civic life are denounced by the syllabus. The document is above all remembered for its final condemnation of the hope that the Papacy can be reconciled to progress, liberalism, and modern civilization.

A similar theological conservatism is evident in the question of papal infallibility endorsed by the Vatican Council of 1869-1870. The pope was not well served by an unauthorized and imprudent article in a Jesuit publication suggesting that the doctrine would be presented in council and accepted without debate. This was by no means the intention, but it offered an opportunity to anti-Catholic forces to claim that the pope was in the hands of the Jesuits. The result was that the question was debated at inordinate length, but its ultimate ratification by a vast majority of the assembled bishops was a personal triumph for Pius.

Taken together, these three questions of dogma illustrate the major concerns of Pius IX at a time when the Church, under fire from progressive and secular forces, sought to assert doctrinal unity behind the authority of God's appointed vicar on earth in order to keep a hold on the faith of its followers and to lead them into the modern era. Pius himself was not implacably opposed to every aspect of modern life; as pope, however, he saw his first duty as consolidating the power of the Church around the issue of faith and his second as securing a permanent place for the Church among the nation states of the new age.

Bibliography

Corrigan, Raymond. *The Church and The Nineteenth Century.* Milwaukee: Bruce Publishing Co., 1938. A pro-papal view by a Jesuit historian of Pius' career and his struggle with the major historical events of his reign, the challenge of republican and monarchical government. There are separate chapters on the unification of Italy, the doctrine of the Immaculate

Conception, and the Syllabus of Errors.

Hales, E. E. Y. *The Catholic Church in the Modern World*. New York: Hanover House, 1958. Hales returns to the central episodes referred to in his biography, here treated with more specific historical detail and discussion. Chapters 7 through 11 deal with the major themes and struggles of Pius' reign, while his career as a whole is set in the broader history of the Church from the French Revolution to Italian fascism and the postwar democracy.

_____. *Pio Nono*. London: Eyre & Spotiswoode, 1954. The fullest study of the pope's career in English and essential reading for the student or scholar. This is a political biography written as a defense of Pius' position vis-à-vis contemporary liberalism, the Roman republic, and Catholic progressives. Informative on his relations with Cavour, Victor Emmanuel, and Napoleon III.

John, Eric, ed. *The Popes, a Concise Biographical History*. New York: Hawthorn Books, 1964. An encyclopedia of the lives of all the popes, each one written in all essential detail. The tone is pro-Catholic but not unctuous. The section on Pius IX is full, complete, and objective, while presenting an essentially sympathetic portrait of a troubled pontiff.

Kelly, John N. D. *The Oxford Dictionary of Popes*. New York: Oxford University Press, 1986. The pages on Pius are concise and detailed, very clear on the major doctrinal contributions made by Pius to Catholic thinking. A useful introduction which will send students on to the complete biographies.

Rendina, Claudio. *I papi, storia e segreti*. Rome: Newton Compton, 1983. Another encyclopedia of papal biographies, this one written from a more skeptical point of view, underlining occasional scandals within the Papacy and those reactionary positions undertaken by all popes that aroused indignation in the opinion of non-Catholic Europe. Rendina's commentary on Pius IX, as in other cases, is enlivened by quotations from contemporary satirists in verse or prose.

Harry Lawton

FRANCISCO PIZARRO

Born: c. 1495; Trujillo, Spain
Died: June 26, 1541; Lima, Peru
Area of Achievement: Exploration
Contribution: Pizarro was a sixteenth century Spanish conquistador who experienced many frustrating years in the New World in search of fame and fortune before discovering and conquering the Incan Empire of Peru.

Early Life

The details of Francisco Pizarro's early life are not clear. He was probably born around 1495 in Trujillo, a city in the province of Estremadura, Spain, from which came many of the famous conquistadores. Pizarro was one of several illegitimate sons of Gonzalo Pizarro, an infantry officer. His mother, Francisca Morales, was a woman of plebeian origin about whom little is known. He received little attention from his parents and was, apparently, abandoned in his early years. He could neither read nor write, so he became a swineherd and was so destitute that, like the prodigal son, he was reduced to eating the swill thrown out for the pigs. He probably needed little encouragement to abandon this ignoble profession to go to Seville, gateway to the New World and fame and fortune.

The circumstances under which Pizarro made his way across the Atlantic Ocean to the island of Hispaniola in the early years of the sixteenth century are not known. By then in his thirties, Pizarro was in his prime, yet his most productive years lay ahead. Contemporary portraits depict him as tall and well built with broad shoulders and the characteristic forked beard of the period. He possessed a noble countenance, was an expert swordsman, and had great physical strength. In 1510, he joined Alonso de Ojeda's expedition to Uraba in Terra Firma, where, at the new colony of San Sebastian, Pizarro gained knowledge of jungle warfare. When the colony foundered and Ojeda was forced to return for supplies to the islands, Pizarro was left in charge. He remained in the doomed colony for two months before death thinned the ranks sufficiently to allow the survivors to make their way back to civilization on the one remaining vessel. Shortly thereafter, Pizarro entered the service of Vasco Núñez de Balboa and shared in the glory of founding a settlement at Darien and the subsequent discovery of the Pacific Ocean in 1513. Yet when Balboa fell from favor and was accused of treason by the governor of Panama, Pedrarias, Pizarro was the arresting officer. In the service of Pedrarias, there were new adventures, but at an age approaching fifty, old for that day, Pizarro had only a little land and a few Indians to show for his years of labor in the New World.

Life's Work

In 1515, Pizarro crossed the Isthmus and traded with the natives on the

Pacific coast. There he probably heard tales of a mysterious land to the south rich beyond belief in gold and silver. The subsequent exploits of Hernán Cortés in 1519-1521 and an expedition by Pascual de Andagoya in 1522, which brought news of wealthy kingdoms, gave impetus to further exploration and greatly excited the cupidity of the Spaniards. To finance an expedition, Pizarro formed a business triumvirate with Diego de Almagro, a solider of fortune, and Hernando de Luque, a learned ecclesiastic.

Pizarro's first foray, launched in December, 1524, took him down the coast of modern Colombia, where he encountered every hardship imaginable and soon returned quietly to Panama. Under the guidance of Bartolomé Ruiz, a famous navigator and explorer, Pizarro's second expedition set sail in early 1526. The voyage took them beyond modern-day Ecuador into the waters south of the equator, where they found evidence of an advanced Indian civilization. An inadequate number of men, dwindling provisions, and hostile natives forced Pizarro and part of the company to take refuge first on the island of Gallo and later on Gorgona while Almagro returned to Panama to seek assistance. The governor, however, refused further help and sent a ship to collect the survivors. Audaciously, Pizarro and thirteen others refused to return. They endured seven months of starvation, foul weather, and ravenous insects until Almagro returned with provisions and the expedition was resumed. At length, they discovered the great and wealthy Incan city of Tumbes on the fringes of the Peruvian Empire. After a cordial stay with the natives, Pizarro returned to Panama with some gold, llamas, and Indians to gain support for an ever greater expedition. The governor remained uninterested, so the business partners decided to send Pizarro to Spain to plead their case.

Charles V and his queen were sufficiently impressed with Pizarro's exploits and gifts to underwrite another expedition. In July, 1529, Pizarro was given extensive powers and privileges in the new lands, among them the titles of governor and captain-general with a generous salary. Almagro received substantially less, which caused a rift between the two friends. Before leaving Spain, Pizarro recruited his four brothers from Estremadura for the adventures ahead.

In January, 1531, Pizarro embarked on his third and last expedition to Peru. With no more than 180 men and three vessels, the expedition charted a course to Tumbes, which, because of a great civil war in the country, they found much less hospitable. Even so, the Spaniards' arrival was fortuitous in that the victor, Atahualpa, had not yet consolidated his conquests and was now recuperating at the ancient city of Cajamarca. In September, 1532, Pizarro began his march into the heart of the Incan Empire. After a difficult trek through the Andes, during which they encountered little resistance, they entered Cajamarca on November 15, 1532. Finding the Incan king at rest with only a portion of his army, Pizarro, pretending friendship, seized Atahualpa after a great slaughter of Indians. Atahualpa struck a bargain with his captors. In return for his release, he promised to fill a large room with gold. A second, smaller room was to be filled with silver. Fearing revolt, however, the captors carried out a summary trial, and the Inca was condemned to death.

Meanwhile, Almagro and his men had arrived in February, 1533, and loudly demanded a share of the wealth. The gold and silver vessels were melted down and distributed among the conquerors, while Almagro's men received a lesser amount and the promise of riches to come. Hernando Pizarro, Francisco's only legitimate brother, was sent to Spain with the royal one-fifth portion. From Cajamarca, Pizarro and his company pushed on to Cuzco. After encountering some resistance in the coutryside, the conquistadores entered the city on November 15, 1533, where the scenes of rapine were repeated again.

After the conquest of Cuzco, Pizarro settled down to consolidate and rule his new dominion, now given legitimacy and the name of New Castile in royal documents brought back from Spain by Hernando Pizarro. A new Inca, Manco Capac II, was placed on the throne, and a municipal government was organized after the fashion of those in Iberia. Most of Pizarro's time, however, was consumed with the founding of a new capital, Lima, which was closer to the coast and had greater economic potential. These were difficult years. In 1536, the Manco Capac grew tired of his ignominious status as a puppet emperor and led the Peruvians in a great revolt. For more than a year, the Incas besieged Cuzco. After great loss of life and much destruction throughout the country, the siege ended, although the Incas would remain restive for most of the sixteenth century.

In the meantime, a power struggle had developed between Almagro, who had returned from a fruitless expedition into New Toledo, the lands assigned him by the Crown, and Pizarro for control of Cuzco. On April 6, 1538, Almagro's forces were defeated in a great battle at Las Salinas. Almagro was condemned to death. In the three years that followed, Pizarro became something of a tyrant. On June 26, 1541, the Almagrists broke into Pizarro's palace in Lima and slew the venturesome conquistador.

Summary

There are, perhaps, two possible ways in which the career of Francisco Pizarro might be evaluated. On the one hand, it is easy to regard him as one of many sixteenth century Spaniards, called conquistadores, whose cupidity sent them in search of fame and fortune, specifically gold and silver, in the New World. In a relatively short period of time, Incas everywhere were conquered, tortured, murdered, and systematically stripped of their lands, families, and provisions. Pizarro played a major role in the rapacious conduct of the Castilians. Although this view is not without some merit, it must be understood within the context of Pizarro's world. He was not unlike a medieval crusader who sallied forth against the enemy with the blessings of Crown and Church. The Crown was interested in precious metals and new territorial possessions, while the Church was concerned about lost souls. When his opportunity for fame and fortune finally presented itself, Pizarro had to overcome seemingly insurmountable odds—financial difficulties, hostile natives, harsh weather and terrain, and later the enmity of other conquistadores—to create a Spanish empire in South America. Although his methods cannot be condoned, the empires of Alexander the Great, Charlemagne, and other conquerors were fashioned in much the same way.

Bibliography

Birney, Hoffman. *Brothers of Doom: The Story of the Pizarros of Peru*. New York: G. P. Putnam's Sons, 1942. A well-written study of Pizarro and his brothers from the opening of the age of exploration to the death of Gonzalo Pizarro in 1548. The author purposely eschews footnotes and lengthy bibliographical references. A good introductory work.

Hemming, John. *The Conquest of the Incas*. New York: Harcourt Brace Jovanovich, 1970. A history of the conquest from Balboa's discovery of the Pacific Ocean in 1513 through the disintegration of the Inca Empire, with reference to the life of Pizarro. Includes chronological and genealogical tables plus an excellent bibliography.

Howard, Cecil, and J. H. Perry. *Pizarro and the Conquest of Peru*. New York: American Heritage, 1968. A well-illustrated history of the conquest and the civil wars which followed. Excellent for a younger reading audience.

Kirkpatrick, F. A. *The Spanish Conquistadores*. London: Adam & Charles Black, 1934, 2d ed. 1946. A survey of Spanish exploration, conquest, and settlement of the New World beginning with the voyages of Christopher Columbus. Provides a good overview of Pizarro's career.

Means, Philip Ainsworth. *Fall of the Inca Empire and the Spanish Rule in Peru: 1530-1780*. New York: Charles Scribner's Sons, 1932. A history of the last years of the Inca Empire and Spanish dominion to 1780. Most of the important events of Pizarro's life are mentioned. Includes a scholarly bibliography plus a helpful index and glossary.

Prescott, William H. *The Conquest of Peru*. Revised with an introduction by Victor W. von Hagen. New York: New American Library, 1961. After more than a century and many editions, still one of the best works on the subject. Prescott's style will appeal to readers at all levels.

Larry W. Usilton

KONSTANTIN PETROVICH POBEDONOSTSEV

Born: May 21, 1829; Moscow, Russia
Died: March 23, 1907; St. Petersburg, Russia
Areas of Achievement: Government and politics
Contribution: As Director General of the Holy Synod and tutor to Czars
  Alexander III and Nicholas II, Pobedonostsev was a major contributor to
  the preservation of the autocratic governmental system in Russia against
  the forces of modernization.

Early Life

Konstantin Petrovich Pobedonostsev was born in Moscow, one of eleven
children. His father, son of a Russian Orthodox priest and trained for the
priesthood, became instead a professor of rhetoric and Russian literature at
the University of Moscow. Little is known about Konstantin's mother, except that she was a descendant of an old-service noble family from near Ko-
stroma. Konstantin, educated at home by his father, entered the School of
Jurisprudence in St. Petersburg at thirteen; the school prepared him and
others from gentry families for service in law courts and the judicial and
legal branches of the imperial bureaucracy. Pobedonostsev spoke, read, and
wrote in seven foreign languages and read widely throughout his life in the
classics and in Russian and Western history and literature. While he believed
that an educated Russia must give special attention to Western Europe and
its achievements, there remained a basic tension in him throughout his life
between a fascination with European ideas and a growing admiration for
Russian traditions and institutions.

Upon graduation in 1846, Pobedonostsev returned to Moscow as a law
clerk in the eighth department of the senate. Established by Peter the Great
as the highest state institution to supervise all judicial, financial, and administrative affairs, by the nineteenth century the senate had evolved into the
supreme court for judicial affairs and appeals against administrative acts of
the government. Pobedonostsev's rise in senate employment was rapid and
steady. By 1853, he was secretary of the seventh department; in 1857 he
became secretary to both the seventh and eighth departments; and by 1863 he
was named executive secretary of the eighth department.

His education and training in the senate, along with his numerous publications, singled him out as an unusually promising young scholar, teacher (he
was appointed lecturer in Russian civil law at the University of Moscow in
1859), and administrator. As the government of Alexander II struggled with
reforms following Russia's defeat in the Crimean War of 1853-1856, Pobedonostsev's work singled him out as one who could make an important
contribution. The reforming decade of the 1860's was a turning point in both
Pobedonostsev's career and his thinking.

Life's Work

In 1861, Pobedonostsev was appointed tutor in Russian history and law for the heir to the throne, Nicholas Alexandrovich. Upon the death of Nicholas from tuberculosis in 1865, Pobedonostsev continued as tutor for the new heir, the future Alexander III. This appointment was a key one in Pobedonostsev's life, removing him from the study and classroom and placing him in a position from which he would eventually exercise a profound influence on the course of late nineteenth century Russian history.

From 1866 to 1880, Pobedonostsev's rise through the bureaucracy continued to be steady and rapid. In 1868, he was named a senator, and in 1872 he was appointed a member of the Council of State, the major advisory body to the czar on projected laws and administration of the non-Russian areas of the empire. In April, 1880, he was appointed Director General of the Holy Synod. The synod, also established by Peter the Great, replaced the patriarch as head of the Russian Orthodox church and was one of the most important branches of the central government. As director general, a position he would hold for the next twenty-five years, Pobedonostsev was the czar's representative to this ruling body of the state church. Through this position, Pobedonostsev came to wield considerable influence over such aspects of government policy as education, access to information, social legislation, and civil rights.

The decade of the 1860's, associated with the Great Reforms of Alexander II, was an exhilarating time, but it proved to be the last time the autocratic system attempted to reform itself. While the reconstruction of society was concerned mainly with the emancipation of the serfs, most state institutions were subjected to intense scrutiny that resulted in various degrees of reorganization. Pobedonostsev's numerous studies advocating reform of the judicial system resulted in his appointment to work on the draft of the judicial reform of 1864.

While these early years might be termed his "liberal" period, the Polish uprising of 1863 and the resulting revolutionary unrest in Russia's major cities and towns came as a deep shock. Pobedonostsev began to turn against the introduction of new ideas and institutions, arguing instead that what Russia needed was more, not less, government control and supervision. His scholarly interests soon reflected this overall change in his outlook. Whereas up to 1864 his research reflected a certain criticism of some of Russia's central institutions, Pobedonostsev now devoted more time to the study of Russian civil law. His research resulted in the publication of his most important work, the three-volume *Kurs grazhdanskago prava* (1868-1880; course on civil law), which won for him high repute as a legal scholar. At the same time, Pobedonostsev became increasingly vocal in his belief that Russia must rely on its traditional values and institutions and reject the importation of alien ideas.

The rise of the revolutionary movement, culminating in the assassination of Alexander II in 1881, turned many in government and society against his policies of reform. Pobedonostsev was among those who saw liberalism as a fundamental threat to the principle of autocratic government and advised Alexander III that the czar's duty was to protect his people from the projects of constitutional reform associated with the last years of his father's reign. It was Pobedonostsev who drafted the famous manifesto of April 19, 1881, that ended all serious consideration of political reform in Russia for the next generation. From then on, the tall, thin, balding Pobedonostsev, peering out at the world from behind small, wire-rimmed glasses, was associated with the reactionary policies linked to the reign of Alexander III. His appointment as tutor to the future Nicholas II ensured that the autocratic system would not adjust itself to the new social and political movements of the day.

Pobedonostsev's political philosophy was spelled out coherently and succinctly in his most famous book, the collection of essays entitled *Moskovskii sbornik* (1896; *Reflections of a Russian Statesman*, 1898). Like many reactionary philosophers before and after him, Pobedonostsev vilified human nature as evil, worthless, and rebellious. Therefore, he believed that those who advocated reason instead of faith as the proper guide for human actions were fundamentally wrong. The enormous size of Russia, plus its complex national composition and the ignorance and economic backwardness of its peasantry, all pointed to the folly of introducing any concept of responsible government, freedom of the press, secular education, or laissez-faire economics. Instead, Pobedonostsev believed, society should be based on those traditional values and institutions that had shaped its character over the centuries. Thus Pobedonostsev, although widely read in European and American social and political literature, opposed any and all arguments for their application in the case of Russia.

There was a basic inconsistency in Pobedonostsev's thinking which can best be seen in his attitude toward Russia's minority peoples and religions. While he always insisted that the human being was a product of a historical tradition, Pobedonostsev refused to Russia's minorities the right to defend their cultural and historical form of life against the encroachments and bureaucratic enactments of the Russian state. In this case, he was more interested in the stability and extension of the autocratic system and argued continuously in support of those Russification policies that so alienated the minorities in the empire.

The revolution of 1905 overthrew autocratic government in Russia and established a constitutional monarchy with civil liberties and an extended franchise for a new legislative assembly. Pobedonostsev played no role in this crisis. The results of the revolution, by introducing institutions and values he had consistently resisted, merely confirmed his pessimism about human nature and the future of Russia. In October, 1905, he retired quietly from his position as Director General of the Holy Synod. While he remained on the Council of State, he no longer played a role in government. His last days, filled with illness, were passed quietly in his residence, working on his ongoing project of translating the Bible into Russian. It was there that he died in 1907. He was buried with little fanfare in the garden of Saint Vladimir's, a finishing school for young women planning to marry priests and work in parish schools.

Summary

Konstantin Petrovich Pobedonostsev is an excellent example of the conservative bureaucratic statesman associated with the reigns of the last two czars of Russia. Convinced as he was of the evil and weak nature of human beings, Pobedonostsev believed that the only institutions that might save the Russian people were the state, the Orthodox church, and the family. Of these he believed the state was central. These beliefs were used to justify his support for arbitrary and authoritarian government. Thus, in facing the momentous changes engulfing Western civilization in the late nineteenth century, Pobedonostsev set himself squarely against them all in the name of Russia's traditional values and institutions.

Since Pobedonostsev believed that a people's educational system reflected their society, it is not surprising that he had a deep interest in the educational policies of the empire. He believed that the educational system must remain firmly under the control of the autocratic system and the state church. The system he envisioned had as its first priority the instillation of a firm religious foundation in its students, along with an emphasis on patriotism and love of autocracy. Pobedonostsev bears considerable responsibility for the ruling that kept Russian higher education in shackles until the 1905 revolution restored some semblance of autonomy.

While he was suspicious of higher education as destabilizing for society, Pobedonostsev emphasized the role of the parish school as best suited to serve the interests of order. During his years as Director General of the Holy Synod, he was instrumental in allocating resources to develop the parish school system throughout the country. By 1900, half of all elementary schools were under the control of the synod, while slightly more than a third of all children receiving primary education were enrolled in parish schools, wherein they were taught the proper values of an autocratic society.

As tutor to the last two czars and as Director General of the Holy Synod for twenty-five years, Pobedonostsev was in a position to wield considerable influence on late imperial Russia. His opposition to all elements of liberalism and his support for the Russification of the national minorities made him, in the popular eye, the "grey eminence" behind the reign of Alexander III. Thus Pobedonostsev contributed to those policies that eventually caused a revolution that destroyed the entire imperial order.

Bibliography

Adams, Arthur E. "Pobedonostsev's Religious Politics." *Church History* 22 (1953): 314-326. Pobedonostsev subordinated the Orthodox church to the state in the name of political stability and state security. His efforts to strengthen and to extend Orthodoxy into the non-Russian provinces and among heretics and dissenters was motivated not by a desire to save souls but by a desire to preserve the Russian Empire.

_____. "Pobedonostsev's Thought Control." *The Russian Review* 11 (1953): 241-246. In his effort to control Russia's thought, Pobedonostsev used his official position in the state and Church to persecute those whom he found dangerous to the stability of the system and to promote the careers of those whose views were in harmony with his own.

Byrnes, Robert F. "Dostoevsky and Pobedonostsev." In *Essays in Russian and Soviet History,* edited by John Shelton Curtiss. New York: Columbia University Press, 1962. Explores the close relationship between Pobedonostsev and Fyodor Dostoevski during the decade of the 1870's. While Soviet historians have argued that Dostoevski was influenced greatly by Pobedonostsev, especially in the writing of his later novels, evidence indicates this was not so.

_____. *Pobedonostsev: His Life and Thought.* Bloomington: Indiana University Press, 1968. A standard biography, presenting an account of Pobedonostsev's life along with a discussion and analysis of his major writings and sociopolitical philosophy. Emphasizes his conservatism and his influence both at court and through the Holy Synod to maintain order and stability within the empire.

_____. "Pobedonostsev on the Instruments of Russian Government." In *Continuity and Change in Russian and Soviet Thought,* edited by Ernest J. Simmons. Cambridge, Mass.: Harvard University Press, 1955. Analyzes Pobedonostsev's political philosophy, emphasizing his view that the duty of absolute government was to distinguish between right and wrong, good and evil, and to ensure social stability. The character of the state was formed by its national religious faith and its traditional political and social institutions.

Pobedonostsev, Konstantin P. *Reflections of a Russian Statesman.* Translated by Robert Crozier Long. London: G. Richards, 1898. Reprint. Ann Arbor: University of Michigan Press, 1965. An eloquent and readable plea in support of the values and institutions of traditional Russia. Expounds Pobedonostsev's belief in the evil and perverse nature of the human being and his social philosophy of stability and order through autocratic government and the Orthodox church.

Thaden, Edward C. *Conservative Nationalism in Nineteenth Century Russia.* Seattle: University of Washington Press, 1964. Chapter 13, entitled "Bureaucratic Nationalism," discusses Pobedonostsev's thought and contri-

bution to Russification policies toward the national and religious minorities in the empire. In support of these policies, Pobedonostsev was not
averse to the use of the power of the state to educate and coerce or to the
use of the parish schools to indoctrinate youth in the values of traditional
Russia.

Jack M. Lauber

POGGIO

Born: February 11, 1380; Terranuova, near Arezzo
Died: October 30, 1459; Florence
Area of Achievement: Literature
Contribution: Through his tireless efforts, Poggio discovered and copied manuscripts of classical Latin authors that had been lost for centuries and which, if not for him, might have remained lost forever.

Early Life

Giovanni Francesco Poggio Bracciolini, better known as Poggio, was born in Terranuova, part of the Republic of Florence, in 1380. He received his earliest education in nearby Arezzo, but at the age of sixteen or seventeen moved to Florence to complete his studies and train for the profession of notary. He was taught Latin by John of Ravenna and may have been a student in Greek under Manuel Chrysoloras, although this is disputable because Poggio never gained mastery of Greek. Since he was from a poor family, Poggio copied manuscripts for the book trade to support himself in these endeavors in Florence.

Poggio's knowledge of Latin caught the attention of Coluccio Salutati, a student of Petrarch and Florence's first Humanist chancellor. It was probably at this time that Salutati nurtured in the young Poggio a love for the classics and the determination to search for lost manuscripts. Also at this time, Poggio met and became a close friend of Niccolò Niccoli, a wealthy Florentine with whom he shared a lifelong passion for classical artifacts and classical manuscripts. These two men, along with Leonardo Bruni, Ambrogio Traversari, and Leon Battista Alberti, carried on the intellectual movement begun by Petrarch in the late 1300's and continued by Salutati in the early 1400's.

In 1403, Poggio entered the Papal Curia as a *scriptor* (scribe). He soon advanced to the post of apostolic secretary and, except for an unhappy interlude from 1418 to 1422, when he served Henry Beaufort, Bishop of Winchester, in England, spent the next fifty years in service to five different popes.

During the early years of his career in the Curia, Poggio developed the Humanist style of writing. The letters of this hand, simpler and rounder in formation and easier to read than Gothic, directly imitated the Carolingian script of the eleventh century. The earliest example of Humanist script is in a manuscript of Cicero's letters to Titus Pomponius Atticus in Poggio's own hand and dated 1408.

Life's Work

Poggio's main interest throughout his lifetime was in the area of classical studies—including archaeology, architecture, coins, epigraphy, and statues, as well as manuscripts. Upon entering Rome for the first time in 1403, Poggio was struck by the decay of the once-noble city. He was the first to use a truly scientific approach to the study of the city's ruins. Comparing the sights with descriptions from Livy (Titus Livius), Marcus Vitruvius Pollio, and Sextus Julius Frontinus, Poggio was able to catalog in part the remains of ancient Rome. He accurately assigned to the Republican era a bridge, an arch, a tomb, and a temple. Among the buildings dating to the Empire, he described several temples, two theaters (including the theater of Pompey the Great), the Colosseum, the Column of Trajan, and the mausoleums of the emperors Augustus and Hadrian. His treatise, *De varietate fortunae* (1431-1438; on the vicissitude of fortune), is the most important document for the physical state of Rome in the fifteenth century. Many artifacts which he discovered on his travels were used to decorate his villa outside Florence.

Poggio's most significant contribution to classical scholarship came in the area of ancient manuscripts. It is reported that as early as 1407 Poggio was in the monastery of Monte Cassino looking for lost texts. The Council of Constance in 1414, however, opened up the monastic libraries of the transalpine countries to Italian scholars. The council meetings, designed to establish one single pope in Rome, afforded the apostolic secretary much leisure time in which to explore the monasteries in search of ancient Latin manuscripts.

From 1415 to 1417, Poggio made his most important and most numerous discoveries in the monasteries of France, Germany, and Switzerland. In 1415, at Cluny, Poggio unearthed two previously unknown orations of Cicero. At Saint Gall the next year came his astounding discovery of the entire *Institutio oratoria* (c. A.D. 95; *On the Education of an Orator*, better known as *Institutio oratoria*) by Quintilian, which had previously been known only from a mutilated copy found in Florence by Petrarch in 1350. In the same expedition, Poggio also found most of the first half of Gaius Valerius Flaccus' *Argonautica* (c. A.D. 90) and a ninth century manuscript of Asconius Pedianus' commentaries on Cicero's orations. On other trips in 1417 he unearthed Sextus Pompeius Festus' *De significatu verborum* (second or third century A.D.), Lucretius' *De rerum natura* (c. 60 B.C.; *On the Nature of Things*), Marcus Manilius' *Astronomica* (c. A.D. 14-27), Silius Italicus' *Punica* (first century A.D.), Ammianus Marcellinus' *Res gestae* (c. A.D. 378), Apicius' *De re coquinaria* (late fourth century A.D.; *The Roman Cookery Book*, 1817), and Statius' *Silvae* (c. A.D. 91-95). Also in 1417, Poggio found a manuscript of Cicero's oration on behalf of Caecina, a Roman general.

After his reinstatement as secretary in the Papal Curia in 1423, Poggio brought to light manuscripts of Sextus Julius Frontinus' *De aquaeductibus* (c. A.D. 97) and Firmicus Maternus' *Matheseos libri* (c. A.D. 354). Other ancient authors rediscovered by Poggio included Columella, Vitruvius Pollio, Nonius Marcellus, Marcus Valerius Probus, and Eutyches. In Poggio's mind, the end justified the means, and he was not above stealing to appropriate manuscripts, as he makes clear in his letters.

Poggio is not without his critics in the area of manuscripts. The seeker of lost texts was not especially careful with his discoveries after he had copied them, and many of his manuscripts disappeared shortly after they were found. Manilius' *Argonautica* was copied, then the original was lost. Asconius Pedianus is only preserved in copies made from the manuscript found by Poggio. The codex of Gaius Valerius Flaccus disappeared shortly after it was copied, and Cicero's work on the comedian Quintius Roscius is known only from an apograph of the recovered text. This carelessness has caused great anguish, even anger, among modern paleographers and textual critics who are more interested in the contents of ninth century texts than they are in Poggio's fifteenth century copy.

Poggio's own writings reveal a multitude of interests and range from moral dialogues to indecent satires on clergy and friars. Two of his more important moral essays are *De avaritia* (1428-1429; on greed) and *De varietate fortunae*. *Facetiae* (1438-1452; *The Fables of Poge the Florentyn*, 1484, 1879) paints humorous, often obscene, vignettes of priests, monks, and rival Humanists. Of most historical value are Poggio's letters, published in three separate works. Addressed to 172 correspondents, the nearly six hundred epistles reveal not only Poggio's own life but also the activities of a number of popes and various rulers throughout Europe, and especially in Italy.

In 1435, at the age of fifty-five, Poggio married the eighteen-year-old Vaggia Buondelmonti. He seems to have been quite happy with his well-born bride, even though the marriage forced him to forsake his mistress, with whom he had had fourteen children. In 1453, he left the papal court to become Chancellor of Florence and devoted the rest of his life to continuing Leonardo Bruni's *Historiarum Florentini populi* (c. 1415; history of the Florentine republic). Poggio died in 1459 and was buried in the Church of Santa Croce, where a statue by the artist Donatello commemorates him.

Summary

Poggio's contribution to classical studies is threefold. His development of the Humanist script, which was refined by the succeeding generation of scribes, became the prototype for the Roman font when the art of printing was introduced into Italy from Germany. The Roman type, which was easier to read, gradually supplanted the Gothic. Because of Poggio's calligraphic efforts, books became more legible. His collection of Latin inscriptions, which he compiled in 1429, evolved over centuries into the modern *Corpus inscriptionum Latinarum*, an ongoing reference work listing all known Latin inscriptions. This reference work provides Latin linguists, Roman historians, Latin philologists, and other scholars with crucial information about early, even pre-Republican, Rome.

Poggio's most lasting achievements, however, lie in the area of manuscript recovery. Petrarch, initiating the intellectual movement called Humanism, had begun the efforts to find and copy ancient texts, and his work had been carried on by Giovanni Boccaccio. In the next generation, Salutati, who espoused the same philosophy of the importance of the classics, continued their work. In addition, he transmitted his beliefs to a number of his most gifted students, Poggio among them.

Poggio, however, eclipsed both predecessors and contemporaries in the amount and importance of his discoveries. In continuing activities begun by Petrarch, he was advancing the Humanist movement, but, more important, he preserved for posterity classical works which might have disappeared forever. Although succeeding centuries have produced far fewer revelations of ancient manuscripts, scholars continue to devote their lives to searching for lost texts. It is in part because of Poggio's successes that they do so.

Bibliography
Baron, Hans. *The Crisis of the Early Italian Renaissance: Civic Humanism and Republican Liberty in an Age of Classicism and Tyranny.* 2 vols. Princeton, N.J.: Princeton University Press, 1955. Still-useful portrayal of the political, intellectual, and cultural atmosphere of the early 1400's. Includes exhaustive notes probably useful only to the advanced reader.
Bracciolini, Poggio. *Two Renaissance Book Hunters: The Letters of Poggius Bracciolini to Nicolaus de Niccolis.* Edited by Phyllis Walter Goodhart Gordon. New York: Columbia University Press, 1974. This English translation of the Latin reveals Poggio's excitement and problems at finding and copying old manuscripts. The introduction chronicles Poggio's life. Includes copious notes (though in places incorrect) and an extensive bibliography.
Holmes, George. *The Florentine Enlightenment: 1400-50.* New York: Pegasus, 1969. The author, writing in a straightforward style, provides a clear picture of the social, political, and religious atmosphere of Florence before, during, and after Poggio's time. There is no bibliography, and the footnotes are of limited help. Illustrated.
Salemi, Joseph S., trans. "Selections from the *Facetiae* of Poggio Bracciolini." *Allegorica* 8 (1983): 77-183. Published in a bilingual format, this study is a translation of forty of Poggio's fables, as well as the introduction and conclusion. Provides insight into Poggio's cynical view toward most of humanity. The footnotes are helpful. Illustrated.
Symonds, John Addington. *Renaissance in Italy, Part II: The Revival of Learning.* New York: Henry Holt, 1881. The research is dated, but the lively anecdotes of Poggio's feuds will entertain and educate.
Trinkhaus, Charles. *The Scope of Renaissance Humanism.* Ann Arbor: University of Michigan Press, 1983. Contains a careful survey of Humanists,

how they interacted, and what they contributed. The abundant notes, often in a foreign language, will be useful mainly to the advanced reader.

Ullman, Berthold L. *Ancient Writing and Its Influence*. New York: Cooper Square Publishers, 1963. Ullman discusses Poggio only as the developer of the Humanistic script, but the photograph of a manuscript in Poggio's own hand makes the book worthwhile.

Joan E. Carr

HENRI POINCARÉ

Born: April 29, 1854; Nancy, France
Died: July 17, 1912; Paris, France
Areas of Achievement: Mathematics and physics
Contribution: Poincaré was one of the most important mathematicians of the late nineteenth century. He developed the theory of automorphic functions (a method for expressing functions in terms of parameters), did extensive work in celestial mechanics and mathematical physics, was a codiscoverer of the special theory of relativity, and his writing style was so clear that he wrote books about the philosophy of science that were read widely by the general public and translated into many languages.

Early Life

Henri Poincaré was born April 29, 1854, to one of the most distinguished families of Lorraine. His father, Leon, was a physician, and one of his cousins, Raymond, became President of the French Republic during World War I. Henri and his sister were adored by their mother, and she devoted herself to their education and rearing. When he was five, Henri contracted diphtheria, and the resulting weakness may have influenced his entire life. Since he was unable to join the other boys in their rough play, Henri was forced to entertain himself with intellectual pursuits. He developed a remarkable memory so that he could even cite page numbers for information in books that he had read many years earlier. In addition, because his eyesight was very poor, he learned most of his classwork by listening, since he could not see the blackboard. Thus, he was forced to develop the ability to see spatial relationships in his mind at an early age.

Although he was a good student in his early years, there was no indication of his impending greatness until he was a teenager. He won first prize in a French national competition and in 1873 entered the École Polytechnique, where he exhibited his brilliance in mathematics. Upon his graduation, Poincaré entered the École des Mines in 1875 to study engineering. Although he was a careful student, who did his work adequately, Poincaré spent much of his time pursuing mathematics as a recreation. He continued his practice of mathematics during his apprenticeship as a mining engineer.

Poincaré was not an extremely attractive man; he had thinning blond hair, wore glasses, and was short in stature; he was known for being absent-minded and clumsy. Nevertheless, he maintained a happy personal life. He married at age twenty-seven, fathered four children, whom he adored, and never wanted for friends, because he was by nature humble and interested in other people.

Life's Work

In 1879, Poincaré submitted the doctoral thesis in mathematics that he had written during his work as an engineer, and he received his degree that same year. The subject was the first of his great achievements: the theory of differential equations. His first appointment was as a lecturer of mathematical analysis at the University of Caen in 1879, and in 1881 he was invited to join the faculty at the University of Paris. He continued this appointment until his death in 1912, although by then his responsibilities had expanded to include mechanics and physics.

During his tenure, he was elected to the Académie des Sciences in 1887 and the Académie Française in 1908. This second appointment is most unusual for a mathematician, for it is given to honor literary achievements and is thus a sure indication of his lucid writing style. He was named President of the Académie des Sciences in 1906. Other awards included a Fellowship in the Royal Society in 1894, the Prix Poncelet, Prix Reynaud, and Prix Bolyai, and gold medals from the Lobachevsky Fund.

Much of Poincaré's early work was in differential equations, a branch of calculus which is linked directly to the physical world. It was natural, then, for him to turn his attention from pure mathematics to physics and celestial mechanics. Yet in his pursuit of solutions of physical and mechanical problems, he often created new tools of pure mathematics.

Poincaré was first drawn to celestial mechanics and astronomical physics by the classical three-body problem, which concerns the gravitational influence and distortions that three independent bodies in space would exert on one another; it held his interest throughout his life. Poincaré published partial results in his early years at the Sorbonne and later published work broadening the number of objects from three to any number. His results won for him a prize that had been offered by King Oscar II of Sweden.

In celestial mechanics, Poincaré was the first person to demand rigor in computations. That is, he found the approximations used commonly at the time to be unacceptable, since they introduced obvious errors into the work. Consequently, more powerful mathematics had to be developed. This work was not centered on any one branch of mathematics but instead included calculus, algebra, number theory, non-Euclidean geometry, and topology. In fact, the field of topology was begun in large part with Poincaré's study of orbits. He published much of this work in *Les Méthodes nouvelles de la mécanique céleste* (new methods in celestial mechanics), in three volumes between 1892 and 1899.

Poincaré's other early achievement was in the theory of automorphic functions, a study in mathematical analysis. These are functions which remain relatively unchanged though they are acted on by a series of transformations. He found that one class of these, which he called Fuchsian (for German mathematician Immanuel Fuchs), was related to non-Euclidean geometry, and this became an important insight. Indeed, there was some argument over priority in this development between Poincaré and German mathematician

Christian Felix Klein; however, scientific historians agree that Poincaré was the developer of these theories.

It seems that all branches of mathematics held Poincaré's interest. Poincaré was essential to the development of algebraic geometry. Of particular importance is his development of a parametric representation of functions. For example, the general equation of a circle $x^2 + y^2 = r^2$ can be rewritten as two equations that describe the variables x and y in terms of some angle A. The equations $x = r$ sine A and $y = r$ cosine A are the equivalent of the original equation since $x^2 + y^2 = r^2$ sine^2 $A + r^2$ cosine^2 $A = r^2$ (sine$^2 A +$ cosine$^2 A$), which in turn equals r^2 since sine^2 + cosine^2 = 1. Many problems can be solved using parameters that do not yield to any other methods.

Poincaré is equally important in physics. Although Albert Einstein is generally known for his theory of relativity, the special theory of relativity was discovered independently by Poincaré. He and Einstein arrived at the theory from completely different viewpoints, Einstein from light and Poincaré from electromagnetism, at about the same time (Einstein's first work was published in 1905, and Poincaré's was published in 1906). There can be no doubt that both men deserve a share of the credit. When Poincaré became aware of Einstein's work, he was quite enthusiastic and supportive of the Swiss physicist even though most scientists were skeptical. Max Planck, who developed quantum theory, was another physicist who was recognized by Poincaré, while he was being scorned by others. In addition, Poincaré developed the mathematics required for countless physical discoveries in the early twentieth century. An example is the wireless telegraph. He also developed the theory of the equilibrium of fluid bodies rotating in space.

Poincaré had a rare gift for a mathematician: He was able to write clearly and to make mathematics and science exciting to people whose educations were directed toward other fields. One of his most widely known works in the philosophy of science, *Science et méthode* (1908; *Science and Method*, 1914), is devoted to a study of how scientists and mathematicians create. Poincaré believed that some things in mathematics are known intuitively rather than from observation or from classic logic. His articles and books in the philosophy of science were avidly read and translated into most of the European languages and even into Japanese.

Poincaré continued in relatively good health until 1908, and in 1912 he died of an embolism following minor surgery. The church Saint-Jacques-de-Haut-Pas, the site of his funeral several days later, was filled with eminent persons from all fields who had come to pay a last tribute to his greatness.

Summary

Henri Poincaré was clearly one of the great mathematicians of his time. In fact, some believe that he had no peer. He won virtually every mathematical prize available, and he also won several scientific awards. His work entered every field of mathematics at the time, and he created at least one new branch called algebraic topology. His discoveries inspired other mathematicians for years after his death. In addition, Poincaré did first-rate work in celestial mechanics and was a codiscoverer of the theory of relativity.

The more than thirty books and five hundred papers that Poincaré published are a testament to his prolific career, especially since he died during his productive years. In addition, his writings on the philosophy of science sparked public interest in mathematics and the physical sciences and foreshadowed the intuitionist school of philosophy. These works have helped define the way human beings think about mathematical and scientific creation and will continue to do so for years to come. The practical applications of Poincaré's work are numerous. Differential functions are the primary mathematics used in engineering and some of the physical sciences; his work in celestial mechanics was completely different from past works and altered the field's course. In addition, he offered many new ideas in pure mathematics.

Perhaps the most articulate tribute to Poincaré was given in the official report of the 1905 Bolyai Prize written by Gustave Rados: "Henri Poincaré is incontestably the first and most powerful investigator of the present time in the domain of mathematics and mathematical physics."

Bibliography
Bell, E. T. "The Last Universalist." In *Men of Mathematics*. New York: Simon & Schuster, 1937. This book is a series of twenty-nine chapters, each introducing a different mathematician from the early Greeks to the early twentieth century. Its account of Poincaré focuses on three areas: the theory of automorphic functions, celestial mechanics and mathematical physics, and the philosophy of science. Biographical information is also included.
Nordmann, Charles. "Henri Poincaré: His Scientific Work, His Philosophy." In *Annual Report of the Board of Regents of the Smithsonian Institution*. Washington, D.C.: Government Printing Office, 1913. Nordmann includes not only a summary of Poincaré's work and philosophy as the title indicates but also a considerable amount of biographical information.
Poincaré, Henri. *The Foundations of Science*. Translated by George Bruce Halsted. New York: Science Press, 1913. Contains a preface by Poincaré and an introduction by Josiah Royce. It argues Poincaré's philosophy of science.
_____. "The Future of Mathematics." In *Annual Report of the Board of Regents of the Smithsonian Institution*. Washington, D.C.: Government Printing Office, 1910. This article represents Poincaré at his best. After a brief introduction, he guides the reader through most of the prominent fields of mathematics and predicts what he believed was to come. His

explanations are excellent.

_____. *Mathematics and Science: Last Essays*. Translated by John W. Balduc. Reprint. Mineola, N.Y.: Dover, 1963. Another work in the philosophy of science.

Slosson, Edwin E. "Henri Poincaré." In *Major Prophets of Today*. Freeport, N.Y.: Books for Libraries Press, 1968. Slosson chose several representatives from the modern era whom he viewed as having lasting prominence. His article on Poincaré includes biographical information as well as a discussion of Poincaré's work in mathematics and philosophy.

Celeste Williams Brockington

ALEKSANDR STEPANOVICH POPOV

Born: March 16, 1859; Turinskiye Rudniki, Perm, Russia
Died: January 13, 1906; St. Petersburg, Russia
Areas of Achievement: Invention and engineering
Contribution: A Russian pioneer in the invention of radio and its application, Popov also contributed to the development of X-ray photography. Outside Russia, he contributed to the development of radio in France.

Early Life

Aleksandr Stepanovich Popov was born in the village of Perm (modern Krasnoturinsk), located in a marshy area of northeastern Russia, just west of the Ural Mountains. Despite its relative isolation, Perm was an area of ancient Russian settlement, first made famous by Saint Stephen of Perm. Saint Stephen converted the pagan Permians after he proved incombustible when they attempted to burn him at the stake. For many generations, the clergy provided Perm's only intelligentsia. Popov was the fourth child in a priest's family of seven children. Though Popov left his village, he loved Perm and in later life took numerous photographs of his native landscape, which form an important collection.

By Popov's time, copper and iron mines, as well as a few factories, were in operation near his village. As a child, he is supposed to have built models of factory and mining equipment. He was educated in seminaries and seemed destined to enter the priesthood, but at the age of eighteen he decided instead to pursue his growing interest in mathematics and physics. He moved to St. Petersburg to attend the university, which was then nearing the apogee of its reputation in science. Among Popov's distinguished teachers were the chemist Dmitry Mendeleyev and the physicists Fyodor Petrushevsky and Orest Khvolson. The University of St. Petersburg was one of the first to offer courses on the physics of electricity and magnetism and had a fine physics laboratory run by Popov's mentor Vladimir Lermantov.

While a student from 1878 to 1882, Popov always worked, not only to support himself and to contribute to the support of his siblings but also to support his wife, Raisa Gorbunov, whom he married before graduating. Gorbunov pursued medical studies and eventually became a physician. Popov found most congenial employment with a newly founded St. Petersburg company, Elektrotekhnik, which built and maintained small electric stations around the city.

As a student, Popov took part in the world's very first electrical exhibition, in 1880, organized by a branch of the Russian Technical Society, which had just founded a new journal, *Elektrichestvo*. The exhibition was intended to raise money to fund the new publication and was a great success; it ran for a full month, attracting thousands of visitors. Popov worked as a guide throughout the exhibition, explaining the new marvels of technology to the public—a role that he was later to continue in public lectures and demonstrations, overcoming his initial shyness. A photograph of him from his student years shows a handsome, rather delicate-looking youth; later, he suffered from heart problems.

Popov was graduated from the faculty of mathematics and physics of the University of St. Petersburg with the degree of candidate (equivalent to a doctorate without a dissertation). His earliest research papers, published in *Elektrichestvo*, focused on the generation of electricity and the conversion of thermal energy into mechanical energy. He was trained in the spirit of concrete application of science, not for personal gain but for the good of others.

Upon graduation, Popov accepted a position at the Russian navy's most prestigious training institute, the Mine Officers' (or Torpedo) School in Kronstadt, on the Gulf of Finland, where he worked from 1883 to 1901. The Kronstadt facility had Russia's most advanced physics laboratory, and Popov was soon in charge of it. He also gave free public lectures, in which he shared his advanced knowledge, delighting in finding ways to make technology accessible to the average person. He had only the most limited funds at his disposal and learned cabinetmaking and glassblowing in order to construct innovative apparatuses himself. Every summer, he supplemented his income by running the electrical power plant for the annual fair at Nizhni-Novgorod (modern Gorky).

Life's Work

At the Mine Officers' School in 1889, Popov reproduced Heinrich Hertz's experiments with electromagnetic waves. In the same year, in order to popularize both the Hertz oscillator and the field of electrical engineering in general, Popov gave a series of public lectures on the recent research done on the relationship between light and electric phenomena. These lectures made him see the need for an apparatus to demonstrate, before a large audience, the presence of the waves generated by the Hertz oscillator.

Popov constructed a better detector of electromagnetic waves, which led to his invention of a lightning-storm detector and a radio in 1895. He began with the electromagnetic-wave detector (later called a coherer), invented by the French physicist Édouard Branly and improved it so that it could be used reliably outside laboratory conditions. By the beginning of 1895, Popov had evolved the primitive coherer into a complete radio receiver. By the spring of 1895, Popov had a radio transmitter ready to complement his receiver; it was based on a modified Hertz oscillator excited by an induction coil. Using the two devices, he conducted radio communication experiments in the physics laboratory and in the garden of the Mine Officers' School. In the course of these experiments, he added a new element of his own, the radio antenna.

Popov successfully demonstrated his system of wireless communication and presented a formal paper to an audience of scientists from the Russian Physics and Chemistry Society on May 7, 1895. A report on his demonstration appeared in the Russian press on May 12, 1895, followed by other reports in late 1895 and early 1896. It is on the basis of this work that Russia claims primacy for the invention of wireless radio communication, although the young Italian physicist Guglielmo Marconi secured a patent on his own radio in the summer of 1896, won the Nobel Prize in 1909, and superseded Popov's achievements.

Initially, the components of Marconi's radio, being tested by the British Telegraph Agency in 1896, were kept secret. When the structure of Marconi's radio was finally revealed in 1897, however, it was identical to Popov's: an enhanced coherer with antenna and Hertz oscillator excited by an induction coil. The detailed description of Marconi's invention was published in the British professional engineering journal, *The Electrician*, in 1897. Popov and other Russian engineers read it and were shocked by the coincidence. Popov declined to accuse Marconi of theft, saying in an address to the First All-Russian Electrotechnical Congress in 1900: "Was my instrument known to Marconi or not? The latter is very likely more probable. At any rate my combination of the relay, tube, and electromagnetic tapper served as the basis of Marconi's first patent as a new combination of already known instruments."

Popov had no interest in a vainglorious contest for primacy but did wish his achievements to be acknowledged. In an 1897 article published in *The Electrician*, he took exception to a lengthy article just published by the British journal on the subject of the coherer and the radio, in which Popov's contribution was not even mentioned.

From May of 1895 onward, Popov continued to work with his wireless system, to lecture, and to give demonstrations. Noting that the device was sensitive to lightning discharges, he set it to record oscillations on paper, clearly indicating the approach of storms. From the summer of 1895, Popov's lightning-storm detector was put to effective, long-term use by the Russian Forestry Institute.

On March 24, 1896, Popov sent the world's first wireless message in Morse code across a distance of 250 meters, between two buildings. The message consisted of two words: "Heinrich Hertz." The witnesses were scientists of the St. Petersburg Physics Society, holding a meeting at the University of St. Petersburg.

Unfortunately for his future fame outside Russia, Popov was distracted from his radio work by his curiosity about the latest scientific phenomenon, X rays, discovered by Wilhelm Röntgen late in 1895. Popov was drawn to investigate these in 1896 and was the first in Russia to take X-ray photographs of objects and human limbs.

Newspaper reports of Marconi's patent broke in the fall of 1896, spurring

Popov to fresh efforts. Popov increased the distance of radio communication. He achieved ship-to-shore communication across six hundred meters in 1897; by 1901, he had expanded that to 150 kilometers. His work was simultaneously experimental and practical, being applied in rescue missions at sea almost immediately. He experimented with wavelengths lying on the boundary between the decimeter and meter ranges. He predicted the development of broadcasting and the possibility of detecting the directionality of radio waves.

Popov was energetic about making foreign contacts and broadening his expertise. In 1893, he attended the Chicago World's Fair, where he delivered a lecture; he witnessed the Third International Electrical Congress being held in Chicago at the same time. In a letter sent from the United States, he expressed a strong intention to visit Thomas Edison's laboratory, but it is not known whether he actually did so. He visited New York and Philadelphia. In the late 1890's, he made several trips to France and Germany to examine radio stations there. In Russia, he was much in demand as a consultant on the establishment of electrical power plants and civilian wireless telegraph stations.

In 1899, Popov built a headphone message receiver and then went to Paris to work with the French engineer Eugène Ducretet. As a result, Popov's headset (patented in 1901) was manufactured in Russia and France from 1901 to 1904 and was widely used. In 1900, he returned to Paris to collaborate with Lieutenant Tissot, one of the pioneers of French radio, on numerous improvements in radio design.

While civilian use of wireless radio was expanding, the Russian navy was slow to apply it. Because of Popov's on-site work, Russia's Baltic Fleet, harbored at Kronstadt, was supplied with both radios and trained personnel. Under the prodding of Vice Admiral Stepan Makarov, a commander based in Kronstadt who took an interest in Popov's work, Popov began to receive modest funding. Unfortunately for Russia, there was no radio equipment aboard its Pacific fleet at the outbreak of the Russo-Japanese War of 1904-1905.

At this point, Popov was at last given a position worthy of his standing and achievement. Having been a professor at the St. Petersburg Electrotechnical Institute since 1901, he was unanimously elected rector in late 1905. Two weeks after his election, his entire faculty passed a resolution condemning "any forcible interference by the authorities in the life of the institute," referring chiefly to police searches of student dormitories and to student arrests.

Popov, who suffered from a weak heart and high blood pressure, was summoned to the office of the St. Petersburg governor for a stormy interview. He refused to back down and returned home in a shaken state. He died of cerebral hemorrhage a few days later, at the age of forty-six.

Summary

Aleksandr Stepanovich Popov belongs to the long line of Russian scientists not much appreciated by their government in their lifetimes. There is a consistent succession, from Paul von Schilling-Cannstadt, who in 1832 installed one of the world's first telegraph connections (which ran between the Communications Ministry and the czar's Winter Palace but was never used), to Dmitry Mendeleyev (who was dismissed from his university post under government pressure), to Andrei Sakharov (who wasted years in the closed city of Gorky for political reasons). While the rest of the world raced to master the wireless radio and its applications, funding teams of researchers, the Russian government—of which Popov was an employee—let Popov work alone, in his limited spare time. On two occasions, in 1925 and again in 1945, the Soviet government remembered Popov and effusively honored him. The regime had so little credibility on other fronts, however, that such honors added nothing to, and may have actually harmed Popov's international repute.

Popov—who did invent a wireless radio, the components and operating principles of which were in essence the same as those of the Marconi radio patented a year later—disparaged suggestions that he had been copied, modestly noting that he had simply put together components that individually were already known. In a time of intense scientific interest in electromagnetic waves, the hour was ripe for such an invention, whose appearance was perhaps inevitable. Popov was content to be part of the world of scientific discovery and to share his knowledge even with the nonscientific public.

He belonged to the first wave of what became the substantial, proud, and little-understood caste of Russia's early twentieth century engineers. Like the highly educated characters in the plays of his scientifically trained contemporary Anton Chekhov, Popov and other members of the technical intelligentsia looked forward to a humane, enlightened future that they did not expect personally to see.

Bibliography

Popov, Alexander. "An Application of the Coherer." *The Electrician*, 1897. Popov's article translated into English, reflecting his precise mind and talent for educating.

Radovsky, M. *Alexander Popov: Inventor of Radio*. Translated by G. Yankovsky. Moscow: Foreign Languages, 1957. The most comprehensive study of the life and work of Popov. This work is intended for the general reader as part of the Men of Russian Science series. Contains abundant footnotes to sources but no bibliography. Photographs of persons, equipment, and sites are included.

Smith-Rose, R. L. "Marconi, Popov, and the Dawn of Radiocommunication." *Electronics and Power* 10 (1964): 76-79. This article presents the

British view that Marconi should be given primacy.

Süsskind, Charles. "Popov and the Beginnings of Radiotelegraphy." *Proceedings of the Institute of Radio Engineers* 50 (1962): 2036-2047. Reprinted as a separate pamphlet by the San Francisco Press in 1962 and 1973, this article utilizes Soviet sources and is favorable to the Russian view of Popov's primacy.

D. Gosselin Nakeeb

NICOLAS POUSSIN

Born: 1594; near Les Andelys, Normandy, France
Died: November 19, 1665; Rome
Area of Achievement: Art
Contribution: Poussin was among the greatest French painters of the seventeenth century and one of the most influential artists of the Baroque era. His work reflects those qualities of rationality and high moral purpose which were so admired by the French classicists, and it profoundly influenced the subsequent development of painting, both in Rome, where he spent most of his life, and in France.

Early Life

What little is known of the circumstances of Nicolas Poussin's birth and early life depends almost entirely on the accounts published by his seventeenth century biographers. He was born in 1594, in a hamlet not far from the Norman town of Les Andelys. His father, Jean Poussin, may have originally been a member of the minor nobility, but, after fighting in the Wars of Religion, he went to Normandy, where he supported himself by working the land. His mother was Marie Delaisement, the daughter of a municipal magistrate and the widow of an attorney.

Nothing is known about Poussin's early education. He may have had some instruction in Latin, but he is said to have neglected his studies in order to devote more time to drawing. In 1612, a mediocre painter named Quentin Varin arrived in Les Andelys, where he executed a number of paintings, some of which are still in place. He is said to have encouraged the young Poussin to try to convince his parents to let him follow an artistic career; when they opposed his plans, Poussin left home. He was eighteen years old.

He went first to Rouen and then to Paris. His activities for the twelve or so years between his arrival in Paris in 1612 or 1613 and his departure for Rome in late 1623 cannot be determined with any certainty, but by the time he left Paris he had acquired some measure of success as an artist, working for the Queen Mother, Marie de Médicis, as well as the Archbishop of Paris. He had access to the royal collections, where he had a chance to study the incomparable examples of antique sculpture and Italian Renaissance paintings, from which he drew far more inspiration than he did from the work of his contemporaries.

Poussin also became friendly with the Italian poet Giambattista Marini, who became his patron and for whom he executed a series of drawings illustrating the Roman poet Ovid's *Metamorphoses* (before A.D. 8). Poussin's goal during those years was to go to Rome, the acknowledged center of the arts, and he made several attempts to reach the city. On one occasion he got as far as Florence before being forced to return to France. A second attempt got him no farther than Lyons. On his third attempt, he finally succeeded, and in March of 1624 he arrived in Rome.

Life's Work

Except for a brief trip to Paris in 1640-1642, Poussin remained in Rome for the rest of his life. He was thirty years old when he arrived, and although he was almost immediately introduced to important patrons, very few commissions came his way. He spent some time working in the studio of the Bolognese painter Domenico Zampieri, known as Il Domenichino, who was one of the leading classicist painters, but it was not until 1628 that he was given a chance to produce a major altarpiece for an important church. This was an enviable opportunity, for the painting of large-scale altar pictures was the stock-in-trade of Roman artists and the surest way to achieve success and recognition. The painting, *Martyrdom of Saint Erasmus*, was intended for an altar in the church of St. Peter's. Unfortunately, it was not well received. A year or two later, Poussin became very ill, and his illness, coupled with the unpopularity of his *Martyrdom of Saint Erasmus*, seems to have brought on an emotional crisis. He realized that his talents lay elsewhere, and he gave up the attempt to compete with the Roman artists by creating altarpieces or large frescoes. The *Martyrdom of Saint Erasmus* was the only large, public commission he ever completed in Rome.

For the next ten years, Poussin worked almost exclusively for a rather select group of Roman clients who shared his consuming interest in Roman antiquity. He was a friend of Cassiano del Pozzo, the secretary to Cardinal Francesco Barberini, and a man whose great interest was the formation of a collection of drawings recording all aspects of Roman antiquity. Poussin was closely associated with Pozzo in this project, and his paintings of the early 1630's reflect the strong antiquarian interests of Pozzo's circle.

By the middle of the decade, Poussin had begun to create the works that are among his greatest contributions to Western art. *The Adoration of the Golden Calf* exemplifies these new developments in style and subject matter. The theme is of epic stature, the composition carefully controlled and rigorously organized. Furthermore, Poussin tried to reveal the emotions of the protagonists in his painted drama through their gestures and facial expressions. This rigorously intellectual approach to pictorial problems was henceforth to be one of the major characteristics of his work. At the end of the decade, he painted some of his finest religious works, among them the paintings representing the *Seven Sacraments* which were commissioned from him by Pozzo.

Poussin was much admired in France, and in 1636 Cardinal de Richelieu commissioned him to execute a series of *Bacchanals* for the Cardinal's château near Orléans. The cardinal and Louis XIV wanted Poussin to return to France, and he finally agreed. In 1640, he left Rome and went to Paris, but the trip was not a success. He was commissioned to execute several paintings and to plan the decoration of part of the Louvre Palace, but none of the commissions was really suited to his talents and the results were disappointing. Poussin was back in Rome by September of 1642, and the principal result of his trip was that it allowed him to make contact with a number of men who were to become his most important clients during the later part of his life. Most of them were well-educated, middle-class bankers, merchants, and civil servants to whom the seriousness and moral earnestness of Poussin's work had a great appeal. It was for this group that Poussin executed the paintings that are considered to be among the finest examples of French classicism. One of Poussin's most important clients was a civil servant named Paul Fréart de Chantelou, who took care of Poussin while he was in Paris and with whom the artist conducted an extensive correspondence when he returned to Rome. It was for Chantelou that Poussin painted his famous *Self-Portrait*, which is now in the Louvre.

In 1644, Poussin began working on a set of paintings illustrating the *Seven Sacraments* for Chantelou, who had wanted Poussin to make copies of the paintings of the same subject which he had executed earlier for Pozzo. Poussin refused and the paintings are quite different, revealing Poussin's deepening sense of the tragic in the severity of their composition. The strange and haunting allegory of *The Arcadian Shepherds* of about 1650 is even more moving, as the shepherds remain motionless to hear the message on the sepulchral monument deciphered for them: Even in Arcadia, there is death.

In the late 1640's, Poussin began painting what are in effect pure landscapes. The *Landscape with the Gathering of the Ashes of Phocion* is based on an incident in the ancient Greek historian Plutarch's *Parallel Lives* (105-115), in which the widow of the general whom the Athenians have put to death is allowed to gather up his ashes. It is the lucid arrangement of the landscape, however, that is the principal expressive element. The principles of organization which he had applied to figural compositions he now used to create an image of an ordered and harmonious nature. It is a vision of the natural world in perfect harmony with human concepts of rational order.

The final years of Poussin's life were marred by illness, and he seems to have isolated himself from the art world, seeing only a few friends and devoting himself to his painting. His late paintings, such as the *Four Seasons* in the Louvre, are some of his most personal creations, works in which the formal elements of art—light and shadow, color and texture—often seem to be his real subject. Finally, after a long decline, Poussin died in Rome on November 19, 1665.

Summary

Nicolas Poussin has often been called the "Painter-Philosopher." While it is certainly true that in his paintings he tried to give expression to his ethical concepts and religious views, he was certainly not unique in this respect. What is so unusual about Poussin's work is that he was able to evolve a language of artistic forms through which these ideas could be expressed with great clarity. Unlike most seventeenth century artists, he was deeply interested in philosophical concepts, particularly the writings of the Stoic philosophers of antiquity, whose ideal of indifference to feelings or emotion he found particularly appealing and from whom he seems to have learned to interpret classical myths as allegories of eternal truth. His subjects from classical history are often those in which the heroes achieve a moral victory through self-sacrifice, and there are numerous parallels between Poussin's paintings and the work of the French seventeenth century playwright Pierre Corneille. Both try to concentrate the action and eliminate any elements that might distract the spectator from the moral lesson. Both favor the rigidly conventional expression of human emotions and work within a self-imposed set of rigidly conventional forms. Their works form the cornerstones of French seventeenth century classicism.

Poussin has always been considered a master of classical composition, above all in nineteenth century France, where he was equally admired by the classicist Jean-Auguste-Dominique Ingres and the postimpressionist Edgar Degas. Paul Cézanne was also greatly influenced by him and tried to fuse the intensity and clarity of the color of the French Impressionists with the formal order of Poussin. Even the early cubist painters have acknowledged their debt to Poussin, and to artists for whom the expressive implications of pictorial order are major concerns, he will always be an important source of inspiration.

Bibliography
Arikha, Avigdor. *Nicholas Poussin, "The Rape of the Sabines" (The Louvre Version)*. Houston: Museum of Fine Arts, 1983. A catalog of a loan exhibition focusing on the painting which Poussin executed for Cardinal Aloisio Omodei in the late 1630's. Includes detailed investigations of subject matter and technique, and a discussion of Poussin's art theory.
Blunt, Anthony. *The Drawings of Poussin*. New Haven, Conn.: Yale University Press, 1979. A general introduction to Poussin's graphic work.
——————. *Nicholas Poussin*. 2 vols. New York: Pantheon Books, 1967. A most important publication on Poussin, written by a noted scholar of Baroque art who devoted the greater portion of his life to the study of Poussin. Part of the Bollingen series, A. W. Mellon Lectures in Fine Arts.
——————. *The Paintings of Nicholas Poussin: Critical Catalogue*. London: Phaidon Press, 1966. The standard catalog of Poussin's work. Includes a complete survey of the literature on the artist.
Friedlaender, Walter. *Nicholas Poussin: A New Approach*. New York:

Harry N. Abrams, 1966. A general study that provides an excellent introduction to Poussin's work and art theory.

Hibbard, Howard. *Poussin: The Holy Family on the Steps*. London: Allen Lane, 1974. A detailed stylistic and iconographic investigation of a version of the *Madonna on the Steps* held in Washington, D.C. (there is another, and perhaps better version, in the Cleveland Museum of Art). Hibbard's book is also an excellent introduction to the study of the artist.

Oberhuber, Konrad. *Poussin, the Early Years in Rome: The Origins of French Classicism*. Foreword by Edmund T. Pillsbury. New York: Hudson Hills Press, in association with the Kimball Art Museum, Fort Worth, Texas, 1988. A catalog of an important loan exhibition of Poussin's work. The catalog entries are a rich source of information and incorporate much modern research on the first phase of Poussin's career.

Poussin, Nicolas. *Drawings: Catalogue Raisonné*. Edited by Walter Friedlaender and Anthony Blunt. 5 vols. London: Warburg Institute, 1939-1974. The standard catalog of Poussin's drawings.

Wright, Christopher. *Poussin Paintings: A Catalogue Raisonné*. New York: Hippocrene Books, 1985. A good, general book by an author who is primarily concerned with the artistic qualities of Poussin's work. Contains excellent illustrations.

Eric Van Schaack

PIERRE-JOSEPH PROUDHON

Born: January 15, 1809; Besançon, France
Died: January 19, 1865; Paris, France
Areas of Achievement: Philosophy and economics
Contribution: Proudhon's greatest activity was as a journalist and pamphleteer. Hailed by his followers as the uncompromising champion of human liberty, Proudhon voiced the discontentment of the revolutionary period of nineteenth century France.

Early Life

Pierre-Joseph Proudhon was born on January 15, 1809, in the rural town of Besançon. Although the political and social climates were important influences on Proudhon's life, the experiences he had as a child growing up in a working-class family shaped his philosophical views in even more important ways. Proudhon's father, who was a brewer and, later, a cooper, went bankrupt because, unlike most brewers, he sold his measure of drink for a just price. Penniless after the loss of his business, Proudhon's father was forced to move his family to a small farm near Burgille. Between the ages of eight and twelve, Proudhon worked as a cowherd, an experience which forged in him a lifelong identity with the peasant class.

Proudhon's formal education began in 1820, when his mother arranged with the parish priest for him to attend the local college, which was the nineteenth century equivalent of high school. The stigma of poverty suddenly became very real to him when he contrasted his clothes with those of his wealthier comrades. Smarting from the insults of the other children, Proudhon protected himself from further pain by adopting a surly, sullen personality. During his fourth year at school, Proudhon read François Fénelon's *Démonstration de l'existence de Dieu* (1713; *A Demonstration of the Existence of God*, 1713), which introduced him to the tenets of atheism. Proudhon then ceased to practice religion at the age of sixteen and began his lifelong war against the Church.

Proudhon's life changed drastically on the eve of his graduation. Sensing that something was wrong when neither of his parents was present, Proudhon rushed home to find that his father, who had become a landless laborer, had lost everything in a last desperate lawsuit. Years later, Proudhon used his father's inability to own farmland as the basis for his belief that society excluded the poor from the ownership of property.

At the age of eighteen, Proudhon was forced to abandon his formal education and take up a trade. He was apprenticed to the Besançon firm of the Gauthier brothers, which specialized in general theological publications. Proudhon became proud of his trade as a proofreader because it made him independent. At home among the printers, who were men of his own class, he found that he had traded the isolation of the middle-class school for the comradely atmosphere of the workshop.

The printshop also enabled Proudhon to continue his studies, in an informal way, for it was there that he developed his first intellectual passions. His budding interest in language was cultivated by a young editor named Fallot, who was the first great personal influence on Proudhon's life. It was there too that Proudhon was introduced to the works of the utopian thinker Charles Fourier. Fourier's position that a more efficient economy can revolutionize society from within is reflected in the anarchical doctrines of Proudhon's greatest works.

Another lesson Proudhon learned at the printshop was that mastering a trade does not guarantee a living, as it would in a just society. His apprenticeship came to an end as a result of the Revolution of 1830, which overthrew the restored Bourbons. Although Proudhon hated to be out of work, he was infected with the spirit of revolution, which stayed with him throughout his life.

His friend Fallot persuaded Proudhon to move to Paris and apply for the Suard scholarship. During their visit to Paris, Fallot provided Proudhon with moral and financial support, because he was convinced that Proudhon had a great future ahead of him as a philosopher and a writer. When Fallot was stricken with cholera, however, Proudhon declined to accept his friend's generosity any longer and began seeking employment in the printing houses of Paris, but to no avail. Discouraged, Proudhon left Fallot to convalesce by himself in Paris.

Life's Work

A turning point for Proudhon came with the publication of his book *Qu'est-ce que la propriété?* (1840; *What Is Property?*, 1876). The book was actually a showcase for the answer to this question—"Property is theft"—and it gained for Proudhon an immediate audience among those working-class citizens who had become disillusioned with Louis-Philippe, a king who clearly favored the privileged classes. Ironically, though, Proudhon was a defender of public property; he objected to the practice of drawing unearned income from rental property. This book represented a dramatic departure from the popular utopian theories embraced by most socialists of the day in that it employed economic, political, and social science as a means of viewing social problems.

Among the people who were attracted to Proudhon's theories was Karl Marx. In 1842, Marx praised *What Is Property?* and met Proudhon in Paris. Since Proudhon had studied economic science in more depth than Marx had, Marx probably learned more from their meeting than did Proudhon. Two years later, though, Marx became disenchanted with Proudhon after the publication in 1846 of Proudhon's first major work, *Système des contradictions économiques: Ou, Philosophie de la misère* (1846; *System of Economic Contradictions*, 1888).

Proudhon hoped that the Revolution of 1848 would bring his theories to fruition by deposing Louis-Philippe. He became the editor of a radical journal, *Le Représentant du peuple* (the representative of the people), in which he recorded one of the best eyewitness accounts of the Revolution. That same year, he was elected to the office of radical deputy. Surprisingly, Proudhon did not ally himself with the socialist Left. During his brief term in office, he voted against the resolution proclaiming the "right to work" and against the adoption of the constitution establishing the democratic Second Republic. His chief activity during his term in office was the founding of a "People's Bank," which would be a center of various workingmen's associations and would overcome the scarcity of money and credit by universalizing the rate of exchange.

The feasibility of such a bank will never be known, because it was closed after only two months of operation when Proudhon's career as a deputy came to an abrupt end. In 1849, Proudhon was arrested for writing violent articles attacking Napoleon III and was sentenced to three years in the Saint-Pelagie prison. Proudhon fled to Belgium but was promptly arrested when he returned to Paris under an assumed name to liquidate his bank, which had foundered in his absence.

Proudhon's imprisonment was actually a fortunate experience. It afforded him ample time to study and write; he also founded a newspaper, *Le Voix du peuple* (the voice of the people). In *Les Confessions d'un révolutionnaire* (1849; the confessions of a revolutionary), written while he was in prison, Proudhon traced the history of the revolutionary movement in France from 1789 to 1849. In *Idée générale de la révolution au XIXe siècle* (1851; *The General Idea of the Revolution in the Nineteenth Century*, 1923), he appealed to the bourgeois to make their peace with the workers. *La Révolution sociale démontrée par le coup d'état du 2 décembre* (1852; the revolution demonstrated by the coup d'état), which was published a month after the release of Proudhon from prison, hailed the overthrow of the Second Republic as a giant step toward progress. Proudhon also proposed that anarchy was the true end of the social evolution of the nineteenth century. Because Proudhon suggested that Napoleon III should avoid making the same mistakes as Napoleon I, the book was banned by the minister of police. Still, the book created a sensation in France.

The most important event that occurred while Proudhon was in prison was his marriage to Euphrasie Piegard, an uneducated seamstress, whose management skills and resilience made her a suitable mate for a revolutionary. By marrying outside the Church, he indicated his contempt for the clergy. Marriage was good for Proudhon, and his happiness convinced him that marriage was an essential part of a just society.

The three years following Proudhon's release from prison were marked by uncertainty and fear. By the end of 1852, Napoleon III's reign was in crisis, and any writer who opposed him or the Crimean War was immediately ostracized. Proudhon's attempts to start a journal through which he could persuade the regime of Napoleon III to move to the Left against the Church was thwarted by the Jesuits. With his journalistic career at an end, Proudhon began a series of literary projects.

The year 1855 saw a significant shift in Proudhon's philosophical outlook. He arrived at the conclusion that what was needed was not a political system under which everyone benefited but a transformation of man's consciousness. Proudhon's new concern with ethics resulted in his *De la justice dans la révolution et dans l'église* (about the justice of the revolution and the church) in 1858. This three-volume work, which ranks as one of the greatest socialist studies of the nineteenth century, attacks the defenders of the status quo, including the Catholic church.

Although the book enjoyed great success, the anger that Proudhon had exhibited in this manifesto of defiance outraged the government and the Church. Once again, Proudhon was given a fine and a prison sentence. Proudhon submitted a petition to the senate, but to no avail; he was sentenced to three years' imprisonment and ordered to pay a fine of four thousand francs; his publisher received a fine as well. Proudhon again fled to Belgium, where he settled as a mathematics professor under the assumed name of Durfort.

Though Proudhon's publisher refused to accept any more of his political works, Proudhon continued to write. The last of Proudhon's great treatises, *La Guerre et la paix* (war and peace), appeared in 1861. This two-volume work explored Proudhon's view that only through war could man obtain justice and settle conflicts between nations. Proudhon also held that women must serve the state only as housewives and mothers in order to ensure a strong, virile nation. In response, Proudhon was branded a reactionary, a renegade, and a warmonger by both citizens and journalists.

Proudhon was forced to flee Belgium when his opposition to the nationalist movement, which he had expressed in various newspaper articles, created a furor. A large segment of readers objected to a statement in one of these articles that seemed to favor the annexation of Belgium by France.

After returning to France, Proudhon threw himself into his work, producing four books in only two years. This final burst of creativity was his last attempt to persuade the workers to abstain from political activity, while the imperial administration continued to distort the workings of universal suffrage. *La Fédération de l'unité en Italie* (1863; the federal principle and the unity of Italy) contains what is considered by many to be the best explanation of the federal principle that has ever been written. *De la capacité politique des classes ouvrières* (1863; of the political capacity of the working classes), inspired by the workers' refusal to support the candidates of the Second Empire in the legislative election of 1863, reflects Proudhon's new confidence in the proletariat. He now believed that the workers could be a viable force for achieving mutualism.

Although Proudhon's mental faculties remained sharp, his health deteriorated rapidly in the last two years of his life. He died of an undetermined illness on January 19, 1865.

Summary

Pierre-Joseph Proudhon was a radical thinker who was incapable of identifying completely with any single political ideology. Early in his career, Proudhon was a revolutionary who denounced the established political and economic institutions. As he grew older, he began to absorb some of those bourgeois values that he had scorned in his youth, such as the importance of the family and the inheritance of property. Thus, he is best described as a man of contradictions, a radical, a realist, and a moralist. In fact, he was viewed as a dissenter by other dissenters of the day: liberals, democrats, and republicans, as well as his fellow socialists.

Proudhon's influence on French politics extended well into the twentieth century. In the Paris Commune of 1871, Proudhon's political views carried more weight than did those of Marx. By the end of the nineteenth century, however, Proudhon's teachings seem to have been overshadowed by the Marxists. Through anarchism, Proudhon's influence was transferred to revolutionary syndicalism, which dominated French trade unionism into the twentieth century. The syndicalists favored a violent approach to the class struggle and employed the general strike as a weapon. Just before World War II, though, French trade unionism turned away from Proudhon as it began to cater to various political factions.

Bibliography

Brogan, D. W. *Proudhon*. London: H. Hamilton, 1934. A short but complete biography which includes summaries and critiques of Proudhon's work. The first half of the book does an excellent job of outlining those influences which shaped him as a writer and a thinker.

Dillard, Dudley. "Keynes and Proudhon." *Journal of Economic History*, May, 1942: 63-76. A fine introduction to Proudhon's economic and political philosophy. In his comparison between Proudhon and J. M. Keynes, who seems to have formulated his theories after Proudhon's, Dillard highlights the most important points in Proudhon's work, thereby clarifying some of Proudhon's more difficult concepts for the average reader.

Hall, Constance Margaret. *The Sociology of Pierre Joseph Proudhon, 1809-1865*. New York: Philosophical Library, 1971. A penetrating analysis of Proudhon's political philosophy and the effects it had on nineteenth century France. The brief biographical sketch in the beginning of the volume is an excellent introduction to Proudhon's life and times.

Ritter, Alan. *The Political Thought of Pierre-Joseph Proudhon*. Princeton, N.J.: Princeton University Press, 1969. An in-depth study of Proudhon's political views which explains the historical events that spawned his ideas and describes how Proudhon's theories have been interpreted in various times. Also demonstrates how Proudhon attempted to integrate revolutionary, realistic, and moral concepts into a cohesive political theory.

Schapiro, J. Salwyn. "Pierre Joseph Proudhon, Harbinger of Fascism." *American Historial Review*, July, 1945: 714-737. Theorizes that Proudhon was an intellectual forerunner of Fascism. Concentrates primarily on those radical elements of Proudhon's works which seem to have influenced National Socialism. Also contains a brief but useful sketch of Proudhon's life.

Woodcock, George. *Pierre-Joseph Proudhon*. New York: Macmillan, 1956. A standard biography of Proudhon's life, combining voluminous details of his personal life with a discussion and critique of his writings and philosophical views. Provides invaluable insights into the turbulent historical period of which Proudhon was a product and shows the role that he played as a catalyst in these events. Emphasizes Proudhon's willingness to suffer as a result of his devotion to his principles.

Alan Brown

SAMUEL VON PUFENDORF

Born: January 8, 1632; Dorfchemnitz, Saxony
Died: October 26, 1694; Berlin, Prussia
Areas of Achievement: Law and philosophy
Contribution: Pufendorf's teachings on jurisprudence, theology, and ethics made possible significant advances in the development of natural law theories in the Western world of the early modern age.

Early Life

The family background of Samuel Pufendorf has been described as extending over four generations of Lutheran clergy, who had practiced that calling for about a century. Relatively little has been recorded, however, about Samuel's father, except that he was a pastor of relatively modest means. When Samuel was born, as the third of four children, on January 8, 1632, the family resided in Dorfchemnitz, a village in Saxony. During the next year, they moved to Flöha, about five miles from Chemnitz. Because of the promise and academic aptitude Samuel and his elder brother Esaias had shown, they received financial support from a wealthy nobleman, which enabled them to attend the well-known Prince's School in Grimma. The education that was received there consisted of lessons in grammar, rhetoric, logic, Bible reading, and Lutheran dogma; while he later complained of excessive rigidity and dullness among his teachers, Pufendorf maintained with some satisfaction that he availed himself of the ample free time that was allowed students to make himself familiar with works of classical Greek and Latin writers. After attending this secondary school between 1645 and 1650, he was enrolled at the University of Leipzig; though his father had hoped and expected that his son's education there would prepare him for the ministry, Pufendorf, again following the example of his brother, turned away from theology, which both of them regarded as a discipline that was presented in an overly conservative manner. Among the subjects that did interest him were history, jurisprudence, philology, and philosophy; this eclectic bent, bordering sometimes on indiscriminate erudition, may have foreshadowed traits of this sort in his later writings.

In 1656, Pufendorf went on to the University of Jena, where in two years he earned the degree of *Magister.* He read works on mathematics and studied modern philosophy; he devoted special attention to the writings of Hugo Grotius and Thomas Hobbes. Moreover, with the encouragement of Erhard Weigel, a professor of mathematics who subsequently was to become known as one of Gottfried Wilhelm Leibniz's early mentors, Pufendorf became impressed with the notion that ethical principles could be adduced with the rigor of mathematical logic. Although schematic conceptions of that sort did not gain Pufendorf's unwavering adherence, a confluence of ideas evidently was taking form by which the conception of natural law guided by natural reason had become foremost.

Shortly after he left Jena, Pufendorf, with the assistance of his brother Esaias, obtained a position as tutor to the family of Peter Julius Coyet, the Swedish minister in Copenhagen. Yet when Sweden, which previously had been at war with Denmark, broke off peace negotiations to reopen hostilities, Danish authorities put the minister's staff and attendants under arrest. During a period of eight months when Pufendorf was imprisoned, he had the opportunity to compose his first work on the principles of law. In 1659, he left for the Netherlands, where Coyet had resumed his diplomatic work in The Hague, and in 1660 Pufendorf's *Elementorum jurisprudentiae universalis libri duo* (English translation, 1929) was published. At the University of Leiden, he was able to pursue further studies in classical philology. He also obtained a recommendation from Pieter de Groot, a son of Hugo Grotius, who was an agent in the Netherlands for Karl Ludwig, the Elector of the Palatinate. Pufendorf had arranged to have his book dedicated to the elector, and in 1661 he was offered a position, the first of its kind in Germany, in philology and international law at the University of Heidelberg.

Life's Work

Pufendorf's appointment was to the faculty of philosophy, rather than law, and his disenchantment with the place he actually received may have been reflected in a trenchant and polemical, but also bold and insightful, study of the law and constitution of the Holy Roman Empire. His *De statu imperii Germanici, ad Laelium fratrem, dominum Trezolani, liber unus* (1667; *The Present State of Germany*, 1690), published abroad under a pseudonym, was banned by the imperial censor. In this work, Pufendorf attacked pretense and empty formality in the imperial constitution. In a famous passage, he contended that the empire, being neither a monarchy nor a democracy nor yet an aristocracy, resembled a monstrosity of irregular proportions; sovereignty on behalf of the state had been compromised, according to Pufendorf, by conflicting forms of authority exercised by its constituent rulers within the empire. The outcry which attended the circulation of this work, taken with Pufendorf's continuing dissatisfaction with his academic lot, left him open to offers from other patrons of learning. Although he had married Katharina Elisabeth von Palthen, a wealthy widow, in 1665, he felt sufficiently uneasy about his position in Germany that he accepted another appointment, advanced on behalf of King Charles XI of Sweden, to take up a full professorship at the University of Lund. Some of Pufendorf's later publications dealt once more with problems of the German constitution but conceded in effect that easy resolutions were not at hand.

More theoretical, and of greater importance for Pufendorf's subsequent reputation, was the major work *De jure naturae et gentium libri octo* (1672;

Of the Law of Nature and Nations, 1703), of which *De officio hominis et civis juxta legem naturalem libri duo* (1673; *The Whole Duty of Man According to the Law of Nature*, 1691) provided a condensed version for the general reading public. Great controversy arose over his effort to treat natural law at some distance from theological doctrines. According to Pufendorf, while Christianity could be regarded as ordained by the law of God, citizenship was ordered by the law of the state. Although natural law was derived from both rational and religious principles, it imposed obligations of a civic and moral sort, which could not be subsumed with respect to church or state. Pufendorf maintained that every individual, by virtue of intrinsic human dignity, had a right to freedom and equality; while he regarded man as a social being, he rejected Aristotle's contention that slavery, in distinction to contractual agreements of master and servant, could be upheld on any rational basis. The impact of Hobbes's thought could be found in many places, for, like Hobbes, Pufendorf took a presumed state of nature as a starting point in his arguments on moral and political relationships; he opposed the notion that by disposition people were hostile to one another, though he seemed to grant that individual self-interest was the wellspring of action in society. He also took issue with the English writer's conception of authority, even as he accorded similar notions an important place in his own works. Whereas early in his career Pufendorf had endeavored to defend Grotius' views, his interpretation of Hobbes had prompted him as well to counterpose his own positions with respect to Grotius' ideas. Pufendorf had come to oppose any notions of the transfer of natural rights, and instead he contended that self-defense and the preservation of property could be asserted in ways that were not provided for in Grotius' thought. On the international level, where Grotius had maintained that natural law of a special sort was binding upon states, Pufendorf was likely to posit rights and interests of separate sovereigns as principles affecting international relations.

In its outlines, Pufendorf's system of natural law was a vast and, on some counts, imperfectly defined edifice, which encompassed ethics, government, jurisprudence, government, and social thought. Whereas some critics have maintained that the very scope of this enterprise may have blunted Pufendorf's purposes, more specific objections have centered on ways by which he sought the reconciliation of opposing postulates by adopting a middle course, which left certain issues murky or incompletely resolved. He upheld the principle of sovereignty as a source of government and argued that self-sufficiency and self-determination were necessary for the existence of any state. His notion of authority led to a justification of actions undertaken for reasons of state; he did not, however, defend the unbridled exercise of power for its own sake, nor did he maintain that encroachments upon the rights of individuals should be permitted at will. Much of the argument he advanced on this front had to do as well with the delimitation of authority between church and state. In some of his later writings, he set forth positions concerning the authority of the state in civil affairs and the power of the Church over ecclesiastical matters, in ways by which he maintained that freedom of conscience could be observed with respect to individuals. In his own day, Pufendorf was roundly denounced by many theologians for his restrictive views on the province of the Church; in many respects, however, his thought was aimed at the promotion of toleration; indeed, his most notable work on theology also justified the Elector of Brandenburg's acceptance of Huguenot refugees after France had revoked the Edict of Nantes in 1865.

After Danish forces, during a further war with Sweden, had captured Lund, Pufendorf went on to Stockholm. In 1677, he became royal historiographer, with the rank of secretary of state; he was allowed access to government archives. He became concerned particularly with relatively recent historical problems, notably those involving the position of Sweden during and after the Thirty Years' War. Although his voluminous writings in this area have enjoyed relatively little vogue subsequently, his methods— which often consisted in the paraphrase of, or indeed wholesale quotation from, original documents—occasionally have been cited as suggesting an approach which would allow firsthand materials to elucidate the unfolding of great events. It would appear, however, that he made little effort to allow for any elements of bias that may have arisen in relying upon sources from one side, and his historical writing sometimes exhibited a pronounced moderation in dealing with delicate political matters affecting Sweden or Prussia.

The portraits of Pufendorf that exist show a dignified man of a sober and pensive bearing; to artists, he showed a steady and deliberate gaze. He had a long straight nose and a firm mouth above a relatively small chin; in some representations, he was depicted with somewhat rounded features and thick, fleshy cheeks. Toward the end of his career, Pufendorf was honored by two courts. In 1688, he left Sweden to become historiographer for the Elector of Brandenburg, and while he was in Berlin he produced several works, including studies of Hohenzollern rulers. In the last year of his life, Pufendorf received a baronetcy from the Prussian ruler, thus adding the "von" to his name, and, during a visit to Stockholm, he was similarly ennobled by the Swedish crown. The state of his health had been difficult for some time, and, upon his return to Berlin, he died from an embolism, on October 26, 1694. A work that was published posthumously the following year developed further his ideas on ecclesiastical law and put forward a proposal for Protestant unity.

Summary

It was the peculiar fate of Samuel von Pufendorf's thought to be widely discussed and probably more often praised than condemned, for about a century after his death; subsequently, his works were relegated to an obscurity into which few, save scholars and intellectual historians, have ventured. In part this result came about because doctrines of secular law became more widely accepted, while, with the development of modern jurisprudence, natural law theories increasingly were regarded as artifacts of an earlier age. In any event, while it lasted, interest in Pufendorf's writings involved some public men of note. Although Leibniz disparaged him as "a poor jurist and a worse philosopher," John Locke preferred Pufendorf's works to those of Grotius; important theorists who continued in the natural law tradition included Christian Thomasius and Christian von Wolff. Numerous editions of Pufendorf's works and translations into several languages appeared during the later seventeenth and eighteenth centuries. In one form or another, his influence was cited in works of Sir William Blackstone and of Montesquieu. Jean-Jacques Rousseau and Denis Diderot found Pufendorf's writings admirably suited for instruction and education. At opposite ends of the Western world, Peter the Great of Russia commissioned a translation of one of his famous works, and Pufendorf's writings evidently were consulted in the composition of Catherine the Great's legislative instruction; in the American Colonies, the clergyman and publicist John Wise referred liberally to the German jurist, and other American leaders paid homage to Pufendorf's thought. All the while, however, other thinkers, by moving beyond those points where Pufendorf had been most cogent, in effect consigned him to a lesser status over the long term; perhaps because his thought was neither entirely consistent nor strictly innovative, his reputation waned to the point that he has been remembered partly because of the influence he exercised rather than because of the various merits of his original writings.

Bibliography

Gierke, Otto. *Natural Law and the Theory of Society, 1500 to 1800.* 2 vols. Translated by Ernest Barker. Cambridge: Cambridge University Press, 1934. This topical study of major themes and conceptions deals with Pufendorf's thought, on the whole rather favorably, and suggests comparisons with the ideas of other theorists.

Gross, Hanns. *Empire and Sovereignty: A History of the Public Law Literature in the Holy Roman Empire, 1599-1804.* Chicago: University of Chicago Press, 1973. The author, in providing a chronological survey of pertinent works, discusses Pufendorf's writings on the imperial constitution in a balanced fashion, while dealing as well with the broader context of such publications.

Krieger, Leonard. *The Politics of Discretion: Pufendorf and the Acceptance of Natural Law.* Chicago: University of Chicago Press, 1965. As the only full-length study of Pufendorf in English, this work discusses in turn biographical facts, political and moral thought, legal doctrines, and writings on history and theology. The author, dealing largely with the philosophical merits as such of Pufendorf's teachings, concludes on an unfavorable note that rather little may be found in the way of coherence or logical rigor.

Nutkiewicz, Michael. "Samuel Pufendorf: Obligation as the Basis of the State." *Journal of the History of Philosophy* 21 (1983): 15-30. This study maintains that, by eschewing mechanistic analogies, Pufendorf was able to arrive at ethical theories, utilizing conceptions that were different from those employed by well-known contemporaries such as Hobbes or Baruch Spinoza.

Phillipson, Coleman. "Samuel Pufendorf." In *Great Jurists of the World*. Edited by John Macdonell and Edward Manson. Boston: Little, Brown, 1914. This sympathetic exposition of Pufendorf's ideas, while partly cast in the context of later controversies over legal positivism, points out ways in which theories of natural law were significant for seventeenth century thought and indeed were of great influence even in areas where later thinkers turned away from such notions.

Schneewind, J. B. "Pufendorf's Place in the History of Ethics." *Synthese* 72 (1987): 123-155. In decrying the neglect that has befallen Pufendorf's ideas among historians of moral philosophy, the author contends that his thought is worthy of further study, both in its own right and as a means of dealing with the later effects of Pufendorf's works.

Tuck, Richard. *Natural Rights Theories: Their Origin and Development*. Cambridge: Cambridge University Press, 1979. In this survey, which considers developments since late medieval times, Pufendorf is discussed toward the end in the light of works in which, at various turns, he upheld but subsequently repudiated the ideas of Grotius.

J. R. Broadus

ALEXANDER PUSHKIN

Born: June 6, 1799; Moscow, Russia
Died: February 10, 1837; St. Petersburg, Russia
Areas of Achievement: Literature and historiography
Contribution: Revered by generations of Russian writers, Pushkin's largest
legacy is in poetry, and his literary memory is compounded by the fact
that his works inspired internationally celebrated operas, ballets, and
films.

Early Life

Alexander Pushkin was born in Moscow to a father who was a tenant of a
ministerial steward and to a mother descended from the Abyssinian black
who became the adopted godson and personal secretary of Peter the Great.
Sergey Lvovich, Alexander's father, was more interested in drawing rooms
and theaters than in his estate, which he left to the mismanagement of his
wife, Nadezhda Osipovna Hannibal.

With curly, chestnut-colored hair, Alexander was a sallow, thick-lipped,
and dreamy-eyed child. Neglected by his parents, who preferred his younger
brother Leo and his elder sister Olga, he turned to his nanny, Arina Rodionovna, who regaled him with legends and songs about wizards, princesses, knights-errant, and elves. He also enjoyed the company of his maternal grandmother, Marya Hannibal, and it was at her country estate that
Pushkin learned to love his native language.

As soon as he was old enough to read, he had a number of tutors, but he
was a poor student. In 1811, he entered the lyceum in Tsarskoye Selo, a
school instituted and sponsored by imperial decree, where he studied everything from religion and philosophy to swimming and horsemanship. At age
fourteen, Pushkin published his first poem, "To a Poet-Friend," in the well-
respected *European Herald.* His official entry into the literary world occurred on January 8, 1815, when, as part of his qualifying examination for
the upper school, he recited his own poem "Recollections of Tsarskoye
Selo" before distinguished guests. His remarkable use of language, rhythm,
onomatopoeia, and references to myth established him as a prodigy.

During 1817, Pushkin's last year at school, he befriended hussars sta-
tioned at Tsarskoye Selo and joined them in bouts of drinking and gambling.
After his graduation, he was appointed to the Ministry of Foreign Affairs,
but in 1818 he joined the Society of the Green Lamp, a literary club with
liberal political leanings. The next year, he was suspected of collaborating
with revolutionaries. Further complications arose with the publication in
1820 of his long poem *Ruslan i Lyudmila* (*Ruslan and Liudmila,* 1974). This
poem created enormous controversy, winning praise for its epic quality but
drawing condemnation for, among other things, its atheism. Pushkin was

forced into exile on Ascension Day, May 6, 1820. He spent the next few years in the south of Russia, especially in Yekaterinenshtadt, the Caucasus, and Kishinev.

Life's Work

Befriended by Nicholas Raevsky, the younger son of a general celebrated for his exploits in the Napoleonic Wars, Pushkin was invited to holiday with the Raevsky family in the Caucasus, which fueled his imagination for his poem *Kavkazskiy plennik* (1822; *The Prisoner of the Caucasus*, 1895). Raevsky's elder brother Alexander was the model for the poet's sneering Mephistophelean hero in "The Demon" of the same year.

As his literary fame increased, so did his social notoriety. He continued to be extravagant in misconduct, surviving a duel against an officer whom he had accused of cheating at baccarat and using the incident in his short story "Vystrel" (1831; "The Shot"). Pushkin finally resigned from the government in 1824, but the emperor transferred him to the Pushkin estate in the deserted province of Mikhailovka, near Pskov. There he lived in sparse, unheated quarters, without books or his customary amusements. He wrote to friends requesting copies of works by William Shakespeare, Friedrich Schiller, Johann Wolfgang von Goethe, Lord Byron, Miguel de Cervantes, Dante, Petrarch, John Milton, and Cornelius Tacitus.

Engrossed in his own idiosyncratic activities, he neglected the family farm. During this period, he completed *Tsygany* (1827; *The Gypsies*, 1957), a verse tale based on his experiences in Bessarabia, a story of defeated egotism. Strong on description, it had affected, bombastic dialogue. *Graf Nulin* (1827; *Count Nulin*, 1972), a thin, rather banal response to Shakespeare's *The Rape of Lucrece* (1594), shocked readers with its sexual frankness. Pushkin wrote many lyric poems in the same year, including "André Chenier," about the poet-martyr of the French Revolution. Its theme of heroic independence was regarded suspiciously by government censors, who deleted all references to the Revolution. Pushkin's political consciousness was further exercised in his drama *Boris Godunov* (1831; English translation, 1918), a powerful story of ambition, murder, and retribution. Never produced in Pushkin's own time, the play was savaged by critics, who thought it massively disorganized because it shifted focus from Czar Boris to the Impostor Dmitry.

This professional setback was coupled with trouble ensuing from Pushkin's friendship with several conspirators in the Decembrist Revolt on December 4, 1825, against Czar Nicholas I, who had ascended the throne after Alexander I had died suddenly in November. Sick with fury and shame for having had to plead for compassion over his friendship with a key conspirator, Pushkin was escorted to the emperor, who appointed himself the writer's censor and commanded the court to take note of the new, repentant Pushkin.

In Moscow, Pushkin lived with a friend and was invited to salons and parties of the famous, but the secret police watched him diligently. The czar wanted the poet supervised continually and tested Pushkin's loyalty and liberalism by both subtle and unsubtle means. Pushkin grew tired of Moscow and left for St. Petersburg, where he saw little of his parents. He was investigated rather belatedly for his authorship of *Gavriiliada* (1822; *Gabriel: A Poem*, 1926) and later was reprimanded for traveling without authorization.

His writing remained calm and controlled, though his life was not. In October, 1828, he began *Poltava* (1829; English translation, 1936), a poem on Peter the Great. Also that year, his beloved nanny Rodionovna died in St. Petersburg, and he met sixteen-year-old Natalya Goncharov in Moscow in the winter, falling victim to her youthful beauty. Natalya was to be his victimizing "madonna," for she was a vain, shallow creature. He became engaged to Natalya on May 6, 1830, but a cholera epidemic forced him to Boldino, where he composed *Povesti Belkina* (1831; *The Tales of Belkin*, 1947), his first sustained fictional work, and almost completed his masterpiece *Evgeny Onegin* (1825-1833; *Eugene Onegin*, 1881), which he had started in 1823.

Written as a novel in sonnet sequences, *Eugene Onegin* was modern in its devastating sociological criticism amid the doomed Romanticism of the central characters. Technically, the story was in eight cantos, each stanza in four-foot iambics, alternating between masculine and feminine rhymes. It was the first occasion that Pushkin had used a regular stanzaic arrangement for a long poem, and the "Onegin" stanza with its final rhymed couplet was probably derived from Byron's *ottava rima*. It was the figure of Onegin, however, that sealed the importance of the work, for the melancholy Romantic had affinities with such figures as Goethe's Werner and Byron's Childe Harold, and he stands as the first hero of Russian realism.

Pushkin's marriage to Natalya in September, 1831, was followed by a move to St. Petersburg, where he served as historiographer and where his mounting debts compounded his anxieties. The next five years were solid successes as far as his literary achievements were concerned. In 1837, he was elected to the Russian Academy.

The final four years of Pushkin's life marked a transition from poetry to prose. In 1834, he produced *Skazka o zolotom petushke* (*The Tale of the Golden Cockerel*, 1918) in verse, but he found more renown with the novella *Pikovaya dama* (1834; *The Queen of Spades*, 1896), which bore comparison with *Eugene Onegin*. Its themes of destruction, death, and madness were underlined by subtle symbolism in a manner reminiscent of his great French contemporary Stendhal.

Pushkin's final masterpiece was *Kapitanskaya dochka* (1836; *The Captain's Daughter*, 1846), a historical novella set during the period of the

Pugachev Rebellion. The hero is a young officer loyal to the queen, who runs the gamut of happiness, pain, and vindication both in love and in honor. In this work, Pushkin conjoins story and history, fashioning a thoroughly credible romance while also creating an interesting portrait of the rebel leader Emelyan Ivanovich Pugachev by presenting him through the sensitivities of less important characters. The alternation of scenes of love and domestic calm with scenes of battle and camp precedes Leo Tolstoy's orchestration of similar scenes in *Voyna i mir* (1865-1869; *War and Peace*, 1886), although Pushkin's scale is smaller.

Despite his literary prowess, Pushkin found himself caught up in a spiral of destructive passions. His wife, though by now the mother of his four children, was still a flirt. Besides being the emperor's special interest, she became the object of Baron Georges-Charles D'Anthès' admiration, the adopted godson of Baron Heckeren. On November 4, 1836, Pushkin received an anonymous "diploma," designating him a member of the "Order of Cuckolds." In response, Pushkin challenged D'Anthès to a duel, which was avoided by skillful manipulation on the part of Heckeren. On his friend's advice, D'Anthès married someone else and tried unsuccessfully to make peace with Pushkin. Matters came to a head with a duel on January 27, 1837, in which D'Anthès suffered a superficial rib injury while Pushkin was mortally wounded. Howling in agony, Pushkin turned to his wife to absolve her of any guilt for his death. He died on February 10.

Summary

There is no critical disagreement over Alexander Pushkin's legacy to succeeding generations of Russian writers in prose and poetry. His mature work drew on a variety of genres and influences, and he can no more be limited by the term "Romantic" than the term "realist." He was not a rebel by nature, so his Romanticism remained a force of circumstance. His most outstanding successes, *Eugene Onegin*, *The Queen of Spades*, and *The Captain's Daughter*, show a tension between a Romantic emotionalism and a cool intellect that moderates his tendency toward excess.

Although the tone of his writing varies almost as much as his inconstant temperament in life, the total body of his writing is charged with satirical humor and implicit sociological criticism. The most explicit evidence of this lies in works such as *Ruslan and Liudmila*, *Gabriel*, *Count Nulin*, and *Eugene Onegin*. Versatile in everything from verse epistles to lyrics and narratives, from historical studies to Romantic tragedies, Pushkin was preeminently a poet and novella writer.

The paradox of Pushkin was that he was intensely Russian even when he was derivatively French. His landscape was thoroughly indigenous, as were his most memorable characters. His plays (of which only *Boris Godunov* has the scope and intensity of a major work) follow history's course even as they move into man's inner world of mind, spirit, and will. While at first there is little that is Slavic about Pushkin, his work evokes some of the most cherished memories of Russia's past and his own times.

Bibliography

Bloom, Harold, ed. *Alexander Pushkin*. New York: Chelsea House, 1987. Edited with an introduction by Harold Bloom, one of the major postmodernist critics, this is a representative selection of some of the best academic criticism on Pushkin. Opens with an introductory critical essay by Bloom and a note that comments on the eleven individual essays that follow. Includes discussions of Pushkin's poetry, prose, language, imagination, and image as a Russian national poet. Contains a chronology and a bibliography.

Mirsky, D. S. *Pushkin*. New York: E. P. Dutton, 1926. A critical biography that is sometimes unsatisfyingly brief in its treatment of many works, but it sheds light on Pushkin's psychology.

Simmons, Ernest J. *Pushkin*. Cambridge, Mass.: Harvard University Press, 1937. A well-documented account of Pushkin's life, but it contains no rigorous discussion of his work.

Troyat, Henri. *Pushkin*. Translated by Nancy Amphoux. Garden City, N.Y.: Doubleday, 1970. A massive but compelling biography that is richly evocative of Pushkin's life and times, while giving detailed analyses of all of his significant writing. While highly laudatory of the artist, it never forgets to present the man in all of his emotional mutations.

Vickery, Walter N. *Alexander Pushkin*. New York: Twayne, 1970. A useful guide for nonspecialist readers that conforms to a house style favoring much plot description and generalized comment. Its main focus is on Pushkin's themes and poetic personality.

Keith Garebian

FRANÇOIS RABELAIS

Born: c. 1494; La Devinière, near Chinon, France
Died: April, 1553; Paris, France
Area of Achievement: Literature
Contribution: Rabelais, although a physician by trade, is best known for his
writings, which satirize the Church and its officials while capturing the
spirit of the Renaissance through grandiose characters who have an insa-
tiable thirst for knowledge. Rabelais' strong challenge to spiritual authority is representative of a new period in literary thought and action.

Early Life

François Rabelais was most likely born in 1494 or 1495 in the Loire valley
of France, at La Devinière, near Chinon, in the province of Touraine. His
father was a lawyer, a prominent member of the landowning middle class.
Little is known of his youth and, in fact, scarcely a date in his biography is
beyond dispute. At some point, he entered the Franciscan monastery of La
Baumette at Angers as a novice. Since his subsequent actions and especially
his writings suggest the opposite of the stereotypical monastic temperament,
Rabelais, the scholars surmise, entered the order so that he might study
ancient texts. By the age of twenty-seven, Rabelais is known to have been a
monk in the monastery of Puy-Saint-Martin at Fontenay-le-Comte, where he
was immersed in Greek and other "new" humanistic studies. The faculty of
theology at the Sorbonne was opposed to the study of Greek (eventually
proscribing such study in France), and the head of the monastery was hostile
to it as well. As a result, Rabelais petitioned Pope Clement VII for a transfer
to the more liberal and scholarly Benedictine Order. His request was granted
in 1524, and the rest of his life was a step-by-step return to a secular status.

Little is known about the next six years of Rabelais' life. He must have
found even the Benedictine monastery unsatisfactory, for he left it in 1527 or
1528. It is believed that he did considerable traveling over the next three
years or so, principally because his books would later show evidence of wide
travel. In September, 1530, he entered the University of Montpellier as a
medical student and earned a bachelor's degree in medicine; the extreme
brevity of his residence and his knowledge of Parisian student types, as
exhibited in his writings, suggest that he had previously studied medicine in
Paris. Early the next year, Rabelais was giving public lectures on Galen and
Hippocrates, the ancient Greek physicians. In 1532, he moved to Lyons and
was appointed a physician in the city hospital of the Pont-du-Rhône. Hence-
forward, medicine was Rabelais' trade. The Church did not object, so long
as he retained his priestly garb and abstained from the practice of surgery.

Life's Work

Rabelais was an outstanding Greek scholar. He was a lecturer on anatomy,

using the original Greek treatises. He received his doctorate of medicine at
Montpellier in 1537 and for the last two decades of his life was highly
regarded as a skilled physician. He was an intimate of the learned and
powerful. It was not until he began his literary career at almost forty years of
age, however, that he won lasting fame.

In 1532, Rabelais was working for a Lyons printer, editing Greek medical
texts. During that summer, he read *Grandes et inestimables cronicques du
grant et énorme géant Gargantua* (1532; great and inestimable chronicles of
the great and enormous giant Gargantua), a newly published book by an
anonymous author. This crude tale was an adjunct to the Arthurian legends,
employing a character who had been present in French folklore for centuries.
Rabelais was moved to write a sequel, greatly superior to the original in both
style and content. *Pantagruel* (English translation, 1653), the literal meaning
of which is "all-thirsty," was published in the autumn of 1532. It is the story
of Gargantua's son, a boisterous and jovial drunkard, who is the gross per-
sonification of the tippler's burning thirst. A visit by Rabelais to his home
province during a time of severe drought also may have been an inspiration
for the book. *Pantagruel*'s author was identified as Alcofribas Nasier, which
was an anagram of François Rabelais. The book was an immediate success
with the public but was censured by the theological faculty of the Sorbonne
as obscene. Also in 1532, Rabelais published a tongue-in-cheek almanac,
Pantagruéline Prognostication, which survives only in fragments.

Rabelais met Jean du Bellay, Bishop of Paris and subsequently a cardinal,
in 1533. By the next year, Rabelais was the bishop's personal physician and
was attending him during a trip to Rome. In Rome, Rabelais requested
absolution for leaving the Benedictine monastery without permission, but the
pope declined to grant it. Later in 1534, back in France and still under the
protection of his powerful patron, he published *Gargantua* (English translation, 1653), the main episode of which (concerning the Picrocholine War)
was based upon his father's dispute with a neighbor over fishing rights. The
events of *Gargantua* precede those of *Pantagruel*; *Gargantua* would eventually become book 1 of the combined work. This volume was more satiric
than the first, and Rabelais made his enemies, the theologians at the Sorbonne, the objects of scorn and derision.

Rabelais' satire of Scholasticism, the Church's official intellectual system
for the previous two hundred years, roused such prejudice against him that
he went into hiding for a time. By 1536, however, he was back in Rome,
again traveling as a member of Jean du Bellay's party. This time, his petition
was successful. The pope granted him absolution, and later in the year, after
his return to France, he gained the status of a secular priest. For the rest of
his life, Rabelais avoided the official censure of the Church. He continued to
travel during the years that followed, and he acquired further protection from
his academic enemies by winning a minor post at the court of King Francis I.

In all, Rabelais made four documented visits to Italy, under the protection either of Jean du Bellay or Jean's older brother Guillaume. The third sojourn in Rome lasted until 1541 and put Rabelais in frequent contact with the most learned and powerful men at the courts of the French ambassador and the pope. During these years, Rabelais was regarded as a greater physician than writer—he was famed for his dissection of cadavers and for the number of amazing cures he had effected.

Also in 1541, a new edition of Rabelais' work, *Gargantua and Pantagruel* (which combined the two earlier publications), appeared. Rabelais edited the work so as to soften somewhat its satirical treatment of theologians. The Sorbonne was not, however, in the least mollified; it forbade the sale or possession of the book.

During the 1540's, relations between the temporal and spiritual authorities were severely strained in France as elsewhere, so Rabelais maintained a low profile. Eventually, Rabelais used his court connections to publish the next installment of the giants' adventures. Book 3 of *Gargantua and Pantagruel* (1546) was dedicated to Queen Marguerite of Navarre, sister to the king. In fact, in 1545, Rabelais had secured official permission from the king to publish the book. Still, the faculty of theology at the Sorbonne condemned book 3. In this volume, the central character is really Panurge. In the loose narrative of the earlier works, Gargantua has sent Pantagruel to Paris to be educated. There the giant falls into the company of Panurge, who is about thirty-five years of age at the time they meet. Panurge (literally "all-doer" or "knave") is the stereotypical perennial college student: He lives by his wits and is sly, mischievous, lascivious, and debauched.

Rabelais made his fourth and final visit to Rome in 1548, and in his absence opposition to *Gargantua and Pantagruel* grew steadily. Nevertheless, in 1550 he again obtained the king's permission to publish further. In 1552, he brought out book 4, as well as revised and corrected versions of the first three books. Not unexpectedly, the Sorbonne banned book 4 immediately upon its publication. In 1551, Rabelais had been appointed to the two curacies of Saint-Martin-de-Meudon and Saint-Cristophe-de-Jambet. He resigned both appointments early in 1553. Some scholars believe that he was forced to give up the curacies as a result of having published book 4; others speculate that poor health was his motivation. According to tradition, Rabelais died in April, 1553, in the rue des Jardins, Paris.

From 1562 through 1564, a fifth book was assembled. Few accept book 5 as being totally the work of Rabelais. Critical opinion ranges from the belief that it includes only sketches and fragments by Rabelais to the belief that it is essentially his work, edited and expanded by the hand of another.

Summary

François Rabelais has been afforded the greatest honor which can be bestowed upon any literary man or woman—his name has become an adjective. The term Rabelaisian is often applied too narrowly, to mean simply a story which graphically features copulation and the bodily functions. Still, the origination of that adjective is an acknowledgment that Rabelais' work is so singular as to be described only on its own terms.

It has been suggested that no writer better captures the spirit of the Renaissance. His giants represent the grandiosity of his age. Their appetite for life is as huge as their bodies, and they thirst for knowledge as well as wine. Few passages in literature contrast the medieval and the Renaissance attitudes so strikingly as do chapters 21 through 24 of book 1. Gargantua's tutor, Ponocrates, an advocate of the "new learning," saves the giant from the slothful and ineffective instruction of his former teachers, the worst of whom is the Sophist and Scholastic master, Tubal Holofernes. The demanding regimen of Ponocrates turns Gargantua into a complete man, physically, mentally, and spiritually—what the moderns have come to call the Renaissance man.

Also, few examples of the Humanist ideal can match Rabelais' utopian Abbey of Thélème (book 1, chapters 52 through 57). The rule of Thélème is the obverse of that of Saint Benedict, which Rabelais himself had finally fled. Only the brightest and most beautiful are admitted to the abbey. There, members of both sexes freely mingle, wearing beautiful clothes and engaging in exhilarating conversation. Their behavior is virtuous not because of codes and admonitions but because of their natural high-mindedness. The only rule at Thélème could serve as the motto of the Renaissance: "Fay ce que vou dras" (do what you wish).

Bibliography
Bakhtin, Mikhail. *Rabelais and His World*. Reprint. Translated by Hélène Iswolsky. Bloomington: University of Indiana Press, 1985. A reprint of the English translation first published by the Massachusetts Institute of Technology Press in 1968; the Russian edition was published in 1965. Bakhtin's widely influential study considers Rabelais in the context of the "carnival" tradition: a rich and subversive vein of folk humor and comic festivities evident throughout the Middle Ages and the Renaissance.
Brown, Huntington. *Rabelais in English Literature*. Reprint. New York: Octagon Books, 1967. A reprint of Brown's study, first published by Harvard University Press in 1933. Argues that since the Renaissance, Rabelais has been better appreciated in England than in his own country and that his influence upon English literature has been very marked. Brown traces this influence in Ben Jonson, Sir Thomas Browne, Jonathan Swift, Laurence Sterne, Tobias Smollett, and others.
Coleman, Dorothy Gabe. *Rabelais: A Critical Study in Prose Fiction*. Cambridge, England: Cambridge University Press, 1971. This study examines

the first four books of *Gargantua and Pantagruel* in nine chapters and some 230 pages of text. The author excludes discussion of book 5 on the grounds that its authenticity has not been established in four hundred years and may never be. She has used the English version (a very free interpretation) of Sir Thomas Urquhart of Cromarty (1611-1660) for the first three books and that of Peter le Motteux for the fourth. She quotes Rabelais directly when a more accurate rendering is required. Contains a chronology and a select bibliography.

Kaisar, Walter. *Praisers of Folly: Erasmus, Rabelais, Shakespeare.* Cambridge, Mass.: Harvard University Press, 1963. Begins with a prologue, discussing the fool in Renaissance literature. Part 2 is devoted to Rabelais' Panurge. He is compared to Desiderius Erasmus' Stultitia (part 1) and to William Shakespeare's Falstaff (part 3). Includes an extensive bibliography.

Rabelais, François. *Rabelais: A Dramatic Game in Two Parts.* Edited by Jean-Louis Barrault. Translated by Robert Baldick. New York: Hill & Wang, 1971. A play adapted from the five books of Rabelais. The playwright attempts to capture and project Rabelais' essential psychic health and love of life. Part (act) 1 is devoted to Gargantua and Pantagruel; part (act) 2 is devoted largely to Panurge. Each of the famous incidents is dramatized: part 1, scene 5, "Medieval Education"; part 1, scene 6, "Humanist Education"; part 1, scene 7, "Picrochole"; part 1, scene 8, "The Abbey of Thelema"; and the epilogue, "The Death of Rabelais." Includes nine photographs from the play in performance.

Tilley, Arthur Augustus. *Studies in the French Renaissance.* New York: Barnes & Noble Books, 1968. A reprint of a work first published by Cambridge University Press in 1922. Three chapters are devoted exclusively to Rabelais: chapter 3, "Rabelais and Geographical Discovery," chapter 4, "Rabelais and Henry II," and chapter 5, "Rabelais and the Fifth Book." Fully indexed.

Patrick Adcock

JEAN RACINE

Born: December, 1639; La Ferté-Milon, France
Died: April 21, 1699; Paris, France
Areas of Achievement: Theater and drama
Contribution: Combining psychological insight, poetic power, and a profoundly pessimistic view of human life, Racine wrote the finest tragedies in French literature.

Early Life

Jean Baptiste Racine was born in the village of La Ferté-Milon, near Soissons, France, and was baptized on December 22, 1639, presumably shortly after his birth. His mother was Jeanne Sconin Racine, and his father was Jean Racine, a minor local official. When Jean Baptiste was a year old, his mother died in childbirth. Although his father remarried a year later, he too died, in 1643, leaving Jean Baptiste and his sister penniless. His grandparents took the two babies; Jean Baptiste's sister went to his mother's family, and he went to live with his father's parents. When Jean was nine, however, his paternal grandfather died, and his grandmother entered the Convent of Port-Royal des Champs, southwest of Paris, where her sister was a nun and her daughter was a postulant.

Port-Royal was the center of Jansenism, an austere doctrine, based on Cornelis Jansen's interpretation of Saint Augustine, arguing that man was predestined to be saved by grace alone, not by works. After its introduction at the Cistercian convent of Port-Royal in 1634, Jansenism began to spread throughout France, partly because its emphasis on rectitude appealed to those who were disillusioned with the moral corruption around them and partly because its proponents were the outstanding scholars and educators of their day. Realizing the threat which Jansenism posed to their intellectual and educational monopoly, the Jesuits opposed it bitterly and in 1653 obtained the condemnation of its doctrines by Pope Innocent X. Throughout its existence, Port-Royal, its nuns, and its scholars were subject to persecution. The opponents of Jansenism finally succeeded in having the convent abolished in 1708.

Like many other young men of his time, Jean Racine was educated by the Jansenists. Indeed, except for two years in a Jansenist college in Beauvais (1653-1655), he was at the center of Jansenism, Port-Royal des Champs, from 1649 to 1658, reading the literary classics, learning Greek and Latin, studying philosophy and theology, and absorbing the somber view of life which was held by his mentors. For the orphaned boy, Port-Royal was home as well as school. In addition to his aunt, grandaunt, and grandmother in the convent, he had other kinfolk nearby. His grandmother's sister had married M. Vitart, and the Vitarts, too, were ardent Jansenists. Racine's feeling for

Port-Royal is evident: Even after his school was closed by royal decree in 1656, he remained at Port-Royal, studying independently. Later, he was to defend the Jansenists as much as he dared; to write a short history of Port-Royal, which was not published even in part until 1742 and not in full until 1767; and to request burial at Port-Royal.

In 1658, Racine went to the Collège d'Harcourt in the University of Paris to study law. The following year, he lived with and was employed by his grandmother's nephew Nicolas Vitart, the steward of the Jansenist Duc de Luynes. From his base in the Hôtel de Luynes, Racine ventured into the brilliant, sophisticated world of Louis XIV's France. He became a boon companion of the ecclesiastical amorist, the Abbé le Vasseur, and of Jean de La Fontaine, who was to write the immortal *Fables Written in Verse* (1668). He attended the theater, socialized with actors and actresses, and indulged in a number of love affairs. He also began to write, first light verse, then an ode dedicated to Louis' new queen. This was Racine's first published work.

Because of his association with performers, however, Racine was also developing an interest in writing for the theater. Encouraged by an actress, he wrote his first play, which was never produced and is lost; encouraged by an actress of another troupe, he began a second play that may not have been finished and certainly was never performed.

Although Racine was enjoying himself in Paris, he was sinking deeper and deeper into debt. Furthermore, his family disapproved of his activities. At their insistence, in 1661 he went to Uzès, where a maternal uncle hoped to find the young man a sinecure in the Church. A year later, unsuccessful, Racine was back in Paris. Events had made the decision for him: He was to make his mark not in the Church but in the theater and at court.

Life's Work

As Racine's letters reveal, the playwright was a complex person. From the Jansenists, he had absorbed the conviction that human beings are at the mercy of emotions over which they have no control and that therefore they have very little control over their lives. As a sensitive human being, he felt compassion for these creatures, yet as an artist he could view their anguish with detachment. Racine liked to think of himself as a scholar-poet; yet he was ambitious, and he planned the political moves which would ensure his success at court. A sketch by his eldest son emphasizes both his confidence and his capacity for detachment. A dark-eyed, dark-wigged man with a prominent nose, rounded features, and an unimpressive chin, Racine looks out at the world with a slight smile, as if he is taking its measure for his plays and for his purposes.

Racine's career as a playwright lasted only thirteen years, from 1664 to 1677. During that time, he produced eleven tragedies and one comedy, rose to social eminence, and, by winning royal favor, gained wealth and a title of nobility. It was the great actor-manager and comic playwright Molière who produced Racine's first tragedy at the Palais Royal on June 20, 1664. Entitled *La Thébaïde: Ou, Les Frères ennemis* (1664; *The Theban Brothers*, 1723), it was the account of the struggle between the two sons of Oedipus, Eteocles and Polynices, for the throne of Thebes. Although the play lacks the sureness of touch which would later be evident, it does have the typical situation of a Racine tragedy: an emotional obsession, in this case the mutual hatred of two brothers, which cannot be controlled, but which results in the destruction of those who are obsessed and of all those who are involved in their lives.

In his second tragedy, *Alexandre le Grand* (1666; *Alexander the Great*, 1714), Racine followed the footsteps of Pierre Corneille, who had for some time been the monarch of French tragic theater. Although it was successful, the play of love, rivalry, and betrayal at the court of Alexander the Great lacks the stature of later plays. Surprisingly, after it had been performed by Molière's troupe, Racine took the play, along with Molière's beautiful leading lady, Marquise Du Parc, to the rival company of the Hôtel de Bourgogne. Biographers have attempted to justify what must be classified as ingratitude by noting that the realistic acting style of Molière's company, so effective in comedy, did not do justice to the raptures and passions of seventeenth century tragedy. At any rate, all of Racine's later plays were presented by the *Comédiens du Roy* of the Hôtel de Bourgogne.

Racine's success in the theater scandalized his relatives and friends at Port-Royal, who hoped to save him and France from the domination of the theater. When in 1665 the Jansenist Pierre Nicole called novelists and dramatists the poisoners of souls, Racine viciously attacked him in print, thus joining himself to the enemies of Port-Royal. Although Racine has been accused of opportunism at a time when the Jansenists were increasingly unpopular, it may be that he had tired of the Jansenists' unceasing castigation of the art form he loved. In the preface to *Phèdre* (1677; *Phaedra*, 1701), Racine addressed his old teachers in more measured tones, urging them to realize that his tragedies were essentially as didactic as their sermons.

In November, 1667, Du Parc played the lead role in *Andromaque* (*Andromache*, 1674), a superb play about Hector's heroic widow who is doomed by Pyrrhus' obsessive love for her. With this play, Racine had reached the level of tragic grandeur that he was to maintain until the end of his career as a playwright. Although in 1668 he tried his hand at comedy with *Les Plaideurs* (*The Litigants*, 1715), an adaptation of Aristophanes, he soon returned to his own métier and wrote two fine tragedies on subjects from Roman history, *Britannicus* (1669; English translation, 1714) and *Bérénice* (1670; English translation, 1676). With these plays, Racine unseated Corneille from the throne of tragedy and became the recognized monarch.

Racine was never afraid to explore new subject matter. In 1672, he pre-

sented *Bajazet* (English translation, 1717), a violent play set in contemporary Turkey; in *Mithridate* (1673; *Mithridates*, 1926), Racine wrote a moving story about an Oriental ruler who could defy Rome but who could not
subdue his own passion for a young Greek woman. Of all Racine's plays,
this was Louis' favorite.

At this point in his career, Racine's fortunes were at their height. Every
play seemed to increase his standing with the king and with the public. The
fact that the critics were equally enthusiastic was reflected in his election in
1673 to a seat in the Académie Française, the French society of men of
letters. The once-penniless orphan was now well-off. Since his second ode
in 1663, he had been awarded pensions from the king, and in 1674 he was
given a lucrative post as Treasurer of Moulins, which automatically raised
him to the ranks of nobility. Ironically, he was only three years away from
abandoning the theater, to which he owed everything he had won.

During those three years, however, Racine produced two more masterpieces, this time modeled on those of the Greek playwright Euripides. They
were *Iphigénie* (1674; *Iphigenia in Aulis*, 1700), the story of Agamemnon's
daughter who was sacrificed for Greek success in the Trojan War, and *Phaedra*, the tale of Theseus' wife, whose desperate desire for her stepson destroyed both him and her.

The year which began with the performance of *Phaedra* marked a turning
point in Racine's life. In June, he was married to Cathérine de Romanet, a
well-connected, pious young woman in her mid-twenties, who had never
read one of his plays but who was to give him seven children. During that
year, too, he accepted an extremely profitable post as king's historiographer.
Whether ambition dictated that he consolidate his position at court by severing his theatrical connections, or whether, as his son and biographer insists,
a religious conversion turned the playwright against his genre, after 1677
Racine wrote no plays for the commercial theater. In 1689, however, at the
request of Madame de Maintenon, Louis' wife, he wrote *Esther* (English
translation, 1715), a religious tragedy, and he followed it in 1691 with
Athalie (*Athaliah*, 1722), which was also based on biblical material. Both
plays were presented at a girls' school at Saint-Cyr. Racine's final works
were the *Cantiques spirituels* (1694), four songs based on biblical texts, and
the secretly written history of Port-Royal, published long after his death.
During the last two years of his life, Racine seems to have once again
embraced Jansenism and as a result to have fallen from the king's favor.
Racine died in Paris on April 21, 1699. At his request, he was buried at Port-
Royal des Champs. When the king had Port-Royal destroyed in 1710, Racine's remains were moved to a churchyard in Paris.

Summary

Following Corneille, Jean Racine established French neoclassical tragedy.

Like his predecessor, Racine emphasized heroic deeds and heroic language, and like him he elevated the human conflict of love and duty to an almost Olympian level. Yet even their contemporaries realized that Racine had surpassed Corneille. Understanding that the simplicity and the compression of Greek tragedy could produce a maximum effect, Racine mastered the conventions of those earlier plays, producing works in which no character, line, speech, or scene seems superfluous. Furthermore, writing from his Jansenist background, Racine created a world essentially more tragic than that of Corneille. In Racine's world, divinity created human beings whose passions were uncontrollable and then warned them that they would be destroyed if they did not control them. For three centuries the audiences at Racine's plays have experienced intensely tragic emotions—pity for his trapped creatures and fear that all human beings at some time may be similarly destroyed.

Although new neoclassical plays are seldom written, the seven tragedies of Racine's maturity, from *Andromache* to *Phaedra*, are all frequently presented at the Comédie Française and throughout the world. Along with four of Corneille's tragedies and the comedies of Molière, they are some of the finest plays from France's golden age of drama.

Bibliography

Abraham, Claude. *Jean Racine*. Boston: Twayne, 1977. A survey of Racine's work, helpful for its overview of his importance in his genre. Interesting analyses of the major plays.

Barthes, Roland. *On Racine*. Translated by Richard Howard. New York: Hill and Wang, 1964. Two of its three essays are useful. "Racinian Man" deals with the Racinian hero from a structural and psychoanalytic point of view, and "Racine Spoken," originally a review of *Phaedra*, discusses the problems in acting Racine plays.

Brereton, Geoffrey. *Jean Racine: A Critical Biography*. New York: Harper & Row, 1973. An important biography by a major critic. Brereton goes beyond the facts to assess Racine's situation realistically in order to ascertain his motives for those actions which have been too easily criticized.

Clark, A. F. B. *Jean Racine*. Cambridge, Mass.: Harvard University Press, 1939. Reprint. New York: Octagon Books, 1969. A well-written chronological study, with valuable sections on the age of Racine and on the development of the French classical tradition up to his time. Contains a full treatment of both biblical plays.

Mourgues, Odette de. *Racine: Or, The Triumph of Relevance*. Cambridge: Cambridge University Press, 1967. A critical work which carefully places Racine within the context of his historical period.

Tobin, Ronald W. *Racine and Seneca*. Lincoln: University of Nebraska Press, 1973. Explores the influence of the Roman tragedian on Racine's plots and themes. An important book because this relationship has been neglected by many critics, who have assumed that Racine followed only Greek models.

Weinberg, Bernard. *The Art of Jean Racine*. Chicago: University of Chicago Press, 1963. An invaluable book on Racine's development as a dramatist, particularly emphasizing structure. Sensibly organized, with one chapter on each of Racine's eleven tragedies.

Rosemary M. Canfield Reisman

JEAN-PHILIPPE RAMEAU

Born: 1683 (baptized September 25); Dijon, France
Died: September 12, 1764; Paris, France
Area of Achievement: Music
Contribution: Rameau was the outstanding French composer of his time.
Particularly important as a composer of music for the stage, he was also
an important theorist and can be said to have established the modern
concept of harmonic practice.

Early Life

Jean-Philippe Rameau was the seventh of eleven children born to Jean
Rameau and his wife, Claudine (née Demartinecourt). His father was an
organist of the collegiate Church of St. Étienne, as well as of the Abbey of
St. Bénigne, and his mother was a member of the lesser nobility. His younger brother, Claude, also became a professional musician, serving as organist for various churches in Dijon and Autun. Jean-Philippe was intended for
the law and to that end was sent to the Jesuit Collège des Godrans, where he
apparently spent more time singing and writing music than studying and was
asked to leave. At the age of eighteen, he was sent by his father to Italy to
study music, but he traveled only as far as Milan, where he spent a few
months before returning to Dijon.

In January, 1702, Rameau was appointed temporary organist at Avignon
Cathedral, and in May of that year he signed a contract to serve for six years
as organist of the cathedral in Clermont, seemingly prepared to embark on
an unexceptional career as a provincial church musician. By 1706, however,
he was in Paris, where he published his first collection of harpsichord music,
Premier Livre de pièces de clavecin, consisting of a single large suite in a
markedly conservative style. In March, 1709, he succeeded his father as
organist at the Church of Notre Dame in Dijon. In July, 1713, he was at
Lyons, where he directed the music in celebration of the Peace of Utrecht
and where he was also employed as organist by the Jacobins. In April, 1715,
he returned to Clermont as cathedral organist, signing a contract to serve for
twenty-nine years; he remained for only eight.

Nothing is known of Rameau's time in Clermont, but either there or at
Lyons he is thought to have written his five surviving motets and a similar
number of cantatas. He also undertook the research and writing of his first
book, *Traité de l'harmonie* (1722; *Treatise on Harmony*, 1971), which was
published in Paris shortly before he relocated there permanently. He was
then in his fortieth year and virtually unknown in the French music world.

Life's Work

During his first years in Paris, Rameau was considered primarily a theorist and teacher, largely because of the success of the *Treatise on Harmony* and of his next work, *Nouveau Système de musique théorique* (1726; *New System of Music Theory*, 1974). He continued to compose, contributing music to productions of the Fair theaters (Théâtres de la Foire) and publishing his second and third collections of harpsichord music, *Pièces de clavecin avec une méthode pour la mécanique des doights*, in 1724, and *Nouvelles Suites de pièces de clavecin*, probably in 1728. Both contain a mixture of dances and genre pieces, organized by keys but not forming suites.

On February 25, 1726, Rameau married Marie-Louise Mangot, the daughter of a musician from Lyons in the service of the French court and herself an accomplished singer and harpsichordist. They had four children, two of whom survived Rameau. In 1727, he competed for the position of organist of the Church of St. Paul, but Louis-Claude Daquin was selected instead. In the same year, he wrote to the writer Houdar de la Motte and obliquely requested a libretto for an opera, but nothing came of the request.

Around this time, Rameau was introduced to the financier Le Riche de la Pouplinière, an avid patron of music and the arts, who from about 1731 maintained a private orchestra under Rameau's direction which gave performances at his house in the rue Neuve des Petits-Champs. The meeting with la Pouplinière was to be the most significant event in Rameau's career. Although from at least 1732 to 1738 he was organist of the Church of Ste. Croix-de-la-Bretonnerie and from 1736 to 1738 also organist at the Jesuit Novitiate, most of the remainder of Rameau's life was spent under the patronage of la Pouplinière both as a theorist and as a composer of music for the stage.

Rameau's first opera, a *tragédie en musique* (or *tragédie lyrique*) entitled *Hippolyte et Aricie* (1733), was written to a libretto by Abbé Pellegrin based on Euripides' and Jean Racine's treatments of the Phaedra myth. In the tradition of Jean-Baptiste Lully's operas, it consisted of a prologue and five acts, each interweaving *divertissements* of dance and singing into the dramatic narrative. *Hippolyte et Aricie* was premiered privately at la Pouplinière's in July, 1733, and presented at the Paris Opéra on October 1, 1733, shortly after Rameau's fiftieth birthday, and was an immediate and overwhelming success.

Hippolyte et Aricie was virtually the first *tragédie en musique* to succeed at the Opéra since the death of Lully some forty-five years earlier. Although it was condemned by the conservative *lullistes* as being too Italianate, too contrapuntal, and too modern, the *ramistes*—who included most of the younger musicians—praised it extravagantly. The elderly composer André Campra remarked that "there is enough music in this opera to make ten of them; this man will eclipse us all." Following upon the success of *Hippolyte et Aricie*, Rameau began composing a sacred opera to a libretto written for him by Voltaire. The work, entitled *Samson*, was largely completed by

October, 1734, when a concert performance was given, but it never reached the stage and Rameau never again set such a distinguished librettro. Some of the music was apparently reused in *Les Fêtes d'Hébé* (1739), *Castor et Pollux* (1737), and *Zoroastre* (1749).

Rameau then began a remarkable period of activity in which he completed nearly twenty operas or ballets over the course of the next twenty years. Rameau also continued his theoretical studies, which he considered at least as important as his efforts at composition. Among his many works of theory, the clearest and most readable is *Démonstration du principe de l'harmonie* (1750; *Demonstration of the Principle of Harmony*, 1976), on which he may have received help from Denis Diderot. As he approached his sixty-fifth birthday, Rameau was at the height of his fame. He had been granted a pension and the title of Compositeur du Cabinet du Roi in May, 1745, and would be granted a further pension in 1750. Objections to his music from the conservative *lullistes* had begun to recede, and some Frenchmen, including Diderot, could admit to recognizing strengths in both composers.

Rameau's tall, thin figure and angular features were familiar to visitors to the gardens of the Tuileries and the Palais Royal, where he often walked alone. His physical resemblance to Voltaire was noted by his contemporaries and became more pronounced as both men grew older. Never a sociable man and always noted for his short temper, Rameau became even more acerbic in his later years. Despite accusations of avarice, however, he seems to have remained generous to his family and as open-hearted to his few friends as he was implacable to his more numerous enemies in the field of music theory.

In 1752, an event occurred in Paris which had a startling effect on musical life in that city: a traveling troupe of Italian musicians performed Giovanni Pergolesi's comic intermezzo *La serva padrona* and ignited the so-called War of the Buffoons over the relative merits of French and Italian music. Rameau, although he took no active part in the quarrel, was naturally cast in the role of representative of French music—and a particularly conservative representative at that. Shortly after this event, la Pouplinière, who had separated from his wife, an ardent Rameau supporter, in 1748 took a new mistress, who rapidly dismissed many of the old faces, including Rameau. La Pouplinière, whose tastes ran to the lighter Italian style, acquiesced in the dismissal, and Rameau left in 1752, soon to be replaced as music director by Johann Stamitz.

Rameau was now seventy, and for the remaining twelve years of his life he was to continue to produce operas and ballets, though at a slower rate. His last completed work was a five-act *tragédie lyrique* entitled *Abaris: Ou, Les Boréades*, a remarkable achievement for a man of eighty. It was in rehearsal at the Opéra when Rameau died on September 12, 1764. It was replaced by a revival of an earlier work by André Campra and had to wait more than two hundred years for its premiere performance.

Summary

Jean-Philippe Rameau's works for the theater form the culmination of the tradition of French Baroque opera begun by Lully. They also contain much of his greatest music. His first opera, *Hippolyte et Aricie*, is also his masterpiece, as it successfully combines a truly dramatic plot with the traditional French love of spectacle and dance, and incorporating the chorus as a participant in the action. He also created authentically dramatic characters in Theseus and, to a lesser extent, Phaedra. *Castor et Pollux* also succeeds dramatically, even though the plot may not be said to be truly tragic, and again the *divertissements* are integrated into the action. The overall effect is gentler and more nostalgic than that of the earlier work.

In many ways, the most remarkable aspect of Rameau's stage works is the astonishing variety of the instrumental music. He was an adept orchestrator, and this is shown most clearly in the descriptive symphonies such as those accompanying the appearance of the monster in *Hippolyte et Aricie* or the summoning of the winds in *Abaris*. His most appealing music is found in his *symphonies de danse*, which include examples ranging from courtly dances such as the gavotte to the newly popular *contredanse* and *tambourin*. In his overtures, he soon broke with the traditional Lullian slow-fast formula and composed programmatic overtures which presaged those of the nineteenth century.

Both Rameau's harpsichord works and his *Pièces de clavecin en concerts* (1741) have remained in the repertoire, and he is especially remembered for his descriptive pieces such as *Le Rappel des oiseaux* and *Les Cyclopes* and his portraits of friends such as *La Forqueray* and *La Cupis*. Many of his keyboard dances reappeared for orchestra in his stage works. His sacred works and cantatas are less important, although they contain much fine music.

Rameau was perhaps more important in his own time as a theorist, and his works made a lasting impression on musical thought. He derived from a study of acoustics the principle of the fundamental bass, whereby each chord possessed a fundamental tone or root whose function was not determined by the lowest sounding pitch. This led to the concept of harmonic inversions, which could be applied either to intervals or to chords, and to the idea of chord progressions, which led in turn to the concept of functional harmony involving tonic, dominant, and subdominant chords and their substitutes. He also had much to say concerning the construction of the seventh chord and the liberal use of dissonance; the presence of both is what gives his own music much of its character. In his later years, he became increasingly fractious and pedantic, but his theories served as the basis for modern views of harmony in Western music.

Rameau seems to have been a man both of his age and apart from it. His theories are clearly the product of the Age of Reason, yet he continued to refer to the earlier concept of "good taste" (*bon goût*). His stage works embody Baroque grandeur dressed in less substantial rococo garb. Throughout his music, there is a sense of detachment, even disillusion, which probably reflects his own philosophy; yet there are moments of deep passion in nearly all of his major works. He was the dominant French musician of the High Baroque and is worthy to stand with Johann Sebastian Bach and George Frideric Handel as the greatest composers of that era.

Bibliography
Anthony, James R. *French Baroque Music from Beaujoyeulx to Rameau.* Rev. ed. New York: W. W. Norton, 1978. A good introduction to the subject. This work actually ends with the rise of Rameau but includes brief discussions of some of his works.
Ferris, Joan. "The Evolution of Rameau's Harmonic Theories." *Journal of Music Theory* 3 (1959): 231-256. A useful overview of the subject, to be read in conjunction with Jacobi's prefaces in Rameau below.
Girdlestone, Cuthbert M. *Jean-Philippe Rameau: His Life and Work.* 2d rev. ed. New York: Dover, 1969. The standard biography of Rameau in English. Contains a detailed discussion of his life and works, musical examples, and a lengthy bibliography. Girdlestone's discussion of the music, based largely on his acquaintance with the scores, is especially insightful, although some of his judgments need modification in the light of subsequent performances.
Girdlestone, Cuthbert, and Albert Cohen. "Jean-Philippe Rameau." In *The New Grove Dictionary of Music and Musicians.* Edited by Stanley Sadie. London: Macmillan, 1980. The standard music-reference article on Rameau. Contains a complete list of works and an extensive bibliography, both compiled by Mary Cyr. This article has Girdlestone's last thoughts on the composer he had so long championed and should be read in conjunction with his biography listed above.
Rameau, Jean-Philippe. *Jean-Philippe Rameau: Complete Theoretical Writings.* Edited by Erwin Jacobi. Rome: American Institute of Musicology, 1967-1972. A facsimilie edition of Rameau's theoretical works in six volumes, with extensive prefatory material in English.
Sadler, Graham. "Rameau's Singers and Players at the Paris Opéra: A Little-Known Inventory of 1738." *Early Music* 11 (October, 1983): 453-467. The most useful article in a volume of the journal devoted largely to Rameau.

Graydon Beeks

LEOPOLD VON RANKE

Born: December 21, 1795; Wiehe, Thuringia
Died: May 23, 1886; Berlin, Germany
Area of Achievement: Historiography
Contribution: Ranke is considered the father of modern historial scholarship and a founder of the German idea of history. His historial works rank as classics of modern historiography.

Early Life

Leopold von Ranke's father, Gottlob Israel Ranke, was a lawyer, but the Lutheran ministry was the traditional profession of the family. Ranke's parents expected him, the eldest of nine children, to follow a career in the Church. After an early education in local schools, he was sent to Schulpforta, a famous German public school known for the quality of its humanistic, classical curriculum. Ranke studied philology and theology at the University of Leipzig and received a doctoral degree in 1817 for a dissertation on the political ideas of Thucydides.

As a student, Ranke adopted the critical philological method of Barthold Niebuhr, a statesman and scholar whose *Römische Geschichte* (1811-1832; *History of Rome*, 1828-1842) reconstructed the historical origins of the Roman state. Ranke admired Niebuhr's history but not his clumsy prose. A master stylist himself, he was early influenced by the German of Martin Luther and Johann Wolfgang von Goethe. Although he remained a devout Lutheran, Ranke declined to enter the ministry. The classics and philology interested him more than dogma. In 1818, he became a master of classical languages in the *Gymnasium* in Frankfurt an der Oder. Entrusted with the teaching of history, Ranke was led to write his first book, *Geschichte der romanischen und germanischen Völker von 1494 bis 1514* (1824; *History of the Latin and Teutonic Nations from 1494 to 1514*, 1887), in which he applied his philological training to the field of modern history. Ranke was called in 1824 to the University of Berlin, where he taught until 1871.

Ranke's students left a vivid vignette of their master. He is described as a slight figure with dark, curly hair, a low voice, a lively speaking manner, penetrating blue eyes, and a serene temperament. He, in turn, took a paternalistic interest in his students, who eventually filled almost every chair of history in Germany. Surrounded by his children and grandchildren (he married Clara Graves, daughter of an Irish barrister, in 1843, and the couple had two sons and a daughter), he would say that he had another and older family, his pupils and their pupils.

Life's Work

In the programmatic preface to *History of the Latin and Teutonic Na-*

tions from 1494 to 1514, Ranke gave a new direction to historical studies by declaring that it was not the duty of the historian to judge the past for the benefit of the present or the future. It was only "to show what actually occurred." This matter-of-fact statement was directed against the historiography of the Enlightenment, which had given history an abstractly defined end and viewed it as an ascending process in which a later age was superior to an earlier one. According to Ranke each age was unique, "each period is equally close to God."

In the appendix of his first book, Ranke added that he had found traditional histories untrustworthy; they did not correspond with the evidence he found in contemporary documents. For his history, he wrote, he had relied only on original sources, critically sifted and cross-examined. Ranke's ambition to use only "the purest, most immediate documents" led him to the Italian archives in 1827. In Italy, where he gratified his "archival obsession" for three years, Ranke became the first scholar to examine the famous *relazioni*, secret reports Venetian ambassadors had submitted to their government after diplomatic missions to the courts of Europe. In such materials, Ranke believed, the historian could divine the core and secret of human events. Upon his return to the University of Berlin, where he became a full professor in 1836, Ranke created the historical seminar and instructed advanced students in *Quellenkritik*, the critical study of the sources.

Ranke spurned the schematic history of the philosophers but he was, nevertheless, a generalist. Through the perception of the particular, the historian was to grasp the inner connection and complete whole of history. As a devout Christian, Ranke believed that the unity and tendency of the historical experience were an expression of divine purpose—the "hand of God" was evident in the particular and the universal.

Divine action in the historical world was largely realized through nations or states, Ranke contended, a theory he developed in "Political Dialogue" (1836) and "The Great Powers" (1833), famous essays written while he was editor of the political journal *Historisch-politische Zeitschrift* (historical-political review) from 1832 to 1836. Ranke argued that there was no ideal political constitution. States developed their own genius and institutional forms: that was the task set them by God. Accordingly, power embodied in the nation-state was ethically good: It was an expression of God's will. This conception or idea of history, reflected in all of Ranke's historical studies, affirmed the importance of the great powers and identified the state as an ethical institution whose interests were in harmony with the general good.

While on his tour of the Italian archives, Ranke outlined the course of his future studies: first Italian, then French, English, and German studies. He turned to German history before the French and English, but otherwise the early outline of his life's work was followed faithfully. The national histories were capped by nine volumes of world history, *Weltgeschichte* (1881-1888;

partial translation as *Universal History*, 1884), begun in his eighty-sixth year.

Ranke's Italian project, published from 1834 to 1836 in three volumes, was *Die römischen Päpste in den letzten 4 Jahrhunderten* (*The History of the Popes During the Last Four Centuries*, 1907), considered by many his finest work in form and matter. Ranke approached the popes as a historian fascinated by their role in world history, but they were also a subject in which he found the "thought of God." The history of the popes was followed by *Deutsche Geschichte im Zeitalter der Reformation* (1839-1847; *History of the Reformation in Germany*, 1845-1847), a six-volume history received in Germany as a national classic, although Ranke himself thought it inferior to his study of the popes. As the first of the Reformation volumes appeared, Frederick William IV recognized Ranke's eminence as a scholar and appointed him, in 1841, historiographer of the Prussian state. Ranke was ennobled, thereby adding "von" to his name, in 1865.

In the two decades after his study of the Reformation, Ranke wrote his massive histories of the great powers, all focusing on developments from the fifteenth to the eighteenth century. *Neun Bücher preussischer Geschichte* (nine books of Prussian history), a study later expanded to twelve books, appeared in 1847-1848, and *Englische Geschichte, vornehmlich im 16 and 17 Jahrhundert* (*A History of England Principally in the Seventeenth Century*, 1966) was issued in six volumes between 1859 and 1868.

In Ranke's opinion, the most important features of history between 1492 and 1789 were the creation of the modern state, the rise of the great powers, and the establishment of the state system. He appreciated the role of ideas in history and suggested that historians should pay attention to population, churches, agriculture, industry, and transportation. In practice, however, he was a political and diplomatic historian, and he focused almost exclusively on courts and chanceries. Later historians, with a greater interest in the evolution of society, assigned ideas and social and economic forces far more important roles in historiography. On the other hand, while he was the motive force behind the creation of an encyclopedia of German national biography, Ranke himself wrote little biography; exceptions were short biographical studies of Frederick the Great and Frederick William IV. For Ranke, the individual was important only when he played an active or leading role in general history.

It is not surprising that Ranke elected to spend his final years, although infirm and unable to read or write, preparing a world history. He was able to produce eight volumes, taking his story to the end of the fifteenth century, before his death in May, 1886, at the age of ninety-one. The universal history, although incomplete, was a fitting conclusion to Ranke's career: To comprehend the whole while obeying the dictates of exact research, he had written in the 1860's, was the ideal goal of the historian.

Summary

Leopold von Ranke is commonly identified as an empirical, nonphilosophical historian, the founder of the "scientific school" of history. This image is one-sided but not invalid. Ranke sought to write history as it actually happened, free of philosophical presuppositions, and he contributed a critical method which emphasized the use of documentary sources. He suggested that national cultures and periods of history should be examined on their own terms. German historians, however, also appreciated Ranke as a contemplative thinker, and most of his successors accepted his emphasis on the central role of the state and of foreign affairs in the European experience. Many, too, adopted his concept of the spiritual character of power, a theme that runs through Ranke's writings. It was only after World War II that leading German historians concluded that Ranke had been insufficiently pessimistic regarding power and the state.

Ranke's own works, and he published a large number of historical classics, are still valuable. They are largely free of bias and show an insight and style that make them profitable reading for modern students of history.

Bibliography

Gay, Peter. "Ranke: The Respectful Critic." In *Style in History*. New York: McGraw-Hill, 1974. A perceptive and gracefully written essay on Ranke as dramatist, scientist, and believer.

Geyl, Pieter. "Ranke in the Light of the Catastrophe." In *Debates with Historians*. Groningen, the Netherlands: J. B. Wolters, 1955. A strong indictment of Ranke's idea that power was an expression of divine activity in the historical world.

Gooch, G. P. "Ranke." In *History and Historians in the Nineteenth Century*. London: Longmans, Green, 1913.

_____. "Ranke's Critics and Pupils." In *History and Historians in the Nineteenth Century*. London: Longmans, Green, 1913. Two of the best brief studies in English on Ranke.

Higham, John, Leonard Krieger, and Felix Gilbert. *History*. Englewood Cliffs, N.J.: Prentice-Hall, 1965. A useful discussion of Ranke's influence in the professionalization of history in Europe and the United States.

Iggers, Georg G. *The German Conception of History: The National Tradition of Historical Thought from Herder to the Present*. Middletown, Conn.: Wesleyan University Press, 1968. A valuable interpretative survey of the theoretical presuppositions and political values of German historians. Ranke is identified as a founding father of a school that not only adopted the critical method but also viewed the state as an ethical good.

_____. "The Image of Ranke in American and German Historical Thought." *History and Theory* 2 (1962): 17-40. A survey of divergent images of Ranke held by German and American historians.

Van Laue, Theodore H. *Leopold Ranke: The Formative Years*. Princeton, N.J.: Princeton University Press, 1950. This book traces the development of Ranke's historical ideas in the context of contemporary Germany from 1795 to 1836. It includes Ranke's essays "Political Dialogue" and "The Great Powers" in translation as well as a useful bibliographical essay.

J. A. Thompson

RAPHAEL
Raffaello Sanzio

Born: April 6, 1483; Urbino, Tuscany, Italy
Died: April 6, 1520; Rome
Areas of Achievement: Art, architecture, and archaeology
Contribution: With Leonardo da Vinci and Michelangelo, Raphael was part
of the great trio of High Renaissance masters. He became the most prolific
and most widely celebrated painter of his time.

Early Life
Raffaello Sanzio, known as Raphael, had the good fortune to be born in
the mountain town of Urbino, where Federico da Montefeltro maintained a
ducal court manifesting splendor, pomp, elegance, and the new learning.
Raphael's father, Giovanni, a minor painter and versifier, had access to the
court; from his youth, Raphael was introduced to the ongoing works of Piero
della Francesca, Sandro Botticelli, Paolo Uccello, and other contemporary
masters. Giovanni died, however, when Raphael was eleven; at this age, he
may already have been apprenticed to Perugino in Perugia. There he rapidly
moved to the head of that artist's busy workshop, which won so many
commissions that the master had to develop an elaborate atelier system, in
which assistants did much of the preliminary work on projects. By the age of
sixteen, Raphael was already influencing local artists, and from this time his
hand is detectable in Perugino's works.

Raphael's earliest independent paintings both date from 1504. The first,
Marriage of the Virgin, shows both his indebtedness to Perugino—the disposal of figures, the use of a temple as background, and an array of colors
are all drawn from him—and the introduction of what are to become signature characteristics—the supple, resilient posture of the figures, their un-
earthly serenity of expression, and the rhythmic organization of the composition. The second, *Saint George and the Dragon*, is a small panel that was
commissioned by the Duke of Urbino to present to Henry VII of England.
The influence of Leonardo da Vinci's *Battle of Anghiari* (1503) is evident
here, as it is in all subsequent mounted battle paintings. Again the dominant
element is rhythmic organization: The mounted knight on his diagonally
placed steed intersects the massed landscape, so that all the tension of the
painting drives through the lance, pinning the wriggling monster to the earth.
The spiral coil of the horse's body generates much of the accumulated tension; yet the animal itself is surprisingly static, betraying the artist's inexperience. The painting abounds in finely observed, meticulously rendered
details; the young artist seems to be showing off the facility of his technique.
These two paintings constitute the auspicious beginning of an ambitious
career.

Life's Work

Raphael's fifteen-year career falls into two phases, Florence and Rome. He settled in Florence in 1505, stepping into a void created by the withdrawal of both Leonardo and Michelangelo, at a time when the appetite for painting had been stimulated by their examples. Raphael's facility soon proved prosperous. Within three years, he finished seventeen still-extant Madonnas and Holy Families, besides several other major works. That kind of activity makes both Michelangelo, productive as he was, and Leonardo, who failed to complete one painting during that period, look like monuments of indolence. Part of the reason for this difference derives from Raphael's method of working. Unlike either of his fellow giants, Raphael did not approach painting as a series of solutions to technical problems of representation. Instead, he made preliminary sketches—many of them preserved—which show him testing variables in the relationship of forms. Only in the painting itself would he settle on one moment in the flow of forms. That allowed him to produce paintings that merely glossed over problems which would have hamstrung either of the other two. That is, Raphael painted for his patrons, not for his peers.

The *Madonna of the Meadows* (1505) is one of the best of the markedly similar items in the series. As before, much of the design and the framing landscape derives from Leonardo's examples, and much of the iconography, from Michelangelo's. Yet the rhythmical organization, the sinuous upward coiling, is distinctly Raphael, as is the countermovement in the downward glance of the Virgin. Yet the truly astonishing feature is the Virgin's face. Though both Fra Angelico and Fra Filippo Lippi had anticipated this clarity of line and simplicity of form, the viewer is still struck almost dumb by this representation of incarnate grace and superhuman serenity.

Raphael also produced for his patrons a remarkable series of portraits, in the process raising the portrait to a new level. At the same time that he was idealizing the features of his sacred work, he reversed the practice with his portraits. With them, he became the dispassionate observer, coolly recording the essential character of his subjects. The result is a gallery of distinct personalities, caught in moments of self-revelation. In doing this, he became the most successful portraitist of all time.

Around 1509, the twenty-six-year-old Raphael was called to Rome by Pope Julius II to embark on the major phase of his career, which would last for eleven years. His first commission from the pope was to take over the official decorations of the Vatican apartments (called *Stanze*, or rooms) from Sodoma. He started with the Stanza della Segnatura; in it, he determined to depict the ideals of the new pope's regime and, in the act, create frescoes of unprecedented refinement and harmony of form. His plan included two major wall frescoes facing each other and a complementary lunette: the *Dispute over the Sacrament* (1510-1511), the misnamed *School of Athens*

(1510-1511), and the *Cardinal Virtues* (1511). The first is an attempt to represent the entire doctrine of the Eucharist, from its origin in Heaven to its veneration by the people. In the cloud scene above, Raphael portrays the ordered harmony of divine Providence, in sharp contrast to the fierce contention of theologians from various disciplines on the earth below. The grandeur and rhythmic energy of the composition surpass anything yet attempted in art—or would, if Michelangelo were not simultaneously at work on the Sistine Chapel ceiling a few barricaded corridors away. Even so, the scene is colossal.

The medallion inset above the *Dispute over the Sacrament* depicts Theology; opposite it is that for Philosophy. The fresco below, the *School of Athens*, attempts to do for that field what the *Dispute over the Sacrament* does for theology—that is, represent all the leading figures in classical philosophy engaged in debate. This painting is Raphael's best-known work; it provides the textbook example of the High Renaissance ideals of integral unity and spatial harmony. The figures circulate in depth around the central figures of Plato and Aristotle, all set within a great vaulted dome in the classical manner, impractical but magnificently proportioned. This beautifully rational frame establishes the perfect setting for the debate of abstract problems; the figures surge beneath the stable, solid dome. The philosophers themselves are wonderfully individualized, yet each is playing an ensemble role in the total composition. The only modern figure slumps prominently in the foreground, dressed in stonecutter's work clothes: He turns out to be Michelangelo, the single man alive whom Raphael considered worthy of a place in the company of the ancients. The painting thus constitutes Raphael's statement of the relationship of the Renaissance to antiquity. Further, the lunette of the *Cardinal Virtues* demonstrates what Raphael had learned from Michelangelo; for his figures there suddenly take on the monumentality of that master, though transformed by Raphael's characteristic sweetness, organic rhythm, and grace.

This transition in style, from balanced serenity to dramatic expressiveness, culminates in the second apartment, the Stanza d'Eliodoro, which contains two full-wall frescoes and two window surrounds: the *Expulsion of Heliodorus* (1512), the *Expulsion of Attila* (1513-1514), the *Mass of Bolsena* (1512), and the *Liberation of Saint Peter from Prison* (1512). These combine harmony of organization with new, vibrant coloring and dramatic tension, so that the images seem almost to seethe with motion and sing with color. They show Raphael raising his unique style of spiral rhythmic organization to a new height: His figures gain weight and tension, and energy explodes in their dynamic interconnection. The artist seems to be moving toward a mode of representation beyond the capacity of the High Renaissance. His work here has been termed proto-Baroque for this reason. The *Expulsion of Heliodorus* is typical of this new sense of the dramatic. In it

Raphael shows that he was secure enough in his habits of rational organization to test them to their limits. His figures take on the mass and muscle of Michelangelo's; they vibrate with energies that threaten to tear apart his rationally organized scheme. Everything still harmonizes, but only barely.

Raphael's *Sistine Madonna* (1513) created a vision of the Madonna which totally eclipsed all of his former efforts. If any painting crystallizes the essence of the High Renaissance, this one does. This work defines rhythmic organization: Its broad spiral curves and delicately balanced masses, counterpointed by the two often-excerpted putti at the bottom of the frame, almost look like a demonstration piece for a painting class. Furthermore, the Virgin is the quintessential Virgin, perhaps the loveliest woman ever painted. Among other portraits of this period which confirm his reputation as a portraitist are those of *Baldassare Castiglione* and *Pope Leo X with Cardinals*. They have never been excelled.

Raphael's most ambitious pictorial project was to design ten massive tapestries, for which he produced full-size watercolor cartoons as models. These were intended to continue the iconographic cycle on Christian religious history begun by Michelangelo. This is Raphael's largest work, and it exhibits his dramatic intensity raised to its highest power. At the same time, Raphael was busy with architectural projects, the grandest of which is the Villa Madama in Rome; though unfinished at his death and never completed, the fragment is exquisite in design and proportion and elegant in its imaginative detail. His final great painting, completed by assistants, is the *Transfiguration of Christ* (1517). Here Raphael matches the level he had reached in the *Expulsion of Heliodorus*; color, design, and rhythm fuse in a drama that swirls off the canvas, and the figures pulse with real breath and warmth. Moreover, this painting generates a religious intensity far removed from the serene, rational indifference of the early Madonnas. Unfortunately, Raphael had little time to develop this mystical strain, for he died after a brief illness on April 6, 1520.

Summary

Raphael is the Renaissance artist ideal, or at least the embodiment of one half of the Renaissance standard of excellence. In his *Il cortegiano* (1528; the courtier), Raphael's friend Baldassare Castiglione had defined the essential quality of the refined gentleman as *sprezzatura*, an untranslatable term which means something like making difficult things look easy. Raphael certainly had the technical facility for that. Perhaps no other painter possessed equal talent. Raphael could do things effortlessly with brush or pen that artists of normal ability could produce only with monumental labor. Moreover, this effortlessness comes through in his work: Everything he does looks easy, natural, right; his figures seem not to be figures but simply themselves. In many ways, he taught his viewers what it meant to see. In the paintings, this ease of technique translates itself into ineffable grace.

Yet in his early works Raphael pays a price for this facility. He produced so much so easily that it is possible to accuse him of creating by mechanical formula. Further, instead of solving technical problems, he merely brushes by them; in this respect, he falls short of another Renaissance ideal, to make human intelligence the norm by which everything knowable was to be measured. As a result, a premium was placed on meeting the difficult head-on; problems were meant to be solved, and the man of true genius used reason to find a solution. Raphael's talent was so great that he ran the risk of becoming merely facile.

His encounters with Leonardo and Michelangelo changed that. Not that he became a great innovator, though much of his work did establish formal precedents, especially in portraits and in group narratives. Rembrandt, for example, copied Raphael's canvases with care and imitated his poses, and Nicolas Poussin and Jean-Auguste-Dominique Ingres are almost unimaginable without his examples. His work for the Vatican, however, clearly ranks with the greatest paintings of all time. In them, the early grace and serenity take on weight, mass, and energy, and a dynamic intelligence informs the whole. In these respects, Raphael becomes the incarnation of the High Renaissance ideal. As a portraitist he is supreme; his perfectly balanced, perfectly poised figures seem to occupy a moment in time, so that one can imagine a gallery of them carrying on civilized conversation when no one is in the room. His real genius, however, appears in the Vatican group compositions, in which he seems to create his own heroic universe, electric with its own energy and populated with entirely plausible though larger-than-life characters. There Raphael seems to reach the limits of the natural. It is small wonder that painters succeeding him were forced to grotesque distortions to represent superabundant energy; only Raphael could cage such forces within his cosmos of radiant and dynamic calm.

Bibliography

Beck, James. *Raphael*. New York: Harry N. Abrams, 1976. This is an excellent, thorough study of Raphael and his times, with much technical information. Intended mainly for specialists, it is surprisingly approachable and packed with a wealth of detail and good reproductions.

Fischel, Oskar. *Raphael*. Translated by B. Rackham. 2 vols. London: Kegan Paul, 1948. Fischel presents the authoritative, old-fashioned account of Raphael's life and works. Though somewhat dated, Fischel is indispensable, partly because critical opinion on Raphael has not changed much since the publication of this work.

Freedberg, Sydney J. *Painting in Italy, 1500-1600*. Rev. ed. Baltimore: Penguin Books, 1975. The reproductions in this small-format book do little justice to Raphael's large-scale works, but then no reproductions can. The text, intended for the general reader, is appealingly informative and nontechnical, making this a useful general reference.

Hartt, Frederick. *History of Italian Renaissance Art: Painting, Sculpture, Architecture*. 3d ed. New York: Harry N. Abrams, 1987. Hartt provides the most accessible brief introduction to the work of Raphael, in clear, nontechnical language and with good reproductions, though mostly in black and white. He is particularly good at summarizing iconography and analyzing formal qualities.

Jones, Roger, and Nicholas Penny. *Raphael*. New London, Conn.: Yale University Press, 1983. This nonspecialist text is a fine source for the general reader, placing Raphael squarely in his historical and social setting and including brilliant reproductions of entire works as well as blow-ups of details.

Raphael. *The Complete Works of Raphael*. Edited by Mario Salmi et al. New York: Reynal, 1969. As the title indicates, this is the only work available which attempts to catalog and reproduce everything that Raphael accomplished. Yet, since he produced so much work which has been preserved, it is impossible to reproduce everything in one volume, so the title misleads somewhat. Still, this volume offers more than any other, and the documentation is thorough.

Vasari, Giorgio. *Lives of the Most Eminent Painters, Sculptors, and Architects*. 10 vols. Translated by Gaston du C. de Vere. London: Medici Society, 1912-1915. Though not always accurate, Vasari is the best near-contemporary source for Raphael's life and his contemporary reception and reputation. Vasari's work is full of entertaining anecdotes and much miscellaneous information, all gathered at second hand. He is better on Raphael than on some, perhaps because he identified so closely with him.

James Livingston

RAMMOHAN RAY

Born: May 22, 1772; Rādhānagar, Bengal
Died: September 27, 1833; Bristol, England
Areas of Achievement: Religion and social reform
Contribution: Ray's writings have become the putative source for almost all India's social and religious reformist ideals. Known as "the father of modern India," Ray saw the Hinduism of his day as a debased form of a purer monotheism practiced in India during a prehistoric Golden Age. He also found many social customs of his own day—the forced suicide of widows and child marriage, for example—as decadent, medieval accretions on the noble patterns of the Vedic age.

Early Life
Among Bengalis of the eighteenth and early nineteenth centuries, priests (Brahmins) of the Kulin class ranked only slightly lower than the gods. Their inferiors customarily addressed them as "Lord" (*Thakur*). They also emulated the Kulin's dialect of Bengali and almost everything about their style. Kulin boys were much in demand as husbands and often had more than one wife. Rammohan Ray was born into a Kulin family and married twice while still in his early teens.

His father's ancestors had long before assimilated themselves into the culture of India's Muslim rulers and had served in many governmental posts. His father was a landowner (*zamindar*) who fell on hard times in later life. In 1800, his father was jailed for debt and died in poverty in 1803. Ray's mother's family had not moved so close to Indo-Islamic culture and supported themselves as ritual specialists.

As a boy, Ray studied Arabic and Persian and was sent to Patna in Bihar, which, as a center of Muslim learning, offered better instruction than his hometown school. That was a common practice among Hindus who adopted the cosmopolitan culture of Muslims. Ray acquired a knowledge of Islamic doctrine as well as an interest in the mystical teachings of the Sufis. These two philosophies may have been responsible for his lifelong iconoclasm. According to his own autobiographical notes, while still a teenager he criticized his father's devotion to images of the gods and was thrown out of the house. Ray seems to have romanticized his recollections of the next decade of his life, claiming a journey to Tibet to study Buddhism and a lengthy stay in Benares to learn Sanskrit. Because in later life he wanted to be considered an authority on ancient Hindu religious texts, he may have exaggerated his knowledge of the classical language.

Between 1797 and 1802, Ray seems to have spent much of his time in Calcutta, the burgeoning capital of Bengal and British India, where he acted as a moneylender. Many of his clients were young Englishmen employed by the East India Company. In this way his name became known in government circles, and he received an appointment in the Revenue Department. He eventually became a deputy district collector, the highest civil post an Indian could hold. During his active career, he invested in real estate, and by his early forties he had an ample fortune which allowed him to retire to Calcutta in 1815.

Life's Work

Beginning in the 1770's, a number of Englishmen began to expand their knowledge of India's non-Muslim traditions. Sir William Jones and Henry Colebrooke, among others, acquired a better-than-rudimentary knowledge of Sanskrit. As they discovered that an enormous body of literature existed in that tongue, they conceded to ancient Indian civilization a classical status analogous to that of Greece and Rome in Western tradition. Their efforts in the reconstruction of the history of India earned for them the sobriquet "Orientalist."

The work of the Orientalists had two institutional foci. The first was the Asiatic Society of Bengal, founded in 1784, and the second the College of Fort William, established in 1800. While the former was a typical learned society of the period which met regularly to hear papers by members on a variety of subjects published in the society's journal, the second was an unprecedented attempt to train the East India Company's servants in the languages of the peoples they expected to govern. Few of those young men proved to be able scholars, but the professors of the College of Fort William, with the help of numerous Indian assistants, kept extending their knowledge of Sanskrit and the texts written in it.

During his earlier stays in Calcutta, Ray had contacts with Englishmen active in the college. He began to learn English and became fluent in the language. He was not, however, alone in his interests and contacts with the British. A number of other Bengali intellectuals had similar connections and concerns. They imbibed a number of ideas which had originated with British scholars such as Jones and Colebrooke. One of the most important of these was the notion that Hindu civilization had enjoyed a Golden Age during which India produced a lofty and subtle religiophilosophical system every bit as valuable as that of the Greeks and Romans. They also believed that, in that halcyon time, India's society was well organized and featured a balance between the various classes.

For the Orientalists, as well as for such Indians as Ray who subscribed to their ideas, a major problem was explaining how the Golden Age had disappeared to be replaced by the polytheism, idolatry, and caste inequalities of their own day. Following the British lead, Ray and others saw Muslims as the cause of that decline. Despite a Muslim presence in the subcontinent of more than nine hundred years' duration, as well as the prominence of Hindus in Muslim governments from the very beginning of their rule, they began describing Muslims as foreign tyrants whose oppression brought on Hindu decadence. Since Ray maintained close personal ties to Muslims—in 1831, he became the Mughal emperor's first ambassador to the Court of Saint James—perhaps he espoused this opinion only as a way of inspiring his coreligionists, never thinking that the notion would have so long a life or such ultimately fatal consequences.

In 1815, Ray published *Translation of an Abridgment of the "Vedant": Or, Resolution of All the Veds, the Most Celebrated and Revised Work of Brahminical Theology*. In this book, he emphasized monotheist religious views, claiming that a pure monotheism was the true doctrine taught by Indian religious texts, especially the *Upanishads*, also known as the "End of the Vedas" (*Vedanta*). To reinforce these assertions, Ray translated several of the more than three hundred *Upanishads*. In his emphasis on monotheism—belief in a personal God—rather than monism—the assertion that all reality is an impersonal, featureless "One"—Ray seems to be reflecting his dependence not on the original Sanskrit texts but on Persian translations of them ordered by the Mughal prince Dara Shikoh. The *Upanishads* tended to stress monism, but as a Muslim Dara slanted his translations toward monotheism in order to make it seem that the texts were closer to Islam. Some of Ray's more perceptive critics pointed out that his interpretations proved that he did not have the Sanskrit learning required to give authoritative explanations of sacred literature. Ray's other concerns also provoked opposition.

As did most other religious critics in India's history, Ray soon became embroiled in controversies over social practices. He made the fate of Bengali women his special cause. At the time, women were uneducated, treated as weak creatures subject to the whims of their brutish husbands, and never allowed to leave their homes. Ray supported many measures to protect them. He championed attempts to outlaw the burning of widows on their husbands' funeral pyres. Though followed by only a few high-status families, the custom dictated that a woman volunteer for this fate, thus proving herself a "virtuous female" (*satī*). In practice, relatives used the occasion to avoid, through murder, having to support an unwanted female. He also opposed the practice of child marriage, which sometimes created widows who were eight or nine years old. Even though they were not consigned to the mortuary fires, these girls were forced to lead dreary lives either as the celibate servants of their in-laws or as unmarriageable burdens on their own parents and brothers.

Though many of his views derived ultimately from the Orientalists, Ray did not invariably support all of their schemes. For example, when some proposed the establishment of a Sanskrit college, he opposed the move, believing that it was better to teach English to Indians than to immerse them in an archaic language. In this instance, he seems to have anticipated the anti-

Orientalist reaction which arose in the government of India in the 1840's and which dominated educational policy throughout the British period.

Ray's interest in religion blossomed in Calcutta. He became a defender of his purified version of Hinduism against attacks by missionaries. He found himself drawn closer to the teaching of the Unitarians, who were emerging in the 1820's as a distinct and, to the minds of most Christians, heretical sect. Their monotheism, iconoclasm, and refusal to assert the absolute superiority of Christian revelation attracted Ray. He began corresponding with leading Unitarians in England and the United States; at one point, he contemplated finishing his life in the United States in order to be close to William Ellery Channing. *The Precepts of Jesus, the Guide to Peace and Happiness*, published in 1820, displayed the Unitarian influence. In it, he selected only those passages of the *New Testament* that contained some moral injunction and ignored those mentioning miracles or that contained assertions of Jesus' divinity. Although Ray often said that his heart was with the Unitarians, he never formally joined their church, preferring always to be known as a Hindu.

In 1828, Ray and a few associates founded the Brahmo Sabha (later called the Brahmo Samaj), or "Society of God." In general, this church was supposed to promulgate reformed religious and social principles. The Brahmo Sabha had little time to evolve as an organization before Ray in 1831 accepted the post of Mughal ambassador to England and left Calcutta forever. After his departure, the organization became moribund until it was revived some nine years later. By the time he left the city, Ray's staunchest friends were either Muslims or British Unitarians. Most of his fellow Hindus either condemned or ignored him. In England, his health ebbed and his fortune dwindled. He became a much-revered figure among English Unitarians and died in one of their homes. A Unitarian minister preached his funeral sermon.

Summary

Though today universally acknowledged as the father of modern India, Rammohan Ray was not fully recognized while he lived. The work of providing him with this identity began in the years following his death. Debendranath Tagore revived the Brahmo Sabha (calling it the Brahmo Samaj) in the years 1840 through 1842 and realized that the society required a spiritual leader to give it cohesion. Tagore, whose family produced several of Bengal's leading intellectual and literary lights, began to edit Ray's Persian, English, and Bengali writings. After K. C. Mitra published a biography of Ray in the *Calcutta Review* of 1845, the practice of crediting Ray for the invention of everything modern and progressive became common. Ray's importance, however, may well have been in his being typical of an era when Indians of many faiths and Englishmen cooperated in securing European recognition of India's civilization as one of the world's most influential and important traditions.

Bibliography
Bhattacharya, Haridas, ed. *The Cultural Heritage of India*. Vol. 4, *Religions*. Calcutta, India: Ramakrishna Mission, 1969. The last volume in a series of books cataloging many aspects of the religious and social traditions of Indian life. Shows that Hinduism is a term loosely connecting a number of very different religious tendencies. The essay on the Brahmo Samaj describes Ray's influence on this group and its place in nineteenth and twentieth century India.

Basham, A. L., ed. *A Cultural History of India*. Oxford, England: Clarendon Press, 1975. Contains thirty-five essays discussing almost every aspect of India's history from ancient times to the present. By judicious reading, a beginner will be able to discover the broader intellectual and social context in which Ray and other reformist thinkers worked.

Farquhar, J. N. *Modern Religious Movements in India*. Reprint. Delhi, India: Munshiram Manoharlal, 1967. Originally written by a sympathetic Christian missionary. The many reprintings of this book demonstrate its value as an introductory text. It has a clear style easily accessible to students. While a number of its views should be modified by reference to the work of modern scholars, notably David Kopf's books listed below, it remains a readable introduction to Ray and his era.

Hay, Stephen N., ed. *Sources of Indian Tradition*. Vol. 2, *Modern India and Pakistan*. 2d ed. New York: Columbia University Press, 1988. A valuable anthology of translations from primary sources, introductory essays, and comments on the sources. Places brief selections from Ray's writings in the context of his own time as well as relating them to the work of later generations of reformers.

Heimsath, Charles H. *Indian Nationalism and Hindu Social Reform*. Princeton, N.J.: Princeton University Press, 1964. Makes the vital connection between religious/social reform, its critics, and India's nationalist movement. The programs of both reformers and their critics must be understood as part of India's long drive for independence. Also has the merit of covering reformist movements in all the major cultural regions of the subcontinent.

Kopf, David. *The Brahmo Samaj and the Shaping of the Modern Indian Mind*. Princeton, N.J.: Princeton University Press, 1979. Together with the book cited below, this work provides a comprehensive and insightful history of Bengali intellectual life from the late eighteenth century to the early twentieth century. The first chapters give a succinct and penetrating appraisal of Ray's influence on modernizing Bengalis. Also describes Tagore's role in establishing Ray as the father of modern India.

—————————. *British Orientalism and the Bengal Renaissance: The Dynamics of Indian Modernization, 1773-1835*. Berkeley: University of California Press, 1969. This valuable work demonstrates the complex interchanges between Englishmen and Indians which added a new dimension to Bengali intellectual life. Provides a history of the College of Fort William and places Ray's career in the context of Orientalist labors. Also charts the anti-Orientalist reaction of the 1830's and 1840's.

Gregory C. Kozlowski

REMBRANDT

Born: July 15, 1606; Leiden, the Netherlands
Died: October 4, 1669; Amsterdam, the Netherlands
Area of Achievement: Art
Contribution: Generally considered to be the greatest portrait painter of all time, Rembrandt is also renowned for his etchings and drawings. His works reflect his masterful ability to create realistic images which invite the viewer into his world, composed primarily of lower-class subjects living simple lives.

Early Life
Rembrandt van Rijn was born on July 15, 1606, in Leiden, the son of Harmen van Rijn, a miller, and Neeltgen Willemsdochter van Zuidbroeck, the daughter of a baker. After seven years in Latin school and a very brief period at the University of Leiden, he studied for three years with Jacob van Swanenburch, a pedestrian painter, and for about six months with Pieter Lastman, who influenced his treatment of mythological and religious subjects, particularly with respect to the use of vivid expressions, of lighting, and of the high gloss that appears on many of his earliest works.

Rembrandt's earliest known dated painting, the *Stoning of Saint Stephen* (1625), is a work that brims with action. The saint's face is tilted up toward a central figure, who stands with a large stone raised over his head in both hands, his arms forming a triangle that defines the space around the kneeling saint. Within this space are several men with stones in hand, whose arms and twisted bodies form powerful diagonals in contrast to the saint's own outstretched, diagonally positioned arms. The vividly realized faces and the skillful composition of a large crowd (with numerous faces peering through outstretched arms) suggest Rembrandt's early mastery of both large subjects and individualized figures.

By his early twenties, Rembrandt was working in Leiden as an independent master, making his living by painting portraits but also devoting considerable time to biblical and mythological subjects. He was attracted to the faces of the anonymous poor, often using them to portray philosophers and biblical characters. *Two Scholars Disputing* (1628) is a fair example of his penchant for presenting scenes that seem like a slice of life yet are unconventional and not easily defined. There is nothing particularly symbolic or representative about the scene. It seems rather about an attitude toward life, an intimate observation of two men—one of whom is seen only from the back and side as the other focuses his eyes on him and points to a particular page in the text over which they are evidently arguing. As in much of the artist's later work, there is a sense of something having been left out, of the painting concealing as much as it reveals about its subjects. They share something that is precisely what the viewer is not able to recover from the painting.

The etchings Rembrandt did of himself in 1630 suggest a man of considerable humor and anger. In the 1630's, Rembrandt enjoyed a happy marriage that was marred by the deaths of his first three children. By the time he had moved to Amsterdam and had wed Saskia van Uylenburgh (who became the model for many of his works), he had already produced great art, such as *The Anatomy Lesson of Dr. Tulp* (1632), a powerfully dramatic painting, with a poised Dr. Tulp able to command the attention and wonder of seven observers, each of whom gazes fixedly on the cadaver's forearm as the doctor proceeds, scissors in hand, to make his demonstration. As in *Two Scholars Disputing*, Rembrandt accomplishes the uncanny feat of suggesting that the viewer is witnessing the scene at first hand and not merely observing from the outside.

Life's Work

The Presentation of Jesus in the Temple (1631) is an early, commanding example of Rembrandt's poised skill in representing biblical subjects. As Michael Kitson suggests, this is a picture about looking—the high priest, the rabbis, the large collection of worshipers are angled in positions that emphasize their excited observation of the Christ child. What is more difficult to see in the reproduction of the painting is the smooth finish of Rembrandt's technique, the way soothing, polished color is applied to this quiet yet epic scene. Although the temple ceiling is very high, the illumination of the central group rivets the viewer's attention.

Saskia died in 1642, leaving a tremendous void in Rembrandt's life. Yet he managed to paint a masterpiece, *The Company of Captain Frans Banning Cocq and Lieutenant Willem van Ruytenburch*, more popularly known as *The Night Watch* (1642)—an erroneous eighteenth century title that was abandoned when the painting was cleaned, revealing a dramatically lit portrayal of eighteen militiamen. What makes the painting so appealing are Rembrandt's characteristic small touches—the children wandering among the armed men, the dog scampering about, the men in varying stages of readiness, checking their rifles, conferring in small groups, and in general inspecting their equipment. Utterly absent from the scene is any sort of staginess or self-conscious presentation. In its sense of depth, of shadow and light, of strong vertical, horizontal, and diagonal lines, the painting moves the eye just as these figures are moved by their preparations. Somehow Rembrandt puts his viewers in sync with the rhythms of his subjects.

What is extraordinary about such pictures is their lack of subject or theme. On the face of it, such paintings do not have any particular message to convey. They do not commemorate some specific event, and they do not invite viewers to take a specific attitude. Yet such works are authentic and intriguing, as though the figures have just stepped into the artist's frame.

In the 1640's, Rembrandt turned toward religious painting, perhaps in response to the death of his wife. *The Holy Family with Angels* (1645) presents an almost homely looking, full-figured Mary bending over the cradle of Jesus as Joseph works on a piece of wood in an interior scene of comforting domesticity. Rembrandt's landscapes and etchings during this period suggest his enormous talent for evoking a place in a few strokes and with great originality, always emphasizing the individuality of scenes.

Toward the end of the 1640's, Rembrandt took his servant, Hendrickje Stoffels, as his mistress. A clause in Saskia's will made it impossible for him to marry again, but his depictions of Hendrickje in his art rivaled his deep feelings for Saskia. Hendrickje seems to be the subject of *Woman Bathing* (1654), a lovely illustration of Rembrandt's later manner, where patches of color blend together and human faces have a shaded suggestiveness to them, an expression they seem to have for themselves when they are all alone. Such figures convey the feeling of being seen from the inside out, as though the artist is rendering their feelings and not those of an eavesdropping observer.

Similarly, *An Old Man Seated in an Armchair* (1652) has been described as one of Rembrandt's most poetic paintings, with reds, orange-browns, and yellows that blend together and fracture the precise color schemes of earlier paintings. The result is a new fluidity and grace, an artful vigor that is in curious contrast with the aged man's obvious weariness as he rests his right hand against the side of his head and casts his eyes downward.

When Rembrandt reached middle age, he was declared insolvent and his great art collection was sold to satisfy his creditors. He remained a respected figure in Amsterdam but also something of a recluse who did not recover his full powers until the 1660's, when he produced some of his greatest works, including *The Syndics of the Drapers' Guild* (1661), a painting that presents a probing analysis of cloth merchants who seem to have been caught in a moment of business. They have what might be called seasoned faces—eyes, in particular, that gaze out from the painting in various guises of watchfulness and inquiry. The viewer feels the weight of their stares and senses what it must be like to do business with these formidable men.

Although Hendrickje died in 1663 and Titus (Rembrandt's only surviving child by Saskia) in 1668, the artist continued to produce great work—not the least of which were his self-portraits, begun in his youth and continued to the very year of his death. His self-portrait of 1640 presents a handsomely clothed and composed figure—obviously a successful and self-confident artist. His self-portrait of 1650 seems less open, perhaps more reserved, and the one of 1652 offers a man, hands on hips, toughened by experience. Later self-portraits suggest an aging but durable figure, with one (c. 1660) composed of very heavy brushstrokes and a roughened texture that indicates the pain and weariness of his later years. There is, however, a majesty in some of these portraits—particularly in the one of 1669, in which old age and experience may have given depth to the eyes but no trace of the weariness Rembrandt painted in the countenances of other old men.

Summary

In the very year that Rembrandt died, he produced a self-portrait that is massive in its philosophical attitude. No portrait painter has equaled the depth and range of his work or had the technique to rival his surface polish and attention to detail. Often, Rembrandt's portraits seemed to be grooved with life—a result, in part, of his using the butt end of the brush to apply paint. His touch was as bold as it was delicate, but in his own time he was faulted for picking lower-class subjects and for not staying within the sublime limits of great art. More modern critics, on the other hand, have welcomed him as a contemporary, who has shown that it is not the artist's choice of subject but what he does with his material that is most important. Rembrandt could make a philosopher of a beggar, and he could turn a painting about businessmen into a work of art that gives the viewer a palpable sense of what it means to transact business with the painter's subjects. Rembrandt's perceptions, in other words, grow out of his subject matter but, in doing so, transcend the subjects of his paintings. In the end, his painting, like his etchings and drawings, exists for its own sake, creating rather than merely reporting its subject matter.

Bibliography

Clark, Kenneth. *Rembrandt and the Italian Renaissance*. New York: New York University Press, 1966. An elegant study by one of the century's great art critics, this volume includes 181 black-and-white plates, a short bibliography, notes, and an excellent index.

Goldscheider, Ludwig. *Rembrandt: Paintings, Drawings, and Etchings*. London: Phaidon Press, 1960. A superb set of 128 plates, thirty-five in color, with an introduction by Goldscheider and three early biographical accounts reprinted in their entirety. Extensive notes and an index make this a very useful volume.

Haverkamp-Begemann, E. *Rembrandt: The Nightwatch*. Princeton, N.J.: Princeton University Press, 1982. A historical and critical study of one of Rembrandt's most famous paintings. With more than ninety illustrations, including a handsome foldout color plate, this is an excellent example of scholarly thoroughness.

Kitson, Michael. *Rembrandt*. London: Phaidon Press, 1969. A succinct study of Rembrandt's life and art, divided in sections evaluating his art, his "subject pictures," portraits, and landscapes. An "outline biography" gives the most important dates in the artist's life and forty-eight large color plates provide a handsome and representative sampling of his work.

Rosenberg, Jakob. *Rembrandt: Life and Work*. Rev. ed. Ithaca, N.Y.: Cornell University Press, 1964. A revised edition of the classic 1948 comprehensive study of the artist's life and work, with separate chapters on portraiture, landscape, biblical subjects, Rembrandt in his century, and style and technique. Heavily footnoted and well indexed. The bibliography is of limited usefulness, since it refers mainly to untranslated European sources.

Wallace, Robert. *The World of Rembrandt, 1606-1669*. New York: Time-Life Books, 1968. A very useful study of the life, the times, and the art of Rembrandt, including chapters on the legend and the man, Rembrandt's Holland, and styles. A rich selection of black-and-white and color plates cover all phases of the artist's career and include comparisons with the work of his contemporaries and models. A chronology of the artists of Rembrandt's era, an annotated bibliography, and an index make this an essential text.

Carl Rollyson

ERNEST RENAN

Born: February 28, 1823; Tréguier, Côtes-du-Nord, France
Died: October 2, 1892; Paris, France
Areas of Achievement: Religious history and philosophical criticism
Contribution: Renan's writings encompass the areas of religion, history, science, and morality. His controversial biography of Jesus Christ illustrates Renan's ongoing theme of resolution of contradictions by emphasizing the problem of reconciling the historical and the spiritually divine Jesus.

Early Life

Joseph-Ernest Renan was born in Tréguier, a town in Britanny that was in many respects a religious center. His youth was shaded by a veil of devout Catholicism, to which he, in accordance with his mother's most intense wishes and his own strong inclinations, was committed. His father, Philibert, was a grocer and seaman. His mother, Magdelaine Féger, was widowed when Ernest was five years old, her husband having drowned—it has not been determined whether accidentally or otherwise—at sea. Ernest Renan had a brother, Alain, born in 1809, and a sister, Henriette, born in 1811. His sister was profoundly influential in his life, and his attachment to her is lyrically expressed in *Ma Sœur Henriette* (1895; *My Sister Henrietta*, 1895), which was initially published in a limited edition of one hundred copies in 1862 as *Henriette Renan: Souvenir pour ceux qui l'ont connue* (Henriette Renan: a remembrance for those who knew her) and reprinted posthumously.

From 1832 to 1838, Renan was a student at the Ecclesiastical School in Tréguier, while his sister, having failed to establish a private school for girls, accepted a teaching position in Paris. In 1838, Renan moved to Paris and studied rhetoric at the seminary of Saint-Nicolas du Chardonnet. After three years, he moved to the seminary of Issy-les-Moulineux outside Paris, where his study of philosophy began to bring about his wavering in religious faith. His sister, with whom he was to maintain an ongoing correspondence, had moved, during this time, to Poland, where she found employment as a governess. From Issy-les-Moulineux, he moved in 1849 to the parent seminary of Saint-Sulpice and entered upon his study of theology.

In his academic progression from rhetoric to philosophy to theology, the normal pattern of seminary education in France, Renan developed a devotion to literature, a skeptical turn of mind, and a sense of alienation in his separation, first, from Britanny and, later, from his mother. He remained firmly within his faith, however, and in 1844 became a tonsured cleric in evidence of his call to the priesthood. After a year, he came to realize that he lacked belief sufficient to this vocation, and his rationalism and scientific propensity led him to abandon the ecclesiastical for the secular life. His sister Henriette supported him in his decision and commended his firmness of purpose and strength of will.

He then set his life's course toward reconciling the two worlds which, as he assured his mother in her disappointment, were not, to his mind, separate. The world of Jesus (the world of religion) and the world of science contradicted each other but were not mutually exclusive. To his own way of thinking, he had departed from Jesus so as to be better able to follow Jesus.

Life's Work

In 1845, at the age of twenty-two, Renan, believing that his own emotions and his own thoughts were his God, became a tutor, an ultimately successful candidate for the *baccalauréat* and *licence* (roughly equivalent to the B.A. and M.A. degrees in the United States), a friend of the chemist Marcellin Berthelot, and a student of the Semitic languages (of which he was soon to become a professor). Two years later, he won the Volney Prize for his essay on the history of the Semitic languages. His friendship with the scientist, which proved to be lifelong, and his own predilection for science, along with his Semitic studies, adumbrated his major contributions to intellectual history and to the history of ideas; these are his *Histoire des origines du christianisme* (1863-1882; *The History of the Origins of Christianity*, 1890) and *L'Avenir de la science* (1890; *The Future of Science*, 1890). Renan completed his work on *The Future of Science* in 1849, three years before the publication of his doctoral dissertation, *Averroès et l'Averroïsme* (1852). Segments of the text of *The Future of Science* appeared in journals, periodicals, and other of his books, but its full publication, with only minor revisions of the original, materialized only two years before his death.

One of the prime focuses of *The Future of Science* is criticism, a subject which he had initially expounded in his *Cahiers de jeunesse* (1845-1846; youthful notebooks). Renan's views on criticism as an intellectual activity anticipated much of the direction that was to be taken by post-World War II critical theorists. For him, true criticism was universal in character and was decidedly not to be limited to literary criticism and even more decidedly not to be identified with judgment and measurements against standards of form and composition. He believed that beauty was open-ended and not subject to the closure that is implied by the concept of an absolute. He saw criticism as a creative use of the powers of interpretation and a conceptual conjunction of history, topography, philosophy, and morality. Like the deconstructionists of the twentieth century, he disregarded the demarcations of disciplines and sought to reconcile the disciplines through comparativism, eclecticism, and synthesis; comparison served him in science, literature, and religion as the great tool of criticism. *The Future of Science* begins with the very simple statement, "Only one thing is necessary." The one thing proves to be, after all syntheses have been unified, science as that religion which comprises human feeling and human thought.

H. W. Wardman recognizes in *The Future of Science* the idea that "philosophy is a human science born of the union of philology and historical sympathy," and this prompts him effectively to conclude that Renan's philosopher is "a kind of seer fitted by his insight into human nature to take over from the Church the spiritual leadership of mankind." Philology, according to Renan, is "the science of the products of the human mind."

Renan's notion of history is an extension of Victor Cousin's concept of the three ages: a primary age informed by religion without science, a secondary age informed by science without religion, and a final age informed by both religion and science. The historical process is the development of the divine. In the final age, the development will have been concluded and God will be manifestly whole. The future of science, then, is the fulfillment of religion, that is to say, God.

Renan's masterwork was a seven-volume study, *The History of the Origins of Christianity*. The first of these volumes, *Vie de Jésus* (1863; *The Life of Jesus*, 1864), is the most famous and is the work for which Renan is best known. At the time of its publication, Renan had been married to Cornélie Scheffer for seven years, had become the father of two girls, the first having died eight months after birth, and had, in 1861, lost in death his sister Henriette, to whose soul he dedicated this work.

The life of Jesus, according to Renan, is the focal event of world history; it brought about the spiritual revolution that was the culmination of seven centuries of Jewish history and that in the subsequent three centuries would be established as a religion. This entire period of one thousand years is presented by Renan as embracing the origins of Christianity.

Renan depicts Jesus as a superior, indeed a sublime person but not as a god. His Jesus let his followers believe that He was God as He taught them the ways to fulfill their subjectivity. He holds that Jesus' immediate followers and their successors invented, in belief and desire, the Resurrection: "The life of Jesus ends, as far as the historian is concerned, with his last sigh. But so great was the mark he had made in the hearts of his disciples and several devoted women that for a few more weeks he was alive to them and he consoled them." This passage from chapter 26 is representative of the secular Jesus whom hosts of Renan's critics rejected and protested against. The whole of chapters 26 and 27 was, for example, among the exclusions from the French Book Club's ornately bound and illustrated 1970 abridgment of *The History of the Origins of Christianity*. The Christian clergy and laity assailed the book for its profanation and its author's apostasy. Literary critics frowned upon the idyllic and romantic Galilee that it painted and upon its overly genteel characterization of Jesus. The book became an international best-seller, however, going through eight printings in the first three months of its publication.

The second volume of *The History of the Origins of Christianity* appeared in 1866; it is a historiography of the Apostles, from A.D. 33 to 45, and an investigation into the continuing apotheosis of Jesus by way of visionary presumption, amplification of legend, and adaptation of mythical traditions. His third volume, *La Vie de saint Paul* (1869; *Saint Paul*, 1869), dedicated to his wife, who had accompanied him in his retracing of the travels of his subject, is replete with the topography and accoutrements of epic. Saint Paul is here reminiscent of the Homeric Odysseus: a man of action and purpose. The fourth volume (1873), following the New Testament's book of Revelation as Renan's second and third volumes follow, respectively, the book of Acts and the Pauline Epistles, studies Emperor Nero as the Antichrist. The fifth volume (1877) expatiates upon the second Christian generation and the production of the first four books of the New Testament, the basis of his life of Jesus. He applauds Matthew and Mark as the genuinely divine increment of Christianity, berates Luke as special pleading, and sees John as fraudulent save for its recounting of various of Jesus' teachings. (Only nine of this volume's twenty-seven chapters are included in the above-mentioned French Book Club edition.) The sixth volume (1879) details the defeat of Gnosticism and Montanism and the establishment of the orthodox Christian church. The concluding volume (1881) centers on Emperor Marcus Aurelius (161-180) and the end of the ancient world.

From 1888 to the year of his death, Renan published three of the five volumes of his last historical opus, *Histoire du peuple d'Israël* (*History of the People of Israel*, 1888-1895), the last two volumes of which were published posthumously in 1893. He looked upon this work as his completion of the history of Christianity's origins and as his exposition of the Jewish "subsoil" of Jesus' roots. The ten books of this work trace the development of Jewish monotheism, messianism, and religious mission—a development which entailed the sacrifice of nationalistic power to spiritual identity.

Renan died on October 2, 1892, from pneumonia and cardiac complications. Although his death was painful, it came after he had gained personal satisfaction from completing his life's work.

Summary

Ernest Renan's monuments are *The Future of Science*, *The History of the Origins of Christianity*, and *History of the People of Israel*. His other works are many, and they warrant careful study by anyone seriously interested in his contributions to modern thought. These include, apart from other works already mentioned, his correspondence, his *Souvenirs d'enfance et de jeunesse* (1876-1882; *Recollections of My Youth*, 1883), his *Discours et conférences* (1887; speeches and lectures), his philosophical dialogues, and his four philosophical dramas: *Caliban, suite de "La Tempête": Drama philosophique* (1878; *Caliban: A Philosophical Drama Continuing "The Tem-*

pest" of William Shakespeare, 1896), *L'Eau de jouvence* (1881; the fountain of youth), *Le Prêtre de Némi* (1886; the priest of Nemi), and *L'Abbesse de Jouarre* (1886; the abbess of Jouarre).

Renan is an outstanding example of the thinker whose crisis of spirit is resolved by his work. Like the English poet William Cowper (1731-1800), who adjusted to his unshakable belief that he was damned by engaging in constant literary effort, Renan overcame his loss of faith with a creative scholarship that brought him spiritual contentment.

In his spiritual secularism and his universal criticism, Renan was ahead of his time. His attitudes and ideas anticipated those of certain significant twentieth century theologians (for example, Hans Küng), literary artists (Miguel de Unamuno y Jugo), and critical theorists (Michel Foucault and René Girard), but his twentieth century successors not only found broader and more consistent readerships but also outdistanced him in depth and caliber of expression, though not in exquisiteness of prose.

Renan saw himself as a man of two worlds: religion and science. He belongs as well to two different temporal worlds: the nineteenth century, in which his ideas were uncommon and thereby largely unheeded, and the twentieth century, in which his ideas were largely unheeded because they had become commonplace.

Bibliography

Chadbourne, Richard M. *Ernest Renan*. New York: Twayne, 1968. An admirable and admiring account of the life and works of Renan, touching upon all the qualities that make Renan a "great historian, critic, and artist." This is one of the finest volumes in the Twayne's World Authors series; if one can find time for only one secondary work on Renan, this should be it.

_____. *Ernest Renan as an Essayist*. Ithaca, N.Y.: Cornell University Press, 1957. An approach to Renan through his contribution to the tradition of essay-writing in France. Chadbourne stresses the seriousness of purpose that is to be found in the essays as against the author's propensity for irony, humor, and open-ended play. Considering that he may have made Renan appear overly serious, Chadbourne corrects the impression in his *Ernest Renan*.

Gore, Charles. Introduction to *The Life of Jesus*, by Ernest Renan. New York: E. P. Dutton, 1927. Gore offers an excellent summary of the reception of Renan's *The Life of Jesus* by critics, liberals, and orthodox Christians. He also offers a vindication of Renan as a historian whose estimation of the historical value of the New Testament documents had come to be recognized as essentially correct. Gore's translation, the second into English and the first in international importance, should also be of interest to any reader seeking familiarity with Renan's most famous work.

Gore, Keith. "Ernest Renan: A Positive Ethics?" *French Studies* 41 (April, 1987): 141-154. A concise account of Renan's philosophical adjustment to his break with the Church and to the political situation in France (Second Empire, Franco-Prussian War, Third Republic). Gore claims that Renan's work comes closest to being "positive" in *Cahiers de jeunesse*. In a long footnote, Gore insists, contrary to assertions by H. W. Wardman (in a book written in 1979 in French), that in the ethical sphere, Renan was pragmatic, not metaphysical.

Neff, Emery. *The Poetry of History: The Contribution of Literature and Literary Scholarship to the Writing of History Since Voltaire.* New York: Columbia University Press, 1947. An appraisal of Renan's historiography as the work of a man of letters. Informative comparison of Renan's work to that of Jacob Burckhardt and John Richard Green. Neff states a cogent case for the long-term worth of Renan's distinctive and efficacious mode of historical inquiry. Helpful study of the fabric of historiography, to which Renan made a signal contribution.

Schweitzer, Albert. *The Quest of the Historical Jesus: A Critical Study of Its Progress from Reimarus to Wrede.* Translated by W. Montgomery. London: Adam & Charles Black, 1954. Chapter 13 is devoted to Renan's *The Life of Jesus.* Schweitzer calls Renan's essay on the sources for the life of Jesus "a literary masterpiece" but finds the work inconsistent in its estimate and use of the Fourth Gospel and in its thoroughgoing "insincerity." Passing attention is accorded to Renan in other chapters.

Wardman, H. W. *Ernest Renan: A Critical Biography.* London: Athlone Press, 1964. The emphasis in this biography is upon Renan's life and work in the context of his times. Wardman offers a consistent characterization of Renan, noting, for example, Renan's fear of his work's becoming outdated or being proved wrong by posterity, as well as Renan's metaphysical anxieties.

Wilson, Edmund. *To the Finland Station: A Study in the Writing and Acting of History.* New York: Harcourt Brace, 1940. Reprint. New York: Farrar, Straus & Giroux, 1972. Places Renan within the revolutionary tradition in Europe. Part 6 of chapter 1 discusses Renan in the context of the decline of the revolutionary tradition and praises *The History of the Origins of Christianity* as "a masterpiece—perhaps the greatest of all histories of ideas." Elsewhere in his text, Wilson suggests that Renan's moral force diminishes in proportion to his urbane tolerance of error and his diplomatic dissimulation.

Roy Arthur Swanson

PIERRE-AUGUSTE RENOIR

Born: February 25, 1841; Limoges, France
Died: December 3, 1919; Cagnes, France
Area of Achievement: Art
Contribution: One of the major French Impressionists, Renoir painted in the
   open air, handling the paint loosely, dissolving masses, and abandoning
   local colors. He differed, however, from most of the other Impressionists
   in his concentration on the human figure and in his strong interest in portraiture.

Early Life
   Pierre-Auguste Renoir's father Léonard, a poor painter, moved his family
from Limoges to Paris in 1845, when the painter-to-be was four years old.
There the young Renoir, who displayed talent for music as well as for drawing, was enrolled in the choir school of the parish church of Saint-Roch. His
elder sister Lisa first exposed him to painting at the age of nine by taking
him to the Louvre. He would doodle in his exercise books in school, and he
was later encouraged in art by Lisa's fiancé, the illustrator Charles Leray. At
the age of thirteen, Renoir was apprenticed to the Lévy Frères firm of porcelain painters, for whom he painted decorative bouquets on dishware in an
eighteenth century style. During his lunch periods, he hurried to the Louvre,
where he practiced his drawing; later, in 1860, he was given official permission to copy there. After losing his job in the porcelain atelier in 1858, when
the firm went bankrupt, he painted fans for a living, copying on them pictures of the rococo artists François Boucher, Jean-Honoré Fragonard, Nicolas Lancret, and Antoine Watteau. The sense of joy and gracefulness en-
capsulated in that phase of French painting would later be found in Renoir's
own work.
   Renoir enrolled in 1862 in the academically oriented studio of Charles
Gleyre, a mediocre Swiss painter, where he met Jean Frédéric Bazille,
Claude Monet, and Alfred Sisley. At gatherings at the home of a relative of
Bazille, he met the painter Édouard Manet, the poet Charles Baudelaire, and
the novelist Théophile Gautier. Leaving Gleyre's studio the next year, Renoir
painted with his friends in the Fontainbleau Forest in order to sketch the
landscape and move toward greater naturalism. They stayed at Chailly, near
the encampment of the Barbizon painters, and Renoir met there the Barbi-
zonist Narcisse Virgile Diaz de La Peña. The major influence on Renoir's
work from 1867 to 1870 was exerted by Gustave Courbet, whose heavy
modeling, massive figures, and use of the palette knife can be seen reflected
in Renoir's rendering of the nude in *Diane Chassereuse* (1867). In that
picture there can be discerned, too, the influence of Manet in the use of an
obviously contemporary figure to pose for a mythological scene.

Life's Work

In the spring of 1868, Renoir and Bazille moved to a studio in the rue de la Paix, where Monet would occasionally join them. In the evenings, they often went to the Café Guerbois, where there would be much talk of painting, with Manet as the presiding figure, the painter Paul Cézanne, the printmaker Félix Bracquemond, Henri Fantin-Latour, Constantin Guys, and Sisley, and the novelists Émile Zola and Gautier.

Renoir's leap into full-blown Impressionism occurred in 1869 with his paintings of *La Grenouillière*, the bathing place and floating restaurant at Bougival on the Seine. His intention was to combine the sense of poetry of the rococo with a motif from contemporary life. His strokes are broken. About half of the painted surface is given to the shimmering water, and light and atmosphere have become the unifying elements. Renoir and Monet painted side by side at that spot, and their compositions and placement of boats and figures on water-surrounded platforms are almost identical, except that Renoir gives somewhat more prominence to the figures.

During that time, as the supporter of his mistress Camille and her son Claude, Renoir struggled to make ends meet and often would borrow from Bazille. In 1870, he was drafted for the Franco-Prussian War. He believed that it was his duty to serve and was sent first to Bordeaux and later to Tarbes. Back in Paris by March 18, 1871, Renoir continued in the Impressionist manner through the 1870's. In his work he gave no indication of the political unrest of the times; his most ambitious paintings of the next years were of streets filled with leisurely strollers and of beautiful young people enjoying their carefree existence in the open air. *Dancing at the Moulin de la Galette, Montmarte* (1876) shows couples dancing at a popular open-air spot while other people converse and drink at the outdoor tables, a custom on Sunday afternoons. The crowd swirls about, with Renoir focusing on no single person or couple, giving a sense of randomness. Some figures are cut by the edge of the canvas. All seem to be enjoying themselves to the utmost, with no hint of anything troubling. Renoir once said, "The earth as the paradise of the gods, that is what I want to paint."

In 1874, Renoir took an active part in the organization of the Impressionist group and participated in some of the group's exhibitions. In spite of his adherence to what was then stylistically avant-garde, he also exhibited more conservative paintings at the salon and was commissioned, to do portraits of prominent people. His portrait *Madame Charpentier and Her Children* (1878) was dignified and can be considered to be related to Impressionism mainly in the casual postures of the sitters. In the Charpentier circle he met Zola once again, as well as the author Alphonse Daudet, the critic Edmond de Goncourt, and the diplomat-banker Paul Bérard, who was to be a steadfast patron. From the mid-1870's, as Renoir began to obtain portrait commissions and as his pictures began to be collected, his circumstances improved.

In the spring of 1881, Renoir traveled to Algiers and then in the fall to Venice, Rome, and Naples, where he was impressed by the works of Raphael and by Pompeian frescoes. He became disaffected with his Impressionist involvement, convinced that he had lost much of his ability to draw. He said to the dealer Ambrose Vollard, "There is a greater variety of light outdoors than in the studio . . . because of this, light plays far too important a part, you have no time to work out the composition." Throughout the 1880's he gave figures a much firmer outline instead of partially dissolving them in light. He made preparatory drawings and grouped figures according to deliberate schemas, sometimes based on a specific monument of the past. The three sculpturesque nudes in *Les Grandes Baigneuses* (c.1887) are based on a seventeenth century relief by François Girardon at Versailles. From 1888 on, his nudes became heavier, with broader hips, longer torsos, more-rounded legs, and smaller breasts, as he tried to capture something of the monumentality of the antique. In 1895, becoming interested in the plays of the ancient Greeks, he painted a series dealing with the Oedipus story.

Renoir, who so admired health, robustness, and joie de vivre, in later life had to cope with serious illness. In 1888, he visited Cézanne at Aix; Cézanne cared for him while he was ill. Arthritis combined with rheumatism became his chief affliction. In 1894, he began to walk with two canes. He traveled to various spas in the hope of finding a cure and wintered in the south. In 1913, he was confined to a wheelchair. Fortunately, after 1892 he had no financial worries, as a large one-man show that year at Durand-Ruel's proved a turning point. (Monet had introduced him to the dealer in the summer of 1872, and Durand-Ruel had done much in the 1880's to further the prices of Renoir's paintings.) Renoir also married rather late in life. His marriage with Aline Charigot in 1882 produced three sons: Pierre was born in 1885, Jean, in 1893, and Claude in 1901.

In his children, Renoir found a new subject matter, yet he also continued to paint his radiant nudes, which in the 1890's were painted outside any environmental context and seemed to glow from within. Toward the end of Renoir's life, for example, as in the painting *Judgment of Paris* (1914), the nudes became bulbous and awkwardly heavy, perhaps reflecting the artist's own hampered mobility. Renoir also became engaged in sculpture from 1907. He was encouraged in this direction when he was visited that year by the sculptor Aristide Maillol, who did a bust of him. Renoir's sculptures are improvisations on his late paintings, with massive figures in slow movements. These include the *Judgment of Paris* (1916) and *Blacksmith (Fire)* (1916). As he was crippled and had little dexterity in his hands, Renoir made drawings for the design, and an assistant, adding and subtracting according to his directions, built up the model in clay. In 1918, Renoir because completely immobilized and had to be carried. Yet, before his death the next year, he made a last visit to the Louvre to see the old masters.

Summary

Although usually considered as one of the inner group of the French Impressionists, Renoir was in important ways atypical. Like the other painters, he portrayed (at first glance) the life of the times, but actually what he presented were young men and women in modern clothes acting as though they were in an arcadia devoid of the stresses of the day. In his evocation of a never-never land, he is as close, in spirit, to the rococo painters of the eighteenth century as he is to the Impressionists. Unlike the other Impressionists, Renoir makes little use of open spaces, sometimes expanding or contracting to convey the tensions of modern life. Nor did he much explore flattenings, unusual perspectives, or cutting of figures (a device sometimes found in Renoir's paintings but seldom made much of). Renoir is perhaps best known for his paintings of figures rather than landscapes, unlike the other Impressionists. His paintings of nudes, especially, gained for him recognition, and his later nudes, with the unusual use of pigments providing a glowing, curiously weightless look, have provoked much interest.

Bibliography

Barnes, Albert C., and Violette De Mazia. *The Art of Renoir.* New York: Minton, Balch and Co., 1935. By the noted and eccentric collector who amassed some two hundred paintings by Renoir. Barnes sees Renoir as an artist of the first rank. The text, however, is full of flowery phraseology and vague terminology. Barnes makes comparisons with Cézanne and others in his attempt to fit Renoir into a quasi-abstract mold.

Renoir, Auguste. *Pierre Auguste Renoir.* Introduction by Walter Pach. New York: Harry N. Abrams, 1950. Includes large, excellent color plates. Discusses Renoir's handling of his subjects, his use of color, and his composition.

Renoir, Jean. *Renoir, My Father.* Translated by Randolph Weaver and Dorothy Weaver. Boston: Little, Brown, 1962. The artists's son, a film director, recounts his father's life, touching on the artist's friends, travels, tastes, and beliefs. The reproductions are few and in black and white, but the volume includes photographs of the artist and his family, and pictures of Manet, Camille Pissarro, and Cézanne.

"Special Section: A Renoir Symposium." *Art in America* 74 (March, 1986): 102-125. Includes the responses of various scholars to the 1986 Renoir retrospective held at the Grand Palais in Paris, the National Gallery in London, and the Museum of Fine Arts in Boston. Suggests that Renoir's reputation seems either to be on the wane or undergoing a major reassessment (with greater importance, for example, accorded the late glowing nudes).

Wadley, Nicholas, ed. *Renoir: A Retrospective.* New York: H. L. Levin, 1987. This authoritative work has contemporary accounts and evaluations.

Wheldon, Keith. *Renoir and His Art*. New York: Hamlyn, 1975. A brief but readable account of the life and development of Renoir's art. Includes commends from such scholars as John Rewald and Fritz Novotny. About half of the 102 plates are in color and some are full-page reproductions.
White, Barbara E. *Renoir: His Life, Art, and Letters*. New York: Harry N. Abrams, 1984. White's work is useful because of its color illustrations, but its chief value lies in its use of Renoir's correspondence. White sees much of Renoir's work as derived from Monet and others.

Abraham A. Davidson

CARDINAL DE RICHELIEU
Armand-Jean du Plessis

Born: September 9, 1585; Paris, France
Died: December 4, 1642; Paris, France
Area of Achievement: Politics
Contribution: As cardinal, prime minister, and head of the royal council of
   Louis XIII, Richelieu was the architect of centralized, absolutist govern-
   ment in France. In addition, his brilliant diplomacy in the Thirty Years'
   War helped to make France the foremost power in Europe.

Early Life
   Though he was to rise to be the most powerful person in France, Armand-
Jean du Plessis, Cardinal de Richelieu, had relatively humble origins. As
a result of a fortunate marriage, his family had risen to upper-middle-class
status and had gained the seigneury (title) to the estates of Richelieu in
the western province of Poitou. Richelieu's father, François du Plessis, was
King Henry III's chief magistrate in Paris, where the future cardinal was
born, on September 9, 1585. His mother, Suzanne de la Porte, was the
daughter of a member of the Parlement de Paris, and it has been said that Richelieu's intelligence, instinct for hard work, and administrative talent derived from these middle-class origins.
   The estates of Richelieu's family were devastated during the French Wars
of Religion, which raged from 1565 to 1598 between Huguenots (French
Calvinist Protestants) and Roman Catholics, and the young Richelieu grew
up determined to restore them. When Richelieu was five, his father died and
his mother removed her five children from Paris to begin rebuilding the
family fortunes. Richelieu, however, was later sent to school in Paris, where
he was enrolled in a military academy, despite the fact that he was pale, thin,
and sickly.
   Among the ruined family possessions was the vacant bishopric of Luçon,
near La Rochelle. In 1606, Richelieu journeyed to Rome to obtain a papal
dispensation which would allow him to be consecrated as a bishop below the
required age of twenty-six. Apparently, his intelligence and charm impressed
the pope, and Richelieu was ordained a priest and consecrated as Bishop of
Luçon on April 17, 1607. As bishop, Richelieu immediately set to the work
of restoring the morale of the parish priests and the obedience of a recalcitrant cathedral chapter. He became the first bishop in France to implement the reforms decreed by the Council of Trent in 1563; these sought to
restore strict moral discipline over the clergy and to educate them in church
doctrine. Richelieu himself was a brilliant student of theology, and he wrote
many papers on this subject, including an influential catechism used throughout the seventeenth century.

In fact, writing was, for Richelieu, the only effective channel for his ambitions and his need to control events around him. Throughout his life, he often suffered ill health, and only immense self-discipline allowed him to accomplish his tasks. Though he could be charming when absolutely necessary, he preferred to avoid emotionally taxing personal confrontations by arguing issues on paper. To many of his contemporaries, therefore, he appeared to be a remote and sinister figure enmeshed in a web of secrecy and intrigue. Actually, he was conscientious, hardworking, and dedicated to the elimination of forces which he believed threatened the social and moral order and unity of France.

These forces threatened once again to throw the state into bloody anarchy in 1610, when King Henry IV, who had succeeded to the throne after the murder of Henry III in 1589, was himself assassinated. Henry IV, originally a Protestant, had won the crown by converting to Catholicism and ending the Wars of Religion through judicious compromises with both sides. In 1599, he had issued the Edict of Nantes, which guaranteed both religious and political rights to the Huguenots as well as the ability to protect them by maintaining garrisons in all the major cities they controlled. In effect, the Huguenots became a kind of separate republic within the kingdom.

Such an arrangement was bound to create tensions, and religion became the excuse used by prominent groups of nobles in their efforts to reduce the authority of the king and reassert the independence they had enjoyed during the Middle Ages. When Henry IV was killed, his son, Louis XIII, was only nine years old, and the nobility saw their opportunity in attacking the regency of the queen mother, Marie de Médicis. Rather than risk an open war, they engaged in threats and protracted negotiations with Marie and her government. At one point in these negotiations, Richelieu was asked to serve as an intermediary, and this led to his being chosen as a delegate to the Estates General of 1614.

Speaking for the Church, Richelieu offered a brilliant plea for the reestablishment of strong royal authority, vested in the regent, to prevent the destructive divisions that had previously torn France apart. Though the assembly broke up without reaching any substantial agreements, Richelieu had won the attention and affection of both the young king and his mother. A few months later, he was appointed chaplain to the new queen, Anne of Austria, an office with great political promise. Richelieu's star had begun to rise.

Life's Work

Richelieu has often been accused of seeking advancement through flattery of the queen mother, but this was a universal practice in the seventeenth century; apparently, Richelieu's detractors were simply jealous of his superior skills. In fact, it was these skills, used in negotiations with a disobedient faction of nobles, which led to his appointment as Secretary of State in 1616.

For the next ten years, his fortunes were tied to those of Marie de Médicis. When her Italian lover Concini, who was also the virtual ruler of France, was murdered by a cabal of nobles, Richelieu went into exile to the papal enclave of Avignon. When Louis XIII, who then took over the reins of government, decided to be reconciled with the queen mother, Richelieu was again recalled to conduct the negotiations. For his success, in 1622, Richelieu was awarded the cardinal's hat. Two years later, he was appointed to the royal council.

In 1624, Richelieu was called upon to resolve his first foreign policy crisis. For more than a century, France had been intermittently at war with the Habsburg dynasty, which ruled areas on three sides of France: Spain, the Holy Roman Empire, and the Netherlands. In addition, Spain controlled nearly all of Italy, which was broken into several smaller kingdoms and provinces. The Spanish now moved to capture the Valtelline, an important mountain pass through the northern Italian Alps to Habsburg Austria, from the Protestant Grisons, a Swiss community under a treaty of protection from France. Invoking the treaty, Richelieu astounded and impressed Europe by sending a French army in a lightning strike against the papal troops holding the pass for Spain.

Richelieu's successful action alienated many Catholics within the queen mother's faction who had been sympathetic to the Habsburgs. The cardinal had won the confidence of the king, however, and Louis appointed Richelieu head of the royal council, a post which made him essentially the prime minister. From this point onward, Richelieu used all of his talents to weaken the Habsburgs and strengthen the French position in Europe. Since France was not, at this time, as militarily strong as the Habsburgs, the accomplishment of this goal required a persistent program of small victories in a variety of situations—a chess game on a grand scale.

The board on which Richelieu played included virtually all of Europe, engaged in the Thirty Years' War, the last of the great religious wars between Protestants and Catholics. Richelieu was largely responsible for transforming this long and complex conflict into a political rather than a religious confrontation. He began by giving diplomatic support and subsidies to the enemies of Spain: In 1625, he arranged for Louis XIII's sister to marry Charles I of England; in Italy, he assured that a French duke would inherit the Duchy of Mantua to deny Spain a military route to Austria; perhaps most important, he supported the Dutch Protestant rebels against their Spanish rulers and gave immense subsidies to the Swedish Lutheran King Gustavus II Adolphus, who had gone to war against the Habsburg Holy Roman Emperor.

At the same time, Richelieu reorganized the French army and created a French navy virtually from nothing. After 1640, French armies won consistent victories against the Habsburgs. With the new navy, he sent colonial expeditions to Africa and Canada, chartered royal companies to develop the new colonies, and encouraged missionaries to convert the natives to Catholicism. He also attempted to strengthen the French economy by supporting export industries and eliminating the domestic trade barriers. Nevertheless, throughout his career, his primary efforts were centered on diplomacy, and he, or the army of agents he employed, were constantly negotiating alliances and treaties throughout Europe. He even supported the Muslim Turks of the Ottoman Empire against Austria. Ultimately, all of these efforts resulted in the end of Habsburg domination and the rise of France as the foremost power on the Continent.

As Richelieu sought security and power for France in international affairs, so also did he seek stability and order in France itself. He did everything he could, first, to reduce the ability of the nobles to cause civil conflict and, second, to create a royal bureaucracy that would be able to oversee the nobility and provide for consistent administration regardless of who was the head of state. To achieve these ends, Richelieu created a web of spies who ferreted out plots of discontented nobles, several of whom were beheaded. The power of the Parlement de Paris, which had attempted to control royal authority by modifying edicts before it registered them as laws, was forcibly limited. Peasant revolts in the provinces, often encouraged or supported by local nobles, were ruthlessly crushed. Richelieu also persuaded Louis XIII to enforce the laws making dueling—a major source of civil disturbances—punishable by death. Finally, Richelieu expanded the role of officers called intendants, who were sent throughout the kingdom to keep an eye on provincial governments and nobility. Thus, Richelieu was kept constantly informed of conditions throughout France. Eventually, the use of intendants was to evolve, as Richelieu planned, into a system of provincial governors and administrators directly controlled by the Crown. Richelieu's efforts created a principle of centralization which not even the French Revolution could destroy.

Religion continued to be another source of division and disorder in French society. While Richelieu realized that to end religious toleration could lead to a major civil war, he also believed that the military and political power granted to the Huguenots by the Edict of Nantes was a constant threat to the stability of the state. Richelieu did not attempt to convert the Protestants forcibly; rather, he simply limited their political rights and eliminated their military power.

Toward the end of his life, Richelieu, a profoundly pious man, found himself in conflict both with Pope Urban VIII over French policy in the Thirty Years' War and with the hierarchy of the French church, who disagreed with Richelieu's allocation of church revenues to support the war efforts. Even in his last months, he was not freed from the conspiracies of his enemies, and he was forced to send one of the royal favorites, the Marquis de Cinq-Mars, to the block for treason. On his deathbed, Richelieu continued to work on the development of a stable civil government. After nominating his protégé, Jules Mazarin, to succeed him, he died, in the Palais Royal, on December 4, 1642.

Summary

Cardinal de Richelieu is remembered primarily as the architect of French power in Europe and centralization in royal government. In the area of foreign policy, he was instrumental in destroying the hold of the Habsburgs over European affairs. Through his intricate diplomacy and military successes, he brought France to the brink of leadership of the European powers. In so doing, he also raised the "reason of state" to primacy as the principle of relations between European states.

Richelieu applied the *raison d'état* as thoroughly in France itself as in his foreign policy. He did not hesitate to use whatever means he believed were necessary to build and maintain the strength of his government and that of France. Yet, respecting history and tradition, he did not seek to overturn completely the accepted structures of administration. A true practical politician, he surprised friends and foes alike with his pragmatism and ability to compromise. He could also be ruthless and seemingly cruel; he justified the state use of force and even the circumvention of the law in matters of national security by insisting that the peace and welfare of the state were simply too important to be confined by the morality applied to personal behavior.

The theoretical vehicle through which Richelieu implemented state power was absolutism, and he is usually given credit for instituting this theory as the principle of authority in France. Louis XIV and other kings would later attempt to transform absolutism into a visible reality. Richelieu's view of royal government was based on his theology, which supported the divine-right concept, in which the monarch was a sacred person who received his crown and powers from God alone. Thus, while bowing to the Papacy in spiritual matters, Richelieu insisted that only the king could be supreme in the secular realm. From this, his devotion to the stability and good order of the state led him logically toward all of those measures designed to curb the nobles and the Huguenots, and to increase the power of the central government.

Bibliography

Bergin, Joseph. *Cardinal Richelieu: Power and the Pursuit of Wealth*. New Haven, Conn.: Yale University Press, 1985. This is a scholarly work based on financial records of Richelieu's personal estates. In addition to providing an interesting perspective on Richelieu's use of political office for personal gain—a practice both accepted and very common in his period—it offers fascinating detail on the management of landed estates and the conduct of business in the seventeenth century. Extensive bibliography and genealogical charts.

Burckhardt, Carl J. *Richelieu and His Age*. 4 vols. Translated by Bernard Hoy. London: Allen & Unwin, 1967-1972. Though somewhat lengthy for the general reader, this is by far both the best biography of Richelieu and the clearest explanation of French politics of the period. Burckhardt's style is highly entertaining yet balanced and scholarly. Volume 4 is devoted to a bibliography, notes, and an analysis of the sources.

Church, William F. *Richelieu and Reason of State*. Princeton, N.J.: Princeton University Press, 1972. A detailed discussion of the conflict between political expediency and moral principles in policy-making in seventeenth century France. Church examines the growth of the idea of the reason of state as it evolved in the policies of Richelieu.

Friedrich, Carl J., and Charles Blitzer. *The Age of Power*. Ithaca, N.Y.: Cornell University Press, 1957. This is a classic introduction to the general development of Europe in the seventeeth century. Though brief, it is extremely well written and offers the student a clear picture of the great historical movements of this age. Unlike many general texts, it is not burdened with lists of names and dates; the authors have chosen to be highly selective, and this makes the book both coherent and comprehensible. Includes an excellent annotated bibliography.

Marvick, Elizabeth Wirth. *The Young Richelieu: A Psychoanalytical Approach to Leadership*. Chicago: University of Chicago Press, 1983. This is a specialist study which attempts to psychoanalyze Richelieu's personality and to discern how incidents in his youth influenced his approach to policy decisions and administration. As is true with most psychohistory, the author's method assumes that it is possible to psychoanalyze a long-dead historical figure; this is, at best, a highly questionable procedure. It is, nevertheless, an interesting work, useful for the detailed information provided about Richelieu's early years.

O'Connell, D. P. *Richelieu*. Cleveland: World Publishing, 1968. A comprehensive biography. O'Connell views Richelieu as an intensely religious man who was forced to deal with the tension between policies that were necessary for the good of France and his own religious morality. The author asserts that Richelieu quieted his conscience by creating an effective double standard: strict morality in the perfunctory administration of justice, but a broader, looser view where the security of the state was at issue. Contains an excellent bibliography.

Perkins, James Breck. *Richelieu and the Growth of French Power*. New York: G. P. Putnam's Sons, 1908. This is a standard and very detailed examination of Richelieu's life and career, concentrating on his methods of administration and the changes he brought which helped to centralize the French royal government.

Treasure, Geoffrey R. R. *Cardinal Richelieu and the Development of Abso-*

lutism. London: Adam and Charles Black, 1972. A standard work by a well-known expert in seventeenth century France. Treasure views Richelieu not as the cold architect of absolutist monarchy but, rather, as a long-suffering minister, fighting for survival in a highly competitive arena of domestic and international politics. Outstanding annotated bibliography.

Thomas C. Schunk

ARTHUR RIMBAUD

Born: October 20, 1854; Charleville, France
Died: November 10, 1891; Marseilles, France
Area of Achievement: Literature
Contribution: Rimbaud became one of the most influential of the French Symbolist poets through his vigorous writings and his dramatic personal history.

Early Life

Jean-Nicholas-Arthur Rimbaud was born in Charleville, near the Belgian border, the family's second son. His parents were Frédéric Rimbaud, a career army officer, and Vitalie Cuif, an austerely devout and conscientious woman of peasant stock. Captain Rimbaud was seldom at the family home in Charleville. In September, 1860, after several violent clashes with his wife, he left the family forever.

Madame Rimbaud reared her children to be examples of propriety and devoted herself to the complete control of their thoughts and actions. The eldest child, Frédéric, was slow, but Arthur showed early promise. The boys entered school together in 1861. In 1865, they were transferred to the Collège de Charleville. Arthur soon outstripped his brother academically, met outstanding success in all studies but mathematics, and won an overwhelming list of year's end prizes.

The young Rimbaud is described as angelic, with blue eyes and round cheeks—an ideal schoolboy. Madame Rimbaud separated her sons from the other boys at school, but eventually they found a long-term friend in Ernest Delahaye, later to be Rimbaud's biographer. Rimbaud's skill in French prose composition and Latin verse won for him the respect of his classmates. The principal of the *collège* indulged him, lent books to his prodigy, and enjoyed Rimbaud's success in academic competitions.

By early 1870, Rimbaud was leading a double life. Outwardly obedient, he read voraciously in all periods and points of view and formed a global view based on revolution against middle-class norms. He hoped to become a journalist and escape his mother, with whom he identified all civil and religious restrictions. He shared long walks with Delahaye, with whom he read and discussed poetry. Several of his Latin poems had already been published when his first long piece of French verse appeared in January, 1870. In the same month, Georges Izambard joined the faculty of the *collège* as a teacher of rhetoric. Izambard was very young, a political liberal, and a poet in his own right. He encouraged Rimbaud, lent him books, and discussed poetry with him. Through him, Rimbaud met Paul Bretagne, a friend of the famous poet Paul Verlaine. The boy was intoxicated by this link with Paris and found an outlet in poems celebrating nature and poetic aspirations as well as satires on the good bourgeois of Charleville.

On July 18, Napoleon III declared war on Prussia. When classes ended, Izambard left Charleville. Rimbaud's older brother ran away to follow the army. Delahaye was his only resource. Isolated, disgusted by bourgeois patriotism, and determined to rebel, Rimbaud ran away. On August 29, he made his first attempt, which ended with imprisonment in Paris for traveling without a ticket. Izambard posted bail and returned him to his mother. Between October, 1870, and April, 1871, he ran away three more times. Many poems written during this period are violent, revolutionary attacks on bourgeois society and the national government. The sixteen-year-old Rimbaud was probably in Paris in late April, 1871, during the last days of the Paris Commune, but left before the Thiers government retook the capital in the "bloody week" of May 7-14. During this stay, the runaway schoolboy witnessed wild scenes and possibly suffered homosexual rape. He also knew hunger and exposure and returned home ill and filthy. His personality and behavior had undergone a dramatic change. He was now determined to break his own ties to normal life.

Life's Work

On May 13 and 15, 1871, Rimbaud wrote his "Lettre du voyant" ("Seer Letter"), tumbling verses and exhortations as he described his ideal visionary poet. The Seer must reach new visions by a reasoned dismantling of all senses and create a new language, in which the senses join to shape material and poetic futures. No suffering or self-sacrifice is too great to reach this end, and other horrible workers will carry on after the individual's death. In a catalog of French poets of the past, Rimbaud heaps scorn on most but names Verlaine a Seer and true poet. Although Rimbaud had not yet met Verlaine, in September, 1871, he twice sent him poems and confided in him as an admired master. Verlaine, who was twenty-seven years old, married, and soon to be a father, was living with his in-laws. He took up a collection, sent for Rimbaud, and offered him temporary lodging with his wife's family. Rimbaud's single most famous poem, "Le Bateau ivre" ("The Drunken Boat"), was written as an introduction to Parisian poets before he left Charleville.

The inflexible young poet was immediately recognized by Verlaine's circle as a sort of evil angel and genius. He bent all of his energies to fulfilling his ideal of the Seer in his own life and Verlaine's. He provoked a series of violent confrontations with Verlaine's friends and family, moved from lodging to lodging, occasionally on the streets, returned to Charleville, but always urged the older man to free himself from his settled life. On July 7, 1872, the two poets left Paris for Belgium and continued to London, where they installed themselves and began to learn English. Their relationship was marked by frequent violent quarrels, separations, and Verlaine's illness. In the course of the year ending July, 1873, the older poet saw himself hopelessly alienated from his wife and the French literary world. In her suit for legal separation, Mathilde Verlaine accused him of homosexuality, a charge he always denied. Leaving Rimbaud penniless in London on July 3, 1873, Verlaine went to Brussels, with the plan either to reconcile with his wife or kill himself. He was joined in Belgium by his mother and Rimbaud. On July 10, Verlaine shot Rimbaud in the left arm. He was arrested on Rimbaud's complaint and spent eighteen months in Belgian prisons. He was released in January, 1875.

Most of Rimbaud's major verse works were written during the two years spent in close contact with Verlaine. Those years were spent in the hardest kind of living, supported by money from Verlaine's mother, with alcohol and hashish used as tools in a deliberate dismantling of his mind for poetry's sake. He had begun work on prose poems, which Verlaine would later publish as *Les Illuminations* (1886; *Illuminations*, 1932). He had written a major piece, "La Chasse Spirituelle" (the spiritual chase), now lost. During a period in Charleville, he had begun *Une Saison en enfer* (1873; *A Season in Hell*, 1932). Verlaine's arrest shook him, and he tried unsuccessfully to withdraw charges; he then retired to his mother's farm in Roche, where he finished *A Season in Hell*. This work, published in October, 1873, is the only book Rimbaud ever saw into print. He obtained at the printer's only a dozen copies; the rest of the printing was discovered in storage there in 1901. He left one copy at Verlaine's prison and embarked for Paris with the intention of distributing the rest in the hope of favorable reviews.

Although Verlaine was older and known as a violent drunk, Rimbaud was blamed for his imprisonment and was ostracized by Parisian literary circles. Their hostility led him to burn his copies of *A Season in Hell* when he returned to Roche. Many believe this to be the end of his literary life. Evidence suggests, however, that he continued working on prose poems after the publication of *A Season in Hell*, during a stay in London with the Provençal poet Germain Nouveau in the spring of 1874. This partnership ended abruptly when Nouveau realized the degree of ostracism awaiting Rimbaud's friends. Verlaine and Nouveau both were involved in copying Rimbaud's works, and it is almost entirely through Verlaine's efforts that Rimbaud's verse and *Illuminations* were published.

Sometime during the months following the departure of Nouveau, Rimbaud stopped writing literature. From 1875 to 1880, the former poet traveled. He studied German in Stuttgart, crossed the winter Alps on foot, visited Austria and Italy, and wandered with a Scandinavian circus. He went as far as Java in the Dutch colonial army, then deserted and worked his way to Europe on ship. Illness sent him home more than once. He studied piano and foreign languages, and even taught. He worked as an overseer for an engineering firm on Cyprus in 1878. In the end, he became a merchant working out of Aden and Harar in Africa, first as an agent for a French firm (beginning in 1880) and eventually on his own, trading in gold, coffee, skins, guns, and small goods for local consumption. He was one of the first white men to travel into the Shoa region of Ethiopia. The facts of his African years have less impact than the aura of adventure they lend his life. When he died of generalized carcinoma in Marseilles, the phenomenal spread of his literary reputation had just begun, and his absence from the scene enhanced public appreciation of his work.

Summary

Arthur Rimbaud's role as a literary meteor, a sort of fallen angel, was enough to guarantee for him a place as an icon of modern poetry. A large school of admirers, among them the great Christian poet Paul Claudel, saw him as a supreme example of spiritual adventure, a poet who pushed the quest for faith to its ultimate limits. An equally ardent school of thought sees the young poet as an unrepentant, Luciferian rebel. The study of Rimbaud's writings, with their shattering power of imagination, involves the reader in an absorbing enigma—the contemplation of language pursued into silence. Even though his work spanned barely five years, it can hardly be matched. Few walk away from Rimbaud in indifference.

Bibliography

Fowlie, Wallace. *Rimbaud*. Chicago: University of Chicago Press, 1965. This elegantly written work is especially focused on *Illuminations*. It gives an outline of Rimbaud's life, coupled with detailed literary and psychological analysis of key Rimbaud texts. Includes a selected bibliography.

Petitfils, Pierre. *Rimbaud*. Translated by Alan Sheridan. Charlottesville: University Press of Virginia, 1987. The most complete of the Rimbaud biographies available in English. A thoroughly scholarly, yet accessible work . which argues for an essential unity in Rimbaud's years as a poet and his mature life. The author does not analyze Rimbaud's writings as literature, but as evidence in the study of his life. An extensive bibliography is included.

Rimbaud, Arthur. *Complete Works, Selected Letters*. Translated with an introduction by Wallace Fowlie. Chicago: University of Chicago Press, 1966. This is the translation of Rimbaud's poems used by Pierre Petitfils in his *Rimbaud*, reposing on the solid basis of Fowlie's long studies of the poet and his period.

St.-Aubyn, F. C. *Arthur Rimbaud*. Boston: Twayne, 1975. Part of Twayne's World Authors series, intended for undergraduate student research. Includes a chronology, a short biography, and an annotated bibliography.

Starkie, Enid. *Arthur Rimbaud*. Winchester, Mass.: Faber & Faber, 1938. Rev. ed. New York: W. W. Norton, 1961. The standard English Rimbaud biographer for many years, Starkie writes from an intimate psychological viewpoint about the works and life of the poet. A short bibliography is included.

Wilson, Edmund. *Axel's Castle: A Study in the Imaginative Literature of 1870-1930*. New York: Charles Scribner's Sons, 1936. The prominent American literary critic relates the life and work of Rimbaud to the literary movements of his day. The French poet is thus juxtaposed to William Butler Yeats, T. S. Eliot, and Gertrude Stein. Somewhat dated but still valuable.

Anne W. Sienkewicz

NIKOLAY RIMSKY-KORSAKOV

Born: March 18, 1844; Tikhvin, Russia
Died: June 21, 1908; Lyubensk, St. Petersburg, Russia
Area of Achievement: Music
Contribution: One of the greatest and most prolific of Russian composers, Rimsky-Korsakov embodied in his music the nationalist spirit which was so important an element in late nineteenth century Russian culture. He composed fifteen operas, in addition to symphonies, concerti, chamber music, and solo pieces for piano and voice.

Early Life
Nikolay Rimsky-Korsakov was born into a gentry family in the town of Tikhvin (then in the government of Novgorod) on March 18, 1844. Although he demonstrated an early aptitude for music, family tradition required that he pursue a service career, and in 1856 he entered the Imperial Russian Navy, remaining on active duty until 1865. Somehow, however, he managed to compose. He had early made the acquaintance of Mily Alekseyevich Balakirev and, in time, sent him the manuscript of a first symphony, for which the latter arranged a public performance in December, 1865.

From 1865 onward, Rimsky-Korsakov lived almost continuously in St. Petersburg, displaying an enviable ability to compose with an ease and rapidity which would characterize his entire career, for there was little of the artist's angst in him. He soon became one of the group known as "the Five" or "the Mighty Handful"—the others were Balakirev, Aleksandr Borodin, César Antonovich Cui, and Modest Mussorgsky—all of whom were dedicated to the creation of a distinctly Russian musical idiom. With the premiere of his first opera, *Pskovityanka* (1873; *The Maid of Pskov*), Rimsky-Korsakov's place among contemporary Russian composers was assured. Two years earlier, in 1871, he had been appointed the professor of composition and instrumentation at the St. Petersburg Conservatory, a position which he would occupy, except for a few months in 1905, for the remainder of his life. In 1874, he took over from Balakirev as director and conductor of the Free School Concerts, an arrangement which continued until 1881, and between 1886 and 1900 he was conductor of the newly established Russian Symphony concerts. By then, however, Rimsky-Korsakov had emerged as indubitably the most prolific of the Mighty Handful. He was blessed with a creative energy, a fluency of invention, and a melodic prodigality which, together with his devotion to traditional Russian folk song and folk melody, made him the embodiment of that phase of late nineteenth century Russian culture in which so many writers, artists, and musicians sought a return to a pre-Petrine Slavic heritage.

Rimsky-Korsakov experimented with most forms of musical composition, and although the bulk of his output was operatic, he wrote three symphonies, several symphonic suites, concerti for various instruments, a respectable corpus of chamber music (including three string quartets), solo pieces for the piano, choral works, and many songs. *Antar* (his second symphony, composed in 1868), *Skazka: A Fairy Tale* (1879-1880), *Capriccio espagnol* (1887), *Scheherazade* (1888), as well as the *Russian Easter Festival Overture* (1888) have remained perennial favorites. All exemplify Rimsky-Korsakov's qualities as a composer—melodic inventiveness, strong rhythms, and brilliant orchestration.

Life's Work

It is primarily as a composer of operas that Rimsky-Korsakov occupies his prominent place in Russian music. He completed fifteen operas, and, of these, only three have non-Russian subject-matter: *Mozart and Salieri*, based upon Alexander Pushkin's poem (first performed in Moscow in 1898); *Servilia*, based upon a Roman play by the popular contemporary dramatist Lev Mey (first performed in St. Petersburg in 1902); and *Pan Voyevoda*, with a Polish setting (first performed in St. Petersburg in 1904). His first opera, *The Maid of Pskov*, was also based upon a play by Mey. *The Maid of Pskov* is based upon a true episode, Ivan the Terrible's visitation upon the city in 1569, and the czar himself is one of Rimsky-Korsakov's most successful character roles. It was a favorite role with the famous bass Fyodor Chaliapin, and Rimsky-Korsakov thought him inimitable in it.

His second complete opera, *Maskaya noch* (*May Night*), based upon a story by Nikolai Gogol, was well-received at its premiere at the Maryinsky in 1880. Two years later, in 1882, the Maryinsky witnessed the opening of what is perhaps his best-loved opera, *Snegurochka* (*The Snow Maiden*). Rimsky-Korsakov himself was extremely pleased with this work, in which he believed he had achieved for the first time a smooth-flowing recitative and in which the vocal writing as a whole constituted an advance upon his earlier work. *The Snow Maiden* was followed by *Mlada* (1892), *Christmas Eve* (1895), based upon a story by Gogol, and the magnificent, sprawling *Sadko* (1898), constructed from material taken from the *bylini*, the epic songs of medieval Russia, all three exemplifying his love of fantasy, folklore, and the fairy tale. In 1898, he returned to the subject matter of his first opera, *The Maid of Pskov*, and set to music Mey's original prologue, *Boyarinya Vera Sheloga*. It received its premiere in Moscow later that same year.

Rimsky-Korsakov now felt himself ready to fulfill a long-standing ambition, the composition of an opera based upon the subject matter of Mey's play, *Tsarskaya nevesta* (*The Tsar's Bride*). For this, he seems to have intended something rather different from his earlier operas. "The style of this opera," he declared, "was to be cantilena par excellence; the arias and soliloquies were planned for development within the limits of the dramatic situation; I had in mind vocal ensembles, genuine, finished and not at all in the form of any casual and fleeting linking of voices with others. . . ." *The Tsar's Bride* was given its premiere in Moscow in 1899. Moscow was also the location for the opening nights of *Skazka o tsare Saltane* (1900; *The Tale of Tsar Saltan*), based upon a poem by Pushkin, and the rarely performed *Kashchey bessmertny* (1902; *Kashchey the Immortal*). By then, however, Rimsky-Korsakov was absorbed in the composition of what is widely regarded as his greatest work, *Skazaniye o nevidimom grade kitezhe i deve Fevroniy* (1907; *The Legend of the Invisible City of Kitezh and the Maid Fevronia*), a story linking the thirteenth century Mongol invasion of Russia, the legend of Saint Fevronia of Murom, and the pagan animism of pre-Christian Russia on which he had previously drawn for *The Snow Maiden*. The result was a work of profound spirituality, which has been called, not inappropriately, the Russian *Parsifal*. It had its premiere at the Maryinsky in 1907, while the composer was at work upon his last opera, *Zolotoy petushok* (1909; *The Golden Cockerel*).

Among Soviet audiences, Rimsky-Korsakov's operas (of which *The Snow Maiden*, *Sadko*, *The Legend of the Invisible City of Kitezh and the Maid Fevronia*, and *The Golden Cockerel* may be regarded as the most original) enjoy enormous popularity. Outside the Soviet Union, they have not traveled well and are best known in the West through a series of brilliant orchestral suites (those of *Mlada*, *Christmas Eve*, *The Tale of Tsar Saltan*, and *The Golden Cockerel*).

Summary

Nikolay Rimsky-Korsakov's role in the development of Russian music was seminal, for in addition to his numerous compositions which now occupy a secure niche in the concert halls and opera houses of the Soviet Union and the world, he left his mark upon Russian music in two other ways. Because he possessed a temperament which did not feel threatened by creativity in others and because of his genuine interest in the work of fellow composers, he willingly undertook the completion of a number of important works by others left unfinished at the time of their deaths. No less significant for the future, his many years as a teacher at the St. Petersburg Conservatory meant that, for the last three decades of the nineteenth century and for the opening years of the twentieth, few young Russian instrumentalists or composers did not have firsthand exposure to him both as an instructor and as a generous, nurturing mentor.

A man of great personal integrity, a liberal, and a staunch opponent of the virulent anti-Semitism which flourished during the reigns of the last two czars, Rimsky-Korsakov found himself increasingly alienated from a regime in which reaction had replaced reform. In March, 1905, he sent a letter to the periodical *Rus* urging the case for the autonomy of the conservatory from the control of the Imperial Russian Musical Academy. He also sent an open letter to the director of the conservatory protesting police surveillance of the students. As a result of these actions, he was summarily dismissed from the professorship which he had held for thirty-four years. That was not the end of the matter, however, for his dismissal prompted the resignation from the faculty of, among others, Aleksandr Glazunov and Anatoly Lyadov. Before the end of the year, the conservatory attained sufficient independence to elect Glazunov its new director and, shortly thereafter, Rimsky-Korsakov was reinstated.

This episode does not seem to have interfered with Rimsky-Korsakov's habitually busy schedule. During the summer of 1905, he revised and supervised the printing of *The Legend of the Invisible City of Kitezh and the Maid Fevronia*, which had its premiere in 1907, and during 1906-1907 he worked on *The Golden Cockerel*. Then the censor intervened, ordering the omission of the entire introduction, the epilogue, and forty-five lines of the text. It has been suggested that the ban was motivated by the opera's subject matter, that the misadventures of the foolish King Dodon could be interpreted as a satire on the czar's court or his disastrous mismanagement of the Russo-Japanese War of 1905, but it is more likely that it was retribution for his publicly expressed liberal sentiments. Rimsky-Korsakov never saw *The Golden Cockerel* staged, for he died on June 21, 1908. Its first performance was given in Moscow in October, 1909.

Bibliography

Abraham, Gerald. *Essays in Russian and East European Music*. Oxford, England: Clarendon Press, 1985. The relevant essays in this collection are "*Pskovityanya*: The Original Version of Rimsky-Korsakov's First Opera," "Satire and Symbolism in *The Golden Cockerel*," and "Arab Melodies in Rimsky-Korsakov and Borodin."

_____. *Studies in Russian Music*. London: William Reeves, 1935. This earlier collection of Abraham's essays includes "Rimsky-Korsakov's First Opera," "Rimsky-Korsakov's Gogol Operas," "Snegurochka (Snow Maiden)," "Sadko," "The Tsar's Bride," "Kitezh," and "The Golden Cockerel."

Borovsky, Victor. *Chaliapin: A Critical Biography*. New York: Alfred A. Knopf, 1988. This definitive biography of the great Russian bass describes how Chaliapin interpreted the roles of Ivan the Terrible in *The Maid of Pskov* and Antonio Salieri in *Mozart and Salieri*.

Calvocoressi, Michel D., and Gerald Abraham. *Masters of Russian Music*. New York: Alfred A. Knopf, 1936. The best general account of Rimsky-Korsakov's life and work. Both scholarly and readable.

Ridenour, Robert C. *Nationalism, Modernism, and Personal Rivalry in Nineteenth-Century Russian Music*. Ann Arbor, Mich.: UMI Research

Press, 1981. A scholarly investigation of Rimsky-Korsakov's circle and their critics to 1873.

Rimsky-Korsakov, Nikolay Andreyevich. *My Musical Life*. Translated by Judah A. Joffe. New York: Alfred A. Knopf, 1942. Essential reading for understanding the outlook and personality of the composer.

Seroff, Victor I. *The Mighty Five: The Cradle of Russian National Music*. New York: Allen, Towne, & Heath, 1948. A popular account of Rimsky-Korsakov's circle of colleagues and friends.

Taruskin, Richard. *Opera and Drama in Russia as Preached and Practiced in the 1860's*. Ann Arbor, Mich.: UMI Research Press, 1981. An important study of the theatrical background to the theory and practice of opera as developed among the Mighty Handful.

Gavin R. G. Hambly

ALBRECHT RITSCHL

Born: March 25, 1822; Berlin, Prussia
Died: March 20, 1889; Göttingen, Germany
Area of Achievement: Religion
Contribution: Ritschl contributed to the liberalizing of nineteenth century Protestant theology by moving its concerns away from the speculative, neo-Scholastic abstractions that the faithful could not understand toward a renewal of a practical examination of the life of Jesus Christ as revealed in the New Testament. Since Christ was the perfect manifestation of the love of God, believers could have a model upon which to make proper value judgments.

Early Life

Albrecht Ritschl came from a solid religious background. His father, Carl Ritschl, was a bishop and general superintendent of the Lutheran church in Pomerania, and the boy grew up in the town of Stettin. He was an excellent student throughout his preuniversity career, excelling in languages and science. His mind welcomed complex information, because it gave him an opportunity to see how complexity grew and came together to formulate antithetical arguments that endlessly repeated the process. It was no doubt his penchant for synthesis that drew him early to the revolutionary work of Georg Wilhelm Friedrich Hegel, the leading professor at the University of Berlin during the first part of the nineteenth century.

Ritschl pursued his education at a number of prestigious universities during the years from 1839 to 1846. He studied at the University of Bonn and Halle, where he received his Ph.D. in 1843 and then pursued postdoctoral work at Heidelburg and Tübingen, where he studied church history with one of its leading scholars, Ferdinand Christian Baur. Baur became, for the next ten years or so, Ritschl's major mentor and influence. Ritschl's earliest scholarly works came out of the deep influence of Baur and his Tübingen school, which was an amalgamation of theologians and biblical scholars and historians that had been highly influenced by Hegel and his so-called conflict model of human history. This model proposed that history, like all other components of naturalistic process, works itself out in terms of the convergence of conflicting elements which then fall into necessary opposition and then form a new synthesis of meaning. History, like everything else in nature, operates within the laws of process, and Hegel had delineated the terms of those laws in his famous model of thesis, antithesis, and synthesis.

It was this Hegelian method of Baur and the Tübingen school that had informed Ritschl's first major scholarly work, *Das Evangelium Marcions und das Kanonische Evangelium des Lucas* (1846; the Gospel of Marcion and the canonical Gospel of Luke), and the success of this work established his career at the University of Bonn, where he became a full professor in 1859 at the age of thirty-seven. While this early work on the Gospel of Luke broke no new scholarly ground, it was an intelligently reasoned and lucidly written examination done within the mode of the Tübingen school of radical New Testament criticism.

It was Ritschl's next book, however, that broke all ties to Baur and his followers. During the years following the publication of his highly abstract book on the Gospel of Luke, Ritschl became increasingly disillusioned and disturbed at the intensified metaphysical approaches that theological and biblical studies were following. With each new theoretical-speculative volume emerging, the laity, the community of Christian believers, was being left behind, buried in the impossibly complex language and heady intellectualism of German scholarship.

Ritschl had found, however, an anchor and antidote to the cause of the increasing abstraction, Hegelian historical process, and he discovered it during the writing of his next book, which concerned the intellectual and spiritual ethos of the early Christianity of the first and second centuries. He performed a simple process of laying the emphasis on the first word, the adjective "historical" and removing it from the word "process." He found that the solid ground of history could save him from involvement in the endless speculative abstractions of the Hegelian dialectic. His next study was of the early Church Fathers and led him, historically, to the earliest forms of Christianity. He found that the closer Christianity came to the temporal and physical proximity of Jesus Christ—and to the earliest apostles and Church Fathers, the roots of the faith—the simpler and more pristine the message of Christianity became. History, then, stopped the Hegelian cyclic process and led him back linearly to the essential simplicity of the message of the Gospels. Once Ritschl disengaged himself from this cyclic model of history and attached himself to a linear model, he found relief in the bedrock of history.

In the second edition (1857) of his *Die Entstehung der altkatholischen Kirche* (1850; the rise of the old Catholic church), he announced the dramatic break, both personal and intellectual, with his mentor Ferdinand Baur. The move was a shattering blow to his former teacher. Two years later, Ritschl was appointed a full professor at the University of Bonn, rejecting similar offers from such prestigious schools as Strasbourg and Berlin. He became, then, the principal founder and exponent of what would be known as the liberal Protestant theological school that took root and flourished until just after World War I.

Life's Work

Ritschl's work after his major break with Baur proceeded with a serious redirection and reevaluation of the whole Christian enterprise. Once he found the anchor of hope in reinstating the historical Jesus Christ as the principal model for a Christian life-style and direction, a linearly sanctioned one at that, he was able to develop the major tenets of his revolutionary project. His basic working premise was the adaptation of a view regarding the moral nature of man that was new within the basic beliefs of Christianity: "In every religion what is sought, with the help of the superhuman spiritual power reverenced by man, is a solution of the contradiction in which man finds himself as both a part of nature and a spiritual personality claiming to dominate nature." Although this was his definitive statement of his views on man's moral nature made in his next work, the monumental three-volume study *Die christiliche Lehre von der Rechtfertigung und Versöhnuns* (1870-1874; *The Christian Doctrine of Justification and Reconciliation*, 1872-1900), his lectures and publications from 1857 through the 1860's thoroughly embodied this view.

What Ritschl had done, in effect, was to move Christianity away from its persistent and losing battles with two of its primary demons: the overly intellectualized speculations of natural philosophy on one hand, and the emotionalism of Pietism, on the other. Indeed, Ritschl's second major three-volume work was his definitive attack on such emotional subjectivism. Ritschl had to concede Immanuel Kant's proposition that man was unable to show evidence of or prove through any rational arguments the existence of God and, therefore, what a Christian's duty is to God. Therefore, he was forced to discard the overly neat proofs of God's existence simply because they started from outside personal Christianity and built on general ideas unconnected either with biblical revelation or with a living Christian faith.

What was left for the sincere Christian was the other end of the philosophical spectrum: subjectivism and its expression, mysticism. Without rational proof of God's existence and influence in the world, the seeker after God is left with his own subjective responses and feelings about his experiences and, therefore, runs the risk of mistaking the knowledge of his own religious consciousness for some kind of valid knowledge of God. Ritschl, having found a way back to the authentic roots of Christianity via history, leaps over the mystical and rationalistic barriers and exhorts the Christian to return to the original message of the New Testament as it was presented by Martin Luther himself. The original message is available, he argued, in the life and revelation of Jesus Christ directly observed through a rigorously historical examination of the texts themselves.

In short, what Ritschl offered was an enfreshened vision of the very purpose of Christianity. Religion should stop engaging in fruitless searches for direct knowledge of God. Kant proved such efforts hopeless. Man must also admit that he is part of nature and, therefore, a divided being who must constantly war with his natural impulses. Yet he is also gifted with two qualities that lift him above mere beast consciousness: self-consciousness and the ability to assign value to his actions. He is capable of making moral and ethical choices which the lower animals are not. Those gifts qualify him, then, to assume moral domination in the world which, as a Christian, he is obliged to do.

In positing these enlightened views on the moral nature of man, Ritschl does away with several key Christian beliefs. He reveals unmistakably Romantic views when he dismisses the Calvinist view of man's innate depravity. Man, he believes, is basically good but must continually war with his animal impulses. With one dramatic gesture, Ritschl does away with Satan, original sin, and innate depravity. Man is, however, a divided being who needs the example of Jesus Christ, who bridged the gulf between his animal and spiritual impulses. Out of man's recognition of his plight, he derives his sense of obligation to rule over the natural world, to take dominion and stewardship over it, and to attempt to shape it into what he called the "Kingdom of God on earth."

Ritschl, in his magnum opus, *The Christian Doctrine of Justification and Reconciliation*, changed the older, guilt-laden term "justification," which had earlier meant the "forgiveness of sins," to mean the lifting of "guilt-consciousness" and a consequent bridging of the gulf between God and man. The second stage of the transforming operation he called "reconciliation," God's free act of mending the split between God and man through the life example and death of Jesus Christ. It was the original intention of the great Protestant Reformers, he claims, to restore "justification and reconciliation" to their previous central positions within early Christianity and to tap its infinitely vital energies and use them to renew the original force and meaning of Christianity.

The first volume of the work delineated the various propositions he used to make his points. The third volume lays out what the results and effects of the reorganization of the entire Christian enterprise will be. If Christianity returns to the early pragmatic interpretation of "justification and reconciliation" based upon replacing the knowledge about God with the practical revelations made in the life of Jesus Christ and recoverable through a historical study of the New Testament, the possibility of an ethical human community comes into being.

By 1864, Ritschl had moved to the University of Göttingen as a full professor, where he finished his two major works and taught not only biblical subjects but also dogmatics and ethics. His last twenty-five years at Göttingen brought forth his full powers as both a thinker and a writer. He died quietly there on March 20, 1889.

Summary

The achievement of Albrecht Ritschl was so significant in the late nineteenth and early twentieth centuries that theologians have invented a term called "Ritschlianism." Unquestionably, Ritschl became the most famous proponent of the new liberal Protestant theology during those years. His major works, *The Christian Doctrine of Justification and Reconciliation* and *Geschichte des Pietismus* (1880-1886; the history of Pietism), brought Protestant theology into the modern era by denying the validity of its endless oscillations between highly abstract, speculative debate over whether God can be known and how He can be known and the overly subjective, emotional, and mystical avenues into the divine mystery. Before Ritschl could approach these seemingly insurmountable projects, he first had to admit that Kant had been correct and that Christianity was forced to discard any remaining vestiges of natural philosophy. History must replace metaphysical speculation as an avenue to certainty, but a certainty only verified through action, not ideas. Jesus Christ's life and death immediately, simultaneously, and permanently effected justification and reconciliation and created the possibility of an ethical human community.

Bibliography

Barth, Karl. *Protestant Thought: From Rousseau to Ritschl.* Translated by Brian Cozens. New York: Harper & Brothers, 1959. Although renowned for a brutal attack on Ritschl and other liberal Protestant theologians, Barth nevertheless delivers a brilliant summary of all the various theological schools leading up to Ritschl and places him at the conclusion of a tradition that was summarily destroyed by World War I.

Heron, Alasdair I. C. *A Century of Protestant Theology.* Philadelphia: Westminster Press, 1980. In a chapter devoted to Friedrich Schleiermacher and Ritschl, the author clearly distinguishes their unique contributions but shows that Ritschl was forced to reject the older theologian's overemphasis on what came to be called "the theology of feeling." Succinct and highly informative.

Lotz, David W. *Ritschl and Luther: A Fresh Perspective on Albrecht Ritschl's Theology in the Light of His Luther Study.* Nashville: Abingdon Press, 1974. Lotz devoted much time and energy to shedding light on exactly what Ritschl derived from his own deep study of Martin Luther's major contributions to theology, particularly Luther's interpretations and explanations of the terms "justification and reconciliation."

Mackintosh, H. R. *Types of Modern Theology: Schleiermacher to Barth.* London: Collins, 1964. The first and, perhaps, still the most comprehensive treatment of Ritschl that is not an entire book. Mackintosh clearly places Ritschl in a nineteenth century tradition and shows how he emerges from Schleiermacher, corrects him, and creates the way for other important theologians. There are many points in Ritschl's approach that clearly disturb Mackintosh, but he explicates him with fairness and equanimity. Highly recommended.

Richmond, James. *Ritschl, a Reappraisal: A Study in Systematic Theology.*

London: Collins, 1978. Richmond shows how theologians are reviving Ritschl since he seems to have so closely adumbrated the more existential modern theologians. This is one of several correctives to certain Barthian neoorthodox criticisms.

Tillich, Paul. *Perspectives on Nineteenth and Twentieth Century Protestant Theology.* Edited with an introduction by Carl E. Braaten. New York: Harper & Row, 1967. Although he does not offer a comprehensive treatment of Ritschl, Tillich discusses Ritschl's influence on American theology long after it seemed dead in Germany. He credits the Ritschlians with introducing Kantianism into theology and labeling Kant the philosopher of Protestantism. Highly informative and intelligent.

Patrick Meanor

ROBESPIERRE

Born: May 6, 1758; Arras, France
Died: July 28, 1794; Paris, France
Area of Achievement: Government
Contribution: Alone among the leaders of the French Revolution, Robespierre was identified with every stage of the Revolution. In addition, he most clearly enunciated the ideals upon which the Revolution was to be based and fought most vigorously for its success.

Early Life

Maximilien-François-Marié-Isidore de Robespierre was born at Arras, in the province of Artois, on May 6, 1758. He was the eldest of four surviving children of Maximilien-Barthélemy, a third-generation lawyer, and Jacqueline-Marguerite, née Carraut, de Robespierre. Maximilien was only five years old when his mother died in childbirth, and, soon after, his father abandoned his children and left them to the care of first their maternal grandfather and later their aunts. These events undoubtedly had a profound impact on the young boy. From an early age, he was forced to assume adult responsibilities and to suffer privation. His childhood instilled in him certain distinctive features of his personality, including serious-mindedness, studiousness, and an appreciation of what it meant to be poor.

Robespierre's education was provided by charitable foundations. Following four years at a church-sponsored school in Arras, he won a church scholarship to the prestigious College of Louis-le-Grand of the University of Paris, where for twelve years he studied classics and law and was first exposed to the writings of his later philosophical idol, Jean-Jacques Rousseau. Robespierre excelled as a classical scholar and was chosen, in 1775, to deliver a Latin address of welcome to the newly crowned king, Louis XVI, and his queen, Marie Antoinette, on their return trip from Reims to Versailles.

In 1780, Robespierre was awarded a law degree and, in 1781, was admitted to practice before the nation's premier court, the Parlement of Paris. After winning a monetary prize from Louis-le-Grand and being allowed to pass on his scholarship to his only brother, Augustin, Robespierre returned to Arras to care for his only surviving sister and to practice law. For the next eight years, he enjoyed the life of a middle-class provincial lawyer inclined, because of his commitment to altruistic principles, to champion the causes of the poor and humble against their social superiors.

Robespierre's life as a country lawyer moved toward its end in 1788, when Louis XVI, under pressure from the nobility, called for a meeting of the Estates General to address the problem of taxation, which had brought the kingdom to the brink of bankruptcy. The nobility, which comprised the

First Estate, intended to join forces with the clergy, the Second Estate, to outvote the rest of the people, the Third Estate, who agreed with the Crown regarding the necessity of taxing the nobility. Election of representatives was authorized, and an outburst of pamphleteering and the drafting of *cahiers de doléances* (lists of grievances) reflected popular enthusiasm and anticipation. Robespierre wrote a *cahier* for the local cobblers' guild, authored a pamphlet in which he called for equal representation, and won election as one of the eight deputies to represent Artois in the Third Estate of the Estates General. On May 5, 1789, he appeared at Versailles with his fellow deputies to begin work on an anticipated regeneration of France.

Life's Work

On June 20, in the face of obstructionism by the first two estates and vacillation by the king, the Third Estate, with the adherence of a few nobles and clergymen, took the revolutionary step of proclaiming themselves the National Constituent Assembly and taking an oath not to disband until they had drafted a constitution for France. During the tumultuous summer of 1789, Robespierre played only a modest role. The fall of the Bastille, the peasant uprisings and the resulting August Decrees which abolished feudalism, and the danger of royalist counterrevolution which forced the removal of the royal family to Paris in October were all events that momentarily made the deliberations of the assembly secondary. Robespierre delivered several speeches, including addresses favoring freedom of the press and limitations on the king's veto power, but his main activities came after the assembly followed the king to Paris. Robespierre was politically astute to court the support of the people of Paris by opposing the imposition of martial law. During the next two years of relative tranquillity, Robespierre emerged as one of the leaders of the leftist faction of liberal democrats and fought for a democratic franchise and for the granting of civil rights to Jews, Protestants, and actors. Robespierre also became increasingly active in the Jacobin Club, which was to become a major base of his support in Paris and the provinces. During 1790 and 1791, he was in constant attendance in the assembly, delivering 125 recorded speeches in 1790 and 328 in the first nine months of 1791. Here and at the Jacobin Club, he emerged as the apostle of Rousseau. He envisioned a nation whose laws and institutions would be founded on ethical and spiritual ideals which represented the sovereign will of the people, who were by nature instilled with the virtues of patriotism and selflessness. In conformity with his philosophy, Robespierre opposed the death penalty, censorship, and the distinction between active and passive citizens in establishing property qualifications for voting. Although favoring a constitutional monarchy at this time, he demanded severe limitations on the king's veto power and on his power to declare war. He also demanded that all male citizens be allowed admittance to the National Guard without property qualifications. It was also Robespierre who, in May, 1791, introduced the "self-denying" ordinance by which members of the National Constituent Assembly disqualified themselves for election to the Legislature Assembly provided in the constitution of 1791. By September, 1791, when the National Constituent Assembly disbanded, Robespierre had emerged as the Revolution's popular hero. He was garlanded and carried in triumph through the streets. Already known as "the Incorruptible" because of his high principles, modest life-style, and refusal to accept financial rewards, Robespierre strengthened his ties to the people by moving to the home of a carpenter, in the rue Saint-Honoré, where he could be close to the Legislative Assembly and the Jacobin Club. Following a brief return to Arras in October, he was to remain there under the doting protection of the carpenter's family, who idolized him, for the remainder of his life.

The new constitutional monarchy with its one-house Legislative Assembly was to survive from only October, 1791, to August, 1792. The king had already signified his lack of commitment to the constitution when he attempted to flee France to join the émigrés and the Austrian army in June, 1791. In the assembly, a leftist faction developed under the leadership of Jacques Brissot, known as the Brissotins, and later, in the convention, as the Girondins. This faction called for war against the crowned heads of Europe to extend the benefits of the Revolution beyond France's frontiers, to force compliance from the king, to divert the lower classes in Paris from the preoccupation with food prices, and to open new markets for the commercial middle class. Robespierre, through the local Jacobin Club, took a great political risk by almost alone opposing the war. The war went badly for France, and Austrian and Prussian troops crossed the frontier in early August, 1792, dooming the Crown and the constitution of 1791. In the insurrection of August 10, 1792, the king was toppled from the throne and removed, with the royal family, from the Tuileries to the Temple prison. Robespierre, in the Jacobin Club, had played a role in this insurrection and was elected to the general council of the Paris Commune, which had been created on August 9. He now called for the election, by universal male suffrage, of a constitutional convention to draft a new republican constitution. He does not, however, appear to have played a direct role in the gruesome September Massacres of Parisian prisoners precipitated by the Austro-Prussian invasion.

Robespierre was elected a delegate from Paris to the National Convention, which began its deliberations in September. He emerged as the leader of the leftist faction of Jacobins known as the "Mountain," who primarily espoused the interests of Parisians. They were opposed by the Girondins, who had their political base in the provinces. The two factions differed heatedly over a variety of issues. Robespierre and the "Mountain" called for the trial of the former king, to which the Girondins acceded. They differed, however, over the imposition of the death penalty. Robespierre prevailed, and Louis was guillotined in January, 1793. Girondin ascendancy prevailed, however, so long as the war went well, as it had done again after August, 1792. In April 1793, however, the tide turned again. England had now joined the coalition which, after driving the French from Belgium, threatened to invade France. Working-class fears, exacerbated by rising prices and food shortages, resulted in the expulsion of the Girondins, the arrests of their leaders, and the flight of those remaining to the provinces to raise the banner of federalist counterrevolution. The "Mountain" was now in control of the convention.

The convention and the Revolution were in grave danger. Foreign armies and their émigré royalist allies were at the gate. In the West, especially in the Vendée, peasants who detested the Revolution's religious policy and who remained loyal to the monarchy were in violent revolt. Thus, the convention was faced with the unenviable task of repressing civil strife and counterrevolution, mobilizing the nation's people and resources to win the war against the allies, and giving France a new constitution. To assist in the tasks, the convention established the Committee of Public Safety, including among its most influential members Robespierre and his close associates Louis de Saint-Just and Georges Couthon and the "organizer of victory" Lazare Carnot.

Robespierre soon emerged as the leading spokesman of the committee before the convention. It was he who justified the establishment of the instruments of the Reign of Terror. Defining terror as prompt, severe, and inflexible justice, he argued that a combination of virtue (patriotism) and terror was necessary in a time of revolution. On June 10, 1794, under Robespierre's sponsorship, the convention passed the notorious Law of the Twenty-second Prairial, which expanded the Revolutionary Tribunal, provided for the imposition of the death penalty for all those convicted, expanded the number of kinds of condemned conduct and the types of evidence that could be used, and disposed of the necessity of calling witnesses. As a result, the number of executions increased. Robespierre overextended himself in his support of this law, and the fear that this generated among fellow terrorists contributed to his fall. Robespierre had also frightened his colleagues by his elimination of the leftist Hébertistes in March and by his role in the condemnation of Georges Danton, a popular fellow Jacobin who favored a moderation of the Terror, and his associates in April. Robespierre and the committee also succeeded on the war front. By the summer of 1794, the allied armies were in retreat and the French Republican army was on the offensive and pushing into the Low Countries. At the height of his power in June, 1794, Robespierre attempted to institute a civic religion. In the farcical Festival of the Supreme Being over which Robespierre officiated on June 8, he naïvely hoped to reconcile devout Catholics and freethinkers to the new order. Having succeeded in his basic goals and outgrown his usefulness, and having frightened several terrorists whose excesses he intended to punish, Robespierre was outlawed and arrested by the convention on July 27, 1794; he mounted the scaffold the following day with several of his associates, including his brother, Saint-Just, and Couthon.

Summary

With Robespierre died the popular hope for a truly democratic revolution. The reaction which followed was a betrayal of most for which the Revolution's most indefatigable leader had fought. The shelved 1793 democratic and republican constitution which Robespierre had helped to draft was never tried. Robespierre emerged unjustly as the bloodthirsty ogre of the Revolution—the vain man with catlike features and a cold and morbidly suspicious nature, who attempted to eliminate all who stood in the way of his ambition for popular adulation. With time has come increased objectivity. Although Robespierre cannot be relieved of any responsibility for violent excesses during his tenure on the Committee of Public Safety, it must be remembered that he was attempting to rule a nation, fight a foreign war and a civil war, control leftist extremism, and draft a constitution at the same time. In a less tumultuous time, he might well have realized, at least partially, his dream of a society and nation based on ethical and spiritual principles.

Bibliography

Cobban, Alfred. *Aspects of the French Revolution*. New York: George Braziller, 1968. In two oustanding essays in this compilation, the author delineates Robespierre's fundamental ideas and traces the changes that took place in the subject's attitudes as the Revolution moved into its most critical and violent stages.

Gallo, Max. *Robespierre, the Incorruptible*. New York: Herder and Herder, 1971. This is a well-intentioned but naïve psychobiography. Although unacceptable to the serious historian, it is entertaining and provocative.

Korngold, Ralph. *Robespierre and the Fourth Estate*. New York: Modern Age Books, 1941. This is a sympathetic treatment of the subject, in which the author argues that a major factor in Robespierre's overthrow and execution was his championing of the proletariat, the Fourth Estate. Korngold's sympathy for Robespierre was partially caused by the collapse of the Third Republic in 1940, which suggested the problems of the First Republic which Robespierre worked assiduously to save.

Palmer, R. R. *Twelve Who Ruled: The Year of the Terror in the French Revolution*. Princeton, N.J.: Princeton University Press, 1941. This is the only scholarly treatment of the Committee of Public Safety in English. It is most useful in understanding the motivations of Robespierre during the last and most important year of his life.

Rudé, George. *Robespierre: Portrait of a Revolutionary Democrat*. New

York: Viking Press, 1976. Although the author provides a useful biography of Robespierre, his main contribution is to trace the changing attitudes of historians toward the subject, from the Revolution to the present. Contains a helpful bibliographical note, a useful glossary, and a concurrent chronology of the main events in the Revolution and in Robespierre's life.

Thompson, J. M. *Leaders of the French Revolution*. London: Basil Blackwell and Mott, 1929. This series of short literary protraits of eleven revolutionary figures by the historian who was to become recognized as the leading authority on Robespierre contains a perceptive account of the subject with special emphasis on the features of his contradictory and enigmatic personality.

_____. *Robespierre*. 2 vols. New York: Basil Blackwell, 1935, rev. ed. 1939. This biography is generally regarded as the best in English and perhaps in any language. As such it is indispensable to the serious student.

_____. *Robespierre and the French Revolution*. New York: Collier Books, 1952. An important contribution to the Teach Yourself History series, this book is especially useful to the beginning student because it treats Robespierre within the broader context of the Revolution.

J. Stewart Alverson

AUGUSTE RODIN

Born: November 12, 1840; Paris, France
Died: November 17, 1917; Paris, France
Area of Achievement: Art
Contribution: One of the greatest sculptors of all time, Rodin has been hailed for both the monumentality and the psychological penetration of his sculpture. Much of his work has a kinetic quality, a dynamism that takes over the solid material of his sculpture, transforming it into the expression of a towering personality.

Early Life

Born the youngest of two children in a working-class home, Auguste Rodin was educated with great care under the supervision of his uncle in a friar's school until he was fourteen. By the age of ten, he had already shown an interest in drawing, and it was thought that he would become an artisan. His teachers were impressed with his dedication and talent and encouraged him to believe that he would one day become a fine artist. Yet his early years were not full of success. Indeed, he failed three times to gain acceptance at the École des Beaux-Arts, where he had hoped to study sculpture.

Working as a craftsman, Rodin studied on his own the work of Antoine-Louis Bayre (1795-1875), who was famous for his lifelike depictions of animals. He also assisted Albert-Ernest Carrier-Belleuse (1824-1887) in his studio, beginning in 1864, and closely followed developments in the world of contemporary sculpture. His early sculptures, one of his father (c. 1860) and one of Father Pierre-Julien Eymard (1863), already exhibit his dexterous and precise sense for the human face. Father Eymard, the superior of the Societas Sanctissimi Sacramenti, profoundly impressed and touched Rodin, who had stayed briefly in a cloister before deciding that the religious life did not suit him.

Still largely unacknowledged, Rodin traveled to Italy in 1875 to study the sculpture of Donatello and Michelangelo. Not being able to afford a long trip, he soon returned to France with great enthusiasm for the Italian masters, which resulted in his sculpture, *The Age of Bronze*, a work that was so lifelike he was accused of having taken a mold of a live model. Other artists came to his defense in what was to be the first of many controversies concerning Rodin's techniques and choices of subject matter.

By the late 1870's, the state was acquiring sculptures such as *Saint John the Baptist Preaching*, which were every bit as realistic as *The Age of Bronze*, for by now the temper of the age was beginning to swing Rodin's way, valuing precisely his uncanny ability to render the human figure in bronze as if it were alive. Rather than accepting traditional sculpture with stereotypical gestures, Rodin had accustomed his contemporaries to a startling, almost photographic depiction of the individual, of a peasant-faced Saint John, for example, crooking one finger of his extended right arm while dropping his left arm, slightly flexed, to his side. This portrait of man in action, in mid-stride, with a body that reflected an inner psychological life and purposiveness, was a stunning achievement.

Life's Work

Now a figure of considerable influence, Rodin was courted and given many commissions, including one which involved the decoration of a door for the future Museum of Decorative Arts. Inspired by Dante's *Inferno*, Rodin chose to create *The Gates of Hell*, a work of enormous ambition which he never finished and perhaps never could, for as William Hale notes, the sculptor took as his subject the creation of chaos itself. Kept in his studio until his death, the work reflects the artist's constant experimentations with style and his engagement with all the inchoate human desires that are never quite fulfilled.

Seated atop this magnificent work is the world-famous statue *The Thinker*. He is at once a perfectly realized and enigmatic figure. With his chin resting on his bent right hand, and his upper body leaning forward in somber meditation, he is evocative of a powerful human intellect but also of a brooding, perhaps dissatisfied nature for whom thought itself does not suffice. Various commentators have noted that this powerfully muscled figure is out of proportion—a deliberate ploy to increase the tension of the pose, to use physical power to suggest mental strength. Behind the thinker, in the tympanum, are the vacant-faced figures of the damned, engaged in their ghastly dance of death while other falling figures suggest horror and the frustration of failed lives. On the twenty-one-foot-tall door (thirteen feet wide and three feet deep), the artist uses the size of human figures (ranging from six inches to four feet) to portray the differentiated scale of a world of human sufferers.

Rodin repeatedly flouted his society's notion of what was dignified and presentable. His commissioned sculpture of Victor Hugo was rejected because he produced a seated rather than a standing figure. Even more bitterness was occasioned by his monument to Honoré de Balzac, which many of his contemporaries considered to be grotesque, a violent and swollen piece that was called "an obscenity," "a toad in a sack," "this lump of plaster kicked together by a lunatic," and the like. Rodin was aiming, however, not for a faithful likeness of his subject but for a visceral rendering of his extraordinary imagination and body of work. The sculptor pursued his subjects like a biographer, and in the case of Balzac went so far as to visit the places where the novelist's fiction was set. Balzac had died at the age of fifty-one, his body exhausted from having produced his novels so intensely and rapidly. Rodin contacted Balzac's tailor to get a measure of his clothes, he checked accounts of the writer's physical appearance, and he exercised his conception of the writer by sculpting more than twenty studies of his head and body. Many of these preliminary efforts were realistic portraits, as though Rodin preferred to work with the outward facts and burrow more deeply into his subject's interior life. The result was a huge figure with a bull neck, a distorted face, and an immense torso—the point being that here was an artist whose very physical presence was magnificently marked by the lives he had imagined. The statue was like a thing of nature, with the figure's features erupting from the surface like volcanic life itself.

Rodin's work in marble—*The Kiss* (1886), for example—has been more accessible and a great favorite with the public. A highly erotic man and artist, Rodin has accentuated the effect of the embrace by the angle he has chosen, which has the woman's right leg thrusting forward while the man's fingers touch her thigh. There is an equality in the embrace, a mutuality (emphasized by the touching of their feet and the entwinement of their legs) that seems perfect.

By 1900, Rodin was recognized as the foremost sculptor of his period. Soon he would travel to do a bust of George Bernard Shaw (1906) and sculptures of English and American notables. In 1905, forty-two of his works were exhibited in the Luxembourg Museum. He continued to innovate, creating human figures which emphasize his interest in the motion and position of bodies. By fragmenting these sculptures, taking away certain physical features, expressions, and bodily parts, he accentuated his art. His *Walking Man* is headless, because nothing must distract from his study of the shift in weight, the rhythm of musculature, and the placement of the feet— all of which contribute to an appreciation of how a man walks. Rodin believed in the principle of leaving out something, of an understatement that allows other features or themes to be seen more clearly.

Summary

Auguste Rodin was both a great scholar and a creator of art. No artist of his stature has exceeded his ability to learn from his predecessors. He was also very much a man of the nineteenth century, taking a profound interest in individual lives, treating his preparations for portrait sculpture the way a modern psychological biographer does his or her research and writing, amassing evidence but also probing for the heart of the subject. He welcomed new tools—the camera, for example—not only to record his work, to help him in modeling and studying his subjects, but also to assist him in capturing reality from new points of view.

There are many accounts of Rodin working in his studio. The biography by Fredric V. Grunfeld contains many passages that show how carefully Rodin studied the nude human body—not simply to attain accuracy of presentation but also to use physical details, the tone and the play of different muscle groups, to suggest mental and spiritual life. Rodin knew that he had to imbue outward forms with a sense of inner life. His statues are not static. They have the dynamism of Renaissance forms, of the works by Donatello that Rodin admired so profusely, but Rodin's work has something more: the pulsing of muscles that reflect interior energies. It is as if the sculptor makes what is invisible visible.

Notoriously slow in executing his commissions, Rodin was known to keep works many years past their deadlines, half-finished, awaiting his inspiration and his maturing conception of what the work could yield to him. In some cases, as in his work on Victor Hugo, he never did find the right form, the appropriate means of expression for his subject. In others, as with his work on Balzac, he was determined to shape a figure that revealed all he had to say about this titanic figure of literature.

Perhaps more than any other sculptor, Rodin concerned himself with sculpture and its relationship to nature. His pieces are renowned for the way they take the light, for the artist's realization that the meaning of form depends upon how it reacts with its environment. A work that has no context, or does not create a context for itself, is a work that is only half-realized. Few great artists have matched Rodin's exquisite sense of the wholeness of art, of the perfect work that creates its own standards, its own way of measuring itself and the world around it.

Bibliography

Champigneulle, Bernard. *Rodin*. New York: Harry N. Abrams, 1967. A sound biographical and critical study, with superb black-and-white and color plates, notes, and a list of illustrations. No bibliography and only an inadequate index.

Elsen, Albert E. *In Rodin's Studio: A Photographic Record of Sculpture in the Making*. Ithaca, N.Y.: Cornell University Press, 1980. A fascinating study of the way Rodin used and was influenced by photography in the creation of his work. Photographs of Rodin and his studio, as well as of his work in various stages of composition, make this an extraordinarily valuable study.

Grunfeld, Frederic V. *Rodin: A Biography*. New York: Henry Holt, 1987. The first full-scale biography of Rodin to appear since 1936. Grunfeld has found and taken advantage of many new sources. His huge book is well written, copiously illustrated, and enhanced by a very full bibliography, extensive notes, and a comprehensive index. Written for both scholars and a larger, general audience, this biography is essential reading.

Hale, William Harlan. *The World of Rodin, 1840-1917*. New York: Time-Life Books, 1969. A copiously illustrated, life-and-times approach to the artist's life which includes a chronology of artists, a bibliography, a comprehensive index, and "A Guide to The Gates of Hell," detailing the architectural features and figures of this complex masterpiece.

Rodin, Auguste. *Rodin Sculptures*. Selected by Ludwig Goldscheider. London: Phaidon Press, 1970. Large, handsome black-and-white reproductions of Rodin's most important works. This work is enhanced by detailed notes on plates and succinct introductions to the artist's life and work.

Carl Rollyson

PIERRE DE RONSARD

Born: September 11, 1524; near Couture, Vendômois, France
Died: December 27, 1585; Saint-Cosme, France
Area of Achievement: Poetry
Contribution: Ronsard enriched French poetry by adapting classical genres and styles to his native language. He wrote historically significant odes, hymns, and lyrics and one of the most important sonnet sequences in the history of literature.

Early Life

Pierre de Ronsard was born into a noble family in the Vendômois area of France. His father, Louis, was made a chevalier by Louis XII a few years before the poet was born. At the age of twelve, Ronsard was placed as a page in the French court, which put him in a position to become an important courtier or functionary in the royal household. His father wanted him to pursue a legal career, then the path to preferment, but Ronsard performed poorly at each school he attended. He was bored with the subjects that were taught but fascinated by the Latin poetry he read, and he nurtured the ambition of becoming a poet.

After the death of his father in 1544, Ronsard took a crucial step in becoming a poet. He placed himself under the tutelage of Jean Dorat, an early French Humanist. He studied Latin and Greek language and literature under Dorat with his friend Jean-Antoine de Baïf. This rigorous training provided him with classical models in form, genre, and style that he believed were superior to the existing medieval models, which were primarily romances and religious works. Ronsard and his friends Joachim du Bellay, Baïf, and others, formed a group that supported the aims of the new poetry and became known as the Pléiade. Ronsard was determined to become not merely another poet but also the poet who would change the tradition by incorporating classical models, elegance, and rigor into French literature. In 1550, three years after completing his studies with Dorat, he published *Odes* and was hailed as the French Pindar.

Life's Work

Ronsard's *Odes* were well received at the time, but later criticism has tended to disparage them, and a nineteenth century critic, Charles-Augustin Sainte-Beuve, called them unreadable. They were historically important in introducing classical forms and myths into French literature, and some can still affect readers today. One of the problems later readers faced was that Ronsard followed the metrical and stanzaic patterns of Pindar—primarily a short poetic line and stanzas grouped into triads—and he transferred some of the subject matter from Pindar directly into poems that seemed distant from sixteenth century France. The odes that imitated Horace were more successful; Horace's structure was looser, the style more urbane, and the world they represented had some analogies to those of Ronsard.

The first poem of the third book of odes, in which he announces his vocation as a poet, is a good example of Ronsard's celebration of his classical models. After announcing that he has become "the gods' mortal companion" because the Greek Muse of poetry, Euterpe, has lifted him up to that state, he now can scorn common pretenders since the "Muse loves me. . . ." At the end of the poem, he describes his poetic position as directly linked to Greece and Rome: "Making me part of high Athens' glory,/ Part of the ancient wisdom of the Romans." The common pretenders would be those still mired in the older forms of poetry or those writing merely love lyrics, while Ronsard has become one of the ancients.

Ronsard's next major work was *Les Amours* (1552). Petrarch, who was Ronsard's poetic model for this work, was closer in time. Ronsard wrote sonnets that followed and varied the Petrarchan structure and metaphors. These poems have remained popular through the years and to most people are the quintessential Ronsard. The first part of *Les Amours* deals with the poet's love for Cassandra. In poem 20, he desires to be rain that falls "one golden drop after another/ Into Cassandra's lovely lap. . . ." He then metamorphoses into a white bull who will take her when she passes. Finally, he becomes a narcissus and she a spring so he can plunge into her. After suggesting metaphorical and mythical ways to unite, the last three lines speak of a union at night with a desire to suspend the approach of dawn. The poem varies slightly from Petrarchan conventions, since it speaks directly about the union with the beloved.

In 1554, Ronsard offered a less ambitious but delightful collection, *Le Bocage*. These poems deal more directly with the countryside, nature, and contemporary events. There is, for example, a poem on the frog "La Grenouille"; Ronsard celebrates the ordinary frog above other animals and even calls her a goddess. In addition, the frog is not subject, as man is, to hard times. He also asks, in a personal touch, that the frog not disturb "the bed or study/ Of my good friend Remy Belleau." The tone is playful and clearly different from the *Odes*. The most interesting poem from that collection, however, is on famine. It asks God to relieve His people and compares the situation of the French to the Israelites. Near the end, he asks that this hardship be visited on barbarians, Scyths, Tartars, and Turks. The last request is the only classical allusion in the poem; the poet asks for a return to the age of precious gold, a common allusion in Ronsard, where people lived naturally and freely.

Also in 1554, Ronsard began the frustrating attempt to produce a national epic of France, *La Franciade* (1572). The poem was to be modeled after

Vergil's *Aeneid* and deal with the legendary founding of France. He published fragments of the poem over the years and one book for the royal family; however, even though he wished to master all poetic forms including the epic, as the greatest poets did, the ambitious work was never completed and seems to have been alien to Ronsard's genius. His gift was for the lyric, not the epic.

In 1555, Ronsard found a form midway between the lyric and the epic in the first book of *Les Hymnes* (1555-1556). The subjects for these poems were lofty and general. For example, there is a hymn to eternity and one on philosophy. Later, he wrote a sequence on the four seasons. The most interesting poem in this collection is, perhaps, "Hymne des astres," a long poem on the mythic history of the stars.

In 1556, he published the *Nouvelle continuation des amours* and the second book of hymns. In the new *Nouvelle continuation des amours*, Ronsard wrote poems on a mysterious rural woman called Marie. These poems use many of the familiar strategies of the sonnet tradition, including the *carpe diem* motif. They are, however, more immediate and intense in their approach to the beloved. For example, in one poem Ronsard urges Marie to rise and join nature, which is already active. At the end, the poet states that he will teach her through kisses on her eyes and breast. There is no Petrarchan coyness here.

In 1559, Ronsard finally achieved the preferment for which he had wished in order to make his life less precarious. He was appointed *counseiller* to King Henry II, and he dropped *Nouvelle continuation des Amours* for poems on political and religious subjects. He defended the royal cause and the Catholics against the Protestants. In 1561, he wrote *Discours des misères de ce temps*, appealing to Catherine de Médicis to heal the division within the country. Yet the religious conflict continued, and, although Ronsard defended the Catholic cause, he was moderate and always counseled peace and toleration. In 1563, he wrote *Remonstrance au peuple de France*, scolding his countrymen for their failure to be reasonable and preserve peace. He also tried to influence the new king Charles IX by writing a plan for his education and training. Ronsard's strong desire for harmony is a reflection of the structure and themes of his poems.

Ronsard also continued his sonnet writing during this period and created one of his finest works, *Sonnets pour Hélène* (1578; *Sonnets for Helen*, 1932). The poems have an intensity and feeling about the experience of love that goes beyond the mythic approach of the Cassandra sonnets. In "Quand vous serez bien veille" ("When You Are Old"), he warns Hélène that she will grow old and live only in the memory and blessing Ronsard's poems will give, an important theme in William Shakespeare's sonnets. The final lines turn from a warning to a plea, "take me, living, now."

In 1574, after the triumph of *Sonnets for Helen*, Ronsard completed *Les*

Derniers Vers, which marked a change in tone and approach. They do not speak of love but of a rejection of the body. Appropriately, one of his last poems is to his soul; his soul, which had been his body's hostess, at death will be purged of remorse and rancor. The last lines are a farewell: "Ladies and gentlemen, my talk/ Is finished: follow your/ Fortune. Don't trouble/ My rest. I will sleep now."

In his last years, Ronsard's health failed. He suffered from a variety of ailments, including gout. He died at Saint-Cosme in 1585, at the age of sixty-one.

Summary

Pierre de Ronsard remains an important historical figure in the development of European literature. He transformed the rediscovered texts and myths of the Greeks and Romans into new French poems. The poetic tradition and the range of allusion and reference could not be the same after his poems. He wrote extensively in every available poetic genre of his time. In addition, he wrote some of the finest lyrics and one of the most influential sonnet sequences of the period. French and European poetry would not have been the same without Ronsard.

There is no doubt that Ronsard wrote too much; there are a huge number of poems, and many are of interest only to students of the period. In addition, he tended to lean on classical mythology to do the work of structuring many of his poems. The job of a critic or reader is to separate the poems that are permanent and valuable from those that are ephemeral or dated, so that we might once more see the value of a poet who was exalted in his own lifetime and still deserves careful and proper attention.

Bibliography

Bishop, Morris. *Ronsard, Prince of Poets*. New York: Oxford University Press, 1940. An old-fashioned but readable biography of the poet. The author can be annoying by claiming knowledge of Ronsard's inmost thoughts, but he does provide some important background information.

Cave, Terence, ed. *Ronsard the Poet*. London: Methuen, 1973. An excellent collection of essays on Ronsard's poetic art. Cave's essay "Ronsard's Mythological Universe" is especially good. There are useful essays on Ronsard's conception of beauty and on the last poems.

Jones, K. R. W. *Pierre de Ronsard*. New York: Twayne, 1970. An excellent introduction to the life and works of Ronsard. Jones places more emphasis on the poems than the life, but he does give the necessary facts. Contains a chronology and a bibliography.

McGowan, Margaret M. *Ideal Forms in the Age of Ronsard*. Berkeley: University of California Press, 1985. McGowan connects the poetry of Ronsard to structures found in the art of the period. This is an excellent interdisciplinary study with illustrations of paintings and sculpture. The book is learned but not leaden.

Wilson, D. B. *Ronsard: Poet of Nature*. Manchester, England: Manchester University Press, 1961. Deals fully with one of the most important subjects of Ronsard and connects Ronsard to the tradition of the descriptive poem in that period. Good discussion of Ronsard's use of landscape and his typical strategies in using nature as subject and context.

James Sullivan

GIOACCHINO ROSSINI

Born: February 29, 1792; Pesaro
Died: November 13, 1868; Passy, France
Area of Achievement: Music
Contribution: Rossini was one of the greatest composers of Italian opera in the nineteenth century. In almost forty works for the operatic stage, Rossini composed some of the last and finest specimens of the *opera buffa* and also numerous serious operas which laid the foundation for the ensuing generation of Italian Romantic composers. His brilliant overtures have enjoyed a separate life as concert pieces.

Early Life

Gioacchino Rossini was the son of musicians: His father, Giuseppe, was a hornist, and his mother, Anna (née Guidarini), was a soprano who, though musically untutored, sang minor roles in provincial theaters. Rossini's childhood coincided with Napoleon I's Italian campaigns, and his hometown of Pesaro on the Adriatic changed hands numerous times; the elder Rossini, an enthusiastic republican, was briefly imprisoned by papal authorities in 1800. Despite vicissitudes, Rossini's early life was not unhappy. Tradition has it that the young Rossini was unusually high-spirited and prankish, early manifestations no doubt of a drollery that was to remain with him in maturity.

The Rossini family settled in Bologna in 1804. For Rossini, this was a stroke of good fortune: He was able in 1806 to enter the Liceo Musicale, one of the finest music schools in Italy. That he had already acquired considerable prowess as a musician is attested by his election in the same year to the Accademia Filarmonica of Bologna, a remarkable honor for a fourteen year old. At the conservatory, Rossini's studies in counterpoint were directed by Padre Stanislao Mattei, a strict traditionalist whose rigorous method helped Rossini attain a well-regulated and fluent compositional technique.

Rossini's studies at the Liceo continued until 1810. By this time he had already completed his first opera, a serious work entitled *Demetrio e Polibio*, which would receive its first performance in 1812. Rossini's actual public debut as an opera composer was with a comic work, a one-act farce entitled *La cambiale di matrimonio* presented at the Teatro San Moisè in Venice in November, 1810. The opera was a triumph. Already the eighteen-year-old composer displayed evidence of the élan and wit which were to be the hallmarks of his later works. The success of *La cambiale di matrimonio* propelled Rossini into a mad whirl of opera composition: In the next twenty-six months, he composed six more comic works and established himself in the front rank of young composers. By age twenty-one, Rossini was a veteran of the operatic wars and a national celebrity; he was poised on the brink of international acclaim.

The larger-than-life Rossini personality had also begun to emerge. Witty and gregarious, Rossini cut a wide swath in society. Precocious in his interest in the opposite sex, he paid a price for his indulgences: Several venereal infections led to chronic urological problems in his middle years. Rossini was slender and attractive as a young man but soon fell prey to baldness and corpulence; all extant photographs show him well fleshed and bewigged.

Life's Work

Rossini emerged as a composer at a time when Italian opera was in transition. The *opera seria* (serious opera) as it had been cultivated in the eighteenth century was moribund; its rigidly conventionalized formality and its reliance on artificial mythological or classical plots caused it to wilt in the hotter artistic climate of the nineteenth century. *Opera buffa*, as it had been cultivated by Wolfgang Amadeus Mozart, was still a vital genre, but it had entered its final phase; it, too, was ultimately an expression of eighteenth century sensibilities. While Rossini remains most closely identified with *opera buffa* through the continuing appeal of works such as *The Barber of Seville* (1816), the clear majority of his operas after his apprentice phase were tragic or heroic works which may be viewed as attempts to recast the *opera seria* in nineteenth century terms. Ironically, Rossini himself remained ambivalent about the emerging Romantic style. Though he helped to shape the Romantic taste in librettos, and though he virtually invented the formal structure of the Romantic melodrama, he was reluctant to succumb fully to the wholesale emotional intensity of the Romantic style.

Nevertheless, the work which first brought Rossini international fame was the proto-Romantic *Tancredi*, a serious opera which was first performed at the Teatro La Fenice in Venice in February of 1813. The libretto, drawn from Voltaire and Torquato Tasso, presents a costume drama of no particular distinction, but it afforded Rossini the opportunity to experiment with new methods of formal organization. Most of the formal conventions which sustained Rossini in later works are here present at least in embryonic state. These forms include the opening choral introduction interrupted by a solo, the multipart ensemble finale, and the extended *scena* for principal characters. A large measure of *Tancredi*'s success had to do, however, with its sheer tunefulness. *Tancredi*'s act 1 cavatina "Di tanti palpiti," for example, became an international hit by nineteenth century standards.

The decade following the premiere of *Tancredi* in 1813 marked the peak of Rossini's productivity as a composer of Italian opera. Rossini completed twenty-five operas in this span, including comic gems such as *L'italiani in Algeri* (1813), *The Barber of Seville*, *La cenerentola* (1817), and dramatic or tragic works such as *Otello* (1816), *Mosè in Egitto* (1818), *La donna del lago* (1819), and *Semiramide* (1823). As Rossini moved from triumph to triumph, he attained a celebrity that was virtually without precedent in the music world. Stendhal was guilty of only modest exaggeration when he wrote of Rossini in 1824: "Napoleon is dead; but a new conqueror has already shown himself to the world; and from Moscow to Naples, from London to Vienna, from Paris to Calcutta, his name is constantly on every tongue."

The Barber of Seville was undoubtedly Rossini's comic masterpiece. Although the work was first given under the title *Almaviva* in order to discourage comparison with a popular opera on the same subject by Giovanni Paisiello, Rossini's work soon eclipsed the older opera in popularity and has remained his most frequently given stage work. The opera stands in the older *opera buffa* tradition, but it has a quality of manic humor which is uniquely Rossinian.

From late 1815 until 1823, Rossini made Naples the base of his operations; ten of nineteen operas produced during this span were written for Neapolitan stages. At Naples, he became romantically involved with one of his prima donnas, the soprano Isabella Colbran. Rossini and Colbran were married in 1822, but the union was not enduring, and separation followed quickly.

The enormous and unbroken popularity of *The Barber of Seville* has obscured the fact that most of Rossini's operas in the Neapolitan period were serious. Of particular note were *Otello* and *La donna del lago*. The former was Rossini's only Shakespearean opera, and though the libretto lamentably perverts William Shakespeare's drama, the score is one of Rossini's most ambitious efforts to synthesize music and text. The entire last act presents itself as a musicodramatic unit rather than as a string of pieces; Rossini himself considered it to be one of his finest achievements. *La donna del lago*, based on Sir Walter Scott's *The Lady of the Lake*, demonstrates Rossini's interest in the literature of his day and was evidently the first of the many nineteenth century operas inspired by the writings of Scott.

In the final phase of his career, Rossini was drawn to Paris. While three of his four operas with French texts were in fact revisions of earlier Italian works, Rossini's last opera, *Guillaume Tell* (1829), was newly composed and is his largest, and arguably his greatest, work. The tale of the Swiss patriot William Tell loosely follows Friedrich Schiller's play of that name and provided Rossini with a grand canvas on which to work. He responded with some of his finest music. The overture, whose electrifying gallop at the close has become a cliché, is nevertheless a superb inspiration.

After *Guillaume Tell* came the so-called great renunciation: Rossini simply ceased to compose operas. Numerous explanations have been adduced to account for his abrupt retirement: that he had said all that he had to say, that he was uncomfortable with the advent of unbridled Romanticism, that he deplored the decline of vocal standards, that he was suffering from ill health. In all probability, each of these factors contributed to Rossini's decision.

The early years of Rossini's retirement were plagued by ill health. During this period, he was nursed solicitously by his new mistress, the former courtesan Olympe Pélissier, whom he married in 1846. In the mid-1850's, Rossini settled permanently in Paris. For the remainder of his life, Rossini was treated like a *grand seigneur*; his salon was a magnet for young composers, and his pungent observations and jests were widely circulated.

Only a few compositions date from the long retirement. The two most impressive are sacred works: the highly dramatic *Stabat Mater* (1832) and the *Petite messe solennelle* (1853). Rossini also composed numerous epigrammatic and parodistic works for piano which he called *Péchés de vieillesse* (1835; sins of my old age).

Summary

Of the great nineteenth century Italian opera composers, only the mature Giuseppe Verdi surpassed Gioacchino Rossini in sheer compositional inspiration. In style, wit, originality, brio, and technical fluency, Rossini was abundantly endowed. Where Rossini was able to concentrate these gifts—in the comic operas and the overtures—he was able to achieve both critical and popular success. Ironically, Rossini did his most original work in a genre— the romantic *melodrama*—for which he was not fully suited by taste and temperament. In works such as *Otello*, *La donna del lago*, and *Guillaume Tell*, Rossini charted the course for the next generation of opera composers. Yet Rossini himself was reluctant to cross the threshold into the new age. His legacy is nevertheless substantial: His thirty-nine operas form a trove which has not yet been fully brought to light.

Bibliography

Gossett, Philip. "Gioacchino Rossini." In *The New Grove Masters of Italian Opera*. New York, W. W. Norton, 1983. Gossett's seventy-page essay, together with a full list of works, constitutes a reworking of his earlier entry for *The New Grove Dictionary* and is perhaps the most reliable and up-to-date account of Rossini generally available.

Stendhal. *Life of Rossini*. Translated and annotated by Richard N. Coe. New York: Orion Press, 1970. Stendhal's famous biography has the merits of contemporaneity and literary brilliance. It was, however, a work of polemical journalism, not of scholarship, and it is marred by many inaccuracies.

Till, Nicolas. *Rossini: His Life and Times*. New York: Hippocrene Books, 1983. This lavishly illustrated work is perhaps the best short introduction to Rossini's life and work for the general reader. Till provides excellent descriptions of Rossini's social and professional milieu and offers intelligent critical judgments couched in highly readable prose.

Toye, Francis. *Rossini: A Study in Tragi-comedy*. New York: Alfred A. Knopf, 1947. First published in 1934, Toye's work engagingly championed Rossini and his works at a time when the composer's stock among music critics was low. Though perhaps overly reliant on the three-volume study by Giuseppe Radiciotti in Italian, this genial work remains valuable.

Weinstock, Herbert. *Rossini: A Biography.* New York: Alfred A. Knopf, 1968. The most exhaustive account of Rossini's life in English, Weinstock's work is the product of impressive research and contains extensive notes, appendices, and a lengthy bibliography.

Steven W. Shrader

THE ROTHSCHILD FAMILY

Mayer Amschel Rothschild

Born: February 23, 1744; Frankfurt am Main
Died: September 19, 1812; Frankfurt am Main

Amschel Mayer Rothschild

Born: June 12, 1773; Frankfurt am Main
Died: December 6, 1855; Frankfurt am Main

Salomon Mayer Rothschild

Born: September 9, 1774; Frankfurt am Main
Died: July 27, 1855; Paris, France

Nathan Mayer Rothschild

Born: September 16, 1777; Frankfurt am Main
Died: July 28, 1836; Frankfurt am Main

Carl Mayer Rothschild

Born: April 24, 1788; Frankfurt am Main
Died: March 10, 1855; Naples, Kingdom of the Two Sicilies

James Mayer Rothschild

Born: May 15, 1792; Frankfurt am Main
Died: November 15, 1868; Paris, France
Area of Achievement: Business
Contribution: The Rothschild family developed one of the most successful banking and investment companies of all time. By locating branches in a number of major cities while keeping the business a family matter, they were able to coordinate international operations and provide services to clients and governments that were unavailable elsewhere.

Early Lives

Mayer Amschel Rothschild was born in the Frankfurt ghetto in 1744. His parents died only eleven years later of smallpox, but traveling with his peddler father had already had an impact on the boy. In the patchwork of principalities making up the eighteenth century Holy Roman Empire, even a minor trader might visit several countries in a day or two. Mayer Amschel was thus introduced at an early age to the mysteries of money exchanging. Although his parents had enrolled him in a Jewish religious school that prepared students to be scholars, after their deaths he was able to convince relatives that he would be better off in a business career. In 1757, an apprenticeship at the Oppenheimer Bank in Hannover was arranged. He returned to Frankfurt in 1763.

Mayer Amschel had become a dealer in rare coins, and in 1765 a connection made in Hannover arranged for him to display his wares for Prince William of Hesse, whose avarice was legendary. For four years, Mayer Amschel sold coins at bargain prices to the prince, getting little for his trouble. Later, however, he was able to buy the house the family had been renting, which became his home and office. He had an illustrated catalog printed. Most important, he married Gutle Schnapper in 1770. The union was fruitful: Five sons and five daughters grew to adulthood. The sons— Amschel, Salomon, Nathan, Carl, and James—would build the family business into a worldwide concern.

Mayer Amschel continued to court William, who was combining enterprises such as renting mercenaries to England for use in America and an inheritance to become enormously wealthy. His break came because of a friendship with Carl Buderus, William's chief financial adviser. Mayer Amschel had given Buderus a valuable coin, and, upon making a second visit to William in his new establishment in Kassel, Mayer Amschel got his first commission. This was the beginning of a relationship that proved extremely profitable to all concerned. By the 1790's, the family was comfortably well off and about to embark on the enterprise that would make it an international financial force.

Life's Work

Annoyed by the haughtiness of an English cotton salesman, the twenty-one-year-old Nathan resolved to go to England and conduct business for the family; he would become the most successful of the entire clan. The stocky, powerful Nathan was round-headed with coarse features; his speech was crude, and he never lost his German accent. Interested in little but business, he was soon established as a major financier and trader in a variety of commodities, taking good advantage of the demands created by the French Revolutionary Wars. On the Continent, the Rothschilds were of enormous service in concealing valuables from the emperor's rapacious agents, but in England Nathan, at least at times, used the funds transferred for investment in bonds in more speculative investments. When he had to account for sums, he bought the requested bonds, making up the interest so that William of Hesse earned as much as if the bonds had been bought when ordered. This was all arranged in partnership with Carl Buderus, who helped hide the operation from William and became rich in the process.

The Rothschild firm was now extremely successful, thanks to its financial manipulations. Another factor was the increased business provoked in London and Frankfurt by the French blockade, which forced the opening of new markets as well as shifting old ones to Rothschild advantage. In 1810, the firm was renamed M. A. Rothschild and Sons, with Mayer Amschel and the four sons still in Frankfurt having shares—Nathan, in enemy territory, could get nothing legally but was promised his share when the political situation made it possible.

Nathan had, the year before, established his own bank in England and was beginning to be brought into government financial arrangements. In 1814, he had a hand in the very profitable process of collecting loans and transferring the funds to the Duke of Wellington in the Peninsula. In addition, he created an excellent system of couriers, carrier pigeons, and other means of communication, which usually meant that he had information about European events before his competitors and often was able to buy or sell government bonds to advantage. While Nathan was expanding the holdings of the English branch, his brothers were spreading family institutions around Europe. James had settled in Paris, where he had had some opportunity to help with Nathan's efforts to supply money to Wellington in Spain.

In 1819, a wave of liberal-nationalist feeling broke over the German Confederation, threatening the Rothschilds both as bankers who supported the conservative policies of Metternich and as Jews. The family was urged to abandon Frankfurt for Paris. Upon hearing of this, Metternich sent word that the Rothschilds would be welcome in Vienna, and subsequently he arranged for the Rothschild bank to raise an enormous loan for the Austrian government. Despite some troubling moments and charges of corruption, the bonds involved proved profitable for the bank and a good investment for purchasers. As the loan required much attention, Salomon opened a branch of the bank in Vienna. In 1821, Carl, the least forceful of the brothers, became the agent for the bank to raise a loan in Naples to help the Austrian government with the cost of maintaining an occupation to prevent revolution. His success not only improved the standing of the family in Vienna but also resulted in his remaining to open a new branch. In 1822, Metternich requested that the emperor bestow baronies on the five brothers.

Amschel, the only brother to be orthodox or slim, remained in Frankfurt, eventually becoming treasurer to the German Confederation and extremely influential in the financial policy-making of the Prussian government. The Rothschilds had become part of the economic and social elite.

Trouble arose when the Revolution of 1830 toppled the Bourbon government, for James Rothschild, deeply involved with government finance, did not believe the government was in trouble. Initial losses were serious, but the excellent communications system maintained by the family allowed Nathan and Salomon to sell French securities early and to rebuy at great profits. James's dependable, fiscally conservative management soon caught the attention of the July Monarch, Louis-Philippe, and James was brought back into a major role in French government finance.

The death of Nathan, while in Frankfurt to attend the 1836 wedding of his son Lionel, left James in Paris as the head of the family. Increasingly involved in the finances of both the government and Louis-Philippe personally, James's fortune approached fifty million pounds. His circle of friends included both aristocrats and intellectuals such as George Sand and Honoré de Balzac. Always pressed to support one cause or another, James gave generously only to be criticized for meanness by the rejected and unsatisfied.

In the middle of the century, the Rothschild business interest turned to railroads, resulting in much profit in Austria, Italy, and France. Efforts were also made to support international peace, as in 1840 when in Paris and Vienna the governments were soothed so that war would not destroy prosperity. In 1848, Carl persuaded the government of Naples to make liberal concessions to the revolutionaries and defuse the threat that in so many places led to violence.

In Paris, revolution again proved expensive. Not only was money invested in government securities at risk but also James's villa in the Bois de Boulogne was burned by the mob. In Vienna, Salomon had to abandon his house to the mob; Salomon went to Frankfurt, never returning to Vienna. James clung to his base in Paris and, by attaching himself to Eugène Cavaignac, Minister of War in the new revolutionary government, was soon back in the thick of politics and finance. Having been the bitter foes of Napoleon I, the Rothschilds were hardly eager for the advent of another. Their hopes were frustrated, however, when Louis-Napoleon Bonaparte was elected President of the Second Republic and then in 1852 declared himself Emperor Napoleon III.

In England, Lionel (1808-1879), already prominent in the business when his father died, became senior partner aided by his brothers, Mayer, Anthony, and Nathaniel. The second English generation began to move the family into traditional English upper-class patterns. Estates were purchased; Rothschilds were also becoming known for charity, art collecting, and hunting. Although the patriarch might not have approved of his sons' charitable impulses or artistic and sporting avocations, he would have been warmly in favor of their efforts to further the removal of civil and social disabilities from Jews. Although few Rothschilds felt much affinity for the outward forms of religion, they remained sensitive to their heritage.

Lionel, who devoted himself to the business, was urged by his friend, the great conservative politician Benjamin Disraeli, to seek a seat in the House of Commons. As members had to take an oath "on my true faith as a Christian," Jews were barred. In 1847, Lionel was elected to Parliament as a Liberal candidate for the City of London (the business district of the metropolis); although Commons passed a bill to allow him to take his seat, the bill was rejected by the House of Lords. Six times over the next eleven years,

Lionel was reelected only to be turned away, despite the support of Disraeli. Finally in 1858, after a seventh electoral triumph, the Lords yielded, and Lionel became the first practicing Jew to be a Member of Parliament.

Membership in Parliament was only one element of becoming prominent in English society. The upper classes were tied together by relationships forged in public schools (the equivalent of private preparatory schools in the United States) and the two universities. As the University of Oxford had a religious test for graduation, the University of Cambridge was the institution for those of nonorthodox religious opinions; Cambridge did, however, require attendance at Anglican chapel. Although exceptions had been made for Lionel's brother Mayer and at least one other Jew, the requirement was not dropped by the university until 1856, and even then individual colleges could retain it. The change facilitated the matriculation of Lionel's son Nathan Mayer (called Natty) in 1859. Having distinguished himself socially at Cambridge and certainly having no lack of wealth, Natty made himself a force in Liberal politics and in 1885 became the first Jewish peer. His cousin Hannah married the Earl of Rosebery, a future prime minister, in 1878. Thus by the end of the nineteenth century, the Rothschilds were not only among the most wealthy of the English but also were firmly ensconced among the social and political elite.

On the Continent, Rothschild fortunes were more mixed during the middle years of the nineteenth century. In 1855, three of the original five brothers died: Carl of Naples, Salomon of Vienna, and Amschel of Frankfurt. The family was not quickly welcomed into the confidences of Napoleon III's government, although James's personal tie to the Empress Eugénie prevented complete ostracism. Although the French Rothschilds were frozen out of the organization of the Crédit Mobilier, a new French financial institution which, with government support, was enormously successful, Anselm, son of Salomon of Vienna, took the lead in developing the Kreditanstalt, a similar business in Vienna. By the late 1850's, a third generation—Alphonse of Paris (James lived until 1868), Anselm of Vienna, Lionel of London, and Mayer Carl of Frankfurt—were cooperating as well as the original brothers had. The Italian War of 1859-1860 strained the Crédit Mobilier, resulting in a cosmetic reconciliation between the emperor and the Rothschilds. The same war began Italian unification, and, with the collapse of Naples as an independent state, the Rothschild Bank there was closed. It would not be reopened.

A growing public role was common for the family in the late nineteenth century. The Franco-Prussian War (1870-1871) did the Rothschild business no real harm and, since the bank managed the payment of the French indemnity, in the long run resulted in a profit. In England, Alfred Rothschild was appointed a director of the Bank of England in 1868, and, when Natty became a peer, his cousin Ferdinand replaced him in Parliament.

The end of the century found Rothschilds still running the family business but pursuing widely divergent nonbusiness interests. For example, Edmond devoted his time and money to supporting the establishment of colonies of poor Jews in Palestine; Lionel Walter (1868-1937) became well known as a naturalist; and Henri (1872-1947) was a successful physician and playwright.

Summary

The Rothschild family holds an extraordinary place in the world of international finance. In less than fifty years, the family went from poverty in the Frankfurt ghetto to control of one of the richest and most powerful banks in the world. Further, the family held its place throughout the turbulent nineteenth century. The Rothschild Bank was an early example of an international company with the twist that its branches were all controlled directly by family members and operated with an eye to the benefit of the entire clan. It is not surprising that, with their wealth and excellent communications system, the family was involved in the public financial operations in all the countries in which they had banks. More unusual is that, despite some use of bribery, the Rothschilds do not seem to have enriched themselves via corruption. The members of the family have generally been committed to serious public service as well as to profit-making.

Rothschilds have also done much to eliminate discrimination against Jews. Never stinting in the use of money and renown in the cause of coreligionists, they accomplished much. Elimination of restrictions on Jewish property holding in Habsburg territories, access to the Parliament, university, and peerage in England, and membership in the social elite of France are only some of their achievements. If noblesse oblige can be applied to the status of wealth, then it seems appropriate for the four generations of Rothschilds between 1758 and 1900.

Bibliography

Corti, Count Egon Caesar. *The Rise of the House of Rothschild*. Translated by Brian Lunn and Beatrix Lunn. London: Victor Gollancz, 1928. An account of the early years of the Rothschild rise to prominence and wealth. Its focus on the first generations makes it particularly useful, since the early years are generally less well known.

Cowles, Virginia. *The Rothschilds: A Family of Fortune*. New York: Alfred A. Knopf, 1973. A popular family history recounting the story of the Rothschilds from their origins in eighteenth century Frankfurt to multinational prominence in the mid-twentieth century. The book is well written and corrects some of the most common myths about the Rothschilds, but it does leave other legends untouched.

Davis, Richard. *The English Rothschilds*. Chapel Hill: University of North

Carolina Press, 1983. The author, an excellent scholar, based this book on the Rothschild family papers and an in-depth knowledge of the period; the style makes it a volume for both the general reader and the serious student. For the English branch of the family, there is no better source of information or bibliography.

Morton, Frederic. *Rothschilds: A Family Portrait*. New York: Atheneum, 1962. Useful account of the family's history. The general focus makes it particularly desirable for the study of the family rather than of individual members.

Roth, Cecil. *The Magnificent Rothschilds*. London: Robert Hale, 1939. Long the standard general history of the family, this book, while still valuable, is dated. It is a complete, well-researched, and well-written account.

Fred R. van Hartesveldt

JEAN-JACQUES ROUSSEAU

Born: June 28, 1712; Geneva
Died: July 2, 1778; Ermenonville, France
Areas of Achievement: Education, literature, and political science
Contribution: Rousseau helped transform the Western world from a rigidly stratified, frequently despotic civilization into a predominantly democratic civilization dedicated to assuring the dignity and fulfillment of the individual.

Early Life

Jean-Jacques Rousseau was born of middle-class parents in the fiercely independent Protestant municipality of Geneva. His mother, the former Suzanne Bernard, died within days of his birth, and he was reared until age ten by his watchmaker father, Isaac Rousseau, with whom the precocious boy shared a passion for romantic novels, a passion which helped to shape Jean-Jacques' emotional and highly imaginative nature. Young Rousseau and the irresponsible Isaac often neglected sleep as they devoured their beloved romances, an escapist reading regimen which Rousseau supplemented with more substantial works by such writers as Plutarch and Michel Eyquem de Montaigne.

This earliest phase of Rousseau's life came to an abrupt end when his father was forced to flee from Geneva to escape imprisonment for wounding a former military officer during a quarrel in the autumn of 1722. Left in the care of a maternal uncle, Rousseau was soon placed, along with his cousin Abraham Bernard, in the home of the Lambercier family, a Protestant minister and his sister, in the village of Bossey, a few miles outside Geneva.

The essentially carefree two years spent with the Lamberciers were followed by a short period of distasteful employment with the district registrar, and a longer apprenticeship to an engraver. Petty thefts and other breaches of discipline earned for Rousseau, now in his teens, a series of beatings which in no way altered his recalcitrant behavior but which augmented his hatred of authority. After nearly three years of these confrontations, in March of 1728 he abandoned his apprenticeship and, with it, his native city.

Rousseau was introduced to twenty-nine-year-old Madame de Warens, eventually to be one of the great loves of his life, who sent the destitute and still-directionless teenager to Turin's monastery of the Spirito Santo, where, within a few days of his arrival, he found it expedient to embrace the Catholic faith. Released into the streets of Turin with little money, Rousseau held several jobs but eventually returned, probably by mid-1729, to Madame de Warens.

Rousseau's duties as record keeper to Madame de Warens were light enough to allow him ample time for wide reading, but his genius had still not manifested itself, and after his patron had left on a journey to Paris, the aimless youth took the opportunity to add to his ample store of life adventures. At Lausanne, he attempted, despite insufficient knowledge of music, to conduct an orchestral work of his own composition; the performance was a fiasco.

Succeeding months saw Madame de Warens establish herself as Rousseau's mistress and Rousseau busy himself with the study and teaching of music. Over the next several years, Rousseau also undertook the intensive study of most other branches of human knowledge in an eminently successful effort to overcome the handicap of his earlier haphazard education.

Life's Work

By 1740, Rousseau had begun serious attempts to write, but he remained essentially unknown. His first minor recognition came in 1742, during his second visit to Paris, when he suggested a new method of musical notation to the Academy of Science. Although the method was judged inadequate, Rousseau's presentation earned for him the respect of and eventual introduction to several figures of importance in the French intelligentsia, most notably Denis Diderot. In 1743, at the salon of Madame Dupin, Rousseau widened his circle of influential acquaintances, and eventually he became Madame Dupin's secretary.

Then, while traveling to Vincennes to visit Diderot, who had been imprisoned in 1749, Rousseau happened across an essay competition which would assure his lasting fame. Had the advancement of science and art, the Academy of Dijon wished to know, improved the moral state of mankind? Rousseau argued in the negative, and his essay *Discours sur les sciences et les arts* (1750; *A Discourse on the Arts and Sciences*, 1751) was awarded first prize on July 10, 1750. Rousseau's central contention, that modern advances in the arts and sciences had produced an abandonment of primitive sincerity and simple virtue, inspired a plethora of attacks and defenses and helped prepare the way for the Romantic reaction against Enlightenment rationalism.

Rousseau's next success was the composition of an operetta, *Le Devin du village* (1752; *Cunning-Man*, 1766), which gained for him some financial security and was honored with a command performance before the French court on October 18, 1752. By refusing an audience with the king and then entangling himself in a dispute over the relative merits of French and Italian music, however, Rousseau almost immediately lost the regal favor he had just gained.

Following this unpleasant interlude, Rousseau achieved another of his great intellectual triumphs with the publication of *Discours sur l'origine et les fondements de l'inégalité* (1755; *A Discourse upon the Origin and Foundation of the Inequality Among Mankind*, 1761), again written in response to a topic proposed by the Academy of Dijon. An analysis of the beginnings of human inequality, this work continues Rousseau's theme of the relative superiority of primitive to civilized man. Distinguishing the irremediable inequality produced by natural circumstance from the imposed inequality encouraged by artificial social convention, Rousseau attacks many of the assumptions underlying the political and social order of mid-eighteenth century Europe.

With the publication of *Julie: Ou, La Nouvelle Héloïse* (1761; *The New Héloïse*, 1761), Rousseau's career took a new turn. An epistolary novel of sentimental love, *The New Héloïse* focuses on the passionate relationship of the aristocratic Julie d'Étange and her tutor Saint-Preux, a relationship doomed by the disapproval of Julie's intolerant father. The novel's emotional intensity, its portrayal of the corrupting influence of the city, and its association of sublime sentiment with the beauty and grandeur of nature engendered tremendous popularity and established a model for emulation by Romantic writers of the ensuing one hundred years.

More in keeping with his previous publications, *Du contrat social: Ou, Principes du droit politique* (1762; *A Treatise on the Social Contract: Or, The Principles of Political Law*, 1764) is Rousseau's fullest statement on the proper relationship between a nation's government and its people. *A Treatise on the Social Contract* admits that, in practice, any of the range of governmental structures, from pure democracy through aristocracy to monarchy, may be the most appropriate for a particular state, but he insists that the source of sovereignty is always the people and that the people may not legitimately relinquish sovereignty to despots who would subvert the general will. If a government acts contrary to the will of the people, the people have a right to replace it.

Published in the same year as *A Treatise on the Social Contract*, *Émile: Ou, De l'éducation* (*Emilius and Sophia: Or, a New System of Education*, 1762-1763) contains his most influential statements on education and religion. The book insists that the developing child be allowed adequate physical activity and that the pace of the child's education be determined by the gradual emergence of the child's own capacities and interests. A slow and deliberate individualized education is infinitely preferable to an education which rushes the child toward an identity which subverts his natural inclinations. Furthermore, the purpose of education should not simply be the acquisition of knowledge but the formation of the whole human being, whenever possible through life experiences rather than through heavy reliance on books.

From the beginning of his career as a writer and thinker, Rousseau had been the center of perpetual controversy. With his publications of the early 1760's banned in some areas of Europe and burned in others, he found himself again becoming an exile. He left Paris in June of 1762 to avoid imminent arrest and spent the next eight years living for varying periods in Switzerland, England, and France, sometimes driven by actual persecution and sometimes by a growing paranoia. Much of his literary effort during this period went into the composition of the posthumously published *Les Confessions de J.-J. Rousseau* (1782, 1789; *The Confessions of J.-J. Rousseau*, 1783-1790), among the most intimately detailed and influential of all autobiographies. A remarkable experiment in self-revelation, his confessions helped to establish the vital relationship between childhood experience and the development of the adult psyche. The work also inspired countless self-analytic memoirs emphasizing their various authors' growth toward a unique individuality, despite Rousseau's belief that he would find no imitators.

By 1770, Rousseau was able to return to Paris, where he supported himself largely as a music copyist and wrote two further experiments in self-revelation, the defensive *Les Dialogues: Ou, Rousseau juge de Jean-Jacques* (1780, 1782) and the more serene *Les Reveries du promeneur solitaire* (1782; *The Reveries of the Solitary Walker*, 1967), both published posthumously. On July 2, 1778, Rousseau died at Ermenonville, just outside the French capital. In 1794, his remains were transferred to the Pantheon in Paris in honor of the influence of his ideas on the French Revolution.

Summary

Jean-Jacques Rousseau is one of those rare individuals whose life and career epitomize the transition from one historical epoch to another. He was a man perpetually at odds with the world around him, a world dominated by ancient privilege and entrenched power. Through the eloquence of his words, he helped to transform that world. Whatever he might have thought of the various revolutions which swept away the old social order, those revolutions would not have occurred so readily without his ideas to justify them. Nor would the constitutions of the new nations which replaced the old have been framed exactly as they were if he had not written on government and popular sovereignty. His hatred of despotism and of a conformity enforced by authoritarian rule shaped a world in which equality and individuality, if not universally to be encountered, were at least more frequently possible than they once had been. Furthermore, his emphasis on allowing the individual to develop according to his own nature rather than according to some externally imposed standard had a profound effect on how modern societies educate their children.

Bibliography

Copleston, Frederick C. "Rousseau." In *A History of Philosophy*. Vol. 6, *Wolff to Kant*. Westminster, Md.: Newman Press, 1961. A detailed explication of Rousseau's philosophy by a prominent Jesuit scholar. Copleston places Rousseau against the backdrop of the Enlightenment, suggesting both his affinities and his points of disagreement with his philosophical contemporaries.

Crocker, Lester G. *Jean-Jacques Rousseau: The Quest (1712-1758)*. New York: Macmillan, 1968. A thoroughly researched biography which places heavy emphasis on Rousseau's eccentric psychological development. A necessary corrective to the distortions and omissions of the confessions.

_____. *Jean-Jacques Rousseau: The Prophetic Voice (1758-1778)*. New York: Macmillan, 1973. This companion volume to Crocker's earlier study further supplements the confessions, narrating the years of Rousseau's deepest psychological disturbance, as well as covering the thirteen-year period omitted from the autobiography.

Grimsley, Ronald. "Jean-Jacques Rousseau." In *The Encyclopedia of Philosophy*, edited by Paul Edwards, vol. 7. New York: Macmillan, 1967. An overview of Rousseau's life and thought, emphasizing the interrelatedness of his educational, political, and religious theories. Grimsley sees Rousseau's belief in the need to free mankind's natural goodness from corrupting restraint as his central philosophical assumption.

Havens, George R. *Jean-Jacques Rousseau*. Boston: Twayne, 1978. A concise account of Rousseau's life and career, with analyses of the major works. Like the other volumes in Twayne's World Authors series, this book contains the essential facts about its subject without attempting exhaustive detail.

Rousseau, Jean-Jacques. *The Confessions*. Translated and introduced by J. M. Cohen. Baltimore: Penguin Books, 1953. A standard translation. Despite its distortions and its incompleteness, ending as it does with the year 1765, Rousseau's autobiography is indispensable to any understanding of his life and achievement.

_____. *Jean Jacques Rousseau: His Educational Theories Selected from "Émile," "Julie," and Other Writings*. Edited by R. L. Archer with a biographical note by S. E. Frost, Jr. Great Neck, N.Y.: Barron's Educational Series, 1964. A convenient compendium of Rousseau's statements on education. The introductory material gives a summary of Rousseau's educational theory, and the concluding subject index and general index provide ready access to the book's contents.

Robert H. O'Connor

PETER PAUL RUBENS

Born: June 28, 1577; Siegen, Westphalia
Died: May 30, 1640; Antwerp, Brabant
Areas of Achievement: Art and diplomacy
Contribution: One of the most successful artists of his time, with a huge workshop of artists who completed many of his commissions, Rubens is regarded as the most important creator of Baroque art. As a distinguished diplomat, he used his cheerful personality and broad human interests to work for the cause of peace.

Early Life

Peter Paul Rubens was the son of a Protestant attorney from Antwerp, who moved to Germany to escape religious persecution. Although Rubens was baptized a Calvinist in Germany, he became a devout convert to Catholicism. When his father died in 1587, Rubens and his mother returned to Antwerp, where he apprenticed himself to several local painters. From his last teacher, Otto van Veen (1556-1629), he acquired considerable knowledge of Italian painting. By 1600, Rubens was in Rome, studying and copying the works of the Italian Renaissance and preparing himself to become the first Northern European painter to combine the grandiose and realistic styles of the Italian and Dutch masters.

Very little survives from Rubens' Italian period (1600-1608), but in his *Portrait of the Marchesa Brigida Spinola-Doria* (1606), there is evidence of his early efforts to make his mark in the tradition of international portrait painting. As Jennifer Fletcher notes, the artist's subject came from a family that owned portraits by Titian, who was renowned for his vivid color and expressiveness. The marchesa's exalted social position is suggested by the elegance and amplitude of her luminous dress, the crimson drapery that flows behind her in the center of the frame, and the beautifully sculpted architectural details—all of which convey a richness and harmony of effect. What makes the painting truly remarkable, however, is its liveliness. This is no staid study of a society matron. She looks as though she is about to smile as she moves through the artist's frame. There is energy in her face, in the details of her clothing, and in the setting that makes this scene triumph over the mere reporting of details.

In 1608, Rubens returned to Antwerp but failed to reach his ailing mother in time. He planned to resume residence in Italy, but his success in Antwerp was so immediate and overwhelming (he became court painter to the Spanish viceroys of the Netherlands) and was followed quickly by his marriage in 1709 to Isabella Brant, that he never saw Italy again. His happy marriage is illustrated in a portrait of himself and his wife (1609). They are seated together in a honeysuckle bower, her hand resting gently and comfortably upon his in the center of the frame, his right foot partially underneath her flowing dress. They look out toward the viewer, forming a picture of mutual contentment and intimacy. Most striking is their sense of ease and equality. Although the artist is seated above his wife, he is also leaning toward her— any dominance he might seem to have is mitigated by the fact that his hat is cropped at the top while his wife's is shown in full, making her larger figure command the right side of the frame. When the positioning of their bodies and their clothing is compared, it is clear that Rubens has shown a couple that complement each other in every conceivable way. This dashing portrait reveals a man on the brink of a great career.

Life's Work

The years immediately following Rubens' return to Antwerp were vigorous and innovative. Two large triptychs, *The Elevation of the Cross* (c. 1610-1611) and *Descent from the Cross* (c. 1611-1614), altarpieces for Antwerp Cathedral, confirmed his great ability to create monumental yet realistic works of art. The fifteen-foot central panels create a sense of deep space and perspective while also conveying great struggle and strain. The cross is raised by heavily muscled men in a powerful diagonal movement that bisects one central panel. Below the cross is a dog in the left corner sticking out its tongue in agitation while the trees in the upper right corner seem to rustle in the wind. This is a painting that concentrates on the dynamism of the event, whereas in the *Descent from the Cross* the limp and ravaged body of Christ is carefully taken down by his followers, with each one expressing grief in bodily postures and gestures that concentrate nearly all the emotion of the scene on their reactions. In their bent bodies, outstretched arms and hands, grasping fingers, and intensely focused faces, the coherence of their feelings is evident. They are at one with the event.

Work on such a scale demanded that the artist take on collaborators. While Rubens would work out the conception of a portrait, a landscape, a religious or mythical subject, he often left the details or some part of a painting to his pupils and collaborators. Thus, in a letter Rubens notes that the eagle pecking Prometheus' liver was done by Frans Snyders (1579-1657). That these paintings are animated by Rubens' prodigious imagination is proved by his enormously powerful sketches, such as the one of a lioness (c. 1614-1615) which captures its power and grace from the rear—its huge tail sweeping through the center of the drawing and to the left, with its massive head sweeping from the center of the frame to the left, its huge paw lifted in mid-stride.

Rubens was drawn to exotic subjects such as a *Tigers and Lions Hunt* (1617-1618). Although his animals are anatomically correct (he studied them in the menageries of noblemen), this stirring painting is about the enormous courage of the hunters and the natural ferocity of beasts. Such paintings appealed to a Europe that was still discovering foreign lands and were a form of entertainment. As C. V. Wedgwood observes, many of these paintings are still admired today for their composition and restraint, for Rubens tends to emphasize the self-control of his human figures even as they seem about to be torn apart.

Rubens was a man of great energy (often rising at 4:00 A.M. to work), a devoted family man, a shrewd businessman, and an even-tempered artist. Such qualities made him invaluable as a respected emissary in the courts of Europe. Isabella, Regent of the Southern Netherlands, sent him on diplomatic missions to Spain and England, and he worked tirelessly to bring the Netherlands back into the Spanish Catholic company of nations. Having worked as a commissioned artist all of his life, he understood the importance of compromise, of balancing competing interests.

After seventeen years of happy marriage, Rubens' wife died in 1626. Four years later, he married Hélène Fourment, enjoying another happy marriage that is reflected in his mellow, luscious paintings of the 1630's—for example, *The Three Graces*, in which Venus and her handmaidens frolic in a dancelike rhythm, their arms enfolding one another, their flesh visibly showing the imprint of one another's fingers. Rubens paints human flesh that ripples loosely, is firm and yet pliant, and is exquisitely modulated in many different tones of white, red, and brown. No other artist of his time could convey the same quality of a painting ripening into view.

Summary

In his last years, Peter Paul Rubens returned to landscape painting with renewed vigor. In *Landscape with a Rainbow* (c. 1635), he emphasizes an ordinary country scene—cattle, a pond with ducks, two women walking down a road past a driver and cart—that suggests, in a way, the daily coming and going of a rural scene, of precisely those activities which define a landscape momentarily distinguished by a rainbow. His ploy is the opposite of that of so many of his predecessors, who used rustic settings in a stylized fashion to suggest the sublimity of nature. In *Landscape with a Sunset* (c. 1635), there is a kind of visionary quality, a perfect blending of the land, the trees, the sheep, the building at the far-right edge of the painting, and the individual seated with a dog beside him against a sky turning various shades of gray, purple, and yellow. As in *Landscape with the Château De Steen* (c. 1635), the depiction of nature seems to be an end in itself, an evocation of harmony and balance that expresses the artist's inner nature. Yet the details of these scenes are so sharply realized that they never blur into vague idealizations.

Rubens died in 1640 of a heart attack that was apparently brought on by his gout, a debilitating illness that had crippled him periodically for three years. It did not stop his enormous productivity. If there were days when he could not paint, there were other days when he probably worked faster than any other artist of his time. His lusty spirit was translated into a facility with brushwork that was truly extraordinary. The virility and sensuality of his work has been undiminished by time, though the intensity of his religious devotion may be more difficult to appreciate in a secular world not accustomed to equating the flesh and the spirit as closely as Rubens did in his day.

Bibliography
Fletcher, Jennifer. *Rubens*. London: Phaidon Press, 1968. An excellent introduction to the painter's life and career, discussing his diplomatic experience, society portraits, family portraits, and landscapes. Includes a bibliography and detailed notes on forty-eight full-color plates.
Jaffe, Michael. *Rubens and Italy*. Ithaca, N.Y.: Cornell University Press, 1977. A comprehensive study of the influence of Italian painting on Rubens. This is a revision of a doctoral dissertation that is carefully documented but strangely organized. There is no list of plates, but after the notes section there are indexes of works and persons that are not noted on the contents page. The black-and-white and color plates make this an indispensable if somewhat cumbersome volume to use.
Martin, John R., comp. *Rubens: The Antwerp Altarpieces*. New York: W. W. Norton, 1969. A thorough, copiously illustrated (in black and white) study of Rubens' great triptychs, *The Elevation of the Cross* and *Descent from the Cross*. Martin includes an informative introduction, contemporary documents, important essays by distinguished artists, critics, biographers, and historians as well as a bibliography of books and articles.
_____, ed. *Rubens Before 1620*. Princeton, N.J.: Princeton University Press, 1972. A somewhat specialized collection of essays edited by Martin. Sixty-eight black-and-white illustrations and a catalog provide helpful information on the background, the context, the shape, and the location of Rubens' early work.
Wedgwood, C. V. *The World of Rubens, 1577-1640*. New York: Time-Life Books, 1967. One of the most comprehensive introductions to Rubens' life and work by one of the most distinguished historians of the seventeenth century. Covering all aspects of Rubens' life, including his years in Italy and his diplomatic career, there is no better volume to consult for a sense of Rubens' place in history. A chronology of the artists in Rubens' day, and an annotated bibliography and index make this an indispensable study.

Carl Rollyson

SAIGŌ TAKAMORI

Born: January 23, 1828; Kagoshima, Kyūshū, Japan
Died: September 24, 1877; Kagoshima, Kyūshū, Japan
Areas of Achievement: Government and politics
Contribution: Saigō's military leadership and political support were instrumental in the events leading to the demise of Japan's last feudal government in 1868, while his championing of samurai ideals, culminating in the failed 1877 Satsuma Rebellion, during the early Meiji reform era earned for him the reputation as one of the last supporters of an honorable but outdated value system he ironically helped destroy.

Early Life

The Tokugawa Bakufu military government was a feudal polity controlling from its capital at Edo (modern Tokyo) about 260 hereditary *han* (domains) ruled by local daimyo lords. Former enemies of the Tokugawa clan were included in this arrangement as *tozama* (outside lords), and their lands were latent repositories of anti-Bakufu sentiments. Satsuma, on the southern island of Kyūshū, was a *tozama* domain ruled by the Shimazu clan. Saigō Takamori was born there in 1828 in the Kajimachi section of Kagoshima, the domain's castle town. Saigō was the eldest of seven children of a low-ranking samurai, serving as head of the Satsuma accounts department. Once proud fighting men, many samurai, as a result of the Pax Tokugawa, had become bureaucrats, assisting their lords in various administrative capacities. Saigō's father was such a retainer. Proud of his warrior heritage, yet reduced to the role of a fiscal manager, he struggled to supplement his low salary by farming.

Saigō, a heavyset boy with a thick neck, bushy eyebrows, and penetrating eyes, was reared among memories of his family's samurai heritage and his domain's proud history. During his youth, Saigō was trained in the fighting arts and had inculcated in him the principles of *Bushidō*, the code of samurai ethics. His formal learning occurred at the *Zōshikan*, the Satsuma clan school. There he received a traditional education grounded in neo-Confucian ethics, the activist moral philosophy of the Ming Chinese philosopher Wang Yang-ming, complemented by swordsmanship, Zen meditation, the nativist Shinto beliefs, and regular school subjects. He had a reputation for being a mischievous, headstrong, inarticulate, yet brave and charismatic young man. His burly stature and weight stood him well in sumo wrestling matches, but it also made him the butt of classmates' jokes. Upon finishing school at sixteen, he became an assistant clerk in the county magistrate's office.

Saigō became politically active when he became involved in a succession dispute within the domain's ruling family by siding with Shimazu Nariakira, who became daimyo in 1851, two years before Commodore Matthew C.

Perry steamed into Uraga Bay near Edo with a squadron of "black ships" to demand an end to the self-imposed seclusion policy begun in the 1630's.

In recognition of his crucial support for his lord's rise to power, Saigō was taken into Nariakira's service. His presence at Nariakira's Kagoshima headquarters gave him entrée into the inner circle of Satsuma political discussions and policy-making. Saigō, from 1855 to 1858, traveled to Edo and Kyoto as Nariakira's private emissary in the complex political maneuvering among shogunate, imperial court, and daimyo over a commercial treaty that had been proposed by American consul general Townsend Harris and the naming of an heir to the childless shogun Takugawa Iesada.

Nariakira's political star eclipsed in 1858, when his preferred Hitotsubashi line candidate for shogun was rejected in favor of the Kii line. The victory of the Kii proponents brought to power Ii Naosuke, who became great elder in the summer of 1858. Ii signed the Harris treaty without court approval in July and launched the Ansei purge (1858-1860) to oust those opposing him and the shogunal policy of *kaikoku* (open the country).

Nariakira died in August, 1858. In despair at the loss of his patron and now on the political outside, Saigō resolved to commit suicide; he was dissuaded from doing so by Gesshō, a proimperialist Buddhist monk, who was also on Ii's purge list. Together they fled from Kyoto to Satsuma, where the authorities would not give them protection. They decided in a joint suicide pact to drown themselves in Kagoshima Bay. Gesshō succeeded; Saigō, however, was retrieved from the water and, after recovering, banished to Amami Oshima in the Ryukyu Islands.

Nariakira's half brother Hisamitsu had become regent for his son Tadayoshi, the new Lord of Satsuma. Hisamitsu, persuaded by Saigō's boyhood friend Ōkubo Toshimichi, decided to send troops to Kyoto to support the emperor and then march on Edo to force reforms on the Bakufu. Ōkubo interceded with Hisamitsu for Saigō's return. On March 12, 1862, Saigō was recalled to Satsuma and soon consented to head an advance party of Satsuma troops to Kyoto. He irked Hisamitsu by holding discussions in Kyoto with radical *rōnin* (masterless samurai) wanting to overthrow the Bakufu. Consequently, he was ordered into a second exile (only six months after his pardon) to the islands south of Satsuma. Saigō spent his second banishment (1862-1864) brooding over his failure to avenge his honor through suicide, practicing his calligraphy, wrestling, writing poetry, and starting a family with a commoner, by whom he had two sons (he would take an official wife, Itoko, in 1865).

Life's Work

Again at the urging of Ōkubo, Saigō's second exile ended on April 4, 1864. After Ii Naosuke was assassinated by samurai extremists in March, 1860, the weakened shogunate tried to reach an accommodation with the proemperor, antiforeign forces in Kyoto. Given the title of war minister, Saigō was sent to Kyoto to serve as a Satsuma watchdog. There he faced plotters from the *tozama han* Chōshū (a Satsuma rival), maneuvering to overthrow the Bakufu elements at court. Saigō and his men helped pro-Bakufu Aizu samurai expel the Chōshū troops from Kyoto. Chōshū was declared rebellious, and a punitive expedition was authorized by the Bakufu to chastise this southwestern domain. Saigō was a leader of the December, 1864, Chōshū expedition that forced the domain to apologize, surrender some land, disband its militia, and have some leaders commit suicide. Saigō was instrumental in preventing a harsher treatment of Chōshū.

By 1865, however, Chōshū was rebuilding itself after an internal revolt by midrank samurai. Satsuma was now concerned that the Bakufu was becoming more powerful. Saigō and others began aiding loyalists such as Sakamoto Ryōma, a young Tosa (another outside domain) samurai, and certain Kyoto nobles allied with Iwakura Tomomi, an important court official. Saigō also met Great Britain's first envoy to Japan, Sir Harry Parkes, to try to persuade the English from wholeheartedly supporting the Bakufu. These efforts impressed Chōshū: the two *han*, burying differences in favor of a united front against the Bakufu, their common enemy, entered an alliance in March, 1866. A powerful *tozama* coalition, soon augmented by Tosa, was in place to challenge the Tokugawa. When a second punitive Bakufu-led army (without Satsuma participation, at Saigō's insistence) was launched against Chōshū in the summer of 1866, the strengthened Chōshū domain had no trouble repelling them.

The ascendancy of Tokugawa Yoshinobu to the shogunate late in 1866 revived the central government; reforms were initiated and Western military matériel was secured. In the face of Satsuma opposition, however, the shogun had to agree in the fall of 1867 to a Tosa compromise requiring him to step down and join the daimyo ranks as the head of a power-sharing council. There was fear that the Tokugawa, still the strongest of the daimyo, might reassert its right to national rule; to counter this threat, Satsuma troops entered Kyoto, where Saigō and others, with the support of Iwakura, formulated a proclamation to be issued in the name of the fifteen-year-old emperor Mutsuhito, declaring the restoration of imperial rule.

On January 3, 1868, this proclamation was made in the context of a *coup d'état* in Kyoto led by Saigō. The office of shogun was officially ended; the Tokugawa were ordered to surrender all lands and titles, a demand that Yoshinobu refused. Saigō, a junior councillor in the new provisional government, led loyalist troops against holdout Bakufu forces, winning the Battle of Toba-Fushimi. His troops continued mop-up campaigns, which lasted until Edo castle was surrendered and the last Bakufu naval forces were defeated. Victorious in battle, Saigō spared most of his enemies, including the ousted shogun. The emperor, his reign title changed to Meiji (enlightened rule), was nominally restored in 1868, but the political future of the new government, transferred to the former Tokugawa seat of power, renamed Tokyo (eastern capital), was in the hands of a small coterie of young middle- and low-rank samurai from the domains of Satsuma, Chōshū, Tosa, and Hizen.

As the fighting diminished in 1868, Saigō returned to Kagoshima along with many of his soldiers. Whereas his colleague Ōkubo stayed in Tokyo to launch the Meiji regime, Saigō entered semiretirement, working as a clan counselor. He was a national military hero. The court offered him the third rank junior grade to recognize his contributions to the restoration, but he declined in self-deprecating tones, since such an honor would have put him at a rank higher than his daimyo. Realizing that Saigō's nonparticipation in the government and his influence at home could be troublesome, Iwakura, serving as an imperial messenger and accompanied by Ōkubo and Yamagata Aritomo, called on Saigō in January, 1871, with a direct order from the emperor, requiring his participation in the Tokyo government. Ever loyal, he acquiesced to the imperial command, becoming a chief counselor of state. He thus joined Ōkubo, Kido Kōin (Chōshū), Itagaki Taisuke (Tosa), and Ōkuma Shigenobu (Hizen) in a coalition government representing the leading pre-Meiji restoration *han*.

In 1871, confident that their reforms had firmly established them in power, Iwakura led more than half of the government's leaders on a year-and-a-half-long trip to observe at first hand the United States and Europe and to convince the Western powers to revise the unequal treaties. Saigō, Itagaki, and Ōkuma were left in charge of a caretaker government bound by written promises not to initiate any new policies while the Iwakura Mission was abroad. In the area of foreign policy, however, independent action was contemplated. When Korea, under Chinese suzerainty, rejected Japanese overtures to recognize the Meiji government, Saigō wanted to go to Korea alone and provoke the Koreans to kill him, thus forcing Japan into war. Earlier, when fifty-four Ryukyuans were attacked by Taiwanese aborigines in 1871, he had called for a punitive expedition against Formosa. Saigō favored a foreign war to create a role for the many samurai who had been replaced by the new conscript army of commoners and who looked to him for leadership.

Before Saigō could have his permission to go to Korea confirmed by the emperor, Iwakura returned and persuaded Ōkubo to head the opposition to Saigō's plans. Ōkubo, the pragmatic realist, and Saigō, the romantic idealist, clashed over the *seikan* (conquer Korea) issue, ending their decades-long friendship. Iwakura followed Ōkubo's efforts by forcing Saigō and his pro-war partisans out of the government. To save face, it was announced that Saigō and many Satsuma supporters were leaving the government because of poor health. This was his irreversible break with the Meiji government, now dominated by the Ōkubo faction.

His retirement was outwardly peacefully spent romping in the Kagoshima woods with his dogs and composing poetry; there was, however, a political dimension to his retirement as well. He founded several private schools to train Satsuma youth in the fighting arts and traditional ethics. Elsewhere, as samurai were being stripped of their class privileges and becoming impoverished by the financially strapped government's reduction of their stipends, resentment turned into rebellion. In 1874, two thousand Saga samurai revolted unsuccessfully under Etō Shimpei, who had left the government when Saigō had. There were similar failed samurai uprisings in Kumamoto and Hagi two years later.

Wary of what Saigō might do, police informants watched for signs of disquiet in Kagoshima. The government decided to remove by ship a cache of arms from Kagoshima to prevent Saigō's followers from arming themselves. Hotheaded young samurai attacked the imperial arsenals to forestall the arms' removal, precipitating the 1877 Satsuma Rebellion. Saigō, probably aware of the futility of the rebellion, backed his followers, reaffirming his allegiance to the emperor while berating the evil politicians who surrounded him. Saigō's twenty-five thousand men faced at least three times as many government forces. A disastrous battle over Kumamoto castle depleted the rebel army, and its remnants were pursued throughout Kyushu. In a cave at Shiroyama, Saigō rejected a request from Yamagata to surrender. As he was attempting to escape, he was wounded by a bullet. A samurai to the end, Saigō, to avoid capture and shame, committed ritual disembowelment on September 24, 1877.

Summary

Ending his life a traitor to the state he had helped to found, Saigō Takamori became a hero in death. In 1890, the Emperor Meiji pardoned him posthumously and restored his titles. This apotheosis, coming at a time when the Meiji oligarchy was secure in its power, reflected the popular verdict that Saigō had been a sincere, patriotic hero representative of samurai values nostalgically celebrated in a modernizing Japan that was struggling for an accommodation with its feudal past. The Satsuma Rebellion and Saigō's suicide for the cause were not only his but also the country's last backward glance at a consciously discarded tradition, the lofty virtues of which still resonated in the hearts—if not the minds—of many Japanese.

Saigō's life bracketed the sweeping changes that in a short period ended a feudal regime and established a centralized nation-state in its place. While the majority of the Meiji restoration leaders looked forward, Saigō clutched at a past symbolic of the pure samurai motives his political activism espoused. For later eras, Saigō's life and deeds would be a manipulatable legacy, often with altered facts, that would provide a model for jingoistic foreign adventurers, right-wing nationalists, and out-of-power political dissidents, who would claim him as their source of inspiration. Saigō's life was so complex that liberals, Westernizers, and other more progressive elements could similarly adopt the Satsuma warrior as their own.

Bibliography
Beasley, W. G. *The Meiji Restoration*. Stanford, Calif.: Stanford University Press, 1972. The most comprehensive treatment of the late Tokugawa to early Meiji period, with useful glossaries and a bibliography. Saigō's role in the important events of the time are woven into this factual and analytical narrative.
Buck, James H. "The Satsuma Rebellion of 1877." *Monumenta Nipponica* 28 (Winter, 1973): 427-446. A thorough account of the samurai uprising and Saigō's participation, emphasizing the military and political maneuverings of the rebel and imperial forces.
Iwata, Masakazu. *Ōkubo Toshimichi: The Bismarck of Japan*. Berkeley: University of California Press, 1964. A biography of Saigō's Satsuma compatriot, with numerous references to Saigō's life where it intertwined with Ōkubo's. Provides an overall view of Satsuma politics and the domain's role in the restoration movement and early Meiji government.
Jansen, Marius B. *Sakamoto Ryōma and the Meiji Restoration*. Stanford, Calif.: Stanford University Press, 1961. Though focusing on this Tosa loyalist samurai, numerous references to Saigō are interlaced in this biographical narrative, describing the downfall of the Tokugawa shogunate.
Mayo, Marlene. "The Korean Crisis of 1873 and Early Meiji Foreign Policy." *Journal of Asian Studies* 31 (August, 1972): 793-819. An analysis of the background of and the reasons for the aborted Korean plan of Saigō and the political maneuvering which defeated it, placed in an overview of emerging Meiji diplomatic concerns.
Morris, Ivan. *The Nobility of Failure: Tragic Heroes in the History of Japan*. New York: Holt, Rinehart and Winston, 1975. Chapter 9, "The Apotheosis of Saigō the Great," is an excellent English account of Saigō's life, analyzed as part of the Japanese fascination for failed heroes. Very useful notes contain additional biographical details.

William M. Zanella

LOUIS DE SAINT-JUST

Born: August 25, 1767; Decize, France
Died: July 28, 1794; Paris, France
Areas of Achievement: Government and politics
Contribution: An acute political theorist and insightful orator, Saint-Just dominated the executive councils of the National Convention at a time when internal anarchy and military invasions threatened social order in France.

Early Life

Louis Antoine Léon de Saint-Just was born in Decize, a town along the Loire River, but he grew up in southern Picardy, the native province of his father, a retired military officer who had purchased property at Blérancourt. The mother of Saint-Just, Jeanne-Marie Robinot, was the daughter of an established notary. She advocated egalitarian principles; after her son completed his education at the Collège of Saint-Nicolas under the direction of the Oratorian Fathers, she used her influence to obtain a position for him as a clerk in the office of the public prosecutor of Soissons. As a student, Saint-Just was self-indulgent and often impudent. At the age of nineteen, he ran away with some of the family silver, which he sold in Paris. He was arrested and placed in a reformatory for six months; after this episode, he entered the University of Reims, where he studied law, receiving a degree in 1788.

Saint-Just began to frequent the political clubs of Soissons; soon he gained a reputation as an enthusiastic orator, and he was elected lieutenant colonel of the national guard in Blérancourt. In July of 1790, he led the federates from Blérancourt to Paris for "La Fête de la Fédération." When he returned home, he learned that some of his constituents were planning to seize the open markets of Blérancourt; he then wrote an impassioned letter to Robespierre, a lawyer and deputy to the Legislative Assembly from Arras, in which he encouraged economic equality as a step toward improving the living conditions of the working class. This letter, which greatly impressed Robespierre, marks the beginning of a political relationship that transformed the destiny of France. Both men were obstinately serious, ambitious, and austere, but Saint-Just—with Machiavellian hauteur and tireless energy—was more impetuous and self-righteous.

Life's Work

In 1791, Saint-Just hoped to run for election as deputy to the National Assembly. His rivals, however, succeeded in removing his name from the list of candidates. In preparation for this campaign, Saint-Just had written *Esprit de la révolution et de la constitution de France* (1791; spirit of the revolution). This work is composed primarily of provocative epigrams that follow the ideas of Jean-Jacques Rousseau. In order to serve the poor and the peasants better, Saint-Just recommended that the French Revolution move beyond benevolent and patriotic activity toward the construction of a new society. According to Saint-Just, the French were not yet free because sovereignty of the people was not possible until everyone was just and rational. In his visionary ardor, he misrepresented Rousseau's intentions and blurred the contours of his philosophy. As the political career of Saint-Just advanced, it became increasingly difficult for him to distinguish between prescriptive theories and irrevocable laws.

On September 22, 1792, France declared itself a republic. The fall of Louix XVI provoked the invasion of the country by the Prussian and Austrian armies. The National Assembly called for new elections of deputies from the newly formed *départments*, and Saint-Just was chosen to represent Aisne. By January of 1793, the king had been indicted; the Girondins, or moderates of the National Assembly, expressed the view that he should be given a trial, whereas the Jacobins, or extremists, demanded an immediate execution. In this debate, Saint-Just emerged as the most forceful and challenging prosecutor against the king. His cold, implacable logic was an indicator of the rigor he expected from others.

Saint-Just argued against the inviolability of the king according to the ideas of Rousseau's *Du contrat social: Ou, Principes du droit politique* (1762; *A Treatise on the Social Contract: Or, The Principles of Political Law*, 1764). He postulated that a king is a usurper who has stolen the absolute sovereignty that belongs only to the people. Law is an expression of the people's common will. Therefore, the king, as a criminal guilty of tyranny, is an outsider and not a citizen. For this reason, he has no access to the law. Saint-Just concluded that the king must die in order to safeguard the republic. In demanding the death of Louis XVI, Saint-Just relied on the rhetoric of revolution as apocalypse; despite the utopian zeal of his formulations, he was promoting a new order of absolutism, with its own assortment of ingenious and exalted crimes.

After the execution of Louis XVI, Saint-Just rose to prominence as an advocate of national patriotism in the service of a strong, centralized government. He proposed a constitution that would subordinate military affairs to civil power, and he opposed the creation of municipalities favored by the Girondins. In May of 1793, he was asked to join the Committee of Public Safety in order to prepare new constitutional laws. Within two months, he became a definitive member of this heterogeneous and powerful group of twelve.

Because of a drastic drop in the volume of foreign trade, the needs of war, inflation, and exploitation by profiteers, the Committee of Public Safety, under Robespierre's direction, began to push for exclusive regulatory privileges. The committee persuaded the National Assembly, by means of Saint-

Just's compelling arguments, that the provisional government of France remain revolutionary until peace with France's enemies was unilaterally acclaimed. This proclamation of October 10, 1793, superseded the constitution of June and announced the creation of exceptional measures to force merchants to adhere to the Law of the Maximum, an economic expedient approved by the convention in September of 1793. The result was an intensification of fear. In order to prepare the way for unprecedented coercion, the Revolutionary Tribunal, or Paris Commune, carried out a spectacular series of trials that virtually eliminated the Girondins; at this time, Marie-Antoinette was condemned and executed.

In November of 1793, Saint-Just embarked on a series of military enterprises that led to the high point of his career. He was sent to Alsace as supervisor of the Army of the Rhine, which had suffered numerous setbacks, leaving the officers and soldiers demoralized and inefficient. Saint-Just and his friend and colleague Philippe Le Bas ignored the other nine representatives from the convention already active in Alsace and proceeded to intimidate local authorities in Strasbourg in order to obtain supplies and to check the advances of aristocratic agitators. Saint-Just insisted on unswerving discipline among the troops and galvanized them with imperious commands. In December, the Armies of the Rhine and Moselle were united, and Saint-Just led a victorious assault against the Austrian forces, lifting the siege of Landau. The following month, in much the same manner, he reorganized the Army of the North on the Belgian front.

When Saint-Just returned to Paris, he initiated a series of purges, with Robespierre's compliance, designed to eliminate traitors among the ultra-Montagnards, an anarchist group responsible for the "dechristianization" of France. Saint-Just emerged as a ruthless enemy of those who either provoked agitation or favored moderation. He was responsible for the execution of Georges Danton and Camille Desmoulins, heroes of the earlier phase of the Revolution. Saint-Just insisted that the elimination of Danton and his followers would pave the way for a pure republic composed of single-minded patriots.

With Danton's death, the Revolution entered the period known as the Reign of Terror. In June of 1794, Robespierre drafted the Law of Twenty-two Prairial, which defined in conveniently vague terms the enemies of the people and denied them right to counsel. Saint-Just disapproved of this measure because the sansculottes, or proletariat, were deprived of power; he declared: "The revolution is frozen, every principle has been attenuated."

Saint-Just returned to the Army of the North and was instrumental in forcing the Prussians to surrender their garrison at Charleroi. That led to the confrontation between the French and the Austrians near the village of Fleurus in Belgium. Despite heavy losses, the French were victorious; refusing accolades, Saint-Just left immediately for Paris. He had been informed by Robespierre that the Committee of Public Safety was hopelessly divided. In such matters, Saint-Just generally favored reconciliation. Robespierre made a speech before the convention, however, condemning his opponents as a league of conspirators. Out of loyalty to Robespierre, Saint-Just prepared a report that would incriminate Robespierre's rivals on the committee. At the same time, moderates, known as "Thermidorians," who were uncomfortable with Robespierre's attempt at hegemony, united to overthrow him. On July 27, Saint-Just, Robespierre, and about twenty of their supporters were denounced as tyrants and proscribed; they were executed on the following day.

Summary

In March of 1794, Louis de Saint-Just was chosen president of the convention for a fortnight. At this time, he composed notes and observations published posthumously as *Fragmens sur les institutions républicaines* (1800; republican institutions), a work that laid the foundation for a communal society. The "immortal, impassive Republic of Virtue," energized by permanent revolution and sheltered from human temerity, would provide education for all. Saint-Just classified and sharpened Robespierre's theories. In a democratic republic, civic virtue made legalistic bureaucracies obsolete; institutions were the social means for producing responsible republicans. Censorship was condoned as an administrative control over unreliable elements.

At the height of his power, Saint-Just proposed the Laws of Ventôse, by which the convention voted in favor of confiscating the property of counter-revolutionaries in order to assign it to "indigent patriots" (these laws were never put into effect). In addition, the Cadet School of Mars, which emulated Spartan standards, was inaugurated to educate three thousand youths as disciplined patriots who would increase the collective efficiency of the state. As a follower of Rousseau, Saint-Just was consistent in activating Enlightenment ideals, but in order to purify the republic and to execute the Laws of Ventôse, he created a General Police Bureau, whose existence inverted democratic liberties.

The personality of Saint-Just offers a wide range of contradictions. The swiftness with which he consigned authority to himself is impressive, but his collusion with Robespierre added to the apprehension created by his virulent, doctrinaire speeches. Known as the "Panther" or "Angel of Death," Saint-Just often revealed chinks in his armor. In Strasbourg, while addressing a Jacobin club, he broke down in tears when referring to the vandalism of churches and desecration of the Blessed Sacrament. His impeccable habits and stoical demeanor suggest a puritan strain that was not pursued in private. His Blérancourt mistress visited him regularly in Paris, and his fiancée, the sister of Le Bas, accompanied him on one of his missions to Strasbourg. He once stated that a man who struck a woman should receive the death penalty.

He was given to peremptory and sententious speech but displayed a genuine solicitude for soldiers in the lower ranks and for the poor and needy. He was not autocratic; he accepted the sovereign will of the people implicitly. For this reason, when he was indicted, he did not appeal to the sansculottes to challenge the convention.

The rhetoric of Saint-Just anticipates twentieth century forms of totalitarianism; however, his confidence in democratic institutions was pristine. As commissioner of the armies, Saint-Just successfully mobilized the resources of France in order to defend the revolutionary government against an allied front directed by the monarchs of Europe. Military victories were preliminary steps toward the complete regeneration of society. Saint-Just sought to create a nation made up of communities with a common interest that would safeguard the principles of the French Revolution.

Bibliography
Béraud, Henri. *Twelve Portraits of the French Revolution.* Translated by Madeleine Boyd. Boston: Little, Brown, 1928. The thirty-page chapter on Saint-Just contains information excluded from subsequent biographies. The presentation of Saint-Just is occasionally melodramatic and there are some factual inconsistencies, but the overall portrait is illuminating.
Bouloiseau, Marc. *The Jacobin Republic, 1792-1794.* Translated by Jonathan Mandelbaum. New York: Cambridge University Press, 1984. The second of a three-volume series designed to provide a synthesis of twentieth century attitudes toward the French Revolution. Bouloiseau studies the economic and social history of the Jacobin organizations to the detriment of political developments. The contribution of women's societies is also explored. Contains a chronology, a bibliography, and an index of names.
Bruun, Geoffrey. *Saint-Just: Apostle of Terror.* Reprint. Hamden, Conn.: Shoe String Press, 1966. This short but perceptive study appraises the contributions of Saint-Just to policies enacted by the Committee of Public Safety. Bruun analyzes the images of Saint-Just as a fanatic, a designation given him by French Royalist émigrés throughout Europe.
Curtis, Eugene. *Saint-Just: Colleague of Robespierre.* Reprint. New York: Octagon Books, 1973. This exhaustive study uses original documents and manuscripts, including Saint-Just's correspondence, to examine the missions to Alsace, dominated by Saint-Just, to counteract Royalist insurgents. An objective and far-reaching study of the reasons behind the Reign of Terror.
Fisher, John. *Six Summers in Paris, 1789-1794.* New York: Harper & Row, 1966. Richly detailed and wide in scope and investigation, this work chronicles the factionalism that developed among the splinter groups that sustained the momentum of the Revolution. Brilliantly conceived but un-

necessarily cynical. Excellent bibliography and use of unpublished material from the National Archives in Paris.

Lefebvre, Georges. *The French Revolution from 1793 to 1799.* Translated by John Hall Stewart and James Friguglietti. London: Routledge & Kegan Paul, 1964. The second part of Lefebvre's comprehensive history, originally published in 1951. The text is well produced and duplicates Lefebvre's metholodogy. An informative, valuable study that clearly outlines Saint-Just's efforts to offset the economic crisis and to mold a national platform of systematic reconstruction.

Loomis, Stanley. *Paris in the Terror: June, 1793-July, 1794.* New York: J. B. Lippincott, 1964. A colorful account of the domestic and foreign intrigue that created a climate of suspicion and panic during the Great Terror. The historical scholarship continues the tradition established by Pierre Gaxotte and Louise Madelin. The biographical sketches of Saint-Just place him above and beyond the fray of partisan politics. A list of secondary sources is provided.

Palmer, R. R. *Twelve Who Ruled: The Year of Terror in the French Revolution.* Rev. ed. Princeton, N.J.: Princeton University Press, 1969. A revised edition of the 1941 text by a distinguished translator and authority on France during the Revolution. Palmer demonstrates Saint-Just's political foresight, but the urbane style depicts him in a patronizing way. Although occasionally impressionistic, this is a vivid study of the conflicts within the Committee of Public Safety. Contains notes and references instead of a formal bibliography and an extensive index of surnames only.

Robert J. Frail

GEORGE SAND
Amandine-Aurore-Lucile Dupin, Baronne Dudevant

Born: July 1, 1804; Paris, France
Died: June 8, 1876; Nohant, France
Area of Achievement: Literature
Contribution: Sand contributed to nineteenth century French literature a pro-
digious number of important romantic novels, travel writings, and politi-
cal essays.

Early Life

In many ways, George Sand's early life reads like one of her more improbable romantic novels, with her socially mismatched parents, her eccentric aristocratic grandmother, her unorthodox tutors, her flirtation with Catholicism, her unfortunate marriage, her idealistic quest for love, and her
close proximity to the political upheavals of her age.

She was born Amandine-Aurore-Lucile Dupin, in Paris, in 1804, the year
of Napoleon I's coronation. When Aurore was only four years old, her
father, Maurice Dupin, a dashing officer in Napoleon's army, and a grandson
of the illustrious Marshal of Saxe, was thrown from a Spanish stallion and
died instantly. Aurore was left alternately in the care of her mother, Sophie,
the lowborn daughter of a tavern keeper, and her fraternal grandmother,
Mme Dupin de Francueil, a woman of aristocratic background and tastes.

Aurore endured the constant emotional and social friction between her two
guardians until 1817, when she was sent to the Couvent des Anglaises in
Paris to finish her education. At the convent, she was much appreciated by
the nuns, despite her somewhat headstrong ways, and even felt the mystical
attractions of a religious vocation. In 1820, to circumvent her taking the
veil, Mme Dupin de Francueil brought Aurore home to the family estate at
Nohant in Berry. There she learned to ride cross-saddle with her brother
Hippolyte Chatiron, began to wear men's clothing for riding, and was taught
to shoot by Stephane Ajasson de Grandsagne.

In the summer of 1821, Aurore's grandmother had a severe stroke, and
Aurore nursed Mme Dupin de Francueil, an unusually difficult patient, until
her death in December of the same year. Shortly afterward, in September of
1822, Aurore married Second Lieutenant Casimir Dudevant, bringing him a
large estate of 400,000 francs. Her first child, Maurice Dudevant, was born
in June of 1823. Her second child, Solange, probably fathered by Stephane
Ajasson de Grandsagne, was born in September of 1828, and signaled the
continued deterioration of her hasty marriage to the then-financially depen-
dent and increasingly unpleasant Casimir.

In 1831, Aurore left her husband, and Nohant, for Paris, where she lived
with her literary mentor, Jules Sandeau. Together, they coauthored articles

for the French publication *Le Figaro* and, under the pen name Jules Sand, published an apprentice novel, *Rose et Blanche* (1831). In the early 1830's, Paris was in turmoil, in the aftermath of the July Revolution, and Aurore Dudevant was writing her first independent novel, to be published under the pseudonym George Sand.

Life's Work

In May of 1832, *Indiana* (English translation, 1881) was published. It was an immediate popular and critical success, launching a distinguished literary career which was to flourish unabated for forty-four prolific years. Sand followed up her first triumph rapidly, in only six short months, with an equally relished novel, *Valentine* (1832; English translation, 1902). This short period of time between novels was a good indication of the famous, almost notorious, fluency with which Sand was to write throughout her life. In 1832, she published *Lélia* (English translation, 1978), and these three early works, along with the ones that followed, *Jacques* (1834; English translation, 1847) and *Mauprat* (1837; English translation, 1870), were typical of Sand's characteristic concerns: the relationship between men and women, class differences in French society, marriage laws and conventions, and the romantic quest for passionate love. There is no question that Sand, when writing these early novels, was drawing on the experience of her own socially mixed parentage, her unhappy union with Casimir Dudevant, and her passionate but troublesome affair with the poet Alfred de Musset.

Critical interest in Sand's life and loves has always competed with interest in her works, and this is not surprising when one considers how much they are intertwined. It was, in fact, her ill-fated trip to Venice with Musset in 1833 that provided the material for her highly acclaimed *Lettres d'un voyageur* (1837; *Letters of a Traveller*, 1847), as well as the later novel *Elle et lui* (1859; *She and He*, 1902). *Consuelo* (1842-1843; English translation, 1846), the story of a charming prima donna, which evokes so beautifully the musical world of the eighteenth century, was written during her long liaison with Frédéric Chopin. With George Sand, life and art seem always to imitate each other.

The works of her second period, probably influenced by the socialist prophet Pierre Leroux, take a religious tone and concern for the common people, which were already present in Sand's earlier works. *Spiridion* (1839; English translation, 1842), which is a mystical story set in a monastery, and *Le Meunier d'Angibault* (1845; *The Miller of Angibault*, 1847), which has a man of the people for its hero, are typical of the novels of this political period, in which she was also establishing the socialist *Revue indépendante* (1841) with Pierre Leroux and gaining the reputation which would make her the unofficial minister of propaganda after the abdication of Louis-Philippe in 1848. As much as her heart was in the Revolution, and as hard as she worked for government reforms in her own province of Berry, she was sorely disillusioned by the reckless and often-irrational behavior of both the proletariat and the bourgeois participants. After the Coup of 1851, Sand focused her political work on interceding with Napoleon III on behalf of numerous imprisoned or exiled republicans. His fortunate admiration for her work made her an unusually successful advocate.

La Mare au diable (1846; *The Devil's Pool*, 1850), *François le champi* (1850; *Francis the Waif*, 1889), and *La Petite Fadette* (1848-1849; *Little Fadette*, 1850) are Rousseauesque paeans to the beauties of nature and the essential goodness of plain, simple peasants, no matter how hard their lives might be, or what difficulties circumstance might put in their way. These novels are a direct and startling contrast to her intense involvement in French politics, and are often considered her most beautiful and authentic works. The characters in these novels are clearly modeled on the Berrichon peasants, whom she had known from childhood.

In the 1850's, Sand's son Maurice had become fascinated with puppet theater, an interest that soon captivated Sand and eventually resulted in her writing a number of plays for the Paris theater. Her fluent, almost poetic, style was not suited to the theater of the day, however, and her plays did not bring her the popularity or the financial rewards of her earlier writings. In the last twenty-five years of her life, Sand continued to publish novels with remarkable felicity, at least partly to support her estate at Nohant. The jewel of her later years is undoubtedly her autobiography, *Histoire de ma vie* (1854-1855; *History of My Life*, 1901), written to finance her daughter's dowry and to settle a number of pressing debts. This enormous work, of close to half a million words, first ran in 138 installments in the Parisian newspaper *La Presse*. It is not exactly an autobiography in the modern, or conventional, sense of the word: since more than one-third of the book is really about her editing of her father's correspondence with her grandmother; since it is quite restrained about the private details of her relationships with such interesting and renowned artists as Prosper Mérimée, Jules Sandeau, Alfred de Musset, Frédéric Chopin, and Alexandre Manceau; since it was written fully twenty-one years before her death; and since it is full of seemingly unrelated digressions and didactic passages. Yet this amorphous tome is an unparalleled source of information about Sand's early life and fundamental ideas.

In her final two decades, Sand's literary output was primarily miscellaneous, with one of the outstanding features being a copious correspondence with other important writers, such as Gustave Flaubert. Sand was a diligent letter writer; more than twenty thousand of her letters are still extant.

George Sand died on June 8, 1876, of an intestinal occlusion, but not before she had seen the dawn of the republic in France, and not before she had spent her early morning hours writing as usual. She was buried at her beloved Nohant, and her funeral was attended by such notables as Prince Jérôme Bonaparte, Alexandre Dumas, *fils*, and Gustave Flaubert, as well as by the grief-stricken peasants of the district of Berry.

Summary

Ivan Turgenev said of George Sand, "What a brave man she was, and what a good woman!" Sand's androgyny, which expressed itself sometimes in her smoking and masculine clothing, and sometimes in the motherly solicitude with which she cared for her friends and lovers, is only one of the many dichotomies which are so characteristic of her life and work. It is important to remember that Sand was a woman with aristocratic blood and a family estate, who wrote socialist novels and worked for the republic. She was an idealistic, sometimes even mystical, novelist, who was, nevertheless, throughout her life, the practical and financial center of her family. She was a famous Parisian and an avid traveler, who loved the quiet countryside of Berry with an almost spiritual devotion. She was a woman who had high respect for marriage but who also wrote some of the most damning criticism of the institution ever written. She was in all ways a woman, and a writer, who captured, in both her life and her works, the conflicted spirit of her age.

Bibliography
Barry, Joseph. *Infamous Woman: The Life of George Sand*. New York: Doubleday, 1977. An enthusiastic biography of George Sand by an author who sees her as "our existential contemporary." Especially useful for its long quotations from her correspondence, and for its well-chosen illustrations; for example, a manuscript page in Sand's own hand from her diary dated August 21, 1865.
Cate, Curtis. *George Sand: A Biography*. New York: Avon Books, 1975. This is the definitive biography of Sand for English-speaking readers. Cate follows the personal, literary, social, family, and economic life of Sand from her birth and the crowning of Napoleon in 1804, to her death and the rise of the republic in 1876.
Crecelius, Kathryn J. *Family Romances: George Sand's Early Novels*. Bloomington: Indiana University Press, 1987. A study of George Sand's early novels, with an emphasis on Sigmund Freud's concept of the Oedipal struggle.
Dickenson, Donna. *George Sand*. New York: Berg Publishers, 1988. In this largely feminist analysis of Sand's life and work, Dickenson attempts to reinterpret some of the staples of the George Sand myth. She argues, for example, that Sand was a more professional and careful writer than critics, who look only at her prolific output, are usually willing to admit. She also combats the image of Sand as an omnivorous, devouring lover.
Glasgow, Janis, ed. *George Sand: Collected Essays*. Troy, N.Y.: Whitson

Great Lives from History

Publishing, 1985. This collection of essays, in both French and English, is an unusual example of Franco-American scholarly cooperation.

Sand, George. *My Life*. Translated by Dan Hofstadter. New York: Harper & Row, 1979. Because the French original was exceedingly large and rambling, because it focused so much on Sand's family before her birth, because it was written long before Sand's career was completed, and because it was not especially frank about her liaisons with other famous artists, Hofstadter has wisely abridged his translation of Sand's autobiography for English readers.

_____. *She and He*. Translated by George B. Ives. Chicago: Cassandra Editions, 1978. This clearly autobiographical novel is a fictionalized account of Sand's stormy affair with the artist Alfred de Musset. Thérèse's and Laurent's sojourn in Italy and Laurent's near-fatal illness closely resemble the events of Sand's life with Musset from 1833 to 1835.

Thomson, Patricia. *George Sand and the Victorians: Her Influence and Reputation in Nineteenth Century England*. New York: Columbia University Press, 1976. Thomson explores the connections between George Sand and Jane Carlyle, Elizabeth Barrett Browning, Charlotte and Emily Brontë, Matthew Arnold, George Eliot, Thomas Hardy, and Henry James. There is an especially good chapter entitled "George Sand and English Reviewers."

Cynthia Lee Katona

JOSÉ DE SAN MARTÍN

Born: February 25, 1778; Yapeyú, La Plata
Died: August 17, 1850; Boulogne-sur-Mer, France
Area of Achievement: The military
Contribution: San Martín, against great odds, led the military forces that secured independence from Spain in Argentina, Chile, and Peru.

Early Life

José Francisco de San Martín was born on February 25, 1778, in the village at Yapeyú on the Uruguay River in what is modern northeastern Argentina, where his father, Juan, a career army officer, was administrator. José, the youngest of four sons, was educated in Madrid following his father's transfer there in 1785. Two years later, following in the footsteps of his father and older brothers, he requested a cadetship in the Spanish army.

His first military experience began at the age of fifteen in Morocco, against Algerian princes. He also fought in the French Revolution and the Napoleonic Wars. In 1808, Napoleon I sent French troops into Spain in order to reach Portugal, which had traded with France's archenemy Great Britain in defiance of Napoleon's wishes. This invasion, along with Napoleon's removal of the Spanish king, caused a furor among the Spanish, who mounted a guerrilla war against the French invaders. San Martín joined the fight against the French by enlisting in the service of the Spanish provisional government (junta), which had been established at Seville. San Martín distinguished himself in battle, receiving a medal and promotions.

For more than twenty years, San Martín served his king with faith and dedication. He had gained valuable experience and had received recognition for his distinguished service. It has been speculated that he did not believe that he had been adequately recognized and, for that reason, he decided to return to his native land and participate in revolutionary events there. San Martín was a Creole, a Spaniard born in the New World, and there was discrimination against Creoles in favor of Spanish-born Peninsulars. Also, in Spain, he had formed friendships with English officers who had imbued him with the revolutionary ideas of the Enlightenment. In 1812, he refused a promotion and returned to Buenos Aires to embark on an enterprise that would gain for him everlasting fame—the independence of South America.

Life's Work

The thirty-four-year-old San Martín returned to Buenos Aires, which in 1812 was in the middle of revolutionary activities. Creoles in Argentina had created a provisional government in the name of the deposed Spanish king Ferdinand VII. Realizing that San Martín would be a valuable member of their military forces because of his experience in Spain, the government gave him command of the army of Upper Peru, which had been defeated by Royalists and was recuperating in Tucumán. San Martín's military genius shone as he improved the soldiers, who lacked discipline and training.

Although not all biographers agree, many have asserted that San Martín founded a secret pseudo-Masonic society, the Lautaro Lodge, whose members dedicated themselves to the independence of South America from Spain. At any rate, San Martín was strongly dedicated to his native country's independence, and he believed that the provisional government should declare independence and abandon any pretense of loyalty to Ferdinand.

In 1814, San Martín asked to be relieved of his command, declaring that he was in poor health. He was then appointed governor-intendant of the province of Cuyo, which enjoyed a better climate than his previous residence in Tucumán. The real reason for this change, however, was San Martín's secret plan to defeat the Spanish in South America by attacking their stronghold in Peru, not through Upper Peru as the provisional government proposed but by creating a small, well-disciplined army in Mendoza, the capital of Cuyo, to cross the Andes Mountains and defeat the Royalists in Chile and then proceed to Lima, the capital of Peru, by sea. Mendoza was located at the eastern end of a strategic pass leading across the Andes to Chile. San Martín believed that independence would not be accomplished until the Spanish stronghold of Lima was captured.

For three years, San Martín devoted all of his considerable energy to his bold and daring plan—recruiting, training, and equipping his army of the Andes. The years in Cuyo were in many ways the happiest years of his life. Shortly after his arrival in Buenos Aires, he had married fifteen-year-old María de los Remedios Escalada, the daughter of a wealthy Creole merchant. Their only child, Mercedes, was born in 1816, during his governorship in Cuyo. San Martín was an efficient administrator, accomplishing much for the people of Mendoza. He was very popular there, proving to be charming and persuasive with the people even though he never pretended to be a politician. He was a tall, broad-shouldered, handsome man with a large aquiline nose, thick black hair, and large, bushy whiskers. His complexion was dark, and he had dark, piercing eyes. He looked every inch the soldier, with a commanding presence.

In 1816, San Martín persuaded the Buenos Aires government to assist him in his bold scheme. Juan Martín Pueyrredón, head of the government, appointed him commander in chief of the army of the Andes. By January, 1817, San Martín's army of more than three thousand soldiers was ready to march across the snow-covered Andes and fulfill its mission. His soldiers successfully traversed the rugged mountains and, twenty-one days later, appeared before the astonished Spaniards on the Chilean side of the Andes. This amazing feat has been compared to Napoleon's march across the Alps in 1800 and Hannibal's similar march in the Punic Wars. San Martín's feat, however, had a greater effect on history, since it prepared the way for the independence of Chile and Peru from Spain.

San Martín's forces inflicted a decisive blow against the Royalist army on February 12 at Chacabuco, which opened the way to Santiago, the Chilean capital. Two days later, his army jubilantly entered Santiago unopposed. Declining offices and promotions from the grateful Chileans, he continued with his plan to attack Lima by sea from some fifteen hundred miles away. To accomplish that, a navy was needed. There were still substantial Royalist forces in Chile, and another battle had to be fought to secure Chile's independence. This battle, fought in April, 1818, at Maipú, near Santiago, ended any further Royalist threat.

A year later, in preparation for his expedition against Peru, San Martín was appointed brigadier general of the Chilean army, projected to be some six thousand strong. In the meantime, a navy was being created in Chile for the upcoming invasion. The Chileans had enlisted the valuable assistance of Thomas, Lord Cochrane, a former English naval officer, who was made the commander of Chile's navy. San Martín's plans, however, were almost thwarted by events in Argentina, where political leaders were arguing over what form the government should take. Many favored a monarchy, as San Martín did, but agreement could not be reached. Amid this discord, the Argentine government ordered San Martín and his army to recross the Andes and return to Argentina. He refused but left his resignation up to his men, who insisted that he remain their commander. The Chilean government reinforced this revolutionary act by appointing San Martín commander in chief of liberation.

In August, 1820, the invasion of Peru, the last stronghold of Spanish power in South America, began. San Martín made it clear to his soldiers that their objective was to free, not to conquer, their Peruvian brothers. Upon his arrival in Peru, Spanish officials in Lima attempted to negotiate a compromise with San Martín, who insisted that Spain recognize the independence of Peru. San Martín proposed that a junta govern Peru for the time being; ultimately, he envisioned a constitutional monarchy for South America, with a king or emperor from the Spanish royal family. Soon, however, the negotiations broke down.

Peruvians in the north had been influenced by San Martín's writings and speeches calling for independence, and it was undoubtedly their demand for independence that caused the viceroy to evacuate the loyalist troops from Lima and the coast, leaving the way clear for San Martín to occupy the capital, which he quietly did on June 12, 1821. The independence of Peru was proclaimed officially on July 28, 1821, amid jubilation. Events, however, would soon turn against San Martín. In August, 1821, he announced that he would assume the title of protector of Peru, with full military and civil power, in order to deal with counterrevolutionary plots and the opposition of the powerful elite in Lima to San Martín's social reforms. Although he declared that he had no ambitious motives, many of his followers voiced criticism. There were also rumors that he wanted to be king. Matters were exacerbated when Lord Cochrane quarreled with San Martín and left Peru with his squadron of ships. San Martín was struck with a sudden illness which confined him to bed. Meanwhile, a large Royalist army gathered near Lima, challenging San Martín to a battle which he refused to join because of his smaller force.

Amid this unhappy state of affairs, San Martín announced that he would meet with Simón Bolívar, the liberator of Colombia, at Guayaquil to discuss plans for the complete liberation of Peru. The famous meeting of the two giants of South American independence took place on July 26 and 27, 1822. It has never been clear exactly what transpired at the meeting, but after it San Martín abruptly withdrew from public life. It is possible that San Martín withdrew because he saw that Bolívar possessed the greater resources necessary to win the final victory over the powerful Royalist army in Peru.

San Martín returned to Argentina, where he received the news of his wife's death. He left an indifferent and hostile Argentina with his young daughter and spent the remainder of his life in exile in Europe, where he suffered from poor health, poverty, and bitterness. He died in Boulogne-sur-Mer, France, on August 17, 1850, unaware that history would elevate him to legendary stature.

Summary

José de San Martín's claim to fame emanated from his bold and daring plan to cross the Andes, liberate Chile, and establish a base from which to attack Peru by sea and thus complete the liberation of southern South America. He was a great leader of men, inspiring them to great feats of endurance. He was a man of action rather than of reflection; he won battles and left other matters to statesmen. At the same time, it should be noted that he was a man who reflected the spirit of his age, since he was a believer in the ideals of the eighteenth century Enlightenment as evidenced in his ideas of independence and his strong support of education and social reforms. He was a rational man who correctly reasoned that South America was not ready for the republican type of government found in the United States. He supported monarchy as the solution to the chaos he saw emerging around him.

San Martín altered the course of history with his bold movements in Argentina, Chile, and Peru. A lesser man would never have accomplished what he did. He truly deserves to be remembered alongside other liberators in the New World, such as George Washington and Simón Bolívar.

Bibliography

Metford, J. C. J. *San Martín: The Liberator*. New York: Philosophical Library, 1950. A very readable, well-balanced, and scholarly account of San Martín's life. The author attempts to separate the man from the legend.

Mitre, Bartolomé. *The Emancipation of South America*. Translated by William Pilling. London: Chapman & Hall, 1893. A translation and condensation of Mitre's exhaustive multivolume *Historia de San Martín y de la emancipación sud-americana* (1887-1888), which is considered a classic. Poetically written. Combines a helpful index and a map.

Robertson, William Spence. *Rise of the Spanish-American Republics as Told in the Lives of Their Liberators*. New York: D. Appleton, 1918. Contains an excellent chapter on San Martín. Offers a well-written and well-researched summary of San Martín's role in the independence of Argentina, Chile, and Peru.

Rojas, Ricardo. *San Martin: Knight of the Andes*. Translated by Herschel Brickell and Carlos Videla. New York: Doubleday, Doran, 1945. A very sympathetic, very readable biography. The author believes that San Martín belongs to the "race of armed Saints" that includes Lohengrin and Parsifal. Helpful backnotes and an index.

Schoellkopf, Anna. *Don José de San Martín, 1778-1850: A Study of His Career*. New York: Boni and Liveright, 1924. A small volume, taken almost entirely from Mitre's works, including several verbatim quotations. Contains several illustrations and a helpful map of South America.

James E. Southerland

JACOPO SANSOVINO
Jacopo Tatti

Born: July 2, 1486; Florence
Died: November 27, 1570; Venice
Areas of Achievement: Art and architecture
Contribution: Sansovino was the first architect to bring Renaissance classical ideas of architecture into a successful conjunction with the Venetian Byzantine-Gothic style, resulting in buildings in the Piazza San Marco which were to confirm its reputation as one of the greatest architectural developments in the world.

Early Life

Jacopo Sansovino was born in Florence. His original name was Jacopo Tatti, but he later took the name Sansovino in honor of his master, the sculptor Andrea Sansovino, whose wall tombs were deeply admired and imitated throughout the sixteenth century. Jacopo Sansovino's early training was, therefore, as a sculptor, and his early reputation was confined to that discipline. He worked in Florence and, particularly, in Rome and was a close associate of many of the great artists of the high Renaissance, many of whom were adept in more than one artistic discipline. It was not, in fact, unusual at the time for an artist to work with considerable distinction at painting, sculpture, and architecture, and Sansovino's contemporaries, who included Raphael, Michelangelo, and Donato Bramante, would provide the model for a young sculptor eager to try his hand at other forms of artistic expression. Sansovino had done some architectural work in Florence at the Duomo in 1515, but it was only for a temporary, decorative façade to mark the visit of Pope Leo X to the city. In Rome, he began two churches, San Marcello al Corso and San Giovanni di Fiorentini, but he did not finish either of them. He completed one important private residence, the Palazzo Gaddi, and showed considerable skill in handling Renaissance architectural ideas. The site for the Palazzo was not an easy one with which to work, but Sansovino solved the problems with elegance and style, anticipating the way in which he would deal with architectural troubles in his Venetian career.

In 1527, at the time of the sack of Rome, Sansovino went to Venice, intending to return to the south when political turmoil had eased. He was forty-one years old, and his reputation was mainly as a sculptor. He gained a commission to restore the domes of St. Mark's Basilica, and he did so with marked competence. His appointment as the *proto*, the supervising architect for the Procurators of St. Mark, a body of prominent Venetian citizens responsible for the maintenance of the buildings in St. Mark's Square, was the factor that kept him in Venice. He joined them on April 7, 1529, and held that office until his death in 1570.

Life's Work

Architecture is, perhaps, the least independent kind of art form, and Sansovino's work as the *proto* was not confined to keeping existing structures repaired; he was to provide a complete renewal of one side of the Piazza San Marco to extend around the corner of the piazza into the smaller piazzetta facing the Doge's Palace, immediately to the south of the basilica. This was a task of major urban renewal, all the more important because the piazza, the piazzetta, the basilica, and the Doge's Palace were, together, the center of Venetian religious and political life. Any changes or additions had to reflect that sense of importance. It was decided that the buildings on the south side of the square were to be razed and a library built to house the world-famous Venetian collection of Greek and Latin manuscripts; the building would also house the procurators. This project continued throughout Sansovino's life, and parts of it were not finished until after his death. It was the major test of his skill, not only as an architect but also as a negotiator, compromiser, and manager. The main difficulty was designing a building which would be both a visual exemplification of Venetian power and grandeur and a residence for important local politicians, while remaining commercially viable. Long-term leases with merchants in the existing buildings had to be renegotiated, and the new structure had to be able to accommodate shops which would provide income for the procuracy.

Sansovino managed to overcome all the complications to produce what Giorgio Vasari called a building without parallel; Andrea Palladio, the greatest architect of the period, proclaimed it the richest and most ornate building since antiquity. Venice had longed to make the piazza something that Rome would envy. Sansovino gave it to them in a building which makes ample use of Renaissance architectural ideas but lightens them, opens them up to the Venetian tradition of lavish encrustation and lively sculptural decoration. The use of the local Istrian stone, easy to carve, responding in its bright whiteness to the sparkling light flashing off the lagoon, makes the building typically Venetian, while the use of the classical orders, Doric below, Ionic on the second floor, topped by a balustrade upon which sculptural figures seem to float in the air, gives it a sense of both majestic solidity and ethereal lightness. The library was to be Sansovino's greatest work.

Sansovino completed two other projects in the San Marco complex. The campanile had, until Sansovino's time, been tucked into a corner of the buildings, losing much of its visual power in a jumble of shops and commercial structures. Sansovino adjusted the line of the library to allow space around the tower, giving it the sight line from all sides which makes it one of the major points of interest in the piazza. He also rebuilt the loggia, a small meetinghouse at the base of the campanile. Prior to his work, the building had no particular aesthetic appeal; when Sansovino was done, it had become a tiny gem of rich red-and-white marble, appropriate for its place at the base of the tower. It is, as Deborah Howard has suggested, not so much a building as a piece of sculpture.

On the lagoon side of the library, Sansovino had another problem, the rebuilding of the Venetian Mint, or Zecca, and again he displayed a capacity for compromise which allowed him to make art out of impossible situations. Something had to be provided for the cheese merchants who had always had shops immediately in front of the proposed site. The multiple bays of the ground floor, heavily rusticated in the Renaissance tradition of acknowledging the classical heritage of Italian architecture, provide an appropriate fortresslike base for a building in which the coin of the realm was cast and stored. The Zecca has become part of the library; in its time, the bays led into the separate shops of the cheese sellers without compromising visually the importance or aesthetic unity of the structure. The upper stories, Doric on the second floor, Ionic on the third, are formidable in their use of column, lintel, and window surround. The Zecca reflects the practice of mirroring a building's function in its façade—the lower floor suggesting its impregnability, the upper levels, particularly the second floor, with its massive protruding lintels, exaggerating the same idea of sudden closure.

Sansovino's career was not confined to the piazza. He was allowed to take private commissions, and he provided an interesting building for the Rialto market area, still extant and still used in the twentieth century. The Fabbriche Nuove again incorporates the Renaissance use of the orders into the long, three-storied building. Sansovino also undertook the more modest problem of a residence for destitute women; the success of the inexpensive stucco building lies in its tasteful proportions and some very witty chimney pots.

Sansovino also designed several churches, probably six in all, but only three of them survive, one of them with a façade by Palladio. The façades of the other two, San Martino and San Giuliano, have interesting mannerist inclinations. San Giuliano in particular manifests the mannerist tendency to eccentric manipulation of architectural motifs. Sansovino usually eschewed variations that were too idiosyncratic in his use of the Renaissance architectural vocabulary, but the narrow site of San Giuliano, and the determination of his patron to be publicly recognized, led to the mounting of a statue of the patron, seated on a sarcophagus, on the front of the church. The statue reminds one of Sansovino's beginnings as a pupil of Andrea Sansovino, the master of tomb sculpture (sculptures usually only mounted on the interior of a church). It is a stunning façade, clearly original in conception and execution.

Sansovino also designed two palazzos of considerable distinction. The Venetian palazzo was used not only as a residence but also as a place of business, since so many of the great Venetian families were traders. Their palazzos were proof of business success, but they were also used as warehouses and offices and often sheltered several generations of the family at once. The first floor was, therefore, designed not only to store goods but also to take in and distribute the goods from the door facing immediately onto the canals. Other floors housed the extended family, and the façades of the buildings, often right on the canal, were required to be as handsome as money could make them. Palazzos were usually in an established style that was partly Byzantine, partly Gothic. Sansovino's Palazzo Dolfin was built to serve in the old way as a home and place of business, but there was no need for a large central entrance on the canal, since there was a small stream down one side of the building which could be used to enter the residential areas of the palace. That allowed Sansovino to use on the ground level six Doric arches in a regularized Renaissance pattern leading to six separate warehouses. The second and third floors made use of Ionic and Corinthian decoration, but Sansovino kept the common Venetian arrangement of windows to achieve another successful mix of the old and the new.

Sansovino's second, grander commission was for a family of political consequence, and again, on a much larger scale, Sansovino put the classical orders into play, especially in a generous inner courtyard. Vasari called it the finest palace in Italy in its time, and it displayed the sense of amplitude and richness of design that Sansovino seemed peculiarly able to manipulate without vulgarity.

Sansovino remained active until his death. Vasari writes that he was a handsome and charming young man, well-built and red-bearded. In his old age, he retained his charm, but the beard was white. Tintoretto painted him, bright-eyed and wary, and Vasari notes that in old age he dressed elegantly, kept himself well-groomed, and took pleasure in the company of women.

Summary

Jacopo Sansovino was not a great architect, but he was a very good one, and he produced a handful of major projects which are as good as anything produced in Venice. He was able to break the hold that the Byzantine-Gothic tradition had on Venetian architecture and develop a new kind of style which was thoroughly modern and committed to the dignity and calm weight of Renaissance classicism, yet also retained the lively, decorative lightness of the island mode. He showed other architects how to bring Venice forward into the Renaissance without repudiating the peculiar history or virtues of the old style.

Sansovino was also able to make architectural compromise work without debasement of standards; he worked with the complicated Venetian committees, demanding a certain amount of tradition within a mercurial political and economic climate. He was, in a sense, the ideal architect—learned, modestly imaginative, sensitive to local prejudices, capable of playing the game, able to nurse major projects along despite constant threats of setbacks and changes of mind. His contributions to the Piazza San Marco alone entitle him to be considered one of the finest architects of urban renewal.

Bibliography
Fletcher, Sir Banister. *Sir Banister Fletcher's History of Architecture.* Rev. ed. New York: Charles Scribner's Sons, 1975. The architecture student's basic reference text. Provides good illustrations and puts Venetian architecture, Renaissance Italian architecture, and Sansovino's version of both in context.
Howard, Deborah. *Jacopo Sansovino: Architecture and Patronage in Renaissance Venice.* New Haven, Conn.: Yale University Press, 1975. A very sensible and easily understood study of how Sansovino went about making art in the context of a social and political structure that foiled many lesser men. Howard is good on the history of Venice and its architecture and shows how Sansovino adjusted to the rules.
Lowry, Bates. *Renaissance Architecture.* New York: George Braziller, 1962. A substantial essay on the subject of Renaissance architecture. Includes a generous selection of photographs.
McCarthy, Mary. *Venice Observed.* New York: Reynal, 1956. A famous essay by one of America's finest writers. Venice is a work of art and should be understood as such. McCarthy and other literary figures, such as Hugh Honour, Jan Morris, and Henry James, are able to make that phenomenon sensible.
Norberg-Schulz, Christian. *Meaning in Western Architecture.* New York: Praeger, 1975. This text does not speak directly of Sansovino but examines how architects make buildings illustrate the ideals of a society, a skill at which Sansovino was particularly good.

Charles Pullen

SANTORIO SANTORIO
Sanctorius Sanctorius

Born: March 29, 1561; Capodistria, Venice
Died: February 22 or March 6, 1636; Venice
Area of Achievement: Medicine
Contribution: Santorio was in the vanguard of innovators in the late sixteenth and early seventeenth centuries in physiology, applied medicine,
and medical instruments. By quantitative experimentation, he encouraged
the use of mathematics and experimentation as analytical tools in the
study of physiology and pathology. He also worked against the strong cult
of astrology in Italy, which had blocked progress in the advancement of
medicine for centuries.

Early Life

Santorio Santorio's father, Antonio, had settled in Capodistria (modern
Justinopolis) as an important official in the Venetian Republic, the Chief
Steward of Ordnance. Antonio Santorio married Elisabetta Cordonia of Capodistria, a noblewoman, the couple first producing Santorio and then Isi-
doro followed by two daughters.

Santorio was initially educated at Capodistria and then sent to Venice,
where he lived with the high-ranking Morosoni family, friends of the San-
torios. The young man, whose first and last names were the same, was given
the best of tutors who were educating the Morosoni sons. As a result, Santorio acquired an unusually firm grounding in classical languages, philosophy, mathematics, and literature.

At fourteen, Santorio entered the Archilyceum of Padua, where he studied
philosophy and then medicine, the usual sequence. In the late sixteenth
century, the University of Padua was known throughout Europe as one of the
best universities, with a distinguished faculty. Famous professors such as
Andreas Vesalius, Realdo Colombo, and Gabriello Fallopio had been acade-
micians there. Santorio's scholars and professors include Giacomo Zaba-
rella, a professor of physics, Bernardino Paterno in medicine, and Girolamo
Fabrici. Having completed his medical degree in 1582, Santorio spent three
years in clinical work and then began to practice medicine.

When the King of Poland purportedly asked Paduan administrators to send
a brilliant medical doctor to Poland, biographers and commentators disagree
on whether Santorio was sent, but this question persists. He may have gone
there for as many as fourteen years, but he was consistently appearing in
Hungary and Croatia (part of modern Yugoslavia) as a medical consultant;
he also returned to Venice for months at a time.

It was in 1607, when Santorio happened to be in Venice, that hired killers
assaulted Fra Paolo Sarpi, an eminent intellectual who was a state counselor

in Venice, and left him near death. Sarpi had incurred the wrath of the Papacy when he blocked Pope Paul V's efforts to wrest Venice into the papal jurisdiction. Santorio and Fabrici were summoned to treat Sarpi's brutal wounds, and, when it was known that the assassins escaped to the papal territory, Sarpi is reported to have said, "I recognize the style of the Roman curia." Many biographers of Santorio cite this episode, since Sarpi protected the University of Padua from papal control. The Venetian Republic was kinder to intellectuals and men of genius than was the Papacy. It is well known that Galileo had the misfortune of developing many of his scientific investigations in territory ruled by the Papacy.

Life's Work

One of Santorio's first important books was published in 1602 in Venice, with the ungainly title *Methodi vitandorum errorum omnium qui in arte medica contingunt* (method of combating all the errors which occur in the art of medicine), a work essentially dealing with differential diagnosis of various diseases, considered brilliant by contemporaries. The book brought instant fame to Santorio as a clinician and a consultant and with it high respect by the Venetian intellectuals. Although based largely on Santorio's own experiments, it contains references to the work of Hippocrates, Galen, and Avicenna, three illustrious names in the history of medicine. In this treatise Santorio discusses the "pulsilogium," an instrument used to track the motion and rest of the artery, asserting that everything can be measured exactly, observed, and kept in mind for comparison. It is believed by many authorities that the "pulsilogium" was invented by Galileo but that Santorio utilized the instrument and popularized its value. This particular instrument, along with others, forged new standards in observations in physiology and pathology.

Ultimately, this innovative book led to the appointment of Santorio, in 1611, to a professorship of theoretical medicine at the University of Padua for six years, a term which was eventually renewed for another six years. Students, especially from Germany, came from all over Europe to attend lectures; Santorio's classes were popular and crowded. Galileo, the unrivaled father of experimental science, had taught mathematics at the University of Padua from 1593 to 1610. Both Galileo and the brilliant philosopher Giordano Bruno were Santorio's close friends. The preeminent William Harvey from England, who discovered the theory of the circulation of the blood, had been a student at Padua too, although he never met Santorio. At Padua the professors of the theory of medicine were expected to make commentaries on the aphorisms of Hippocrates, Galen's art of medicine, and Avicenna's first *Fen* (an Arabic word meaning part). Santorio's commentaries on these works became the bedrock of his lectures and subsequently his books.

A decade following the appearance of Santorio's first book, he published his *Commentaria in artem medicinalem Galeni* (1612; commentary on the art of medicine of Galen). In addition to following traditional paths, the respected physician made his first mention of the air thermometer. In the history of medicine, it has been discussed at length whether Galileo or Santorio invented the thermometer; evidence points to Galileo as the conceptualizer of a kind of thermometer and to Santorio as the discoverer of a variant and the first physician to utilize the thermometer and discuss it in publications.

With a heavy schedule of medical practice and university lecturing, which also drew prominent physicians, Santorio still found time to publish *Ars de statica medicina sectionibus aphorismorum septem comprehensa* (1614; *Medicina Statica: Or, Rules of Health in Eight Sections of Aphorisms*, 1676), the book that seems to have captured the imagination and attention of more contemporaries and subsequent medical professionals than any other of his publications. This relatively short work discusses weight variation experienced by the body from ingestion to excretion, with weighing procedures after purgation. Experiments that were made over twenty-five years on more than ten thousand subjects were discussed, using scales and other instruments of measurement. The main thesis is that "insensible perspiration" (as opposed to actual perspiration) is capable of systematic recording or weighing, more than all forms of combined sensible body wastes, and is variable according to sleep, cold, fever, and sexual and other activity. Having caused a sensation, *Medicina Statica* engendered twenty-eight Latin editions, translations into many other languages, along with four Latin editions with commentaries by Martin Lister, the well-known physician to Charles I of England. The book led many to cite Santorio as "the father of the science of metabolism." Many other physicians were inspired to study "insensible perspiration" and to write books on their own experiments. Santorio was now at the apex of his accomplishments and fame. He was deluged with requests for consultations, and in 1616 he was appointed President of the Collegio Veneto in Padua, a new center founded to eliminate abuses in the medical faculty.

When Santorio resigned his academic post at the end of his second term as professor, the Venetian Senate, recognizing his enormous contributions to medicine, to the university, and to the republic, granted him a lifetime title of professor and also his full salary for life. Despite invitations by the University of Bologna and those at Messina and Pavia, he rejected them all and returned to Venice.

Now in his mid-sixties, Santorio published *Commentaria in primam fen primi libri canonis Avicennae* (1625; commentaries on the first part of the first book of the Canon of Avicenna), which pleased his contemporaries because of its practicality and which remains a classic medical text. The book emphasized precision instruments in medical practice, a technique which helped physicians to sharpen observations and diagnoses. He discussed the thermometer and the "pulsilogium," among other instruments. In the commentary on the Avicenna book, Santorio shows the importance of humidity in disease treatment and depicts three types of instruments for humidity measurements. The lack of specific recordings of pulse rates or temperatures of people is conspicuous. Future medical specialists were to work on statistics, while Santorio merely explains the instruments.

Another part of the book on the *Fen* of Avicenna is given much attention—Santorio's attack on astrology and astrologers. Padua at this time was a virtual nest of astrologists, and there were several astrologers on the faculty of the University of Padua. In fact, their influence throughout the Venetian Republic was powerful, and their attack on medical science and on Santorio was ferocious; still, the venerable doctor survived the counterattacks of the diviners. Santorio's practice flourished along with his reputation, and some of the most important people came to his office.

Santorio was appointed president of the Venetian College of Physicians, and, when Venice was besieged by plague in 1630 he was pressed into service as chief health officer, subsequently making a report to the health officer of the city, a document which still exists and is preserved in the General State Archives in Venice.

Never married, Santorio was considered to be a misogynist. He was known to be frugal, and biographers agree that he was interested in amassing a fortune and did succeed in becoming wealthy. An engraving by Giacomo Piccini shows the celebrated physician to have had an elongated face, a long goatee, and a furrowed brow. His skeletal remains indicate that he was tall. His style in lectures which were published and in conversations with his brilliant friends indicate that he was archly ironic—contemporary writers agree that he possessed an unusually high level of critical intelligence. All agree on his substantiated contributions to medicine.

Santorio died of a disease of the urinary tract and was buried in the Church dei Servi, which ultimately was destroyed by Napoleon I. A casque containing his bones (together with the bones of others) was given to a professor of anatomy at Padua. He buried the bones but preserved the skull, which today rests in the Museum of Anatomy of Padua. Santorio left a number of bequests to his immediate family and to other relatives. He also granted money to establish a medical college at Padua, to be named "Santorio," and a sum to the Medical College of Venice to have a Mass said yearly for his soul on Saint Luke's Day, an annual celebration of the patron saint of medicine.

Summary

The history of medicine began in the seventeenth century when Galileo,

Giordano Bruno, and Santorio Santorio, among others, helped to free science from dogma. Santorio helped to construct the foundation on which modern medicine is based—the necessity to experiment, the measurement of research through observation and instruments, and the need for determination of positive, provable data.

Santorio's contribution in the virtually unknown field of the amelioration of the condition of invalids advanced medicine in a significant area and signaled to future generations of physicians the need to work further on its theory and practice. Santorio's invention, modification, and employment of instruments provided his profession with measuring devices so that future practitioners could develop resources in recording data for the treatment and the prevention of diseases. Santorio's commentaries on past generations of scholars and his own innovative theories and practice in physiology and pathology significantly advanced medical knowledge. His book on static medicine, apart from William Harvey's theory of blood circulation, was of quintessential importance to medicine. Trained exhaustively in the humanities as well as in the sciences, Santorio developed concepts and techniques of diagnosis well ahead of his time. His researches contributed to the advancement of medicine throughout Europe, especially in the first third of the seventeenth century, and have continued to serve medicine in its attempt to treat and to prevent the development of diseases throughout the world.

Bibliography
Drake, Stillman. *Galileo at Work: His Scientific Biography.* Chicago: University of Chicago Press, 1978. An excellent biography of Galileo that also encompasses his relationships with other scientists, including Santorio. There is a discussion of the pulsilogium and the thermoscope, both of which instruments advanced the course of science and which involved studies and practical application by Santorio.
McMullin, Ernan, ed. *Galileo, Man of Science.* New York: Basic Books, 1967. The book is a compilation of essays by worldwide authorities on Galileo. Considerable attention (with illustrations) is paid to medical instruments, including the thermoscope and the pulsilogium, a milestone in the history of medical instruments. The contributions of Galileo and Santorio are evaluated in chapter 13.
Major, Ralph H. "Santorio Santorio." *Annals of Medical History* 10 (September, 1938): 369-381. A concise treatment of the life and work of Santorio, especially of his books on Herodotus, Galen, and Avicenna. Delves into the medical instruments associated with Santorio, with illustrations and careful descriptions of their design and use.
Mitchell, S. Weir. *The Early History of Instrumental Precision in Medicine.* New Haven, Conn.: Tuttle, Morehouse, and Taylor, 1892. An overview of the development and use of medical instruments in the seventeenth

century, acknowledging Santorio's considerable importance in medicine and the instruments that his innovations utilized.

Sigerist, Henry E. *The Great Doctors*. Translated by Eden Paul and Cedar Paul. New York: W. W. Norton, 1933. Discusses contributions of Santorio in the history of medicine. Sigerist claims that Harvey's circulation of the blood theory became more important than Santorio's "insensible perspiration" theory because Harvey's language use was more concise and better organized.

Julia B. Boken

FRIEDRICH KARL VON SAVIGNY

Born: February 21, 1779; Frankfurt am Main
Died: October 25, 1861; Berlin, Prussia
Area of Achievement: Law
Contribution: Savigny was a leading historian of Roman law. In the field of
legal philosophy, he is considered generally to be either the founder or the
leading exponent of the so-called historical or Romantic school of jurisprudence, which means that the content of a given body of law can only
be understood through a process of historical research.

Early Life
Friedrich Karl von Savigny, who was thin, with thick dark hair and a kind
and generous face, descended from a wealthy Protestant noble family which
had emigrated from Lorraine to Frankfurt. Savigny, whose family name
came from the castle of Savigny near Charmes in the Moselle valley, was
educated at the Universities of Göttingen, Jena, Leipzig, Halle, and Marburg; at Marburg, he studied under Philipp Friedrich Weiss, a specialist in
medieval jurisprudence, and Anton Bauer, whose reputation was gained in
activities keyed toward the reform of German criminal law. Receiving his
degree in 1800, Savigny determined to spend his life in scholarly pursuits.
Personally wealthy, he was probably the first of the ruling classes to take up
teaching as a career, a field that, because of its low pay and accordingly poor
social standing, had hitherto largely drawn its members from the lower-
middle classes. As privatdocent at Marburg, where he lectured in criminal
law and on the Pandects of the Roman law, he published *Das Recht des
Besitzes* (1803; *Treatise on Possession: Or, The Jus Possessionis of the Civil
Law*, 6th ed. 1848), which he allegedly wrote in seven months and which
gained for him offers of two chairs, one at Greifswald and one at Heidelberg. Savigny also published in 1803 a brief article in a short-lived English
periodical, *The Monthly Register*, in which, after an assessment of German
universities at that time, he declared that only four of almost forty universities in Germany were of more than local importance. In 1804 Savigny
married Kunigunde Brentano, so he declined both university offers in favor
of a honeymoon that included searching the libraries of France and Germany
for manuscripts that would aid him in writing a proposed history of Roman
law in the Middle Ages.
    Savigny did, however, advise the government of Baden, one of the many
independent German states, on the reorganization of the University of Heidelberg, which helped to make Heidelberg one of the important seats of
learning in Europe. In 1808, Savigny went to the University of Landshut in
Bavaria as professor of Roman law, and, in 1810, he not only took a significant share in the foundation of the University of Berlin but also was the first

to be elected rector, or vice chancellor. He helped to organize the university on lines similar to those employed at Heidelberg, but with perhaps greater success. Savigny remained at the University of Berlin until March of 1842.

Life's Work

In 1817, Savigny became a member of the Department of Justice in the Prussian Privy Council and, in that same year, a member of a commission for organizing the Prussian provincial estates. In 1819, he became a member of the Berlin Court of Appeal and Cassation for the Rhine Provinces, in 1826 a member of the commission for revising the Prussian code, and in 1842 chairman of the newly established department for revision of statutes. In 1842, he was also appointed *Grosskanzler* (high chancellor), or head of the juridical system in Prussia, a post he held until the Revolution of 1848, after which he devoted himself to his writing and research, holding no more government positions.

In 1806, Napoleon I promulgated the Code Napoleon, which provided a uniform body of rules for the French nation; many Germans looked upon this code enviously as an example of what should and could be done for the German people. In 1814, a professor of civil law at the University of Heidelberg, Anton Friedrich Justus Thibaut, wrote an article arguing that the law of the German people be codified both as a means of unifying the German states and as a means of applying a universally held logic or rule of reason to the law. Savigny objected strenuously in his famous pamphlet *Vom Beruf unserer Zeit für Gesetzgebung und Rechtswissenschaft* (1814; *Of the Vocation of Our Age for Legislation and Jurisprudence*, 1831), theorizing that law, like language, arises out of the customs, traditions, needs, and spirit of a particular people or community (*Volkgeist*) and that law cannot be imposed on a people or community arbitrarily. Something that is logical and reasonable for the French or English mind may be entirely illogical for the German. Rather than arbitrarily impose a mass of legislation upon a people, one must research the particular history of that people to determine the law that suits it best. This exaltation of customary law, as distinguished from law as a universal rule of reason, was derived from the worldview of the Romantics. It proved, whether intended so by Savigny, to be not only the glorification of things German but also a recognition of distinctions between one German state and another. Furthermore, this concept of Savigny argued against the codification of the law of any particular people at any particular time, because, according to Savigny, the law, wherever located, was always in the process of evolving and neither could nor should reach a point where codification was possible. In 1815, with Karl Friedrich Eichorn and Johann Friedrich Ludwig Göschen, he founded the *Zeitschrift für geschichtliche Rechtswissenschaft* (journal of historical jurisprudence), a periodical voicing the ideas of the historical school.

Savigny's theories, therefore, were the heart of the Romantic branch of the historical school of jurisprudence, which tended to dominate the German universities until his death and which were powerful enough to delay until 1900 the codification of German law—well after German unification in 1871. Nevertheless, despite Savigny's emphasis on the historical approach, he was not an advocate of natural law. In his *Juristische Methodenlehre, nach der Ausarbeitung des Jakob Grimm* (wr. 1802-1803, pb. 1951; legal methodology as elaborated by Jakob Grimm), delivered as a lecture at Marburg, Savigny voiced the view that the historical approach should be systematic, so that the result contributes to a clearly defined system of legal science.

A second aspect of Savigny's work dealt with the study and research of Roman law. His *Geschichte des römischen Rechts im Mittelalter* (1815-1831, 1834-1851; partial translation as *The History of Roman Law During the Middle Ages*, 1829) remains the definitive work on the subject. Although Roman law, which he admired, had been codified, Savigny tried to demonstrate that, despite the codifications, Roman law was actually administered as customary law, bringing it into conformity with the historical school of thought. Apart from this, Savigny's scholarship eliminated much of the incongruity that had clouded the understanding of Roman law during the period from the fall of the Roman Empire until A.D. 1100. *System des heutigen römischen Rechts* (1840-1849) presents in its eighth volume Savigny's theories of private international law and the first modern systematic presentation of this phase of the law. The eighth volume also shows that Savigny was acquainted with the work of Joseph Story, an associate justice of the United States Supreme Court. In 1850, Savigny published *Vermischte Schriften* (miscellaneous writings), a collection of various pieces on the law. *Das Obligationenrecht* (1851-1853; the law of contracts), which is a furtherance of *System des heutigen römischen Rechts*, emphasizes freedom of contract, which proved of great use after the unification of Germany in the rise of industrial capitalism prior to World War I.

Although Savigny opposed a codification of German law, he nevertheless approved the application of the Roman law code to Germany, avoiding this contradiction by stating that Roman law during the Middle Ages had been so generally applied to and used by the German people that it had become in many respects part of the German customary law and thereby reflective of the German *Volkgeist*. Savigny's thinking is weak in that codification is not necessarily an imposition of arbitrary law upon an unwilling people; it may be a mere memorial of a people's customary law, and codification may thus be a plateau in the natural evolution of a people's customary law. Further, as Julius Stone has noted, the *Volkgeist* doctrine "probably exaggerated the role in legal development of popular consciousness as distinct from the consciousness of small groups, either of specialists or of a dominant class," as well as "the element of conscious attitudes . . . which lies behind a people's relation with its law."

Summary

Friedrich Karl von Savigny's contribution to law lies in his objection to codifications and in his scholarship in Roman law. He connected these two aspects of his work by maintaining that there had never really been a codification of Roman law but merely a development of customary law by an evolutionary process natural to the Roman people and the Roman Empire. This spirit of nationhood in the law was contrary to the nineteenth century efforts of the codifiers to press upon the German people an arbitrary set of laws unnatural to it. At the time of his writing, Savigny was very popular; those who wanted greater democracy were delighted with the concept that the people and not the nobility were the real makers of the law, and the nobility or aristocracy was happy to have found a way to avoid needed reforms. In the end, the results were not entirely salutary, for Savigny's emphasis on the *Volkgeist* tended to strengthen the concept of German mysticism, to glorify the superiority of German law, to stifle reforms, to inhibit the development of a badly needed code for a unified people, and perhaps even to set another stone in the edifice of corrupt nationalism. Savigny's major contribution to the law, it would appear, remains his scholarly work in laying open the field of Roman law, his insistence that the practice and theory of jurisprudence must be one and the same, his recognition of the evolutionary process in law, and his elevation of the profession of teaching and scholarship.

Bibliography

Allgemeine Deutsche Biographie. Leipzig, Germany: Duncker and Humblot, 1875-1912. The article on Savigny, in this fifty-six-volume biography of prominent Germans, presents a clear and sometimes provocative presentation of Savigny's life and doctrines. In German.

Jones, J. Walter. *Historical Introduction to the Theory of Law*. Reprint. New York: A. M. Kelley, 1969. Chapter 2 discusses the legal codes in France and Germany, Thibaut, and Savigny's criticism of the codes, together with excellent material on the pros and cons of the historical school of legal thought. The concepts of other legal historians of the period are brought to bear upon the historical school so that the reader obtains a fair view of the thinking on the subject during the nineteenth century.

Kantorowicz, Hermann U. "Savigny and the Historical School of Law." *Law Quarterly Review* 53 (July, 1937): 326-343. Presents some of the facts of Savigny's life but largely deals with the meaning of the historical school. Kantorowicz believes that it is Savigny's scholarship and research in Roman law that constitute his real contribution to legal science. The article, however, is difficult reading for the layperson.

Montmorency, James E. G. de. "Friedrich Karl von Savigny." In *Great Jurists of the World*, edited by John Macdonell and Edward Manson, vol. 2. Boston: Little, Brown, 1914. Deals with biographies of great jurists from Gaius through Rudolph von Ihering. In the selection on Savigny, Montmorency gives a general picture of Savigny's concepts of the historical school of law. Montmorency does not discuss the essential contradiction between Savigny's glorification of the evolutionary law of a particular people and his desire to impress Roman law upon the Germans, a point that is well discussed in the work by Stone, cited below.

Stone, Julius. *The Province and Function of Law.* Sydney, Australia: Associated General Publications, 1946. Chapter 18 is probably the best brief study of Savigny's ideas. Concisely presents Savigny's opposition to a code for Germany and gives a fine overview of his work in the Roman law of the Middle Ages in Europe and as applied to Europe in his own time. Also treats the essential conflict between Savigny's insistence on an evolutionary customary law, his demand for an acceptance of the codified Roman law, and his attempt to resolve the conflict.

Robert M. Spector

GIROLAMO SAVONAROLA

Born: September 21, 1452; Ferrara
Died: May 23, 1498; Florence
Areas of Achievement: Religion and government
Contribution: Savonarola set in motion the greatest religious revival of his
  day, turning a materialistic and worldly city into a democratic theocracy.
  He inspired many Florentines with a new, simple faith. He began the tide
  of Reformation soon to sweep over Europe.

Early Life
  Girolamo Savonarola was the third son of Niccolò di Michele della Savonarola and Elena Bonacossi. His mother was a descendant of the Bonacossi
family who had been lords of Mantua. The Savonarolas were a merchant
family with an aristocratic-military background. The boy's grandfather, Michele, had been a well-known physician and teacher at the University of Padua, and had become personal physician to Niccolò III d'Este. This grandfather was the primary influence on the boy—a pious, ascetic, aged, and
scholarly man, he had much of the medieval schoolman in him, and passed
this characteristic along to his grandson, who became, partly because of this
influence, somewhat out of his time.
  Savonarola's family intended that he become a doctor, but he studied
many disciplines, including art, music, poetry, and philosophy (Aristotelian
and Thomist). Savonarola did study the sciences and medicine, but he eventually turned instead to theology and close study of the Bible.
  Pious and inflexible, from a very early age, Savonarola seemed wounded
by the corruption of the time. On April 24, 1475, he left home and his
medical studies, which he had begun after taking his degree in the liberal
arts, and entered the Dominican Order at Bologna, which had a famous
school of theology. At the monastery, Savonarola wished to live humbly as
one of the brothers, to rid himself of his philosophy, and to be obedient and
at peace. The superiors of the order, however, did not wish to waste such a
fine education and wanted him to become a priest. His theological studies
began in 1476. In 1479, he was sent to complete his studies in Ferrara. Sustaining a disputation there, Savonarola impressed his superiors sufficiently to
be elected to the office of lecturer at the Convent of San Marco in Florence.
He first arrived in that city on foot that May. Florence was at that time in the
hands of Lorenzo de' Medici, patron and poet of the Humanism so hated by
Savonarola.

Life's Work
  Arriving at Florence in 1482, Savonarola took up his post of lecturer at
San Marco. A great biblical scholar, he taught the Bible to novices at the
monastery. The Old Testament was his specialty, especially the canonical

books. He was a very learned teacher but was primarily concerned to move his students. He inspired a quiet religious revival at San Marco during his tenure there. His first sermons in Florence, preached at small churches such as the Murate and Orsanmichele, were not successful. His sermons were not to the sophistical taste of the Florentines, who admired the art of rhetoric, and they also found his Ferrarese accent laughable. Nevertheless, in 1484, he preached at one of the main churches in the city, San Lorenzo, the parish church of the Medicis. He had no more success there. It was not until he began preaching sermons based on his apocalyptic revelations, at the Church of San Gimignano during Lent of 1485 and 1486, that he began to wield influence as a preacher. Perhaps the reason for his success then was that the theme of his sermons—the need for church reform, his prophecy that the Church would be scourged and renewed—struck an urgent chord after the election of the pope with the ironical name of Innocent VIII. On August 12, 1484, Sixtus IV had died. He had not been a virtuous pope, but his successor was far worse.

In 1487, Savonarola left Florence, having been appointed master of studies at the Studium Generale of San Domenico in Bologna, his own illustrious school. After the year of his appointment was over, he was sent to preach in various cities. In 1488, he went to Ferrara to see his mother and sisters (his father had died during Lent in 1485); he stayed two years at the convent of Santa Maria degli Angeli in that city and traveled to other towns on foot preaching. By this time, Count Giovanni Pico della Mirandola, a famed scholar and linguist, had become a great admirer of Savonarola and requested of his patron and friend Lorenzo de' Medici that he use his influence to bring Savonarola back to Florence. This Lorenzo did, and in 1490, Savonarola was back again in Florence, at the request of the very family to whom he was to be such a scourge. In August of that year, Savonarola began preaching his sermons on the Apocalypse, which continued until 1491. His rough style began to gain favor with the people, though his adherents were the pious, the poor, and the malcontents, not the city's elite. His themes were based on real abuses: the confiscatory taxes and corruption of the Medicis, and their looting of the dowry foundations (the *monte del doti*) set up for the marriages of poor girls. In 1491, he preached the Lenten sermons at Santa Maria del Fiori, the principal church of the city.

Lorenzo began to awake to the danger that these revolutionary sermons posed and warned Savonarola not to prophesy or stir up unrest. Savonarola did not take this advice and continued to vilify Lorenzo and the city government for abuses. His popularity continued to increase as Lorenzo's health failed. In 1491, Savonarola was elected Prior of San Marco. He began to be seen as a saint. Poets, philosophers, and artists became his adherents at about this time. His Lenten sermons of 1492 had a more markedly prophetic tone than ever before. Soon after this, Lorenzo lay dying and sent for Savonarola to ask his blessing. Contrary to an apocryphal story, eyewitness accounts have it that Savonarola did indeed give his blessing to the dying man and that Lorenzo was greatly consoled by it. Medici rule did not long survive Lorenzo, largely because his son and successor, Piero, was not a competent leader.

In 1492, Pope Innocent VIII died, fulfilling one of Savonarola's prophecies. His successor was the notorious Borgia pope Alexander VI, who was almost certainly an atheist, had droves of children whose fortunes he aggrandized, had reportedly committed incest with two of his daughters, and had openly purchased the Papacy. At this time, Savonarola had a vision: An arm with a sword appeared to him. A voice spoke, inviting conversion, speaking with "holy love," warning that a time was coming when conversion would no longer be possible. Clouds of angels appeared, dressed in white, carrying red crosses, offering the same accoutrements to all. Some accepted, some did not, and some prevented others from accepting. The sword then turned down, and thunder, lightning, darkness, plague, war, and famine began.

During this time, Savonarola had been engaged in the reform of cloistered life. He told his monks of San Marco that he had had a vision wherein it had been revealed to him that of the twenty-eight monks who had died in the last few years, twenty-five were eternally damned for love of possessions. The monks then brought him all their private goods, which were sold for the benefit of the poor. He changed the dress and diet of the monks, and wanted to found a new, very austere convent outside Florence. He also battled to separate San Marco from the Lombard Congregation and to start a new congregation along with the Convents of Fiesole and Pisa. Savonarola eventually accomplished this goal.

The French invasion of Italy, the event that proved the end, for the time, of Medici administration in Florence, occurred in 1494. The French were opposed by the Aragonese of Naples and the pope; Piero de' Medici sided with them against Florence's traditional ally, France. In 1492, Savonarola had predicted the French invasion and its success; now, with the approach of Charles VIII and his army, Piero's administration was imperiled. It did not help that he was arrogant, openly tyrannical, and a less-than-clever politician. Piero panicked when it became obvious that he could not raise funds for the defense of the city, and he went to treat directly, on his own authority and not that of the Signoria (the Florentine Senate), with the French king. He conceded all the Florentine strong points to the French, and the French entered the city and began to mark houses for the billeting of troops. The citizens were angry, and a group was appointed, among them Savonarola, to negotiate with Charles. All during this time, Savonarola had been preaching apocalyptic sermons on the theme of Noah's Ark and invoking his earlier prophecy. He now played an important part in negotiations with Charles, hailing Charles as a prophesied deliverer, but warning him to be careful of

Florence and admonishing him not to abuse the city.

When Piero de' Medici returned to Florence after his disastrous private embassy, he was baited and ridiculed. He fled; Florence became a republic once more, with Savonarola as its de facto ruler. Savonarola advocated the republican form of government and was not personally ambitious. His goal was to found the City of God in Florence which would then act as a model for reform throughout Italy. In the difficult days after the end of Medici rule, with the French occupying the city and the citizens beginning to align along traditional factional lines, Savonarola's constant preaching of moderation, forgiveness, and calm prevented any outbreaks which could have set off civil war. He rejected vengeance against Medici adherents and rebuked the people for executing a particularly hated tool of the Medicis, Antonio Bernardo. There were no more executions, and Savonarola's government grew in popularity.

Nevertheless, there were opponents. The Arrabbiata (the enraged), the opposition faction, began to ally themselves with the opponents of the King of France: the Duke of Milan, the pope, and the other members of the Holy League, the Italian anti-French alliance. The Holy League saw Savonarola as the main obstacle preventing Florence's joining them, and the pope began to use his authority over Savonarola as head of the Church to bring him to heel. He summoned Savonarola to Rome, praising him for his wonderful works; Savonarola was justly suspicious and pleaded illness as an excuse for not going. Alexander sent a second brief vilifying him and ordered him to Bologna under threat of excommunication. Savonarola replied respectfully to this brief but did not comply, pointing out mistakes in its formulation. A third brief arrived a month later, forbidding him to preach. Several months later, admitting the political reason behind the ban on Savonarola's preaching, which Savonarola had obeyed, Alexander gave a Florentine embassy a verbal revocation of the ban. Savonarola then preached his 1496 Lenten sermons on Amos, in which he continued to criticize the Church and vilified Alexander's private life. Despite this impolitic behavior, a college of theologians convened to examine the propriety of Savonarola's preaching found nothing to criticize in it. He was allowed to continue.

The pope, however, tried other angles: He offered a cardinal's hat as a bribe and tried to incorporate San Marco into another congregation, in which Savonarola would have no authority. The incorporation was ordered on pain of excommunication. Savonarola protested but obeyed—and the order was not put into effect; he could continue his course. Just before Lent in 1497, during Carnival season, Savonarola's authority and popularity reached a kind of peak with "the burning of the vanities," when bonfires were made of those possessions deemed sinful by the new regime. Bands of children went about the city encouraging the destruction of these "vain things." Soon afterward, Savonarola's grip on the city began to fail. His own faction, the

Frateschi, or brothers (termed pejoratively "the Piagnoni" or the weepers), lost control of the government to the Arrabbiata, who bought a bull of excommunication from Alexander VI. It was secret, and marred by errors; the pope himself disowned it. Nevertheless, it was not withdrawn. The Arrabbiata began to foment riots against Savonarola. The Florentine government tried to get the bull of excommunication revoked; Rome offered to do it if Florence joined the Holy League. At this point, Savonarola took a hand in his own defense and began to preach on Exodus; these Lenten sermons of 1498 were to be his last. The city was threatened with an interdict, and Savonarola was forced to stop preaching.

His final downfall was caused, indirectly, by one of his own supporters in a rather ludicrous episode of failed heroism. A Franciscan monk had challenged to an ordeal by fire anyone who maintained that the pope was not correct in excommunicating Savonarola. A loyal adherent, Fra Domenico da Pescia, took up this challenge. The Franciscan did not show up. Even though, by the terms of the trial, this meant that Savonarola's team had won, the city was disappointed in the lack of a miracle, and the following day Savonarola and two followers were arrested.

His trial for heresy was marked by confessions extracted under torture. His testimony is very touching in its frankness, and it is evident that the verdict was unjust. He was found guilty by the papal commissioners and was hanged and burned by the civil authorities. He received the pope's absolution and plenary indulgence before his death. A cult soon grew up around him, and until the nineteenth century flowers were found on the spot of his execution every May 23, left by devotees in the night. Miracles that he performed were recorded, and occasionally his name was brought up as a candidate for sainthood.

Summary

Girolamo Savonarola's primary importance was as a reformer. In a time that had become corrupt, he reawakened the possibility of virtue, both in religion and in civic life. His remarkably direct and simple approach to right action brought together the life of the spirit and the life of the body, religious life and civil life, in a time when these aspects of life were becoming more separate—when life was becoming, actually, what one would recognize as modern.

That, after all, is the oddity of his life. He was a reformer, a voice of the new, a revolutionary even; yet the source of his ideas was archaic. In living out perhaps the last medieval life in Renaissance Italy, in resisting the alienation of personal life from the eternal that marked the beginning of the modern, he opened the door to attacks on the centralized authority of the Church. Reared in the aura of his grandfather's fourteenth century education and finding his own time too relativistic, too "advanced," he revolutionized his society in the attempt to archaize it. The life of Savonarola shows the difficulty, for interpreters of history, in the consistent application of the idea of "progress." He is remembered now for his incorruptibility and for his championing of the humble against the great, for his devotion to the Church and his opposition to its human incarnation, and for his effect on certain of the thinkers and artists of his day, such as Michelangelo and Pico della Mirandola.

Bibliography
Butters, H. C. *Governors and Government in Early Sixteenth-Century Florence, 1502-1519*. Oxford, England: Clarendon Press, 1985. A thorough examination of the political aftermath of Savonarola's rule of Florence. Chapter 1, "Florentine Politics and Society at the End of the Fifteenth Century," covers the period of transition and reorganization. The details of political and economic life ignored by nineteenth century Romantic historians are here included. Good index and an appendix of principal actors in the various aspects of the state.
Lucas, Herbert. *Fra Girolamo Savonarola*. 2d rev. ed. St. Louis: B. Herder, 1906. An account of Savonarola's life, copious but rather dry, in which special attention is paid by its Jesuit author to points of theology and canon law. The author takes great pains to present a balanced view of both Savonarola and his enemies. Contains an index.
Ridolfi, Roberto. *The Life of Girolamo Savonarola*. Translated by Cecil Grayson. London: Routledge & Kegan Paul, 1959. Probably the best general life of Savonarola. Written with grace and scope, this is an account of the events that strives for balance. The author has a wide, cultured grasp of the Florentine spirit and history.
Rowdon, Maurice. *Lorenzo the Magnificent*. Chicago: Henry Regnery, 1974. A chatty, heavily illustrated look at the Florence of Lorenzo, which includes material on Savonarola's career. His earlier life as a prophet and reformer of influence in the days of Lorenzo is fairly well covered; his three-year period of rule is cursorily dismissed. Many maps, paintings, and photographs. Offers a sound introduction to the period for a not-too-demanding student. An index is provided, as well as a bibliography for further study and a list of illustrations.
Villari, Pasquale. *Life and Times of Girolamo Savonarola*. Translated by Linda Villari. New York: Charles Scribner's Sons, 1888. This is the commonly cited authoritative biography before the Ridolfi work. A copious treatment but outdated. It has perpetuated some factual errors. A sort of apology for Savonarola, it tells what has become the classic account of his life, heroicizing it in opposition to the wickedness of the times. A thorough index is provided.

Ann Klefstad

JOSEPH JUSTUS SCALIGER

Born: August 5, 1540; Agen, France
Died: January 21, 1609; Leiden, United Provinces
Areas of Achievement: Literature and historiography
Contribution: Educated by a learned father and through study with leading
   scholars, Scaliger became the foremost scholar of Greek and Latin in his
   time. His editions of Latin authors set high critical standards; his research
   on ancient chronology established the study of ancient history on a firm
   foundation and introduced to Europe the literature and history of Byzantium.

Early Life

In 1525, the physician Julius Caesar Scaliger accompanied the Italian
nobleman M. A. de la Rovère to Agen, a small town in western France,
where the nobleman would serve as bishop. The physician claimed a remarkable record. Julius Caesar Scaliger was descended from the family (the della
Scala) that once had ruled Verona. He had studied art (with Albrecht Dürer),
medicine, theology, natural history, and classical literature. He had earned
military distinction during seventeen years of service under his kinsman the
Holy Roman Emperor Maximilian I. Now the physician devoted himself to
other pursuits. His medical practice at Agen flourished, and in 1528 he married an adolescent orphan of a noble family, Andiette de Roques Lobejac.
From this union came fifteen children.

The physician studied Greek and Latin in his leisure. He circulated a
brilliant (if misguided) polemic against Desiderius Erasmus' criticism of
contemporary Latin in 1531, from 1533 to 1547 wrote volumes of his own
Latin verse, which would be critically disparaged but read widely and reprinted often, and composed his own Latin grammar in 1540 and a notable
treatise on Latin poetry (published in 1561 after his death). His major work
was a massive commentary on the ancient Greek tradition of natural history
as understood by Hippocrates, Aristotle, and Theophrastus. This great study
was completed in 1538 but not published until after the author's death, when
Gottfried Wilhelm Leibniz praised it as the best contemporary guide to Aristotle.

Julius Caesar Scaliger's love of classical learning bore its greatest fruit in
his third son (and tenth child), Joseph Justus. Educated at home to age
twelve, Joseph was then sent, with his brothers Leonard and John, to the
College of Guyenne at Bordeaux. There they read standard Latin authors and
learned Greek by using the fashionable new grammar of the Protestant educator Philipp Melanchthon. Plague erupted in Bordeaux in 1555, and the
three boys returned to Agen to be educated again by their father. The elder
Scaliger required of his sons daily composition and declamation in Latin—

studies in which Joseph excelled: By age seventeen, he had composed an original Latin drama (*Oedipus*), of which his father approved and of which he himself remained proud in his old age.

His father, however, did not instruct his son in Greek. Therefore, after Julius Caesar's death in 1558, Joseph Scaliger set out for the University of Paris. There he attended the lectures of a contemporary master of Greek, Adrian Turnèbe, but soon realized that he knew insufficient Greek to profit from the course. Scaliger thereupon dedicated two years to reading basic Greek authors and, in the process, compiled his own Greek grammar. He then went on to study Hebrew and Arabic to a good level of proficiency. Scaliger's formal education at Paris ended in 1563, when another Greek professor, Jean Dorat, was sufficiently impressed by Scaliger's learning to recommend him successfully as companion to the young nobleman Louis de Chastaigner.

Life's Work

Scaliger's position as companion to Chastaigner provided secure employment and other advantages: extensive travel, access to learned men and to scholarly collections throughout Europe, and, what was of especial importance in an age of turmoil (for these were the years of religious and dynastic wars in France), freedom to study and write. Thus, in 1564, Scaliger published his first work, *Coniectanea in M. Terentium Varronem de lingua latina*, a wide-ranging discussion of textual problems and the etymologies of Latin words in the *De lingua latina* (first century B.C.; *On the Latin Language*, 1938) by the Roman scholar Marcus Terentius Varro. The book attracted scholarly attention, because here Scaliger demonstrated his profound knowledge of classical and Near Eastern languages and revealed what would become a deep interest in archaic (before 100 B.C.) Latin. Thus, as well, Scaliger accompanied Chastaigner on several journeys to Italy, where he met the great French Humanist and textual critic Marc-Antoine Muret, who introduced Scaliger to Italian scholars and their libraries. Chastaigner and his companion next traveled to England and Scotland, where Scaliger disliked the insularity, ignorance, and vulgarity of the scholars he encountered but found time to continue his studies on Varro and record his impressions of Mary, Queen of Scots (negative), and Queen Elizabeth (positive). The years from 1567 through 1570 Scaliger spent with the Chastaigner family, moving from place to place in France to avoid the ravages of civil war.

From 1570, Scaliger lived for two and a half years at Valence with the great scholar of Roman law Jacques Cujas. Cujas provided an introduction to a wide range of scholars (with whom Scaliger would correspond in years to come), expert instruction in the study of Roman legal texts, and a library of more than two hundred Greek and Latin manuscripts and instruction in how to discriminate among them. Cujas' influence and the texts he placed at

Scaliger's disposal encouraged Scaliger to concentrate his energies on the manuscript sources for individual ancient authors and the ancient sources for specific topics. Thus, in 1573, Scaliger published an edition of the late, difficult Latin poet Ausonius, based on his own scrutiny of an important ninth century manuscript that Cujas possessed.

The Saint Bartholomew's Day Massacre—the slaughter of Huguenots in France in 1572—caught Scaliger en route to Poland on a diplomatic mission. Scaliger had been reared as a Roman Catholic, but in Paris he had taken instruction from Calvinists and, by the time of his sojourn in England, had declared himself a Protestant. He therefore fled to Calvinist Geneva, where he was given a professorship of philosophy. He lectured on Aristotle and Cicero but did not enjoy his subjects. His private tutorials were more successful.

At the first opportunity, in 1574, Scaliger returned to France to live with Chastaigner. Intermittent wars made the next twenty years far from comfortable; Scaliger several times had to serve in the military. Nevertheless, with the financial support of Chastaigner, Scaliger produced important studies of individual Latin authors in which he demonstrated his skill at textual emendation (the correction of the received text of an author). Scaliger's breadth of knowledge and technical skill at evaluating manuscripts changed emendation from a common and popular practice of haphazard guesses to a rational procedure founded on principles consistently applied.

In this same period (1574-1594), Scaliger produced works that established the study of ancient chronology on a solid basis. Scaliger's 1579 edition of the poetry of the Latin astrologer Manilius was in fact a treatise on astronomy as understood by the ancients and served as preface to Scaliger's *De emendatione temporum* (1583; on the correction of chronologies), in which Scaliger argued that a correct understanding of ancient history must be based on a comparative, critical, and analytic study of the surviving fragments of ancient chronological systems (king-lists, calendars, and the like) and a correct understanding of how the ancients reckoned the passage of time. Furthermore, Scaliger in a sense here created a new discipline, ancient history, by establishing comparative chronologies not only for Greek and Roman civilization but also for the societies of the ancient Near East (Egypt, Mesopotamia, Judaea). These studies were the foundations of Scaliger's most important work: *Thesaurus temporum* (1606; treasure of chronologies), a collection of the known Greek and Latin fragments on chronology and a reconstruction of the great *Chronicon* (fourth century A.D.) of Eusebius. Eusebius had compiled a comparative chronology of Greek, Roman, Christian, and Jewish events back to the time of Abraham, but his chronicle was known only from Saint Jerome's and other Latin versions. Scaliger's reconstruction of Eusebius was so good that some later scholars have mistaken Scaliger's work for Eusebius' own text. Later study and discovery of other manuscripts confirmed the accuracy of Scaliger's reconstruction.

In 1594, Scaliger accepted a position at the University of Leiden, where, with no teaching responsibilities, he dedicated his time to scholarly correspondence and encouraging a new generation of scholars who, in their own ways, would carry on his work. He enjoyed complaining of his accommodations and the climate at Leiden but enjoyed even more the honor in which he was held at this Protestant university. His energies, however, were sapped by dispute. Leiden recognized his claim of descent from the Princes of Verona. Assorted Jesuits and lay scholars, for whom Scaliger's historical and textual criticism was perceived as a threat, did not. They attacked Scaliger's scholarship and religious beliefs by questioning his ancestral pedigree. A few months after completing a pamphlet in his own defense, the embittered scholar died at Leiden, on January 21, 1609, in the company of his colleague and student Daniel Heinz. Scaliger was buried four days later in Saint Mary's, the church of the Huguenots in Leiden.

Summary

A typical scholarly production of Joseph Justus Scaliger's time was the *Adversaria*: a miscellany volume wherein an author offered his observations, argued his criticism, and proposed his emendations on a variety of classical texts. Scaliger often affirmed that, while he could have written volumes of *Adversaria*, he preferred to work on complete scholarly editions of classical authors. Indeed, when his contemporaries saluted Scaliger as among the most learned of any age, they cited as evidence his skill at emendation exhibited in his editions of, for example, Catullus and Manilius. Later generations acknowledged the worth of those editions but recognized that Scaliger's studies of ancient chronology were more significant. Furthermore, the breadth of his chronological studies was the manifestation of Scaliger's firm belief that as broad a knowledge of antiquity as possible was the prerequisite for a proper understanding of ancient texts. Scaliger thus anticipated the nineteenth century German scholarly ideal of *Altertumswissenschaft*—"a science of (all of) antiquity." In addition, Scaliger's study of the sources for ancient chronology drew attention to an entire field of history and literature previously unrecognized in Western Europe. In the nineteenth century, students of Byzantine history and literature looked back to Scaliger as their master and as the founder of their discipline.

In retrospect, Scaliger may be recognized as the first of a new breed of scholar. That scholarship ought to impart skills and values was a basic principle of Renaissance Humanism. That principle, in turn, was founded on a tradition stretching back to the Greek historian Polybius and beyond: The ideal historian was the man of political involvement who brought to his studies the experience of life; those studies would then instruct others to lead more effective lives. Scaliger's father was a man of this mold. Scaliger, however, thought otherwise: "Scholars should not teach practical politics." The scholar should, in Scaliger's estimate, devote himself to scientific study; knowledge should be pursued for purely intellectual, not practical, ends. In this emphasis on "value-free" studies, Scaliger asserted an educational and academic principle that would not be widely recognized until two centuries later and still remains a topic of considerable debate.

Bibliography
Grafton, Anthony. *Joseph Scaliger: A Study in the History of Classical Scholarship*. Vol. 1, *Textual Criticism and Exegesis*. Oxford, England: Clarendon Press, 1983. This study (the first of a projected two-volume biography) takes its subject up to 1579. Grafton treats well Scaliger's early education and assesses Scaliger's early writings in their contemporary context. Detailed notes, no bibliography; adequate index. This study should be supplemented with the following item.
Grafton, Anthony, and Lisa Jardine. *From Humanism to the Humanities*. Cambridge, Mass.: Harvard University Press, 1986. A fine study of education and the emergence of scholarly disciplines in Europe during the fifteenth and sixteenth centuries. Documents and discusses the education that Scaliger and his brothers received at Bordeaux. An excellent index and full bibliographic footnotes compensate for the lack of a bibliography.
Hall, Vernon, Jr. *Life of Julius Caesar Scaliger (1484-1558)*. Philadelphia: American Philosophical Society, 1950. This is the best single discussion of the elder Scaliger's life and literary works. Contains information on the education the Scaliger sons received at home and at Bordeaux. Includes reference notes, a bibliography, and a full index. Hall's discussion of the elder Scaliger's early (pre-1525) career should be supplemented with Paul Oskar Kristeller's discussion in *American Historical Review* 57 (1952): 394-396.
Pattison, Mark. *Essays by the Late Mark Pattison*. 2 vols. Edited by Henry Nettleship. Reprint. New York: Burt Franklin, 1964. Volume 1 contains two essays that constitute an excellent sketch of Scaliger. Pattison emphasizes both Scaliger's scholarly work and the circumstances of his life. Volume 2 contains a brief index.
Pfeiffer, Rudolf. *History of Classical Scholarship from 1300 to 1850*. New York: Oxford University Press, 1976. A standard discussion, with emphasis on Scaliger's place in the history of classical philology. Pfeiffer offers sound critical judgments on Scaliger's scholarly works and places those works in their contemporary intellectual context. Contains bibliographic footnotes and a full index.
Sandys, John Edwin. *History of Classical Scholarship*. Vol. 2, *From the Revival of Learning to the End of the Eighteenth Century*. Cambridge: Cambridge University Press, 1908. Reprint: New York: Hafner, 1964.

Features a straightforward, brief literary biography of Scaliger, with little analysis. Contains bibliographic footnotes and a full index.

Scaliger, Joseph Justus. *Autobiography of Joseph Scaliger with Autobiographical Selections from His Letters, His Testament, and the Funeral Orations by Daniel Heinsius and Dominicus Baudius.* Edited and translated by George W. Robinson. Cambridge, Mass.: Harvard University Press, 1927. The brief (five-page) autobiography takes Scaliger to Leiden in 1594; the selection of letters illustrates Scaliger's personality; the will offers information on the scholar's family, library, and other worldly goods. Contains an adequate index, a fine bibliographical introduction by Robinson, and two contemporary portraits of Scaliger.

Paul B. Harvey, Jr.

ALESSANDRO SCARLATTI

Born: May 2, 1660; Palermo, Sicily
Died: October 22, 1725; Naples
Area of Achievement: Music
Contribution: Scarlatti was the outstanding Italian composer of operas and cantatas active at the end of the seventeenth and beginning of the eighteenth centuries. His work brought fame to Naples as a center for operatic composition and performance, and provided the foundation for the so-called Neapolitan school of composers, though he and his musical style had little direct influence on them.

Early Life

Pietro Alessandro Gaspare Scarlatti was the second of eight children of Pietro Scarlata (or Sgarlata) and his wife, Eleanora d'Amato, and the eldest to survive infancy. Nothing is known of his childhood, although he may have studied music with the *maestro di cappella* of Palermo Cathedral, Don Vincenzo Amato, a presumed relative of his mother. In June, 1672, at the age of twelve, he was sent to Rome with his two young sisters, Anna Maria and Melchiorra Brigida, presumably to live with relatives. Again, nothing is known of his education at Rome, although he may well have attended a choir school connected with one of the large churches or seminaries. Presumably he would have performed and heard the music of the older composers active or recently active in Rome, including Giacomo Carissimi (with whom he is traditionally held to have studied), Antonio Cesti, Alessandro Stradella, and Bernardo Pasquini.

Scarlatti seems to have acquired patrons among the Roman nobility at an early age, and by 1677 was composing a short opera, as yet unidentified, for an evening gathering in a private home. By this time, he must have been earning a living, for he was married on April 12, 1678, to Antonia Anzalone, a native of Rome whose family may also have come from Sicily. Scarlatti was then just short of his eighteenth birthday and prepared to launch his career as a composer. A portrait of Scarlatti painted by Lorenzo Vaccaro and probably dating from the 1680's shows a young man very much of the seventeenth century, dressed in court finery, with a serious mien, an elongated face, a prominent nose, and penetrating eyes. When he was painted again by an unknown artist near the end of his life, in sober attire and wearing a cross, his face had rounded and his features softened, but the penetrating eyes remained. He seems to have been essentially a serious man, concerned equally with his own music and with the welfare of the large Scarlatti clan of which he had become head after the death of his father.

Life's Work

The year 1679 marked the beginning of Scarlatti's public career as a composer, although he had undoubtedly composed a number of cantatas and other smaller works as a student. Early in the year, the Arciconfraternita del San Crocifisso commissioned him to compose an oratorio, which was probably the one performed for them on February 24, 1679, but otherwise unidentified. His earliest known opera is the *commedia in musica* entitled *Gli equivoci nel sembiante*, privately premiered in early 1679 because of the severe restrictions imposed upon public performances by the reform-minded Pope Innocent XI. The opera, which requires a cast of only four and limited staging, was an immediate success and was performed a number of times at Rome in 1679 and subsequently at Bologna, Naples, Monte Filottrano, Vienna, Ravenna, and Palermo.

Perhaps more important to Scarlatti, his first opera earned for him the patronage of Queen Christina of Sweden, living in Rome after her abdication from the Swedish throne and acting as one of the city's major patrons of the arts. Scarlatti immediately became her *maestro di cappella* and dedicated to her his next opera, *L'honestà negli amori*, premiered during Carnival, 1680. He also acquired other influential Roman patrons, foremost among them being Cardinals Benedetto Pamphili and Pietro Ottoboni, with whom he maintained contact even during his two separate stays at Naples from 1683 to 1702 and from 1709 to 1718. Between 1680 and 1683, Scarlatti wrote at least three more operas, six oratorios, and a number of cantatas for performance in Rome. He may also have been employed at one or more churches, including San Gerolamo della Carità. By 1681, the Scarlatti household consisted of the composer, his wife, two infant children, his sister-in-law, a nurse, and his younger brother Giuseppe.

Scarlatti was a successful young composer in the Rome of the early 1680's, but he had already irritated papal authorities by participating in the annual attempts to bypass the pope's regulations concerning operatic performances. It must have seemed both a politic move and a good opportunity when in 1683 the Marquis del Carpio, formerly Spanish ambassador to the Vatican and newly installed Spanish Viceroy of Naples, invited Scarlatti to become his *maestro di cappella*. Since Naples was then the most populous city in Italy and Sicily was also under Spanish control, Scarlatti may have believed that the new position would provide better opportunities both for himself as an opera composer and for the entire Scarlatti family, and he promptly accepted the offer.

In the event, Scarlatti's tenure in Naples was marked by further controversy. Nevertheless, he remained in charge of the viceroy's chapel until 1702 and during that time was the dominant composer in the city. As at Rome, Scarlatti made his principal impact at Naples as a composer of operas. Over a twenty-year period, he composed more than half of the new operas performed at Naples and adapted and supplemented the majority of the operas by a variety of composers which were imported from Venice and elsewhere.

For Naples he composed the first of his serenatas—large-scale works for soloists, instruments, and occasionally chorus generally written to celebrate specific occasions—and continued his output of cantatas, at least sixty-five of which date from these years. He was also responsible for the composition and performance of music for the Viceregal Chapel.

Opera at Naples was under the direct patronage of the viceroy, and new works were generally premiered in the theater at the Viceregal Palace before being transferred to the public theater of San Bartolomeo. Scarlatti may have had a hand in the composition and performance of as many as eighty of these, the most successful of which were *Il Pirro e Demetrio* of 1694 and *La caduta de' Decemviri* of 1697. These works and others carried Scarlatti's fame as a composer and Naples' renown as a center of operatic activity throughout Italy and as far abroad as Germany and England. As with the Roman operas, the subject matter was generally based very loosely on historical figures and events, history being freely altered to provide suitable opportunities for dramatic encounters between characters (generally conveyed in the form of recitative) and reactions by one and occasionally two of the characters to these encounters (generally conveyed in the form of arias or duets).

By the end of the 1690's Scarlatti appears to have felt overworked by the viceroy and underappreciated by the Neapolitan public. He was certainly worried about his financial situation, since his salary was being paid irregularly and the onset of the War of the Spanish Succession in 1700 promised hard times and possibly extensive warfare for the city of Naples. In addition, he was concerned with the future of his son Domenico, the sixth of his ten children and an exceptionally talented keyboard player and composer. In June, 1702, father and son left Naples for an approved absence of four months which stretched to six years for Scarlatti.

Scarlatti and his son went first to Florence in the hope of obtaining an appointment in the service of Prince Ferdinand de' Medici, a great patron of music. No appointment was forthcoming, and father and son returned to Naples before Scarlatti moved to Rome. Over the next six years, Scarlatti sent Ferdinand oratorios, church music, and at least four new operas, the latter completely lost, apparently hoping that the Florentine prince would be interested in more serious fare than was acceptable at Naples. Meanwhile, at the end of 1703 Scarlatti became assistant *maestro di cappella* of the Church of Santa Maria Maggiore in Rome and probably entered the service of his earlier patron Cardinal Ottoboni, already a patron of Arcangelo Corelli and soon to be the same for George Frideric Handel.

The years 1704-1707 were not banner ones for Scarlatti. The Roman public theaters had been closed since 1700, so operas were seldom performed. Aside from the lost operas sent to Florence, he wrote only the two five-act *tragedie per musica* for performance at Venice in 1707. Of these, *Il Mitri-*

date Eupatore, based on the Orestes legend, is generally considered one of his greatest works. Instead of operas, Scarlatti produced during this period a stream of cantatas, serenatas, and oratorios written for old and new Roman patrons. He was elected to the Arcadian Academy in 1706 together with Pasquini and Corelli. In 1707, he was promoted to *maestro di cappella* of Santa Maria Maggiore, but his financial worries continued and Domenico's career was aparently not flourishing at Venice. Naples, which did not suffer extensively during the War of the Spanish Succession, was ceded to the Austrians in 1707, and in 1709 Scarlatti accepted an invitation from Cardinal Grimani, the first Austrian viceroy, to return as viceregal *maestro di cappella*.

For the next decade, Scarlatti remained at Naples while retaining his Roman contacts. He wrote at least eleven operas for the viceroy, the most famous being *Il Tigrane* of 1715 and one of the most interesting being *Il trionfo dell'onore* of 1718, his only late opera designated *commedia in musica*. He also began to compose purely instrumental music, most notably his twelve *Sinfonie di concerto grosso*, begun in 1715.

Scarlatti had attained the status of a famous and revered composer, even receiving a patent of nobility from Pope Clement XI in 1716 that allowed him to employ the title "Cavaliere." His music, however, was rapidly falling from favor, and his essentially serious operas could not compete with the simpler, livelier style of the younger composers such as Domenico Sarri, Francesco Mancini, or Leonardo Vinci. Even his most famous operas were seldom revived.

In 1718, Scarlatti once more obtained leave from Naples and returned to Rome. He may have anticipated supervising the career of his son Domenico, then serving as *maestro di cappella* of the Cappella Giulia at St. Peter's Basilica, but the younger Scarlatti had apparently had enough of his father's interference and succeeded in securing an order of legal independence in early 1717. In August, 1719, Domenico gave up his appointments in Rome and left, arriving by September, 1720, in Lisbon. He spent the rest of his life in Portugal and Spain, returning to Italy only three times and visiting his aging father only on the second of those visits in 1725.

Alessandro was in Rome by Carnival, 1718, to direct his new opera *Telemaco*. He added the operas *Marco Attilio Regolo* in 1719, *La Griselda* in 1721, and two more operas whose music does not survive. He also composed an oratorio, several cantatas, and some large-scale sacred works, including his *Il martirio di S Cecilia* (1708; mass for Saint Cecilia) and several related vespers psalms and motets written in 1720. Several of these later works employ larger orchestras and display more interesting use of instrumentation than his earlier compositions. Even in those scored for soloists with string orchestra alone, the vocal line is independent from that of the first violins, producing a thicker and more complicated texture.

Scarlatti returned to Naples in 1722, where he spent his last years writing some music, entertaining guests, including the younger composers Johann Adolph Hasse and Johann Joachim Quantz, and gradually passing from the public memory. He died on October 22, 1725, and is buried in the Santa Cecilia chapel at the Church of Santa Maria di Montesanto.

Summary

By his own count, Alessandro Scarlatti composed 114 operas between 1679 and 1721, but this may include his additions to operas by others. He also composed more than six hundred cantatas, most for a single voice accompanied only by a basso continuo, and was the most prolific composer of this genre and the last to make a significant contribution to it. He also wrote at least thirty-five serenatas, forty oratorios, and a substantial body of church music. Only in the area of instrumental music did he fail to make a significant contribution, despite a flurry of interest in his last years, which produced some eighteen concerti and a variety of chamber sonatas and keyboard pieces.

Scarlatti was easily the most prolific vocal composer of his generation and probably the most famous. His greatest success came at Naples in the 1680's and 1690's. As he grew older, his fame remained, but his post-1700 operas, though admired, were seldom popular successes. Although he brought fame to Naples, his own essentially conservative and contrapuntal style had little direct influence on the famous Neapolitan composers of the eighteenth century. His operas and cantatas illustrate the development of musical forms and styles in the late seventeenth century, but his own influence was not substantial. His last operas were clearly underwritten by his loyal Roman patrons and received scant critical or popular acclaim, being too old-fashioned even for so conservative a city. By the time of his death, he was largely forgotten.

Scarlatti's posthumous reputation has suffered much from hearsay and legend. Very little of his music was actually known by succeeding generations. The music to more than half of his operas is completely lost, and more than half of the remainder survive in fragmentary form. Only since 1974 have a handful of his operas been available in reliable modern editions, and even fewer have been performed. The cantatas survive in profusion, but only a very few are available in modern editions and only one, *Su le sponde del Tebro*—an atypical work for soprano, trumpet, strings, and continuo—is at all well known. The same holds true for the serenatas. Perversely, several of the less important genres have fared somewhat better, and ten of the oratorios have appeared in reliable modern editions since 1953, as have all the madrigals and a small number of the instrumental and sacred works.

In the late eighteenth and the nineteenth centuries, Scarlatti was mistakenly seen as the founder of the Neapolitan school of opera composers and the teacher of many of its earliest members. In fact, he should more appropriately be seen as a composer of the seventeenth century, whose works mark the culmination of the Italian traditions of opera and cantata composition of that century. His main contributions were to the expansion of the dimensions of arias, the standardization of the use of the *da capo* form, and the more active participation of the orchestra in vocal accompaniments. It was his misfortune to have written some of his greatest works in the eighteenth century, when a newer, lighter style prevailed.

Bibliography
Dent, Edward J. *Alessandro Scarlatti: His Life and Works*. 2d rev. ed. London: Edward Arnold, 1960. The pioneering biography of Scarlatti and, although brief, still the best single-volume work in English. Dent and Frank Walker, who revised this work, were both perceptive students of Scarlatti's life and works, and the former's comments on the music are particularly useful.
Grout, Donald J. *Alessandro Scarlatti: An Introduction to His Operas*. Berkeley: University of California Press, 1979. A brief but very clear introduction to the subject drawn from the Ernst Bloch lectures given by Grout at the University of California at Berkeley in 1975-1976. Includes several extended musical examples but no bibliography.
Grout, Donald J., and Edwin Hanley. "Alessandro Scarlatti." In *The New Grove Dictionary of Music and Musicians*, edited by Stanley Sadie. London: Macmillan, 1980. The standard music reference article on Scarlatti. Contains a complete list of works and an extensive bibliography, both compiled by Malcolm Boyd.
Robinson, Michael F. *Naples and Neapolitan Opera*. New York: Oxford University Press, 1972. Although primarily concerned with events of the later eighteenth century, this book places Scarlatti in context and is a valuable study of the tradition he was long held to have established.
Smither, Howard E. *A History of the Oratorio*. Vol. 1, *The Oratorio in the Baroque Era: Italy, Vienna, Paris*. Chapel Hill: University of North Carolina Press, 1977. An exhaustive treatment of the subject, especially valuable for the discussion of the social context. Pages 335-342 are especially relevant. Contains an extensive bibliography.
Westrup, Jack A. "Alessandro Scarlatti's *Il Mitridate* (1707)." In *New Looks at Italian Opera: Essays in Honor of Donald J. Grout*. Edited by William W. Austin. Ithaca, N.Y.: Cornell University Press, 1968. A brief introduction to Scarlatti's serious opera of 1707, which retells the Orestes myth under different names. Regarded as one of Scarlatti's greatest works, *Il Mitridate Eupatore* was long championed by Westrup.

Graydon Beeks

GERHARD JOHANN DAVID VON SCHARNHORST

Born: November 12, 1755; Bordenau, Lippe
Died: June 28, 1813; Prague, Bohemia, Austrian Empire
Area of Achievement: The military
Contribution: Scharnhorst's modernization of the Prussian army made it the
    model for the armies of the nineteenth century. Among the reforms which
    he either initiated or helped to push through were the development of the
    general staff, the abolition of army corporal punishment, a scheme for
    training large numbers of recruits, and the overhaul of Prussian tactical
    training.

Early Life
    On November 12, 1755, Gerhard Johann David von Scharnhorst was born
in Bordenau, a small town in the principality of Lippe, one of the sleepy,
minor German states of the time. The son of an independent small farmer,
Scharnhorst was born a commoner whose connections to the aristocracy were
limited to two uncles who sold fish and other supplies to the kitchen of the
Elector of Hanover. Nevertheless, Scharnhorst's father had served in the
artillery of the Hanoverian army as a sergeant major, and it was a military
career that the young boy would pursue.
    Scharnhorst had the good fortune to be enrolled at the Military Academy
of the Count of Schaumburg-Lippe, a cadet school which provided an education far above what was commonly taught at such provincial institutions.
Commissioned as an officer-cadet in 1778 and made second lieutenant in the
artillery in 1784, Scharnhorst, like Napoleon I, took advantage of new open-
ings in the military for men of the middle class. Recent inventions had made
the artillery technologically the most advanced arm of the European armies,
and its officers were necessarily chosen on a basis of proficiency rather than
of noble birth.
    Despite its incorporation of technological progress in its military hard-
ware, the army in which Scharnhorst served was still grounded in the military philosophy of the era which effectively ended with the American War of
Independence in 1776 and the advance of the armies of the French Revolution after 1792. In both campaigns, the old European armies, which relied on
a small, perfectly drilled body of professional soldiers able to move with
mathematical precision to the orders of its commander, were beaten by an ill-
trained but highly motivated mass army which replaced chessboard strategies
with a revolutionizing reliance on open fire and massive offensive punches.
    Since the European aristocrats had decided to fight revolutionary France,
Scharnhorst first fought on the battlefields of Belgium and distinguished
himself both as a courageous tactical leader and as a valuable chief of staff.
In order to share his new insights into modern warfare, Scharnhorst took on

the editorship of an influential military journal and began his lifelong career as a military writer. The Hanoverian army, however, was not an adequate vehicle for Scharnhorst's ambitions, and the forty-five-year-old major began to look for advancement elsewhere.

Life's Work

In 1801, Scharnhorst offered his services to King Frederick William III of Prussia; however, he attached three conditions to his coming: He asked to be made lieutenant-colonel, to be raised to the nobility, and to be allowed to transform the Prussian army into a modern fighting force which could therefore withstand the onslaught of France. As further proof of his qualifications, the Hanoverian officer attached three essays on military topics.

In December, 1802, when Scharnhorst was actually ennobled, the Prussian king had answered all of the young man's requests and had made him director of the War Academy in Berlin. Physically, Scharnhorst did not quite fit one's idea of a Prussian staff officer: A portrait by Friedrich Bury shows an intelligent face framed by soft brown hair; Scharnhorst's expressive eyes gaze over a long, fleshy nose, and his mouth seems to be trying to suppress an ironic smile. His contemporaries noted an absence of stiffness in Scharnhorst, and, on the parade ground, his was not an impressive figure; when he addressed the troops, his voice failed to inspire them. On the other hand, his writings were exceptionally clear, witty, and persuasive. All in all, the Prussian king had obtained an officer who stood out of the crowd of his mostly noble and aging colleagues.

From his very first year in Prussian service, Scharnhorst gathered around him an impressive body of students, among whom was the young Carl von Clausewitz, whose ideas would later revolutionize military thought. At the same time, Scharnhorst communicated actively with fellow reformers in and out of the military; to create a forum where the reform of the army could be discussed, he founded the Military Society of Berlin in July, 1801. Soon, young and enlightened officers joined to express their ideas and to put them on paper in the society's publications.

Meanwhile, the triumphs of Napoleon began to draw the eyes of the Prussian reformers to his military machine. The movement and organization of large masses of soldiers required immense organizational support, and the French had designated that task to a still-rudimentary general staff. The idea caught on with the Prussians, and in 1803 the old quartermaster-general's staff was enlarged and reorganized. As a result, Scharnhorst was made general quartermaster-lieutenant for Western Germany (the Prussian possessions west of the river Elbe) and at once began to order such revolutionary activities as field trips for staff officers and peacetime reconnaissance and mapping of potential grounds of conflict.

War came in 1806, and Scharnhorst tested his theories of modern military leadership when he served as a staff aide to the charismatic General Gebhard Leberecht von Blücher; however, the two men could not save the generally poorly led Prussian army. Captured with Blücher and released later, Scharnhorst fought valiantly at Preussisch Eylau in the East, but his superiors failed to use this tactical gain in order to engineer a strategic reversal. In 1807, Prussia had to admit defeat and sign the Peace of Tilsit.

In the aftermath of defeat, the king appointed an Army Reform Commission, which, headed by Scharnhorst, would examine the wartime conduct of every Prussian officer. As a final result of these examinations, only two of the generals who had served in 1806-1807 would still be on active duty in 1813. Furthermore, the king ordered the institution of a Ministry of War. Scharnhorst was appointed head of its General War Department and thus was put in charge of overseeing the army as a whole.

In his new position, Scharnhorst began to draft energetic proposals for reform. Central to his thoughts was the idea of a standing army in which all male citizens would serve their nation for a certain time. An important step toward this goal was taken on October 9, 1807, when Scharnhorst's civilian counterpart, the great reformer Baron Heinrich vom und zum Stein, moved the king to proclaim the abolition of serfdom in Prussia as of November 11, 1810. By this, the people of Prussia were freed to serve the state rather than their landowners.

The French limit on Prussia's army, however, which was to be kept to forty-two thousand men, prohibited the building of a larger force of conscripts and volunteers. Here, Scharnhorst found an ingenious way out when he proposed his famous *Kruempersystem*, or "shrinkage system." According to this scheme, regular soldiers of a regiment were sent on leave, while fresh recruits took their place and received a quick but thorough training. Although the effect of this system has been overestimated, Prussia had at hand about sixty-five thousand trained soldiers in 1813, and some of the surplus came from the *Kruempersystem*.

Before the suspicious French effected his removal from the General War Department in 1810, Scharnhorst had also worked on the opening of the officer corps to members of the middle class. Meanwhile, for the common soldier, Scharnhorst was coinstrumental in abolishing humiliating forms of corporal punishment, such as scourging or "running the gauntlet." While he stayed with the emerging general staff, Scharnhorst gave the Prussian army its modern organization into brigades and divisions which would each consist of a combination of infantry, cavalry, and artillery. The need for modernized tactical training did not escape his view; the army training regulations of 1812 bear witness to his influence in their placing of a new emphasis on operational flexibility and common sense, fire power, and the formation of a strong attacking force. Soldiers were increasingly trained in the field and on the rifle range, while the parade ground became less important.

When France forced Prussia into war against Russia in 1811, Scharnhorst removed himself to a remote outpost in Silesia until fortunes changed and Prussia, now an ally of Russia, declared war on France on March 16, 1813. The new war brought to fruition all the reforms for which Scharnhorst and his colleagues had struggled. Universal service was proclaimed on February 9, and the idea of a militia was realized with the formation of the *Landwehr* and *Landsturm*. Volunteers rushed to the Prussian recruitment centers, and Scharnhorst found himself appointed chief of staff to General Blücher. Together, they engaged the French in two battles. At Grossgörschen, Scharnhorst received a foot wound which developed gangrene and ultimately killed him on June 28, 1813, while he was waiting in Prague on a mission to win Austria's entry into the war against France.

Summary

At a crucial moment in Prussian history, Gerhard Johann David von Scharnhorst succeeded as a leading military reformer who laid the foundations for the survival and ultimate triumph of the Prussian army in the war with France after 1813. His idea of a well-organized citizen army backed by the logistical help of a general staff would find its ultimate expression in the victories of the Prussian armies in 1866 and 1871. Scharnhorst's ideas thus proved essential for the creation of the German Empire by Otto Bismarck and Kaiser William I.

Throughout his years in the service of the Prussian state, Scharnhorst stressed the importance of education and individual dignity and responsibility for all reforms. This emphasis links Scharnhorst's military work to the struggles of his civilian counterparts, reformers such as Stein and Prince Karl von Hardenberg; it also makes him exemplary of the zeitgeist of a new era in Prussia and Germany, which drew inspiration from thinkers such as Immanuel Kant and Georg Wilhelm Friedrich Hegel.

In his reforms, Scharnhorst was always led by a deep humanism as well as a sincere appreciation of the individual soldier. As a practicing Christian, Scharnhorst also rejected the idea that army and warfare fell completely within the private sphere of the ruler. Like his pupil Clausewitz, the great reformer firmly believed in a political, rather than a personal, purpose of a nation's defense forces.

Bibliography

Dupuy, T. N. *A Genius for War: The German Army and General Staff, 1807-1945*. Englewood Cliffs, N.J.: Prentice-Hall, 1977. Dupuy, a retired air force colonel, views Scharnhorst as a brilliant thinker who, together with an influential group of reformers, laid the groundwork for Prussia's emerging superiority in army organization and operational leadership. Very readable and richly illustrated. Contains useful maps.

Feuchtwanger, E. J. *Prussia: Myth and Reality.* Chicago: Henry Regnery, 1970. Covers the Prussian state from its origins to its abolition in 1947 and contains a valuable chapter on the reform era. Describes Scharnhorst's accomplishments in detail and places them in the context of a broad reform movement. Depicts the obstacles which were laid in the path of the reformers by opposing elements of the old establishment. Readable, with four maps.

Goerlitz, Walter. *History of the German General Staff, 1657-1945.* Edited and translated by Brian Battershaw. New York: Frederick A. Praeger, 1953. An extremely useful look at Scharnhorst in his role as a military reformer who would prove crucial to the development of the German war machine. Contains a personal view of the man, his general environment, and his supporters, friends, students, and opponents. Very readable; illustrated.

Kitchen, Martin. *A Military History of Germany from the Eighteenth Century to the Present Day.* Bloomington: Indiana University Press, 1975. Centers on the democratic aspects of Scharnhorst's reform work. Places him in the framework of Germany's military history. Gives some background information on the Prussian state and its army. Well written and persuasive.

Koch, H. W. *A History of Prussia.* New York: Longman, 1978. A detailed account of Scharnhorst's struggles with the Prussian establishment. Contains valuable extracts of Scharnhorst's writings in translation that are not generally available in English. Contains maps and tables. Somewhat scholarly and dry in its approach but useful for further studies.

Reinhart Lutz